PALESTINE

ABOUT THE AUTHOR

Professor Nur Masalha is a Palestinian historian and a member of the Centre for Palestine Studies, SOAS, University of London. He is also editor of the *Journal of Holy Land and Palestine Studies*. His books include *Expulsion of the Palestinians* (1992); *A Land Without a People* (1997); *The Politics of Denial* (2003); *The Bible and Zionism* (Zed 2007) and *The Palestine Nakba* (Zed 2012).

PALESTINE

A FOUR THOUSAND YEAR HISTORY

NUR MASALHA

I.B. TAURIS
LONDON · NEW YORK · OXFORD · NEW DELHI · SYDNEY

I.B. TAURIS

Bloomsbury Publishing Plc

50 Bedford Square, London, WC1B 3DP, UK

1385 Broadway, New York, NY 10018, USA

29 Earlsfort Terrace, Dublin 2, Ireland

Palestine: A Four Thousand Year History was first published in
1999 by Zed Books Ltd.

BLOOMSBURY, I.B. TAURIS and the I.B. Tauris logo are trademarks
of Bloomsbury Publishing Plc

First published in Great Britain 2021

Reprinted 2021

Reprinted by I.B. Tauris in 2022, 2024 (five times)

Copyright © Nur Masalha 2018

Nur Masalha has asserted his right under the Copyright, Designs and Patents
Act, 1988, to be identified as Author of this work.

Cover design © De Agostini Picture Library/Getty

A catalogue record for this book is available from the British Library.

A catalog record for this book is available from the Library of Congress.

ISBN: PB: 978-0-7556-4942-6
HB: 978-1-78699-272-7
ePDF: 978-1-78699-274-1
eBook: 978-1-78699-275-8

Typeset by Deanta Global Publishing Services, Chennai, India
Printed and bound in the United States of America

To find out more about our authors and books visit www.bloomsbury.com
and sign up for our newsletters.

CONTENTS

Acknowledgements

Any credit for this book should be shared with a large number people who provided me with documents, archival and material sources, logistics, ideas, comments and moral support. These include Thomas Thompson, Rosemary Sayigh, Hamdan Taha, Hussein Hamzah, Emanuel Beška, Ghalib Anabsi, Maysa Hamzah, Raja Khalidi, Marie Antoinete, Salim Tamari, Sherna Berger Gluck, John Docker, John Rose, Saad Chedid, Gilbert Achcar, Yosefa Loshitzky, Bernard Regan, Ismael Abu Saad, Nahla Abdo, Asia Zrike, Hassan Hakimian, Ehab Masalha, Peter Mayo, Laura J. Khoury, Hatem Bazian, Faiha Abdulhadi, Niels Peter Lemche, Ella Shohat, Nadera Shalhoub-Kevorkian, Maryse Gargour, Ilan Pappe, Issa Jubrael Sarie, Khalil Nakhleh, Adrian Beidas, Oren Ben-Dor, Rashid Khalidi, Ghada Karmi, Khalil Hindi, Iman Saca, and Ahmad Sa'adi. My special thanks go to Professors Thomas Thompson and Haim Bresheeth for their extraordinary generosity and insightful comments and to the two anonymous reviewers for their time and helpful advice. My family and friends have also been an ongoing source of inspiration and encouragement and this book could not have been completed without the support my wife Stephanie and my daughter Maryam; to both I owe enormous gratitude. At Zed, I am particularly grateful for the comments and practical help of the Commissioning Editor Kim Walker, Production Director Amy Jordan and Project Manager Linda Auld. Needless to say that, while all the above have contributed directly and indirectly to this work, thus enabling the book to come to fruition, any mistakes or shortcomings in this book are entirely mine.

Introduction

PALESTINE AS A NAME COMMONLY USED THROUGHOUT ANCIENT HISTORY

First documented in the late Bronze Age, about 3200 years ago, the name Palestine (Greek: Παλαιστίνη; Arabic: فلسطين, Filastin), is the conventional name used between 450 BC and 1948 AD to describe a geographic region between the Mediterranean Sea and the Jordan River and various adjoining lands. This work explores the evolution of the concept, histories, identity, languages and cultures of Palestine from the Late Bronze Age to the modern era. Moreover, Palestine history is often taught in the West as a history of a land, not as *Palestinian history* or a history of *a people*. This book challenges colonial approach to Palestine and the pernicious myth of *a land without a people* (Masalha 1992, 1997) and argues for reading the history of Palestine with the eyes of the indigenous people of Palestine. The Palestinians are the indigenous people of Palestine; their local roots are deeply embedded in the soil of Palestine and their autochthonous identity and historical heritage long preceded the emergence of a local Palestinian nascent national movement in the late Ottoman period and the advent of Zionist settler-colonialism before the First World War.

Friedrich Nietzsche argued that history is always written from and with a particular perspective and the past looks different from different perspectives, although some perspectives are empirically more truthful or less distorting than others. This work is not aimed at creating a grand narrative or a metanarrative for Palestine, as a way of mirroring or mimicking the foundational myths of Zionism. However, considering alternative and

1

critical perspectives and looking for proof and empirical evidence are also central to critical historical writing. Using a wide range of contemporary evidence, testimony and sources, this book applies a multiple-perspective approach to the history of Palestine across time, while always keeping in mind the realities of the country and its indigenous people. It further argues that multi-linear evolution of the conceptual experience of Palestine, with its unanticipated twists and turns over time and space, centre on the general and concrete ideas which represent the historical and fundamental characteristics and lived experiences of Palestine and its indigenous people. The geo-political unit and contextualised representations (and indigenous framing) of Palestine are deeply rooted in the collective consciousness and empirical experiences of the indigenous people of Palestine and the multi-cultural and shared ancient past.

The name Palestine is the most commonly used from the Late Bronze Age (from 1300 BC) onwards. The name is evident in countless histories, 'Abbasid inscriptions from the province of Jund Filastin (Elad 1992), Islamic numismatic evidence maps (including 'world maps' beginning with Classical Antiquity) and Philistine coins from the Iron Age and Antiquity, vast quantities of Umayyad and Abbasid Palestine coins bearing the mint name of Filastin. As we shall see below, the manuscripts of medieval al-Fustat (old Cairo) Genizah also referred to the Arab Muslim province of Filastin (Gil 1996: 28–29). From the Late Bronze Age onwards, the names used for the region, such as Djahi, Retenu and Cana'an, all gave way to the name Palestine. Throughout Classical and Late Antiquity – a term used by historians to describe a period between the 3rd and 8th centuries AD, a transitional period from Classical Antiquity to the Middle Ages in the Mediterranean world, Europe and the Near East – the name Palestine remained the most common. Furthermore, in the course of the Roman, Byzantine and Islamic periods the conception and political geography of Palestine acquired official administrative status. This work sets out to explain and contextualise the multiple beginnings and evolution of the concept of Palestine, geographically, culturally, politically and administratively. It also seeks to demonstrate how the name 'Palestine' was most commonly and formally used in ancient history. It argues that the legend of the 'Israelites' conquest of Cana'an' and other master narratives of the Old Testament (or 'Hebrew Bible') – a library of books built up across several centuries – are myth-narratives designed to underpin false consciousness, not evidence-based history which promotes truth and understanding. It further argues that academic and school history curricula should be based on contextualised historical facts, empirical evidence, archaeological and scientific discoveries, not on conventional opinions or the fictional narratives of the Old Testament and religio-political dogmas repeatedly reproduced in the interest of powerful elites.

The celebrated English historian and Enlightenment author Edward Gibbon, writing in 1776, noted that 'Phoenicia and Palestine will forever live in the [collective] memory of mankind'. Gibbon also astutely observed that the Romans, Persians and Arabs wanted Palestine for the extraordinary fertility of its soil, the opulence and beauty of its cities and purity of its air (Gibbon 1838, Vol. 1: 40; 1840, Vol. 5: 173).

Today the idea of a country is often conflated with the modern concept of 'nation-state', but this was not always the case and countries existed long before nationalism or the creation of metanarratives for the nation-state. The conception of Palestine as a geo-political unit and a country (Arabic: *bilad* or *qutr*), with evolving boundaries, has developed historically and continues to do so. The identity and cultures of Palestine are living organisms: they change, evolve and develop. This work explores the representation of Palestine over time as a mixture of the perceived and conceived and the lived realities of the country. The evolving idea of Palestine is framed here within five basic assumptions which also centre on the principles of human agency, context and lived experiences:

- Palestine is the individual and collective *bilad* (country) – in modern terms: *watan,* or *mawtin* ('homeland') – of the Palestinian people: the indigenous people of historic Palestine (*Filastin al-Tarikhiyyah*) and the indigenised immigrants in Palestine. The Palestinian people (individually and collectively) have a multifaith and multicultural heritage and a multi-layered identity deeply rooted in the ancient past (Farsoun 1997).
- Palestinian history is *a house of many mansions* – to echo an expression coined by the late Lebanese historian Kamal Salibi in connection with the modern history of Lebanon. The cultural pluralism of Palestine and the multi-tier identity of the Palestinians (as individual and collective

agencies) must be situated within their evolving social, cultural and political context and actual historical circumstances.

- The multicultural dimensions of Palestianness and the textured polity of Palestine are grounded here in the living history and living experiences of the indigenous people of Palestine and the Palestinised immigrants in the country.

- Of particular interest here are the urbanisation processes, the emergence of early city city-states and state formation in Palestine. Contrary to the claims about the tribal organs of the state in the Arab Middle East, this book argues that early state formation in Palestine and the wider Near East was a product of urbanisation processes. These processes began in the Early Bronze Age at around 3200 BC and were associated with the emergence of great urban centres in Palestine – stratified urban social spaces in comparison with the somewhat smaller and more egalitarian Chalcolithic localities in the country (4000–3200 BC). In the course of the Early Bronze Age urbanisation in the great urban centres in the country, each about 100–400 *dunums* in size, was accompanied with the appearance of the Semitic alphabet, stratified society, public buildings, palaces, temples, towers and fortification systems. Some of urban centres which emerged in Early Bronze Age Palestine were represented in Jericho, Gaza, Tell al-Ajjul, Tell al-Sakan, Tell al-Tell, Jerusalem, Tell Dothan, Tell Taannek and Tell al-Mutasallim – the latter being the archaeological site of the powerful city-state of Megiddo which emerged during the Bronze Age (Taha 2017: 6–11; De Vaux 1966). The work will also explore the interaction of Palestinian cities across history with their surrounding rural life and the wider regional context. In this respect, Henri Lefebvre's three constituents of the social production of urban spaces – perceived, conceived and lived experiences (Lefebvre 2011) – are relevant to the way multicultural urban Palestine – Caesarea-Palaestina (also known as Caesarea Maritima; Arabic: Qaysariah), Gaza (Ghazzah) Ascalon ('Asqalan), Nablus, al-Ramla, Jerusalem, Acre (Arabic Akka; Greek: Ptolemais) Nazareth, Jaffa, Tiberias, Beisan, Safad – evolved historically. Greek, Roman and Byzantine urbanisation processes and urban planning were maintained under Islam in the Middle Ages and this urban planning is still visible today in the Arab Islamic medieval

Old City of Jerusalem, a city whose urban planning and architecture are among the best surviving medieval cities in the world.

Some Arab writers and artists promoting the political and national cause of Palestine or pan-Arabism create metanarratives to depict Palestinian national identity or Arab nationalism as being more ancient than they actually are. Moreover, until the advent of anachronistic European political Zionism at the turn of the 20th century the people of Palestine (Arabic: *sha'b Filastin*) included Arab Muslims, Arab Christians and Arab Jews. Being a rendering of the Israeli Zionist/Palestinian conflict, historically speaking the binary of Arab versus Jew in Palestine is deeply misleading. The Palestinian people experience their country of Palestine individually and collectively. Although Zionist settler-colonialism violated their indigenous right to self-determination in their historical homeland and they live either under settler-colonial occupation or exiled and rarely allowed to speak for themselves, they continue to speak of *Biladuna*[1] *Filastin* ('Our Country, Palestine';[2] vernacularly: *bladna Falastin*) or *Filastinuna* ('Our Palestine'[3]). Even Palestinian citizens of Israel often speak of *al-blad* or *bladna* ('Our Country') as a patriotic way of mentally or representationally avoiding the term Israel and connecting with historic Palestine and the Palestinian people as a whole. The terms *bilad* or *biladuna* are medieval Arabic terms which have been in common use for many centuries and are deeply rooted in people's daily lives. In the second half of the 19th century the medieval Arabic term *watan* ('homeland') was impacted by the European term *patria*, and *watan* became more closely associated with the rise of modern forms of patriotic homeland nationalism (*wataniyyah*) in Palestine and throughout the Arab world.

PALESTINE AS AN OFFICIAL ADMINISTRATIVE ENTITY

The British occupied Jerusalem in December 1917 and historians often argue that Palestine did not exist as an official administrative unit until the creation of Mandatory Palestine by the British in 1918. In fact, as we shall see below, Palestine existed as a distinct administrative unit and a formal province for over a millennium. This was first as the joint Roman province of 'Syria Palaestina' (135–390 AD) and subsequently, as a province separate from Syria, in the form of the three administrative provinces of Byzantine Palestine: Palaestina Prima (Палестина Прима), or Palaestina I, Palaestina Secunda (Палестина Секунда) and Palaestina Salutaris or Palaestina Tertia (Палестина Терция). Moreover, these three provinces were effectively governed politically, militarily and religiously from Palaestina Prima as a 'three-in-one' polity from the 4th century until the early 7th century. And once again Palestine existed as a separate administrative entity in the form of the administrative Arab Muslim province of Jund Filastin. This administrative province of Jund Filastin (Arabic: جند فلسطين) existed for nearly four and half centuries from the Muslim conquest of Palestine in 637–638 until the Latin Crusader invasion of 1099 AD.

Distinction between Filastin, al-Sham, Bilad al-Sham and present-day Syria: Palestine as an administrative Muslim province, al-Sham as an Islamic geographic region

For nearly half a millennium from the 630s until the Crusader invasion of Palestine in 1099, and the creation of the first Crusader Latin Kingdom of Jerusalem (1099–1187), the official Arab Islamic administrative province of Jund Filastin existed within the wider geographic region of al-Sham. In Muslim geography and cartography, al-Sham ('the North') was a geographic region (*iqlim*: al-Maqdisi 2002: 135–162) – a vast region which included the territories of present-day Syria, Palestine/Israel, Lebanon, Jordan and south Turkey. For several centuries, al-Sham consisted of several administrative Muslim provinces, Palestine included. In 1890 Guy Le Strange (1854–1933), a scholar of Arabic and Persian at Cambridge University, published an important work entitled: *Palestine under the Moslems: A Description of Syria and the Holy Land from AD 650 to 1500*, published in London by the Committee of the Palestine Exploration Fund. Translating extensively from the works of the medieval Arab geographers, Le Strange conveniently and mistakenly rendered all geographic Arabic references to 'al-Sham' into 'Syria'. Subsequently further confusion was added to this automatic conflation of the al-Sham region with modern Syria by some historians of the modern Middle East and by the fact that the city of Damascus, the capital of present-day Syria, was also historically called al-Sham. This historic city of al-Sham became synonymous with the capital city of the Muslim province of Dimashq (Damascus) in the Middle Ages.

Yet today anyone who is familiar with the works of medieval Muslim geographers and Arab historians knows that the region of al-Sham consisted of a vast geographic region, from southern Turkey in the north to Palestine in the south, and several provinces (al-Maqdisi 2002: 137–138). Al-Sham, in medieval Islamic geography and history works, was not synonymous with present-day Syria. This vast 'northern' region became the basis of the medieval Islamic term for the geographic area of Bilad al-Sham (بِلَاد الشَّام), which often referred to the two Muslim provinces of Damascus and Aleppo.

Under Arab Islam the Greek and Latin forms of the name (Palaistinê and Palaestina) were rendered in Arabic into Filastin and the Arab Islamic province of Jund Filastin existed for nearly half a millennium from the 630s to the late 11th century. Before Islam the al-Sham region was partly populated by Monophysite Arabs and Miaphysite Christians, including Ghassanid Arabs and Aramaic-speaking Christians. While Palestine became an administrative province under Islam, al-Sham was never a single administrative province; the Muslim province of Dimashq (Damascus) in the Middle Ages was only one of the five provinces of the al-Sham region, one of which extended deep into present-day southern Turkey. In any case Filastin and al-Sham were neither synonymous nor mutually exclusive. The province of Filastin was part of wider region of al-Sham (al-Maqdisi 2002: 165–162). However, of all the neighbouring countries, Palestine's historic links with al-Sham under Islam were the closest and most enduring (al-Maqdisi 2002: 165–162). However, it would wrong to argue that the Arab Islamic term al-Sham made the perception of Palestine anachronistic under both the Mamluks and Ottomans. As we shall see below, the two geo-political terms coexisted throughout the Middle Ages and modern period and the term Filastin was viewed as a component of the wider region of al-Sham. And Palestine's strategic and geographic location between Egypt and al-Sham ('countries of the north') had a lasting impact on its history, arts and culture as well as identity as a geo-political and administrative unit.

Being Palestine, becoming Palestine: reimagining Palestinian territorial identity, from regional to national

The history of Palestine, unlike the myth-narratives of the Old Testament, has multiple 'beginnings' and the idea of Palestine has evolved over time from these multiple 'beginnings' into a geo-political concept and a distinct territorial polity. The concept of Palestine is often approached in an abstract or ahistorical way, rather than as a contextualised representation of an entity whose (physical, administrative, territorial and cultural) boundaries have evolved and changed across three millennia. But there are no pure ideas or an ideal concept of Palestine per se; empirical evidence and human experience are fundamental to the formation of ideas and knowledge about Palestine. Crucially, we do not know Palestine only 'from without' through perceptions and generalisations but also 'from within' through embodied experiences and affections. The classical Greek scholars – who were among the first to popularise the concept of Palestine – conceived of time in two distinct ways: *khronos*, the way human beings measure time quantitatively and chronologically: days, months, years, centuries; and *kairos*, the way human beings experience and remember particular moments or events from and with a particular perspective. Following this distinction between the two different notions of time, this work explores the multi-linear evolution of the conception of Palestine and the experiences of Palestine through time and across time. While putting the highest value on synchronic (contemporary) evidence and testimony, this work analyses the conception of Palestine across time both synchronically and diachronically.

Although there are multiple beginnings and multiple meanings to the idea of Palestine, the important question is not so much about the 'origin' of the idea of Palestine, or where the idea came from, but how the identity of Palestine evolved and experienced through and across time. Also, to borrow from Martin Heidegger's notions of *Being and Time* (2010) and temporality (past, present and future) and the way human beings experience the world through time, ideas, terms and discourses on Palestine should be explored synchronically and diachronically as well as the human experiences of Palestine time. Furthermore, terms and concepts evolve multi-linearly and discursively and are experienced differently by different people – to borrow from Ludwig Wittgenstein's (2001) discourse on 'family resemblance' and multiple meanings.

From *Ahl Filastin* to *Sha'b Filastin*: from indigenous to modern national collective consciousness

In Palestine, the indigenous collective consciousness of, and Arabic terminology for, 'the people of Palestine' (*Ahl Filastin, Abnaa Filastin* or *Abnaa al-Balad*) long preceded, but also followed, the modern Arabic nationalist terms *Sha'b Filastin* (the 'people of Palestine') or *al-Sha'b al-Filastini* (the 'Palestinian people'). Of course, the actual connotations of terms and representations of social and collective identities have evolved and changed historically and the evolution of the multicultural identity for the people of Palestine is no exception. The Islamic reference to the Arabic term *sha'b*, people or nation, is enshrined in the Quran and the term is described positively and pluralistically: 'O mankind! We created you ... and made you into nations [pl. *shu'ub*] and tribes [*qabail*], that ye may know each other'. Thus, social pluralism became fundamental to the way collective identities were framed throughout Islamic history. Of particular relevance to the evolution of the indigenous concept of Palestine are the self-representation of the people of Palestine in indigenous Palestinian Arabic writings between the 15th and 20th centuries. These representations are framed as follows: the Arabic terms *Ahl Filastin* and *Ard Filastin* ('people of Palestine' and 'land of Palestine') were repeatedly used by indigenous Palestinian Arab writers in the 10th–18th centuries, long before the emergence of a nascent Palestinian national movement in the late 19th and early 20th centuries. In the second half of the 19th century the Arabic term *Ahl Filastin* evolved into *Abnaa Filastin* and *Abnaa al-Balad* – the (indigenous) 'sons and daughters of Palestine' and the 'sons and daughters of the country' respectively; and these terms evolved into *Sha'b Filastin* – the nation or people of Palestine – in the early 20th century; and again into *al-Sha'b al-Filastini* and *al-Kiyan al-Filastini* – the Palestinian people/nation and the Palestinian entity – in the second half of the 20th century. All these terms (*Sha'b Filastin, al-Sha'b al-Filastini* and *al-Kiyan al-Filastini*) refer to the articulation and consolidation of the collective identity of the Palestinian nation under the impact of modern Palestinian territorial nationalism; but, read flexibly and not literally, these collective terms are also deeply rooted in a premodern indigenous collective consciousness centred around *Ahl Filastin*, *Ard Filastin* and *Abnaa al-Balad*.

The ancient term Palestine (country, *Balad* or *Bilad*) and modern Palestinian nationality are not identical or synonymous; the latter has existed for millennia while the former has come into a modern use and was the product of the emergence of modern Palestinian nationalism. This critical distinction between Palestine as a country and Palestinian nationality should also be kept in mind when reflecting on the fact that some historians of modern Palestinian nationalism have overlooked the links between land and country (and Palestine-based territorial consciousness) which was evident in the works of Palestinian Muslim scholars and writers such al-Maqdisi (Shams al-Din Abi 'Abd Allah Muhammad ibn Ahmad al-Muqaddasi, محمد بن أحمد شمس الدين المقدسي (1866, 1994, 2002), Mujir al-Din al-'Ulaymi (c. 1495), Khair al-Din al-Ramli (1585–1671) and Salih ibn Ahmad al-Tumurtashi in the 10th–17th centuries and the reimagining of Palestine in modern Palestinian territorial nationalism. As we shall see below, these Muslim writers of the 10th–17th centuries displayed a sense of, and pride in, Palestinian regional-territorial identity, though of course within the context of the multiple identities Palestinians at the time possessed (religious and local identities included). Reading the history of Palestine through the eyes of the indigenous people, this work argues that the reimagined modern Palestinian *people* as a national community (Palestinian-framed nationalism) along the lines suggested by Benedict Anderson (1991) should also take into account the literature and social memory of historic Palestine bequeathed to us by indigenous Palestinian authors between the 10th and late 17th centuries: al-Maqdisi, al-Ramli, Mujir al-Din and al-Tumurtashi. All these writers produced a rich literature with extensive description of the medieval territorial and administrative Arab province of Filastin.

Late 19th century Palestine saw a cultural and educational renaissance coupled with incipient local nationalism. An important distinction made in this work is between this nascent Palestinian national identity or local Palestinian nationalism of the late Ottoman period, under the impact of modernity and through the literary works and journalism of Palestinian writers such as Khalil Beidas, Ruhi al-Khalidi, Yousef al-'Issa, 'Issa al-'Issa,

Khalil al-Sakakini and Tawfiq Cana'an, and Palestinian territorially based regional consciousness of historic Filastin. Although regional consciousness is found in the writings of Josephus in 1st century AD Roman Palestine and the works of the celebrated authors Prokopios (Procopios) and Eusebius of Provincia Palaestina in the 4th and 6th centuries, by the 19th century Palestine had for centuries been an Arab country with Arabic and the symbols of Islam being key markers (and signifiers) of its identity. In fact, territorially based consciousness of Filastin as a distinct Arab region/country (*bilad*), with Arabic and Islam being key markers of identity, is also evident in the works of al-Maqdisi, Mujir al-Din al-'Ulaymi, Khair al-Din al-Ramli and Salih ibn Ahmad al-Tumurtashi in the period between the 10th and late 17th centuries. The territorially based multi-faceted regional identity articulated by Palestinian Muslim authors was partly derived from the cultural and religious heritage of the Arab Islamic province of Filastin, an administrative province which existed for several centuries.

This work makes a third distinction between historic Palestine (Late Bronze Age to 1917) and Mandatory Palestine (1917–1948). Palestinian territorial nationalism has evolved since the late Ottoman period and, like all modern nationalisms, it continues to renew itself. However, historians, who tend to focus on the boundaries of British Mandatory Palestine, have overlooked the evolution of Palestinian territorial nationalism from the late Ottoman period into the British Mandatory period (1917–1948). While Palestinian nationalists of the late Ottoman period draw inspiration from historic Palestine – including greater Palaestina under the Byzantines and the Arab province of Filastin under Islam – Palestinian nationalism has since 1918 been fixated symbolically on the territorial map of Mandatory Palestine as a key marker of territorial nationalism. The political and cultural geography of Palestinian nationalism has had a major impact on the evolution of the modern geo-political concept of Palestine. For instance, traditionally different styles of embroidery by and for women were a signifier of regional identities within Palestine. Today embroidery (as well as necklaces, and many other forms of art work produced in Palestine) repeatedly reproduces the territorial map of Mandatory Palestine, with the names of its historic Arab cities, as a powerful symbol of Palestinian national identity.

Of course, the issue of historic Palestine and the rise of modern Palestinian nationalism is a complex one. However, a discussion about the histories and shared memories of Palestine has to address the emergence and becoming of the Palestinian national identity which has emerged since the late 19th–early 20th centuries. The evolution of this modern national identity, which will be explored in chapter nine, will be addressed within the conceptual and methodological framework of 'being Palestine, becoming Palestine' proposed by, among others, Mahmoud Darwish. For Darwish, in particular, being and becoming is a lifelong process of learning, development, self-discovery and the opening up of possibilities, something which is central to the pluralist social traditions of Palestine. These pluralist, multifaith and shared traditions were woven into the fabric of modern Palestinian national identity as conceived by the Palestinian 'national' poet. Darwish's conceptualisation of 'being Palestine, becoming Palestine', of formation and transformation of Palestinian identity, was not a binary or two-tier conception; it is rather in line with the multidimensional and textured identity of Palestine and the Palestinians. Moreover, the modern national conception of Palestine did not totally displace and/ or completely replace older conceptions of Palestine; on the contrary, the nationalist idea did not come out of the blue and was, as I argue here, deeply rooted in the ancient past. In fact, the new nationalist idea of the nation-state simply added further modern overarching layers to the already multi-layered identity and histories of the country.

The current debate about the one-state or two-state solutions in Palestine is beyond the scope of this work. However, it will explore the conceptual experiences of Palestine both 'from within' and 'from without'. It will make a clear distinction between Palestine as a country and 'regional territorially based consciousness' of Palestine, on the one hand, and Palestinian nationality and 'national, territorially based consciousness' of Palestine, on the other. Palestinian nationalism and nationality, like all other nationalisms and nationalities, are a modern phenomenon. The emergence of modern Palestinian national identity along the lines of reimagined communities (to paraphrase Benedict Anderson 1991) has been explored by Rashid Khalidi (1997: 171–190, 1998), Muhammad Muslih (1989, 1991) and others. Yet Palestine as a country (with its shifting boundaries) has existed across more than three millennia and this historical reality was bound to produce forms of territorially based consciousness. Evidence of this regional territorially based consciousness of Filastin as a country under Muslim rule can be found 'from within' Palestine. As we shall see below, the shared memories of territorially based consciousness of a distinct Arab region called Filastin, with clear boundaries extending to Rafah in the south to the district town of al-Lajjun (in Marj Ibn 'Amer) in the north, is shown clearly in the works of four Palestinian Muslim scholars and writers: al-Maqdisi, Mujir al-Din al-'Ulaymi and Khair al-Din al-Ramli and Salih ibn Ahmad al-Tumurtashi in the 10th–17th centuries, as well as in the records of the Islamic Sharia Court (*Sijillat al-Mahkamah al-Shari'yyah*) of Jerusalem in the 18th–19th centuries. In the 17th century both al-Ramli, of al-Ramla, and al-Tumurtashi, of Gaza, called the country where they were living Filastin and unquestionably assumed that their readers would do likewise. What is even more remarkable is al-Ramli's use of the term 'the country' and even 'our country' (*biladuna*), which is exactly how Palestinians today describe Palestine.

Of course, there are multiple ideas (and representations) of being Palestine and being Palestinian – ancient, medieval, modern, nationalist. The nationalist framing of Palestinian identity have been dealt with by many scholars (Khalidi, R. 1997: 171–190, 1998; Suleiman 2016, Masalha 2012; Muslih 1989, 1991; Kimmerling and Migdal 1993; Said 1980). As Rashid Khalidi (1998) and Muhammad Muslih (1989, 1991) have shown, a distinct Palestinian national identity anchored in the land of Palestine emerged in the late 19th–early 20th century. However, much of Palestinian national identity is derived from attachment to the past and to Palestine as a country. Moreover, throughout the world countries existed long before the emergence of modern nationalism, the nation-state or modern national identities, and the existence of Palestine for over three millennia is no exception. The idea that Palestinian national identity emerged out of the blue, or was created *ex nihilo*, in the late 19th–early 20th century is completely untenable. Viewed from the perspective of this work, and of the multi-layered identity of historic Palestine, the impact of the features and historic heritage of the country, which has evolved across millennia, on modern Palestinian national identity construction can hardly be overstated.

However, there are three ways of juxtaposing the old notions of Palestine with the emergence of modern Palestinian national identity. These ways can be explored through (a) essentialising, (b) nominalising or (c) conceptualising strategies:

(a) All these evolving ideas of Palestine are essentially the same; they only differ in appearances, manifestations, attributes.
(b) Although nominally the same, and despite the similarities in appearance, all these perceptions of Palestine are fundamentally different.
(c) The conceptualising strategy applied in this work is related to Wittgenstein's (2001) idea of 'family resemblance', although sharing many features of old Palestine, modern Palestinian national identity is *distinct*.

Furthermore, much of the millennia of history of Palestine as a country, narrated in a tapestry of stories which explored the evolving multi-textured, embroidered identity of the country, has nothing whatsoever to do with the Palestinian–Zionist conflict which in historical terms is a relatively recent development of late 19th–early 20th century. Furthermore, the conception and historic identity of Palestine should not be confounded or automatically conflated with the reframing and reconfiguration of modern Palestinian national identity, although clearly the latter would have a major impact on the perception, representational experiences and evolution of modern Palestine from the late Ottoman period onwards. The themes of imported modernities, nationalism, ethnicity and the nation-state are some of the key preoccupations of historians of the 'modern Middle East'. But historians often reproduce their own preoccupation with identity politics and imported nationalism and modernities and the millennia of Palestinian history cannot just be treated as a footnote to modern nationalism or the idea of a modern nation-state in Palestine. Moreover, the millennia of Palestinian history cannot be an appendage to the 'Israel–Palestine' conflict or subsidiary to the debates on identity politics in Palestine-Israel.

It is impossible to talk about Palestine intelligently without having a concept of the real Palestine in the same way as we cannot talk about Britain or China without having a concept of these two countries. Concepts are better understood not in the abstract or nebulously, but from the ground up: from the real, concrete and historical to the representational, from the observations and experiences to the concept, from the particular to the general. However, Israeli historians often seek to belittle Palestine and minimise the fact that the conceptual experiences of Palestine are deeply rooted in the ancient past. In her Introduction to *Islamic Art and Archaeology in Palestine*, Myriam Rosen-Ayalon (2006: 15), Mayer Professor of Islamic Art and Archaeology at the Hebrew University of Jerusalem, argues: 'As a geographical entity, the concept of Palestine is relatively modern and it is somewhat difficult to find references to it in historical sources'. She then goes on to contradict herself by referring to some of the 'historical sources':

> The Muslim conquerors translated the Roman terms 'Palestina prima' and 'Palestina secunda' as 'Jund Filastin' and 'Jund al-Urdun' to designate the two parallel strips of land that divided the country from north to south. They made Ramla the capital of Jund Filastin to replace Caesarea, and Tiberias the capital of Jund al-Urdun to replace Baysan ... The division adopted later by the Ottomans was more or less identical. (Rosen-Ayalon 2006: 15; see also Avni 2014: 41)

The conventional wisdom that the conception of Palestine is a modern, artificial construct is not confined to Israeli academics or opinion formers in the West; it is also shared by some influential Palestinian intellectuals. In fact, it is not just Israeli authors who continue to propagate the myth of the recent provenance of the idea of Palestine. Palestinian and pan-Arab intellectual 'Azmi Beshara has also repeated the claim in interviews in the Israeli Hebrew media that the idea of Palestine and 'Palestinian nationality' are 'colonial inventions'. For instance, Beshara had this to say long before he was forced to leave Palestine for exile in Qatar in 2007:

> I don't think there is a Palestinian nation at all; No, I think there is an Arab nation [ummah 'arabiyyah] ... And I always thought like that. I didn't change my opinion. I don't think there is a Palestinian nation I think 'Palestinian nation' is a colonial invention. When were any Palestinians? When was this? ... Despite my strong struggle against the

occupation, I'm not a Palestinian nationalist, never. I think Palestine until the late 19th century was greater southern Syria.[4]

In fact, contrary to the claims made by Beshara, not only did colonialism not create Palestine or Palestinian nationalism; British colonialism and Zionist settler-colonialist nationalism gave birth to the Israeli state and brought about the destruction of much of Palestine and expulsion of the Palestinians from their homeland in 1948 (Masalha 1992, 2012; Pappe 2006). Furthermore, while the term (*'ummah 'arabiyyah'*)is just over 100 years old, the term 'Palestine' is more than three millennia old. Working from a particular type of collective memory (and forgetfulness) and pan-Arab nationalist identity construction, rather than the actual histories of Palestine and the region, Beshara failed to acknowledge that all nationalisms (French, Arab, Indian, Egyptian, Palestinian, Turkish, Iranian, Jewish, Scottish) are 'invented traditions' and that the idea of an 'Arab nation' (*'ummah 'arabiyyah*) was also a late 19th century form of reimagining; the concept was reconfigured by Nahdah (reawakening) intellectuals as a form of secularisation of the religio-medieval representations of the 'Islamic ummah' (ummah islamiyyah). Some pan-Arab intellectuals have failed to come to terms with the emergence of *wataniyyah* (or a two-tier 'homeland nationalism') over the last century. This two-tier nationalism which has emerged in Palestine, Iraq, Syria and other Arab countries in the course of the last century was in part the outcome of the influence of European nationalist ideas and the colonial legacy. In large measure, it was the product of the multi-layered Arab Islamic identity which is deeply rooted in the cultural history and political geography of this region.

Moreover, as we shall show, contrary to Beshara's ahistoricism and Rosen-Ayalon's self-contradiction, the conception of Palestine as a country and a geo-political unit is deeply rooted in the political history, cultural geography and heritage of the country from the late Bronze Age onwards. Furthermore, in fact it was the Christian Byzantines, not the pagan Romans, who in Late Antiquity created the administrative provinces of Palaestina Prima and Palaestina Secunda, and the Arab Islamic provinces of Jund Filastin and Jund al-Urdun to the north-east were no parallel or equal strips; in fact, the province of Jund Filastin encompassed both Byzantine

Palaestina Prima and Palaestina Salutaris (the Third Palestine Province) in the south and south-east. Moreover, geographically the Arab province of Jund Filastin, which was four to five times the size of Jund al-Urdun, effectively encapsulated the core of Byzantine Palaestina. Also, if the Muslim conquerors came from Arabia to the south and south-east of Palestine, why would they want to divide Palestine 'from north to south', rather than 'from south to north' (Jund Filastin and Jund al-Urdun respectively)? Crucially, as we shall see below, the perception of Palestine is deeply embedded in the ancient past and extensively grounded in ancient, medieval and early modern historical sources.

The evolution across time of the country of Palestine as a distinct political geography – with its own distinct and diverse traditions and a melange of styles – is deeply rooted in the local psyche and consciousness; the toponym (place name) of Palestine is deeply rooted in the ancient past from the Late Bronze Age onwards. The name is found in numerous and diverse sources for the Ancient Near East throughout the last 3300 years. The name Palestine was used by the ancient Egyptians and Assyrians, classical Greek writers, Romans, Christian Byzantines and Medieval Arabs. The toponym Palestine is also evident in countless inscriptions, histories, 'world maps', ecclesiastical histories, chronicles, letters, coins and encyclopaedias from Classical and Late Antiquity, medieval and modern Palestine. For a millennium and a half of Classical Antiquity and Byzantine Christianity as well as under Islam in the Middle Ages the term Palestine also acquired official administrative status.

This book sets out to chart and explain the historical beginnings and ancient roots of the name 'Palestine' within the multifaith and shared settings of the country. It also presents a list of major ancient and medieval sources for and references to the name Palestine and to its cognates and manifestations in various Semitic and European languages – such as Peleset, Palashtu, Pilistu, Παλαιστίνη, Палестины, Palaistinē, Palaestina, Philistia, Filastin/فلسطين, פְּלִשְׁתִּים/Plishtim, פלשתינה, פלסטין – throughout the ancient, medieval and modern history of the region. Different Assyrian spellings are Pilishti, Pilishte, Palashtu, Pilishtu, Pilistu, Pilisti, Pilistin and Greek and Latin-Roman forms are: Palaistinê and Palaestia. The silver coinage of Philistia (Gaza, Ascalon, Ashdod) of late 600 and 500–400

BC (see below) shows that the process of peaceful and gradual 'Hellenisation' of Palestinian place names, which also became closely associated with cosmopolitanism, started long before the conquests of Alexander the Great in 332 BC. These processes were revived under and after Alexander, accelerated in Late Antiquity and lasted for 1000 years. The English name 'Palestine' comes from the Old French name Philistin, which comes from the classical Latin Philistinus (Palaestina) which in turn comes from the late classical Greek-speaking Philistinoi. Interestingly, the pronunciation of the medieval/modern Arabic toponyms Filastin (standard Arabic) and Falastin (vernacular Palestinian Arabic) are close to the Old French pronunciation, Philistin, and the classical Greek term Philistinoi.

The work also seeks to demonstrate how the name Palestine (rather than the term 'Cana'an') was most commonly and formally used in ancient history, in a wide range of sources including material evidence, toponymy, maps, coins produced 'in Palestine', famous texts and inscriptions from the Levant and the wider Mediterranean region. The book further argues that academic and school history curricula should be based on historical facts/empirical evidence/archaeological discoveries and evidence-based historical research – not on religious belief or Old Testament sacred narratives and religio-ideological myth-narratives (e.g. 'Israelites' conquest of Canaan') (Numbers 13: 1–16; Joshua 1:1–18; 2:1–5:15; 2:1–24; 3:1–17; 4:1–5:1; 6:1–12:24; 9:1–27; 10:1–43; 11:1–23).

FROM PALESTINE-FOCUSED BIBLICAL ORIENTALISM TO THE NEW HISTORIES OF ISRAEL

> No need to hear your voice when I can talk about you better than you can speak about yourself. No need to hear your voice. Only tell me about your pain. I want to know your story. And then I will tell it back to you in a new way. Tell it back to you in such a way that it has become mine, my own. Re-writing you I write myself anew. I am still author, authority. I am still colonizer the speaking subject and you are now at the center of my talk. (Hooks 1990: 243)

History and collective memory are often a tapestry of stories woven by social elites, with disregard for the voices of ordinary people and self-representation of the oppressed, colonised, indigenous and marginalised. Much of the histories of Palestine are written by powerful elites and those who are in the service of conquerors and colonisers. However, today there are three types of writings on Palestine influenced by three distinct traditions: (1) scriptural geography and Israeli settler-colonialist writings; (2) the discourses of the 'New Histories' of Israel in which the millennia-long history of Palestine is treated as a mere appendix to modern Israel; and (3) indigenous and decolonisation scholarship informed by a people's history of Palestine, 'history from below', subaltern studies, indigenous self-representation and the classical writings of Edward Said and Frantz Fanon on the coloniser and colonised. This work comes under the third category of writings. It prioritises giving Palestine and the Palestinians a voice and allowing Palestine to speak for itself. The other two discourses are challenged in this book:

- *Orientalist, biblicist and colonialist writings*: this literature of history/collective memory has been largely produced and circulated by Western or Israeli Zionist biblical geography on behalf of powerful social elites, with little regard for the autochthonous Palestinian agency and voices. Furthermore, obscuring the history of the country, historical approaches to Palestine are often constructed through the chronologies of empires and through imperial conquest or dynastic chronologies (Roman, Ottoman, British and so forth) and 'from without'. There is very little appetite among historians, often dependent on funding by powerful elites, to record the voice of Palestine 'from within', independent of biblical myth-narratives or imperial possession, or as having its own agency and shaping its own destiny.
- *The New Histories of 'Israel'*: the Zionist liberal coloniser has often sought to combine 'settler-colonisation' with 'democracy' – two contradictory projects – and this tendency has in recent decades contributed to the emergence of the 'New Histories' of Israel. These new histories have also been backed by the generously funded 'peace process' industry – an industry which has spawned 'new' academic elites, drawn for the most

part from the same powerful social classes, and repackaged discourses which have sought to subsume Palestine and obscure its millennia-long history of the country under the rubric of 'Israel-Palestine'. One of the most revealing aspects of this new peace industry of 'Israel-Palestine' is found in the much-hyphenated 'Israel-Palestine', with Israel constructed as a core (primary) political entity and Palestine as a (secondary, marginalised, subordinate) appendage to Israel. These New Histories of Israel are designed to micro-manage, rather than challenge, the impact of ongoing settler-colonialism in Palestine. This anachronism is deployed even when the entire work focuses on Ottoman Palestine (1516–1917) or Mandatory Palestine before the State of Israel came into existence. Israel itself was created in 1948 by ethnic cleansing the indigenous people of Palestine and founded on the ruins of a country. Works published on the history of Ottoman or Mandatory Palestine are often now packaged as 'New Histories' or 'New Perspectives' on Israel, without the liberal colonisers of these New Histories of Israel bothering to explain why a new state (Israel), which was created in 1948, should come before the name of a country (Palestine) which has existed for millennia. The Zionist New Histories of Israel often claim to 'speak for' and 'represent' everyone, while ignoring that the asymmetry of power and experiences of 'colonised' (Palestine) are fundamentally different from the experiences of the 'coloniser' (Israel). In a famous 1998 article in *Al-Ahram* online, entitled: 'New History, Old Ideas',[5] the late Edward Said challenged the Zionist 'New Histories' of Israel, which seek to create artificial symmetry between 'Israel' and 'Palestine' and, on the face of it, bridge the 'narrative gap' between the coloniser (Israel) and colonised (Palestine). In effect, however, the New Histories of Israel seek to represent Palestine and speak for the Palestinians, rather than allowing the indigenous people of Palestine to speak for themselves.

In his seminal work *The Invention of Ancient Israel: The Silencing of Palestinian History*, Keith Whitelam (1996) shows how the term 'ancient Israel' was invented as ahistorical religious dogma. He links the problems of the modern biblical discipline to the Palestine question and examines the political implications of the terminology of biblical scholarship chosen to represent this area. Whitelam shows how the naming of the land implied control and possession; how the religious term 'the land of Israel' – a late religio-literary fiction that does not relate to any particular period in the actual history of the land – has been invested with secular political meaning in both Western and Israeli scholarship. He also argues that in Western and Israeli biblical scholarship the term Palestine has no intrinsic meaning of its own, no history of its own; but provides a background for the history of Israel. Commensurate with this lack of history is also the absence of the indigenous Palestinian inhabitants of the land. The history of Palestine and its inhabitants in general is subsumed and silenced by the concern with, and the search for, 'ancient Israel' (Whitelam 1996: 40–45).

Inspired by the works of Edward Said, *Orientalism* (1978) and *The Question of Palestine* (1980), Whitelam argues powerfully that specific Palestine-focused biblical Orientalism have been part of and an extension of the hegemonic Orientalist discourse and representation in the West, which has been written without any 'Oriental' subject in view. For both Said and Whitelam, in this Orientalist–biblical discourse the local cultures of Palestine and Palestinians were presented as incapable of unified action or collective memory. Whitelam develops Said's arguments further, showing that the history of ancient Palestine has been ignored and silenced by the discourse of biblical studies, which has its own agenda: 'Western scholarship has invented ancient Israel and silenced Palestinian history' (Whitelam 1996: 1, 3). Ancient Palestine, Whitelam insists, has a history of its own, and needs to be freed from the grasp of romantic biblical Orientalism and scriptural geography:

> The problem of Palestinian history has remained unspoken within biblical studies, silenced by the invention of ancient Israel in the image of the European nation state. Only after we have exposed the implications of this invention will Palestinian history be freed from the constraints of biblical studies and the discourse that has shaped it. (Whitelam 1996: 36)

As we shall see below, modern romantic biblical Orientalism and Protestant Restorationism were two of the ideological catalysts for supporting

Zionism in the West and for backing the creation of the Israeli state. Specific Palestine-focused biblical Orientalism also led to the concoction of the pernicious myth that Palestine was 'a land without people for a people without land' and the long development of Christian Zionism laid the foundation for a concept of Palestine without Palestinians (Kamel 2014: 1–15, 2015; Masalha 1997). In the modern period, European writers adopted the *terra nullius* concept for territorial and colonial conquests. Variants on the theme of Palestine being *terra nullius* were popularised in Zionist Jewish settler culture (Wolfe 2006: 391; Masalha 1992, 1997).

Collective religious memory versus evidence-based history: polytheistic Palestine, pluralism and the archaeological evidence

In Palestine multifaith and polytheism went hand in hand and for millennia the country was a multifaith/polytheistic polity; the multitude of religions and cultures in Palestine is one of its most striking and characteristic features. This multitude of faiths in the country and the role of Palestine (and Arabia) as the birthplace of the three monotheistic traditions is a major topic of this work, which argues that religious pluralism has always been at the heart of the pluralist identity of Palestine, well before monotheism. Writing in the 5th century BC, Herodotus was the first historian to describe vividly a multifaith country located naturally (geographically) between Phoenicia and Egypt, and to denote a geographical region he called Palaistinê (Παλαιστίνη) which was larger than ancient Philistia. He also reported that Palestine was deeply polytheistic. Today the findings of archaeology, including recent archaeological excavations in Philistia, which are central to the ways in which the ancient history and heritage of Palestine are understood and taught in Western universities and schools, confirm Herodotus' account of polytheistic Palestine and contradict the grand narratives of the Old Testament. In fact monotheism evolved gradually (not in a revolutionary fashion) through a centring strategy of representation from polytheism (many pagan gods) to monolatrism,[6] and from 'mono-polytheism' (pagan 'God of gods') to strict monotheism, focusing on one God and one authority, under Islam in the early Middle Ages.

The terms holy 'Bible' and 'biblical' as signifiers meant different things to different people across the centuries. Today it is widely recognised that the 'Bible' is not a single book; it is a library of books. While Christianity distinguishes between two traditions, Old Testament and New Testament, the Quran identifies three distinct traditions, or holy books, associated with the Bible: the Tawrah (or Torah) attributed to Moses, the Injil, the Arabic name for what Muslims believe to have been the original Gospel of Jesus, and Zabur (or the Book of Psalms), attributed to David. The diversity of traditions and sources associated with the evolution of the 'Bible' is central to any scholarly understanding of the evolution of 'biblical' narratives.

Furthermore, the 'biblical' narratives are literary imagination, adaption, theology and officially sanctioned memory – not history. Its stories and narratives were derived from conventional wisdom, which was produced and circulated by educated elites and opinion formers of the time, which may or may not contain facts. Much of the new research on the Old Testament focuses on its Babylonian conventional wisdom and recreated Babylonian social memory (Masalha 2007), but also evidently recreated Greek religious memory, and Hellenistic imagination and representations are adapted in the stories of the Old Testament (Hjelm and Thompson 2016). The adaptation and reimagining of Hellenistic representations are also evident in the 'mono-polytheism' of the Old Testament. The impact of 'Hellenisation' on the literary imagination and representations of the Old Testament and the representation of the divine in the post-Alexander era should not be underestimated. Hellenistic allegorised representations had constructed a hierarchical pantheon of 'King of gods' – a supreme absolute deity (Zeus) at the head of 'twelve Olympian deities'. This pagan Greek 'mono-polytheism' was represented by Zeus as 'God of gods' ('Representation of representations'). The Greek term *theós* was later conflated with *deós* ('to the gods'), although etymologically the word is not related to Latin *deus*, which comes from a different root. However, in spite of these etymological differences, in Latin *deus* and *theos* became inescapably linked.

In the Christological debates and controversies of Late Antiquity, which hugely affected Palestine and the Near East, the predominantly Greek-speaking Orthodox Christianity adapted and reconceptualised that Hellenistic ideas about 'essence' and 'existence' as well as allegorised and analogous representations of divinity. These adaptations and representations were reflected in the Trinity, 'three individual persons in one nature', and in

Christology of the 'god-man', 'one person in two natures', and of Jesus born from a human mother. The Greek forerunner of this latter idea was Dionysus, son of Zeus. These complex Christian representations of divinity brought Aristotelian Maimonides (1138–1204) to contrast sharply with the purity and simplicity of monotheism in Islam in the Middle Ages. Under impact of the strict Oneness and Unity of God in the holy Quran, Maimonides came to believe that the doctrine of Trinity ('three persons in one nature') under-mined true monotheism. Interestingly, in modern times, under the impact of Quranic monotheism, Scottish Orientalist and scholar of Islam William Montgomery Watt came to interpret radically the 'three in one' idea of Trinity. Like the ninety-nine names/attributes of God in the Quran, Mont-gomery Watt believed the 'three in one' were not 'three individual persons on one nature', but three attributes, faces or personas of 'one' God.[7]

Race and ethnicity are problematic terms: they were both invented and constructed in modern times on the basis of myths, whether physical or national myths. There is no race without racism, while the myth of common ancestry is fundamental to the conception of ethnicity. Being Arab Jewish himself, Maimonides' conception of Judaism had nothing to do with the modern conception of race or ethnicity. His conception of Jewish identity is highly relevant to the multicultural notion of identity in historic Palestine and the analytical framework of this book. For Maimonides, Judaism was rooted in and based on faith; it had nothing to do with modern ideological constructs of race or ethnicity. Originally, being Jewish was one of the many regional identities within Palestine; it simply meant an inhabitant of Judaea. The latter derives from the name Judah which dates from the 8th century BC and refers to the region of the southern highlands, foothills and adja-cent steppe lands at some stage in the course of the 8th–early 6th century BC. The inhabitants of Judaea became associated with what subsequently became known as the 'Israelites', who, as a group, appeared in Assyrian inscriptions at one point in Iron Age II in the 9th–8th centuries BC.

For Maimonides, however, the ancient 'Israelites' were not a race or an ethnicity – but a community of faith. And in post-exilic Judaism, and for many centuries before and after Maimonides, being Jewish meant belonging to a community of faith, the Jewish faith. Things began to change ideologically and radically in the 19th century under the impact of European racial theories and social Darwinism, when being Jewish was reinvented into a racial identity. This racial framing of Jews persisted until the Nazi Holocaust. In the post-Holocaust era, and following the horrors of Nazism, being Jewish was reinvented again into a single ethnicity. Today the Arab Jews of Iraq, Morocco and the Yemen, together with the Amharic-speaking Falasha Jews of Ethiopia and the Russian, German and Polish Jews are all treated as having a single ethnicity, if not a single race, by the Israeli Zionist regime. In fact, until the advent of European Zionism, members of the Arabic-speaking Jewish minority of Palestine, known locally and fondly as 'the Jews sons of the Arabs' ('al-yahud awald al-'arab'), were an integral part of the Palestinian people and their Arabic language, culture and heritage – all of which are related to the heritage of Maimonides – and were also destroyed by the European Zionist settler elite. The double reinvention of the 'Jewish people' in the modern era is often overlooked by critical scholars, Shlomo Sand (2009) included (Masalha 2007). The relatively more recent ethnicisation of the Jewish people, often by Israeli and Zionist Jewish academics, is designed to homogenise multicultural and multi-ethnic Jewish identities, recasting it in a softer and more palatable – yet no less misleading – notion of historic Judaism than the racial theories of the 19th century (Masalha 2007). However, within the wider analytical framework of this work, being a Palestinian Jew (whether Aramaic- or Arabic-speaking), simply means being a member of the Jewish faith community in Palestine.

Furthermore, historically, holy mountains played a key role in the sacred histories of diverse religious traditions as well as in the mega-narratives of Greek and biblical divinities. Creative biblical social memory, conventional wisdom, reimagined traditions and recreated Hellenic representations also found their way into the collective religious memory of Palestine. Mount Olympus was notably known in Greek religion as the home of the Greek gods. This reimagined and reconfigured social memory is found in the imaginative Exodus story of the Ten Commandments and Mount Sinai. Mount Sinai (Quran: *Tur Sina*) is referred to in the Quran in several *surahs*, but the Quran does not assert its exact location. In the religio-social terminology of officially Greek-speaking Palestine of the 4th century AD Itabyrium ('Mount Tabor', the name based on Psalm 89:12) in Lower Galilee became the fixed site of the Transfiguration of Jesus tradition, a key story of the New Testament. However, for many centuries Itabyrium has been designated by the local Palestinian Muslims and Christians as Jabal al-Tur and this indigenous social toponymic memory is similar the Quranic designation of Tur Sina (Mount Sinai). As we shall see below, during the Byzantine era the region of Mount Sinai was part of the Byzantine province of *Palaestina Salutaris* (late 4th century to early 7th century). In indigenous toponymic social memory, 'al-Tur' ('mount' in Aramaic and Arabic) is a common designation of holy mountains in Palestine and the Quranic designation of 'Tur Sina' was probably aimed at differentiating this holy mountain from other holy mountains in Palestine. Jabal al-Tur is also a name used by Palestinians to refer to Mount Grezim near Nablus; al-Tur is also a Palestinian neighbourhood on the Mount of Olives (which is holy for Christians) in East Jerusalem located on a hill about 150 metres from the Old City. .

Religio-social memory and the Christological debates and controversies of Late Antiquity deeply affected Palestine and the whole Near East. These debates emerged from Christian Neo-Platonism – an influential Hellenistic tradition of philosophy that arose in the 3rd century AD, which was greatly influenced by Plato – and the attempt to synthesise Neo-Platonism with biblical (Old and New Testament) ideas. Founded by Plotinus (c. 204/5–270), Hellenistic Neo-Platonism conceived the derivation of the whole of reality from a single principle, 'the One'; hence the Christological doctrines of Jesus being 'Two in One' and the Trinity doctrine of 'Three in One'. Synthesising Platonic and Aristotelian notions, Neo-Platonism remained hugely influential throughout the Middle Ages and many of its ideas were integrated into the philosophical and theological traditions of some of the most important medieval Muslim, Jewish and Christian thinkers. With the evolution of strict monotheism in the Middle Ages, the rationalist Muslim philosophers, in particular, adhered to the principle of the reality of 'many' deriving from the single monotheistic principle of the Almighty (eternal, absolute) 'One' (or 'One in One').

Interestingly, however, the Septuagint, the first translation of some of the Old Testament stories, was made in the 3rd century BC in Koine Greek (the 'common dialect'), a prevalent language in Palestine and Egypt throughout this time. This translation survived in fragments. Koine Greek was a dominant language which was spoken and written during Hellenistic and Roman Antiquity and the Byzantine era of Late Antiquity. It had evolved from the spread of Greek following the conquests of Alexander the Great in the 4th century BC and had served as the lingua franca of much of the Mediterranean region and the Near East in the course of the following centuries. The Septuagint was aimed at Greek-speaking audiences. In it the term *Elohim* (plural for 'gods') in the Old Testament was rendered into Greek *theós* (Θεός), the supreme God at the top of the divine hierarchy. *Elohim* can be read in both monolatrist and Hellenistic mono-polytheistic ('representation of representations') terms. The allegorised Greek deity of 'twelve Olympian deities' headed by Zeus ('Twelve of One' or 'Twelve in One') were adapted and synthesised with Near Eastern legends and allegorised in the form of the stories of Genesis including the 'twelve sons of Jacob' and 'twelve tribes of Israel'.

Read in these evolutionary terms, representations of deity from polytheism to 'mono-polytheism' ('God of gods') to austere monotheism evolved out of the local cultures of ancient Palestine and the surrounding Near East (Gnuse 1997), but also under the impact of forms of Hellenisation in the regions. Adaptations of mono-polytheistic representation of deity continued to evolve in Palestine and the Near East many centuries after Herodotus had visited deeply polytheistic Palestine in the 5th century BC. As we shall see below, many aspects of polytheism and pagan temples can still be found in Late Antiquity Palestine – for instance, in Gaza in the early 5th century – a millennium after Herodotus had visited the country.

The Genesis story of Moses leading the 'Israelite tribes' from Egypt to 'Cana'an' is a late literary construct that does not necessarily relate to any historical period or actual, evidence-based history; but it is also central to the myth-narrative (and mega-narratives) of the Samaritan Pentateuch[8] and the Old Testament. There is also a distinct story of Moses (Arabic: *Musa*) in Egypt in the Quran (sura 19, Maryam, ayat 51–53). Medieval Islam admired the 'people of the book' (*ahl al-kitab*), adapted the classical traditions and developed its own strong and distinct tradition of bibliophilia: of book writing, book translation, calligraphy and libraries of knowledge. Its medievalist view of religious pluralism brought it to recognise formally the religious and social autonomy of four 'monotheistic' religious traditions:

Majusiyyah (Zoroastrianism) or Majus (Greek: *magos*; practitioners of Zoro-astrianism), Sabaeanism, Christianity and Judaism, and accorded them the status of autonomous and protected communities (*dhimis*); Samaritanism in Palestine was treated as a 'type' of Judaism and given the same status as an autonomous, protected community (al-Maqdisi 2002: 40). However, generally speaking, the Abrahamic traditions (Islam, Christianity, Samar-itanism and Judaism) have shared traditions as well as distinct narratives. Crucially the empirical archaeological and diverse historical evidence is different from elite 'sacred texts' or elite 'sacred collective memory' which produces 'one story from many' and allows a prosopography (group narra-tive) of power elites to emerge. In the last two centuries, ancient Egypt has been scientifically and systematically excavated (perhaps more than any other country on earth) and no empirical or archaeological evidence was uncovered to substantiate or validate this Old Testament story of Egypt. This does not mean that there was no Moses; it simply means there is no empirical historical evidence or facts to corroborate positively the Old Testa-ment Exodus text. Moreover, these elite narratives are interpreted today by theologians and biblical scholars using a variety of methods and the texts are read more as theology than as accurate history. Therefore, the collective 'sacred literature' is more likely to be taught today in academic departments or programmes of theology and biblical studies.

Also, crucially, after more than 150 years and thousands of biblical excavations carried out in and around the Old City of Jerusalem, there is still no material history or archaeological or empirical evidence for the 'Kingdom of David' from 1000 BC. The reason for the lack of any material or empirical evidence for the 'United Kingdom of David and Solomon' and other mega-narratives of the Old Testament is simple: these are invented traditions (Masalha 2007, 2013). The 'Kingdom of David' as a large and influential polity was probably based on a small tribal leader in Judaea – the latter is a name which appears in the Assyrian sources in the course of 8th–early 6th century BC. This lack of material or empirical evidence for a 'United Kingdom of David and Solomon' is almost univer-sally recognised by archaeologists in the West and also by some leading Israeli archaeologists. Broadly speaking, the collapse of the historicity of the events described in the Old Testament about the 'United Kingdom of

David and Solomon' – Iron Age II (around 1000 BC) – over the last four decades has been the result of two interrelated factors: empirical archaeological evidence, and critical textual and literary criticism (Masalha 2007; Sturgis 2001; Thompson 1992, 1999, 2003).

Material histories and the archaeological revolution (or paradigm shift) of recent decades centres on the ancient history of Palestine (Masalha 2007: 241–262) and the new ways in which this history should be read independent of Old Testament stories by scholars and history students alike. Zeev Herzog (Professor of Archaeology at Tel Aviv University, and the Director of its Institute of Archaeology from 2005 to 2010), in an article in the weekly magazine *Haaretz* entitled 'Deconstructing the walls of Jericho', wrote:

> Following 70 years of intensive excavations in the Land of Israel, archaeologists have found out: The patriarchs' acts are legendary, the Israelites did not sojourn in Egypt or make an exodus, they did not conquer the land. Neither is there any mention of the empire of David and Solomon, nor of the source of belief in the God of Israel. These facts have been known for years, but Israel is a stubborn people and nobody wants to hear about it. (Herzog 1999: 6–8)

Herzog went on to explain that the empirical and critical archaeology of modern Palestine has shown that the Old Testament narratives of 'Exodus' and 'Joshua's conquest of Cana'an' could not have happened:

> This is what archaeologists have learned from their excavations in the Land of Israel: the Israelites were never in Egypt, did not wander in the desert, did not conquer the land in a military campaign and did not pass it on to the 12 tribes of Israel. Perhaps even harder to swallow is the fact that the united monarchy of David and Solomon, which is described by the Bible [Old Testament] as a regional power, was at most a small tribal kingdom. And it will come as an unpleasant shock to many that the God of Israel, Jehovah [Yahweh], had a female consort [see below] and that the early Israelite religion adopted monotheism only in the waning period of the monarchy and not at Mount Sinai. Most of those who are engaged in scientific work in the

interlocking spheres of the Bible, archaeology and the history of the Jewish people – and who once went into the field looking for proof to corroborate the Bible story – now agree that the historic events relating to the stages of the Jewish people's emergence are radically different from what that story tells. (Herzog 1999: 6–8; see also Sturgis 2001)

The Old Testament is not actual history but imaginative fiction, theology, sacred literature, ethics and wisdom. The Jewish contribution to the multi-faith, pluralist heritage and long history of Palestine is undeniable. But the genres of fiction and storytelling of the Old Testament may or may not contain some historical facts. Herzog argues that the archaeology of Palestine has completed a process that amounts to a scientific revolution in its field; archaeology – which has become an independent professional discipline with its own conclusions and its own observations – presents us with a picture of a reality of ancient Palestine completely different from the one which is described in the Old Testament. Palestine archaeology is no longer using the Old Testament as a reference point or a historical source; the biblical archaeology is no longer the ruling paradigm in Palestine archaeology. For the critical archaeologists, the Bible is read as literature which may or may not contain some historical information (Herzog 1999: 6–8; 2001: 72–93).

Although academic departments of theology will continue to teach and explore these distinct narratives of Solomon and David in the Old Testament and the Quran, today, as a result of more than 150 years of critical biblical scholarship and critical archaeological excavations, there are very few archaeologists or historians in the West who treats these stories literally or as actual 'historical facts' (Masalha 2007, 2013).

Interestingly the diverse Abrahamic prophetic traditions of the Old Testament, New Testament and the Quran all argue that the ideology of 'kingship' (*malchoot* in Old Testament Hebrew, *malakut*, from the verb *malak* 'to own' in Quranic Arabic) belongs to the 'One Almighty God'. The claim by mainstream biblical scholars that 'absolute kingship' was in theocratic form in 'Israel' under Saul, David, Solomon and their successors is ahistorical and completely unfounded. The Old Testament stories of Saul, David and Solomon are imagined traditions (fiction, literary invention and theology) not proven historical facts. The primary aim of these post-exilic literary invention and fictional stories (about the 'kingdom' of Saul, David and Solomon) was to construct ideo-political and theocratic justification and legitimisation for the (originally Persian Šahanšah, 'King of Kings', or Emperor) idea of 'absolute kingship'. Interestingly, the Gospel of John's hierarchical Hellenistic representation of this theo-political doctrine of 'absolute kingship' is to argue that Jesus of Nazareth is 'King of Kings', the 'Son of God' and 'King of the Judaeans' (John 19: 3). The Quranic representation of this debate is to reject the Trinitarian notion that Jesus is divine or the literal 'Son of God' (Quran 4: 171–172). The Quran furthermore narrates that Jesus was backed by Ruh al-Quds (the 'sacred spirit') and was a human prophet; 'kingship' (*malakut*) belongs exclusively to the 'One Almighty God', not to humans. The Islamic Caliphate, therefore, began as a non-monarchical tradition, but often developed into a hereditary form of government. It rejected absolute monarchy and vested political legitimacy in the *Jama'a* (group or people) – in principle a form of Islamic social and political pluralism.

The strict monotheistic theology of the Quran further teaches that the 'One Almighty (Maximum Absolute) God' has sent messengers and prophets to humanity, at different times and places, to communicate His message. There are twenty-five prophets and messengers (all men) mentioned by name in the Quran. All, in essence, are equal and all taught the message that the Quran communicated to Prophet Muhammad, known to Muslims as the 'Holy Prophet' and the last prophet sent by God to mankind. The Quran and Islamic traditions link Prophet Muhammad and several prophets (messengers) – Ibrahim (Abraham), Musa (Moses), Dawud (David), Suleiman (Solomon), Jesus ('Isa) – directly and indirectly to Palestine and to al-Quds (Aelia Capitolina/Iliya/Bayt al-Maqdis/Jerusalem) in particular. The Quran and the theological traditions of Islam offered an inclusive, multi-religious representation of the shared heritage of Jerusalem.

While many evangelical Christian fundamentalists (mostly in the US and some in Europe) and Zionists (both Christians and Jews) continue to read these biblical stories literally, today mainstream academics who teach Old Testament and biblical studies in the West tend to treat these stories metaphorically and allegorically or as 'sacred literature' or 'sacred texts', while historians and archaeologists treat them as literature and social memory which evolved across many centuries, rather than as actual accurate history.

Evidence-based history – unlike officially sanctioned sacred literature – requires a scientific approach, critical thinking, empirical and material evidence and accurate facts. Scholarly approaches to history require proven evidence, 'facts' or refutation. Scholarly historical research should not be conflated or equated automatically with 'sacred literature' or with specific religious beliefs and traditions. Religious traditions often evolved from social memory and across many generations. The Old Testament mega-narratives, in particular, were often derived from the evolving oral traditions and from the repackaging of Near Eastern epics and legends such as Gilgamesh rather than being accurate historical events of the past. While the beliefs and religious sensitivities of Muslims, Christians and Jews should be respected and people are entitled to their beliefs and religious traditions, critical scholarship and academic and school history curricula and textbooks should be grounded in scientific research, critical methodology, historical facts and evidence-based historical and archaeological research on ancient Palestine – not on meta-narratives or religious-ideological orientations.

Furthermore, it can be shown empirically and based on material and documentary evidence that the name Palestine is continuously and uninterruptedly found in ancient, medieval and modern histories and historical sources, including: (a) ancient Egyptian and Assyrian inscriptions and texts (Assyrian: Palashtu, Pilistu, Palastu, Pa-la-as-ta-a-a); (b) classical Greek texts and literature (Παλαιστίνη); (c) Roman and Byzantine administrative divisions of the region and sources (Palaestina); (d) medieval Arabic and Islamic Arabic sources on Palestine; (e) modern Hebrew (Peleshtina); (f) and all modern European languages and sources.

The ancient history and heritage of Palestine are the study of the past in the region of Palestine generally defined as a geographic region in Western Asia between the Mediterranean Sea, the Jordan River and the Red Sea. Palestine is the name most commonly used from the Late Bronze Age (from 1300 BC onwards) to the modern period to describe this distinct geographic region between the Mediterranean Sea, the Red Sea and the Jordan River and various adjoining lands.

The region of Palestine was among the earliest in the world to see human habitation, agricultural communities, material civilisation and eventually sophisticated urbanisation in the Early Bronze Age. With the beginning of the Middle Stone Age (Mesolithic period) in about 12,000 BC humans in Palestine began to raise animals and farm the land. The Neolithic period consolidated agricultural practices in Palestine, in Jericho, circa 11,000–8800 BC. The modern Palestinian city of Jericho is believed to be one of the oldest continuously inhabited cities in the world, with archaeological evidence of settlement dating back to 9000 BC, providing important information about early human habitation in the Middle East.

It is widely recognised by historians and archaeologists that Palestine had a remarkably stable population from the end of the Neolithic period, some 6000 years ago, when the Mediterranean economy was first established in the region. In the 1980s biblical scholars Thomas Thompson (Copenhagen University), Francolino Goncalvez and Jean-Marie van Cangh (1988) completed a pilot toponymic project on two regions in Palestine, the Plain of Akka (Acre) and the Jerusalem Corridor, which was published in 1988 in a monograph entitled *Toponomie Palestinienne*. This study brought out the many names of hills, *wadis*, springs and wells, but only those on maps. However, this project was limited in its scope and has not directly worked with the oral tradition. Thomas Thompson's works *Bronze Age Settlements of Sinai and the Negev* (1975) and *The Bronze Age Settlements of Palestine* (1979) have a very useful list of antiquity sites with the corresponding modern Arabic names (see also Ra'ad 2010).

Furthermore, the *Tubingen Bible Atlas* (2001), based on the *Tubingen Atlas of the Near East* (TAVO), documents the ancient historical and cultural geography of Palestine in a unique way in twenty-nine high quality maps and extensive indices. Although the question of the Arab Muslim heritage of Palestine in the toponymic memory of the region is one which the *Tubingen Bible Atlas* project never took up directly, many maps of Palestine in the *Tuebinger Bible Atlas* and TAVO archives are important historical and geographical sources on ancient Palestine. More recently, Salman Abu-Sitta's *Atlas of Palestine 1917–1966* (2010) also provides useful maps and indices on the modern Palestinian Arabic place names of the region.

On the theme of the charting of maps and the production and dissemination of knowledge on Palestine in the medieval and ancient periods, Robert North's *A History of Biblical Map Making* (1979) is an important source. North's volume on early historical maps of Palestine had its basic foundation in the archives of the Vatican library, Rome. In addition, there are some cartographic materials on Palestine in the libraries of Istanbul. There are three kinds of maps:

- Maps such as the Carte Jacotin; The British Mandate map 1:20.000; the Map of Israel 1:10.000 (although many sheets are classified secret by the Israeli military) and 1:50.000 (this entire map (including Sinai) has been declassified.
- Scholarly geographically and historically analytical maps, such as those in the Atlas of Israel 1967 and other atlas studies such as Salman Abu-Sitta's *Atlas of Palestine 1917-1966* (2010).
- The TÁVO maps, both the A and B series.

POLITICAL AUTONOMY, INDEPENDENCE AND STATEHOOD IN PALESTINE OVER THE LAST THREE MILLENNIA

Conventional wisdoms are often articulated by powerful elites; they are not always based on facts. The conventional wisdom is that Palestine never in its history experienced self-government, political or cultural autonomy, not to mention practical sovereignty and actual statehood. Nothing is further from the truth. As we shall amply demonstrate in this work, over three millennia from the late Bronze Age and until the establishment of the Israeli state in 1948, Palestine enjoyed a great deal of social, political and economic autonomy and also experienced statehood through six distinct, though not mutually exclusive, ways – ways which had a profound impact on the evolution of the ideas of Palestine across the millennia:

- *Autonomous economic and monetary systems and the issuing of Palestinian currency*: the institution of independent monetary policies and the minting of distinct Palestinian currency were evident in the cases of the coinage of Philistia or Philisto-Arabian in the 6th–4th centuries BC (discussed in chapter one) and the minting of Arab currency 'in Filastin' throughout early Islam (discussed in chapter six).

- *Imperial patron–protégé systems*: the construction of patron–client systems and the rise of local and autonomous regional and urban elites in Palestine, as was in the case of the 'urban notables' of Ottoman Palestine. But ultimately, as we shall see in chapter eight, these Ottoman urban elites in Palestine were rule-takers not rule-makers and rule-breakers.

- *Administrative, provincial and military autonomy*: this is evident throughout the Roman and Byzantine periods in what became widely known as *Provincia Palaestina* or the Dux Palaestinae, the 'military commander of Palestine' (discussed in chapter four), *Mutawalli Harb Filastin* ("متولي حرب فلسطين", Military Governor of Palestine) (discussed in chapter six) and in late Ottoman period Palestine with the creation of the autonomous administrative Mutasarrifate of Jerusalem as the key province of Palestine (discussed in chapter nine).

- *Palestinian client states*: the emergence and creation of several Palestinian client states, partly based on the same patron–client relationships. Although the types of client states in Palestine and the degree of their subordination to imperial or powerful states varied significantly, the kings of Philistia throughout much of the Iron Age, the client King Herod the Great under the Romans in the 1st century AD (discussed in chapter four), the Ghassanid tribal Arab federate kings (supreme phylarchs) of Palaestina Secunda, Palaestina Prima and Palaestina Tertia in the 6th and early 7th centuries (discussed in chapter five) and to a lesser extent the autonomous regime of Ahmad Pasha al-Jazzar in the 18th century were cases in point.

- *Palestinian practical sovereignty and statehood*: this was achieved by Daher al-ʿUmar following his successful rebellion against Ottoman rule in the middle of the 18th century (discussed in chapter eight).

- *Ecclesiastical independence and autocephaly*: this was achieved by the Church of Aelia Capitolina and Provincia Palaestina from the mid-5th century following the Council of Chalcedon (discussed in chapter four).

In addition to all the above arguments and distinctions already made, seventeen points are central to the argumentation of this work on the evolution of the conception of Palestine across time:

1. Before the Late Bronze period (before 1300 BC) we have names of towns, but none for the particular (Palestine) region as a whole, although the name 'Cana'an' (*ka-na-na, kinahhu*) does occur earlier, in the Late Bronze Age in New Kingdom inscriptions (1400s BC) and in the cuneiform tablets known as the Amarna Letters. The latter primarily consisted of diplomatic correspondence spanning thirty years between the Egyptian administration and its representatives in 'Cana'an' and Amuru (north-western Syria and north Lebanon) during the New Kingdom of Egypt.

2. 1350s–1330s BC: in the inscriptions of this period the name Cana'an refers primarily to the northern coastal regions of Lebanon, much as it is used in 5th century Greek texts and later. In the Late Bronze age, the normal name for the region of Palestine in Egyptian texts is not Cana'an, but Djahi, which is used to designate the southern part of the greater region of Tehenu.

3. It is true that the name Peleset first occurs in the 13th century BC and is not witnessed in any earlier historical source. So it would be historically inaccurate to use the name Palestine for the region before the 13th century. However, to be historically accurate one should point out that the name of the region of Palestine prior to the Late Bronze Age is simply unknown.

4. From the Late Bronze Age onwards, the names used for the region of the southern Levant, such as Djahi and Retenu or Cana'an, *all* gave way to the name Palestine, the name which thereafter is the most commonly used throughout ancient history and Classical Antiquity,[9] as well as in the period of Byzantine Christianity.

5. No other early toponym from the Late Bronze Age, such as (a) Retenu (1500s–1200s BC); (b) Djahi (1500s–1200s BC); or (c) Cana'an (1400s–1300s), is used as the name of the region in the Iron Age I (c. 1200–1000 BC) and later. One or other form of the name Palestine is used from the 12th century BC through the Roman period. This is

also the most common name for this region from the end of the 18th century AD to the present, which includes the British Mandate period, when Palestine was the internationally recognised name of the country. No other historically known toponym is used. One perhaps should also point out the 'official' administrative toponym of Provincia Palaestina, which was consolidated in Classical and Late Antiquity and revived officially in the modern period.

6. The toponymic use of the name Judah dates from the 8th century and refers to the region of the southern highlands, foothills and adjacent steppe lands *only* at some stage in the course of 8th–early 6th century BC. Similarly, the name Israel exists first in the 9th century BC and is used until the 4th quarter of the 8th century BC, when this name gives way to the name of the Assyrian province of Samerina.

7. The modern conception of Palestine as a geo-political unit and a distinct country is deeply rooted in the ancient history, culture and material and intellectual heritage of the land. Already in the course of the Iron Age (1200 to the Assyrian conquest of 712 BC) Philistia evolved not only into a distinct political geography but also as a separate geo-political entity. This fact would have a long-term impact on the evolution of the ancient, medieval and modern representations of Palestine.

Palestine as a country (*balad* or *bilad*) with a distinct history, physical and cultural geography, evolving boundaries, shifting capital cities (al-Quds/Aelia Capitolina/Iliya/Jerusalem, Caesarea-Palaestina, al-Ramla-Filastin), regional capitals (Gaza, Tiberias, Scythopolis/ Beisan, Safad, Acre, Nablus) existed for millennia; a country may or may not be a sovereign state; Palestine as a country (like Scotland, Wales, Catalonia, Andalus/Andalusia, Kurdistan, the Basque region, Chechnya or Kashmir) should not be automatically conflated or equated with modern Palestinian nationalism or any modern national representations of the 'nation-state of Palestine'.

8. Archaeological evidence shows that urbanisation and most of the Palestine towns and cities that are known in historic times existed throughout the Early Bronze Age in the 3rd millennium.[10] Moreover, while ancient literature and the physical remains of cities in Late Antiquity attest to the power that urban cultures held over the lives of their inhabitants

as well as over the rural communities in which the majority of people lived, archaeological excavations demonstrate the continuing interdependence of urban centres and rural contexts.

9. Historical evidence indicates that the toponymically Hellenised Palestinian cities of the Byzantine era: Caesarea Maritima (Arabic: Qaysariah), Aelia Capitolina (Jerusalem; Arabic: liya, al-Quds) Lydda (Greek: Diospolis/Georgiopolis), Beisan (Greek: Scythopolis), Gaza, Tiberias, Nablus (Greek: Neapolis), Jaffa, Arsuf (Greek: Apollonia) 'Amwas (Emmuas), Rafah, Beit Jibrin (Greek: Eleutheropolis), Acre (Greek: Ptolemais), Ascalon (Arabic: 'Asqalan), Aelas (Arabic: Aylah modern-day 'Aqabah) continued to function as major urban centres under Islam and some kept their ancient place names. Andrew Petersen's *The Towns of Palestine under Muslim rule: AD 600–1600* (2005), which focuses on urban sites from Byzantine to early Ottoman times, provides important archaeological evidence about the continuities and recycling of material objects and art forms in urban regeneration and development. Petersen's study also includes a detailed investigation of al-Ramla, which was founded by the Umayyads within the first century of Muslim rule, and cites the archaeological discovery of Byzantine-style mosaics and motifs in the city. Interesting also are the architectural forms of early urban Islamic Palestine: in Jerusalem, Jericho Hisham Palace (Khirbat al-Mafjar), al-Ramla and Khirbet al-Minyar, near Tiberias; all exhibit continuities and an exquisite mélange of Islamic and Greco/Roman/Byzantine styles and modes of organisation. The adaption of ideas and art forms from Late Antiquity Palaestina continued under Islam throughout the Middle Ages and this was combined with new Islamic architectural forms, thus creating a mix of Islamic and Greco/Roman/Byzantine styles. The recycling of ideas, material objects and art forms of ancient Palestine persisted into the modern period. For instance, some of the building materials, marble and granite components, for the spectacular White Mosque of Acre, famously known as al-Jazzar Mosque – constructed in 1781, with a complex which included an Islamic theological academy with student lodging, an Islamic court and a public library – were taken from the ancient ruins of medieval Acre, Caesarea-Palestina of Late Antiquity and Castello Pelegrino

(Atlit fortress), to the south of Haifa, one of the largest fortresses built in Palestine by the Latin Crusaders in 1218 and one of the best examples of Crusader military architecture. Modelled on the great mosques of Istanbul, the al-Jazzar Mosque (also known as the 'White Mosque') is a wonderful example of the mixture of styles, Ottoman, Byzantine Palestinian and Persian, incorporating and recycling the extraordinarily rich martial and cultural heritage of Palestine.

10. Until the modern era and the conception of Mandatory Palestine (1918–1948) the perception of what constituted Palestine's eastern boundaries was shifting, although in the course of the classical age and under Islam the boundaries of Palestine often extended to areas lying east of the Jordan River.

11. The classical, post-classical, medieval (Arab Islamic) and modern conceptions of Palestine all went far beyond the original 'land of the Peleset' (*pi-lis-te*, or Pilistu, 'from Gaza to Tantur') of the Late Bronze Age and Iron Age.

12. Seafaring and international trade routes in Palestine and the highly sophisticated urban coastal centres of Philistia (which included Gaza, Ascalon, Ashdod and Jaffa) combined to develop geo-politically as an integrated south in the course of Iron Age II (c. 1000–600 BC) and Philistia was the first to develop political autonomy and an autonomous monetary system in Palestine in the form of silver coins, issued in the late 6th, 5th and 4th centuries BC. This local Palestinian currency, known as the coinage of Philistia, was circulated widely in the Philisto-Arabian region and became known as Philisto-Arabian coins.

13. The official conversion of the Eastern Roman Empire to Christianity in the 4th century and the massive spread of Christianity in the Near East and Roman Provincia Arabia brought about religious, social, intellectual and cultural transformation of the country and the creation of greater Palestine (Provincia Palaestina). At its greatest extent in Late Antiquity, greater Palestine under the Byzantines (from the 4th to the early 7th centuries) was divided into three provinces: Palaestina Prima, Palaestina Secunda and Palaestina Salutaris. But as we shall see below, these were not seen as three totally separate provinces. Politically, militarily, culturally and ecclesiastically they were conceived and

continued to evolve under the Byzantines as 'Three in One' Palestine provinces. With time the (One in Three) Provincial Palaestina under the Byzantines was seen and, indeed, consciously constructed – militarily-strategically, politically and religiously – as a core province: Palaestina Prima, surrounded to the east and south by two 'frontier provinces', Palaestina Secunda and Palaestina Tertia (Palaestina Salutaris). A 'frontier province', Palaestina Salutaris was created in the southern Transjordan in the late 4th century and from the 5th century also became known as Palaestina Tertia. The names Palaestina Tertia and Palaestina Salutaris became interchanged and some documents refer to Petra as the metropolis of 'Third Palestine Salutaris' (Ward 2008: 93). The Third Palestine also encompassed the former Roman Provincia Arabia. The three Palestine provinces included the Naqab (Negev), Beersheba (Bir Sabi'), Nabataea (and its capital Petra) and major parts of Sinai. This greater Palestine also included large parts of Transjordan in the east and the Golan plateau in the north. This was a period of great prosperity and urban expansion, with Palestinian cities such as Aelia Capitolina (Jerusalem), Gaza, Neapolis (Nablus), Caesarea-Palaestina (also known as Caesarea Maritima; Qaysariah), a thriving seaport and the imperial capital of the province of Palaestina Prima, being built. Palestinian social and religious urban centres acquired a great deal of political and religious autonomy and projected classicising cultural influences throughout the Mediterranean region. Scythopolis (later Arab Beisan), the capital of Palaestina Secunda, and Eleutheropolis (Beit Jibrin) reached their peak in population in the course of Late Antiquity, and the diverse population of the 'Three Palestines' may have reached as many as one and a half million.

14. Greater Palestine (the three provinces of Byzantine Palaestina) of the 4th–early 7th centuries AD became a major centre of cultural and intellectual renaissance and classicising in Late Antiquity. The two most famous symbols of classicising Palaestina were the Rhetorical School of Gaza and the Library of Caesarea Maritima, the most extensive ecclesiastical library of Late Antiquity. Caesarea Maritima and Gaza were the two most important cities of Palaestina Prima, which was effectively the dominant political and cultural centre of greater Palestine. As we shall

see below, the 'Three Palestine' provinces had a great deal of religious and cultural autonomy and the All Palestine Church of Aelia Capitolina (Jerusalem) achieved independence from both Churches of Antioch and Constantinople. It was not only one of the most economically prosperous countries in the Mediterranean region, but also – with the highly influential Mediterranean schools of Gaza and Caesarea-Palaestina and the architectural and urban planning work of Julian of Ascalon – one of the most important centres of learning and intellectual activity in Late Antiquity; in effect, Caesarea-Palaestina and Gaza superseded and replaced both Athens and Alexandria as the premier centres of learning for the whole Mediterranean region.

15. In the 3rd–early 7th centuries AD large parts of the 'Three Palestines' were settled by the Ghassanid Arab population that immigrated from Arabia; the Palestine ecclesia integrated these Ghassanid Arabs and large parts of these provinces were gradually transformed in the 5th–6th centuries into Ghassanid Arab phylarchates, or 'frontier kingdoms', under Byzantine patronage and indirect imperial control. Ghassanid influence on Provincia Palaestina lasted for centuries, and their Christian Arab kings (supreme phylarchs) reined until the Islamic conquest of Palestine in the 7th century.

16. Unlike the six regional and neighbouring countries – Egypt, Syria, Iraq, Arabia, Turkey and Iran – throughout its history Palestine never produced empires or mighty imperial cities, although its history was hugely shaped by powerful empires. Its Patriarchs in Late Antiquity became part of the Pentarchy, the five major Patriarchs governing the churches of the Byzantine Empire, largely due to the unique status of the holy city of Jerusalem. As a Mediterranean country, strategically located between Asia, Africa and Europe, and between the Mediterranean Sea and Red Sea, Palestine managed to flourish culturally and economically and achieve a degree of autonomy by relying largely on its soft power: its holy places, academies and libraries (famous examples are the Rhetorical School of Gaza and the Library of Caesarea-Palaestina). Its ability to accommodate and integrate multiple social and cultural groups and its successful synthesis of diverse traditions and a variety of styles became central to its identity.

17. In contrast with the European Zionist settler-colonial project, which is based on old legends and new Social Darwinism – of 'iron walls' and 'survival of the fittest', of the appropriation and erasure of indigenous heritage of the country (see chapter ten) – Palestine and its local heritage have survived across more than three millennia through adaption, fluidity and transformation. The continuities, ruptures, adaption, re-adaption and metamorphosis of Palestine (from Philistia to Palaestina to Filastin) are also exhibited in the medieval Arabic name Philistin (Filastin), which preserved the Latin Philistina or Philistinus, deriving from ancient Philistia – which gave rise to the Roman administrative name of Provincia Palaestina – in turn based on the ancient name preserved in a variety of ancient languages, the Akkadian (Babylonian) Palastu and Egyptian Parusata/Peleset.

FROM THE GEO-POLITICAL TERM PALESTINE TO THE CONCEPT OF PALESTINE: CARTOGRAPHY, PLACE NAMES AND SOCIAL MEMORY

For practical reasons, the historical evolution of *terms and place names* often precedes and follows the evolutions of *concepts*. Although the geo-political term *Palestine* can be traced to the late Bronze Age and the indigenous Philistines, the consolidation of the concept of Palestine can be traced to Herodotus and other Greek historians, ethnographers and geographers of Classical Antiquity. This study intends to link Bronze Age Palestine and Classical Antiquity Palestine with modern times and explore the etymology of Palestine toponyms – the term derives from the Greek words *topos* ('place') and *onoma* ('name') – and their changes through and across time. Modern Palestinian collective memory and place names have evolved from the Neolithic Age into the modern period by embracing multiple traditions and preserving the shared and multi-layered heritage of the land. In a largely peasant society with one of the most fertile lands in the Fertile Crescent, many Palestinian Arab toponyms were based on plant foods (such as varieties of beans, lentils), fruit trees (olive, fig, vine) and natural geographical sites (hills, meadows, springs, streams, *wadis*, valleys and mountains).

By and large the names of Palestinian villages and towns were very stable, but names of provinces and districts were evolving.

Palestine is found on the earliest known world maps beginning with Late Antiquity and the famous 'word map' of Claudius Ptolemy (100–c. 170 AD). Of course, cartography is a practical science and since Ptolemy produced a map of the world known to Hellenistic society in the 2nd century cartography has never been about 'objective' representation of reality. In the Middle Ages cartography was developed by Muslim geographers such as al-Khawarizmi and deployed in the service of the Abbasid state and for practical purposes such as international Muslim trade, navigation and pilgrimage. In modern times cartography and renaming were also central to expanding European trade and empire-building (Bassett 1994: 316–335).

Place names (including human settlements such as villages, towns, cities, streets and countries and natural places such as mountains, hills, valleys, rivers, springs and *wadis*) are meant 'to provide clues as to the historical and cultural heritage of places and regions' (Kearns and Berg 2002: 284). Yet in reality place names are not just spatial references; they are rooted in power relations and struggles over land and resources and the identities of the people that inhabit these places (Kearns and Berg 2002). Struggles over land, toponyms, naming and renaming between indigenous peoples and settler-colonists are common. Examples include Zimbabwe (Rhodesia), Islas Malvinas (the Falkland Islands), Istanbul (Constantinople), Northern Ireland (Ulster; the Six Counties), Azania (South Africa), Aotearoa (New Zealand), Palestine (Israel), al-Quds (Jerusalem) (Masalha 2007, 2012, 2013; Benvenisti 2002; Zerubavel 1995, 1996; Yacobi 2009; Gann 1981; Nyangoni 1978; Abu El-Haj 2001; Ra'ad 2010; Berg and Kearns 1996; Berg and Vuolteenhaho 2009; Nash 1999; Housel 2009; Kadmon 2004). In modern times the drive to rename geographical sites is also about staking claims to a country. This focus on place names in the context of nationalism shows how hegemonic political elites and state authorities use the toponymic process as a way of constructing a new collective memory and 'inventing traditions' (Hobsbawm and Ranger 1996) and as a tactic of land-grabbing as well as an ideological reversion to a supposedly ancient or mythical 'golden age'. State authorities deploy renaming strategies to erase earlier political, social and cultural realities and to construct new notions of national identity (Guyot and Seethal 2007; Nash 1999; Azaryahu and Kook 2002; Azaryahu 1996, 1997).

In view of the Zionist ethnic cleansing of most of Palestine in 1948 and the current reality of coloniser/colonised in the country, the liberal Zionist slogan that the history of modern Palestine centres on the idea of 'one land, two peoples' rings hollow. The asymmetry of power in Palestine informs the works of nearly all Israeli 'New Historians'. This work, by contrast, challenges this 'Zionist nationalism'-based perspective and argues for decolonising methodologies; this work argues that the nationalism perspective serves to camouflage the heart of the conflict in Palestine; it argues further that at the heart of the question of Palestine is the vastly asymmetrical conflict between an eliminationist European settler-colonialist movement, backed by major Western powers (first Britain and now the US), and the indigenous people of Palestine. Furthermore, place-naming cartography and state-sponsored explorations were central to the modern European conquest of the earth, empire-building and settler-colonisation projects, the Zionist enterprise included. Scholars often assume that place names provide clues to the historical and shared heritage of places and regions. This work uses social memory theory to analyse the cultural politics of place-naming in Israel. Drawing on Maurice Halbwachs' study of the construction of social memory by the Latin Crusaders and Christian medieval pilgrims, the work shows Zionists' toponymic strategies in Palestine: their superimposition of Old Testament and Talmudic toponyms was designed to erase the local Palestinian and Arab Islamic heritage of the country. In the pre-Nakba period Zionist toponymic schemes utilised 19th century Western explorations of Old Testament 'names' and 'places' and appropriated Palestinian toponyms. Following the ethnic cleansing of Palestine in 1948 and the ruptures of the Nakba, the Israeli state, now in control of 78 per cent of the land, accelerated its toponymic project and pursued methods whose main features were memoricide. Continuing into the post-1967 occupation, these colonial methods continue to threaten the destruction of the diverse cultural and historic heritage of the land.

The toponyms of historic Palestine derive from a wide range of sources, including Phoenician, Philistine, Aramaic, Greek, Hebrew and Arabic –

toponyms which are representative of the multi-layered cultural identity of Palestine. The social and cultural importance of toponymic memory and geographical rendering of sites and terms in historical writing is evident in many histories from antiquity, medieval and modern Palestine. One classical example is the listing of the name of ancient Palestine in *Histories* (or *The History*, 1987) by Herodotus, written from the 450s to the 420s BC. Herodotus is believed to have visited Palestine in the fifth decade of the 5th century BC. Like the classical tradition of Greek and Roman historiography, Herodotus' work put the greatest value on oral testimony for contemporary history (Robinson, C. 2003: 26). Herodotus was the first historian to denote a geographical region he called Palaistinê (Παλαιστίνη), which was far wider than ancient Philistia. He refers to Palestine or 'Syria', or simply 'Palaistinê', five times, meaning an area encompassing the distinct region between Phoenicia and Egypt (Rainey 2001; Jacobson 1999). Herodotus also mentions the city of Ascalon (Akkadian: Isqalluna; Greek: Ascalon; Arabic: 'Asqalan; Latin: Ascalonia; Hebrew: Ashkelon), a great ancient seaport city which dates back to the Neolithic Age. At the time of Herodotus Palestine was deeply polytheistic and consequently, in contrast to the myth-narratives of the Bible, Herodotus does not mention Jews or monotheism but describes Ascalan as having a temple for Aphrodite and its polytheistic tradition. Although Herodotus' *Histories* is now considered a founding work of history in Western literature, and serves as a key record of the ancient traditions, politics, geography and clashes of various powers that were known in Greece, Western Asia and North Africa, when it comes to Palestine and toponymic memory Western Christian writing relies not on Herodotus' *Histories* but on the myth-narratives of the Bible. Interestingly, however, the Greek toponym for Palestine and Ascalan were preserved in indigenous Palestinian Arab tradition and by medieval Arab historians, geographers and travellers, and 'Ascalon' became known to the Palestinian Arabs from the 7th century as 'Asqalan'.

The emphasis of this work is on the indigenous (individual and collective) agency and the ability of the peoples of Palestine to borrow, adapt, shape and transform outside influences and their own environment. Consequently, the superficial use of the term 'Hellenisation' in Palestine is problematic. This uncritical use marginalises the indigenous agency and over-emphasises the Hellenistic side of the relationship as the primary source of power and legitimacy. However, aspects of the 'toponymical Hellenisation' of Palestinian urban place names are evident. Toponymical 'Hellenisation' of urban Palestine, which began with the conquest by Alexander the Great in the late 330s BC and developed over several centuries, was markedly accompanied by extensive economic growth and development that included urban planning and the establishment of well-built fortified cities. Distance and regional trade and gradual 'cultural Hellenisation' had some impact on Palestine and this was felt in the urban centres and major cities. In addition to the impact of Hellenisation on the historic cities of Gaza, 'Asqalon, Jerusalem and Jaffa, ongoing Hellenisation of place names and renaming of Palestinian cities affected Scythopolis (Beisan), Ptolemais (Akka/Acre), Diospolis (Lydda), Eleutheropolis (Beit Jibrin), Sepphoris (Diocaesaraea/Saffuriyah), Nicopolis (Emmaus), Petra (Greek: rock; Aramaic: Raqmu; Arabic: al-Batra), Philadelphia ('Amman), Antipatris (Surdi fonts/Binar Bashi), Flavia Neapolis (Nablus) and Sebastos (Sabastiyah). Sebastia (Greek: Sevastee) is today a large Palestinian village, located some 12 kilometres north-west of the city of Nablus. Rebuilt in 63 BC, its name derives from Sebastos ('venerable'), the Greek equivalent of the Latin Augustus, a name chosen in honour of Emperor Augustus. For many centuries, the town was the seat of a bishop, first in Palaestina Prima under the Byzantine Empire, then in the province of Jund Filastin under Islam and again a Latin bishop in the Frankish Kingdom of Jerusalem. The original Palestine Orthodox tradition of Sebastia was restored after the defeat of the Latin Crusaders and continued under Islam into the modern era. Since 2005 a leading Palestinian Arab public figure, Atallah Hanna (Theodosios), with a strong commitment to Palestinian Arab national identity, has been the Archbishop Sebastia in the Greek Orthodox Patriarchate of Jerusalem, a religious title which embodies the continuities and the deeply rooted toponymic social memories of historic Palestine.

As for the name of the Palestinian city Nablus, it derives from Greco-Roman name Flavia Neapolis (Νεάπολις) – the 'new city of the Emperor Flavius' – which was given to it by the Roman Emperor Vespasian in 72 AD. Thus Nablus shares its name with the Italian city of Naples. Flavia Neapolis had been founded near Tell Balatah, the site of the remains of an ancient Palestinian city Shechmu, traditionally identified with the Samaritan city of Schechem. The site of Balatah is one of the most ancient localities in Palestine and archaeologists estimate that the towers and buildings at the site date back 4000 years to the Chalcolithic and Bronze Ages. Today Tell Balatah is listed by UNESCO as part of the Inventory of Cultural and Natural Heritage Sites of Potential Outstanding Universal Value in Palestine. Ancient and modern Palestinian cities are closely related not only in terms of toponymic memories. Archaeological evidence shows the historical continuities, interruptions, revival and continuous transformation of the urban centres of Palestine from the Early Bronze Age to the modern period:

> Archaeological data take us beneath and beyond such recitation [of military battles] to gain a glimpse of what life was actually like in Hellenistic Palestine. A presentation of the period's architectural remains, changes in its settlement patterns, and the variety of its material cultures helps us understand how the inhabitants of various parts of the country lived and how their lives changed during the course of these momentous centuries. Peaceful and increasingly wealthy and cosmopolitan lifestyles emerge from the obscuring dust of the historian's preoccupation with battles. (Berlin 1997: Abstract)

Palestine's educated urban elites and thriving urban spaces played an important part in shaping the early idea of Palestine. Both Latin and Koine Greek were the dominant languages of the Byzantine Empire until the 6th century; Latin remained the official language of the government in the 6th century, whereas the prevalent language of merchants, farmers, seamen and ordinary citizens in Palestine was Greek. Also, Aramaic – closely related to Arabic – was a prevalent language among the (predominantly Christian) Palestinian peasantry which constituted the majority of population in the country. In practice, Greek and Latin were the prevalent languages of the educated urban elites of Byzantine Palestine, affecting education, trade, administration, official documents, art and architecture and key place names throughout Palestine and the Eastern Mediterranean. Greek, however, became the lingua franca of late

Byzantine Palestine, shortly before the advent of Islam. Consequently, the Hellenisation of Palestinian toponyms was not uncommon in Late Antiquity. A well-known example of Hellenisation from Late Antiquity is the work of the 1st-century Romano-Jewish historian and translator Josephus (Titus Flavius Josephus 37–c. 100 AD) who spoke Aramaic and Greek and who became a Roman citizen. Both he and Greco-Roman Jewish writer Philo of Alexandria used the toponym Palestine (Robinson, E. 1865: 15). Josephus believed in the compatibility of Judaism and Greco-Roman thought, often referred to as Hellenistic Judaism.[11] He listed local Palestinian toponyms and rendered them familiar to Greco-Roman audiences. In his works *The Jewish War* (1981) and the *Antiquities of the Jews* (2004) which include material about individuals, groups, customs and place names, Josephus almost never refers to Torah-authority Jewish scribes as 'scribes'; instead he refers to them as sophists and elders. Similarly, Josephus refers to Jewish 'sects' (a loaded term) as philosophies or schools. The term he used to refer to Transjordan, Peraea ('the country beyond'), is not found in the Bible, modern 'Amman is referred to by its Greek name, Philadelphia. Medieval Muslims and modern Palestinians preserved Greco-Roman toponyms such *Nablus* (Greek: Neapolis, Νεάπολις), Palestine, Qaysariah[12] (Caesarea; Greek: Καισάρεια), but not Philadelphia. Eusebius' 4th century work on Palestinian topography, *Onomasticon: On the Place Names in Divine Scripture* (Notley and Safrai 2004; Eusebius 1971), refers to 'Amman: this is now Philadelphia'.

In addition to the Hellenisation of many Palestinian toponyms by the Jewish writer Josephus, the Founding Fathers of Christianity introduced religio-political dimensions to Palestinian place names. The role of this religio-social memory in influencing the geographical mapping and toponymic memory of Palestine was widely recognised in the 4th century AD in two famous works: St Jerome's Vulgate translation into Latin and the subsequent work on Palestinian topography, *Onomasticon: On the Place Names in Divine Scripture* by Eusebius of Caesarea (Eusebius Caesariensis; 260/265–339/340 AD) – a historian of Greek descent, a topographer and an exegete and one of the Founding Fathers who became the Bishop of Caesarea about AD 314. Eusebius' work, *Onomasticon* (Notley and Safrai 2004; Eusebius 1971), the first comprehensive attempt to construct and 'locate' these places and names from the biblical narratives, was partly based on Jerome's religio-imperial enterprise which was driven by the fact that Christianity had become an official religion of empire. It was these two works by two of the Founding Fathers of Christianity, Jerome and Eusebius, rather than Herodotus' actual history of Palestine which formed the basis of Western religio-social toponymic memory and the reimagining of Palestine as a Christian Holy Land (Sivan 2008: 57). Eusebius, in *Onomasticon*, provides a list of place names of Provincia Palaestina, with additional geographical, historical and religious commentary partly based on biblical stories. His topography of Palestine was later translated into Latin. St Jerome relocated physically to Judaea in Provincia Palaestina while working on the Vulgate translation. Jerome, a founding father of Christianity and a major contributor to its seminal religious memory, was the first person to go back and translate the Old Testament from Hebrew rather than from the Septuagint (or 'Greek Old Testament').

The evolving multi-layered identity and conception of Palestine since the late Bronze Age has geo-political, secular, administrative and legal connotations. The Byzantine era also added a religious layer to the geo-political, secular conception of Palestine, in the form of the 'Holy Land'. The religio-sacred representations of Palestine, the Holy Land, the 'land of the Gospel' as religious memory and an imagined sacred territory have been embraced and celebrated by the indigenous people of Palestine: Muslims (from the Quranic traditions), Samaritans (based on the Samaritan Pentateuch), Jews (from the traditions of the Old Testament) and Christians (from the traditions of the Old and New Testaments). This multifaith identity of Palestine is universally recognised.

Furthermore, the medieval Western Christian religious memory of, and pilgrimage to, the Terrae Sanctae had a major influence on the modern social memory theory of French sociologist Maurice Halbwachs (1877–1945), whose seminal writings on the sociology of knowledge and the social construction of memory was entitled *Mémoire Collective* (1980). In his work Halbwachs contrasted structured, evolving 'social memory' with actual history and thus established 'collective memory' both as a concept and as a distinct research field. The term 'collective memory' itself is traceable to the founder of modern sociology, Émile Durkheim

(1858–1917), who wrote extensively in *Les formes élémentaires de la vie religieuse* (2003) about organised religion, collective memory, remembering and commemorative rituals. Halbwachs, a student of Durkheim and a positivist sociologist, contrasts 'history' with evolving 'social memory' and argues that an individual's memories and understanding of the past are closely related to group memberships, 'collective memory' and group consciousness. According to Halbwachs (1992), this production of social memory is dependent upon a religious or political 'cadre' as well as the framework within which a group is situated within a society.

Halbwachs' work on the social framing of collective memory and the construction (and reproduction) of social memory began with his landmark study on *Les Cadres Sociaux de la Mémoire* (1925, 1992) and *La Topographie légendaire des évangiles en terre sainte: étude de mémoire collective* (1941, 1992). Halbwachs was preoccupied with religious and nationalist social memory. His work *La Topographie légendaire des évangiles en terre sainte* focuses on publicly available commemorative symbols, rituals and representations. It also examines the religio-social memory of successive generations of medieval Christian pilgrims and Latin Crusaders in the Terrae Sanctae and their geographical subdivision of Palestine, Syria and Arabia, and how these groups 'found' and then 'found' again (reproduced) particular place names from the Gospel narratives.

This work will show how the collective (religio-social) memory of Western scriptural scholars such as Edward Robinson and Victor Guérin (like the medieval Crusaders and pilgrims) 'found' again and (reconstructed) in the 19th century particular place names in Palestine from the biblical narrative – place names which formed the basis of Zionist replacement toponymic projects. Place names, geographical sites and landscape are also – to borrow French historian Pierre Nora's term, *Les Lieux de mémoire* (1996, 1997, 1998) – 'sites of memory' around which social groups consciously construct and cultivate social and cultural memory and individual and collective identities. Underpinned by the social memory theory of Halbwachs, Nora and others, this book also draws on other approaches: the exploration of Israeli archival historical documents; Palestinian oral history and memory accounts; map-making and the cultural production of maps in Palestine–Israel.

In the modern period, and especially during the British Mandate of Palestine (1918–1948), the term 'Palestinian' was used to refer to all people residing in Palestine, regardless of religion or ethnicity, including those European Jewish settlers granted citizenship by the British Mandatory authorities. Earlier, in the second half of the 19th century, the British had set up the Palestine Exploration Fund (PEF) as an imperial project. It was founded in London in 1865 under the patronage of Queen Victoria and coined the terms 'Western Palestine' and 'Eastern Palestine' (the *Survey of Western Palestine* and *Survey of Eastern Palestine*) and mounted geographical map-making expeditions in Palestine in the 1870s. The large number of publications by the PEF included *The Fauna and Flora of Palestine* (Tristram 1884). There was no mention of the expression 'Land of Israel' by the PEF – this was later coined by the founding fathers of Jewish Zionism.

However, one of the key religio-political-strategic objectives of the PEF was clear from its own publication: *Names and Places in the Old and New Testament and Apocrypha: with their Modern Identifications* (Palestine Exploration Fund 1889). The PEF listed more than 1150 place names related to the Old Testament and 162 related to the New Testament. Shortly after the British military occupation of Palestine in 1918, the British Mandatory authorities set out to gather toponymic information from the local Palestinian inhabitants. Following the PEF, the Mandatory authorities assumed that the Palestinian Arabs (Muslim, Christian and Arab Jews) had also preserved knowledge of the ancient place names which could help identify archaeological and biblical sites.

In Palestine, the struggle between the coloniser and colonised over land, demography, power and ownership also centred on representation, misrepresentation and self-representation. The metaphoric self-representation of the European settler-coloniser as a 'return to history' works to uproot and 'detach' the native from history. The settler-coloniser invaded the space and appropriated the heritage of the local Palestinians and simultaneously detached itself from the colonised and disinherited Palestinian. The production of historical knowledge and power by the Ashkenazi Zionist settler-coloniser – a self-referencing ouroboros – resulted in the creation of a range of foundational myths, self-indigenising and self-antiquating strategies, including the myths of 'exile and return' and 'return to history'. But the 'many returns' of Zionism, as Israeli scholar Gabriel Piterberg put it in *The Returns of Zionism* (2008), did not just manifest themselves in the obsessive 'return to history' by the European settler coming to reclaim the land, they were also constructed around erasure, the non-existence of the indigenous people of Palestine and the actual, physical uprooting of the Palestinians and their detachment 'from history'.

Since the mapping and explorations of the PEF and especially since the establishment of an ethnically cleansing Israeli state in 1948, the production of historical knowledge and cultural struggle over the naming (and renaming) of Palestine sites/cities/towns and villages have become major weapons of Zionist settler-colonial nationalism, biblicisation, Hebrewisation and Judaisation strategies that sought to detach the Palestinians from the history of the country. Toponymy itself is a branch of onomastics or onomatology, the study of the origin, history and uses of names of all kinds. Anthroponomastics (or anthroponymy) is the study of personal names. Chapter ten will explore Zionist toponymic, anthroponymic and self-naming strategies. The eliminationist projects of Zionist settler-colonisation in Palestine did not just centre on land-grabbing and the ethnic cleansing of the indigenous people of Palestine. These projects also consisted of self-indigenisation, self-antiquation, biblicisation and Hebrewisation in addition to the Judaisation of the land.

LOCATING PALESTINE: THE METHODOLOGICAL AND INTELLECTUAL FRAMEWORK

This work locates the multicultural identity and shared histories of Palestine in a very long history of the whole region. It locates Palestinian history in the ancient, classical, post-classical, medieval, early and modern histories of the Near East and Eastern Mediterranean. The intention is not to produce an intellectually detached form of history but rather to offer a socially, intellectually, culturally and politically informed and engaged history. While attempting to cover the vast span of history, this work links questions of history from below, social memory, cultural identity and politics.

This is not a 'nationalist history' or a narrative about the Bible to the present for a 'Palestinian nation', although I am fully aware of history's power to create national/political legitimacy in the present. 'Nation' and nationalism are modern inventions and constructions and I am highly sceptical about the utility of a political term such as 'nation' across a vast sweep of history. Of course, the process of 'national invention' and visualisation is not confined to modern Palestine or the Palestinians. It is common to all modern national entities and groupings, and it is an important ingredient both in nationalism and in the creation and maintenance of nation-states. Nation-building and the invention of tradition was a typical European practice of using collective memory selectively by manipulating certain bits of the national and religious past, suppressing others and elevating and mobilising others in an entirely functional way and for political purposes; thus mobilised memory is not necessarily authentic but rather useful politically (Said 1999: 6–7). Competing modes of modern nation-building and nationalist myth-making have received extensive critical reappraisal in the works of Benedict Anderson (1991: 6, 11–12), Eric Hobsbawm (1990; Hobsbawm and Ranger 1996), Anthony Smith (1971, 1984, 1986) and Ernest Gellner (1983). Hobsbawm's most comprehensive analysis of nation-building and myth-making in Europe is found in *Nations and Nationalism since 1780*. Published in 1990 with the subtitle *Programme, Myth, Reality*, his work is about the 'invention of tradition', the creation of national culture, and the construction of national identities from a mixture of folk history and historical myths (Hobsbawm 1990). In *The Invention of Tradition* Hobsbawm and Terence Ranger (1996: 1–14, 263–283) explore the way social and political authorities in the Europe of the mid-19th century set about creating supposedly age-old traditions by providing invented memories of the past as a way of creating a new sense of identity for the ruler and ruled.

Often liberal Israeli Jewish scholars (Sand 2009; Sternhell 1998; Piterberg 2001, 2008; Rabkin 2006, 2010; Ben-Zeev 2014; Greenstein 2014) critique the 'nationalist inventive' traditions of Zionism and the impact of this 'imagined tradition' on the Jewish people, rather than on the catastrophic consequences of Zionism for its main victim, the indigenous people of Palestine. But since this Zionist nation-building and the invention of tradition was typical of European 'nationalist' practices of using collective memory, this scholarly approach places Zionism among the 'normal' European traditions of nationalist invention and myth-making. In effect this 'normalisation' and 'nationalisation' of Zionism is exactly what Zionist ideologues have always argued for. Also, these myth-making strategies of Zionism are hardly its worst aspects. By contrast, reading Zionism from below, from the viewpoint of its main victim, the indigenous people of Palestine, places Zionism within an altogether different tradition: among the forces of modern European settler-colonisation, ethnic cleansing memoricide and cultural genocide (Masalha 1992, 2012; Pappe 2006; Rashed et al. 2014).

Furthermore, as I have argued in *The Bible and Zionism: Invented Traditions, Archaeology and Post-Colonialism in Palestine-Israel* (2007) and *The Zionist Bible: Biblical Precedent, Colonialism and the Erasure of Memory* (2013), Palestinian history as people's history can and should only be written independent of the Old Testament stories. These works have also addressed the ways in which Zionism attempted to validate its colonisation projects and its own 'historical claims' through extensive uses and abuses of the biblical text. This theme has also been explored in Keith Whitelam's seminal work, *The Invention of Ancient Israel: The Silencing of Palestinian History* (1996). This book is not designed to revisit that ground or build on Whitelam's excellent work and his effective dismantling of a Bible-to-independence 'historical continuum' for Israel. It rather seeks to move forward by recovering and narrating a history of Palestine completely independent of the biblical debates and the biblical scholarship. Furthermore, while arguing that the complex history of Palestine is deeply grounded in the ancient Near East and Eastern Mediterranean, there is no attempt here to mimic the Zionist claims of a long, 'unbroken' and neat history of Palestine. On the contrary, as this volume will demonstrate, the multi-layered heritage of Palestine is a history of mixed styles and contradictory traditions; a history full of twist and turns, of memory and forgetfulness, and of suppression and recovery.

Chapter 1

THE PHILISTINES AND PHILISTIA AS A DISTINCT GEO-POLITICAL ENTITY

Late Bronze Age to 500 BC

THE PHILISTINES AS INDIGENOUS PEOPLE: EPIGRAPHIC AND ARCHAEOLOGICAL EVIDENCE FOR *PELESET* AND THE PHILISTINES

The most traditional and earliest toponyms for the area which became known in classical Antiquity as 'Palestine' were not related to Cana'an. They were the toponyms of Retenu and Djahi, which might be seen as traditional names, as used in the 14th century BC Egyptian story of Sinuhe.[1] Retenu was used to refer to the regions along the eastern shore of the Mediterranean and was divided into three sub-regions: Amurru, in the north, Lebanon (sometimes referred to as 'Upper Retenu'), which lay south of Amurru and north of the Litani river, and Djahi, the southernmost part of Retenu, which referred to the regions south of the Litani to Ascalon ('Asqalan, or perhaps Gaza) and as far as the Rift Valley to the east.

The traditional approaches to the Philistines, 'Peleset' and ancient Palestine have been constructed through the eyes of settler-colonisers. New archaeological discoveries and epigraphical evidence can help us read the history of Palestine through the eyes of the indigenous. New archaeological discoveries in Palestine/Israel and epigraphic evidence on ancient Palestine – carved on walls, temples, memorials, gravestones, coins and Philistine graveyards uncovered recently in Ascalon, dating to about 3000 years ago (Ariel 2017) – have all transformed our understanding of the ancient history of Palestine and have resulted in new paradigms which revolutionised our scholarly knowledge on Palestine. A cognate of the name Palestine, 'Peleset', is found on five inscriptions as referring to the settlement of a seafaring people along the southern Palestinian coast from the mid-12th century BC during the reigns of Ramesses II[2] and III of the nineteenth Egyptian dynasty. The 3200-year-old documents from Ramesses III, including an inscription dated c. 1150 BC, at the Mortuary Temple of Ramesses III at the Medinat Habu Temple in Luxor – one of the best-preserved temples of Egypt – refers to the Peleset among those who fought against Ramesses III (Breasted 2001: *24; also* Bruyère 1929–1930), who reigned from 1186 to 1155 BC. Ramesses III's war against the so-called 'sea peoples' (1181–1175 BC) placed Peleset, geographically, in the land of Djahi, that is Palestine. In fact, new archaeological discoveries from a 3000-year-old Philistine graveyard in Ascalon have resulted in a new paradigm on the origins of the Philistines, firmly suggesting that they were not marauding Aegean invaders of the southern Levant or 'sea peoples' that appeared in Palestine in the course of the Late Bronze Age, but an indigenous population of the Near East (Evian 2017; David 2017). Since the 19th century biblical Orientalist scholars have linked the Egyptian cognate Peleset inscriptions with the 'biblical Philistines'. Assyrian inscriptions from the 8th and 7th century refer to this southern coastal region as 'Palashtu' or 'Pilistu'.

Arabic-language epigraphic evidence from Palestine east of the Jordan River is extensive, with some Arabic inscriptions dating from the Roman era and as early as 150 AD. In fact, Palestine is extremely rich in Arabic inscriptions, most of which date from the early Islamic and Umayyad periods. Already in early Islam Palestine acquired particular religious, economic and strategic importance. The historical importance of Filastin is shown in the hundreds of Palestine Arabic inscriptions which cover a huge variety of topics: architecture, Islamic religious (*waqf*) endowments, epitaphs, construction, markets, dedication, Quranic texts, prayers and invocations. A large collection of the inscriptions is assembled in the multi-volume *Corpus Inscriptionum Arabicarum Palaestina* (Sharon 1997–2013; van Berchem 1894).

THE NAME 'CANA'AN' IN THE LATE BRONZE PERIOD

The Old Testament is based on exilic and post-exilic imagination, literary invention and fiction not facts. Its myth-narratives should be read as fiction, theology and literature, not proven facts. The 'Cana'anites' are in fact identical to the Phoenicians. The alphabet of the Phoenicians of the coastal regions of Palestine and Lebanon – conventionally known as the proto-Canaanite alphabet – was given to Greek, Aramaic, Arabic and Hebrew. However, the Old Testament terms 'Canaanites' and 'Israelites' in Palestine do not necessarily refer to or describe two distinct ethnicities. Niels Peter Lemche, an Old Testament scholar at the University of Copenhagen, whose interests included early Israelites and their relationship with history, the Old Testament and archaeology, has suggested that the Old Testament narrative of the 'Israelites' and 'Canaanites' must be read as ideological constructs of the other (as the non-Jews) rather than as a reference to an actual historical ethnic group: 'The Canaanites [of Palestine] did not know that they were themselves Canaanites. Only when they had so to speak "left" their original home ... did they acknowledge that they had been Canaanites' (Lemche 1999: 152).

Literary invention and the fact that exilic Old Testament authors imaginatively coined the term 'Canaanites' – a religio-ideological construct by these authors – does not necessarily indicate that there was a conflict between historical Israelites and Canaanites in Palestine.

However, in the modern era (beginning with the late 19th century) European Zionist leaders appropriated the Old Testament narratives as historical accounts and used them instrumentally to justify their settler project and their conflict with the indigenous people of Palestine. Nevertheless, the Israeli–Palestinian conflict is a modern conflict and should not be confused with the real, historical, ancient Palestine or any subsequent religio-ideological constructs of the Old Testament narratives.

Historically the name Cana'an was indeed used in the Late Bronze Age. But the name did not always refer to the Cisjordan area from Gaza to the Litani River. Nor was it the only term used in connection with this area (between the Wadi Gaza and the Litani). Other names such as Palestine, as well as earlier names, such as Retenu and Djahi, were also used for this area (including, at times, the inland regions of western Palestine and the Transjordan) at some point in the course of the Late Bronze Age. Cana'an referred to a geographical region of varying size, along the Mediterranean coast of Lebanon, Palestine and Syria (and not just Palestine). At times this included regions inland. In the first millennium, however, Phoenicia (modern Lebanon) was the most common name used for the northern coastal region, which had earlier been referred to as Cana'an, while the Assyrian-derived name of Philistia was most often used initially for the southern coast and later for Palestine as a whole. The name Cana'an is found in ancient Near Eastern inscriptions with reference not just to the specific area of Palestine but crucially to Syria from the 15th century BC to the early 9th century BC. The first certain reference to the name Cana'an is found in cuneiform on the statue of Idrimi from Alalakh in northern Syria (c. 1500 BC) in the form Kinahhu.

The name Cana'an is also found sixteen times in Egyptian texts; of these, twelve are from the New Kingdom (Hasel 2009: 8–17). The name is found on some of the Amarna tablets in the form *kn'ny* – about thirty years from the middle of the 14th century BC. In these inscriptions, the ancient port city of Ugarit itself does not belong to Cana'an, but Qadesh does. The name also occurs in Egyptian inscriptions in the form *k3n'n'* from the 13th century Hattusa, Ramesses II and Merneptah inscriptions (this last from c. 1205 BC). On the Merneptah Stele, the town Gaza is referred to as 'the mouth of (that is, "the opening to" *k3n'n*°.

THE NAME PALESTINE TAKES OVER FROM THE LATE BRONZE AGE ONWARDS

The international trade between Palestine and Egypt dates back to the Chalcolithic period (4000–3200 BC), during which Palestine exported copper to Egypt. Also, a large amount of Palestinian ('Canaanite') pottery from this period was discovered in Egypt – pots manufactured in Palestine and transported to Egypt presumably as containers of wine and olive oil (Grainger 2016: 27).

However, the name Palestine first occurs in Egyptian sources from the Late Bronze Age in relation to the Egyptian struggle to control the Philistines during the reigns of Ramesses II and III and of Merneptah (1276–1178 BC). In fact, the name Palestine originally derives from the 3200-year-old documented name Peleset, used to refer to the people in southern Levant, allies of the 'Libyans',[3] who are mentioned in Egyptian inscriptions, including the Merneptah Stele, which celebrates the Egyptian victory over Libya. These allies of the Libyans include a number of peoples besides the Peleset, some of whose names are identifiable. These names include the Shardana (Sardinia), the Ekwesh, the Teresh, the Tjekker, the Lukka, the Kheta (Hatti = Hittite), the Amor (Amurru), the Shasw (Bedouin in the Sinai), including possibly the *Asher* or *Israel* of the Merneptah Stele. Following the integration of the Philistines with other population, the name Peleset succeeded the name Djahi as the dominant toponym for the region as a whole.

From the Late Bronze Age onwards, it should be stressed, the names used for the region of the southern Levant, such as Djahi, Retenu and Cana'an, all gave way to Palestine, the name most commonly used in 8th and 7th century Assyrian inscriptions. Using a 'part for the whole' designation, Palestine came to refer to the greater region (Palashtu, Piliste (or Philistia), literally the 'land of the Peleset' (Greek: Γη των Φυλιστιειμ), of the southern Levant. This wider conception included not only the well-known cities of Philistia: Gaza, Ekron, Gath,[4] Ashdod, Ascalon, Timnah[5] and Tantur, but served also for the interior of the country and gradually as a wider designation for the whole area from Lebanon to Egypt. Interestingly also, almost all the toponyms of the cities of Philistia: Gaza (Ghazzah), Askelon ('Asqalan), Ashdod (Isdud[6]), Tantur (Tantura), Gath (Jat), Ekron ('Aqir) survived into the modern era and were preserved in the modern Palestinian Arabic names and were mostly depopulated by Israel in 1948.

THE NAMES PILISTE AND PHILISTIA IN ASSYRIAN SOURCES

In seven known Assyrian clay tablet and Cuneiform inscriptions from different periods the Assyrians called the region connected with modern Palestine 'Palashtu', 'Palastu' or 'Pilistu', and called the people who lived in this region Palestinians: '*pa-la-as-ta-a-a*', beginning with the King of Assyria Adad-Nirari III (from 811 BC to 783 BC) in the 'Nimrud inscriptions' in 800 BC through to Esarhaddon (who reigned 681 to 669 BC) more than a century later (*Room 2006:* 285; also Smith, G. 1875: 115). The Nimrud inscriptions were discovered in 1854 by William Loftus in his excavations at Nimrud, a major ancient Assyrian city originally known as Kalhu. Located 30 kilometres south of the Iraqi city of Mosul, Nimrud was a strategic Assyrian city between approximately 1250 BC and 610 BC. They are among the best studied of the inscriptions of Adad-Nirari III, since they include a description of early Assyrian campaigns in Palestine and Syria. The text of the Saba'a Stele, the inscription of the reign of Asas-nirari III, was translated by Daniel Luckenbill (1881–1927), an American Assyriologist and Professor at the University of Chicago, as:

> In the fifth year [of my official rule] I sat down solemnly on my
> royal throne and called up the country [for war]. I ordered the
> numerous army of Assyria to march against Philistia [*Pa-la-áš-tu*].
> I crossed the Euphrates at its flood. As to the numerous hostile kings
> who had rebelled in the time of my father Shamshi-Adad and had
> wi[thheld] their regular [tributes], or overwhelmed them [and] upon
> the command of Asur, Sin, Shamash, Adad (and) Ishtar, my trust [in]
> gods ... I received all the tributes ... which they brought to Assyria.
> I ordered [to march] against the country Damascus [Ša-imērišu].
> (Luckenbill 1926: 260–261)

The inscription goes on:

> I subdued [the territory stretching] from the bank of the Euphrates,
> the land of Hatti, the land of Amurru in its entirety, the land of Tyre,

the land of Sidon, the land of Humri, the land of Edom, the land of Palastu, as far as the great sea of the setting sun. I imposed tax (and) tribute upon them. (Grayson 1996: 212; see also Luckenbill 1926; Smith, G. 1875: 115)

The Palestinians are also mentioned in the *Nimrud Letters*, which contain Cuneiform texts of royal correspondence from the reigns of Tiglath-pileser III and Sargon II of Assyria. The correspondence includes the letter of Qurdi-Ashur-lamur to Tiglath-Pileser III, dated c. 735 BC:

Concerning the ruler of Tyre, about whom the king said: 'Talk nicely to him', all the wharves are at their disposal. His subjects enter and leave the warehouses at will, and trade. The Lebanon range is accessible to him; they go up and down at will and bring lumber down. On the lumber they bring down I impose a tax. I have appointed tax inspectors over the customs [houses] of the entire Lebanon range, [and] they keep the watch on the harbour. I appointed a tax inspector [for those who[were going down into the custom houses which are in Sidon, [but] the Sidonians chased him away. Thereupon I sent the Itu'a contingent into the Lebanon range. They terrified the people, [so that] afterwards they sent a message and fetched the tax inspector [and] brought [him] into Sidon. I spoke to them in these terms: 'Bring down lumber, do your work on it, [but] do not deliver it to the Egyptians or Palestinians [*pa-la-as-ta-a-a*] or I shall not let you go up to the mountains'. (Cited in Saggs 2001: 155–157)

Four decades later, the annals of the Sennacherib, a record of improvements in the Assyrian capital in c. 694 BC, mention the Palestinians. The annals speak of the 'the people of Kue and Hilakku, Pilisti and Tyre' ('Ku-e u Hi-lak-ku Pi-lis-tu u Sur-ri') (Luckenbill 1924: 104), while another Assyrian record of his successor, the treaty of Esarhaddon, in 675 BC identifies *du-u'-ri* (Dor or Tantur) 'in the district of *pi-lis-te*'[7] (Pilistu or Peleset). An earlier Assyrian tablet, Sargon II's Prism A, an inscription dating to c. 717 BC, which describes describes Sargon II's campaigns, speaks of the incorporation of the region of Pilistu into the Assyrian Empire. Pi-lis-te or

Pi-lis-tu is the Assyrian name for the Philistines, while Peleset is the Egyptian name for one of the so-called Sea Peoples throughout the reigns of Ramesses II and III. The 'land of the Peleset' is used in an inscription from the reign of Ramesses III. The Egyptian use of *peleset* refers to indefinite areas which possibly include the southern and central coast, but might also include areas inland.

IRON AGE PHILISTIA AS A DISTINCT POLITY: THE COUNTRY OF THE PELESET FROM GAZA TO TANTUR (1200–712 BC)

The Assyrian name pi-lis-te (also pilistu palashtu, pilistu, pi-lis-te, pa-la-as-ta-a-a, pilishti, pilishtu, pilistu, pilisti, pilistin) referred to an area that runs from Gaza to Tantur, and may include much larger areas inland. The Assyrian filisti, filistin and palashtu are Assyrian spellings of this name which are used variously. Perhaps it should be distinguished from the Assyrian provinces of Tantur (Tantur to Akka), Magiddu (مجيدو; in the Jezreel valley/ Marj ibn 'Amer), Samerina (the central highlands) and Sennacherib's Jerusalem (including Lakhish) and possibly other regions. Over a period of six centuries, these names were found on a handful of Assyrian inscriptions.

The Old Testament talks about a 'land of the Plishtim'. In the Bible the Mediterranean Sea was also known as the 'Sea of the Philistines' (Exod. 23:31), named after the people occupying a large portion of the shores of the Mediterranean. The Philistines were known in the Old Testament as Plishtim and their Mediterranean territory as Pleshet: Philistia (1 Sam. 17:36; 2 Sam. 1:20; Judg. 14:3; Amos 1:8). Most American and Israeli biblical scholars identify this Peleset with a somewhat historicised, but ultimately biblical 'land of the Philistines'; that is, at least the coastal region from Gaza to Tantur.

The militant myth-narratives of the Books of Joshua, Deuteronomy and Samuel have provided modern Zionist settler-nationalism with the muscular, militaristic and violent dimensions of the 'conquest of the land of Cana'an' and elimination of its indigenous people. The Book of Judges has also given Zionism another militarist tradition: the 'holy war' stories associated with the (real or imagined) struggle against the Philistines, and the narrative of Samson (an Israelite hero) and cunning Delilah, who betrayed Samson on behalf of the Philistines of Gaza (Judg. 16).

Philistia of the late Bronze Age and Iron Age was dominated by the Philistines and evolved into a distinct geo-political entity with strong international trade links, a distinct economy and a sophisticated urban environment. The Philistines – a highly advanced people who, according to the Old Testament, ruled five famed Pentapoli of Philistia: Gaza, Ascalon, Ashdod, Ekron and Gath (Niesiołowski-Spanò 2011: 38) – have, for centuries, suffered under the weight of their relentlessly negative portrayal in the books and stories of the Old Testament. From Goliath to Delilah, they have personified the intrinsically evil Other in the burgeoning narrative myth of the nation of Israel (McDonagh 2004). In the Old Testament, the Philistines were constructed as a typical ideological scapegoat (McDonagh 2004). Modern European racism and biblical constructs and prejudices towards the Philistines have survived in the derogatory and offensive connotation of the modern Western term: 'a *philistine* is a person ignorant of, or smugly hostile to, culture' (Eban 1984: 45; Rose 2004: 17; McDonagh 2004).

There are recent pro-Zionist sources which seem to suggest that '*p-l-s-t*' ('Peleset'; Philistines) was an area corresponding roughly to today's Gaza region. In fact, contrary to these propagandistic claims, from the Late Bronze Age onwards and the beginning of the Iron Age I (about 1200 BC), the Peleset intermingled with other local populations inhabiting the Mediterranean coastal region of Palestine, from Gaza in the south to Tantur in the north. In all probability, the land of the Peleset extended further north to Mount Carmel. Tantur is the normal international English name for Tantura. This small Palestinian harbour town (depopulated in the Palestinian Nakba of 1948[8]) is located south of Haifa and 8 kilometres north-west of the Israeli town of Zikhron Yaakov (founded in 1882) on the Mediterranean coast, 35 kilometres south of Haifa. Nearby Tantura (Tantur) is the ancient site referred to as Tel Dor, or Dora, by archaeologists. Tantur was the centre of the Assyrian province of Tantura and controlled the coast north to Acre for about a century. Around 1100 BC the Philistines expanded their inland territory eastwards to include the city of Beisan (later Scythopolis), an important strategic city located at the junction of the Jordan River and

the Plain of Esdraelon (Arabic: Marj Ibn 'Amer). The large extent of the
coastal region of the 'land of *p-l-s-t*' ('Peleset', 'Philistines'), from Tantur in
the north to Gaza in the south and including vast areas inland, suggests that
the 'land of the Peleset' was fifteen to twenty times larger than the current
Gaza Strip, encompassing much of greater Tel Aviv, the Israeli metropolitan
area, which includes the cities of Holon and Petah Tikva, the latter known
in Zionist historiography as Im Hamoshavot, the 'Mother of the Colonies'.
Tel Aviv is a city which grew out of and then consumed its parent, the
ancient Palestinian city of Jaffa, whose indigenous inhabitants were driven
out en masse in 1948 (Rotbard 2015). The Tel Aviv metropolitan area, which,
according to Avishai Margalit (of the Hebrew University of Jerusalem), had
never been the historic homeland of the Jewish people (Margalit, A. 1991),
constitutes Israel's largest conurbation with 3,700,000 residents, over 40 per
cent of the country's population.

Overall Israeli settler-colonial collective memory links the ancient
Philistines with the modern Arabic-speaking people of Palestine. Zionist
ethnic cleansing tactics in the 1948 War against the Palestinians evidently
adopted and adapted the legendary narrative of Samson's 'sacred war'
against the Philistines. To do this, the Israelis officially named one of their
key 1948 commando units Samson's Foxes (*Shu'alei Shimshon*); it operated
within the Givati Brigade which took part in the expulsion of the Palestinians. Furthermore, a secret reconnaissance battalion of the same name,
Samson's Foxes, was re-established by the Israeli army in 2002, to back its
occupation of the Gaza Strip, a region to which Israeli (biblicist) collective memory links to the ancient Philistines. The fox logo of the Israeli
Army's Southern Command is also designed to foster the same collective
and Israeli struggle against the indigenous people of Palestine.

THE HIGHLY DEVELOPED CITIES OF PHILISTIA

Throughout much of the Iron Age (c. 1200–600 BC) Philistia flourished
on strong international trade links and, as we shall see below, developed
the first monetary system of Palestine in the late 6th–early 5th century
BC. Terrestrial excavations and underwater archaeology of shipwrecks of

Philistia have revealed that the Philistines were a highly civilised people. They were sophisticated seafarers and highly accomplished architects and urban planners, highly artistic potters and weavers and ivory and metal-workers (Dothan 1992). Like the Phoenicians, the Philistines developed advanced naval technology which probably enhanced their reputation as seafaring people. Although their origin (Aegean or Near Eastern) has been seriously disputed among scholars (Berlin 1997) – with the most recent research suggesting they were an indigenous people of the Levant (Evian 2017) – there are good reasons to assume that the evolution of the highly advanced Philistine city-states in Palestine resembled, to some extent, the evolution of the sophisticated ancient Greek *polis*. In time, and more noticeably during the Hellenic and Roman periods, several cities in Palestine, especially Ascalon in the south and Ptolemais (Acre) in the north, would evolve into typical Greek *poleis*. The Greek term *polis* (plural *poleis*), 'city-state', continued to evolve in the course of the ancient period as the ancestor of city, state and eventually citizenship; the Greek term *polis* (Arabic *madinah*) persisted into the Hellenic, Roman and Byzantine periods and became common to the naming of cities in Roman- and Greek-speaking Byzantine Palestine; it is also found in modern Palestine in the adapted name of the Palestinian city of Nablus (originally Neapolis). However, the historical evolution of Nablus ('new city') and Iliya/al-Quds/Jerusalem into the key Arab Islamic madinas in Palestine did not result in cities very different from the earlier Greco-Roman-Byzantine poleis.

Greek–Roman–Byzantine urban planning flourished under Islam and is still much in evidence today in the Arab Islamic medieval Old City of Jerusalem, one of the best preserved medieval cities in the world. Like Gaza, Caesarea Maritima and other *poleis/madinas* in Palestine, Nablus, Gaza, 'Asqalan, Akka (Acre) and the medieval Islamic City of Jerusalem are classic examples which exhibit both historical continuities and continuous processes of adaption and transformation of the rich urban landscape of Palestine. Furthermore, the Greco-Roman *poleis*, dominated by small urban social elites, evolved and changed with the development of the centre of governance in the city to signify 'state', which included its surrounding villages, and this form of governance (the city with its surrounding villages) is also evident in Byzantine and Islamic Palestine.

However, it should be pointed out that the Greek *poleis* were unlike other primordial ancient city-states in the Near East like Sidon and Tyre, which were ruled by a king or a small oligarchy, but rather were political entities ruled by their bodies of citizens.

The strong tradition of trading and the technological innovation of Philistia during that period, and the nature of Philistine civilisation – a highly developed and influential Mediterranean culture and polity – have all been confirmed by recent archaeological excavations. The archaeology of Philistia has shown that the Philistine city-states had a highly sophisticated culture, in fact far more advanced in urban and technological development (from iron to pottery) than other contemporary regions of Palestine. Israeli-excavated archaeological evidence for this high level of development of the coast of Philistia was found outside the northern border of the modern city of Tel Aviv (the Israeli metropolis – 'mother city' – founded by East European Jewish settlers in 1909 and effectively the capital of the Zionist Yishuv settler colony in Palestine until 1948) in the remains of Tel Qasile, a Philistine town which formed a thriving harbour town through the 12th–10th centuries BC. These archaeological discoveries were deposited in 'the Eretz Israel Museum' on the campus of Tel Aviv University, a historical and archaeological museum in the Ramat Aviv neighbourhood of Tel Aviv. The campus of Tel Aviv University itself was constructed on the ruins of an ancient Philistine town and a modern Palestinian village, al-Shaykh Muwannis, depopulated by the Haganah in March 1948.

Throughout the Iron Age Philistia, with its southern and northern natural borders, emerged as a distinct polity nestling between two powerful trading neighbours, Egypt and Phoenicia, but also cultivated flourishing international trade with the Aegean region in the West and Arabia in the south. This neighbourhood was shrewdly exploited by the Philistines, who used it to develop their international trade links, economy and a distinct geo-political region and material culture (Ben-Shlomo 2010; Thompson 2016). The trade-based economy of Philistia was also a major unifying factor in a country which was shaped by polytheism and cultural hybridity. The Philistines integrated with other local populations and lived in coastal port towns and their surrounding villages. Their key cities were ruled by autonomous kings and their populations were mixed and integrated with other indigenous populations of Palestine. Pottery remains excavated in ancient cities such as Gaza, Jaffa, Ekron, Ashdod, Ascalon and Gath, decorated with stylised birds, provide archaeological evidence for highly developed Philistine cities in ancient Palestine. Ships sailing along the Eastern Mediterranean coast between Egypt and Phoenicia used the harbours of Philistia (Gaza, Ascalon, Ashdod, Jaffa and Tantur/Dor) to replenish supplies and take shelter in stormy weather. Crucially, the cities of Philistia controlled the international trade route of the Via Maris ('Way of the Philistines') and charged the trade caravans tolls for passing through their region (Gallagher 1999: 113).

The great trading cities of Philistia were not only credited with introducing iron weapons and chariots to ancient Palestine, but, as we shall see below, also with the creation of the earliest monetary and coinage system in Palestine in the 5th and 4th centuries BC. Regional and distant trade was a key factor in shaping the history of ancient Palestine and must have contributed to the introduction of the coinage of Philistia, which also became known as Philisto-Arabian coins, struck in the period 538–332 BC (see below);

> [The] integration [of the Philistines] with the indigenous population resulted in the geographically, but hardly ethnically, distinctive region of Philistia, which was tightly linked to the international trade routes. These followed the Via Maris, on the one hand, through the Jezreel and in the direction of northern Mesopotamia, and, on the other hand, continued along the coast to the Phoenician seaports of northern Palestine and southern Lebanon. Under Assyrian patronage, Palestine's expansive trading politics not only dominated the coastal economy but, over the course of the Iron II period, created an integrated South. Arab trade supported the processing of grains, cattle and fruits from the Northern Negev and coastal plain with the sheep and wool, olives and wines from the Judean foothills and highlands. Among the southern coast's most important towns were Jaffa, 'Aphek, Ekron, Ashdod, *Gimti* (Tall as-Safi), Askelon and Gaza. (Thompson 2016: 165)

In 712, after an uprising by the Philistine city of Ashdod, supported militarily by Egypt, the Assyrian King Sargon II (reigned 722–705 BC) invaded Pilishte to oust the King of Ashdod Iamani and annexed the whole region; Philistia was brought under direct Assyrian control, in effect becoming an Assyrian province (Thompson 2016: 165), although the King of Ashdod was allowed to remain on the throne (Gallagher 1999: 115). By the time Sargon II died, he 'had two provinces in Philistia: Dor (Tantur) and Ashdod, a reliable king in Gaza and a clearly defined border with Egypt (Gallagher 1999: 115).

THE 'WAY OF THE PHILISTINES': PALESTINE AS A TRANSIT COUNTRY AND THE HISTORIC ROAD OF VIA MARIS

Palestine as a 'transit country' from North to South and from West to East is another striking feature. The great importance of the country as a juncture of trade, industry, technology and monetarism, as well as agricultural innovation, and the importance of the famous Via Maris (the 'Way of the Sea'), also known as Way of the Philistines, can hardly be overstated. Historically Palestine fully exploited its geo-political position as a 'transit country' serving international trade and linking three different continents. Both the Philistines and Phoenicians controlled much of the Levantine coast of Philistia and Phoenicia (modern Lebanon) and the Way of the Philistines, or Via Maris, was described in Exodus as the 'way of the Land of the Philistines' (Old Testament: '*derech Eretz Plishtim*': 13:17). Much of the evidence concerning this route comes from Egyptian and Assyrian sources. The section connecting cementing Egypt with Palestine via Gaza was described in Egyptian sources as the 'Way of Horus'. It was an important international trade and traffic route running through the country's coastline dating from the early Bronze Age. It was the most important historic route from Egypt to the Levant, and linked Egypt with Palestine and the Fertile Crescent throughout all historical periods; along its route most of the important cities in the country sprang up, including Gaza (ancient Egypt's administrative capital of Palestine), Ashdod (Isdud), Ascalon ('Asqalan), Joppa (Jaffa), Tantur (Tantura) and later Caesarea-Palaestina. It followed the coastal plain of North Sinai and Palestine until

Tantur before veering north-eastwards, with alternative roads through Wadi 'Ara into Marj Ibn 'Amer (the Plain of Esdraelon), then passing by Mount Tabor and northwards towards present-day Syria. One branch continued from Tantur northwards along the Phoenician coast. This international trade highway of Palestine was criss-crossed by other trading routes in the country, including from Jaffa to Jerusalem, from Marj Ibn 'Amer in the north to the Jordan valley in the east and from the rich port city of Gaza in the south to the wealthy trading town of Petra (originally known to its literate Nabataean Arabs as Raqmu) in the east and via the long-distance spice trade and incense route of Arabia and the Yemen. The Nabataean Arab trade flourished across southern Palestine and northern Arabia. Not surprisingly, for practical reasons the earliest form of Arabic script (also known as the Kufi script) – which evolved from the Nabataean Aramaic and proto-Arabic scripts, which, in turn, can be traced to the Phoenician alphabet – evolved under the impact of these important trade routes of Palestine and Arabia and the growing urbanisation of the Arab Near East.

PHILISTO-ARABIAN COINS: CURRENCY, POWER AND AUTONOMY IN PHILISTIA (6TH–4TH CENTURIES BC)

Although coming under imperial (direct and indirect) rule, the highly advanced cities of Philistia (or Philistin) were the first to develop a monetary system in Palestine, and Philistia was the first region in the country to witness a movement from bullion to a coin economy and Palestinian currency struck in Gaza from 538 BC until the occupation of Palestine by Alexander the Great in 332 BC. Subsequently an ancient Greek-style currency, drachma, was struck in several Palestinian cities, including Gaza, Ascalon, Joppa (Jaffa) and Acre. The drachma gave rise to the silver dirham, the Arab Islamic coin whose name derives from the drachma.

The coinage of Philistia of the 6th–4th centuries BC refers to the much-discussed group of silver coins of the 6th, 5th and 4th centuries, minted by the autonomous rulers of the Palestinian cities of Gaza, Ascalon and Ashdod, and these coins represent the earliest and most significant phase of the development of money in Palestine. This monetary development continued in the 4th century until the end of the Achaemenid (Persian) rule over Palestine. Philistia's early coinage consisted of silver and silver-plated coins. Some of the famous and unique pieces of this large collection are housed in the British Museum. The coins issued in Philistia circulated and were traded widely in the Philisto-Arabian region and became known as Philisto-Arabian coins.

The iconography of the coinage of Philistia was influenced by a melange of Greek, Sidonian, Achaemenid, Egyptian and local Palestinian sources and patterns (Hill 1914, 2011; Tal 2016; Gitler and Tal 2006). The presence of Greek Archaic silver coins, with strong Athenian artistic influences, was noted by several authors and the 'most striking influence on the Philistia coinage is notably Athenian. The people of Philistia observed these foreign motifs and frequented adopted and adapted them to local use' (Tal 2016: 253). The iconography also represents the most miscellaneous assemblage of deities of Assyria, Egypt, Greece and Palestine.

Chapter 2

THE CONCEPTION OF PALESTINE IN CLASSICAL ANTIQUITY AND DURING THE HELLENISTIC EMPIRES (500–135 BC)

Palestine was the name used most commonly, consistently and continuously for over 1200 years throughout classical and Late Antiquity, from the highlight of classical Athenian civilisation in 500 BC until the end of the Byzantine period and the occupation of Palestine by the Muslim armies in 637–638 AD.

To substitute the vague and imprecise term Cana'an for the real historical and official toponym Palaestina used during a classical period lasting over a millennium would be tantamount to the elimination of the history of this region and would create major obstacles to an understanding of Classical and Late Antiquity. The substitution of the term Cana'an (known only for a limited period during the Late Bronze Age) for Palaestina would also eliminate the possibility of any real historical knowledge of one of the most important periods in the ancient history of the region, namely early Christianity and Byzantine Palestine. Greek-speaking Byzantine Christianity in Palestine began in the reign of the Roman Emperor Constantine the Great (306–337 AD) and lasted until the beginning of Muslim rule in Palestine in 637–638 AD.

THE GREEK NAME ΠΑΛΑΙΣΤΙΝΗ IN CLASSICAL AND FOUNDATIONAL GRECO-HELLENIC SOURCES

Classical Antiquity and the Hellenistic period from 500 BC to 135 BC is one of the periods when records of life in Palestine were numerous and well-kept. This is also a period in which the first famous historians and authors of Antiquity, including Herodotus and Aristotle, wrote about the country in detail, and the strategic, commercial and cultural importance of Palestine to the various Hellenistic monarchs, military commanders, traders, travellers, cartographers and scientists led to great interest, and close examination of the country and its people.

The term Palestine was also extensively used in referring to the entire area connected with modern Palestine in 5th century BC Ancient Greece. The name Παλαιστίνη (Phalastin) was widely used by the most important ancient Greek historians, cartographers, writers, philosophers and scientists, including Herodotus, Aristotle and Ptolemy. The Greco-Roman-Byzantine name 'Palestine' is commonly found in major classical Greek texts, especially the *Histories* of Herodotus, written near the mid-5th century BC.

THE CONCEPTION OF PALAISTINÊ BY THE FOUNDING FATHER OF HISTORY

Palestine always played a special role in the imagination, sacred literature and historical representations of the West (Said 1980: 9). This began with the earliest classical literature and seminal works of the Greek writers, especially Herodotus and Aristotle in the 5th and 4th centuries BC. It was in the writings of Herodotus (who lived in the 5th century BC (c. 484–425 BC) that the name took on its Greek form Παλαιστίνη (Palaistinê or Phalastin) and was used as the name of the region. Herodotus talks about Palaestine, Palaestine-Syria and the 'Syrians of Palestine' and he distinguishes the Phoenicians from the 'Syrians of Palestine' (Herodotus 1841: 135). He also describes the physical geography of the region which is associated today with the modern Middle East as follows:

The other [region] starts from the country of the Persians, and stretches into Erythraean sea, containing first Persia, then Assyria, and after Assyria, Arabia. It ends, that is to say it is considered to end, though it does not really come to termination, at the Arabian gulf ... between Persia and Phoenicia lies a broad and ample tract of country, after which the region I am describing skirts our [Mediterranean] sea, stretching from Phoenicia along the coast of Palestine-Syria till it comes to Egypt, where it terminates. This entire tract contains but three nations. (Herodotus 1860: 27)

In his geographic representation of Παλαιστίνη (Palaistinê or Phalastin) Herodotus uses the term in its wider sense and not merely in reference to Philistia, or the coastal strip of land from Carmel to Gaza, but also the interior of the country (Herodotus 1841: 135). He and Aristotle, for example, used the term in a way that includes the regions of Transjordan, or 'Eastern Palestine', beyond the Jordan Rift Valley. Herodotus not only mentions Palestine as an autonomous district of Syria but describes it geographically, as the country we know today, but also including some adjoining areas in the Sinai and the north, as well as the area east of the river Jordan. Herodotus also adds that southern Palestine sea ports from Cadytis to Jenysus (or Ienysos, modern Khan Yunis in the Gaza Strip) were occupied by Arabians (Herodotus 1841: 135).

Herodotus' conception of Palaistinê included the Galilee and referred to Palestine in the wider sense. In effect, this conception applied to the region of the 'Levant between Phoenicia and Egypt' (Jacobson 1999). This classical conception of Palestine also influenced modern representations of the country and a map of Palestine in c. 450 BC, according to Herodotus, was reconstructed in 1897 by John Murray, one of the most important and influential publishers in Britain.

Herodotus' wider conception of Palestine also reflected the expansion of the province of Idumaea in the south, following the destruction of Iron Age Edom by the Babylonian Nabonidus. The Idumites were identified by some scholars to be of Nabataean Arab origins. Idumaea's centre, first in Hebron (al-Khalil) and later centred in Lakish, in the southern foothills, created boundaries stretching from the Transjordan plateau to the

Mediterranean. In 132 CE, under the Romans, Idumaea was joined to the provinces of Judaea and the Galilee and the Latin form Palaestina was used to refer to the whole of the southern Levant.

Herodotus was a contemporary of Socrates and is widely referred to as 'the Father of History' (Cicero, 1st century BC). He was the first historian to systematically investigate historical subjects, arranging material into a historical narrative. Herodotus' *Histories* (also known as *The History*, 1987) is one of the most famous historical texts on the origins of the Greco-Persian Wars, a text known to academics, historians and history students throughout the world. *Histories* is now considered a foundational text in the Western academy. It serves as a key record of ancient oral traditions, politics, geography and the clashes of various powers that were known in Greece, Western Asia and North Africa. When it comes to ancient Palestine and toponymic memory, modern Western Christian writing relies partly on Herodotus' classic work (1987).

In this classical text (written from the 450s to the 420s BC), Herodotus writes about a 'district of Syria, called Palaistinê' and lists place names of ancient Palestine. Herodotus himself visited Palestine in the fifth decade of the 5th century BC. He travelled extensively through 'the part of Syria called Palestine, I myself saw',[1] and acquired first-hand knowledge of the country and its people (Jacobson 1999). Herodotus refers to Παλαιστίνη (Palaistinê), Syria, or simply Palaistinê, many times as an area comprising the whole region between Phoenicia and Egypt (see also Herodotus 2014: 724, Map 10).

Herodotus' text includes the description of key towns and ports, the road later to be called Via Maris, and many other places he had seen and recorded. He describes in detail the city of Ascalon, an ancient seaport city which dates back to the Neolithic Age. At the time of Herodotus Palestine was polytheistic and he consequently describes Ascalon as having a temple for Aphrodite Urania. This signified 'celestial love' and the 'spiritual', as distinct from the more earthly aspect of Aphrodite Pandemos, 'Aphrodite for all the people'. The cult of Aphrodite Urania was associated with body and soul and with spiritual love, beauty, fertility, procreation and pleasure, and its sacred doves still flocked on the roofs of the city in Roman times (Lewin 2005: 156). The cult of Aphrodite Urania was also associated with the sea and existed in several Palestinian cities, including the ancient port city of Jaffa, often referred to in Arabic by Palestinians as 'Arus al-Bahr' (Bride of the Sea).

Classical Greek historians Herodotus and Thucydides (c. 460–c. 400 BC), in contrast with the authors of the Old Testament, sought to separate myth (*muthos*) from reality based on reasoned argument (*logos*) and histories of the gods from histories of humans; they disregarded political and myth-narratives in favour of facts on the ground. Their histories were also strongly geo-ethnographic. Geo-ethnography is central to Herodotus' account of ancient Palestine and its inhabitants. Greek historians and geographers were fully conscious of the fact that the Mediterranean and Red Seas were a major route of international trade and a major source of wealth for Palestine. Herodotus refers to the Arabs who occupied Mediterranean sea ports in southern Palestine (Herodotus 1841: 135) and north Sinai and controlled the incense trade route from the Eastern Mediterranean to southern Arabia and via the Red Sea to India – the frankincense road of Antiquity which comprised a network of major ancient land and sea trading routes linking the Mediterranean world with eastern and southern sources of incense, spices and other luxury goods. Stretching from the Mediterranean ports of Palestine and Egypt through Arabia and beyond, and involving the Nabataean Arabs (and Petra at its height at the beginning of the 2nd century AD), the long-distance land trade in incense flourished between the 7th century BC and the 2nd century AD.

Thus Herodotus records his many conversations with the Philistines and other groups he meets, and interesting facts he learnt about their lives, such as the practice of male circumcision (originally polytheistic) learnt from the Egyptians: the 'Syrians called Palestinians' 'confess that they learnt the custom of the Egyptians' (Herodotus 1858, Book II, Ch. 104; 1836, Vol. 1, Book II: 247). Egypt had the oldest documented evidence for male circumcision dating back to 2345–2182 BC (World Health Organization 2007: 3). David Asheri (1925–2000), Professor of Ancient History at the Hebrew University of Jerusalem, Dean of the Faculty of Humanities (1972–1975), in *A Commentary on Herodotus*, Books 1–4, writes:

> the 'Syrians called Palestinians', at the time of Herodotus were a
> mixture of Phoenicians, Philistines, Arabs, Egyptians, and perhaps
> also other peoples ... Perhaps the circumcised 'Syrians called
> Palestinians' are the Arabs and Egyptians of the Sinai coast; at the

time of Herodotus there were few Jews in the coastal area. (Asheri et al. 2007: 402)

Herodotus, who travelled widely in Palestine and Syria and beyond the coastal region, does not mention Judaea or refer to Jews. He does not mention terms such Cana'an or Canaanites or Israelites in Palestine; nor does he describe monotheism in the country. First, as archaeological evidence shows, monotheism was a much later development in Palestine and the Near East (Masalha 2007). Second, also significantly, many of the Old Testament religio-ideological dogmas evolved centuries after Herodotus.

Interestingly the ancient Philistine and Greek toponyms for Palaistinê, Tantur (Tantura) and Ascalon ('Asqalan) were preserved in local Palestinian Arab tradition and by medieval Arab historians, geographers and travellers, and 'Ascalan' became known to the Palestinians as 'Asqalan (or Majdal 'Asqalan), depopulated by the Israel army in 1950 (Masalha 1997). This shows how, by and large, the local names of Palestinian villages and towns were fairly stable throughout the ancient, medieval and modern history of Palestine.

THE NAME PALESTINE IN ARISTOTLE'S METEOROLOGY

Approximately a century after Herodotus, the celebrated Greek scientist, philosopher and historian Aristotle (Aristotélēs, 384–322 BC) talks about 'Palestine' and does not mention the term 'Cana'an' – primarily because 'Palestine' applied to a real historical region, while the term 'Cana'an' was probably derived from a subsequently constructed religio-ideological narrative of the Old Testament with which at the time Aristotle could not have been familiar. The work of Aristotle is foundational for ancient, medieval and modern empirical sciences and philosophy. His work constituted the first comprehensive system of Western philosophy. According to the *Encyclopaedia Britannica*, 'Aristotle was the first genuine scientist in history ... [and] every scientist is in his debt'.[2]

In his famous work, *Meteorology* (Greek: Μετεωρολογικά (340 BC), Aristotle describes the special qualities of the Dead Sea water:

Again if, as is fabled, there is a lake in Palestine, such that if you bind a man or beast and throw it in it floats and does not sink, this would bear out what we have said. They say that this lake is so bitter and salt that no fish live in it and that if you soak clothes in it and shake them it cleans them.

This is widely and logically understood by scholars to be a reference to the Dead Sea (Jacobson 1999: 66–67)

Aristotelian terminology and thought profoundly influenced Arab-Islamic, Arab-Jewish and Christian philosophical thought throughout the Middle Ages. Aristotelian terminology and naming were well known among medieval Muslim intellectuals and scientists and he was widely revered by Muslim scholars as 'The First Teacher'. Throughout the Middle Ages Muslim translators, scholars and scientists became closely acquainted with classical Greek sources, including sources in history, sciences, philosophy and geography. An Arabic compendium of Aristotle's *Meteorology*, called *al-ʿAthar al-ʿUlwiyyah* was produced c. 800 CE by the Arab Christian scholar Yahya ibn al-Bitriq and was widely circulated among Muslim scholars over the following centuries.

PALAESTINA ON THE WORLD MAP OF PTOLEMY: THE USE OF THE TERM PALAESTINA BY GREEK GEOGRAPHERS AND HISTORIANS DURING THE SELEUCID AND PTOLEMAIC EMPIRES

Another giant of the Hellenistic world, the highly influential Alexandrian cartographer and writer Ptolemy: Claudius Ptolemaeus (c. AD 100–c. 170) produced the first known map to describe Palestine; Ptolemy clearly distinguished between the so-called Syria-Coele, Phoenicia and Palestine, proving the latter was conceived and treated as a separate and autonomous entity. The toponym Syria-Coele or Coele-Syria (Greek: Κοίλη Συρία, Koíle Syría; Latin: Cava Syria; English: Hollow-Syria) is often confounded or equated by some historians with the modern invented term 'Southern Syria' (e.g. Cohen 2006: 41). This strategy is partly designed to camouflage the existence of historic Palestine as a geo-political unit, thereby denying the widespread use of the term Palestine throughout Classical Antiquity. Rendered as Coelosyria and Celesyria, Coele-Syria was a geographical designation of a region in Syria in Classical Antiquity. Although the term Coele itself was possibly a transcription of the Aramaic *kul*, all (Arabic *kul*) of the region of Syria, the term actually acquired a different meaning in both Greek and Latin: *Ca*va Syria or Hollow-Syria. Crucially, it was often applied in a narrower sense to the Beqaa Valley of Lebanon (Pliny the Elder's *Naturalis Historia*, Book V (c. 78 AD; Sartre 1988) and later to the Roman province of Syria-Coele in northern Syria.

After the collapse of the Macedonian Empire of Alexander the Great in 323 BC the Hellenistic Seleucid and Ptolemaic kings fought over Palestine. However, the official use of the name Coele-Syria emerged at some stage in the period of the Hellenistic Seleucid Empire (Cohen 2006: 4I), which existed from 312 BC to 63 BC. The Seleucid and Ptolemaic empires began after the collapse of the empire of Alexander the Great and faded away with the rise of Rome in the 1st century BC. The Seleucid Empire, whose capital was Antioch, was a major centre of Hellenistic culture that maintained the pre-eminence of Greek customs where Greek political elites dominated, mostly in the urban areas.

However Greek historians, following Herodotus, by and large made a clear distinction between Coele-Syria and Palaestina, although they were not in agreement as to the exact boundary between the two geo-political units.[3] The term Coele-Syria was used by some historians in Classical Antiquity in a wider sense to indicate 'all Syria' or 'all Syria without Phoenicia' (Cohen 2006: 41) and by Greek geographers and historians to indicate 'all Syria with the exception of Palestine'. This included Ptolemy, to whom later generations of Arab geographers and scientists referred using his name in Arabic: Batlymus. Ptolemy's world map is a map of the world known to Hellenistic society in the 2nd century. It is based on the description contained in Ptolemy's *Geography*, written c. 150. This work, which had been lost to the West for centuries, was known to the Arabs and Byzantines. It was brought to Italy in the late 14th century and translated into Latin in Florence (Edson 2007). Ptolemy's world map made a clear distinction between Palaestina and Syria-Coele, Phenecia (roughly modern Lebanon) as three completely distinct countries. As we shall see below, the new province of Syria-Palaestina created later by Emperor Hadrian in 135 AD was distinct from the Roman province of Syria-Coele created in 193 AD in the north of Syria.

This crucial distinction made by Ptolemy between the three countries, Palaestina, Coele-Syria and Phoenicia, was hugely influential and impacted on the way future historians, geographers, cartographers, travellers, pilgrims and romance seekers would reproduce similar distinctions. In the 2nd century BC this was evident in the work of Agatharchides or Agatharchus of Knidos (in modern Turkey). Agatharchides was an important political figure of his time, and served as a guardian to one of Ptolemy's sons. In composing his speeches Agatharchides was an imitator of Thucydides, whom he equalled in dignity and excelled in clarity. Ptolemy's world map – and the distinction between the countries of Palaestina, Coele-Syria and Phenecia – was cited directly or indirectly by Strabo, Pliny the Elder, Diodorus Siculus, and Josephus and Philo of Alexandria.

As we shall see below, Filastin and Palaestina are also found on the world maps of cartographers Muhammad al-Idrisi, Pietro Vesconte, Marino Sanudo and Fra Mauro in the 12th, 14th and 15th centuries. Of course, 'world maps' were not just about representations of space and reality, they were designed for practical purposes of traffic and navigation and for the use of traders and pilgrims to the holy places; world maps often provided an expression and fulfilment of power and were produced for empires and state-builders. Ptolemy's world map was no exception; it was produced, reproduced and revised to promote the political agendas of different powers across many centuries. The map was first used to expand the Roman Empire. In the 9th century Ptolemy's *Geography* and map were translated from Greek into Arabic and played a role in the corrective cartography of al-Khawarizmi (780–c. 850) in the Mediterranean region, the Middle East, Africa and Asia, and his scientific work and geographic world map was used in the service of the Muslim global trade and the Baghdad-based Abbasid state. In the late 19th century Ptolemy's map was reproduced by Claude Reignier Conder, of the British Palestine Exploration Fund, and used to advance British imperial ambitions in the Near East and Palestine.

Chapter 3

FROM PHILISTIA TO PROVINCIA 'SYRIA PALAESTINA' (135 AD–390 AD)

The administrative province of Roman Palestine

During Roman rule in Palestine, and more specifically between 135 AD and 390 AD, Palestine became one of the *Provincias* of the empire. This is also a period from which many written records were preserved in a variety of languages – Latin, Greek, Aramaic, Hebrew –and also covered in the annals and texts of the new religion of Christianity. By this time the name 'Palestine' was more than a millennium old and had substantial currency. During the Roman period the official/administrative name of 'Palestine' was consolidated and popularised in Latin and Greek, which were the two lingua francas of the Roman Empire and Eastern Mediterranean. These two languages affected trade, administration, education, religion, architecture, diplomacy, coinage and key place names throughout the Eastern Mediterranean.

THE UPGRADING OF PALESTINE BY HADRIAN: THE OFFICIAL DESIGNATION OF THE PROVINCE OF 'SYRIA PALAESTINA' (135–390 AD)

In Roman times, a province (Latin: *provincia*, pl. *provinciae*) was the basic and, until 293 AD, largest territorial and administrative unit of the empire. A Roman *provincia* in the modern sense was a geographically defined official administrative unit. Provinces were generally governed by politicians of senatorial rank, former consuls or top army commanders. The Romans also distinguished between two types of provinces: minor provinces, or procuratorial provinces, such as Judaea in 1st century AD, and major provinces, or proconsular provinces, such proconsular provinces like 'Syria Palaestina' after 135 AD.

In 135 AD, the Roman Emperor Hadrian (Hadrianus; reigned 117–138 AD) officially combined the minor Roman (procuratorial) province of Iudaea (comprising Judaea and Samaria) with the old Philistia, the Galilee in the north and Idumaea in the south to form a new major (proconsular) province of 'Syria Palaestina'. According to some accounts the new province was created following the military defeat of the Jewish revolt of Bar-Kochba in 135 AD. Four years later the official designation of the new province of 'Syria Palaest[ina]' was given in a 139 AD Roman military diploma granted for military service – 'a rectangular bronze tablet' which was 'discovered in Palestine near Nazareth' in the late 19th century and was exhibited at the Louvre Museum (de Ville-fosse 1897). Issued by the Roman Emperor and lodged in the military archive of Rome, these military certificates were inscribed in bronze confirming that the holder was discharged from the Roman armed forces and had received the grant of Roman citizenship with its privileges, as a reward for military service. In addition to this military evidence, the first numismatic evidence for the province of Syria-Palaestina comes from the period of Marcus Aurelius, Emperor from 161 to 180. However, the new province of 'Syria Palaestina' should not be conflated with Roman Syria as a whole – as some historians do – or with either the separate Roman province of Syria-Coele in the northern parts of Syria or Roman Phoenicia (modern Lebanon).

The Roman (and Hadrian's) conception of Palestine had nothing to do with any biblical narratives or the Old Testament narrative of the 'Philistines'. For Hadrian, in addition to a combination of political and military-strategic calculations following the defeat of the Bar-Kochba rebellion in 135, the historical-geographic considerations behind the official upgrading of Palaestina by the Romans in the early 2nd century should also be taken into account. After all, Emperor Hadrian chose the 1000-year-old name of Philistia, the most common geo-political designation for Palestine used by Greek geographers and historians, long before the Old Testament stories were put together; and Hadrian combined Palestine with the southern parts of Syria.

The Greek name for the country Palaistine and the Latin name Palaestina were frequently and repeatedly cited in classical literature and by classical Greek and Roman historians and poets with reference to the country between Egypt and Phoenicia. The metamorphosis of Palestine – from Philistia to Palaestina – is not surprising when considering that the early 1st century Roman poet Ovid, one of the canonical poets of Latin literature, repeatedly invoked the term Palaestina and adjective Palaestino (Palestinian) in *Metamorphoses* and his other epic poems.[1] In Ars Amatoria ('The Art of Love') Ovid also mentioned 'the seventh-day feast that the Syrian of Palestine [Palaestino Syro] observes', with reference to followers of Judaism in Palestine, who were in the 1st century AD one of the many religious groups in the country. Ovid and other Roman writers did not confine the term Palaestina and Palaestino to the coastal region known as Philitia, but included the interior of the country. In c. 90 AD another famous 1st century Greco-Roman author, Dio Chrysostom (c. 40–c. 115 AD), an orator, philosopher, historian of the Roman Empire (born at Prusa, present-day Turkey), was quoted by Synesius – Greek bishop of Ptolemais, in modern Libya, in the early 4th century – referring to the Dead Sea as located 'in the interior of Palestine' (Dio Chrysostom 1951, Vol. 5: 378–379).

Another classical Roman poet of the 1st century AD, Publius Papinius Statius, in the *Silvae*, refers to '*liquores* Palaestini' (Palestinian wine) (Zeiner 2005: 104; Feldman 1996: 565), which was produced in large quantities and was widely known throughout the Mediterranean region. Its fame was partly derived from the application of south Arabian spices and local herbs and the Palestinian aromatic *Balsam*[2] to wine-making in Palestine and the Arab region as a whole, something which Statius called *liquores Arabes* (Zeiner 2005: 104). In the course of the subsequent Byzantine period, large-scale production of *Palaestini liquores* in greater Palaestina led to international commerce in the commodity, and Palestinian wine was exported around the Mediterranean region and in the Near East. Although religiously discouraged, the genre of wine poetry (*al-Khamriyyat*) became a recurring theme in classical Arabic poetry of the Abbasid period in the Middle Ages. Ancient methods of wine-making survived in Palestine into the modern period, while the balsam shrub was reported to be cultivated in the Galilee in the early 19th century (Burckhardt 1822: 323).

The administrative name of the new province, 'Syria Palaestina', was almost certainly inspired by the works of classical Greek and Roman historians, geographers and poets who had contributed so much to the spread and popularisation of the name Palaestina since the work of Herodotus in the 5th century BC. Considered by many to have been a classicising humanist, and one of the greatest and most accomplished of the Roman Emperors, Hadrian was fond of Greek culture, historiography and literature (Birley 1997). During his reign, he travelled extensively with the Roman military and visited nearly every province of the empire, including Palestine. An admirer of cultural Hellenisation, he sought to make Athens the cultural capital of the empire and ordered the construction of many opulent temples in the city. Hadrian had served as the Governor of Syria, giving him an intimate knowledge of the region (Birley 1997: 75). He had travelled through Palestine and visited Gaza – the most powerful city of old Philistia – on his way to Egypt in 130 AD: 'Gaza began dating its coinage by a new era beginning with Hadrian's arrival, which can be narrowed down to July. A "Hadrian festival" was also founded there' (Birley 1997: 234). Hadrian's trip further encouraged the classicising culture of the city and the building of many Greek temples there.

The speed with which the new name of the administrative province of 'Syria Palaestina' was widely adopted is evident in its use not only by establishment Roman historians and geographers who often defended the status quo, but also among Palestine-based early Christian apologists who were often philosophically radical and politically subversive. Greco-Roman historian Appian of Alexandria (c. 95–c. 165 AD), who flourished before, throughout and after the reign of Hadrian, wrote in his Preface to *Historia Romana* (c. 150 AD):

> Intending to write the history of the Romans, I have deemed it
> best to begin with the boundaries of the nations under their sway
> ... Here [after Egypt] turning our course we take in Palestine-Syria,
> and beyond it a part of Arabia. The Phoenicians hold the country
> next to Palestine on the sea, and beyond the Phoenician territory are
> Coele-Syria, and the parts stretching from the sea as far inland as the
> river Euphrates, namely Palmyra and the sandy country round about,
> extending even to the Euphrates itself.[3]

The new genre of early Christian apologetics focused on defending the new religion in philosophical terms and on equating Christianity with Greek philosophy. Early Christian apologists included prominent Palestine-based writers such Justine the Martyr and Origen. Justine the Martyr was born to a pagan family in Flavia Neapolis (Nablus), then a largely Greek-speaking town in the Roman Province of Syria-Palaestina (Parvis 2008). At the time, Flavia Neapolis was also a flourishing centre of Greek philosophy and Platonism. Today Justine is regarded as the foremost interpreter of the concept of the Greco-Christian logos in the 2nd century AD (Rokeah 2002: 22). Following his conversion to Christianity Justine travelled to Rome during the reign of Antoninus Pius (138–161 AD) and started his own Christian philosophical school. Justine was beheaded in Rome. Addressed to Antoninus, his sons and the Roman Senate, his First Apology (c. 155 AD) passionately defended the morality of the Christian faith and provided various ethical and philosophical arguments to convince the Roman authorities to abandon their persecution of the fledgling sect. In the introduction to the First Apology Justin also refers to his native city 'Flavia Neapolis in Palestine'.[4]

Both the official administrative name of the province of 'Syria Palaestina' and the term Palaestina continued for many years to be widely and interchangeably used by native Palestinian and Roman and Greek writers, geographers, historians and imperial administrators to refer to the area between the Mediterranean Sea and River Jordan. The Romans promoted further urbanisation in Palestine and the province of 'Syria Palaestina' itself had a well-organised road network and an efficient traffic system as basic elements of proper imperial administration. The importance of Provincia Palaestina can be seen by the fact that the Romans invested great resources in the urban infrastructure and transport system of the country, in labour and technological skill in road building. During much of this period of Roman Provincia Palaestina Jerusalem served as one of the two administrative and cultural hubs of the country – the other one being the city of Caesarea-Palaestina – and the seat of the Roman Governor and the royal court.

Continuing the long Hellenistic tradition of changing place names and personal names in Palestine – a tradition which was actively pursued internally by Roman Jewish rulers and public intellectuals from King Herodes (Herod) the Great to Josephus – the city of Jerusalem was renamed by Emperor Hadrian (full name in Latin: Publius Aelius Hadrianus Augustus) as Aelia Capitolina (Wilkinson 1975). Capitolina was dedicated to Jupiter Capitolinus, the chief deity of the Roman state religion, while Aelia referred to Hadrian's own second name and to the name of Lucius Aelius Caesar, the father of Emperor Lucius, who was adopted by Hadrian and named heir to the throne, but died before Hadrian. The latter accelerated the Hellenistic tradition of renaming Palestine cities. Subsequently Aelia Capitolina remained the official name of Jerusalem for more than five centuries until 638 AD when the Arabs conquered the city and kept the first part of the name as Iliya. In fact, it seems that the Arabs began to use the name Iliya at a 'very early period', long before the Islamic conquest of the city (Gil, M. 1997: 114). The name 'Jerusalem' almost became extinct; Aelia Capitolina becoming the common name for the city. Its Arabic version, Iliya, was still being used in medieval Arabic sources in the 10th century, together with the other Arabic name for Jerusalem, Bayt al-Maqdis (al-Maqdisi 2002: 135, 144; Drijvers 2004: 2). However, a century later, during the Fatimid period, Muslim traveller Nasir Khusro (Khusrau), who visited Jerusalem in 1047, reported that the people of Palestine and al-Sham as a whole called *al-Bayt al-Muqaddas* (the Holy City) by the name al-Quds (Khusrau 1888). This is also the modern and current name of the city used by the Palestinians.

Aelia Capitolina, due to its centrality under both the Romans and later the Byzantines, served as a starting point for no fewer than seven highways. These seven highways were later broadly reflected in the 16th century Ottoman walls and gates of the Old City of al-Quds. The 'Hadrian Column' can be seen in the Madaba Floor Mosaic Map of the 6th century (see chapter 4). The name has also survived in local modern Palestinian social memory and in the naming of the most spectacular Ottoman Gate of the Old City of Jerusalem: Bab al-'Amud (literally, the 'Column Gate'), also known as Damascus Gate.

FURTHER DEVELOPMENTS: FROM 'SYRIA PALAESTINA' TO PALAESTINA

In the course of time, and especially from Vespasian (Emperor from 69 to 79 AD) onwards, the term Palaestina began to supersede the longer Roman name of the province of 'Syria Palaestina'. The territorial boundaries of Palaestina in the time of the Romans embraced the coastal region of Palestine, Idumaea, Judaea, Samaria, Perasa (northern modern Jordan) and Trachonitis (modern Arab, Lajat), south-east of Damascus. Following Herodotus and classical literature, this Roman conception of Palestine applied to the country in the wider sense: to the area of the southern Levant between modern Lebanon and Egypt. The shift in the terminology from the official Roman province of 'Syria Palaestina' introduced by Emperor Hadrian to more and more emphasis on Palestine is reflected in the works of important Roman writers such as Strabo, Pliny the Elder and Pomponius Mela and classical Jewish authors including Josephus and Philo of Alexandria.

THE 1ST CENTURY GEOGRAPHY OF PALAESTINA BY STRABO, PLINY THE ELDER AND POMPONIUS MELA

Historical and geographical knowledge and power are inextricably linked and the expansion and consolidation of the Roman Empire brought about the rise of encyclopaedic multi-volume works. In the 1st century AD there are three well-known geographical accounts of Palestine by: (a) Greco-Roman geographer and historian Strabo (64–63 BC–c. 24 AD), in his multi-volume work *Geographika* (Strabo 1917) – this encyclopaedic knowledge was based on his extensive travels throughout the Mediterranean region and Near East; (b) Pliny the Elder (23–79 AD) in his work *Naturalis Historia* (c. 78 AD);[5] (c) Pomponius Mela, who was the first Roman geographer and wrote the only ancient treatise on geography in classical Latin, *De Situ Orbis* ('A Description of the World'), written around 43 AD. The accounts of Strabo, Pliny the Elder and Mela all treat the country of Palestine in the wider sense, in the same way as the name applied by the classical Greek writers to the whole country.

Pliny, Strabo and Mela may well derive some of their information on Palestine from earlier Hellenistic sources. Pliny's *Naturalis Historia* (c. 78 AD) is an encyclopaedic book about the natural world written by a Roman author and naval commander who also belonged to Emperor Vespasian's inner circle. The geo-administrative term Palaestina used in *Naturalis Historia*, Book V: Chapters 13 and 14, reflects both the evolving place names of the time and the changes introduced by Vespasian. Geographically Pliny uses Palaestina in two distinct ways: old Palaestina, or old Philistia, and the new Palaestina whose vast expanses reach all way to modern Lebanon and Syria:

> The next country on the coast is Syria, formerly the greatest of lands. It had a great many divisions with different names, the part adjacent to Arabia being formerly called Palestine [Palaestina, or old Philistia], and Judaea, and Hollow Syria, then Phoenicia and the more inland part Damascena, and that still further south Babylonia as well as Mesopotamia between the Euphrates and the Tigris ... Behind Sidon begins Mount Lebanon, a chain extending as far as Zimyra in the district called Hollow Syria [Coele-Syria], a distance of nearly 190 miles. Facing Lebanon [Phoenice], with a valley between, stretches the equally long range of Counter-Lebanon, which was formerly connected with Lebanon by a wall. Behind Counter-Lebanon inland is the region of the Ten Cities [the Decapolis in the Roman province of Syria-Palaestina and later Byzantine Palaestina Secunda] and with it

the tetrarchies already mentioned, and the whole of the wide expanse of Palestine [Palaestina]. (Pliny 1991: Book V)

The work of Pomponius Mela, *A Description of the World* (*Chorographia*), although inferior by the standard of the works of Strabo and Pliny the Elder as well as by modern technical standards, was circulated widely in the course of Europe's Great Age of Exploration from the end of the 15th century to the 18th century, and was translated into English. It remained highly influential throughout the modern period. Published in 44 CE, at the height of the Roman Empire, Mela's work was one of the world's earliest geo-ethnographies and is the earliest surviving geographical work in Latin (Romer 1998). This work was influenced by classical Greek sources and, like Herodotus, Mela describes Palestine in the wider sense: from Phoenicia in the north to Egypt in the south. Unlike Herodotus, however, Mela mentions Judaea but he correctly views it as a small part of the country he calls Palaestina. In 43 AD Mela spoke of 'the Arabs of Palestine' (*Hic Palaestine est qua tangit Arabas*) and describes Syria and Palaestina as follows:

> [Syria holds a broad expanse of the littoral, as well as lands that extend rather broadly into the interior, and it is designated by different names in different places. For example, it is called Coele, Mesopotamia, Judea, Commagene, and Sophene.
>
> It is Palestine at the point where Syria abuts the Arabs, then Phoenicia, and then – where it reaches Cilicia – Antiochia, which was powerful long ago and for a long time, but which was most powerful by far when Semiramis held it under her royal sway. Her works certainly have many distinctive characteristics. Two in particular stand out: Babylon was built as a city of amazing size, and the Euphrates and Tigris were diverted into once dry regions.[6]

It is also fascinating what Mela had to say about Gaza and other important cities of the country he calls Palaestina. In Semitic languages, the name Gaza means 'strong' or 'fierce' (Hebrew: עַזָּה, 'strong'). Etymologically the Greek and Latin name: Γάζα and Gaza, were probably a rendition of the Syriac: ܓܙܐ (*ganzā, gazzā*) which originated from Persian *ganj* ('treasure', 'store', 'granary'). The ancient Egyptians called it Azzati, *the* 'prized city' (Shahin 2005: 414; *Katzenstein 1982*). Mela goes on to describe the Palestine cities of Gaza, Ascalon and Jaffa and refers to both Semitic and Persian connotations of the name Gaza:

> In Palestine, however, is Gaza, a mighty and very well fortified city. This is why the Persians call it their treasury: when Cambyses headed for Egypt under arms, he had brought here both riches and the money for war. Ascalon is no less important a city. Iope [Jaffa] was founded, as they tell it, before the flood. Iope is where the locals claim that Cepheus was king, based on the proof that particular old altars–altars with the greatest taboo–continue to bear an inscription of that man and his brother Phineus. What is more, they even point out the huge bones of the sea-monster as a clear reminder of the event celebrated in song and legend, and as a clear reminder of Andromeda, who was saved by Perseus. (Pomponius Mela, in Romer 1998: 52–53)[7]

THE OFFICIAL DESIGNATION OF PALAESTINA BY CLASSICAL JEWISH SCHOLARS

The same wider territorial concept of Palestine was embraced by classical Jewish writers, especially Josephus (37–c. 100 AD; Hebrew: Yosef ben Matityahu), born in Jerusalem to a priestly family, and Philo of Alexandria (c. 25 BC–c. 50 CE; Hebrew: Yedidia HaCohen; also called Philo Judaeus), the Jewish philosopher and a contemporary of Jesus who lived in the Roman province of Egypt and became the most important representative of Hellenistic Judaism. Philo (whose father had apparently played a prominent role in Palestine before moving to Alexandria[8]), wrote in *Quod Omnis Probus Liber Sit*[9] that 'four thousand' Essenes[10] – a Jewish sect that flourished from the 2nd century BC to the 1st century AD and who gained fame in modern times as a result of the discovery of the Dead Sea Scrolls – lived in 'Palestine and Syria'.[11]

Hellenised Greek-speaking Jewish authors such as Philo and Josephus wrote in standard Greek for educated Jewish classes in the region and for

Roman and Greek audiences. Like Greek and Roman writers and many Jewish Roman citizens, both Josephus and Philo understood and applied the term Palestine to 'greater Palestine' extending from modern Lebanon to Egypt (Robinson 1865: 15; Jacobson 1999), and not just to Philistia, the coastal region of Palestine, or the former 'land of the Philistines' from Gaza to Tantur.

The official Roman designation of the province as Syria-Palaestina existed long before the Jewish revolt of 66–69 AD. However, Vespasian – the patron of Josephus – who was personally involved in subduing the revolt in Judaea, formally widened the territorial boundaries of Palestine and officially designated the whole country as 'Palestine', and this is evident from Roman coins of the period. However, it would be wrong to assume that Roman Provincia Palaestina displaced or replaced Judaea. The latter simply was and remained one of the regions of Provincia Palaestina. Judaea was always seen as representing only a specific and small component of this greater whole, while Palaestina was viewed by classical Greek and Jewish writers and Roman politicians as representative of the whole country from Phoenicia (mostly associated with modern Lebanon) to Egypt.

Writing in the late 1st century, Josephus embraced the Roman patron–protégé system and himself would later write his history works *Antiquities of the Jews*, *The Jewish War* and *Against Apion* in Greek; in these works of history Vespasian is positively remembered by Josephus. Josephus made a clear distinction between Syria and Palestine and endorsed Herodotus' account of Palestine from the 5th century BC.

> Josephus holds Herodotus in high esteem as the founder of historiography, recognizes his authority on ethnographical matters, praises his reliance on autopsy as a basis for knowledge, uses material, vocabulary and themes from the *Histories*, and even uses historical information to 'correct' the Bible. (Priestley and Zali 2016: 6)

Although occasionally Josephus would refer to Palaestina in connection with Philistia and the 'land of the Philistines', by and large he accepted the wider Roman conception of Palestine and used the name within the wider context of the official Roman designation and toponymic representation of the country (Flavius Josephus 1981, 2004, 2013).

As with the iconography of the *Coinage of Philistia* of the 5th and 4th centuries BC (discussed above), for many centuries Hellenistic and Athenian intellectual and artistic creations had exercised considerable influence on the culture of the coastal Palestinian cities of Ascalon, Gaza and Ashdod and their Hellenised intellectuals. The most famous Palestinian academic was Antiochus of Ascalon (130–68/67 BC), by far the most distinguished Palestinian philosopher of the Roman era. Born in the Palestinian city of Ascalon on the Mediterranean coast, Antiochus' compatriot Sosus of Ascalon, a Stoic, played an important part in his philosophical education (Sedley 2012: 11). Antiochus travelled to Athens, at the time the world centre of philosophy, at around 110 BC and became an eminent Platonic philosopher and a friend of Cicero, Rome's greatest politician and orator; the latter was his pupil in Athens in about 78–79 BC. Antiochus was a pupil of Philon of Larisa and succeeded Philon as the head of the New Academy which had been founded in Athens by Plato. After teaching philosophy in Athens, he travelled to Alexandria and later founded his own school of philosophy which 'advocated the possibility of knowledge, thus reversing the sceptical tradition of the recent Academy' (Sedley 2012: 3). He also attempted to reconcile the principles of Platonic epistemology with those of the Stoics and in 87/86 he went on a mission to Alexandria and the Eastern provinces of the Roman Empire to spread his ideas (Gerson 2005: 42).

Antiochus' school of philosophy, especially Antiochian epistemology and ethics, had 'a considerable impact among the Romans of his day', Cicero included (Sedley 2012: 4); 'Antiochus' influence at Alexandria was also considerable' (Sedley 2012: 5). However, there is no evidence to suggest that Antiochus went back to teach in his native Ascalon. Nevertheless, as we shall see below, half a millennium after he led Platonic academies of Athens and Alexandria, another Greek-speaking Palestinian city on the Mediterranean coast, only 20 kilometres to the south of Ascalon, would replace both Athens and Alexandria as the most important centre of classicising Hellenistic philosophy in the Mediterranean region.

THE RISE OF CAESAREA-PALAESTINA

The Romans reoriented Palestine towards the Mediterranean region and this resulted in the establishment and subsequent spectacular rise of the coastal city of Caesarea Maritima (Greek: Parálios Kaisáreia; Παράλιος Καισάρεια), which was also famously known as Caesarea-Palaestina (or 'Caesarea of Palestine'). For centuries Caesarea-Palaestina would serve as the capital of Palestine and one of the most important cultural centres in the Mediterranean region, in effect replacing the two great cities of Athens and Alexandria. Originally a Palestinian/Phoenician village on the Mediterranean coast, Caesarea-Palaestina became one of four Roman settlements (*coloniae*) for demobilised veterans in the province of Syria-Palaestina (Butcher 2003: 230), named in honour of Augustus Caesar. The Roman city and its major harbour were spectacularly expanded by the Roman client king of Judaea in Palestine, Herod the Great (Greek: Horodos), who ruled from 37 to 4 BC. Herod, whose ancestors were Idumites (possibly of Nabataean Arab origins) who had converted to Hellenistic Judaism, became known for his colossal building programme, including the construction of the port at Caesarea Maritima, the Greek-style temple in Jerusalem ('Herod's Temple') and the fortress at Massada. He also constructed or rebuilt several military forts along the Via Maris. The construction of a massive port at Caesarea Maritima signalled the decline of Joppa (Jaffa) in importance as a historic harbour. Two years after the death of Herod, Caesarea Maritima became the seat of a Roman prefect – head of an administrative area – beginning in 6 AD.

To distinguish Caesarea Maritima from Caesarea Philippi (or Caesarea Paneas) – a name which mutated into modern Arab Banyas in the Golan Heights – and Caesarea Cappadocia (modern Turkey), Caesarea-Maritima became famously known throughout the Mediterranean region and Christian world as Caesarea-Palaestina. The reputation of its academy, library and Christian scholars soared throughout the 3rd–6th centuries as it effectively replaced Alexandria as the most important learning centre in the Eastern Mediterranean.

Caesarea-Palaestina was described in detail by the 1st century Roman Jewish historian Josephus in his work *The Jewish War* (1981). As the headquarters of the Roman government in Palestine, Caesarea gradually became the largest and most important city in the country and the economic and political hub of Roman and Byzantine Palestine. Its predominance was elevated further after the Jewish Bar Kochba revolt and war, waged in the course of the later years of the Roman Emperor Hadrian (132–136 AD). The city and its big harbour were extensively rebuilt by Hadrian and at its height the city covered an urban area of nearly a thousand acres – almost five times the size of Jerusalem. Praise for the splendour and physical attributes of Caesarea and other cities of Provincia Palaestina were common in Roman sources. Ammianus Marcellinus, a 4th century Roman soldier and historian, born to a Greek-speaking pagan family in Syria or Phoenicia – whose work was highly regarded by English historian Edward Gibbon – describes Provincia Palaestina in c. 380 AD as follows:

> The last region of the Syrias is Palestine, extending over a great extent of territory and abounding in cultivated and well-kept lands; it also has some splendid cities, none of which yields to any of the others, but they rival one another, as it were, by plumb-line. These are Caesarea, which Herodes built in honour of the emperor Octavianus, Eleutheropolis [Beit Jibrin], and Neapolis [Nablus], along with Ascalon and Gaza, built in a former age. In these districts no navigable river is anywhere to be seen, but in numerous places natural warm springs gush forth, adapted to many medicinal uses. (Ammianus Marcellinus c. 380, Book XIV: 8, 11; cited in Johnson, L. 2000: 36)

From the early 3rd century Caesarea-Palaestina became the civil metropolis of Palestine, and later, when Palestine was divided into three provinces (see below), it remained the capital of Palaestina Prima. In the 3rd and 4th centuries the diverse population of this pluralistic Mediterranean city included Greco-Roman citizens worshipping Greco-Roman deities, Samaritans, Greek and Aramaic-speaking Jews (Donaldson 2000), Greek-speaking Christians, Aramaic-speaking Christians and Arab Christians.

Chapter 4

THE (THREE IN ONE) PROVINCIA PALAESTINA

The three administrative provinces of Byzantine Palestine (4th–early 7th centuries AD)

The Christian Byzantines transformed urban Palestine socially, religiously, economically and architecturally, and this particular period from the 4th to the early 7th century underscored the centrality of Christianity in Palestinian history. The fast spread of the new religion to all countries bordering Palestine made this period important for an additional reason: it was the centre of a strong, confident and growing religion which was born in the country, and continued to consider Palestine as its spiritual centre even after placing the Catholic Church in the capital city of the Roman Empire.

The remnants of the architectural splendour of urban Palestine under the Byzantines can still be seen today. Byzantine Palestine also gave birth to Julian of Ascalon, a native of the ancient Palestinian coastal city, who became a renowned Palestinian architect and whose work on the growth and planning issues of the built environment and on construction and design rules in 6th century Palestine influenced Istanbul's urban planning and endured for more than 1400 years; his work can still be relevant to modern environmental urban planning (Hakim 2001).

After the Christian Byzantines replaced the Romans, Palaestina and its major cities – Caesarea-Palaestina, Jerusalem, Gaza, Neapolis (Nablus), Scythopolis (Beisan), Tiberias and Beit Jibrin (Eleutheropolis) – experienced their greatest growth and prosperity in Antiquity. Throughout the early Christian and Byzantine period, the 4th to the 7th centuries AD, Palaestina remained the dominant and universally applied name for this region. The former Roman provinces of 'Syria Palaestina' were split by the Christian Byzantines, who also redrew the administrative regions of the country. Palaestina was reorganised into three subdivisions. The spread of Greek- and Aramaic-speaking Christianity in the Eastern Mediterranean, Near East and Roman Provincia Arabia[1] and the creation of greater Palestine in the 4th century AD further expanded the early Roman concept of Palestine and the designation employed by classical Greek writers such as Herodotus from the mid-5th century BC onwards. This greater Palestine consisted of Palaestina Prima (in the centre of the country), Palaestina Secunda (much of the Galilee) and Palaestina Salutaris (in the south and south-east).

The Christian Byzantines came up with a major reconfiguration of Palestine. Byzantium itself (renamed Constantinople and later Istanbul) came to the fore upon becoming the imperial residence in the 4th century and the Greek-speaking Eastern Roman Empire came to be known as the Byzantine Empire after 476 AD. The creation of greater Palestine and the official administrative reorganisation of expanded Palestine by the Eastern Roman Empire around 284–305 AD produced 'Three Palestine' provinces whose lingua franca was Greek. These three administrative provinces of Palestine lasted from the 4th to the early 7th centuries:

- Palaestina Prima (combining Philistia, Judaea and Samaria), extending from Rafah in the south to the bay of Haifa in the north, with Caesarea-Palaestina for its capital. In the 630s AD when the Arab Muslim armies took control of Palestine they initially kept Caesarea as the capital of the province of Jund Filastin (the official administrative centre of Palestine). The capital was temporarily moved to Lydda, which was also the temporary capital of Suleiman ibn 'Abd al-Malik, the Umayyad Governor of Filastin (wali Filastin, 'والي فلسطين'), until he built the new city of al-Ramla. Becoming Caliph in 715–717, Suleiman ibn 'Abd al-Malik permanently transferred the capital of Filastin to al-Ramla. Al-Ramla, approximately 20 kilometres south-east of Jaffa, was located strategically on the highway of al-Sham-al-Fustat, Damascus–old Cairo, the latter being the first capital of Egypt under Muslim rule. Al-Ramla remained the administrative capital of the Arab Muslim province of Jund Filastin and an economic hub for the country for over three and a half centuries until the late 11th century.

- Palaestina Secunda (including most of the Galilee and the Golan Heights, parts of *Peraea*[2] and some of the cities of the former Roman Decapolis of Eastern Palestine[3]), with Scythopolis (Beisan) for its capital.

- Palaestina Salutaris (created in the 4th century and later became known also as Palaestina Tertia) included the former Roman Provincia Arabia (Ward 2008), Idumaea, the Naqab/Negev, parts of Sinai, south-west of Transjordan, south of the Dead Sea and Arabia Petraea[4] whose Nabataean capital at the beginning of the 2nd century AD was Petra. It was split from Arabia Petraea in the 6th century AD (Shahin 2005: 8). Petra became the capital of Palaestina Salutaris

Interestingly, the naming of the 'Three Palestines' (Prima, Secunda and Tertia) was inspired by classical and early Christian representation of 'Three in One'. The most famous analogy of this Greco-Byzantine concept was the theological idea of Trinity which was settled and codified at the Council of Nicaea in 325 AD. Crucially the 'Three Palestines' were not conceived as totally separate provinces. Politically, militarily, culturally and ecclesiastically they were conceived and evolved, managed and defended as 'Three in One' provinces of Palaestina. The 'Three Palestines' were closely linked in four different areas:

1. Politically, militarily and ecclesiastically they were dominated by Palaestina Prima. The capital of Byzantine Palestine and of Palaestina Prima was Caesarea-Palaestina, 'Caesarea of Palestine' (von Suchem 1971: 7, 111; 2013; Gilman et al. 1905). This city was also called 'Caesarea by the Sea', or Caesarea Maritima. Since the creation of Israel in 1948 historians in the West have tended to avoid referring to the historic name

of the Palestinian city, Caesarea-Palaestina, and use only the name Caesarea Maritima. But, as we shall see below, the social memory of Caesarea-Palaestina has been preserved in ecclesiastical records and by both the Catholic and Palestinian Orthodox churches.

2. Culturally, they came under the influence of the two most important cultural centres in Palestine and the Eastern Mediterranean: Caesarea-Palaestina[5] (or Caesarea Maritima) and Gaza, which were both also located in Palaestina Prima.

3. Militarily and strategically they were commanded by *Dux Palaestinae*, the 'military commander of Palestine', whose headquarters were in Caesarea-Palaestina and who commanded all Palestine.

4. Ecclesiastically, from the mid-5th century onwards the 'Three Palestines' were united under one single independent all-Palestine Patriarchate of Aelia Capitolina (Jerusalem) with officially recognised religious jurisdiction over the 'Three Palestines'.

Of the three provinces of the country Palaestina Prima was the largest, most powerful economically and most developed culturally. Its bishops of Aelia Capitolina and Caesarea-Palaestina dominated the independent (*autocephalous* or 'self-headed') All Palaestina Church. The *Notitia Dignitatum* ('the List of Offices') is a unique early 5th century imperial chancery document that details the administrative organisation of the Byzantine Empire. It notes that Palaestina Secunda and Palaestina Salutaris were administered by a *praeses*,[6] while Palaestina Prima was presided over by a governor who bore the high rank of proconsul (Ward 2008: 89–90). This should not be confounded with the *Dux Palaestinae*, the 'military commander of Palestine', who was based in Caesarea-Palaestina and commanded the garrison of the 'Three Palestines' in the 5th and 6th centuries (Shahid 1995: 192–193; Röhricht 1890: 7).[7]

Palaestina Prima lasted from 390 AD until the early 7th century. In 614, both Palaestina Prima and Palaestina Secunda were conquered by the Persian Sassanids. The Byzantines lost control of the three Palestine provinces again and irreversibly in 636–638 AD in the course of the Muslim conquest of Bilad al-Sham and Palestine. The urban structure of Palestine and Bilad al-Sham remained largely unscathed by the Sassanid and

Islamic conquests (Walmsley 2000: 273) and the core of greater Palestine, or Provincia Palaestina, under the Byzantines – which combined Palaestina Prima and Palaestina Tertia (Salutaris) – became known as the province of Jund Filastin under Islam.

CAESAREA MARITIMA AS A MEDITERRANEAN CAPITAL OF CULTURE: THE CITY'S METROPOLITAN ELITE

The Christian era of Byzantine Palestine (which refers to this geographic region between the Mediterranean Sea and the Jordan River and various adjoining lands in Transjordan, Nabataea and former Provincia Arabia), with its coastal capital and metropolitan city of Caesarea-Palaestina, was an extraordinary time of cultural flourishing and of great expansion and prosperity in Late Antiquity. New areas were brought under cultivation, urban development increased and the cities of greater Palestine including Gaza, Neapolis (modern Nablus), Jerusalem, Scythopolis (modern Beisan) and Caesarea Maritima grew considerably in population and the diverse population of greater Palestine may have reached as many as one and a half million.[8] Also, monasteries proliferated throughout the country. In fact, the earliest monasteries in Christianity outside of Egypt were built in Palestine during the Byzantine era, notably that of the St Hilarion Monastery, one of Palestine's oldest Christian monuments, today located in the Gaza Strip.[9] At the heart of greater Palestine was the province of Palaestina Prima. Caesarea Maritima was the administrative capital of both Palaestina Prima and greater Palestine. The country consisted of a mixed Greek and Aramaic-speaking population, minorities of Samaritans, Christian Arabs, the Ghassanids, who were the dominant group among the Monophysites and who believed in the single-nature doctrine of Jesus, and Miaphysite[10] Arabs (see also below), Jews and Nabataean Arabs were present as well. Throughout the 6th century and until the Arab Muslim conquest of 638 AD, the Ghassanid Arabs practically ruled Palaestina Secunda (which included parts of the Galilee) and Palaestina Tertia (which included the Naqab/Negev) and, together with Byzantine soldiers, defended and protected the holy sites in Palestine (Shahid 2009, Vol. II, part II: 63–64).

The Louvre Museum in Paris exhibits a masterpiece bronze bowl created in the 4th century AD to commemorate the founding of Caesarea-Palaestina.[11] A flourishing Mediterranean seaport and later the metropolitan city of Palaestina Prima, the city's harbour rivalled the Piraeus of Athens (Barnes 1981: 81). The urban social space of Caesarea is of particular interest. By the 3rd century Caesarea, officially still pagan, had become a cosmopolitan, culturally and socially diverse metropolis, and the largest and most developed city in Roman Palestine; the city contained as many as 100,000 inhabitants of many ethnic and religious backgrounds (Barnes 1981: 82). Caesarea Maritima[12] also became the home of the Founding Fathers of the Church and of prominent Christian intellectuals, missionaries and martyrs. Under the Romans, and more visibly under the Byzantines, *Caesarea* became not only the most powerful city in greater Palestine but also home to the metropolitan, predominantly Greek-speaking, cultural elite of the country. As a major centre of learning and scholarship in the Eastern Mediterranean, it became home to outstanding scholars and theologians and some of the best historians and philosophers of Late Antiquity. This metropolitan cultural elite included Eusebius of Caesarea Maritima and Prokopios of Caesarea Maritima (c. 500–c. 554 AD), in Palaestina Prima. The city also became for many years the home of the Church Father Origen (185–254 AD) and several leading Palestinian Christian theologians who also sought to forge a distinct Palestinian Christian identity based on the unique position of Palestine. Prominent historian Prokopios of Caesarea, a native of Palaestina, had this to write in 560 AD about another compatriot Palestinian:

> Jesus, the Son of God, was in the body and moving among the men
> of Palestine, showing manifestly by the fact that he never sinned at
> all, and also by his performing even things impossible, that he was the
> Son of God in very truth; for he called the dead and raised them up as
> if from sleep, and opened the eyes of men who had been born blind,
> and cleansed those whose whole bodies were covered with leprosy,
> and released those whose feet were maimed, and he cured all the other
> diseases which are called by the physicians incurable. (Prokopios 2005)

But the greatest theologian of Caesarea Maritima was Origen. Born in Alexandria, Origen was later summoned to Provincia Arabia, to give instruction to the governor of that region. Afterward, on account of a great tumult in Alexandria, he left Egypt and went to Caesarea Maritima. St Jerome says that Origen went to Achaia in Greece on account of heresies which were worrying the churches there. His words are: 'Et propter ecclesias Achaiæ, quæ pluribus hæresibus vexabantur, sub testimonio ecclesiasticæ epistolæ Athenas per Palæstinam pergeret' (And for the churches of Achaia, with which many heresies grew throughout Palestine under the ecclesiastical head). He passed through Palestine on his way to Greece, and it was at this time that he was ordained a presbyter by Palestinian bishops.

An avid collector of books, Origen helped create the Library of Caesarea and provided Caesarea Maritima with some of the cosmopolitan charisma and intellectual vigour of large cities such as Alexandria and Antioch. Caesarea became his fixed abode in 232 AD. He also became a catalyst for the phenomenal rise of a Palestinised Greek-speaking cultural elite – an elite which made Caesarea-Palaestina one of the most important cities of classical Antiquity. Palestinised Origen became a prolific Christian author, a philosopher of history and the Father of the Homily. He founded a Christian academy in Caesarea, which included the Library of Caesarea-Palaestina, an ecclesiastical and historical library of 30,000 manuscripts (Carriker 2003; Murphy-O'Connor 2008: 241) and second only to the Library of Alexandria in its heyday. Origen also became known for composing seminal works on Christian Neo-Platonism, including his famous treatise *On First Principles* (1966), a work which had a huge influence on Christian thought and modern Renaissance humanism. Origen wrote *Hexapla* ('sixfold')[13] and other exegetical and theological works while living in Caesarea.

Caesarea-Palaestina has been one of most extensively excavated areas of Byzantine Palestine (Avni 2014: 42). Palestine of the 3rd–6th centuries AD centred on Caesarea, the largest metropolitan city in the whole country:

In the sixth century the city expanded further, beyond its walls, creating extramural quarters with spectacular residences. A large and wealthy agricultural hinterland expanded beyond the urban limits of Caesarea. This urban expansion reflects the constant growth of the urban population, which made Caesarea the largest city in Palestine. (Avni 2014: 42)

Already in the 3rd century AD Provincia Palaestina was centred on its wealthy, largely well-educated and highly developed Mediterranean capital city, Caesarea Maritima. Palaestina was also treated as a distinct country in the writings of its educated urban elites. From the capital Caesarea Maritima, Origen corresponded with the Roman Emperor Philip (Marcus Julius Philippus, or Marcus Iulius Philippus Augustus, who reigned from 244 to 249 AD), also known by his Latin nickname 'Philippus Arabs'. He was born in the northern part of Provincia Arabia, the Roman Arabia Petraea. Inhabited by a mixed population and many Arabs, this region of the Hauran would later become part of Palaestina Secunda and would be in effect ruled by Ghassanid Christian client Arab kings under nominal Byzantine control. 'Philip the Arab' himself went on to become a major figure in the Roman Empire (Bowersock 1994: 122). Among early Christian historians 'Philip the Arab' had the reputation of being sympathetic to the Christian faith. Some later Christian traditions, first mentioned by Eusebius, who was from Caesarea-Palaestina, in his *Ecclesiastical History*, claimed that Philip was the first Christian Roman Emperor (Eusebius 2011: VI.xxxiv). Critics, however, argue that 'Philip the Arab' fared well with ecclesiastical historians because of his religious tolerance and overall sympathetic attitude towards Christians (Shahid 1984: 76–77).

After Origen's death, Palestinian Origenism continued to spread throughout the Near East – until the general condemnation and persecution of Origenism in the mid-6th century – and the theological Library of Caesarea was managed and expanded by St Pamphilus of Caesarea (latter half of the 3rd century–309), who was chief among biblical scholars of his generation and a friend and teacher of the church historian, and Bishop of *Caesarea*, Eusebius (263–339 AD). Eusebius (the 'Father of Church History') was himself born in Caesarea and lived most of his adult life in the city. Pamphilus devoted his life to searching out and obtaining ancient texts for the library, which became one of the most famous and richest in Antiquity. It attracted church historians and theologians from all over the Roman Empire: St Basil the Great (329–379), Gregory of Nazianzus, a 4th century Archbishop of Constantinople and St Jerome (c. 347–420 AD). The latter was a 'Father of the Church' who is best known for his translation of the Bible into Latin. All these famous scholars came to study in Caesarea-Palaestina. Moreover, today the Caesarea text-type is widely recognised by scholars as one of the earliest types for reading the four Gospels (Streeter 1926).

While Christianity continued to play crucial role – not always positive, as cited above only the one case of the persecution of Origen and intellectual followers – in the history of the country and its people, it is this period of its great spread which was the most important for the new religion in Palestine, creating many iconic cultural texts and objects and making Palestine probably the best known country in the world at the time, due to the many descriptions, artefacts, literary, religious and historical works which made it a household name within Christianity and beyond. Some of the iconic texts about the country were produced by the 'Father of Church History', Eusebius of Caesarea, who took pride in in his native country of Palaestina; he repeatedly used the name Palaestina in his works, which later influenced generations of Christian writers worldwide. *De Martyribus Palaestina*[14] by Eusebius (1861) gives us a clear indication of the consolidation of the concept of Palaestina as a country during the early Byzantine period. *The Martyrs of Palestine* relates to the persecution of early Christians in the capital of the country, Caesarea-Palaestina, and the country at large in the early 4th century AD. This account may have originally been composed in Palestinian Aramaic, the language of Jesus of Nazareth. Hebrew at the time of Jesus was largely an extinct language, with the Jews of Palestine speaking Aramaic, and Hebrew being confined to liturgical uses. Closely related to Arabic, Palestinian Aramaic was a language with which Eusebius was well acquainted. At the time, Aramaic was the main vernacular speech of the country and was spoken in the capital, Caesarea-Palaestina.[15] Aramaic would also influence the evolution of Palestinian vernacular Arabic.

Byzantine Palestine also gave birth to the 6th century world's most important historian, Prokopios of Caesarea Maritima, an illustrious scholar from Palaestina Prima, the principal historian of the 6th century Byzantine

Empire and of the reign of Emperor Justinian. Prokopios travelled extensively throughout the Mediterranean region and the Near East, accompanied the Byzantine general Belisarius as secretary in the wars of Justinian and commented extensively on the Ghassanid tribal Arab kings (top *phylarchs*) of Palaestina Secunda, Palaestina Prima and Palaestina Salutaris. In his multi-volume work, *The Wars of Justinian* (c. 560), Prokopios wrote:

> The boundaries of Palestine extend toward the east to the sea which is called the Red Sea. Now this sea, beginning at India, comes to an end at this point in the Roman domain. And there is a city called Aelas [present-day 'Aqabah] on its shore, where the sea comes to an end, as I have said, and becomes a very narrow gulf. (Prokopios 2014)

Prokopios (Greek: Prokopios ho Kaisareus; Latin: Procopius Caesariensis) added that Chosroes (Khosrow I, 501–579), the Shahanshah (King of Kings) of the Sasanian Empire of Persia from 531 to 579, had a great desire to make himself ruler of Palaestina on account of its extraordinary fertility, its wealth and the great number of its inhabitants (cited in Gibbon 1838, Vol. 1: 40; also Prokopios 2014). Commenting on Prokopios' observation about the fertility of the country, the English historian Edward Gibbon, in his most important work, *The History of the Decline and Fall of the Roman Empire*, published in eight volumes between 1776 and 1788, wrote that the Roman historian Tacitus described Palestine as follows: 'the inhabitants are healthy and robust; the rains moderate; the soil fertile' (Gibbon 1838, Vol. 1: 40). Gibbon added: 'Palestine, and the holy wealth of Jerusalem, were the ... objects that attracted the ambitions, or rather the avarice, of Chosroes [I]' (Gibbon 1840, Vol. 5: 173). He further added that the Muslim Arabs 'thought the same, and were afraid that Omar, when he went to Jerusalem, and charmed with the fertility of the soil and purity of the air, would never return to Medina' (Gibbon 1838, Vol. 1: 40).

During the early Christian period, particularly from the 4th century onwards, the Holy Land – a nebulous, abstract and semi-mythical location – was transformed into a real country called Palaestina, with thriving cities, ports, beautiful churches and numerous monasteries, famous philosophical schools and libraries, an extensive road system, villages and a large, commercially and culturally active population, which added to the interest shown by (Latin-speaking) Europeans. It was in the course of this early Christian period that the Latin term Terrae Sanctae became synonymous in Christian texts with the extensive use of the term Palaestina by Christian pilgrims and local historians. *On the Martyrs of Palestine* (311 AD) was written by the church historian and Bishop of Caesarea-Palaestina, Eusebius (AD 263–339), 'Father of Church History', who composed his monumental work *Historia Ecclesiastica* and his *Onomasticon (On the Place Names in the Holy Scripture)* (1971), a comprehensive geographical-historical study of Palestine, in the city: 'Eusebius states that he compiled *On the Place Names in the Holy Scripture* by working through the Bible piecemeal' (Barnes 1981: 109). This major biblical enterprise has been described by British classicist Timothy David Barnes (1981: 106) as a 'biblical gazetteer which is still the main literary source for the historic geography of Palestine both in biblical times and under the Roman Empire'.

Although his *Onomasticon* was partly based on religiously constructed and officially sanctioned scriptural geography and religious memory, Eusebius uses the name Provincia Palaestina repeatedly and in application to the whole country from Lebanon in the north to Egypt in the south, and this Roman/Byzantine administrative and official use influenced later generations of Christian and European writers. A native of Caesarea-Palaestina, whose language was Greek, Eusebius, in his *Oration in Praise of Constantine*, writes proudly about the special attention given to 'our Provencia Palaestina':

he [Emperor Constantin] has selected two places [for his church-building programme] in the eastern division of the empire, the one in ['our province'] Palestine (since from thence the life-giving stream has flowed as from a fountain for the blessing of all nations), the other in that metropolis of the East which derives its name from that of Antiochus; in which, as the head of that portion of the empire, he has consecrated to the service of God a church of unparalleled size and beauty. The entire building is encompassed by an enclosure of great extent, within which the church itself rises to a vast elevation, of an octagonal form, surrounded by many chambers and courts on every side, and decorated with ornaments of the richest kind.[16]

NICAEA AND HISTORICAL ECCLESIASTICAL REPRESENTATIONS OF PALESTINE: THE ARCHIEPISCOPAL SEE OF CAESAREA

The diocese of Caesarea-Palaestina is ancient – one of the earliest Christian bishoprics ever established. Records of the diocese (Greek: 'administration') date as far back as the 2nd century and its bishopric became a metropolitan see. Under the Byzantines the diocese was the metropolis of Palaestina Prima. It was initially directly subject to the Church of Antioch, one of the five major Christian churches during the early Byzantine period. After the All Palestine ecclesia of Aelia Capitolina was granted by autocephaly and independence in the mid-5th century by the Council of Chalcedon (see below), with top ecclesiastical jurisdiction over the 'Three Palestines', for many centuries the metropolitan Church of Caesarea-Palaestina continued to see itself as a 'mother church' and as 'first among equals' of the churches of Palestine.

The most distinguished bishop of the diocese was Eusebius of Caesarea, who was among the most famous bishops to attend the First Council of Nicaea in 325. Today the historic metropolitan see of Caesarea-Palaestina, or the archiepiscopal see of Caesarea in Palaestina, is preserved by the modern Orthodox Palestinian Church. The Archiepiscopal See of Caesarea-Palaestina is also known as a Latin titular see of the Catholic Church (Segreteria di Stato Vaticano 2013: 867; Riley-Smith 1978). A titular (non-diocesan) metropolitan or archbishop of the Catholic Church is a title used to signify a diocese that no longer functions, often because the diocese once flourished but the land was conquered by Muslims.[17] In later days, 'titular see' was seen by the Catholic Church as important to preserve the historic memories of ancient metropolitan churches such as that of Caesarea Maritima. In the period between the creation of this titular Bishopry of Caesarea-Palaestina in 1432 and 1967 twenty-eight Catholic bishops have occupied this honorary position. From 1975 to 2012 the Eastern Orthodox Metropolitan of Caesarea was Basilios Blatsos, who was also an Exarch of Palaestina Prima, under the jurisdiction of the Eastern Orthodox Patriarchate of Jerusalem (formerly the Patriarchate of Aelia Capitolina).

In Roman Provincia Palaestina Jerusalem was renamed by Emperor Hadrian as Aelia Capitolina. Under the Byzantines the name Jerusalem became largely extinct; officially Aelia Capitolina became the common name for the city (Drijvers 2004: 2). At the Council of Nicaea Eusebius and Macarius, the Bishop of Aelia Capitolina, were accompanied by seventeen other bishops representing all the major cities of Palestine (Palaestina Prima and Palaestina Secunda) (Wallace-Hadrill 1982: 165).[18] In ecclesiastical matters, the elites of urban spaces in Palestine interacted with, and often dominated, their surrounding countryside. In the event, however, the council gave the Bishop of Aelia Capitolina (Jerusalem) the first place among the bishops of Palestine, while leaving the Rites of the Church of Caesarea applicable to the whole of greater Palestine. Caesarea-Palaestina also retained its position as metropolis to the Church of Aelia Capitolina and was directly subject to the Church of Antioch. This ambiguous situation created by Nicaea was subsequently used by the Bishop of Aelia Capitolina, Maximus, to ordain bishops for Palestine and to assemble a council of bishops for the whole country. Inevitably this situation brought about conflicts between the Church of Aelia Capitolina and the older (ancient) Church of Caesarea-Palaestina. The latter persisted and continued to claim for a while ecclesiastical primacy over Palestine (Du Pin and Wotton 2010: 107).

THE EMERGENCE OF INDEPENDENT PALESTINIAN CHURCH: POLITICAL VERSUS RELIGIOUS CAPITALS IN PALESTINE

Politically and administratively a capital city is the city enjoying primary or official status in a country, province or state as a seat of government. The word capital derives from the Latin *caput* ('head'), but in Greek-speaking Byzantine Palestine the Greek term for capital cities was *metropolis*. Some capital cities, such as Jerusalem, were also religious centres. Furthermore, under Islam an arrangement of joint political and administrative capitals existed at the height of the Abbasid Caliphate: Baghdad and al-Raqqa (in modern Syria), under Harun al-Rashid in 796–809 AD.

The first to make a clear distinction between political/administrative capital city and religious capital in Palestine was the Greek-speaking

Idumite King Herod the Great, who developed and expanded Caesarea-Palaestina as his metropolitan political capital, while at the same time continuing to develop Aelia Capitolina as the religious capital of his autonomous kingdom.

Under the Byzantines over time two crucial ecclesiastical developments took place in Palestine:

1. The ecclesiastical autonomy of the three Palestine provinces continued to evolve throughout the 5th and early 6th centuries and the evolution of a *distinct* Palestinian religio-cultural identity benefited greatly from the international organisation of the churches in the East which was conceived as radically different from that in the West.

2. The All Palestine Church of Jerusalem was headed by both Greek-speaking and Arab bishops (Shahid 2006a: 46–48, 193–194, 523) and several Arab bishops of Palestine – including the bishops Elusa, in Palaestina Tertia, Abdelas (Arabic 'Abdallah; Greek Theodulos, which was a translation of his Arabic name: 'Servant of God') and Aretas (al-Harith) – participated in the crucial ecumenical councils of Ephesus and Chalcedon in 431 and 451 respectively (Shahid 2006a: 523; Sharon 2013: 75).

In Palestine and the Near East as a whole the churches began 'from below' as a network of *independent* churches, while the Rome-based (Catholic) Church in the West ultimately evolved into a single, hierarchical structure with sub-churches. In contrast with the Catholic notion that the Bishop (and Church) of Rome was above *all* bishops, in the East the churches adopted the Greek ideas of autocephaly (αὐτοκεφαλία, 'self-headed') and 'first among equals' (Greek: Πρῶτος μεταξὺ ἴσων). These became the guiding principles of the Orthodox churches whose Palestine Patriarchs ('Bishop of Bishops' or Archbishops) did not have to report to any higher-ranking Patriarch, including the Patriarchs of Antioch or Constantinople. These two principles contributed to the consolidation of an *independent* Palestine Orthodox Church with jurisdiction over the 'Three Palestines'. They also contributed to the emergence of a distinct religio-cultural identity in Palestine. Ironically, however, this ecclesiastical independence of the Church of Aelia Capitolina contrasted with the rigid formal power structure of the Byzantine Empire, in which provincial political and military powers in the 'Three Palestines' were ultimately subordinate to the Emperor of Constantinople.

The All Palestine Church of Aelia Capitolina was granted autocephaly and its head bishop, or Patriarch, did not have to report to any higher-ranking Patriarch in Byzantium. This development began with the Council of Chalcedon in 451 AD, which was attended by four Arab bishops including the bishops of Elusa in Palaestina Tertia, Gaza and Neila in Provincia Arabia (Shahid 2006a: 523) and which was a turning point in the history and growing independence of the Palestinian church. This growth in the autonomy and power of Palestine had begun with the increased Christian pilgrimage and growing economy of the country throughout and after the reign of Constantine the Great. The growth in pilgrimage and revenues increased the fortunes of the head bishop of Aelia Capitolina. Already in 325 AD the first ecumenical council of the church, the Council of Nicaea, attributed special honour to the holy city, though without awarding it the 'metropolitan' status, then the highest rank in the church, which went to the metropolitan of Caesarea-Palaestina rather than to the bishop of Aelia Capitolina. Until the creation of the idea of the Patriarchate in 325 AD, the position of metropolitan was the highest episcopal rank in the church. However, in 531 the title of 'Patriarch' of Aelia Capitolina was created by Byzantine Emperor Justinian (reigned 527–565 AD). Yet, in reality, Aelia Capitolina continued to be viewed as a bishopric until 451, when the Council of Chalcedon, the fourth ecumenical council of the church, granted it independence not only from the metropolitan of Caesarea but also from any other higher-ranking bishop, including that of Antioch, in what became known as autocephaly, a self-governing church over the 'Three Palestines'. In the Council's seventh session, the 'Decree on the Jurisdiction' of Aelia Capitolina and Antioch contains the following reference to the three provinces of greater Palestine:

> The most magnificent and glorious judges said: ... The arrangement arrived at through the agreement of the most holy Maximus, the bishop of the city of Antioch, and of the most holy Juvenal, the

bishop of Jerusalem [Aelia Capitolina], as the attestation of each of
them declares, shall remain firm for ever, through our decree and
the sentence of the holy synod; to wit, that the most holy bishop
Maximus, or rather the most holy church of Antioch, shall have under
its own jurisdiction the two Phœnicias and Arabia; but the most holy
Juvenal, bishop of Jerusalem, or rather the most holy Church which
is under him, shall have under his own power the three Palestines
all imperial pragmatics and letters and penalties being done away
according to the bidding of our most sacred and pious prince.[19]

Here the Council of Chalcedon makes a clear geo-political distinc-
tion between the 'Three' provinces of Palaestina, the 'Two provinces of
Phœnicias' (i.e. the two provinces of Syria) and the province of Arabia.
This decree of elevating the Palestine Church led to the Church of Aelia
Capitolina not only becoming an independent Patriarchate, but also to
becoming (a) the dominant ecclesiastical and religious capital of the 'Three
Palestines' and (b) one of the five Patriarchates of Christendom, at the
time known as the Pentarchy (Πενταρχία). In this model, which was
reflected by the laws of Emperor Justinian I (527–565 AD) and received
formal ecclesiastical sanction at the Council in Trullo (692 AD), universal
Christendom was governed by the heads of the five major Patriarchs of the
empire: Constantinople, Rome, Alexandria, Antioch and Aelia Capitolina.
The latter was not among the biggest and most powerful urban centres of
the empire; it was included by virtue of its holiness. Although the Pentarchy came about because of the political and ecclesiastical prominence
of these five Patriarchs, the idea of their universal and exclusive authority
was linked to the increasingly hierarchical administrative structure of the
Byzantine Empire in the 7th century, thus moving the churches further
away from their democratic roots and their status as an association of independent churches. In reality, however, infighting among the Sees, and the
rivalry between Rome and Constantinople, prevented the Pentarchy from
functioning effectively. Yet the extraordinary elevation of the Palestine
Church made it a top international player far beyond its formal jurisdiction over the 'Three Palestines', which were perceived and represented in
Church documents as one country. However, the metropolitan ('mother')

church of Caesarea-Palaestina remained the political, military, commercial and administrative capital of greater Palestine and its metropolitan bishop remained highly influential both politically and religiously.

Furthermore, in the Orthodox tradition, bishops and archbishops exercised both religious and temporal political power. Autocephaly for the Palestine Church and membership in the Pentarchy (the five major Patriarchs of the empire) meant five things:

- Religious autonomy, self-governing, self-legislation and ecclesiastical independence from the Church of Antioch or Church of Constantinople.
- The extension of the religious jurisdiction and temporal power of the Church of Aelia Capitolina over the 'Three Palestines' (Prima, Secunda and Tertia).
- Autocephaly and primacy for the Church of Aelia Capitolina reinforced the distinction between secular and religious capitals in Byzantine Palestine, of Aelia (Jerusalem) versus Caesarea Maritima.
- Autocephaly and independence of the Palestine Church reinforced the unity of greater Palestine. Now the 'Three Palestines' were also officially united ecclesiastically. They were already closely linked commercially and militarily and were commanded by the *Dux Palaestinae*, 'the military commander of Palestine', who was based in Caesarea-Palaestina and commanded the garrison of all three provinces of Palaestina in the 5th and 6th centuries. This all meant that by the early 6th century, in both ecclesiastical-religious-temporal and military affairs, greater Palestine was treated as more than three Palestine provinces of the Byzantine Empire; it was longer treated as separate 'Three Palestines' but had evolved into a single religio-political entity.
- Membership in the exclusive club of Pentarchy provided the Church of All Palestine with an added international prestige and further clout at home.

Interestingly, a medieval document written in the 9th or 10th century, entitled *The Limits of the Five Patriarchates*, describes the five Patriarchates of Christendom in the Middle Ages and treats Palestine as a country. The sequence of the text, which was found appended to some manuscripts of the New Testament, is a variation of the Pentarchy established by ecumenical Councils of Chalcedon and Trullo, with the Patriarchates of Jerusalem moving from fifth to first place. The text, which in some sources is entitled *Knowledge and Cognition of the Patriarchate Sees* (Scrivener 1893: xx), states: 'The first See and the first patriarchate is of Jerusalem ... contains the whole Palestine a country until Arabia' (Πρῶτος θρόνος καὶ πρώτη πατριαρχία Ἱεροσολύμων ... περιέχων πᾶσαν τὴν Παλαιστίνων χώραν ἄχρι Ἀραβίας).

Some of these religious and secular administrative features of Palestine were initially maintained and later adapted under Islam. Following the Muslim conquest in the 7th century the Arab rulers endorsed the principle of Autocephaly, recognised the autonomy of the Church of Aelia Capitolina as the seat of Palestinian Orthodox Christianity and recognised the Patriarch as its leader. For many years, the Muslim Arabs continued to call the city Iliya (Aelia Capitolina) and they initially minted Arab Byzantine style coins with the name Iliya Filastin. Palestinian historian al-Maqdisi and some Muslim writers were still using the name Iliya in the 10th century in combination with other Muslim names for the holy city such as Bayt al-Maqdis (al-Maqdisi 2002: 43, 135, 144; Drijvers 2004: 2; Gil, M. 1997: 114).

However, sometime after the Islamic conquest the Arabic term Bayt al-Maqdis came into common use. And later, largely starting from the 11th century onwards, the current name al-Quds became the most common, supplanting all the other names (Gil, M. 1997: 114). Moreover, for several centuries throughout early Islam (as under the Christian Byzantines), the clear distinction between the political and administrative capital of Filastin (al-Ramla) and the religious capital of the country (Iliya, Bayt al-Maqdis) was maintained.

Throughout early Islam the city of Caesarea continued to thrive as a largely Christian city, led by a Greek-speaking elite. However, the local Christians were predominantly Arab Christians who were connected to the Palestinian Muslim Arabs by language, history and social customs. The powerful metropolitan archbishops of the city kept their autonomy and managed to maintain ecclesiastical ties with the churches of the Byzantine state. However, in the absence of close Byzantine imperial control, the local autonomy of the archbishops of Caesarea (and of Aelia Capitolina) increased significantly under Arab Muslim rule and the See of Caesarea Maritima became the effective local rulers not only of the city but also of its surrounding countryside.

LATIN PALESTINE

The current archaeological knowledge about Palestine during the Islamic period shows that for several centuries the country prospered and grew under its Muslim rulers. This should surprise no one; the similar situation in the Andalus (Muslim Spain) is evidence for the great opulence and innovation of the Muslim regime. Indeed, when the European (Frankish) Crusaders invaded Muslim-majority Palestine in 1099, they found there a cultural and technical level of development unknown in contemporary Europe.

The Catholic Church, reaching the peak of its political power in the High Middle Ages, called armies from across Europe to a series of Crusades against Islam. The Latin Crusaders occupied Palestine in 1099 and founded the Crusader states in the Levant. Following the great East–West schism of 1054 between the Eastern Orthodox and Latin churches and after the arrival of the first Latin Crusaders in Palestine, the Crusaders appointed a Latin Patriarch in Jerusalem. The hierarchical international organisational structure of the Latin Church contrasted sharply with the organisation in the East of a network of independent churches. The Crusaders also dismissed the principles of autocephaly and the independence of the Palestine Orthodox Church. As a result, the Eastern Orthodox Patriarch chose to relocate to Constantinople, in exile until 1187, and returned to the city only after its liberation by Salah al-Din. Furthermore, paradoxically in the Latin Crusader Kingdom of Jerusalem, in the early 12th century the diocese of 'Caesarea in Palaestina' lost its religious and cultural autonomy and was subjected to the direct control of the Latin Patriarchate of Jerusalem which was overseen by the European rulers and settlers of the Latin Kingdom of Jerusalem.

However, the Latin Kings of Jerusalem sought to revive memories of Byzantine Palaestina and the actual diocese system of the All Palaestina

Church was revived in Frankish Palestine. For instance, the 'Archbishop of Petra, in Palaestina' – which in the 6th century was the metropolis of the Byzantine province of Palaestina Tertia (Salutaris) – was established at some stage during the Crusader era and served the diocese of Palaestrina III, the Transjordan area, and traditionally included St Catharine's Monastery on Mount Sinai, although Crusader military protection rarely extended deep into Sinai. Despite the dwindling number of Christians in the Petra region, appointing Archbishops of Petra lingered into the 20th century.

The hierarchy of the Latin Patriarchate of Jerusalem and high-minded elite Frankish crusaders in Palestine, who sought to create a European Latin-speaking colony in the Holy Land, could not prevent the transformation, within a generation or so, of the outlook of many ordinary Latin settlers in Palestine. Some churchy Latin crusaders were deeply concerned that many ordinary European colonists practically went native in Palestine, adopting 'Oriental' styles and local customs. Fulcher of Chartres, a priest who participated in the First Crusade (of which he later wrote a chronicle), then served the Latin Patriarchate of Jerusalem and acted as chaplain to Baldwin, the Latin King of Jerusalem, until 1118, wrote in July 1124:

> For we who were Occidentals now have been made Orientals. He who was a Roman or a Frank is now a Galilean, or an inhabitant of Palestine. One who was a citizen of Rheims or of Chartres now has been made a citizen of Tyre or of Antioch. We have already forgotten the places of our birth; already they have become unknown to many of us, or, at least, are unmentioned. Some already possess here homes and servants which they have received through inheritance. Some have taken wives not merely of their own people, but Syrians, or Armenians, or even Saracens [Muslim Arabs] who have received the grace of baptism ... One cultivates vines, the other the fields. ... Different languages, now made common, become known to both races. (Cited in Heng 2015: 359; also Folda 2001)

This rapid 'Orientalisation' and 'indigenisation' of many ordinary European Crusaders should surprise no one; after all, the levels of social, cultural and technical development in Palestine and the Near East at the time under Islam were superior to those in Europe. However, by the 1120s, Nazareth in Galilee, under the impact of educated Frankish settlers, had become a scholarly centre of some importance and was referred to as a 'famous religious community' in a papal document of 1145 (Riley-Smith 2005: 75): The city provided a living to some literary figures including Rorgo Fretellus of Nazareth and Gerard of Nazareth; its library, the catalogue of which survives, had similarities with European schools. Although Latin settlers in Palestine and the Levant still looked towards Europe for learning and culture, today Palestine and the Levant are considered to have been a channel for the transmission of Arabic learning to Europe (Riley-Smith 2005: 75). In the 1130s, a Frankish archdeacon, Rorgo Fretellus of Nazareth (Fetellus), who had moved to Palestine, wrote a guidebook that was used by pilgrims and scholars. He spoke of Provincia Palaestina in his descriptions of Latin Palestine: 'The city of Jerusalem is situated in the hill-country of Judea, in the province of Palestine' (Fetellus 1892). Jonathan Riley-Smit has pointed to the 'survival in Latin Palestine of the Muslim administration' (1977), and in all probability Fretellus of Nazareth was conflating scriptural geography with the actual Arab Islamic province of Filastin prior to the Latin Crusades.

Overall, following the establishment of the Latin Kingdom of Jerusalem the power and religious independence of the local Palestine Orthodox church were reduced sharply and the two Sees of Caesarea Maritima and Jerusalem were transformed into a Frankish archdiocese, subordinate to the Latin Patriarch of Jerusalem. The Crusaders also confiscated properties and seized key ecclesiastical positions traditionally held by the Greek Orthodox clergy in Palestine (Ellenblum 2003: 505). This policy undermined further the position of the Greek Orthodox clergy in the eyes of the predominantly Orthodox Arab Christians of Palestine. In the early 13th century, following the defeat of the Latin Crusaders by the Ayyubids, the Palestinian Arab town of Qaysariah (Caesarea-Palaestina) was still being described by Arab geographers as a key town in Filastin (Le Strange 2014: 29). In the post-Crusader period, however, Qaysariah and its formerly renowned and powerful metropolitan bishops and scholars never recovered their influential position after the destruction of the first Latin Kingdom by Salah al-Din (Saladin) in 1187 and the eventual elimination of the 200-year Frankish rule from Palestine by the Mamluks in the late 13th century, Although today the formerly powerful Archiepiscopal See of Caesarea-Palaestina is largely symbolic, the social memory and spectacular history of Caesarea-Palaestina are remembered by the Palestinian Christians, and the Eastern Orthodox Metropolitan of Caesarea is represented by an Exarch of Palaestina Prima, under the jurisdiction of the Eastern Orthodox Patriarchate of Jerusalem.

The local Arab Muslim–Christian bonds in Jerusalem can be traced to early Islam. Following the elimination of the European Latin Crusaders from the city, indigenous Arab Muslim–Christian shared traditions of convivencia in Jerusalem were re-cultivated; symbolically, the keys to the Church of the Holy Sepulchre were entrusted to two aristocratic Palestinian Muslim families in the city, the Nuseibeh and Judeh al-Ghoudia. Created by Salah al-Din shortly before his death in 1193, this post-Crusader ceremonial tradition added another widely respected layer of daily rituals to the multi-layered ancient sacredness of the site. Today the ruins of Crusader sites (churches, hostels and castles) are visible throughout historic Palestine and graffiti left by Crusaders can still be seen in the Church of the Holy Sepulchre in Jerusalem.

RELIGIO-CULTURAL AND INSTITUTIONAL MEMORIES OF PROVINCIA PALAESTINA AND MODERN PALESTINE

The structure of the Palestine Church created during this period is still preserved in the structure of the Palestine Church today. The Church in Palestine became an independent body in the 5th century (autocephaly), no longer an appendage of the empire of Byzantium, an important stage in developing the polity of Palestine. Also, the religio-cultural–geographic memories of Provincia Palaestina (greater Palestine) under the Byzantines have been kept alive by the local churches of Palestine. Today the shared memories and indeed actual institutional continuities of the 'Three in One' Palestine is represented in the Eastern Orthodox Patriarchate of Jerusalem, or the Greek Orthodox Patriarchate of Jerusalem (Arabic:

Kanisat Al-Rum al-Ortodoks fi-Quds), the Byzantine Orthodox Church of al-Quds. Originally the Patriarchate of Aelia Capitolina, it is regarded by many Christians as the 'mother' church of all Christendom. Today it exercises ecclesiastical jurisdiction over the predominantly Arabic-speaking Orthodox Christians of Palestine, Israel and Jordan. The headquarters of the Palestine Orthodox Patriarchate is the Church of the Holy Sepulchre in Jerusalem. The church dates back to 4th century Palestine. The name Church of the Holy Sepulchre is derived from the Latin Ecclesia Sancti Sepulchri. The Israeli name, Knesiyat ha-Kever, is derived from the same European tradition which began with the Latin Crusaders. Yet the Arabic name used by Palestinian Christians and Muslims, the Church of the Resurrection, Kaneesat al-Qiyamah, is directly derived from the Orthodox Greek toponym of Byzantine Palestine: Church of the Anastasis (Ναός της Αναστάσεως), named after the 'resurrection' of Jesus. This is another way of showing how Palestinian toponyms and local toponymic memory managed to preserve some of the social and historic memories of 4th century Palestine and the dominant religious traditions of the 'Three Palestines' of Late Antiquity.

Moreover, the religious authority over the Orthodox Christians of Palestine, Israel and Jordan is derived directly from its autocephaly, independence and jurisdiction over the 'Three Palestines' of Late Antiquity. This social memory of historic Palestine is also reflected by the fact that the Church celebrates its liturgy in the Byzantine Rite, whose original language is Koine Greek, the official language of the 'Three Palestines' during the Byzantine period.

Also, today the Orthodox Patriarch of Jerusalem, Theophilos III of Jerusalem is represented as 'Patriarch of the Holy City of Jerusalem and all Palestine'; 'all Palestine' of today, then, is a modern reformulation of the 'Three Palestines' of the Byzantine era. Elected in 2005, Theophilos III could trace his office in Jerusalem to the Council of Chalcedon in 451, an office with historical ecclesiastical jurisdiction over Provincia Palaestina (Palaestina Prima, Palaestina Secunda and Palaestina Salutaris). The Patriarch of Aelia Capitolina is also the religious leader of Eastern Orthodox Christians in the Holy Land/Palestine/Israel and Jordan, who are predominantly Palestinian and Jordanian Arabs. The election was endorsed by

Jordan on 24 September 2005, as one of the 'three governments' whose endorsement is apparently required. Two years later, the Israeli government officially recognised his election on 16 December 2007.

MATERIAL EVIDENCE AND POWERFUL SYMBOLS OF BYZANTINE PALAESTINA (ΠΑΛΑΙΣΤΙΝΗ): THE 1884 ARCHAEOLOGICAL DISCOVERY OF THE MADABA MOSAIC MAP

Urban development and the construction of civil buildings and churches in Palestine reached a zenith in the reign of Justinian (527 to 565 AD) (Burns and Eadie 2001; Walmsley 1996) and the Madaba Mosaic Map is one of the most powerful symbols of this urban Palestine during this spectacular era of Late Antiquity. Discovered in 1884, in the course of the construction of a new Greek Orthodox church in Madaba (present-day Jordan) on the site of its Byzantine predecessor, St George's church, the map is the most famous and among the oldest surviving material evidence for the official use of the name Palaestina in Late Antiquity. Since then more churches with floor mosaics have been discovered in Madaba that are similar to those found in the Holy Sepulchre in Jerusalem. The city contains one of the greatest concentrations of mosaics from the Byzantine and Umayyad periods and these mosaics are also testimony to the spectacular Palestine mosaic industry, ancient, medieval and modern (see chapter seven). Showing Palestine, Egypt and the Mediterranean Sea, and featuring a detailed description of the holy city of Aelia Capitolina (Jerusalem) at its centre, being one of the most significant archaeological discoveries in the study of Byzantine Palestine, the remaining part of the map contains the oldest surviving original cartographical depiction of Byzantine Palaestina. This part also contains details of some of the key cities of Palaestina Prima including Aelia Capitolina, Gaza, Ascalon and Eleutheropolis (Beit Jibrin). Dated 560–565 AD, the map was created originally on a large scale (measuring 15 by 6 metres) and was part of the mosaic floor of the early Byzantine church of St George, Madaba, 30 kilometres to the south-west of 'Amman. The mosaic floor map was created by local Christian artists and was aimed at Christian pilgrims, travellers and theologians. At the time Madaba, part of the administrative Byzantine province of Palaestina Prima, was the seat of a Christian bishop.

The Madaba Map has a famous extract showing 'ὁροι Αιγυπτου και Παλαιστινης' (the 'border of Egypt and Palestine'). There is no mention of the terms 'Cana'an' or 'land of Israel' on this historic map of Late Antiquity Palestine. The map (with the 'border of Egypt and Palestine') is another powerful indication of the fact that the name Palaestina was the official name of the country throughout early Christianity and Late Antiquity.

The Madaba Map shows Eleutheropolis as a walled city with three towers, a curving street with a colonnade in the central part and a large basilica. In the 4th century AD the city had a Christian bishop with the largest territory in Palaestina Prima. Its bishop Maximus attended the First Council of Nicaea which was convened in 325 by the Emperor Constantine I. In December 1964, the Volkswagen Foundation provided funding to the Deutscher Verein für die Erforschung Palästinas (German Society for the Exploration of Palestine) to work on saving the Madaba Map. And, we shall see in chapter nine, this sensational and widely publicised discovery of 1884, which, at the time, also involved the All Palestine Greek Orthodox Church of Jerusalem, would also contribute to reviving memories of historic Palestine among some Palestinian Arab Orthodox intellectuals in late Ottoman Palestine.

THE 'ATHENS OF ASIA' IN PALAESTINA: GAZA AS A MEDITERRANEAN CENTRE OF CLASSICAL LITERATURE AND RHETORIC

Mass literacy in Palestine, as in all countries, is a modern phenomenon. However, looking at the thriving learning centres of Palestine in the 5th and 6th centuries AD, one gets a strong sense of the country's sense of self-identity, its vibrant economy, its relatively widespread education and literacy and its overall confident cosmopolitanism. One of the most important centres of learning in the country during this period was the city of Gaza, which emerges as a seat of classical literature and rhetoric, with a number of famous scholars living and working there, a vibrant and cultured Christian urban centre of the whole Mediterranean region.

Throughout this period the harbour cities of Gaza and Caesarea-Palaestina, linked by sea transport and the highway of the Via Maris, competed and worked together as the two most cosmopolitan urban centres in the country, and both cities had sizeable Arab communities. Also significant is the fact that in 451 AD, at the crucial ecumenical Council of Chalcedon, the city of Gaza was represented by an Arab bishop (Shahid 2006a: 523). In the 530s AD Aratius, Dux of Palaestina Prima, and Archon Stephanus, proconsul of Palaestina Prima are praised in the *encomium*[20] written by a fellow compatriot of Provincia Palaestina, Choricius of Gaza, a philosopher and rhetorician (died in 518 AD), for maintaining law and order and improving the water supply system of Caesarea Maritima by maintenance work, clearing obstructions from the high-level aqueducts (Patrich 2011: 109; also 2001; Prummer 2002: 246). *Encomium* also refers to several distinct aspects of rhetoric for which the classical Gaza School of Rhetoric became very famous in Late Antiquity.

Established more than 5000 years ago, Gaza is one of the oldest cities in the world. Located strategically between Egypt and Asia, at the centre of the ancient road of the Via Maris, and on a beachfront, Gaza has never stopped looking at the Mediterranean Sea. Gaza was also a very ancient port and the closest outlet for Arabia. It treated Petra as its hinterland and the ancient Greeks knew that it was through Gaza they could reach India (Humbert 2000).

In the 12th century BC the Philistines made Gaza the leading city of the Pentapolis of Philistia. As we have seen above, Gaza was always identified with the key cities of Philistia and with the ancient Philistines. Mentioned in the Amarna letters as 'Azzati', Gaza served as ancient Egypt's administrative capital in Palestine. In the 5th and 4th centuries BC the cities of Philistia maintained their international trading links and developed their distinct Philisto-Arabian coins; the city continued to flourish under the Romans and in the 2nd century AD imperial Roman bronze coins were struck in Gaza. In the course of the two long periods of Palestine under the Romans and Byzantines, Gaza expanded and its strategically located Mediterranean port continued to prosper. In 635 AD, Gaza became one of the first cities in Palestine to be conquered by the Arab Muslim army and it quickly developed into a major centre of Islamic jurisprudence. Today the city of Gaza, with a population of over 500,000, is the largest Arab city in Palestine; the majority of Gaza's inhabitants are Muslims, but there is also a Christian Arab minority.

Under the Byzantines, Palestinian society of Late Antiquity was, on the whole, an educated one. Basic education was widely available, sometimes at village level, especially for men. Education was fostered not only in the imperial capital Constantinople but also in schools operating in major centres such as Antioch, Alexandria, Caesarea Maritima and Gaza. The main components of education were rhetoric, philosophy, law and languages (Greek and Latin) with the aim of producing educated leaders and officials for state and church. However, female participation in patriarchal society was not encouraged in the new 'Athens of the Mediterranean'. For instance, the lot of women in classicising Gaza was not much better than the situation of women in the patriarchal classical Athens of the 4th century AD (Sivan 2008: 300).

Today the spectacular classical heritage of Late Antiquity Palestine is not taught in Palestine; educated Palestinians are more likely to recall the classical heritage of the 'House of Wisdom' (*Bayt al-Hikmah*), a major intellectual centre in Baghdad throughout the Golden Age of Islam from the 9th to the 13th centuries, than the classical Rhetorical School of Gaza or classical Library of Caesarea Maritima. Yet the disciplines of rhetoric (the art of discourse) and philosophy were central not only to ancient, classical and post-classical intellectual life but also to the classical heritage of Late Antiquity Palestine. If the capital city of Palaestina Prima, Caesarea, flourished in Late Antiquity, developing into a Mediterranean centre of classicising, learning, theologising and historical writings, the Mediterranean city of Gaza became in the course of the late 5th and early 6th centuries the home of a classicising Christian School of Rhetoric (Kennedy, G. 1994: 255). In the School of Gaza, the classical tradition had become deeply intertwined with the Christian one. Other cities of greater Palestine, such as Ascalon ('Asqalan) and Scythopolis (Beisan), were also profoundly transformed by this post-classical Christian renaissance of Late Antiquity.

Intellectually and culturally influenced by a mix of diverse Hellenistic traditions of Alexandria, Caesarea-Palaestina and Athens, as well as by Christian Neo-Platonism, the extraordinarily relaxed setting and flourishing cultural and intellectual urban environment of Christian-majority Gaza for over two centuries in Late Antiquity brought about the spectacular rise of the Rhetorical School of Gaza, which was headed by Christian philosophers and rhetoricians including Procopius of Gaza (c. 465–528 AD) (Westberg 2009; Kennedy, D. 2008: 169) and his disciple Choricius of Gaza. The latter flourished in the early 6th century AD. In the classical tradition, love for rhetoric and love for theatrical performance went hand in hand and in Gaza, as well as in several other Palestinian cities, a thriving theatre culture arose. The private and public spaces of Christian-majority Gaza nurtured theatrical performances and public rhetorical displays in schools, 'holy theatres' and even public 'baths' (Champion 2014: 21–51). This flourishing cultural space and indeed intellectual revolution in Gaza was described by George A. Kennedy as follows:

> Gaza, on the southern coast of Palestine, was a pleasant and
> prosperous city in the Fifth Century which clung to the old traditions.
> Julian's apostasy was greeted there with enthusiasm. Gregory of
> Naziansus ... and Libanius thought well of its rhetoric schools ...
> Christianity may for a time have inhibited classical studies in Gaza,
> but in the late Fifth and early Sixth Centuries it was the home of a
> series of Classicizing sophists and writers who together constitute
> what is known as the School of Gaza. The most important of these are
> Procopius and Choricius, but brief mention may be made of several
> others. Aeneas of Gaza was the author of a surviving dialogue entitled
> *Theophrastus*. (Kennedy, G. 2008: 169)

For many centuries prior to Late Antiquity, Gaza and Arab sailors and traders had been central to the long-distance spice trade route from India to southern Arabia and then to the Eastern and Western Mediterranean. Gaza had also achieved economic and social prosperity, being at the centre of the traditional King's Highway from Egypt, with routes running through Naqab and Transjordan – a highway which confirmed its status as a major port city. Its port was not only the gateway to the towns and villages of southern Palestine but also for trade goods arriving from southern Arabia and India to the Mediterranean (Hirschfeld 2004: 63). Jennifer Hevelone-Harper, in *Disciples of the Desert: Monks, Laity, and Spiritual Authority in Sixth-Century Gaza* (2005), describes 6th century Gaza as a major economic, intellectual and cultural centre not only for Palaestina Prima but for the whole Eastern Mediterranean region:

> late antique [Antiquity] Gaza was a commanding cultural and economic center ... the sixth-century city was known for its bustling market-places, its lavish theater and baths, its resplendent churches adorned with mosaics and all the other amenities of a prosperous urban center. With its port, Maiouma, a couple of miles away on the coast, Gaza served as a key commercial center, not only for its own province, Palestine I [Palaestina Prima], but for the entire eastern Mediterranean. The city was a major destination for spices, silk and luxury goods coming overland by caravan from the East; these items would then be dispersed by sea to all parts of the western empire. Local products such as wine, dried fruit[21] and flax were exported from Gaza to the rest of the Roman world, while wheat was imported from Egypt to feed the crowded city. Moreover, a road to the northeast led to Jerusalem, the chief center for Christian pilgrimage, only forty miles away. Visitors to the Holy Land from all over the empire made sure to include a trip to Gaza in their itinerary to see the ancient biblical city of Samson's last victory.
>
> In addition to boasting local amenities, the prosperity of late antique Gaza nurtured remarkable intellectual and cultural developments. The school of rhetoric in Gaza was famous throughout the Mediterranean world. Its distinguished orators were instrumental in bringing about a revival of rhetoric in the six century. (Hevelone-Harper 2005: 3)

The Madaba Map – the most famous surviving material evidence for the official and administrative use of the name Palaestina in Late Antiquity, which depicts greater Palestine of the 6th century AD – shows seven large villages and provincial towns between Gaza and Elusa (at one point the capital of Palaestina Salutaris which had several Arab bishops), 23 kilometres south-west of the city of Beersheba. Also, two important roads crossed the region in the Byzantine period, including the route of the 'Spice Road' along which the Nabataean Arabs transported precious cargoes from the East (Hirschfeld 2004: 63–66).

Koine Greek and Latin were the prevalent languages of Late Antiquity Gaza, although the Ghassanid Arabs, who resided throughout Palaestina and in Gaza, spoke Arabic and much of the Palestinian peasantry spoke Aramaic. Procopius (Procopios) of Gaza – who must be distinguished from the aforementioned renowned 6th century Palestinian historian Prokopios of Caesarea-Palaestina – was an original Christian sophist and rhetorician, and one of the most important representatives of the famous Rhetorical School of his native Gaza in Palaestina Prima, a school with a lasting impact on the discipline of rhetoric. Procopius spent nearly all of his life in Gaza teaching and writing philosophical and rhetorical tracts. However, what we know about him comes mainly from his letters and from the encomium (Greek: *enkomion*, literally the praise of a person) of his disciple and successor Chorikios of Gaza. The latter was another major Palestinian rhetorician and a representative of the Gaza School of Rhetoric in the time of Emperor Anastasius I (491–518 AD). The encomium of what became widely known as the Gaza School of Rhetoric also refers to the distinct aspects of rhetorical pedagogy and rhetorical genres of Late Antiquity that developed and flourished. The surviving works of Chorikios of Gaza, which encompass the main genres of post-classical Greek rhetoric, are represented in the elegant style of the Gaza School of Rhetoric with its special features and peculiarly persistent avoidance of hiatus. Chorikios' work became also known for its panegyrical descriptions of two churches in Gaza, descriptions which consist of some of the most prominent early examples of *ekphrasis* – a graphic, dramatic, verbal description of a visual work of art – of church buildings.[22]

Palestine was brought fully under Islam in 637–638 by the third Caliph 'Umar, who expanded the Caliphate (*khilafah*) at an unprecedented rate, conquering the Sasanian Empire and about two-thirds of the Byzantine Empire. In the 690s the Umayyad Marwanid rulers embarked on a colossal building programme in Palestine in general and Iliya (Bayt al-Maqdis/ Jerusalem) in particular. The church architectural styles of Byzantine Palestine and Bilad al-Sham significantly influenced the Islamic architecture of Palestine under the Umayyads, the most celebrated example of which was the exquisite octagonal structure of the Dome of the Rock (Qubbat al-Sakhrah), sponsored by Caliph 'Abdel Malik ibn Marwan in 685–691 AD. It is the oldest extant Muslim monument in the world and Byzantine Palestine influences are evident in its mosaics. Islam and Muslim Palestine inherited the cultural, material, administrative and intellectual heritage of Byzantine Palestine. Archaeological excavations at al-Ramla, the capital of Jund Filastin for over three and a half centuries, discovered mosaics with animals including lions, birds and donkeys (Petersen 2005). Islam also absorbed and developed further the Greek Aristotelian philosophical traditions and Christian Neo-Platonism, a tradition of philosophy that arose in the 3rd century AD and persisted until shortly after the closing of the Platonic Academy in Athens in 529 AD by Emperor Justinian I. However, Byzantine Palaestina of the 4th–6th centuries AD recreated and developed further the Greek traditions in Gaza and Caesarea-Palaestina. Subsequently the Golden Age of Islam also translated these traditions into Arabic and developed them further intellectually and scientifically, first in the Abbasid capital city of Baghdad (from the late 7th century onwards) and later in the Andalus Ummayad capital city of Cordoba (from the 10th century onwards). It is not inconceivable that the extraordinary intellectual, material and scientific heritage of greater Palestine, that is, Gaza, Caesarea-Palaestina, Ascalon ('Asqalan), Jerusalem, Scythopolis (Beisan), provided one of the many cultural routes to the Golden Age of Islam from the 8th to the 13th century.

The Rhetorical School of Gaza was also involved in collating the opinions of commentators of preceding centuries and its work contributed to palaeography, the study of ancient and historical handwriting and of the forms and processes of writing. The most important development that concerned palaeographers was script. This issue is also applicable to the *catenae* (Latin for chain) and its relationship to *scholia*. The term *catenae* is reserved for annotated biblical texts rather than classical texts and the distinction made between *catenae* and *scholia* is that the former makes an attempt to cite the name of the authority, usually before the quotation. In *catenae* the author is more of a compiler and editor with very little to add to the work.

Historian of Byzantuim N. G. Wilson was the first to suggest that *catenae* come from the Palestine School of Gaza in the 5th century. Procopius of Gaza describes his method in the following excerpt from a hypothesis: 'Having been supplied the ability before God, we collected the explanations which were put down from the Fathers and the others into the Octateuch, combining these things from commentaries and different sayings'. From this we learn that Procopius took selections from authorities and added them to the text. This expanded the text but made the corpus of opinions of the Church Fathers more manageable. Zosimus of Gaza was a sophist during the time of Emperor Anastasius. He wrote a rhetorical lexicon according to the alphabet and a commentary on Demosthenes and Lysias. According to 11th century Byzantine historian Georgius Cedrenus, Zosimus of Gaza was put to death during the reign of Zeno in 490 AD. On the one hand, we may have a Zosimus contemporary with Procopius who was involved in *scholia* on classical authors or, on the other hand, there may have been two of that name. It is possible that the scholiast Zosimus of Gaza flourished in the mid-5th century. In that case, he may have been responsible for introducing the practice of entering *scholia* such as is attributed to a Zosimus (Wilson 1967: 254). The School of Gaza did not make a distinction between *scholia* (marginal commentary on classical texts) and *catenae* (marginal commentary on biblical texts). Commenting on the beginnings of *catenae* in Gaza, Timothy Seid writes: 'The evidence suggests that marginal commentary on biblical texts [by Christian theologians] had a beginning in the fifth to sixth century and was probably of Palestinian origins if not the School of Gaza itself'.[23]

POPULAR RELIGION AND THE RELAXED SETTING OF GAZA: THE ROSE FESTIVAL OF GAZA

If Christian classicism and Origenism in Caesarea-Palaestina sought to develop theologies and philosophies of the mind, the classicising philosophers and Christian theologians of Gaza sought to combine high theology and classical rhetoric with popular religion and religious festivals, the most famous of which was the Rose Festival of Gaza. In the relaxed setting of Gaza the Christian rhetoricians Procopius and Coricius participated in the Rose Festival (Kennedy, G. 2008: 171), a spring festival with a long classical history and deep pagan roots. Also John of Gaza wrote two *anacreontic* poems – imitating verses in metre used by the Greek poet Anacreon (c. 582–c. 485 BC) in his poems dealing with love and wine – that he says he presented publicly on 'the day of the roses, and declamations by Procopius'. Poetry by Chorikios of Gaza is also set at rose days (Westberg 2009: 187–189; Talgam 2004: 223–224).

In the 6th century, a 'Day of Roses' was held in Gaza as a spring festival that may have been a Christianised continuation of the Rosalia (Talgam 2004: 223–224; Belayche 2004: 17). In Greece and Rome, floral wreaths and garlands and greenery had been worn by both men and women for festive occasions. Rosaria or Rosalia was a Roman festival of roses celebrated on various dates, primarily in May. The observance is sometimes called a *rosatio* ('rose-adornment') or the *dies rosationis* ('day of rose-adornment'). As a commemoration of the dead, the *rosatio* developed from the custom of placing flowers at burial sites. In classical mythology blood and flowers were linked in divine metamorphosis. Flowers were traditional symbols of rejuvenation, rebirth and memory, with the red and purple of roses and violets felt to evoke the colour of blood as a form of propitiation. When Adonis, beloved of Aphrodite, was killed by a boar during a hunt, his blood produced a flower. Their blooming period framed the season of spring. In some parts of the pagan Roman Empire the Rosalia was assimilated into floral elements of spring festivals for Dionysus, Adonis and Aphrodite (Roman Venus), but rose-adornment as a practice lent itself to Christian commemoration of the dead. The Roman pagan traditions associated with the Rosalia were reinterpreted into Christian terms and early Christian writers of Palestine transferred the pagan imagery of garlands and crowns of roses and violets to the cult of the Christian saints. Roses were in general part of the imagery of early Christian funerary art. Christian martyrs were often described or depicted with flower imagery, or in ways that identified them with flowers. These early Christian traditions of

Byzantine Palestine and Gaza also survived in modern Catholic traditions of Palestine.

A modern incarnation of the Roman Catholic Rosary is found in the Arabic name Rahbat al-Wardiyyah ('Sisters of the Rosary'). In May 2015 the founder of Rahbat-al-Wardiyyah, Sister Marie Alphonsine Danil Ghattas, a Palestinian nun, was proclaimed a saint at a ceremony in the Vatican.[24] Born in Jerusalem, Maryam Sultanah Danil Ghattas (1843–1927) – Marie Alphonsine after she joined the Congregation of St Joseph of the Apparition – founded in 1880 the Rosary Sisters, the first female congregation of nuns devoted to eradicating illiteracy among women regardless of faith, education and social welfare in the Holy Land/Palestine. Today the Christian Arab Sisters of the Rosary, supported by the Latin Patriarchate of Jerusalem, run forty-two schools in Palestine, Jordan and Israel. These schools educate both Muslim and Christian Arab students (Jansen 2006: 59).

MONASTIC SCHOOL OF GAZA AND THE MONASTERIES OF PALAESTINA: THE DESERT FATHERS AND MOTHERS AND THEIR WORLDWIDE IMPACT

> Forgotten, as if you never were.
> Like a bird's violent death
> like an abandoned church you'll be forgotten,
> like a passing love
> and a rose in the night ... forgotten
> when I'm forgotten!
> (Mahmoud Darwish, *Forgotten As If You Never Were*[25])

'Desert theology' and the monasteries of the desert of Late Antiquity Palestine, Egypt and Syria played an influential role in Near Eastern societies, and the 'Desert Fathers' are widely acknowledged today as key figures in the history of Christian theology, spirituality and doctrinal developments (Binns 1994). If the Mediterranean cities of *Caesarea Maritima* and Gaza, with their renowned scholars, libraries and intellectuals, represented

Palaestina of the mind, the monastic traditions of Palaestina represented Palestine of the heart. The latter had a huge impact on the worldwide monastic traditions of both Christianity and Islam and religious mysticism in general. According to Muslim tradition, the Prophet Muhammad met the monk Bahirah (Sergius) in one of the Christian monasteries in the town of Bosra in the Hauran region, then an integral part of Palaestina Secunda. In the 'Three Palestines', Ghassanid Arab Christians belonged largely to monophysitism. If Gaza of Late Antiquity, with its classicising Rhetorical School, became a famous centre for philosophy, rhetoric, drama and law, the region of Gaza also became renowned for its distinct monastic tradition. Indeed, one of the most spectacular chapters in the history of Late Antiquity Palestine was the monastic culture and monastic legacy of Gaza. An intellectual monastic community flourished in the region of Gaza in *Palaestina Prima* from the 4th to the 7th century, creating a distinct Palestinian monastic tradition, shaped by the Christological intellectual battles of the 5th and 6th centuries, and producing a wealth of literary works which might be termed the 'Monastic School of Gaza' (Bitton-Ashkelony and Kofsky 2006).[26]

The earliest known Christian monasticism appeared simultaneously in the deserts of Egypt and Palestine around the 3rd century AD. The famous monastic developments of the Gaza region were intimately connected to both the Palestinian and the Egyptian experiences (Hevelone-Harper 2005: ix). However, by the 4th century greater Palestine effectively replaced Egypt as the centre of desert monasticism. Between the 4th and early 7th centuries Palestine, and in particular the two semi-arid regions of Gaza and east Jerusalem – which became known as the 'desert of Jerusalem' – was 'converted into a city' and became the centre of the global Christian monastic movement.

The legendary Desert Fathers and Desert Mothers[27] were Christian hermits, monks and nuns who had a major influence on the development of Christianity and Christian monasticism worldwide. The monasteries of Palestine were a centre for knowledge preservation and knowledge production, from the preservation of the ancient technology of wine-making (of *Palaestini liquors*) to the copying and archiving of ancient manuscripts. While the art of copying and wide circulation of manuscripts developed considerably under Islam, little is known about the ways in which Muslim philosophies of the heart and Sufi asceticism were directly and indirectly influenced by the desert mysticism of Egypt and greater Palestine. However, the knowledge of the heart or inner insight into Christian monasticism corresponds to '*Ilm al-Ghayb*, or '*Ilm al-Batin* – knowledge of the concealed, hidden or inner truth – in Sufi Islam, whose original inspiration appears in the holy Quran (4: 34, 11:49, 12: 52, 12:102, 25:4–6). While Origenism and outward-looking Mediterranean cities such as Caesarea Maritima, Gaza, Alexandria and Antioch provided the classicising intellectual, rhetorical, speculative and rational underpinnings for early Christianity, the solitude, poverty, austerity, interior silence and 'prayer of the heart' (the Jesus Prayer) of the monastic communities of Egypt, the Gaza region and greater Palestine became the city of the heart. This Palestinian monastic movement combined the way of life of Jesus with a modest and secluded life which included fasts, mortifications and spiritual activities. Above all, at the heart of this Palestine monastic life of simplicity and 'desert escapism' was the desire to shun power and organised religion, and the growing hierarchy of the official, urban-based church.

The early Christian monastic communities in Palestine established autonomous egalitarian communities with an *abba* ('my father' in both Syriac Aramaic and Quranic Arabic) and an *amma* (mother) in charge of the spiritual and social welfare of their monks and nuns. The English term Abbot (its female equivalent is Abbess), meaning father, is an ecclesiastical title given to the head of a monastery in various Christian traditions. The term itself is derived from the Syriac Aramaic *abba*, which is based on this Syriac Aramaic Monophysite tradition of Byzantine Palestine. The title soon became generally accepted in all languages as the designation of the head of a monastery.

By the end of the 4th century there were dozens of monasteries with thousands of monks in Palestine. Palestine desert monasticism evolved from detachment from the world to social and practical engagement with society. Numerous Palestinian monasteries of monks and nuns were established in Gaza region, Bethlehem, Jerusalem, Eleutheropolis (Beit Jibrin), Nazareth and the Galilee with adjacent hospitals and schools to care for the sick and serve their local communities. The social teaching and ethics of these early egalitarian monastic communities survived in modern Palestinian Christian theology. However, their speculative approach and detached way of life gave way to a more engaged and applied theology. This formed the basis of modern contextualised Palestinian liberation theology with its preference for the poor, marginalised subaltern and its struggle against Zionist settler-colonialism and the occupation of Palestine (Masalha and Isherwood 2014). Their social teaching also gave rise to the doctrines developed by the more engaged Christian churches of Palestine on matters of social justice, poverty and wealth, economic and social organisations and the role of the state.

In Palestine monasteries evolved into two distinct types: 'monastery of hermits', or *lauras* (Greek: *lavra*), and 'communal monastery of monks' (*coenobium*[28]). The first *lauras* were founded in Palestine and the Greek term Λαύρα (Greek: path[29]), which referred to the cluster of caves or cells used by the hermits for seclusion, with a church as their weekly meeting centre, was specifically employed from the 5th century for the Palestine semi-hermitical monastic communities in what became known as the 'desert of Jerusalem', where thousands of hermits and monks lived and dozens of *lauras* and communal monasteries were established.

Supported by the Byzantine state, desert monasticism and enlightened philosophies of the heart encouraged the proliferation of monasteries across greater Palestine (Palaestina Prima, Palaestina Secunda and Palaestina Salutaris). Crucially under the Christian Byzantines Sinai, the Nagab (Negev), the Nabataean region and northern Arabia (former Roman Provincia Arabia) were all part of Palaestina Salutaris (Ward 2008: 69). The monastery of St Catherine was built between 548 and 565 as a Palaestina Salutaris monastery dedicated to Saint Catherine of Alexandria. Saint Catherine's monastery lies at the foot of Mount Sinai, which was mentioned in the Quran (Surah al-Tur, Chapter 52, Verses 1–28). For local audiences in the 6th and 7th centuries, Palaestina Salutaris, Sinai and northern Arabia were geographically linked and administratively united.

The Jerusalem desert monasteries developed an extensive system of cisterns built to catch and store rainwater, and, like the Nabataean Arabs before them, they became known for their great ability in constructing efficient water collecting methods in the semi-arid and barren environment.

The numerous monasteries of Palaestina Prima included the famous Euthemius Monastery which was established in 428 to the east of Jerusalem and named after the Armenian monk Euthemius (377–475), who was one of the founders of the 'Jerusalem desert' monasticism of Christian-majority Byzantine Palestine. The monastery of Euthemius would also play an important role in converting to Christianity the Arab tribes that had settled in Palaestina Prima in the 4th and 5th centuries (see chapter five). The site continued to function as a major Christian monastery for centuries under Muslim rule and the Latin Crusaders expanded it further in the 12th century. The monastery was abandoned after the expulsion of the Crusaders from Jerusalem in the late 12th century, and beginning in the 13th century the site began to function as a major Palestinian caravanserai, al-Khan al-Ahmar (the 'Red Inn'), on the Jerusalem–Jericho trade road, until its final desertion at some point during the Ottoman period. A nearby 16th century Ottoman caravanserai, also named al-Khan al-Ahmar, was built to shelter caravans of traders.

Many Byzantine Palestinian monasteries continued to flourish after the Arab Islamic conquest of Palestine in the 630s. Mar Saba's Monastery is located south of Jerusalem in the West Bank. It evolved from a Laura to a communal monastery and continues to function today. Founded in Palaestina Prima in 484, it is dedicated to Saint Sabbas the Sanctified (439–532),[30] a 'leader of Palestinian monasticism' whose impact as founder and abbot has endured from the 5th century to the present (Patrich 1995). Sabbas was a Cappadacian-born Greek monk and priest who lived most of his life in Palaestina Prima and composed the first monastic rule of church services, 'the Jerusalem Typikon', a monastic book to regulate life in monasteries and for guidance of all the Byzantine monasteries. Another famous monastery in Palaestina Prima was Saint Hilarion's, located in today's Gaza Strip and dedicated to Saint Hilarion (291–371). A legendary Desert Father, Hilarion was born in Thabatha, then 5 miles south of Gaza city, in the Roman province of Syria-Palaestina. After he had lived in the wilderness for twenty-two years, this hermit of Palestine became famous throughout Syria-Palaestina and beyond and petitioners started to visit his abode near Gaza seeking his blessing and help.

Sabbas' *Life* was written by one of his disciples, Cyril of Scythopolis (525–559) (modern Beisan) in Palaestina Secunda; also known as Cyrillus

Scythopolitanus, he was a Christian monk and historian of monastic life in Palestine in the early years of Christianity (Kazhdan 1991). Sabbas' relics were taken by the Latin Crusaders in the 12th century and remained in Italy until Pope Paul VI returned them to the Palestinian monastery in 1965 as a gesture of goodwill towards the Orthodox Church. Mar Saba is currently being considered by UNESCO as a World Heritage Site).[31] The numerous monasteries have left their mark on the landscape of Palestine. They have also survived in Palestinian social memory and in some of the modern Palestinian Arabic toponyms which begin with the word *Deir* (Monastery), although the Arabic word *deir* (pl. *diyar*) also means house.

Today the ruins of Euthemius Monastery are located in the Israeli colony of Ma'alie Adumim in the West Bank. The memory of the Palestinian caravanserai was preserved in the name of a small Palestinian Bedouin village, al-Khan al-Ahmar, located between the Israeli settler-colonies of Ma'alei Adumim and Kfar Adumim. This Palestinian village has been threatened with destruction by the Israeli state since 2010 in a plan to expand local Israeli settlements in the West Bank.[32]

Chapter 5

ARAB CHRISTIAN PALESTINE

The pre-Islamic Arab kings, bishops, poets and tribes of Provincia Palaestina (3rd–early 7th centuries AD)

Before the arrival of Islam the Arab Christians of Palestine contributed to the gradual Arabisation of the country as parts of it were transformed into Arab statelets under the influence of the Byzantine court. This protracted process, which began hundreds of years before the rise of Islam, contributed to the spectacular rise of Islam in the early 7th century. The process began when Arabs started migrating as individuals and communities in different waves from the Arabian Peninsula to the Levant region, Palestine included. These waves of migration continued and increased after the triumph of Christianity in the 4th century AD when the new religion was officially embraced by the Roman Empire. The integration of the Ghassanid Arab migrant communities into Palestinian society in general and the Palestine Church in particular was much in evidence. In the *Ecclesiastical History* of the 5th century AD the bishop of Gaza, Sozomen, who was born in present-day Beit Lahia in the Gaza Strip and who was involved in the introduction of Christianity among the 'Saracens' (Arabs), refers to the Ishmaelites (Ghassanid Arabs) in Palestine, who were coming into contact not only with Christians but also with Jews and learning from them about their common descent from Abraham (Hawting 2004: 38).

The history of the birth of Christianity in Palestine and its massive spread in Late Antiquity has been written largely by Western academics either from the perspective of Empire or with the elite Christian (Byzantine) Hellenistic settings in mind. The official narratives of the 'beginnings' of Christianity in Palestine and its doctrinal orthodoxy were all established in the 4th–6th centuries and these narratives have been maintained to this day by the establishments of the Catholic and Greek Orthodox churches. Very rarely was an account of early Christianity and Palestine written from the perspective of the local Aramaic-speaking Christian Arabs or the anti-Chalcedon Christian Monophysite Ghassanid Christian Arabs of greater Palestine. Yet early Christianity was extremely diverse. The Arabic- and Aramaic-speaking Christian Monophysites and Miaphysites of the 'Three Palestines' and the powerful Arab Christian Ghassanid tribal rulers, bishops and poets of Palaestina Secunda, Palaestina Salutaris and Palaestina Prima are a case in point.

In the 4th–6th centuries the three provinces of Palestine went through a gradual process of Arabisation and large parts of them were effectively transformed into Arab vassal states under imperial Byzantine influence. Palaestina Prima, Palaestina Secunda and Palaestina Tertia all acquired Ghassanid Arab Christian kings. This process of gradual Arabisation of parts of Palestine began in the 3rd–4th centuries with the spread of Christianity throughout the Near East and the gradual conversion of many Arabs to Christianity.

Christian Arab communities existed in the 'Three Palestines' throughout the 3rd–6th centuries (Shahid 1989). The Ghassanid Arabs (Arabic: *al-Ghasasinah*) were the biggest Arab group in Palestine. They migrated in different waves in the early 3rd century from the Arabian Peninsula to Palestine and the southern Levant region (Bowersock et al. 1999). The presence of the Ghassanids in what became officially known as Palaestina Salutaris in the 4th century dates back to the 3rd century. The Arabic-speaking Ghassanids converted to Monophysite Christianity before and after their migration to Palaestina Tertia and frequently merged with the Greek-speaking Christian communities of the region. Many of them, adhering to austere Monophysism, were initially hostile to the dominant Nicene Creed ('two natures' of Jesus) and official/elite Chalcedon doctrine of the Orthodox Church. While some Ghassanids converted to Islam from the mid-7th century onwards, the majority remained Christian and joined Melkite and Syriac Monophysite communities of the Levant and greater Palestine. After settling in Palaestina Tertia and Palaestina Secunda, the Ghassanids created client (buffer) states to the eastern Roman (later Byzantine) Empire and fought alongside the Byzantines against the Persian Sassanids and Arab Lakhmid tribes of southern Iraq. Both the Romans and Byzantines found a powerful ally in the Ghassanid Arabs, who acted as a buffer zone and a source of troops for the Byzantine army and controlled parts of Palaestina Salutaris and Palaestina Secunda.

However, from the 4th to the early 7th centuries, the Byzantine Empire constructed a patron–client system and the title phylarch (φύλαρχος: *phylarchus*) was granted to important Byzantine Arab allied rulers. In Greek the terms φυλή and φῦλον meant tribe, clan or race. The Byzantine title phylarch (from phylé and *phylon* and *archein*, 'to rule') meant 'ruler of a large clan or tribe'. This political title was given to the leading princes of the Ghassanids and other Byzantine Arab allies. Many Arab tribes led by phylarchs had been encouraged to settle as *foederati* in the 'Three Palestines'. When discussing the Ghassanid Arab communities of Palestine, historian Prokopios of Caesarea uses the expression *Sarakēnós* and distinguishes between the 'Saracens in Palestine' and territories 'immediately beyond the boundaries of Palestine held by Saracens' (Prokopios 2005). He also defines phylarch as 'any leader of the Saracens federated by treaty to the Romans' (Peters 1994: 61). Originally the *foederati* (sing. *foederatus*) had been Arab allies identified as one of the groups or nations bound by treaty (*foedus*); they were neither Roman colonies nor beneficiaries of Roman citizenship (*civitas*), but they had been allowed and even encouraged to settle on Roman territory. They were also obliged to provide a contingent of military men when trouble arose. From 530 to 585, the individual Arab phylarchs were subordinated to a supreme Ghassanid phylarch ('phylarch of phylarchs') or king (Kazhdan 1991). These supreme phylarchs were appointed as Arab kings of the 'Three Palestines' directly by the Byzantine Emperors of Constantinople (who were 'King of Kings') in the 'Three Palestines': Palaestina Prima, Palaestina Secunda and Palaestina Tertia. The dramatic rise of the Ghassanid princes to Arab kings in the 'Three Palestines' reveals an important development in Palestine and the emergence of the Arabs as key players in the politics of pre-Islamic Palestine. These Ghassanid kings were later to play a major role not only in the Byzantine–Persian Wars but also in the affairs of the Eastern Syriac Monophysite Church.

The first appearance of the Ghassanid kings in connection with greater Palestine is found in a tomb inscription written in Arabic in Nabataean script dating to the 4th century AD. Nabataean Aramaic and Nabataean Arabic had been spoken for several centuries before Islam (Fiema et al. 2015: 396–497). The tomb inscription refers to the Ghassanid King Imru al-Qais, 'king of all the Arabs', who died in Byzantine service in 328 (Sartre 2005: 519). Known in Greek sources as Amorkesos (Αμορκέσος), Imru al-Qais signed a treaty with the Byzantine Empire acknowledging his status as *foederati* and as controlling major parts of Provincia Palaestina. Amorkesos was appointed by the Byzantine Emperor as supreme phylarch of what became known as Palaestina Salutaris and included the Nabataean region and the former Roman Provincia Arabia. Indeed, the lure of greater Palestine for the Ghassanid Arabs is illustrated by the military and political career of Amorkesos and his rise to power in Palestine. This success followed his military achievements and his establishment of a power base in Arabia, and led to his eventual appointment as the Arab king of the region of Palaestina Tertia. Amorkesos had defected from the military service of Sassanid Persia and entered the political service of the Byzantine Empire. Following a visit to Constantinople and royal treatment by Emperor Leo I (Emperor from 457 to 474 AD), Imru al-Qais returned to Palestine having concluded a *foedus* with the Emperor, which endowed him with the overall phylarchate of Palaestina Tertia (Shahid 1989, 2006a: 61–81). Amorkesos preferred to serve in Palestine, eventually becoming king (supreme phylarch) of Palaestina Tertia, rather than be a king in the Arabian Peninsula. All these Ghassanid Arab leaders not only flourished and exercised considerable power under the Byzantines but also preferred the social and cultural environment of Palestine to their former situation in Arabia (Shahid 1989, 2006a: 61–81).

The Byzantine imperial patron–client system worked in both directions: it cemented the Byzantine–Ghassanid alliance and it was used by the Ghassanid Arab rulers to consolidate their domain in greater Palestine. By the late 5th century the Ghassanid kings had dramatically risen to become the powerful supreme phylarchs of Palaestina Tertia and Palaestina Secunda, effectively transforming major parts of two Palestines into two Palestinian Arab vassal kingdoms. Nominally the two Palestines were still imperial provinces, but in reality, under Ghassanid military and political control, they functioned as client monarchical states, having and commanding their own Arab armies, enforcing law and order within their jurisdiction, raising revenue and taxes from the lucrative trade passing through their territories, providing protection to the holy places in Palestine and dispatching ambassadors to foreign countries.

Abu Karib ibn Jabalah (known in Greek as Abocharabus), the Ghassanid supreme phylarch, was made by Emperor Justinian the supreme phylarch of Palaestina Tertia (Shahid 1989: 69, 89; Martindale et al. 1992: 111–112). Abu Karib had received the territories of Palaestina Tertia, including the Negev and parts of the northern Hijaz, from his father Jabalah IV (Gabalas in Greek sources) (Peters 1994: 62), who ruled in Palaestina Tertia from 512 to 529. In 529 AD, Abu Karib was endowed with the phylarchate of Palaestina Tertia by Justinian for the same reason that inspired the creation of the new province, Palaestina Tertia, in the fourth century' (Shahid 2002: 303).

The Ghassanids reached their peak under Abu Karib's brother, the Miaphysite al-Harith V ibn Jabalah (Flavios Arethas, Φλάβιος Ἀρέθας in Greek sources) (Shahid 1995, Vol. 1: 260, 294–297), who reigned from 528 to 569 AD as King of the Ghassanids, was made patrikios and vir gloriosissimus ('most glorious', ἐνδοξότατος) and supported the Byzantines against Sassanid Persia. Gradually, and under the impact of the dominant Nicaea/Chalcedonian creed of greater Palestine, the Ghassanid kings had begun to shift in the early 6th century from austere Monophysitism to Miaphysitism, a doctrine that was perceived to be more amenable to the official creed. Harith V played a major role in the affairs of both Miaphysite and Monophysite churches in the Levant. In 529 AD al-Harith V was given by Emperor Justinian I the highest imperial title available to the senatorial aristocracy of the Byzantine Empire in the 6th century (Kazhdan 1991: 163). Al-Harith became King of the Ghassanids and supreme phylarch of

Palaestina Secunda and Arabia Petraea around 528 after leading a successful military campaign against the Mundhir rulers and their Arab Persian allies in southern Iraq. In the words of historian Prokopios of Caesarea Maritima, in Palaestina Prima, a source hostile to the Ghassanid ruler, al-Harith was promoted by Justinian 'to the dignity of a king', becoming the overall commander of all the Byzantines' Arab allies (*foederati*) in the East with the title patrikios (πατρίκιος καὶ φύλαρχος τῶν Σαρακηνῶν, 'patrician and phylarch of the Saracnes'), although his actual area of political and military control may initially have been limited to parts of Palaestina Secunda and Arabia Petraea (Shahid 1995, Vol. 1: 84–85, 95–109, 225–226, 260, 282–288, 294–297, 337; Martindale et al. 1992: 111–113; Kazhdan 1991: 163; Greatrex and Lieu 2002: 88, 129–130, 135–136).

As supreme Arab king-phylarchs of Palaestina Secunda and Palaestina Tertia, al-Harith and Abu Karib were equal in status, each of them dispatched ambassadors of their own respective vassal states to the Ethiopian ruler of south Arabia, Abraha (Shahid 2009, Vol. 2, Part 2: 44). As the phylarch of Palaestina Tertia, Abu Karib became very famous and rose in stature to the point of becoming a participant in the dispatch of diplomatic representatives to other countries in the Middle East (Shahid 2006b: 90).

> The Diocletiantic enlargement of Palaestina Tertia entailed the addition of the Negev and the part of the Provincia Arabia south of the Arnon River, including Petra. The enlargement thus made the phylarch of Palaestina Tertia, Abu Karib, responsible for more spice route ... Of all the exports of Arabia, the item most significant to the Christian Roman Empire was Frankincense. After first disdaining it as a symbol of pagan worship, the church finally accepted Frankincense in the late fourth century. Produced only in Hadramawt in South Arabia, it was brought to Byzantium by Arab merchants and taxed [in gold and silver] at the frontier by such Arab officials as Abu Karib. (Shahid 2009a, Vol. 2, Part 2: 44, 49)

Saracens (Greek: Σαρακηνός, *Sarakēnós*; late Latin: *Saracenus*; possibly from Arabic: šarqiyyin, 'easterners') became in medieval and modern times a pejorative European term closely associated with Arabs and Muslims. This European negative connotation may be traced to Prokopios' somewhat hostile accounts of the Arab *foederati* and Ghassanid Arabs and their 'upstart' *foederati* Arab kings of the 'Three Palestines'. Also, Prokopios' term *Sarakēnós* may have been largely directed at the non-conformist Monophysite Christian Arabs of the 'Three Palestines'. Prokopios' attitude also betrays class tensions between the metropolitan (Greek-speaking) elite of Palestine and the Arab/Sarakēnó (largely subaltern) communities of the 'Three Palestines', conflicts which have continued to plague the Palestine Orthodox Church in the modern era. Prokopios' account also reveals the class-ridden, stratified society of Provincia Palaestina and the latent class tensions and prejudices that existed in the country. On the one hand, there were the Greek-speaking urban social elites and ecclesiastical (Chalcedon) hierarchy, and on the other, the Aramaic-speaking Palestinian peasantry, the Eastern Arabic-speaking Monophysite (anti-Chalcedonian) Syriac churches, and the Arab ('Saracen') tribes of greater Palestine.

However, with the elevation of al-Harith to king of the Ghassanid Christians in Palaestina II and Arabia Petraea many Arab tribes joined the phylarchate and he became a very popular character in pre-Islamic history, folktales and sagas. The Ghassanids retained their powerful positions as supreme phylarchs, or 'kings', in Palaestina Secunda and Palaestina Salutaris until the Byzantine Empire was overthrown by the Muslim Arabs in the 7th century following the Battle of Yarmuk in 636. In the ancient Middle East kings conducted autonomous foreign policies and dispatched ambassadors to neighbouring countries. Monumental epigraphic evidence from the Yemen shows that the Ghassanid Arab kings and phylarchs of Palaestina Tertia and Palaestina Secunda, Abu Karib and Arithas, pursued independent foreign policies towards Arabia (Shahid 2009, Vol. 2, Part 2: 44).

Byzantine military-strategic plans with regard to the 'Three Palestines' were centred on the army commanded by *Dux Palaestinae*, military commander of all Palestine, whose headquarters were in Caesarea-Palaestina, while relying heavily on Ghassanid federate forces which dominated Palaestina Secunda and Palaestina Tertia and formed a key pillar of the Byzantine frontier defence system. Arab federate troops were also involved in guarding the holy sites in Palestine and the pilgrims' routes to and from the Holy Land. This provided the Ghassanid Arab federate kings of Palaestina Secunda and Palaestina Tertia huge military resources and strategic influence over the 'Three Palestines', an influence which lasted for nearly two centuries.

The Ghassanid Arabs played a key role in protecting the Holy Land from raids of the Arab Lakhmids of Iraq – the security of Palestine from such raids was crucial for the continuation of the pilgrimages on which the thriving economy depended. The religiously devout Ghassanid Arabs prospered in Palestine economically and flourished religiously and culturally, and they engaged in much religious and public building, as evidenced by a spread of urbanisation and the sponsorship of several churches and monasteries. They planted vineyards and other crops, raised livestock, mined the subterranean wealth of their territories for gold, silver and copper and cultivated horsemanship. Their Arab customs officers raised taxes from the lucrative regional and trans-continental trade passing through Palaestina Tertia and Palaestina Secunda. Their economic, social and cultural lives were closely connected to their devout Christianity and close involvement with the pilgrims to the Holy Land. Their Christian Arab soldiers in Palestine provided security for Christian holy places in and Christian pilgrims to Palestine (Shahid 2009, Vol. 2, Part 2: 45, 49, 51):

> More important than the Byzantine influence in their social life was their Christianity, which was required of them once they became Byzantine's *foederat.* This factor revolutionized their social life.
>
> The feasts of the Christian calendar and the liturgical year had distinct social aspects. As devout Christians, the Ghassanids scrupulously observed these feasts, which at the same time became social events; thus these celebrations became part of their cultural life ...
>
> As *foederati* encamped in the Provincia Arabia, Palaestina Secunda, and Palaestina Tertia, they were physically very close to the Holy Land, some of whose *loca sancta* they could even see from their military stations. [Such places were especially visible from Palaestina Secunda, where Christ performed one of his miracles on the woman

with the issue of the blood (Mark 5: 25–34). From Jabiya (in the Golan Heights) and elsewhere the Ghassanids could see the Sea of Galilee, sites of the lakeside of the ministry of Christ, and Mount Tabor, the scene of the Transfiguration, as well as the Jordan, the river of baptism. A verse in one of the poems of their panegyrist al-Nabigha may suggest they even had a presence in northern Galilee].

In addition, they, together with the Byzantine regular troops, were the protectors of the Holy Land and its holy sites from the raids and incursions of the Lakhmids [of al-Hirah in Iraq] ... This role gave their Christianity a military tone – they were literally *milites Christi*.

Just as they were the military protectors of the Holy Land, so too they were the ecclesiastical protectors of the Monophysite church in Oriens, which they had resuscitated around 540, and continued to defend and protect until their own existence as Byzantine phylarchate ended in 636, after the Battle of Yarmuk. (Shahid 2009, Vol. II, Part II: 63–64)

In the 5th century, during the Byzantine period, the Golan Heights formed part of Palaestina Secunda and was populated by Christian Arab Ghassanids. At the end of the 5th century AD, the Emperor Anastasius made use of the Ghassanids, Monophysite Christian Arabs, and they became the rulers of Palaestina Secunda.

Following the Battle of Yarmuk in 636 Islam not only conquered the Ghassanid phylarchates of Palestine, it also inherited the *millet* concept which was used for the autonomous communities of the churches of the East (including the Monophysite Ghassanid) in the Byzantine Empire in the 4th–7th centuries. Even under the Ottomans the term *Millet-i Rûm*, the Greek Orthodox (Byzantine) *millet*, applied specifically to the Orthodox Christian communities of the Ottoman Empire. The head of a *millet* – most often a religious hierarch – was the Greek Orthodox Patriarch. It is not inconceivable that the Arab Islamic word *millah* may have evolved from the metaphorical expression *milites Christi* (soldier for Christ) ,whose beginnings were in early Christianity and the Ghassanid Arab Christian communities of former Provincia Arabia and Provincia Palaestina (Prima, Secunda and Tertia).

ARABIC CLASSICAL POETRY AND BYZANTINE PALESTINE: AL-NABIGHAH ADH-DHUBYANI
النابغة الذبياني (535–604 AD)

By and large Arab pagan society was illiterate, cultivating immensely rich oral/aural traditions and epic stories and prizing, in particular, exquisite oral poetry, the oldest form of Arabic literature. Furthermore, for many centuries before Islam the spread of Arabic in the predominantly oral culture of Arabia and beyond, and the Arabisation of parts of the Levant and Iraq, were carried out through the memorisation of oral/aural traditions, epics, Arabic poetry and classic poems (for instance, the *mu'allaqat*). This pre-Islamic poetry became a major source for the Arabic language and rhetoric and a rich historical record of the political and cultural life of the time. This communication of powerful pre-Islamic oral/aural traditions and poetry and the memorisation of epics were transmitted not only by poets and *rawis* (storytellers) but also by travelling Arab traders, through the annual pilgrimage to pre-Islamic Mecca and poetry competitions at seasonal literary markets (a famous example was Souq 'Ukath, near Ta'if in the Hijaz). In this pre-Islamic Arab culture the poet played the role of oral historian, storyteller, social critic, public intellectual, soothsayer and political agitator.

Arabic poetry and Arabic literacy and the movement from a predominantly oral/aural culture and oral traditions to a more literate Arabic setting and book culture was hugely influenced by the spread of Hellenistic Christianity and later the rise of Islam and by what Islam termed the 'people of the Book' (*ahl al-kitab*). Crucially, this gradual movement from illiteracy and oral/aural traditions to literacy and written culture was also promoted by the Christian Arab courts of the Ghassanid phylarchs of Palestine. These courts generously patronised the arts, especially Arabic poetry. This movement to literacy, together with the important tradition of memorisation of epics and classic Arabic poetry, continued to flourish with the spread of Islam, but crucially it was also accompanied by the reading and memorisation of the holy Quran as a means of spreading standard Arabic and establishing Arabisation and Arabic as the lingua franca in the newly founded Islamic empire. The Arabs of Provincia Palaestina and former Provincia Arabia, with their predominantly oral/aural culture, were also influenced by the literary life of the Arabs in the 5th and 6th centuries and by the tradition of memorisation of classic Arabic poetry by poets, *rawis* and ordinary people.

In pre-Islamic times, there were Christian Arab courts at Hirah, in southern Iraq, and Jabiyah, in Palaestina Secunda, and court poets, such as al-Nabighah adh-Dhubyani (535–604 AD), who played an important role in the spread of classical Arabic poetry. The Ghassanid tribal kings (phylarchs) of Palaestina Secunda, in particular, patronised the arts and entertained some key Arabian poets such as al-Nabighah and Hassasn ibn Thabit (a companion of the Prophet Muhammad who died in 674) at their courts. One possible connection between the Ghassanids of Palestine as protectors of the Christian holy places in the 'land of the Gospel' and the future Islamic holy places in Mecca is related to al-Nabighah, a contemporary of the Prophet Muhammad (570–632 AD). Al-Nabighah (literally 'the genius') was one of the last great Arab poets in the pre-Islamic era who spent most of his time at the courts of the Ghassanid kings in Palestine and the courts of the Christian Arab kings of Hirah, al-Mundhirs. Like Palaestina Tertia and Palaestina Secunda, Hirah was an important major pre-Islamic Arab Christian centre, being a diocese of the church of the East between the 4th and 7th centuries and seat of the Nestorian bishopric by 410 AD. Al-Nabighah became known as by his Christian Arab name 'Ilyas and later 'Ilyas from the Land of the Gospel' (*Ilyas min ard al-Bishara* الياس من أرض البشارة) or the Holy Land, as described by Arab historian al-Maqrizi (1364–1442). Greek was one the two lingua francas of Byzantine Palestine and Ilyas is the Arabic form of the Greek Elias, a name common among Christian Arabs today.

Al-Nabighah/Ilyas is one of the six eminent pre-Islamic poets whose poems were collected before the middle of the 2nd century of Islam, and have been regarded as the standard of Arabic poetry. These poets have written long poems comparable to epic poems, known as *Mu'allaqat* since they were hung on the walls of the Kaaba (a building at the centre of Islam's most sacred mosque in Mecca). The surviving descriptions of the Ghassanid urban centres and courts impart an image of luxury and an active cultural life, with patronage of the arts, music and especially Arab-language poetry. Warwick Ball, writer, archaeologist and former Architectural Conservator in the Department of Antiquities in Jordan, comments:

the Ghassanid courts were the most important centres for Arabic poetry before the rise of the Caliphal courts under Islam, and their court culture, including their penchant for desert palaces like Qasr ibn Wardan, provided the model for the Umayyad caliphs and their court. (Ball 2000: 103–105; also Shahid 2006b: 102)

Samaritan communities were established in practically all the cities of Roman Palestine: Neapolis, Sebaste, Caesarea Maritima, Scythopolis, Ascalon, Ashdod, Gaza, Iamnia, Emmaus, Ashdod and Antipatris (Hjelm 2016), and these communities were also found in most Palestinian cities in the Byzantine period. In fact, demographically the Greek-speaking Byzantine Christians and Samaritans dominated the central region of Palaestina Prima, while the Christian Ghassanid Arabs and Nabataean Arabs dominated Palaestina Secunda and Palaestina Tertia respectively. However, the Samaritan revolts during the 5th and 6th centuries in Palaestina Prima were marked by great violence on both sides, and their brutal suppression at the hands of the Byzantines and their Ghassanid Arab allies (Crown 1989: 72–73; Shahid 2010: 8) contributed to shifting the demographics of the region, making the Christians the dominant group in the province of Palaestina Prima for many decades. Also, many Samaritans converted to Islam from the early 7th century onwards.

The Ghassanid Arabs rose in the 5th century to be become an important ethno-linguistic religious community in Palestine and their Monophysite Orthodox Church became important in Palestine. In the 5th–6th centuries their capital was at Jabiyah in the Golan Heights, located within Palaestina Secunda. 'Gabitha' is mentioned in 520 AD in a Syriac Aramaic letter of Monophysite Bishop Simeon of Bet Arsham. Following the Battle of Yarmouk in 636 AD and the Arab conquest of Palestine and Syria, the Ghassanid town of Jabiyah became the headquarters of the main military camp for the Muslim armies in Syria. Overall the Monophysite Ghassanid Arabs preferred the Muslim Arab conquerors to the Christian Chalcedonians (Wigram 2004). Following the Byzantine military defeat at Yarmouk many of the Ghassanids would have been happy to get rid of the Byzantine Emperor and the Greek-speaking Chalcedonite Church and ally themselves with the rising power of Islam.

Derived from the Quranic Arabic term *millah*, the term *millet* denoted the religious community under Islam. The Ghassanid-dominated Monophysite Orthodox churches may have given the idea of the *millet* system to Islam. This became a principle for non-Muslims, who were given a significant degree of religious and social autonomy within their own community throughout the history of Islamic Palestine and the Near East. Furthermore, according to historians Warwick Ball and Irfan Shahid, the Ghassanids' promotion of a simpler and more rigidly monotheistic form of Christianity in a specifically Arab context can be said to have anticipated Islam (Ball 2000: 105; Shahid 2006b: 102).

The substantial autonomy achieved by the Ghassanid Arab-populated settlements of Palaestina Prima was derived from the fact that their localities acquired the status of both phylarchates, headed by a supreme Arab phylarch (a tribal king), and episcopates, headed by bishops. Petros (or Petrus), a chief of an Arab tribe or group of tribes from Byzantine Provincia Arabia, whose original name was Aspebetos, was the first to be simultaneously appointed as phylarch and bishop in Palaestina Prima (Shahid 2006a: 181; Isaac 2003: 450–451). The colourful career of Aspebetos was remarkable. He started as a military commander in the service of the Persian shah. He then defected to the Byzantines and became the Arab phylarch of Provincia Arabia. He then moved to Palaestina Prima, settling near the monastery of Euthemius, located between Aelia Capitolina (Jerusalem) and Jericho, and served as the Arab phylarch of Palaestina Prima. He and his son Terebon were then converted to Christianity and baptised by Euthemius. He also adopted the name Petros (Greek: rock) which became his baptismal name. Butros, the Arabic form of the Greek name Petros – a name still common among Palestinian and Arab Christians – would be the name used by him and his Arab followers in Palestine. Petros/Butros became first phylarch-bishop of the Palestinian Parembole in around 427 AD. This line of Palestinian bishops survived until the middle of the 6th century. Although his bishopric was based in Palaestina Tertia, he was responsible to the All Palestine Patriarchate of Aelia Capitolina, which later became known as the Patriarchate of Ilya (Jerusalem) under Arab Muslim rule from 637 onwards. The conversion of Aspebetos/Butros was followed by the conversion of his Arab tribe and he became a zealous Christian and for years led his converted Saracen (Arab) Christian community and managed to increase significantly the number of Christian Arabs in Palestine. The climax of his career was his active participation at the ecumenical Council of Ephesus in 431 AD, where he appears not merely as a subscription in the conciliar list but as an active participant in the debates and a delegate of the Council of Ephesus to Nestorius (Shahid 2006a: 46–48, 181–184, 528; 2006b: 128). Members of the house of Aspebetos continued to thrive as the tribal leaders of Arab Palaestina Prima and in the 6th century Cyril of Scythopolis, the historian of monastic life in Palestine, describes Terebon II, Aspebetos' great-grandson, as 'the renowned phylarch in this region': the area between Jerusalem and Jericho (Shahid 1995: 652).

But there were some fundamental differences between the 'autonomous' Arab phylarchs-bishops of Palaestina Prima – a core province – and the fairly independent Ghassanid kings-phylarchs of the two 'frontier provinces' of Palaestina Secunda and Palaestina Tertia: Abu Karib and al-Harith. The latter operated from established and recognised capitals. They also commanded their own substantial professional Arab armies, and not just contingent tribal forces. They enforced law and order within their wider domain and raised revenues and taxes from the lucrative international and regional trade passing through their provinces. They provided protection to the holy places in Palestine and, crucially, they dispatched their own ambassadors to foreign countries – ambassadors who acted in their names rather than representing the Byzantine state.

The year 451 was a turning point for the Church in Palestine. At the Council of Chalcedon, 451, the 'Three in One' Palestine provinces were separated from the jurisdiction of the Patriarchate of Antioch. The ecclesiastical separation of the 'Three Palestines' from Antioch did not have an immediate effect on the Arab church of the federates who remained staunchly Orthodox. With the growth of Monophytism in the Near East in the 6th century, especially after the impetus given by the Emperor Anastasius, the Patriarchate of Palestine remained the stronghold of Greek-dominated orthodoxy in Palestine and this legacy had a lasting impact on Arab–Greek relationships within the Palestine Church (Shahid 2006a: 528). It also opened up internal conflicts which lasted until today;

in the 5th century AD, these internal divisions within the Palestine Church were also reflected in symbols and colour codes:

> The Arab federates of the three Palestines, at least Prima and Secunda, remained staunchly Orthodox, while those outside the jurisdiction of the Patriarchate of Jerusalem, were mostly Monophysites, especially the dominant group, the Ghassanids … The division within the Arab church is reflected in Palestinian historiography, where the image of the [Arab] Orthodox phylarchs of the Parembole in Palaestina Prima is bright and that of the Ghassanids of Arabia is dim. (Shahid 2006a: 528)

Somewhat different in background from all Arab phylarchs of Palaestina Prima, Palaestina Secunda and Palaestina Tertia was Elias, the Arab Patriarch of Aelia Capitolina (Jerusalem), who became head of the All Palestine Church in 494 AD. While the others were federate Arab kings, Elias was a Rhomaic Arab born in Arabia. His ecclesiastical career was no less remarkable. He started as a monk in the desert of Palestine associated with Saint Euthymius the Great (377–473), an abbot venerated today in both Roman Catholic and Eastern Orthodox churches. Elias then drew the attention of Patriarch Anastasius, who ordained him priest of the Church of Anastasia in Jerusalem; finally, Elias became the Patriarch of the holy city, and engaged in an effective administration of his Patriarchate. He devoted time to the improvement of the churches and monasteries and laid the foundation of the Church of the Theotokos in Jerusalem, the spectacular church completed during the reign of Emperor Justinian and dedicated in 543. Possibly Elias was also associated with the translation of a simple liturgy and biblical lectionary into Arabic for the benefit of the various Christian Arab communities scattered in the 'Three Palestines' which came under his ecclesiastical jurisdiction (Shahid 2006a: 193–194).

Chapter 6

THE ARAB PROVINCE OF JUND FILASTIN (638–1099 AD)

Continuities, adaption and transformation of Palestine under Islam

PALESTINIAN SYRIAC ARAMAIC, PALESTINIAN ARABIC AND PALESTINIAN TOPONYMS

Late Bronze Age Peleset and Hellenic/Roman/Byzantine Palaestina were adapted by the Arabs and became Filastin under Islam from 638 AD onwards. In the mid-7th century the population of Palestine was predominantly Christian, mostly Palestinian Syriac Aramaic-speaking Christian peasants who continued to speak the language of Jesus throughout early Islam. However, the earliest Arabic inscriptions found in Palestine go back to the Roman and Byzantine periods, and for several centuries the Arabs were closely linked with the three Byzantine provinces of Palaestina; in fact, under the Byzantines Provincia Arabia itself became part of Palaestina Salutaris, with its capital located in Petra, the old capital of the Nabataean Arabs. Also after the Arabs took over Palestine in the 7th century many place names in Palestine that were used by the Greek-speaking Byzantine administration continued to be used by the Arab administration; hence the emergence of the three Arabic forms of Byzantine Παλαιστινη: Falastin, Filastin and Filistin (Schiller 2009: 85; Sharon 2003).

The presence of Arabs in Palestine was noted by Herodotus in the 5th century BC and Arabic inscriptions in Palestine were discovered from the Roman era. Closely related to Palestinian Arabic is Palestinian Syriac Aramaic, which was part of the north-west Semitic group of languages and was the language of ordinary people in the country. Palestinian Syriac Aramaic continued to flourish at a non-official popular level in Roman and Byzantine Palestine and in early Islamic Palestine and became closely related to the modern Palestinian Arabic colloquial language.

In the 4th–early 7th centuries the Ghassanid Arabs of the 'Three Palestines' were champions and protectors of the Syriac Monophysite Church. Their Arabic-speaking poets, bishops and kings (and phylarchs of Palaestina Prima, Palaestina Secunda and Palaestina Tertia) must have been familiar not only with the lingua franca of the Byzantine Empire (Greek), but also with the Syriac Aramaic dialect of greater Palestine.

Palestinian Aramaic was also spoken by Palestinian Jews during the Roman and Byzantine period (Sokoloff 2003). Today a significant number of Palestinian Aramaic words are found in both standard Arabic and in the vernacular language of many Palestinian villages. Also interestingly, in the early 20th century the European Zionist inventors of modern Hebrew, in pursuit of indigenising and antiquating strategies, borrowed heavily from Palestinian Aramaic and ancient Greek vocabulary.

Palestinian Aramaic has also survived in a large number of modern Palestinian and Arab toponyms including:

- Ramallah (Aramaic 'Ram', meaning height, and 'Allah', the Arabic word for God), a city which is the headquarters of the Palestinian National Authority.
- Al-Rama (height), a Palestinian town in upper Galilee.
- Al-Ram, a Palestinian town north-east of Jerusalem.
- Al-Majdal (meaning fortress), an Arab village near Tiberias depopulated by Israel in 1948.
- Al-Majdal ('Asqalan), the ancient Philistine city.
- Majdal Shams, a Druze Arab town north of the Golan Heights.
- Al-Mujaydil, an Arab village south-west of Nazareth depopulated by Israel in 1948.

- Al-Tur (mountain), the name of three mountainous place names in Palestine.

THE CONTINUITIES AND TRANSFORMATION OF THE PROVINCE OF JUND FILASTIN

Historians tend to conflate Arabisation processes in Palestine with the establishment of Arabic as the lingua franca for Palestine and the Near East. In fact, Arabisation and Islamisation in Palestine and the transformations of religious communities of the country – including the three Palestine provinces: Prima, Secunda and Tertia – were distinct historical processes and should not be automatically conflated or synchronised. Historically, Arabisation processes in greater Palestine (including the existence of Arabic-speaking Palestinian Christians) long preceded Islamisation processes in the country, although the establishment of Arabic as the lingua franca of Palestine went hand in hand with the Islamisation of the country.

As we have already seen, over the course of the Iron Age II (1000–6000 BC) the trading cities of old Philistia (Gaza, Jaffa, 'Aphek, Ekron, Ashdod, Ascalon) created a flourishing integrated south in Palestine by working closely with Arab traders and sailors. The Arabs were powerful traders who linked the distant trade from India and Asia to the Eastern Mediterranean region via the Red Sea, Nabataea, southern Palestine and the seaports of Philistia. This integrated south was maintained under the Assyrian and Persian empires and in the 5th century BC Herodotus describes in detail the presence of Arabs in southern Palestine. A century later, the Nabataean Arabs, who flourished on international trade and local agriculture, began to dominate the Naqab/Negev from the 4th century BC onwards and founded several Palestinian villages and towns, some of which survived until the Palestinian Nakba of 1948.

Al-Khalasa, a Palestinian Muslim village located 23 kilometres south-west of the city of Beershiba and depopulated by Israel in 1948, was founded by the Nabataean Arabs in the early 4th century using the Arabic name 'al-Khalus', and the town became part of the Nabataean

Arab incense route. The Greco-Roman historian and geographer Ptolemy identifies it as a town in Idumaea. In the late Roman period it grew to become the principal town of the western Roman Arabia Petraea province. Under the Byzantines the Palaestina Tertia town became known as 'Elusa', preserving the Arabic name. It also served as an administrative centre in the Naqab desert and was the home of one of three classical schools of rhetoric in Byzantine Palaestina. Under Arab Islam the town continued to function as a major urban centre and became known by its modern Arabic name al-Khalasa, but was abandoned sometime during the late Mamluk period in the 15th century CE. It was repopulated by Palestinian Bedouins in the early 20th century. After the destruction of the Arab village in 1948 the Israelis renamed it Haluza (Hebrew: 'pioneer'), a Hebrew-sounding name based on the Arabic toponym 'al-Khalus'; and more recently UNESCO declared the archaeological site a World Heritage Site, ironically due to its historic importance but, in fact, without acknowledging the centrality of the site to the twenty-four centuries of Arab history and heritage in Palestine.

In early Islam, the combination of strategic-military and administrative considerations for the creation of the four, and later five, Muslim *ajnads* (provinces) system in Bilad al-Sham were influenced by the previous Byzantine strategic configuration of the region. The origins of the *ajnad* system of Bilad al-Sham under Islam are in dispute. However, Irfan Shahid (1986) sees a Byzantine origin for this system. The provinces, or *ajnad*, retained civil and administrative responsibilities for their surrounding districts, including the raising of taxes (Walmsley 2000: 273). The Arab governors of the five *ajnad* (sing. *jund*) of al-Sham region, Damascus, Filastin, al-Urdun, Hims and Qinnasrin, were called *amirs* and, in one case, the Governor (wali) of Jund Filastin, Suleiman ibn 'Abd al-Malik, became the Umayyad Caliph in 715.

Palestine had been brought fully within the Islamic Caliphate in 637–638. In the Islamic theory of governance, a Caliph was a supreme ruler who was chosen by the community to be a successor to the Prophet Muhammad. As political leader of the entire Muslim community, the Caliph was provided with an Islamic reference framework defined by the Quran and the Hadith (the sayings and actions of the Prophet Muhammad) and was obliged to govern through *shura* (consultation, deliberation, advice). The *shura*, a Quranic principle, created a space that enabled the Islamic traditions to negotiate social pluralism and inter-cultural exchanges throughout the vast Islamic empire. In practice, however, many Caliphs were hereditary rulers and they were only as strong as their armies and political alliances made them. The founders of the Umayyad dynasty were also acutely aware of the power/knowledge nexus, to echo Michel Foucault's famous paradigm. They were powerful, shrewd and pragmatic Caliphs and sought administrative advice, political *shura*, scientific knowledge and technological expertise from their Muslim and non-Muslim subjects alike. With the flexibility of the Islamic tradition firmly established, in 661 AD the Umayyad Caliphs took over the Islamic state and made Damascus the capital of the vast Islamic empire.

Material, economic, religious and political evidence shows that under the Umayyad Marwanid Caliphs,[1] who succeeded in expanding the Islamic empire to an unprecedented size, the two provinces (*ajnad*) of Dimashq and Filastin were treated as core provinces (أجناد) of a vast empire, for reasons of religious dogma mixed with realpolitik. After all, Palestine was more strategically important and more tightly controlled by the Umayyad rulers than the deserts of Arabia, as indeed was Syria, so that the centrality and importance of Palestine and Syria under the Umayyad Marwanid Caliphs remained paramount. It also helped the process of homogenisation and Arabisation of the large empire that the peasants of Palestine spoke a local version of Aramaic, a dialect much closer to Arabic than any other language but Hebrew, which had largely been extinct for centuries, so the gradual but steady move to Arabic as the official lingua franca in Palestine and the Near East was neither difficult nor protracted.

Moreover, the Umayyad Marwanid revolution and extraordinary shrewdness and innovation also resulted in the construction by the Umayyad Marwanid Caliphs of a system of exquisite and large palaces in Jerusalem, al-Ramla, near Jericho and near Tiberias which give us a glimpse into the centrality of Palestine within this vast Islamic empire. The reforming Marwanid ruler 'Abd al-Malik ibn Marwan (r. 685–705 AD) is credited with the transformation of Jerusalem, the construction of the Dome of the Rock in the city and the currency reforms, as well as the establishment of Arabic as the official language of the Islamic Caliphate (Ochsenwald and Fisher 2004: 57). For the first six decades of Islam in Palestine, prior to 'Abd al-Malik's linguistic and administrative reforms, much of the local government's work in Palestine was recorded in Koine Greek and many prominent positions in the country were held by Christians, some of whom belonged to families that had served in Byzantine administrations. The linguistic revolution which began with 'Abd al-Malik ibn Marwan and was maintained by subsequent Marwanid Caliphs meant that Arabic became the lingua franca not only of Palestine but the Islamic empire, which, at the time, included more than 30 per cent of the world's population. The linguistic revolution and having Arabic as the single lingua franca for tens of millions of people from Spain to Central Asa was also central to the expansion of global trade under Muslim rule. Throughout the Middle Ages, as in ancient times, regional and distant trade remained a key source for the prosperity of a strategically located Palestine.

Arabic and the Arabisation of Palestine added more cultural layers to Palestine's already rich and complex identity. The Arabisation of Palestine benefited from the fact that the predominantly Palestinian Christian peasantry spoke a Palestinian dialect of Aramaic, a Semitic language closely related to Arabic. However, if under the Romans and Byzantines Koine Greek was the elite language of Palestine and the Levant and Hellenisation was closely associated with cosmopolitanism and high culture, under Islam literary Arabic and Arabisation became a vehicle for globalisation. Literary Arabic and translation into Arabic became closely associated with scientific inquiry and cultural innovation, expanding international trade and cosmopolitanism. Furthermore, Byzantine Palestine had been bedevilled by deep class cleavages reflected in linguistic divisions. If speaking Greek was a key marker of metropolitan and urban elite identity and speaking Aramaic was a key marker of identity for ordinary people and Palestinian peasantry in Christian-majority Byzantine Palaestina, Arabic and Arabisation encouraged egalitarianism in Palestine and became key markers of identity for both urban elites and the increasingly Arabised Palestinian peasantry.

Under Islam, the metropolises of Damascus, Baghdad and Cairo stood out as imperial centres, but their trade and strategic linkages through overland and sea routes tied them to an archipelago of hinterland cities in al-Sham and Palestine and the whole al-Sham region, including al-Ramla, Gaza, 'Asqalan, al-Lajjun, al-Quds, Nablus, Acre and Tiberias. Naturally Arabisation and Islamisation followed trade and political power, and this cultural and linguistic transformation of Palestine was promoted actively and assiduously after the Arab Islamic conquest of Palestine. Islamisation processes in the country followed suit. Filastin became part of the Arab Islamic state following the Battle of Yarmuk (636 AD) in the course the Muslim conquest of Syria and Palestine.

Although the Arab Islamic military conquest of Palestine took place in 638 AD, the practical Islamisation of Palestine was a gradual but radical process which went on for many generations. There is also some evidence of the mass conversion by Samaritans to Islam in Palestine in the course of the early Muslim period (see Levy-Rubin 2000). However, the powerful Arab Muslim impact on Palestine has continued for nearly 1400 years, to the present time. The profound religious, social, cultural and linguistic transformation of the country under Islam is evident throughout the land. But the gradual processes of Arabisation, homogenisation and Islamisation of the country, from a largely Aramaic-speaking majority Christian country to a predominantly Arabic-speaking Muslim majority, and from one monotheistic religion to another – as well as from one Semitic language to another closely related one – was less traumatic culturally and socially less painful than the sudden conversion of a pagan society into a monotheistic polity.

The archaeological evidence on the early history of Islam in Palestine debunks the common perception and insidious myth that the Muslim conquest of Palestine in the 7th century caused a decline in the number of localities and the overall prosperity of the country (Magness 2003: 1–3). On the contrary, the Muslim Arabs ushered in a period of prosperity and religious toleration and religious and cultural autonomy for Christian and Jewish religious communities (Arabic: *millah*) in Palestine and permitted the previous administrative organisation to continue (*The Encyclopaedia of Islam* 1965, Vol. II: 911). The Islamic states, like the Roman and Byzantine empires, also applied a patron–client system in Palestine and this patronage system allowed the emergence of a degree of local autonomy and powerful urban elites.

For largely defensive military-strategic reasons greater Palestine under Islam was reconfigured and reconstituted from two of the 'Three Palestines' of the Byzantines (Blankinship 1994). This military-strategic reconfiguration and reorganisation was also reflected in the actual naming of the country: Jund Filastin, the 'administrative/military province of Palestine'. This reconfiguration was also aimed at addressing some of the fundamental weaknesses of the Byzantine strategic thinking for defending the 'Three Palestines' and other regions in Syria. The Byzantine military was headquartered in the coastal city of Caesarea Maritima and relied extensively on the Ghassanid Arab allies of the hinterland who had effectively controlled Palaestina Secunda and Palaestina Tertia. The Muslim Arab commanders, while still using many Ghassanid Christian troops in Muslim armies, preferred to rely on Muslim commanders. Reducing Jund Filastin from the original Three to 'Two Palestines' (Palaestina Prima and Palaestina Tertia) also made sense in military-strategic terms.

The administrative reorganisation of Palestine during early Islam meant that Byzantine greater Palestine became a combination of a relatively large Jund Filastin province and a small Jund al-Urdun (Jordan province). Governed from Tiberias in Galilee, Jund al-Urdun should not be equated with modern-day Jordan. With the consolidation of Arab Muslim rule in Palestine and the Levant in the mid-7th century, the region was divided into Filastin, al-Urdun and Dimashq (Damascus) and the Arabs (like the Romans) opted for a decentralised administration. During the Umayyad period (661–750 AD) the al-Sham region was divided into *junds* or military/administrative provinces. Jund Filastin was organised soon after the Muslim conquest of Palestine in the 630s. The Umayyads adapted many of the Byzantine toponymic, monetary and administrative traditions and this process of adaptation was evident in many aspects of the province of Jund Filastin.

THE EXTENT OF THE ARAB PROVINCE OF JUND FILASTIN: FROM MARJ IBN 'AMER TO THE RED SEA

For several centuries Aylah, the present-day Jordanian port city of al-'Aqabah on the Red Sea, was part of the Islamic administrative province of Jund Filastin, whose governors (*walis*) were also in charge of looking after the safety of the caravans of Muslim pilgrims from Mecca through Aylah and al-Ramla to Damascus and beyond. Umayyad numismatic and epigraphic evidence shows that Aylah was an early Islamic town in the province of Jund Filastin. Originally a Roman and Byzantine town called Aelas, now the ruins of Aylah lie within the present-day port city of al-ʿAqabah (Ramadan 2010b). 'Aylah in Filastin' ('Aelas in Byzantine Palaestina') was also the reason, within the Israeli settler toponymic project post-1948, for calling the nearby new Israeli settlement Eilat.

Southern 'Aelas' in Byzantine Palaestina, which became 'Aylah' in Islamic Jund Filastin, should be clearly distinguished from the northern 'Ilya-Filastin' (Jerusalem) under Islam (Aelia Capitolina under the Romans and Byzantine). Aylah (Aelas) was a vibrant Palestinian port town under both the Byzantines and Muslims and at the centre of the Indian and South Arabian spice trade. Rising to prominence after the Islamic conquests, Aylah-Filastin, located strategically on the Red Sea – also known to medieval European geographers as Mare Mecca, or the Sea of Mecca, and Sinus Arabicus, or the Gulf of Arabia – developed into a major trading port town and benefited hugely from the annual caravans of Muslim pilgrims to and from Mecca (Lev 2006: 591) and from the linking of the al-Sham region with the Arabian Peninsula and Indian Ocean. Apparently, Umayyad 'Aylah in Filastin' coins were also minted in Iliya-Filastin for the use in the Red Sea town and beyond (Ramadan 2010a, 2010b) and 10th century Palestinian geographer al-Maqdisi, after visiting Aylah-Filastin, described it as 'a port of Palestine on China Sea' (Ramadan 2010a, 2010b). The combination of Arabic written sources, Umayyad numismatic and epigraphic evidence and Byzantine sources gives us a good idea about the way the large Arab province of Jund Filastin emerged out of the combination of two provinces of Palaestina Prima and Palaestina Tertia. In this regard, it is worth noting that Palestinian historian Prokopios of Caesarea Maritima had already written in 560 AD:

The boundaries of Palestine extend toward the east to the sea which is called the Red Sea. Now this sea, beginning at India, comes to an

end at this point in the Roman domain. And there is a city called
Aelas [modern-day 'Aqabah] on its shore, where the sea comes to an
end, as I have said, and becomes a very narrow gulf. And as one sails
into the sea from there, the Egyptian mountains lie on the right,
extending toward the south; on the other side a country deserted by
men extends northward to an indefinite distance; and the land on
both sides is visible as one sails in as far as the island called Iotabe,
not less than one thousand stades distant from the city of Aelas.
(Prokopios 2005)

Aylah-Filastin under Islam gives us some indication of the vastness and
wealth of the province of Jund Filastin which stretched from the fertile
plain of Marj Ibn 'Amer in the north – a rich granary in Palestine and a
region which at the time was considered part of lower Galilee – to al-'Arish
in Sinai and to the trading town of Aylah-Filastin on the Red Sea. In fact,
the province of Jund Filastin encompassed most of Palaestina Prima and
Palaestina Tertia (Avni 2014: 27). Jund al-Urdun (جند الأردن), 'the Mili-
tary/Administrative Province of Jordan', replacing Palaestina Secunda
(Blankinship 1994: 84; Avni 2014: 27), was formed with its capital in the
Palestinian city of Tabariyyah (Tiberias). Founded in Roman Palestine and
known by its Greek name, Τιβεριάς, the city had been the regional capital
of Galilee at the time of Jesus and would remain a key Palestinian centre
of trade, silk industry and leisure activities for several centuries to come.
The city was also a seat of religious learning for Arab-Judaism and ancient
Hebrew – then a language of liturgy (lashon hakodesh) rather than a day-to
day spoken language – was codified in Tabariyyah under the globalising
impact of Arabic and Islam. Under Islam the fame of Tabariyyah as a
multicultural, hedonistic and leisure city –situated in the proximity of
many natural thermal springs and hot health baths – became so great
that the Sea of Galilee became known in Arabic as the 'Sea of Tiberias'
(Bahr Tabariyyah and later Buhayrat Tabariyyah). Like Palaestina Secunda,
Jund al-Urdun included most of the Galilee and some territories in Transjordan. The overall size of Jund al-Urdun was about one-third of modern
Mandatory Palestine. With some minor changes this administrative division of Palestine remained largely unchanged until the Crusader invasion

of the country in 1099, although under the Fatimids Jund al-Urdun was effectively ruled from al-Ramla by the Military Governor of Palestine (متولي حرب فلسطين).

Of course, the medieval Arabs were familiar with the Old Testament and New Testament. But they opted for the real historical and official administrative name of the country: Palestine (Filastin) rather than for the ideological Old Testament term 'Cana'an', and they embraced and cherished the diverse heritage of Palestine and the shared heritage of the Levant. The medieval Arabic toponymy of Filastin was identical to the Old French term Philistin, which came from Latin Philistina or Philistinus or Palaestina which, in turn, derived from the Roman name of the province, Palaestina, based on the ancient name with its memory preserved in the Old Testament and a variety of ancient languages, the Akkadian Palashtu and Egyptian Parusata.

THE SECULAR AND SACRED CAPITALS OF THE PROVINCE OF FILASTIN: THE GRANDEUR OF ILYA (BAYT AL-MAQDIS) AND AL-RAMLA UNDER THE UMAYYADS

> During the season of pilgrimage [Muslim Haj], thousands who cannot travel to Mecca, come to Jerusalem. They approach the sanctuary [al-Haram] and offer sacrifices as is customary. In some years, over 20,000 [Muslim] people fulfil the [Haj] law here ... Christians and Jews come here too, from the land of the Christians. (Nasir Khusro, 1050 AD, cited in Matar 2013: 913)

The Arab Islamic province of Jund Filastin was one of the military/administrative provinces of the Umayyad and Abbasid region of al-Sham, provinces organised soon after the Muslim conquest of the Levant in the late 630s. The official name, Jund Filastin, was universally adopted from early Islam onwards by Muslim rulers and Arab governors of Filastin (*walis*), Arab and Muslim geographers, cartographers, historians, translators, engravers, coiners, pilgrims and merchants. They all relied on the classical heritage of Palestine and the Near East. Arab administrators, historians and geographers also translated and preserved many of the ancient place names of Palestine and much of the classical heritage of Greece and Antiquity in the Levant.

Islamic pilgrimage to Jerusalem began very early and this was enhanced by the grandeur and centrality of the holy city and Umayyad Filastin (661–749), which can hardly be overstated. The Dome of the Rock was the first monumental sanctuary erected by Umayyad Islam between 688 and 691 (Murphy-O'Connor 2012: 27). The Umayyads, like the Romans and Byzantines, promoted urbanisation in Palestine. They also respected the multifaith and shared heritage of the country and continued many of the Byzantines' administrative traditions and architectural styles. For the Muslim Arabs, as for the Byzantine Christians, Palestine (Holy Land: Arabic: al-Ard al-Muqaddasah [al-Maqdisi 2002: 135]; Hebrew: Eretz HaKodesh) and Jerusalem were a special, sacred space. The sanctity and centrality of Jerusalem is enshrined in its very Arabic name: Bayt al-Maqdis (the 'house of the holy') or al-Quds (the 'holy'). According to the traditional Muslim view, the Qibla (Arabic: 'direction'), the direction in which the first Muslims had prayed, originally faced the Noble Sanctuary in Jerusalem. The sacred city was always a focus of intense Islamic devotion and pilgrimage.

The governors of the province of Jund Filastin were appointed by the Caliph. They were in charge of the army commanders, Muslim clergy, religious officials, tax collectors, police and civil administrators in the province. But the Umayyad rulers, especially the Marwani Caliphs, took a personal interest in Palestine. The Umayyad Caliphs, like the Byzantine Christian rulers, made a clear distinction between the 'secular' (political, worldly) and 'sacred' spheres and between the political (secular/administrative/military) and sacred capitals of Palestine. For the Byzantine Christians that distinction, formalised at the Nicaea Council in 325, produced a rather complicated and confused ecclesiastical arrangement between the Archiepiscopal See of Caesarea-Palaestina and the Archbishopric of Aelia Capitolina. However, for the Umayyad rulers the distinction between political/secular/administrative and sacred capitals of Jund Filastin was simpler and more straightforward. Also, subsequent accounts by Arab geographers from the 10th century lends some weight to the secular-administrative versus religious capital ('double capitals') concept in Palestine suggested in this work.

Aelia Capitolina remained the official name of Jerusalem until 638 AD when the Arabs conquered the city and kept the first part of it as Iliya. Iliya (later Bayt al-Maqdis and al-Quds) was the sacred/religious capital of the Umayyad state and of Palestine. The Umayyad Caliphs loved and honoured Jerusalem, and Mu'awiyah (602–680 AD), founder of the Umayyad dynasty, was reported to have had himself proclaimed Caliph in Jerusalem (*The Encyclopaedia of Islam* 1965, Vol. II: 911). The Umayyads devoted a great deal of effort and resources to its expansion and the prosperity of Jerusalem and other Palestinian cities.

Interestingly, the Umayyad Marwanid Caliphs considered relocating their capital from the *secular* capital Damascus to the *holy city* of Jerusalem. Although the move was abandoned for strategic reasons, in preparation they symbolically built their large 'palaces' adjacent to the al-Aqsa Mosque. In excavations carried out by Hebrew University archaeologist Benyamin Mazar in the 1970s, south and south-west of the al-Haram al-Sharif (the Noble Sanctuary) the remains of six massive buildings were uncovered; these buildings were not mentioned in any of the Arabic written sources describing the period. The buildings were labelled 'palaces' as they were probably part of the government complex and the administrative centre of the Umayyad government in Jerusalem. Nothing similar or comparable to this government complex in Umayyad Jerusalem was found in the *secular capital* of Jund Filastin, al-Ramla. The Marwanid Caliphs also renewed and enhanced the centrality of Jerusalem in the Muslim empire. If al-Ramla became the administrative head of Muslim Palestine, Jerusalem became the religious heart of Muslim Palestine, but also of the rest of the Umayyad Empire. Now, added to the Christian pilgrims who continued to arrive, were the convoys of Muslim pilgrims who came to Jerusalem in their thousands from the Maghreb, Iran and even Central Asia.

The largest and most impressive palace at the centre of the magnificent secular Umayyad architecture in Ilya (Bayt al-Maqdis) was near the south-west corner of the al-Haram and was the seat of the Umayyad Caliphs who visited the holy city on a regular basis. The palace was apparently constructed during the reign of the al-Walid ibn 'Abd al-Malik (who ruled from 705 to 715) and is similar to other fortified Umayyad palaces in Palestine (near Jericho and near Tiberias) and Syria. The palace measured 96 by 84 metres and was surrounded by a 3-metre protective wall, constructed of large, trimmed stones. Two main gates, one facing east and one facing west, gave access to the palace. A broad, stone-paved courtyard in the centre of the building was surrounded by rows of columns supporting the roofing of the porticoes. Many of the columns came from Byzantine churches and buildings in Palestine, as evidenced by traces of engraved crosses on them. The rooms around the central courtyard were paved with small stone slabs and mosaic. Plaster, decorated with geometric designs and floral motifs, covered the thick walls. A bridge was built from the roof of the palace to the al-Haram al-Sharif (Noble Sanctuary compound), providing direct access to the al-Aqsa Mosque. The magnificent complex of Muslim buildings was destroyed by the earthquake of 749; evidence of this is the fallen columns and collapsed walls.[2]

The Umayyad undertook monumental building programmes in Jerusalem, the centre of which were the Dome of the Rock (completed in 691 AD) and the al-Aqsa Mosque (completed in 705 AD), both still standing, and both remaining the most potent religious and cultural symbols of Palestine. The al-Aqsa Mosque itself was constructed on the basis of an earlier Islamic mosque built within the Haram al-Sharif compound and with reference to a key Islamic tradition, the Isra and Mi'raj. This tradition, according to Islam, involved Prophet Muhammad's night-time journey to Jerusalem, which took place around the year 621 AD. The Umayyads' magnificent public (secular and religious) rebuilding programmes in Jerusalem and al-Ramla and their large palaces in Jerusalem and near Jericho and Tiberias show the extent to which Palestine had become central to the Umayyad state and early Islam. But the founding of a completely new metropolitan city for Palestine also represented a break from the Byzantine past and a reorientation of Palestine under the Marwanid rulers. This resulted in the creation of a new capital city for the province of Filastin, al-Ramla, an administrative capital founded by Suleiman ibn 'Abd al-Malik, the Governor of Filastin (705–715 AD) and later Umayyad Caliph (715–717). But in the end, and especially during the Umayyad period, the new city of government built at al-Ramla could never rival the location and splendour of the buildings in Jerusalem, or its religiously rich history – a city which, as we shall see in chapter seven, would, once Salah-al Din had recovered from the Latin Crusaders in the 12th century, become the centre of the administration of Muslim-majority Palestine.

According to the conventional wisdom, the name Ramla is derived from the Arabic word *raml*, meaning sand (Palmer 1881: 217). But it is more likely that the new Arab capital was named by Suleiman ibn 'Abd al-Malik not for its sand but in memory of Ramla, a remarkable woman who was the daughter of Caliph Mu'awiyya ibn Abu Sufyan, the founder of the Umayyad dynasty. Ramla's reputation among the Umayyad ruling elite was enhanced by the fact that she also married to a son of Uthman, the third Caliph of Islam (Roded 1994: 57). The likelihood of a major city being named in memory of an important Umayyad woman in the history of the ruling dynasty could easily have been overlooked by the post-Umayyad almost exclusively male (Abbasid-leaning) Muslim historians of the Middle Ages.

In any event, crucially, Suleiman ibn 'Abd al-Malik continued to reside in al-Ramla, and did not move to the imperial capital Damascus after he became Caliph in 715 AD (*The Encyclopaedia of Islam* 1965, Vol. II: 911). He is also 'credited with the construction of a palace, a mosque, an extensive water supply and storage system and the House of the Dyers'; subsequently, and for several centuries, al-Ramla flourished as a fortified city with many cisterns and a highly developed system of rainwater collection and storage (Lev 2006: 590–591). Moreover, throughout early Islam the two political/ secular and sacred cities of al-Ramla and Jerusalem were at the heart of a distinct Palestinian Arab province. Combining the Byzantine provinces of Palaestina Prima and Palaestina Tertia, the Arab province of Jund Filastin included most major Palestinian cities and more than two-thirds of the territory of Mandatory Palestine.

Archaeological finds and place names show the continuities of historic Palestine with toponymic memory and shared culture. They indicate that the major Palestinian cities of Byzantine Palaestina – Lydda, Scythopolis (Beisan), Gaza, Tiberias, Neapolis (Nablus), Jaffa, 'Amwas/Emmuas, Rafah, Acre, 'Asqalan, Ilya/al-Quds/Jerusalem, Eleutheropolis (Beit Jibrin) and Caesarea Maritima (Qaysariah) – continued to function as urban centres in this period. a number of new cities and towns were also built, most notably al-Ramla (which became the administrative and commercial centre of Palestine for several centuries), located inland, away from potential Byzantine seaborne attacks and the Mediterranean battleground between Byzantines and Arabs, while new Arab naval bases and shipyards were established in Palestine (Nicolle 1996: 47). Jerusalem (like Gaza, 'Asqalan, Nablus, Caesarea and Jaffa) was a district (*qada*) and religious capital of the country It was expanded by the Umayyads with new monumental Arab Islamic architecture and the city flourished as the religious centre of the whole country as well as a holy city for Jews and Christians. Moreover, the architectural forms of urban Palestine and Islamic Jerusalem exhibited continuities and adaption and a mélange of Arab Islamic and Byzantine styles.[3]

According to the 9th century Muslim historian al-Baladuri, the principal cities/towns of the province of Jund Filastin included al-Ramla, al-Quds, Gaza, 'Asqalan, Nablus, Yafa (Jaffa), 'Amwas, Rafah, Sabastia, Qaysariah, Tabariyyah, Beit Jibrin, al-Khalil (Hebron), Lid (Lydda) and Yubna,[4] the latter being one of ten towns in Jund Filastin conquered by the Arab army commanded by 'Amr ibn-'Aas in the 630s (cited in Le Strange 1890: 20). Back in the 7th century the Arab-Byzantine coinage of the province of Jund Filastin was minted in Yubna, Jerusalem and Lydda (Goodwin 2004), the initial and temporary capital of Jund Filastin.

Strategic-military considerations and international trade routes were major factors in the conceptualisation of Palestine and in shaping its history under both Byzantium and Islam. The new capital city of the province of Jund Filastin, al-Ramla, was founded by the Arabs c. 705–715 AD and became the capital of Palestine. Al-Quds (Jerusalem) was the religious centre of Palestine and the Umayyad state. Al-Ramla was chosen as the administrative centre of Palestine between 715 AD and 940 AD because of its important strategic location along the historic trade route of the Via Maris ('way of the sea' or 'way of the Philistines') via Gaza to Egypt.[5] At Tantura the old Via Maris veered inland to the right and passed through Marj Ibn 'Amer and then by Mount Tabor northward towards Damascus. Under Muslim rule this route connected to al-Fustat (early Cairo), with the city of al-Sham (Damascus) at its intersection with the road connecting the seaport of Jaffa with holy city of al-Quds (Jerusalem).

However, after the Muslim recovery of Jerusalem from the Latin Crusaders in 1187 and the elimination by the Ayyubids of the first Latin Kingdom of Jerusalem, the administrative capital of Filastin shifted to al-Quds. The Latin Kingdom of Jerusalem had been a Crusader state established in 1099 after the First Crusade. Following the Third Crusade, the kingdom was re-established in Acre in 1192 and lasted until 1291. Overall the Latin Kingdom lasted in Palestine nearly 200 years, from 1099 until 1291, when the last stronghold and capital, Acre, was destroyed by the Mamluks. The position of al-Quds as both the administrative and religious capital of Palestine was reinforced by both the Ayyubids and the Mamluks (1260–1517) in the post-Crusader period.

Earlier under Islam, and for several centuries between the early 8th and late 11th centuries, al-Ramla was the economic and political hub of the province of Filastin and the largest, richest and most powerful trading city in the country. Al-Ramla was at the centre of the north–south and west–east trade routes and the large number of caravanserais (*khans*) which dotted the country, with a distance of approximately 20 to 30 kilometres between them, allowed merchants and pilgrims to rest overnight. These khans were also intended to facilitate the postal service (*barid*) which had been introduced to Palestine by the Umayyads (Rosen-Ayalon 1998: 515) and developed further under successive Muslim dynasties. The other historic cities of the province of Jund Filastin in early Islam were al-Quds, 'Asqalan, Gaza, Lydda, Arsuf (Greek: Apollonia),[6] Jaffa, Beit Jibrin, Nablus, Jericho and Qaysariah, with 'Amman east of the River Jordan. During this period, we can observe both continuities and transformation in the social, cultural, economic, administrative and geo-political identities of Palestine.

Throughout the Middle Ages Muslim pilgrims and travel writers reported that Filastin was equated throughout the Muslim world with the capital city of the country: al-Ramla (Khusrau 1888; Ibn Battuta 2005: 57). Indeed, for centuries throughout early Islam the name of the capital city of Palestine, al-Ramla, became synonymous with the name of the country as a whole, Filastin (Palestine), and the capital city was often called by al-Ramla-Filastin by medieval Arab travellers, geographers and historians, in the same way as the former capital city of Byzantine Palestine, Caesarea Maritima, had become synonymous with the name of the country as a whole, Palaestina, and had often been called Caesarea-Palaestina. Once again we see Islam continuing and pragmatically adapting Palestine traditions and the Byzantine administrative and geo-political traditions of Palestine rather than replacing them completely. This adaption and transformation of Byzantine administrative and geo-political traditions was also influenced by the tendency in Palestine and the Near East as a whole (the Arab Muslim Near East included) to equate countries, provinces or regions with capital cities. For instance:

- The capital cities of Gaza and Ascalon and their hinterland became synonymous with Philistia in the late Bronze Age and throughout the Iron Age.
- Caesarea Maritima, the capital city of Palaestina Prima under the Byzantines became synonymous with Provincia Palaestina as a whole.
- Al-Sham became synonymous with the capital city of the Muslim province of Dimashq (Damascus).
- The first capital of Egypt under Muslim rule, al-Fustat was called Misr al-Fustat and Fustat-Misr (Fustat-Egypt) and the term Misr or Masr (Egypt) became synonymous with Masr al-Qadimah, the capital city of old Cairo.
- As shall we see, the two capital cities of the Latin King of Jerusalem (and Latin Palaestina) under the Frankish Crusaders, first Jerusalem and later Acre, became associated with Provincia Palaestina.
- As shall we see, the capital city of late Ottoman Palestine, al-Quds, and its province: Kudüs-i Şerif Mutasarrıflığı (the 'Mutasarrifate of Noble Jerusalem'), became associated with Filastin as a whole.

International and regional trade was always central to the prosperity of Palestine, being a transit country. While geographically Jerusalem of the period was isolated in a mountainous region, the fact that the secular capital of the province of Filastin, al-Ramla, was strategically and commercially located on the highway leading to the two great capital cities of Islam, al-Sham (Damascus) and Misr al-Fustat and Fustat-Misr (Fustat-Egypt), greatly enhanced the prosperity and international reputation of al-Ramla. Thus Filastin was not only the official name of the province/

country but, for some medieval Arab historians, the name also became synonymous with the capital city of al-Ramla. Strategically, geo-politically and in trade terms located at the centre of the country and linking the holy city of Jerusalem with Jaffa, the main Mediterranean port of Jund Filastin, al-Ramla flourished as the administrative, military and trading hub of the country for more than three centuries (Foster 2016a).

In the late 9th century the province of Filastin was probably at its greatest extent. It was expanded further by the Tulunids, who broke away from the Abbasids and ruled from Egypt as an independent dynasty from 868 until 905. The province of Filastin was enlarged for practical purposes eastwards and southwards, at the expense of Jund Dimashq, to include Bilad al-Sharat, the highlands and highly fertile region in modern-day southern Jordan and north-western Saudi Arabia (Salibi 1993: 18–20; le Strange 1890: 28). Aylah (present-day 'Aqabah) was the first major town in Palestine to be taken over by Muslim forces under the leadership of Prophet Muhammad in 630 AD (9 AH). This is hardly surprising: in his teens, Prophet Muhammad had joined his uncle on Syrian–Palestinian trading caravans and had gained experience in international trade and regional geography. Later in adult life, the Prophet acquired the reputation of being a trustworthy and very successful trader, and he was involved in international trade between the Red Sea and Mediterranean Sea; the Prophet must have also been closely familiar with port cities such as Aylah (present-day 'Aqabah), and Gaza, which, at the time, linked the international trade networks of Palaestina Salutaris and Palaestina Prima. Indeed, throughout early Islam Aylah became the major trading port of Filastin to Asia and China (Ramadan 2010a). The port city of Aylah became a centre of economic activity in southern Filastin and also served as a major stopover for Muslim pilgrims en route to Mecca (Ramadan 2010a; 2010b). As for the Bilad al-Sharat region, its principal city is al-Karak, known today for its Crusader castle, located 140 kilometres to the south of 'Amman and then a site on the ancient King's Highway. At its greatest extent, Jund Filastin extended from the Mediterranean coast to the region beyond the Dead Sea, to include Bilad al-Sharat, and from al-'Arish in Sinai to Marj Ibn 'Amer and Beisan in the north, with most of Galilee being part of Jund al-Urdun (the 'military province of Jordan'). Its predominantly Muslim towns included Gaza, Nablus, Jaffa, Lydda, al-Ramla, Qaysariah, 'Amwas, Yubna, Rafah, Sabastiyah (Sebastia) and Beit Jibrin.

The political capital of Filastin, al-Ramla, became famous throughout the Muslim world for its spectacularly beautiful White Mosque – whose minaret is still standing – and for the fertility of the soil of the district, the abundance of its fruit trees and 'tasty fruits', while the religious capital of Palestine, Bayt al-Maqdis, was renovated not only for its religious significance but also for the beauty of its stone buildings and its exquisite architecture (al-Maqdisi 2002: 34–35). While under the Byzantines Caesarea had for centuries been the largest city in Palaestina, for three centuries under Islam al-Ramla became the largest metropolitan city in the country. Al-Ramla was described in the late 10th century by the Jerusalem-born historian and geographer al-Maqdisi as one of the 'best' cities in the whole Muslim regions (al-Maqdisi 2002: 35). He had this to say:

> Ar-Ramlah is the capital of Palestine [Arabic: Qasbat Filastin]. It is a beautiful and well built city. Its water is light and plentiful, its fruits are abundant. It encompasses manifold advantages ... situated as it is in the midst of virtuous landscape, of pleasant villages and lordly towns and near to holy places. Commerce in it is prosperous and the markers are excellent. There is no finer mosque in Islam than the one in the city ... there are no fruits in Islam tastier than in the city and its surrounding towns ... its hostels are pleasant and its *hammams* [public baths] are elegant ... its houses are large ... its mosques are good, its streets are wide ... its roads lead ... to Bayt al-Maqdis [Jerusalem] road ... Lydda road, Jaffa road, Egypt road, Dajon toad ... The chief mosque in the capital [Ar-Ramlah], located in the markets, is even more beautiful and graceful than that of [the Great Mosque] of Damascus. It is called Al Abyad [the White Mosque]. In all Islam there is found no bigger *mihrab* [prayer niche] than the one here [in Ar-Ramlah] and its pulpit is the most splendid to be seen after that of Bayt al-Maqdis; also it possesses a beautiful minaret built by Hisham ibn 'Abdel-Malik. (Al-Maqdisi 2002: 143–144; also cited in Le Strange 1890: 304–305)

Clearly al-Maqdisi himself was fully aware and indeed proud of his 'Jerusalemite' identity and Palestinian heritage. Interestingly, however, in view of his extensive travels throughout the Muslim world and his multiple occupations, he describes the thirty-six names and designations by which he was called throughout his journeys and these included 'Jerusalemite [*Maqdisi*], Palestinian [*Filastini*], Egyptian, Maghribi, Khurasani ... faqih, sufi ... tourist ... trader, imam ... Iraqi, Baghdadi, Shami ... Hanafi ... teacher, sheikh' (al-Maqdisi 2002: 41).

Al-Maqdisi's account also gives us an insight into the construction of a multi-layered Palestinian identity in the 10th century by a highly educated and extensively travelled individual, a construction which in many ways echoes the construction of a *regional Palestinian identity* by al-Maqdisi, Mujir al-Din al-'Ulaymi, Khair al-Din al-Ramli and Salih ibn Ahmad al-Tumurtashi in the 10th–17th centuries (see below). The identity begins with al-Maqdisi's native city (Jerusalem/Bayt al-Mqdis), a city in the administrative region of Filastin, which is in the greater region of al-Sham, in the domain of Islam (al-Maqdisi 2002: 41, 143–144).

JUND FILASTIN AS THE RICHEST PROVINCE OF AL-SHAM REGION

The changes in the political/religious regime under Islam contrasted with the continuity of Palaestina/Filastin as territory/country and the stability of its economic prosperity and its mainly farming people is striking. For over three centuries the province of Jund Filastin under Islam was a larger and even more prosperous country than the combination of Palaestina Prima and Palaestina Salutaris under the Byzantines, in contradistinction to various ideological histories presenting this period as one of decline. Throughout early Islam the administrative province of Filastin maintained its economic prosperity partly by being strategically located at the centre of regional and distant trade and partly by developing its own distinct monetary system, within the wider monetary zone of Islam. Under Islam, *dinar* coins were minted in gold, *dirham* coins in silver, while *fals* (plural *fulus*) was a copper coin first produced by the Umayyads in the late 7th century.

The name *fals* derives from *follis*, a Roman/Byzantine copper coin. Various Islamic copper *fals* were in production until the 19th century. Today the word *fulus* (or *flus*) is still used in Palestinian Arabic vernacular as a generic term for money and the term has also given rise to the modern Arabic terms *iflas* (bankruptcy) and *muflis* (bankrupt). In the Middle Ages, the monetary system of the province of Palestine included *dinars*, *dirhams* and *fals*, which were minted in several Palestinian cities.

Furthermore, in the 9th century, during Abbasid rule, the province of Jund Filastin was described as the most fertile province in the region of al-Sham. Commenting on the annual tax revenues raised in the province, 9th century Abbasid postmaster and geographer ibn Khordadbeh, the author of the earliest surviving Arabic book of administrative and descriptive geography, *The Book of Roads and Kingdoms* (*Kitab al-Masalik was Mamalik*, c. 870) recorded in about 864: 500,000 gold dinars of taxes from Filastin province. By comparison with other provinces of al-Sham, the Damascus province raised 400,000 dinars, the Hims province 340,000, the Jordan province 350,000 and the two provinces of Qinnasrin and 'Awasim 400,000 dinars (Le Strange 1890: 46; Röhricht 1890: 17; Ibn Khordadbeh 1865). For another comparison, the tax revenues raised in the whole of Palestine (the two provinces of Filastin and al-Urdun) in 864 (850,000 dinars) amounted to more than half of (mainly land) taxes raised in the whole of Abbasid Mesopotamia in 818/819 (Christensen 1993: 42). These annual revenues of the province of Palestine is also evident from the tax figures and revenues collected during this era from the Filastin province both in absolute terms and in comparison with those taxes collected from the other *ajnad*, including the much smaller Jund al-Urdun and the much larger Jund Dimashq (the Damascus province), which included much of present-day Lebanon and territories east of the River Jordan known as al-Balqa region (Le Strange 2010: 43–48; Blankinship 1994: 47–48, 292, note 7). Indeed, Filastin is accounted, by tax figures given in certain sources, to have been the richest province of al-Sham throughout the late Umayyad period (Blankinship 1994: 48).

The works of Arab historians and geographers of the Middle Ages are central to our understanding of the evolving reconfiguration of Palestine and its environs and of the relatively immense wealth and prosperity of the province of Filastin throughout much of the Umayyad and Abbasid periods. Local Palestinian historians and geographers such al-Maqdisi — who uses not just the term *Palestine* (فلسطين) repeatedly but also '*Palestinian*' (فلسطيني) — also began to develop an embryonic sense of regional Palestinian identity. In 985 AD al-Maqdisi, in his work *The Best Divisions for Knowledge of the Regions* (*Ahsan al-Taqasim Fi Ma'rifat al-Aqalim*), gives us a detailed account of all the place names, cities and towns he had visited in Palestine (al-Maqdisi 1994, 2002). Describing in detail his native country and the fertility of its land, al-Maqdisi comments in the 10th century on the agricultural produce and manufactured goods of Palestine:

> within the province of Palestine may be found gathered together 36 products that are not found thus united in any other land ... From Palestine come olives, dried figs, raisins, the carob-fruit, stuffs of mixed silk and cotton, soap and kerchiefs. From Jerusalem come cheeses, cotton, the celebrated raison of the species known as 'Ainuni and Duri, excellent apples, bananas – which same is a fruit in the form of a cucumber, but when the skin is peeled off, the interior is not unlike the water-melon – only finer flavoured and more luscious – also pine-nuts known as 'Kuraish-bite,' and their equal is not found elsewhere; further mirrors, lamp-jars and needles. From Jericho is brought excellent indigo. From Sughar and Baisan came indigo and dates [and rice], also the treacle called *Dibs*. From 'Amman –grain, lambs and honey. From Tiberias – carpet stuffs, paper, and cloth. From Kadas – clothes of the stuff called *Munayyir* and *Bal'isiyyah*, also ropes. (Cited in Le Strange 2014: 18–19; also Le Strange 1890: 16–19; al-Maqdisi 1994)[7]

The economy of Palestine was boosted by the country's strategic location and its international trade, including its long-distance trade with India, China and Europe. An extensive long-distance silk trade from China to the Near East existed from Antiquity. Silk fabric, a natural fibre produced by silkworms, was first developed in ancient China and, because of its texture and lustre, silk rapidly became a popular luxury fabric in the Near East. It was made accessible by both Chinese and Arab traders in Antiquity. Under Islam, Palestine and al-Sham as a whole traded with India and

China via Aylah ('Aqabah) on the Red Sea, 'a port of Palestine on China Sea' (Ramadan 2010a, 2010b). In the Middle Ages, Arab merchants began importing Asian silkworms (Arabic: *dudat al-qazz*) and in Palestine the silk (*harir*) fabric was woven into textiles and helped develop the country's own silk industry. Palestine produced a variety of silk fabrics – including one coarse type of silk fabric mixed with various types of wool and woven into coats, which became known as *qazz* silk, and '*bi-harir*' – which were exported to Arabia and various Mediterranean and European countries (Gil, M. 1997: 238; Goitein 1983: 403, note 141; Lewandowski 2011: 243; Weir 1994: 288). In early modern England, the raw type of silk made in Palestine and known as *qazz*, became known as *gauze* or *Gaza*, the name of the Palestinian city; it was a thin, often transparent woven fabric used in clothing, drapery and surgical dressings (Cannon and Kaye 1994: 196).

Palestine's foreign export and international trade were key contributors to the country's economic prosperity and wealth under Islam. Palestine had begun exporting olive oil and wine to Egypt in the Chalcolithic Age and the export of Palestinian olive oil and *liquores Palaestini* ('Palestinian wine') remained important commodities in Antiquity. Although the export of *liquores* Palaestini declined under Islam, exports continued throughout the Middle Ages and camel caravans transported olive oil from Palestine to the city of Medina in Arabia (Gil, M. 1997: 236). Also, various woven items and textiles and types of *qazz* silk mixed with rabbit wool made in Palestine were loaded onto ships and exported to Mediterranean markets, including Egypt (Gil, M. 1997: 238). Interestingly, many of these key manufactured and exported products, such as cotton, oil, soap, glassware, woven, embroidered and silk items, would still play a role in the Palestinian economy of the modern era.

Also under Islam the religiously autonomous, predominantly urban Arab-Jews of Palestine played an important part in the culture, commerce and manufacturing industries of the country. This was particularly evident in an important international export of Palestine: glassware. Glass-making in the region dates back to Phoenician times, and the mosaics of Hellenic and Roman buildings and Byzantine mosaic floors. In the Middle Ages, Acre, Tyre, al-Khalil (Hebron) and other localities in Palestine became famous for glass-making and the Arab Jews of the country and al-Sham as a whole became known as experts at making glass, which would be exported to various countries including some in Europe (Gil, M. 1997: 238). As we shall see in chapter seven, the industry of exquisite glass-making was further developed by Muslim industrialists in al-Khalil during the Mamluk period.

In one of the most famous encyclopaedic geo-political and geo-ethnographic works of the 10th century, al-Maqdisi describes some of the Mediterranean ports of the province of Jund Filastin:

All along the sea-coast of Filastin are the Watch-stations, called *Ribat*, where the levies assemble. The war-ships and galleys of the Greeks also come into these ports, bringing aboard of them the captives taken from the Muslims; these they offer for ransom – three for the hundred Dinars. And in each of these ports there are men who know the Greek tongue, for they have missions to the Greeks, and trade with them in divers wares. At the Stations, whenever a Greek vessel appears, they sound the horns; also, if it be night, they light a beacon there on the tower; or, if it be day, they make a great smoke. From every Watch-station on the coast up to the capital (Ar Ramlah), there are built, at intervals, high towers, in each of which is stationed a company of men. On the occasion of the arrival of the Greek ships the men, perceiving this, kindle the beacon on the tower nearest to the coast-station, and then on that lying next above it, and onwards, one after another, so that hardly is an hour is elapsed before the trumpets are sounding in the capital, and drums are beating in the towers, calling the people down to the Watch-stations by the sea. And they hurry out in force, with their arms, and the young men of the village gather together. Then the ransoming begins. Some will be able to ransom a prisoner, while others (less rich) will throw down silver Dirhams, or signet-rings, or contribute some other valuable, until at length all the prisoners who are in the Greek ships have been ransomed. Now the Watch-stations of this province of Filastin, where this ransoming of captives takes place, are these: Ghazzah, Mimas, 'Askalan, Mahuz – (the port of) Azdud, Mahuz – (the port) of Yubna, Yafah, and Arsuf. (Cited in Le Strange 2014: 23–24)

Also in the 10th century, Arab geographer and chronicler Ibn Hawqal – who travelled extensively in Asia, Europe and Africa in 943–969 AD and wrote *The Face of the Earth* – describes the Arab province of Filastin. Ibn Hawqal, who may well derive some of his information from earlier Arabic sources, describes the extent of the province of Filastin: from Rafah in the south to the region of al-Lajjun in the north and from the Mediterranean Sea in the west to 'Amman in Transjordan (al-Maqdisi 2002: 138).

Located 16 kilometres north-west of Jenin and 1 kilometre south of Tell Megiddo (also called Tell al-Mutasallim), for many centuries al-Lajjun was an important strategic Palestinian district town, until the turn of the 19th century when it was annexed by the Ottomans to the new district of Jenin. Depopulated and destroyed by Israel in 1948, al-Lajjun was identified with ancient Megiddo, which was one of the strongest and most important Palestinian city-states throughout the Bronze Age and housed one of the most monumental temples of its time in the whole Near East (Wiener, N. 2016). Under the Romans this region was treated as part of the Galilee and in the 18th century al-Lajjun became part of the practically independent Galilee-based Palestinian state ruled by Dhaher al-'Umar. The continuities between the ancient and medieval Arab heritage of al-Lajjun is symbolically present in the name of the medieval Palestinian Arab town Lajjun, which is derived from the Roman name *Legio*, meaning an early Roman legion camp in the province of 'Syria Palestinia'. The site, a strategic point on Palestine's Via Maris and known to Romans as Caparcotna, remained the base of the Legio Sexta Ferrata (Sixth Ironclad Legion), the 6th Roman Legion, between 120 and 300 AD. The Sixth Ironclad Legion was honoured by the Roman Arab Emperor, Philippus Arabs (244–249), who took a close interest in the affairs of the provinces of 'Syria Palaestina' and Arabia and minted coins with the number of this legion.[8]

Under the Abbasids in the 8th–9th centuries, al-Lajjun was an important district town, within the province of Jund Filastin. Throughout the long Mamluk period (1260–1517) it served as an important station in the commercial and postal route and during the early Ottoman period it was the capital of the district (*sanjak*) in Palestine that bore its name. According to some Arabic sources, the two major towns of Beisan (former Scythopolis) and al-Lajjun, were included in the province of Jund Filastin throughout early Islam (see Gil, M. 1997: 111), yet al-Maqdisi (2002: 138) reports that Beisan, al-Lajjun, as well as Acre were part of Jund al-Urdun, something which lends further weight to the argument that, geographically and strategically, Jund al-Urdun remained for several centuries equivalent to the former Byzantine province of Palaestina Secunda.

In the 10th century Ibn Hawqal describes the administrative capital of the province of Jund Filastin, al-Ramla, as the largest town in the country, 'but the Holy City (of Jerusalem) comes very near this last in size' – something which also lends some weight to the two (political/religious) capitals notion existing in Palestine for three centuries under the Byzantines and for nearly four centuries under Islam from the early 8th century until 1099. Ibn Hawqal writes:

> Jund Filastin (Palestine) and its subdistricts. Subordinate to this district were those of the Tih [in north Sinai] and Al Jifar, both lying towards the Egyptian Frontier ... Filastin is the westernmost of the provinces of [al-Sham]. In its greatest length from Rafh [Rafah] to the boundary of Al Lajjun (Legio), it would take a rider two days to travel over; and the like time to cross the breadth from Yaffa (Jaffa) to Riha (Jericho) ... Filastin is watered by the rains and dew. Its trees and its ploughed lands do not need artificial irrigation; and it is only in Nabulus that you find the running waters applied to this purpose. Filastin is the most fertile of the Syrian provinces. Its capital and the largest town is Ar Ramlah, but the Holy City (of Jerusalem) comes very near this last in size. In the province of Filastin, despite its small extent, there are about twenty mosques, with pulpits for the Friday prayer. (Cited in le Strange 2014: 28; also Röhricht 1890: 18; Gil, M. 1997: 111)

Although the perception of the boundaries of the province of Filastin did change over the years, in 1226 the Arab geographer Yaqut al-Hamawi, writing during the Ayyubid period, mentioned that the Arab town of al-Fuleh (present-day Israeli town of 'Afula), which was at the heart of Marj ibn 'Amer, about 12 kilometres to the north of al-Lajjun, as being 'a town in Jund Filastin' (Le Strange 1890: 441).

COINS MINTED 'IN-FILASTIN' ('بفلسطين'): PALESTINE CURRENCY, MONETARY AUTONOMY AND NUMISMATIC EVIDENCE FROM ARAB ISLAMIC PALESTINE

Numismatic and monetary evidence are important sources of knowledge on the economy and degree of political autonomy of Roman, Byzantine and medieval Islamic Palestine. Numismatic evidence of Arab Byzantine coinage of the province of Jund Filastin (the military/administrative province of Palestine in early Islam) in the 7th century (Goodwin 2004) shows the continuities of Palestine, the variety of styles and traditions evolving in the country, as well as some of the distinct traditions evolving within Palestine.

One of the key indicators of economic prosperity and greater regional and economic autonomy under empire was the ability of a particular region or city to issue its own currency. As we have already seen, the earliest phase of the momentary phenomenon in Palestine began in the late 6th and early 5th century BC and took place in Philistia. This phase continued into the 4th century up to the end of the Achaemenid (Persian) rule over Palestine. Throughout much of this period the economically autonomous Palestinian cities of Gaza, Ascalon and Ashdod were able to issue their own silver coins. The monetary phenomenon of silver coinage became widely known as the coinage of Philistia or Philisto-Arabian coins.

However, in the 1st century AD the Roman Empire granted many cities in Palestine the right to mint only bronze and copper coins. Minting prestigious silver coins was confined to a few important cities outside of Rome. Bronze coins were issued by many Palestinian cities, including Gaza, Caesarea, Joppa (Jaffa), Ascalon, Ptolemais (Akka), Tiberias, Sepphoris, Neapolis (Nablus), Antipatris, Diospolis (Lydda), Nicopolis (Emmaus), Aelia Capitolina (Jerusalem) and Eleutheropolis (Beit Jibrin). Antoninus Pius (Titus Fulvus Aelius Hadrianus Antoninus Augustus Pius, 86–161 AD), also known as Antoninus, was Roman Emperor from 138 to 161 AD. His name appears on imperial bronze coins struck in Gaza, Philistia. This tradition of bronze coinage struck in several Palestinian cities persisted into the Byzantine era.

Islam in Palestine pragmatically adapted and combined the Roman/ Byzantine monetary tradition of coinage with the Achaemenid silver coinage in Palestine and encouraged the minting of both silver and gold coins in Palestinian cities. Furthermore, the continuation of this Arab-Byzantine tradition and the continuity of economic growth and prosperous trade in Palestine under Islam is evident in the widespread presence of precious metals and minting of gold coinage in Islamic Palestine. Rare and naturally occurring elements of high economic value and investment, historically precious metals were important in fine jewellery and coinage as currency. The best known precious metals were the Arab Islamic coinage and initially coins were minted in Filastin in copper, and later gold and silver coins were widely minted in several Palestinian cities.

The key elements of the Islamic coins struck in Palestine – materials, words, designs, signs and symbols – evolved significantly from the initial Byzantine-style coinage used in early Islam to the post-reform currency introduced by Caliph 'Abdel Malik ibn Marwan around 696 AD into the coins used during the Abbasid, Tulunid, Ikhshidid and Fatimid periods from the 8th to the 11th centuries (Shamma 1969, 1980). After the Umayyads took over the Muslim Caliphate and made Damascus their capital in 661 AD, the economic and financial stability of their vast Islamic empire was one of their top priorities. Consequently, the Byzantine-style *solidus* – originally a Roman weight unit of a relatively pure gold – influenced the Umayyad gold dinar; the Arabic name of the gold coin derives from *denarius*, a Roman coin. The Arab gold dinar was first issued by the reforming Caliph 'Abdel Malik ibn Marwan around 696 AD, with his own image replacing that of the Byzantine Emperor. However, subsequently the image of the Caliph was removed from the Islamic currency. Greek was the official language of the Byzantine Empire and under the influence of Byzantine-style coinage, the fineness of the gold Arab dinar was measured in *qirat* (carat) which derives from the Greek κεράτιον. The carat as a gold unit of weight still stands today.

The Islamic-style currency reform introduced by this fifth Umayyad ruler was designed to reinforce Umayyad power and provide a standardised Arab Islamic coinage that reflected the new politico-cultural reality of the time (Ramadan 2010b). Using the oldest calligraphic form of the Arabic script, the Kufi script, in addition to 'there is no god but God' and later 'Muhammad is the messenger of God', gold, silver and copper coins struck in Palestine added the Arabic name Filastin.

The economic and monetary prosperity of Palestine in early Islam and the centrality of the coins minted locally in the province of Jund Filastin, especially in the administrative capital al-Ramla, in the first half of the 8th century is evident from the origins of the two hoards of post-reform Islamic coins excavated at Jericho. Currency is about monetary power and the currency minted locally in Palestine gives us a sense of the extent of the local autonomy exercised in the province of Palestine under Islam. Not surprisingly, in view of the location of Jericho and the centrality of the province of Palestine in the Umayyad period, the provinces of Jund Filastin and Jund Dimashq 'provided an almost equal number of coins' excavated from the Jericho site (Walmsley 2000: 338). Originating from a range of mints in Bilad al-Sham, the percentage of these coins were as follows:

- 32 per cent minted in the province of Jund Filastin;
- 35 per cent from the province of Jund Dimashq;
- 20 per cent minted in Jund Hims;
- 6 per cent from Jund al-Urdun;
- 5 per cent from al-Jazirah;
- 1 per cent from Jund Qinnasrin;
- 1 per cent from Egypt (Walmsley 2000: 336–337).

These coins were from the following mints:

- twenty-seven Jund Filastin (twenty-three from the mint of the capital al-Ramla; three Lydda; one Iliya [Jerusalem]);
- twenty-nine Jund Dimashq (all from the mint of the capital Dimashq);
- five Jund al-Urdin (four Tiberias; one al-Urdun);
- seventeen Jund Hims (all from Hims mint)
- one Jund Qinnasrin (Aleppo mint);
- four al-Jazirah (al-Ruha mint);
- one Egypt (Alexandria mint) (Walmsley 2000: 338).

Under Islam, especially from the early 8th century onwards, Palestine also began to develop its own distinct Arab Islamic traditions of weights, measures and coinage; crucially coins were produced in several Palestinian cities with the mint formula 'struck in Filastin' (Gil, M. 1997: 257)[9] and circulated locally, regionally and internationally. The earliest numismatic evidence for the official designation of the country as Palaestina on Roman coins comes from the period of Vespasian (69 to 79 AD) and subsequently for the name 'Syria Palaestina' from the period of Marcus Aurelius, who was Roman Emperor from 161 to 180 AD. In the 1st century AD the Roman Empire also granted many Palestinian cities the right to mint bronze coins. Sir George Francis Hill, the Director and Principal Librarian of the British Museum (1931–1936), produced the British Museum Catalogue of Palestine coins showing sixteen Palestinian cities minting their own coins (Hill 1914).

This tradition of economic autonomy and Palestine city-coins came to an end in the 3rd century AD when the (western) Roman Empire disintegrated, but it was renewed and expanded in Muslim-ruled Palestine in the Middle Ages to include the minting of coins in silver and gold in the Palestine cities of Ilya[10] (Bayt al-Maqdis, al-Quds, Jerusalem), al-Ramla, Tabariyyah (Tiberias), 'Asqalan and others. This autonomous bronze coinage of Palestine cities under the Romans and Byzantines and silver and gold under Islam suggests the development of a considerable degree of regional Palestinian autonomy and of distinct local traditions, away from rigid imperial control:

> The finds of coins indicate that there was an intensive production of coins in Palestine in the following places: Jerusalem, Bet Guvrin [Beit Jibrin], Ramla, Ascalon, 'Amman, Gaza, Lod [Lydda], Yavne [Yubna], Tiberias, Bet Shean [Beisan], Sipphoris [Saffuriyah] and Tyre. Some of these mints were already in existence during the Byzantine era, and it appears that they were again in use during the days of the Damascene Caliphs after 'Abdel Malik. The inscriptions on the coins were Ilyā Filastin [al-Quds Filastin], 'Asqalān Filastin, and the like. From the mint of Bet Shean (Beisan), coins were found with Greek inscriptions, but appear to have been gradually replaced by Arabic. Among those coins from Bet Shean there were some with the Greek inscription 'Skythopolis' together with the Arabic, 'Baysān' or 'Baysan' (Gil, M. 1997: 110).

The history of Islamic Palestine is often read through overall Caliphate chronologies with little consideration for local developments and regional conditions. Under Islam Filastin developed a substantial measure of economic and commercial autonomy. It produced its own coinage and developed its own distinct commercial traditions of weights and measures. Its coins were minted in several Palestinian cities with the inscription 'in Palestine', in the same way as the country of manufacture or production is stated on goods today.

Al-Maqdisi devotes an entire section of his work to these distinct traditions, measures and coins of his native country (Gil, M. 1997: 257). The minting of Islamic coins (*dinar* in gold and *dirham* in silver) in Filastin began under the Umayyads. It was initially halted by the Abbasids but was restarted in al-Ramla under the Tulunids, which was the first independent Muslim dynasty to rule Egypt, Palestine and much of Syria from 868 until 905 AD. Three decades later the Ikhshidid dynasty ruled Egypt and Palestine from 935 to 969 AD:

> [in the 9th century Palestinian] coins began to appear with the
> inscription *bi-filastin* ['بفلسطين', 'in-Palestine']. The first of these were
> produced in the days of Khumarawayh and his son, Harun, from 890
> until 904, and these were gold dinars with the unusual weight of 3.2
> grams. These practices continued during the period when the Abbasids
> reconquered Egypt and Palestine ... The Ikhshidids continued to
> mint coins in Ramla, as previously, but unlike the inferior quality of
> the Palestinian coins produced under the Tulunids, Muhammad ibn
> Tughj, the Ikhshid, ordered the minting of dinars of a finer quality ...
> The mint in Ramla continued working during Fatimid times as well
> ... The mint in Tiberias was also active ... After the conquest of most
> of Palestine by the Crusaders, the mint in Ascalon ['Asqalan] was
> activated. (Gil, M. 1997: 258; see also Album 1998)[11]

RECONFIGURATION OF PALESTINE UNDER THE FATIMIDS: THE PROVINCE OF JUND FILASTIN AND THE MILITARY GOVERNOR OF PALESTINE (متولي حرب فلسطين) (11TH CENTURY)

The Egypt-based Shi'ite Fatimid state invaded Palestine in 970, conquering the whole of country in 972. The Fatimid rule of Palestine was marred by great turmoil and upheavals. During this period al-Ramla was still the official capital of the province of Jund Filastin. But the city suffered badly from its occupation and pillaging by the Bedouins of Banu Tayy in Palestine in late 1024 as well as the two devastating earthquakes in 1025 and 1068. Although the city would recover in the middle of the 11th century and would remain an important strategic and garrison town for many centuries to come, its decline during the Fatimid rule and its subsequent replacement by al-Quds as the administrative capital of Palestine under the Ayyubids would inaugurate a new era in the strategic re-centring of Palestine in the post-Crusader era.

Political and military-strategic considerations played an important part in shaping the Fatimid regime in Palestine. A combination of political and military-strategic calculations were also factors in the reconfiguration of the perception and boundaries of historic Palestine before, during and after the Fatimid rule. These considerations, which were present in radically different historical periods, were evident:

- The creation of the new province of Syria-Palaestina by Hadrian in 135 AD following the defeat of the Bar-Kochba rebellion of that year.
- The fact that the Byzantine Dux Palaestinae, the 'military commander of all of Palestine', commanded all Byzantine forces in Provincia Palaestina (Palaestina Prima, Palaestina Secunda and Palaestina Tertia) from the 4th to the early 7th centuries.
- The creation of the military-administrative *Ajnads* in al-Sham, Jund Filastin included, under Islam from the 630s onwards.
- The secret Ottoman strategic-military plan of Filastin Risalesi, prepared for the officers of the Eighth Army Corps in Palestine at the beginning of the First World War (to be discussed in chapter nine), for the combined defence of the three Ottoman *sanjaks* of Palestine.

- The secret Sykes–Picot Agreement of 1916 between Britain and France which was designed to carve up the Near East between the two imperial powers; an agreement which would contribute to the shaping of the British Mandatory boundaries of Palestine.

Following the deteriorating military–security situation in Palestine and tribal uprisings in the 1020s, strategic-military considerations by the Fatimid state seem to have contributed to the creation by the Fatimids of a new title: Mutawalli Harb Filastin, the 'Military Governor of Palestine' ("متولي حرب فلسطين").

The extent to which the responsibilities of Mutawalli Harb Filastin were separate from those of the traditional civil governor (*wali*) of the province of Jund Filastin is not entirely clear (Lev 2003: 46–47). But, with echoes of the responsibilities of the Byzantine Dux Palaestinae, the Military Governor of Palestine commanded all the Fatimid military forces in the two provinces of Jund Filastin and Jund al-Urdun. Interestingly, a form of this military-strategic innovation, in the shape of the Military Governor of Palestine, with military responsibilities, did survive the end of the Fatimid rule in Palestine. The titles of *mutawalli* (military) and *wali* (civil) are often conflated during the Ayyubid period and in 1193 the title of *mutawalli al-harb bi-Bayt al-Muqaddas*, the Military Governor of Jerusalem, is found in Ayyubid Palestine (Humphreys 1977: 78–79). In any event, however, the conception of the Military Governor of Palestine by the Fatimids and the rise of a Palestinian, Muhammad al-Yazuri, to become *wazir* (chief minister) of the Fatimid state in 1050–1058, together with the evidence we have from the Arab-Jewish al-Fustat Genizah, all give rise to the impression that Filastin was perceived to be a key province of the Fatimid state.

Under the Egypt-based Shi'ite Fatimids in the early 11th century Islam in Palestine remained largely Sunni and senior Fatimid officials of the province of Jund Filastin resided in the capital city of al-Ramla:

Several Fatimid officials resided in Ramla during the Fatimid period (early eleventh century), including the governor, who is referred to as *wali*, meaning apparently the governor of Jund Filastin. The governor, through his military slave[-soldier] (*ghulam*), controlled the police force and kept contact with Cairo [Fustat] through the postal service, or the *barid*. The town was also the seat of the secret police (*ashab al-akhbar*) and the local Fatimid [Shi'ite] propagandist (*da'i*). Two other officials whose presence is attested to in the town were the fiscal administrator (*'amil*) and auditor (*zinumam*), both of which were nominated by the government in Cairo. The social composition of the population in Ramla remains enigmatic, but there was a local Muslim elite made up of notables, judges and court witness ... In Muharram 414/March–April 1023, Anushtakin [al-Dizbari, an elite Turkish slave-soldier in Fatimid employ and a former governor of Baalbeck and Caesarea] was appointed as the governor of Jund Filastin, bearing the title of a military governor (*mutawalli harb Filastin*). The beginnings of his governorship were peaceful and, in April 1024, a large caravan of Khurasani [Sunni] pilgrims from Mecca travelled through Ayla [present-day 'Aqabah] via Ramla and Damascus to Baghdad. (Lev 2006: 591)

However, the security situation in the two provinces of Jund Filastin and Jund al-Urdun deteriorated quickly and, in September 1024, tribal rebellion erupted over the terms of the tax collection (*iqta'a*) system, which had been granted to the Bedouin leader of Banu Tayy, Hassan ibn al-Jarrah, over the Beit Jibrin region in the province of Filastin. In the north of Palestine the Bedouins attacked and looted Tiberias, the capital of Jund al-Urdun. They also occupied al-Ramla, looting property, executing the soldiers of the local garrison and enslaving women and children. After plundering the city and destroying its soap and olive industry, Hassan ibn al-Jarrah set fire to the capital of Palestine: 'The Bedouin conquest of Ramla was a bleak chapter in the history of the town' (Lev 2006: 591). The tribal uprisings in the two provinces lingered sporadically for five years until 1029 and caused hardship and famine.

Although resentment of the Shi'ite Fatimid rule in Palestine was not universal or even evident among the Sunni *ulema* of Jerusalem, this resentment was very strong among the Bedouins of Banu Tayy and the Christian communities – the former for economic reasons and the latter for religious ones. In the early 11th century the Fatimid rule in the country was marred by a series of tribal rebellions, widespread insecurity and famine which, in addition to the severe earthquake of 1025, devastated Palestine (Gil 1996: 22, 25–27). The destruction of the Church of the Holy Sepulchre in Jerusalem and the splendid church of St George at Lydda by the Fatimid Caliph al-Hakim bi-Amr Allah in 1009 was part of general campaign against Christian places of worship in Palestine and Egypt. Fatimid policies adversely affected the province of Filastin and these policies became an impetus not only to local rebellions but also to the invasion of Palestine by the Seljuks in 1073 and the Latin Crusaders in 1099.

In 1029, five years after the Bedouin occupation of al-Ramla and four years after the 1025 earthquake, which badly damaged the city, and at the height of the Fatimid regime in Palestine, the severely affected province of Filastin was referred to in the old Cairo Genizah, a collection of Arab Jewish fragments of manuscripts that were found in the storeroom (*genizah*) of the Ben Ezra Synagogue in al-Fustat, then the capital of Egypt. Written in various languages, especially Arabic, Hebrew and Aramaic, the massive collection, which began during the Abbasid period in 870 AD and covers a millennium, became the largest and most diverse collection of medieval manuscripts in the world and a testimony to the flourishing culture of Arab-Jews under Islam. Al-Fustat was also the home of Ibn Maimun (Maimonides, 1135–1204) the great Andalusian-born Arab-Jewish philosopher, Rabbi and head of the Arab-Jewish community in Egypt. In 1029 the Jerusalem-based Rabbi Solomon ha-Kohen ben Yehosef, in a letter to his son Abraham in Fustat, refers to the damage inflicted by the Fatimids on both the city of al-Ramla and the 'land of Palestine': Rabbi Solomon refers to 'the infliction of famine, for no food is to be found in the land of Philistines [i.e. the Province of Filastin] and there are many poor' (Gil 1996: 28–29).

In 1029, the military commander of all the Fatimid forces in Palestine, Mutawalli Harb Filastin, Anushtakin al-Dizbari, brought an army from Egypt, collected local forces in Palestine and decisively defeated the combined Bedouin army at al-Uqhuwana near the Sea of Galilee (Grainger 2016: 246), an area which was part of the province of Jund al-Urdun. After these military successes, General al-Dizbari was the most powerful Fatimid governor of the whole region of al-Sham, Palestine included. He became fairly popular among the local population by forming alliances with the local notables and he managed to unite the whole region under a single Fatimid authority. Medieval Muslim historians have stressed al-Dizbari's 'just rule and fair treatment of the population in the towns he ruled as governor' (Lev 2003: 55). For the first and last time, all of Palestine and al-Sham was ruled by a single Fatimid governor. He died in Aleppo in 1042. Fifteen years later his grave was relocated to Jerusalem.

Although little is known about the political developments in Palestine in the second part of the 11th century, and prior to the Crusader invasion of 1099, letters from the al-Fustat Genizah show that Muhammad Hassan ibn 'Ali al-Yazuri, from Yazur,[12] a town east of Jaffa in the province of Filastin, and a former Governor of al-Ramla, served in the capacity of vizier of the Fatimid state, the second most important position after the Fatimid Caliph in Egypt, from 1050 to 1058. He was also personally involved in the affairs of the al-Quds (Jerusalem), the religious capital of Muslim Palestine (Gil 1996: 30).[13]

In the middle of the 11th century Muslim traveller Nasir Khusro (Khusrau), who visited Fatimid Palestine in 1047, produced an account of his seven-year journey (*Safarnama*) through the Muslim world of the 11th century (*Diary of a Journey through Syria and Palestine*). He wrote:

> Sunday, the day of the new moon of the month of Ramadan (the 1st of March), we came to Ramlah. From Caesarea to Ramlah is eight leagues. Ramlah is a great city, with strong walls built of stone, mortared, of great height and thickness, with iron gates opening therein. From the town to the sea-coast is a distance of three leagues. The inhabitants get their water from the rainfall, and in each house is a tank for storing the same, in order that there may always be a supply. In the middle of the Friday Mosque, also, is a large tank; and from it, when it is filled with water, anyone who wishes may take. The area of the mosque measures two hundred paces (*Gam*) by three hundred. Over one of its porches (*suffah*) is an inscription stating that on the 15th of Muharram, of the year 425 (10th of December, 1033 A.D.), there came an earthquake of great violence, which threw down a large number of buildings, but that no single person sustained an injury. In

the city of Ramlah there is marble in plenty, and most of the buildings
and private houses are of this material; and, further, … they do most
beautifully sculpture and ornament. They cut the marble here with
a toothless saw, which is worked with 'Mekkah sand'. They saw the
marble in the length, as is the case with wood, to form the columns;
not in the cross; also they cut it into slabs. The marbles that I saw here
were of all colours, some variegated, some green, red, black, and white.
There is, too, at Ramlah, a particular kind of fig, than which no better
exists anywhere, and this they export to all the countries round. This
city of Ramlah, throughout [al-Sham] and the West [al-Maghreb], is
known under the name of Filastin. (Khusrau 1888: 21–22)

In the post-Fatimid period, the first (Crusader) Latin Kingdom of
Jerusalem was created in 1099 and lasted until 1187 and occupied much of
Palestine. Yet the conception of Jund Filastin as an administrative province,
as mentioned by the Muslim historian Ibn Shaddad (1145–1234 AD), a biographer of Salah al-Din (Saladin) and an eye-witness of the Muslim–Third
Crusade battles, survived until the Mongol invasion of Palestine in the
mid-13th century. Its territory also seems to have been expanded from the
10th century onwards both towards the east in Transjordan and in the south-
east (*The Encyclopaedia of Islam* 1965, Vol. II: 911; also ibn Shaddad 2002).

Chapter 7

BETWEEN EGYPT AND AL-SHAM

Palestine during the Ayyubid, Mamluk and early Ottoman periods

PALESTINE ON ARAB AND VENETIAN WORLD MAPS
(12TH–15TH CENTURIES): THE MAPS OF MUHAMMAD
AL-IDRISI (1154), PIETRO VESCONTE, MARINO
SANUDO AND FRA MAURO (1450)

The glories of Arab geography and cartography continued well into the late Middle Ages and in 1154, at the height to the Latin Crusader Kingdom of Jerusalem, Palestine was mentioned on the world map of the Arabic magnum opus, *Nuzhat al-Mushtaq fi'khtiraq al-Afaq* (translated as *The Pleasure of Him who Longs to Cross the Horizons*), produced by Andalusian Arab geographer and cartographer Muhammad al-Idrisi (1100–1165), the foremost geographer of his age. Becoming famous in Latin as the *Tabula Rogeriana* (Arabic: *Kitab Rujar*, The Book of Roger) and *Opus Geographicum*, al-Idrisi's masterpiece of geographical information and a description of the known world included a world map, showing Filastin in Arabic. Bearing in mind that al-Idrisi was working decades after the Crusaders' victory in Jerusalem (he was born a year after), interest in Palestine was at an all-time high, and maps and literature including the country were sought after.

Al-Idrisi had settled in Palermo, then the capital of a rising Mediterranean power and a centre of Christian and Arab Muslim cultural

189

convivencia, and had worked on the commentaries and illustrations of the map for fifteen years at the court of the Norman King Roger II, the founder of the Kingdom of Sicily in the first half of the 12th century, with a mixed cultural heritage, who commissioned the work around 1138 (Houben 2002: 102–104; Maqbul 1992). Al-Idrisi travelled extensively in Europe, North Africa and West Asia and gathered information from Muslim travellers, sailors and merchants. Inspired by Ptolemy's Map of the World (discussed above), al-Idrisi's Map of the World was far more advanced and for the next three centuries geographers treated his map as the most accurate and copied it without alteration (Scott 1904: 461–462; Maqbul 1992; Edson 2007: 42–43).

An abridged Arabic version of *Nuzhat al-Mushtaq fi-Ikhtiraq al-Afaq* was published in Rome in 1592 with title: *De Geographia Universali* (Maqbul 1992; al-Idrisi 1592). Printed by Rome's academic Medic Press, this was one of the first Arabic books to be printed. (Hopkins and Levtzion 2000: 104–131). The most complete Arabic manuscript, which includes the world map and all seventy sectional maps, is kept in Istanbul (Pinto 2006: 140).

A century and a half after Idrisi's world map was produced, Palestine was found on another world map, this time by Marino Sanudo (c. 1270–1343) a Venetian merchant who travelled to Palestine a number of times and drew maps based on his travels. Sanudo was also a public figure and geographer who became widely known for his lifelong attempts to revive the Latin Crusades following the fall of Acre, the last capital of the Latin Kingdom, in 1291. For the Venetians, money-making, maritime trade and crusading for the Holy Land went hand in hand. Suddenly, with the loss of the considerable wealth of Acre (and much of the Galilean and Lebanese coasts), the Venetians, and their European allies, had lost lucrative trade, local harbours, considerable material assets, residential quarters, churches, monasteries and the famous religio-military Orders such as the Templars, Hospitallers and Teutonic Knights in Acre. By 1307 Sanudo had written a book, *Conditiones Terrae Sanctae*, effectively a strategic manual for crusading schemes and for European reconquest of Palestine. A map of Acre was included in Sanudo's book (Edson 2004: 133). Also, a world map appeared in most of Sanudo's manuscripts of the early 14th century. Historian Evelyn Edson writes:

The map of the Eastern Mediterranean ... which shows the
main theatre of operations for Sanudo's proposed campaign, is a
combination of a marine chart and a map of the interior ... Lined up
along the southern coast of Asia Minor, and the shores of Palestine
and Egypt and the island of Cyprus, is a series of names of ports.
On the coast of Palestine these are accompanied by indications of
distances in miles. In the interior, much more vaguely indicated,
are larger features such as the Tigris and Euphrates rivers and the
countries of Mesopotamia, Persia and Chaldea. (Edson 2004: 139)

For nearly three centuries al-Idrisi's world map was treated by Arab and
European geographers, cartographers and historians as the most accurate
and they copied it without alteration (Scott 1904: 461–462; Maqbul 1992:
156–174). In the mid-15th century the *mappa mundi* of Fra Mauro (died
1464), an Italian cartographer and monk who lived in the Republic of
Venice but also worked for the Portuguese kings, came to replace al-Idrisi's
map from the 12th century. In his youth, Mauro had travelled extensively
as a merchant and a soldier and became familiar with the Near East regions.
In 1450 Mauro completed a world map, which became the most detailed
and accurate map of the world up to that time. Among Mauro's sources we
find classical authors and Ptolemy's *Geography* as well as Arab cartographers
and the 12th century maps of al-Idrisi.

Mauro's world map mentions Palaestina for religio-political and practical purposes. If al-Idrisi's map in the 12th century was commissioned by
King Roger II of Sicily and in the service of a trading Mediterranean Christian kingdom with religious connections to Palestine, Mauro's map was
commissioned by King Alfonso V of Portugal in the service of the rising
global Portuguese Empire. But the 'land of Jesus' was central to the Italian
monk and to Christian pilgrims to Terra Sancta. However, the size of Pales-
tine/Terra Sancta is considerably reduced by having to accommodate all
the other places on the map and Mauro feels he had to apologise for this:
'Those who are knowledgeable would put here in Idumea, Palestine and
Galilee things which I have not shown, such as the river Jordan, the sea
of Tiberias, the Dead Sea and other places, because there was not enough
room' (Edson 2007: 151).

The printing revolution in Renaissance Europe and the spread of the press from the late 15th century onwards introduced an era of mass circulation of ideas with considerable impact on the mass representation of the Holy Land/Palestine. In the European and Italian Renaissance era cartographic representations of Palestine/the Holy Land also increased sharply. The map of 'Palestina Moderna et Terra Sancta' was published in Florence around 1480 and was included in Francesco Berlinghieri's expanded edition of Ptolemy's *Geographia* (*Geography*). Berlinghieri, an Italian Renaissance scholar and diplomat, was the first modern European to interpret, expand upon and republish the works of the 2nd century Greek geographer. Apparently the 'Palestina Moderna et Terra Sancta' map was based on the Sanudo–Vesconte map of Palestine, a map produced by Pietro Vesconte (who was active between 1310 and 1330) and Marino Sanudo, first published in Venice around 1320.[1] Vesconte was a Genoese cartographer, geographer and navigational chart-maker who worked in Venice. He also provided a world map, nautical atlas, a map of Palestine and plan of Acre and Jerusalem for inclusion in Marino Sanuto's *Liber secretorum fidelium cruces super terrae sanctae recuperatione et Conservatione*, a work which discusses trade routes and was aimed at encouraging a new Latin crusading campaign, providing a manual for the military reconquest of the Holy Land (Edson 2004: 139; Bagrow 2010: 69–70). Although gradually ideas of new military crusades began to subside, the Sanudo–Vesconte map and the maps of 'Palestina Moderna et Terra Sancta' were destined to project European power and provide modern representational images of Palestine for the Europeans until the 18th century.

The European printing revolution made it possible for dozens of detailed maps of 'Palestina/Palaestina' to be published and circulated in Europe throughout the 18th century. In 1714 *Palaestina ex monumentis Veteris illustrata* by Dutch cartographer, philologist and biblical Orientalist Hadrianus Relandus illustrated the geography of Palestine with maps. In the Ottoman Empire, the printing of books and maps started only in 1729 and in 1803 the Ottoman *Cedid Atlas Tercümesi* (*A Translation of a New Atlas*), published in Istanbul, was partly based on European geographical knowledge as well as European map-making methods of the day. Published within the framework of the 'new system' of the Ottoman administrative and military reforms of the time, the New Atlas included a map of *Filastin* and *bar-Sham* (hinterland of al-Sham) with the Arabic term *Ard Filastin* ('Land of Palestine'; written in a peculiar way: ارض فلاستان) shown in large Arabic script on the bottom left of the map. As we shall see below, the publication of this new Ottoman atlas preceded the publication of 'Jacotin Atlas', which had a map using the Arabic script for 'Palestine' and the 'land of al-Quds' (فلسطين أو أرض قدس) by twenty-three years.

In the 19th century European romantic Crusader revivalism in art, religious fervour and politics and British actual penetration of Palestine were repackaged in the form of a 'peace crusade' and biblical Orientalism. This gradual penetration of late Ottoman Palestine culminated in the pro-Zionist Balfour Declaration of November 1917 and the actual British military occupation of Palestine in 1917.

AYYUBID PALESTINE AND THE RE-ESTABLISHMENT OF ISLAMIC JERUSALEM IN POST-CRUSADE PALESTINE: THE DECLINE OF PALESTINE'S COASTAL CITIES AND RISE OF THE INTERIOR URBAN CENTRES

The defeat of the Latin Crusaders in the 12th century brought about the re-establishment of Muslim rule in Palestine and once again the reorientation of the country. This lasted for seven centuries and consisted of three distinct periods: the Ayyubid (1187–1260), Mamluk (1260–1517) and Ottoman (1517–1917) eras. The economic and political reorientation of Palestine towards Europe under the rule of Dhaher al-'Umar in the 18th century, as well as during the Ottoman reforms of the second half of the 19th century, all contributed to bringing Palestine into the modern era.

The geo-political and strategic reorientation of Palestine in the post-Crusader period away from the Mediterranean coastal region and its strategic location under both the Ayyubids and Mamluks between the al-Sham region and Egypt had a lasting impact on its history, culture and arts as well as identity as a geo-political polity. In medieval Muslim geography, the al-Sham region consisted of the territories of present-day Syria, Filastin (Israel included), modern Jordan, Lebanon and south Turkey. Of the two present-day countries of Egypt and Syria, Palestine's close historic links with the al-Sham region were the most enduring historically and most rooted in modern Palestinian social memory.

The important Ayyubid period in Palestine began with Salah al-Din's spectacular victory over the Frankish at the Battle of Hittin in 1187, a turning point in the history of Palestine. Salah al-Din had been the vizier of the (Shiite) Fatimid state in Egypt before he brought an end to Fatimid rule in the country. Shortly afterwards the Crusader stronghold of Acre was captured by Salah al-Din and in the same year the Ayyubid forces took Nazareth, Saffuriyah, Haifa, Arsuf, Caesarea, Sabastiyah (Sebastia), Jaffa, al-Ramla, Gaza, Beit Jibrin, 'Asqalan and Jerusalem. Most of the Latin Kingdom of Jerusalem fell to the Ayyubids in or shortly after 1187. However, the Crusaders continued to pose a major threat by regaining control of parts of Palestine's coastline in the 1190s and the Frankish enclave in the coastal city of Acre lasted until 1291.

Within less than a century during their relatively short tenure, the Ayyubids ushered in a dynamic period of great cultural flowering of learning (of schools and colleges) and highly original, multi-faceted and marked technological developments in the country and throughout the region (Rosen-Ayalon 1998: 512, 520); developments in science, engineering and medicine, education and architecture pioneered in the Arab and Muslim world, from the Andalus to Egypt and from Palestine and Central Asia, were later either copied by the Latin Crusaders and translated in Europe or inspired further developments during the later Renaissance. The most crucial development was the removal of the European colonial and Frankish domination of Jerusalem and the restoration of Muslim rule in the holy city. The Muslims and Jews of the city had been slaughtered or driven out by the Latin Crusaders and the Muslim holy places on the Haram al-Sharif had been desecrated or converted into Christian temples and offices. The contrast between the behaviour of the Ayyubid and Frankish rulers can hardly be overstated. The re-establishment of Islamic Jerusalem allowed Jews and Muslims to return to the city and permitted Christian access to and worship at their holy places. Also, crucially, under the Ayyubids al-Quds permanently replaced al-Ramla as the political, administrative and cultural capital of Palestine as well as the religious capital of the whole Ayyubid state. Earlier in this work I suggested the theory of a secular-administrative versus religious capital ('double capitals') evolving in Palestine under the Romans, Byzantines and Muslim Arabs. This was illustrated in the cases of Caesarea-Palaestina versus Aelia Capitolina under the Romans and Byzantines and al-Ramla versus Iliya-al-Quds during the first three centuries of Islam in Palestine. This separation between administrative and religious capitals of Palestine was discontinued under the Ayyubids. And the Mamluks, Ottomans and British followed the Ayyubid tradition. The status of Jerusalem as the foremost and capital city of Palestine was to last for the next seven centuries.

The Ayyubids, furthermore, ushered in a new era of intellectual activity and economic prosperity in Palestine and in all the countries they ruled. Islamic *madrasahs* (schools) had existed in Jerusalem since the early Islamic period (Gil, M. 1997). However, the earliest *madrasahs* in Jerusalem after the Frankish period were built by the Ayyubids (Galor and Bloedhorn 2013: 216). The *madrasahs* and patronage provided by the Ayyubids led to resurgence in educational, commercial, architectural and artistic activity not only in Jerusalem but in other urban centres of Palestine (Hillenbrand and Auld 2009). A substantial number of *ribats* (hospices for Muslim pilgrims) were built during the Ayyubid and Mamluk periods (Galor and Bloedhorn 2013: 213). The Crusader period had affected mainly the urban centres of Palestine; it was 'merely an episode in the life of much of the [rural] hinterland which quickly returned to normal conditions with the end of Christian domination' and the advent of the Ayyubids (Rosen-Ayalon 1998: 514). The period was also marked by an Ayyubid process of reinforcing Sunni Muslim domination under their rule by setting up numerous *madrasahs*, sufi lodges (*zawiyas*), *ribats*, public baths, markets and caravanserais (khans) in the main cities, especially in Jerusalem. Over time, nearly a quarter of all institutions and commercial properties in Jerusalem belonged to Islamic *waqf* endowments and Ottoman deed records show this situation was still evident in the late Ottoman period.[2] The surviving monuments in Jerusalem and other parts of Palestine bear witness to the dynamism and prosperity of the Ayyubid period in Palestine.

The Crusaders continued to threaten coastal Palestine via the Mediterranean Sea. Crucially, the Crusaders' abilities to utilise siege techniques

and blockade methods to capture Palestine's and Syria's greatest fortifications 'confirmed the crusaders to contemporaries as successful and
terrifying siege warriors' (Rogers 2002: 39). To prevent attacks from the
sea and pre-empt the eventual return of the Crusaders and siege situations,
the Ayyubids sought to reorient the country strategically from the coastal
region to the hinterland of Palestine and consequently destroyed the walls
of a number of coastal cities (and much of their infrastructure) from Tyre
in the north to Gaza in the south and dumped the rubble in the water in
an effort to block any possible landing in the ports of these cities:

> Obviously, the objective was to prevent any landing from the sea.
> To that end, material of every sort was dumped into the water,
> obstructing access to the ports. The port of Caesarea is blocked by
> the debris until today. Asqalon [sic] was the first city to suffer this
> fate, the order for its destruction being given by Salah al-Din himself.
> The remains of its walls are scarred not far from where they originally
> stood. These walls, which – according to all existing evidence – were
> constructed by the Fatimids, had continued to serve the Crusaders but
> fell victim to the Ayyubid policy of destruction. (Mujir al-Din 1973:
> 422; Rosen-Ayalon 1998: 515)

However, it is not entirely true to suggest that Palestine's coastal cities
were completely destroyed by the Ayyubids. In fact, the evidence contradicts this claim about the existence of a wholesale policy of destruction.
Writing in the early 13th century during Ayyubid rule the Arab biographer
and geographer Yaqut al-Hamawi (1179–1229) – a highly educated former
slave who traded widely and travelled extensively in Palestine, Egypt,
Syria, Persia and Central Asia and became renowned for his encyclopaedic
writings on the Muslim world, published in *Kitab Mu'jam al-Buldan*
(al-Hamawi 1861) – describes the province of Filastin and lists the coastal
cities of 'Asqalan, Gaza, Arsuf and Caesarea among the premier cities of
Filastin, whose capital Jerusalem had replaced al-Ramla. Yaqut writes:

> Filastin is the last of the provinces of [al-Sham] towards Egypt. Its capital
> is Jerusalem. Of the principal towns are 'Askalan, Ar Ramlah, Gazzah,

Arsuf, Kaisariyyah [Qaysariah; Caesarea Maritima], Nabulus, Ariha (Jericho), 'Amman, Yafah [Jaffa] and Beit Jibrin. (Le Strange 2014: 29)

Also, crucially, much of the pre-Crusader Arab geographical terminology of the province of Palestine continued to be used by Arab geographers during and after the Crusader period. For instance, the term 'the province of Filastin' was repeatedly used by Arab geographer Yaqut al-Hamawi (1179–1229), who situates the town of the town of Sabastiyah (Sebastia) in the district of Nablus, in the province of Filastin, whose capital is Jerusalem (Le Strange 1890: 523; also see 441).

However, the Crusader wars and overall insecurities of coastal Palestine brought about the slow decline of the coastal cities and the rise of Palestine's urban hinterland. This period was also marked by the slow decline of the city of al-Ramla, which had been the political and administrative capital of the province of Filastin for over three and a half centuries; the population of al-Ramla decreased and the capital city of Jund Filastin was devastated during the Fatimid period by two major earthquakes in the 11th century (Mujir al-Din 1866: 416; Lev 2006: 592). But the coastal cities of Palestine experienced a more dramatic decline. In fact, coastal cities such as Acre and Jaffa began to recover and experience a socio-economic revival only in the middle of the 18th century. By contrast, the inland city of al-Quds/Jerusalem became once again the most developed metropolitan city of Palestine under the Mamluks throughout the 13th–15th centuries. In the 18th century regional and global trade in cotton, wheat and textiles made Acre and Nablus the biggest and most prosperous cities in Palestine and among the largest cities in the al-Sham region (Doumani 1995; Philipp 2001).

THE LEADING ROLE OF AL-QUDS UNDER THE MAMLUKS: THE CAPITAL OF MAMLUK PALESTINE AND THE 'CITY WITHOUT WALLS' (1260–1517)

Based in Egypt, the Mamluk Sultans maintained and accelerated many of the innovations ushered in by the Ayyubids in Palestine. In fact, the Mamluks were one of the most important Muslim dynasties in the history of medieval Palestine. They gained fame and legitimacy and produced lasting impact in stopping the terrifying Mongol advance into the Near East at the Battle of 'Ain Jalut in Palestine in 1260 – which was the first time that the Mongol army had suffered a major defeat – and for eradicating the Latin Crusader presence in Palestine and elsewhere along the Palestinian, Lebanese and Syrian coasts. The Mamluk's spectacular military successes in Palestine came only two years after the Mongol capture and sacking of Baghdad, the capital of the Abbasid Caliphate.

Although military dynasties are never revolutionary, under the long-lasting Mamluk rulers al-Quds was expanded significantly and remained central to the province of Filastin, which was mentioned by North African historian Ibn Khaldun, who, in his 1377 *Muqaddimah*, reported Filastin province taxes as 310,000 gold *dinars* plus 300,000 *ratls* of olive oil (cited in Le Strange 1890, 2010: 45). Rosen-Ayalon describes the pivotal position of Jerusalem in Mamluk Palestine:

> There can be no doubt as to the predominant role of Jerusalem during the Mamluk period. For nearly three centuries, life developed harmoniously in the city, which became an urban center of varied activity ... Jerusalem became a city of exile to which were banished undesirable [Mamluk] commanders ... Thus, the city profited from much of their personal involvement in its affairs. It was transformed into an organized medieval city, provided with all the necessary installations, services and public buildings. Even today, the 'Old City' – Jerusalem within the walls – reflects the stamp it acquired during the period of Mamluk domination.
>
> Most of the urban fabric of Jerusalem within the walls dates back to the Middle Ages, whose numerous surviving monuments bear witness to the glory of this medieval city ... Apparently, Jerusalem was not enclosed with walls, or, at most, only sectors of the previous walls and gates (destroyed by the Ayyubids) remained, providing a convenient frame around the peaceful city. (Rosen-Ayalon 1998: 518)

The Palestinised (mostly 'exiled'), demonstratively devout Mamluk and highly enterprising elite in al-Quds – with echoes of Origen and the

Greek-speaking elite in Caesarea-Palaestina a millennium earlier – became a driving force in the spectacular rise and phenomenal urban expansion of Jerusalem in the 13th and 14th centuries.

After the Umayyads, the Mamluks had the most lasting impact on al-Quds/Jerusalem, which had, for nearly 300 years, so prospered under Mamluk rule. The latter brought welcome stability to the region, so that the city grew and became a 'city without walls' – with the exception of the walls surrounding the Haram al-Sharif (Noble Sanctuary) – something extraordinary and totally unique for a medieval capital city of the size, importance and centrality of Jerusalem. After the first major defeat of the Latin Crusaders in 1187 the walls of al-Quds had been largely demolished by the Ayyubids as a drastic defensive measure designed to prevent another destructive siege of the city by the Crusaders. However, this medieval 'city without walls' grew confidently and spectacularly under the Mamluks in the 13th and 14th centuries. Although the annual pilgrimage, *Hajj*, to Mecca was always a mandatory religious duty for Muslims, the city of al-Quds had long been a focus of intense Islamic devotion and the centre of Islamic pilgrimage, long before the Crusaders, and in the 10th century al-Maqdisi, the Jerusalem-born Palestinian historian, refers to the city as 'virtuous Iliya' (*Iliya al-Fadila*) (al-Maqdisi 2002: 135). Subsequently the *Fada'il al-Quds* ('Merits or Virtues of Jerusalem') literature also played an important role in the Muslim efforts to defeat the Crusaders and recapture Jerusalem from them.

The Islamic *Fada'il al-Quds* literature and the struggle with the Latin Crusaders heightened the intensity of Islamic devotion, and increased the number of Muslim pilgrims to Jerusalem. Also, for medieval Muslims, clean running water and hygiene, bath houses and fountains had always been among the most important elements in the prosperity of the sacred city. The Arab bath houses are something the Frankish knights picked up and took back to Europe. Under the Mamluks, al-Quds underwent an intensive process of construction and became the focus of urban life and learning in Palestine, with numerous *madrasahs*, architectural splendour, bath houses, beautiful fountains, minarets and hostels for pilgrims. The splendour of Hammam al-'Ayn, one of the most exquisite bathhouses in Jerusalem and the longest to remain in operation, throughout its 700-year history, can still be seen today (Asali 1990). Muslim pilgrims flocked to the city after its liberation from the Crusaders. Architecturally one of the most spectacular eras of Jerusalem's history is that of the Mamluk period, and its distinctive pink, black and white patterned buildings and markets date from this era (Irving 2011: 96).

The massive socio-economic and religious growth of the city under the Mamluks is evident in the expansion of its marketplaces:

> The construction of several markets (*suq*, plural *aswaq*), is indicative of the city's expanding commercial activity. Some of this construction expanded earlier installations, those along the north–south main artery of the city which had developed out of the Roman and Byzantine Cardo ... Other markets were a true creation of the Mamluk period. The most outstanding example is *Suq el-Qattanin* with its magnificent portal opening at Haram al-Sharif. This market, dating from the first half of the fourteenth century, is so well preserved that it presents the most typical, classical formula in architectural terms of the Near Eastern covered suq. In fact, most covered marketplaces initiated this style for several centuries, as was the case with the nineteenth century 'White Market' of Acre, that followed this same plan exactly. (Rosen-Ayalon 1998: 518)

During this long Mamluk period, leading Palestinian Muslim scholars (*ulama*) moved freely between Palestine, Egypt and al-Sham not only to study but also for senior jobs. For instance, Ibn Hajar al-ʿAsqalani (1372–1449) was a leading medieval Shafiʾi Sunni scholar. Born in Cairo in 1372 as Shihab al-Din Ahmad ibn ʿAli, he was the son of the Shafiʾi scholar and poet Nur al-Din ʿAli, but he became famous as 'Ibn Hajar al-ʿAsqalani' because his family had originated in the city of ʿAsqalan in Palestine. Ibn Hajar studied Islamic jurisprudence in Damascus and Jerusalem and he went on to be appointed to the position of Egyptian chief judge (*qadi*). Ibn Hajar authored numerous works on *fiqh* (Islamic jurisprudence) interpretation, history and poetry and Shafiʾi jurisprudence, the most famous of which was his commentary on the Sahih of Bukhari, entitled *Fath al-Bari* (Adamec 2009: 136).

THE SEA VERSUS THE MOUNTAIN: SAFAD AS A NEW REGIONAL CAPITAL OF THE GALILEE

The 'sea versus the mountain' is a key theme in modern Palestinian poetry, especially the poetry of Mahmoud Darwish, cultural writings and 'nativist' geo-ethnography (see e.g. Tamari 2008: 95–98; also Furani 2012). Framing this cultural discourse in geo-political and historical terms, the roots of this idea may go all the way back to ancient and medieval Palestine. Historically, key cities in Palestine were associated with either the sea (Arabic: *bahr*) or the mountain (Arabic: *jabal*). The cities of Gaza, 'Asqalan, Jaffa, Caesarea, Arsuf and Acre were associated with the Mediterranean Sea, while al-Khalil (Jabal al-Khalil), al-Quds (Jabal al-Quds), Nablus (Jabal Nablus) and Safad (Jabal Safad) were all associated with mountains in the Palestine interior.

A significant part of the economy of the mountainous regions of Palestine was the proliferation of thousands of stone quarries and the development of extensive marble and stone quarry industry which supplied the local construction industry with stones and other building materials and exporting marble and quarried white-stones to neighbouring countries. The social memories of the Palestine stone quarry (محجر) was immortalised in Mahmoud Darwish's 1964 poem: 'Identity Card':

> Record!
> I am an Arab
> Employed with fellow workers at a quarry
> I have eight children
> I get them bread
> Garments and books
> from the rocks'.

The marble-producing quarries of Palestine and the white-stone quarries of the Arab province of *Jund Filastin* under Islam (Gil M. 1997: 230) gave the urban centres of the country (Nablus, al-Quds/Jerusalem, al-Ramla, al-Khalil) their distinctive look as 'cities of stone'. This stone quarry industry also left a monumental legacy which can be seen in the Dome of the Rock, the 16th century Ottoman Walls of Jerusalem, the 18th century Walls of

Acre and the city of Petra ('rock'), the old capital of the Nabataean Arabs and the province of *Palaestina Salutaris* under the Byzantines. Furthermore, the construction of monumental mosques, minarets and churches and the economy of Holy Land pilgrimage went hand-in-hand with the economy of stone quarrying and stone masonry. Historically the tradition of holy mountains developed greatly during the Greek, Roman and Byzantine eras; the notion of holy mountains and mountainous cities (Nablus, Jerusalem, al-Khalil, Safad, Mount Tabor, Mount Gerizim, Mount of Olives, Mount Sinai) versus the relatively more relaxed and secular environment of Palestine coastal cities (Caesarea Maritima, Gaza, 'Asqalan, Jaffa, Haifa, Acre) played an important role in the construction of district collective religious memory and identity of the country.

The siege and fall of Acre, a chief port and the capital of the Latin Kingdom, took place in 1291 and resulted in the loss of a Crusader stronghold and last Crusader-controlled city in Palestine to the Mamluks. To modern historians fall of Acre was the end of the Crusades, but to contemporary Muslims, the Latin Crusaders' threat to Palestine and Syria from the Mediterranean Sea persisted. In the post-Crusader era, the Mamluks continued to consolidate the strategic and defensive reorientation of the country towards the Mountain, a policy which began under the Ayyubids. The decline of Palestine's coastal towns and the rise of country's urban hinterland, especially under the Ayyubids and the Mamluks, were also illustrated by the rise Safad in upper Galilee, a town protected by the high Galilean mountains.

Following the recovery of Safad from the Crusaders in 1266, the Mamluks took steps to shift the provincial power in the Galilee from the coastal town of Acre westwards and turn the mountainous town of Safad into the capital of northern Palestine. The fortress town of Safad was renovated and expanded under the Mamluks and served as a regional capital in Palestine for the first time in its history (Luz 2014: 36). Crucially, Safad remained the capital of northern Palestine for several centuries. It all began in 1266 when *Bilad al-Sham* came under Mamluk rule and this vast region was divided into six large administrative provinces, each called a *mamlakat* (literally 'kingdom') or *niabat* ('vice regency'). These provinces were Damascus, Aleppo, Hamat, Tripoli (modern Lebanon), Safad (Palestine),

Karak (Transjordan). The head of each province (or *mamlakah*) bore the title of *naib* (viceroy, or 'little Sultan'). Encompassing much of northern Palestine and consisting of ten districts, the *Mamlakat Safad* (مملكة صفد, 'Kingdom of Safad') (Tarawneh 1982) included not only modern-day Galilee but also Marj ibn 'Amer, including the towns of al-Lajjun and Jenin – both of which were at the time considered part of lower Galilee – and other territories which today constitute the southern parts of modern-day Lebanon. When the Ottomans occupied Palestine in the early 16th century they retained many of the administrative characteristics of the previous Mamluk rule (as we as many of the social, economic, religious and legal institutions of the country). However, the Ottomans changed the name of the administrative province of Safad from *Mamlakat Safad* to *sanjak* (or *pashalik*) of *Safad* (Arabic: *Liwa Safad*).

Although the Galilee remained a 'frontier province' throughout much of the Mamluk and Ottoman periods, after 1266 the new administrative status of Safad brought about urban expansion in the city and the establishment of new buildings, baths, mosques, markets and caravanserais (Drory 2004). The new building programme in the city included the Red Mosque, one of the oldest Mamluk buildings in Palestine still standing today. The building of the mosque in 1276 was attributed to the Sultan Baybars, who ruled the region from 1260 to 1278 and who apparently embarked on a bridge-building programme across Palestine designed to revive its highways and improve its transport system, according to inscriptions above the wooden door at the entrance to the mosque. One of the best known Palestinian judges among the magistrates of Mamluk Palestine was Shams al-Din Muhammad al-'Uthmani (d. 1378), author of the detailed local history *Tarikh Safad*, written in 1378, which has survived in only partial form (Drory 2004: 184). *Tarikh Safad* gives us important information on the villages of the Galilee under the Mamluks and a unique glimpse into the inner workings of the religious and Sufi institutions in the region.

THE SOCIAL MEMORY OF PALESTINE DURING THE MAMLUK AND EARLY OTTOMAN PERIODS: FILASTIN IN LOCAL MUSLIM SOCIAL MEMORY

The historical writing on Palestine is dominated by imperial chronologies and colonising methodologies and history 'from without' approaches. In a similar vein, it has been suggested that the term Palestine had been completely forgotten by local Arabs during the late Mamluk and early Ottoman periods and that it was only brought back to them in the late Ottoman period by local Arab Christians in touch with Europe. In her work *A History of Palestine: From the Ottoman Conquest to the Founding of the State of Israel*, Gudrun Krämer, a German scholar of Islamic history, astutely observes:

> And yet, the widespread view that the term 'Palestine' was only
> revived at the time of the European Renaissance with its conscious
> reference to Greek and Roman antiquity, that it was never used by
> Jews, that it had been entirely forgotten by local Arabs, and that it was
> brought back to them by Arab Christians in touch with Europe, can
> no longer be upheld. (Krämer 2011: 16)

In fact, the memory of historic Palestine was kept alive throughout the Mamluk and Ottoman periods by Palestinian Muslim writers and jurists as well as by Arab and Muslim travellers through Palestine. In the 14th century under the Mamluks the name Filastin was cited by Arab and Muslim travellers, often also in connection with the city of al-Ramla, the former capital of the province of Jund Filastin for several centuries under Islam. Ibn Battuta, the famous Muslim traveller and scholar from North Africa, travelled through most of the Muslim world and visited Palestine in the summer of 1326. He later wrote his account as the *Rihlah* ('Journey' or 'Travels'):

> I journeyed thereafter from Jerusalem [al-Quds] to the fortress of
> Askalon, which is a total ruin. Of the great mosque, known as the
> mosque of 'Omar, nothing remains but its walls and some marble
> columns of matchless beauty, partly standing and partly fallen.

Amongst them is a wonderful red column, of which the people tell that the Christians carried it off to their country but afterwards lost it, when it was found at its place at Askalon. Thence I went on to the city of ar-Ramlah, which is also called Filastin, in the *qibla* of those mosques they say three hundred of the prophets are buried. From ar-Ramlah I went to the town of Nabulus ... a city with an abundance of trees and perennial streams and one of the richest in [al-Sham] for olives. The oil of which is exported thence to Cairo and Damascus. It is at Nabulus that the carob-sweet is manufactured and exported to Damascus and elsewhere ... Nabulus has also a species of melon which is called by its name, a good and delicious fruit ... Thence I went to Ajalun ... passing through the Ghawr, followed the coast to Akka [Acre] which is in ruins ... Akka was formerly the capital and port of the country of the Franks [Crusaders] ... and rivalled Constantinople itself. (Ibn Battuta 2005: 57–58)

But the social memory and political geography of Palestine were kept alive perhaps more vividly by indigenous Muslim Palestinian writers living in the country than by Arab writers travelling through Palestine during the Mamluk period. Writing during the late Mamluk period, Mujir al-Din al-ʿUlaymi (مجير الدين العليمي) (1522–1456), a Palestinian Muslim *qadi*, historian and Jerusamelite, in his comprehensive work *The Glorious History of al-Quds and al-Khalil (al-Uns al-Jalil bi-Tarikh al-Quds wal-Khalil,* c. 1495), extensively refers to his native country as Filastin, a term he repeats twenty-two times. Although he also uses the term Holy Land (*al-Ard al-Muqaddasah*), no other geographical names, such al-Sham, are mentioned. Mujir al-Din divides the al-Sham region into five distinct provinces, two of which are connected with historic and modern Palestine:

- The first Sham is Palestine with the city of al-Ramla at its centre.
- The second Sham is Hauran with the city of Tiberias at its centre.
- The third Sham is the Ghouta with the city of Damascus at its centre.
- The fourth Sham is Hims with the city of Hims at its centre.
- The fifth Sham is Qinnasrin with the city of Aleppo at its centre.

Mujir al-Din constructs a concept of al-Sham which places his own country, Filastin, at its centre as the first region of al-Sham. He also puts Palestine centre stage by proudly quoting other Muslim authors saying: 'what is lacking on earth, increases in al-Sham, and what is lacking in al-Sham, increases in Palestine' (Mujir al-Din 1973). He describes Filastin as stretching from a point in the south near al-'Arish in Sinai to Lajjun in Marj Ibn 'Amer in the north. This territorial conception of Filastin echoes the boundaries of the Arab province of Filastin throughout early Islam (Mujir al-Din 1495; Gerber 2008: 49; le Strange 2014; Khalidi, R. 1998: 216, note 25). This amply demonstrates how the incredibly fertile social, cultural and geographic memories of the medieval Arab Islamic province of Filastin were nurtured by local Muslim Palestinian judges and writers throughout the Mamluk and early Ottoman periods.

In view of the fact that the polity of Filastin was preserved in the social memory and works of two distinguished Palestinian Muslim scholars and jurists, Mujir al-Din al-'Ulaymi, (c. 1495) (see below) and Khair al-Din al-Ramli in the 17th century, it is hardly surprising that the archives of the Islamic Sharia Court of Jerusalem in the 18th century also show that the terms *Filastin, ard Filastin* ('land of Palestine', 'أرض فلسطين') and *ahl Filastin* (the 'people of Palestine', 'أهل فلسطين') – with specific reference to the cities of al-Ramla, Lydda, Jaffa, al-Quds, al-Khalil (Hebron) and Gaza, and within the wider geographical region al-Sham – remained very much alive in local and regional Palestinian Muslim social memory throughout the Mamluk and Ottoman periods.

THE MOSAICS OF HISTORIC PALESTINE, CONTINUITIES AND TRANSFORMATION: THE PALESTINIAN GLASSWORK INDUSTRY OF AL-KHALIL AND THE SCHOOL OF MOSAICS OF AL-QUDS

The Arabic term for mosaics is *fusayfisaa*. The Arab term is a transliteration of the Byzantine Greek term Ψηφιδωτό and mosaic art spectacularly flourished during the Byzantine Empire. Byzantine-style mosaics decorated the churches, synagogues and temples of Provincia Palaestina (Prima,

Secunda and Tertia) which, from the 4th century onwards, were exquisitely embellished with wall, ceiling and flour mosaics. Both the Nea Church (Νέα Ἐκκλησία) in Aelia Capitolina (Jerusalem), erected by Justinian I (527–565),[3] and the Church of the Nativity in Bethlehem, built as a great Constantinian basilica, were decorated with mosaics. The original mosaic floor of the Church of the Nativity, with its typical Roman geometric motifs, is partially preserved today. As we have already shown, the very name of the country Palaestina, in Greek (Παλαιστινη), was found on the famous Madaba Mosaic Map, dated 560–565 AD, in a town which at the time was part of the Byzantine province of Palaestina Prima. Similar Arab Byzantine-style mosaics were found at the Umayyad Hisham's Palace (*Qaṣr Hisham*) at Khirbat al-Mafjar, an important early Islamic archaeological site located 5 kilometres north of the town of Jericho. Many of the finds from the excavations at the site are now held in the Rockefeller Museum (formerly Palestine Archaeological Museum) in occupied East Jerusalem.

The Palestine mosaic (wall, ceiling and floor) industry also flourished and grew further under the impact of the Ayyubid and Mamluk building programmes in Jerusalem. The reorientation and re-centring of Palestine in the post-Crusader era by the Ayyubids and Mamluks towards the interior of the country and the rise again of the cities of the mountain (al-Khalil, al-Quds, Nablus, Safad) as a consequence are reflected in work of Mujir al-Din al-ʿUlaymi, *The Glorious History of al-Quds and al-Khalil*. Mujir al-Din not only repeatedly refers to the term Filastin but also points to the evolution of regional social and cultural identities in Palestine and in particular Palestinian regional arts and identity linked to the cities of al-Khalil (and the area of Jabal al-Khalil) and al-Quds (the area of Jabal al-Quds). These close social, economic, cultural and artistic links between the two cities, which were formed and flourished during the Ayyubid, Mamluk and Ottoman periods, have endured for centuries and survived into the modern period; and they point to the way internal Palestinian factors contributed to the formation of strong regional identities within Palestine, identities which, like the works of Palestinian Muslim writers and *qadis* – Mujir al-Din in the 15th century and Khair al-Din al-Ramli and al-Tumurtashi in the 17th century – contributed greatly to the concept of Palestine by keeping the history and memories of Filastin alive.

During the Ayyubid and Mamluk periods Palestine came under social, cultural and architectural influences from Cairo and Damascus. But also the key Palestinian cities such as Nablus, al-Quds and al-Khalil exported much of their locally manufactured goods to Damascus and Cairo (see, for instance, Ibn Battuta 2005: 57). Unfortunately, however, the internal Palestinian agency and the productive and creative capacities of Palestine are often ignored or glossed over by historians who are frequently preoccupied with imperial chronologies and prefer to comment on the external influences behind the Islamic art and architecture of Ayyubid and Mamluk Jerusalem, failing to see Palestinian history from within or the autonomous agency of the Palestinians. For instance, historians often point to the aesthetics of the Tankiziyyah Madrasah in Jerusalem, whose style resembles the Tankiziyah Madrasah in Damascus (see e.g. Rosen-Ayalon 2006: 119, 155), but fail to see independent Palestinian schools of arts emerging within Palestine. Indeed, distinct Palestinian craft traditions and schools of arts developed during the Mamluk period and these are found in the glass industry of al-Khalil and the Palestinian School of Mosaics. These traditions have survived into the modern period. In the 13th century during the Mamluk period al-Khalil developed a flourishing and highly respected glass industry, including glass jewellery known in Arabic as *zujaj al-khalili*; the Old City of al-Khalil still includes a district named the 'Glass-Blower Quarter' and Hebron glass continues to the present time to serve as a tourist attraction for the city. Traditionally, the glass was melted using local raw materials, including sodium carbonate from the Dead Sea. Stained glass windows and great works of art in glass produced in al-Khalil also adorn the Dome of the Rock in the Old City of Jerusalem (al-Ju'beh 2008). Al-Khalil's glass lamps and glass ornaments were exported to Egypt, Syria, Arabia and Africa. The city became well known for its glass production throughout the Arab world and to Western travellers to Palestine in the modern period. It was also represented with glass ornaments at the World Exposition of 1873 in Vienna.[4]

As in the glasswork industry of al-Khalil, other continuities of historic Palestine can be illustrated by the mosaic art which has a long history in Palestine and the Middle East, starting with palaces and temple buildings in Mesopotamia in the 3rd millennium BC. The ancient mosaic art of the Middle East consisted of patterns and images made from the assembly of small pieces of coloured glass, stone (pebble mosaics) or other materials, used in decorative arts or as interior decoration. Mosaics with patterns and pictures became widespread in classical times.

Islamic Palestine and al-Sham as a whole inherited the material heritage and Byzantine mosaic art of Late Antiquity and this material and cultural heritage was deployed widely in the construction of monumental religious buildings and palaces in Umayyad Filastin and al-Sham. These buildings included the first great Islamic religious buildings in Jerusalem, the Dome of the Rock, completed in 691 AD, and the Umayyad Mosque in Damascus, completed in 715. The Dome of the Rock and the neighbouring Dome of the Chain also embodied some of the most spectacular Islamic heritage of Palestine, a heritage which continued to inspire generations of craftsmen and artists for centuries under the Ayyubids, Mamluks and Ottomans. Katharina Galor and Hanswulf Bloedhorn comment on the emergence of an independent Palestinian school of mosaics and glasswork during the Mamluk period:

> Mosaics of colored and gilded glass, colored paste, turquoise faience, and mother-of-pearl, as well as colored stone and marble, embellished some of the ... Mamluk buildings. The most impressive wall mosaic is located in al-Madrasa al-Tankiziyya. It mihrab is covered with narrow strips of polychrome marble, flanked by reused Crusader columns with capitals, clearly analogous to certain features of Umayyad wall mosaics in the Dome of the Rock, in particular with its mother-of-pearl inlay ... It appears that this late re-emerging art draw its inspiration from seventh-century mosaics in the Dome of the Rock. Historical sources indicate that restorations of wall mosaics were carried out during the Mamluk period in both the Dome of the Rock and the Dome of Chain. Although Syria and Egypt have similar types of wall mosaics, Jerusalem appears to have been the home of a genuine Palestinian school that lasted for centuries. (Galor and Bloedhorn 2013: 230)

The quality of Palestinian glasswork, mosaics and crafts was tightly regulated and this legacy of the Mamluk system of regulation has survived in modern Palestinian vernacular terms such as *Hisbe* and in Palestinian family names such as the Muhtasib, a leading Muslim family in the city of al-Khalil (Hebron). The quality of Palestinian glasswork, mosaics and crafts was tightly regulated and this legacy of the Mamluk system of economic regulation has survived in modern Palestinian vernacular terms such as *Hisbe* and in Palestinian family names such as the Muhtasib, a leading Muslim family in the city of al-Khalil (Hebron). The *muhtasib* system in Islamic Palestine was part of the pre-capitalist 'moral economy' (to borrow an expression by English historian E. P. Thompson), influenced by sharia principles of social justice and the public good and widely promoted in the Near East. The *muhtasib* was an important official appointed by the Mamluk sultan whose duties included the regulation of prices and supervision and inspection of bazaars and trade in Palestine, Egypt and al-Sham. These varied duties also included ensuring that public business was conducted in accordance with the ethical requirements of the sharia (Islamic law). Recurrent epidemics were a regular phenomenon in the urban centres of the Middle Ages and hygienic conditions and the continuous supply of clean water, for public baths and public drinking fountains in the cities, were major achievements of Islamic civil engineering in Palestine throughout the Muslim world. Relying on written official manuals, the *muhtasib* supervised the regulation of hygienic conditions in the bazaars, weights and measures, money, prices of produce and manufactured goods, safety of public places and food sold publicly. They also ensured that craftsmen and builders adhered to the specification set for their craft and construction standards (Ibn al-Ukhuwah 1976; Broadbridge 1999; Hill, D. 1984).

Chapter 8

PALESTINIAN STATEHOOD IN THE 18TH CENTURY

Early modernities and practical sovereignty in Palestine

The Eurocentric analysis of the Arab states has failed to recognise that most of the Arab countries and their borders are closely based on long (pre-colonial) historical precedents, including the naming of states. In the case of Palestine, as in the case of most other Arab political entities, traditionally and throughout the Middle Ages the name Filastin had indicated both an exact geographic location and the identity of the (predominantly, but not exclusively) Arab Muslim population. Moreover, the history of modern Palestine is often studied from and with European, Ottoman and Zionist-settler perspectives; the autonomous agency and voice of Palestine and the Palestinians themselves are seldom recognised. With this imperial and colonial mindset, historians of the modern Middle East also tend to focus on the Ottoman Empire and 'Ottoman reforms', which is also part of a long Western tradition of preoccupation with imperial chronologies of the Near East: Assyrian, Persian, Greek, Roman, Ottoman, British etc. Yet the *dawlah al-qutriyyah*, or the country/state – the Arabic term *qutr* being a 'country' – as a parachronism, and whether traditionally in the form of sultanate, emirate, kingdom, khanate, shaykhdom, wilayat, caliphate or any other name, was one of the most common forms of statehood throughout Muslim history and in Muslim-majority countries; a statehood which often enjoyed practical sovereignty. The Caliphate of Córdoba (929 to 1031 AD), the Emirate of Granada (1230–1492), the Khanates of Central Asia, the Sultanate of Oman (1741 to the present), the Beys of Tunis (1705–1957), the Emirate of Mount Lebanon (1516–1841), the first Saudi state (the Emirate of Dir'iyah, 1744–1818) and the Wilayat of Muhammad 'Ali Pasha of Egypt (1805–1948) are only a few examples of how incredibly widespread this form of statehood was throughout Muslim history. Some *dual qutriyyah*, such as the Mamluk Sultanate of Egypt (1250–1517), were far more powerful than the Muslim Caliphate of Baghdad during the 11th–13th centuries. Far from being an aberration, the *dawlah qutriyyah* became common throughout the Arab and Islamic worlds, especially after the decline of the Abbasid Caliphate in the second half of the 9th century AD and many of these independent states enjoyed a great deal of prosperity and spectacular cultural developments. For instance, the independent Emirate of Aleppo, which encompassed most of northern Syria and parts of western al-Jazirah, was founded in 944 by the Hamdanid princes and became the seat of an independent emirate under Sayf al-Dawlah. It enjoyed a period of great prosperity and became home to the greatest Arab poet, al-Mutanabi, and one of the greatest philosophers of Islam, the polymath al-Farabi, the author of *The Opinions of the People of the Virtuous City*, also known as *The Perfect State* (al-Farabi 1985).

This rich historical legacy of the *dawlah qutriyyah*, whose modern equivalent is the *dawlah wataniyyah* or national state, was a factor in the emergence and construction of a two-tier *watani–qawmi* nationalism in the Arab world and in Muslim-majority Palestine in the early 20th century. Today the Arab world consists of twenty-one states, or *dual qutriyyah*, excluding Palestine. Pan-Arab nationalist ideologues often argue that the failure of Arab unity schemes and the predominance and durability of *al-dawlah al-qutriyyah* in the Arab world are primarily the product of the colonial legacy. But this argument is made in disregard of the historical legacy of statehood under Islam, Arab indigenous agency, the distinct local and regional traditions and the ancient local roots and historical autonomy of many Arab societies. In fact, as we shall see below, European colonialism prevented the creation of a *dawlah qutriyyah* in Palestine.

Moreover, Arabic toponyms such as Palestine/Filastin, Egypt, Syria, Libya, Iraq or the Yemen all have deep and ancient historical roots and indigenous legitimacy of self-definition. Furthermore, the indigenous agency behind the creation of Palestinian statehood, the Emirate of Dhaher al-'Umar, in 18th century Palestine, which was a form of *dawlah qutriyyah*, is a case in point. The revival and spread of ancient toponyms such as Palestine/Filastin in the modern era was derived from the common use of the name in ancient history (from the Late Bronze Age onwards) and throughout Classical Antiquity, Byzantine Christianity and Medieval Islam. Although the colonial legacy and influence of European ideas about the 'nation-state' contributed to the rise of a two-tier (*watani–qawmi*) form of nationalism in the Arab world, local roots and regional historical legacies must be part of the mix of factors for the emergence and domination of the *dawlah qutriyyah* throughout the Arab world.

REVIVALISM AND REDISCOVERY UNDER OTTOMAN RULE: THE ARAB ISLAMIC JURISPRUDENCE OF PALESTINE AND INDIGENOUS MEMORIES OF FILASTIN UNDER THE OTTOMANS (1517–1860S)

Under the Ottoman Empire (1517–1917), Palestine was used both as a general term to describe the predominantly Arab Muslim country in the southern Sham region, and as a social and cultural term among the indigenous people of Palestine. By this stage, Muslim-majority Palestine had developed a strong tradition of Arab Islamic jurisprudence, one of the most crucial requirements of any sense of autonomous polity. The long Ottoman period reinforced the already close historic links between Palestine and the al-Sham region, an Arab Islamic geographic term which had been coined during the early Islamic period and referred to the territories of present-day Syria, Palestine, Jordan and southern Turkey, while al-Sham often referred to the specific capital city of Damascus (al-Sham). Palestine was not an official designation under the Ottomans and some Arabs during this period referred to the area as al-Sham, a term which should not be conflated automatically or exclusively with present-day Syria and the modern myth of Suriyya al-Janubiyyah or, as some Arab intellectuals continue to assert,[1] 'Southern Syria'. The term 'Southern Syria' was invented and popularised in 1919–1920, and was derived from two modern currents: (a) a late 19th century Syrian *qawmi* (nationalist) ideology; and (b) the circumstances surrounding the formation of the pan-Arab nationalist regime in Damascus headed by Emir Faisal in 1919–1920 (see below). Whether or not 'Southern Syria' was also related to the ancient Roman designation Syria-Palaestina is not clear, yet the indigenous, shared memories of medieval Arab Islamic Filastin and Byzantine Palaestina were kept alive throughout the Ottoman period both in Palestine and in Europe.

Modernities in Palestine have multiple beginnings and multiple sources. Although the social and regional roots and markers of modern Palestinian identity are found in the pre-modern period, its distinct modern features evolved gradually, both consciously and unconsciously, from its early beginnings in the 18th century into the 19th and 20th centuries. This evolution was influenced by a range of social and cultural markers including the social memories and cultural heritage of the medieval Arab Muslim province of Jund Filastin (Gerber 1998a, 2008).

Palestine's strong tradition of Arab Islamic jurisprudence and the roots of the modern social, cultural and geographic consciousness of Filastin as a distinct polity and 'regional territorially based identity' can be traced to the works of Khair al-Din al-Ramli (خير الدين الرملي, 1585–1671), one of the most extraordinary Palestinian jurists of all times and a prominent 17th century Islamic jurist, public intellectual and writer in Ottoman Palestine (Tucker 2002; Gerber 1998b). Al-Ramli was a native of al-Ramla, and he was named for the town which was for centuries the administrative secular capital of the province of Jund Filastin and a major garrison town in Ottoman Palestine. Al-Ramli was a landowner and farmer in 17th century Palestine, and his descendants, the Khairis, remained wealthy farmers and prominent figures in the town for nearly three centuries until the 1948 Nakba. During the British Mandatory period, Mustafa Khairi served for four years as *qadi* and a long-time mayor of al-Ramla, and his family owned the only cinema in the town. In the 17th century Khair al-Din al-Ramli became well known for issuing a collection of *fatwas* (religious edicts) known as *al-Fatawa al-Khairiyyah* (الفتاوى الخيرية) – compiled into final form in 1670

– that became highly influential in the Sunni Hanafi school of jurisprudence (*fiqh*) not only in Palestine but throughout the Arab region in the 18th and 19th centuries (Islahi 2008) and his jurisprudence was highly relevant to family *waqf*, landownership and agrarian relations in Palestine.

Filastin itself had developed a strong tradition of Islamic jurisprudence and one of the founders of the four great Sunni schools of Islamic jurisprudence, Imam al-Shafi'i (767–820 AD), was born in Gaza (Haddad 2007: 189–190, 193). A brilliant jurist, al-Shafi'i was known to have been authorised to issue *fatwas* at very young age. In 17th century Palestine *al-Fatawa al-Khairiyyah* had major practical dimensions and offers a contemporary record of the period, giving a complex view of agrarian relations in Palestine, as al-Ramli was a jurist, farmer and landowner. He is known to have amassed a big library. He also imported a variety of seeds from Egypt and introduced them to the district of al-Ramla (Islahi 2008). Al-Ramli's terminology and *al-Fatawa al-Khairiyyah* would also have been known to the administrators of the Sharia Courts in Jerusalem in the 18th and 19th centuries.

The way Khair al-Din al-Ramli, Mujir al-Din al-'Ulaymi and other leading Palestinian Muslim jurists and writers used the term Filastin to refer to the 'country' as Palestine, or to 'our country' (*biladuna*), in the 15th to 17th centuries suggests that the territorial notion of Palestine was still very much alive in Palestinian Muslim social and cultural memory throughout the Mamluk and early Ottoman periods. This also contradicts the unfounded claim that the term Palestine 'had been entirely forgotten by local Arabs, and that it was brought back to them by Arab Christians in touch with Europe' (Krämer 2011: 16). Several scholars used the works of Mujir al-Din and al-Ramli (for instance, Tucker 2002; Gerber 1998a, 2008: 50–51) to trace the pre-modern roots of the emergence of embryonic Palestinian social and territorial consciousness. In *Remembering and Imagining Palestine: Identity and Nationalism from the Crusades to the Present* Haim Gerber explains:

> The term 'Palestine' appears later as well. The next writer to use the name ... lived two and half centuries after Mujir al-Din, an independent mufti and legal scholar in al-Ramla in the seventeenth century, who left for posterity a most important collection of

fatwas (Islamic legal discussions of questions posed by members of the public). A *fatwa* is a public document, to be read and used (sometimes in courts) by all sorts of people, probably literate, and it is my understanding that the language employed could not have been invented by the mufti. Nor was Khyar al-Din al-Ramli an obscure personality. Quite the reverse: all legal jurists from Syria and Palestine after the seventeenth century used this material intensively and unquestionably knew every *fatwa* in it inside out. All this information becomes important if we bear in mind that on several occasions Khayr al-Din al-Ramli calls the country he was living in Palestine, and unquestionably assumes that his readers do likewise. What is even more remarkable is his use of the term ''the country' and even 'our country' (*biladuna*) possibly meaning that he had in mind some sort of a loose community focused around that term. (Gerber 2008: 50; also Gerber 1998a)

The Islamic *Fada'il al-Quds* (Merits of Jerusalem) literature and the works of Khair al-Din al-Ramli, of al-Ramla-Filastin, and another Palestinian Muslim compatriot and writer in the 17th century, Salih ibn Ahmad al-Tumurtashi (died in c. 1715), of Gaza, in Filastin, give us another dimension to the multi-linear evolution of the concept of Palestine in the course of the late Ottoman period. Al-Tumurtashi wrote during the middle Ottoman period an Islamic Merits of Jerusalem work entitled: *The Complete Knowledge in Remembering the Holy Land and its Boundaries and Remembering the Land of Palestine and its Boundaries and al-Sham* (*Al-Khabar al-Tam for Dhikr al-Ard al-Muqaddasah wa-Hududiha wa-Dhikr Ard Filastin wa-Hududiha wa-Sham*) (al-Tumurtashi 1695–1696; al-Turk 1998; Anabsi 1992; Gerber 2008: 50–51). Al-Tumurtashi uses the terms Filastin, the land of Palestine (*ard Filastin*), the people of Palestine (*ahl Filastin*) the boundaries or borders of Palestine (*hudud Filastin*, حدود فلسطين) and memory of Palestine (*dhikr Filastin*, ذكر فلسطين) to describe his own country. Al-Tumurtashi does not create new knowledge on Palestine. In his manuscript – of which four copies based on the original manuscript have survived, including two at the Centre for the Revival of Islamic Heritage in Ab-Dis (Jerusalem) and one at the Süleymaniye Library in Istanbul (al-Turk 1998: 2–4) – he reproduces locally available knowledge and social memories of Arab Islamic Filastin. In the late 17th century al-Tumurtashi uses a 15th century work by another compatriot, Mujir al-Din, *Al-Uns al-Jalil bi-Tarikh al-Quds wal-Khalil*, in his reconstruction of the boundaries of Filastin, which, according to him and Mujir al-Din, extended from al-'Arish/Rafah in the south to al-Lajjun (in Marj Ibn 'Amer) in the north. All this demonstrates that the social, administrative and geographic memories of Palestine among indigenous Palestinians were very much alive in the 17th and 18th centuries. In the 15th–17th centuries among local Palestinians these centuries of lived and living memories of Islamic Filastin would be far more powerful than the historical memories of Islamic Spain (al-Andalus) among Arabs and Muslims today. These lived memories also show that the term al-Sham did not displace the indigenous, deeply rooted idea of Filastin throughout the Ottoman period. In fact, the two geographical terms coexisted in indigenous Palestinian social and cultural memories, and, for practical purposes, complemented each other.

In Europe the printing press revolution made sure that the Latin term Palaestina and English term Palestine increased their circulation at the time of the European Renaissance. The printing and publication revolution accelerated during the Age of Enlightenment with conscious reference to the classical Greek and Roman heritage in general and the classical heritage of Palestine in particular. It has already been shown that during Europe's Great Age of Exploration from the end of the 15th century to the 18th century key classical (Greek and Roman) works, which described the geography, topography and ethnography of classical and Late Antiquity Palaestina as a country from Phoenicia in the north to Egypt in the south, were circulated widely in Europe. The famous classicising Christian Byzantine intellectuals, philosophers and theologians of Palaestina Prima (of Gaza, Caesarea Maritima and Ascalon) and the religio-cultural heritage of Palaestina were also of interest to Renaissance authors.

In fact, in early modern European collective memory the name Palestine (both in Latin and European vernaculars) became the most common designation of the country (see, for instance, Plett 2004: 512). The fact that the name Palestine remained the most commonly used throughout the early modern and modern eras is evident in William Shakespeare's plays. *Syntagma Musicum* (Vols. I–III) was an encyclopaedic work by German musicologist Michael Praetorius (1571–1621), one of the most versatile composers and musical academics of the 17th century. Published in Wittenberg and Wolfenbüttel in three parts between 1614 and 1620, it is one of the most commonly used research sources for music theory of the early modern period (Herbert 2006: 87). Typical of its period, the second volume, *De Organographia*, describes musical instruments and their use, and refers to early instruments of 'Palestine, Asia Minor and Greece' (Vol. II, fol. 4).

Two points are central to modern European mapping of and writing about Palestine:

- Provincia Palaestina remained synonymous with the Christian notion of Terra Santa, or the Holy Land.
- Like the Roman and Byzantine conceptualisation (but unlike the medieval Islamic idea), the conceptualisation of Palestine was always sufficiently wide to include the Galilee and Acre. Indeed, throughout the early and modern periods (especially from the 17th century onwards) dozens of maps and books were printed and published in Europe (in many languages) under the designation 'Palestine' or 'Map of Palestine' and in much of this European literature the country of Palestine included Acre and the Galilee. It was this European notion of Palestine which influenced late Ottoman reconceptualisation and the Ottoman military handbook named *Filastin Risalesi* (see below).

AL-DAWLAH AL-QUTRIYYAH: PALESTINIAN STATEHOOD AND THE REGIMES OF DHAHER AL-ʿUMAR AND AHMAD PASHA AL-JAZZAR IN THE 18TH CENTURY

Scholars of the modern Middle East are often preoccupied with the history and politics of urban elites and with nationalism and modernities imported from Europe in the 19th century. This approach tends to focus on urban centres and reproduce elite narratives, while ignoring peasant and 'frontier societies' and the subaltern and marginalised. This approach also contributes to the silencing of much of Palestinian history and divesting the Palestinians of their own sense of identity and collective agency. Palestine and the Palestinian people are rarely allowed to speak for themselves, argued Edward Said; they have to be represented by authoritative Western or Israeli scholars – Orientalists, biblical archaeologists, scriptural geographers (Said 1980) – or they have to be viewed through the prism of imperial configurations and urban (cosmopolitan) patron–client systems (Mamluk, Ottoman, British).

HISTORY OF URBAN ELITES VERSUS HISTORY 'FROM BELOW': NEW LEADERSHIP, PALESTINE'S COTTON TRADE WITH EUROPE AND THE INDUSTRIAL REVOLUTION

In the 18th and 19th centuries, wheat and cotton shipments from the Palestinian port of Acre to Italy, southern France (Beheiry 1981: 67) and England helped save the growing population of France from famine and fuelled the English Industrial Revolution and the rise of commodity capitalism in Europe. This brought about the rise of a local bourgeoisie in urban Palestine (in Acre, Nazareth, Tiberias, Nablus, Jerusalem and Jaffa) as well as a peasant economy directed towards export to Europe, as this became the more lucrative market. This move during the 18th century transformed Palestinian agriculture and industry from subsistence towards production for the international market, and brought about a new relationship between (larger) cities and towns, and the hundreds of villages where most people lived and worked. This increasing international trade with the growing capitalism of Europe, and the insatiable British demand for cotton for its mills, also ushered in early modernities in Palestine. The conventional wisdom about modernity in the Arab world focus on the elite notable (*a'ayan*) politics, the Napoleonic invasion or the Ottoman state's weaknesses as a mix of factors behind the start of modernisation in the region (Baram 2007a: 16). Furthermore, the conventional wisdom advanced by historians is that early modernities in Palestine were first imported by European missionaries and biblical explorers in the 19th century or disseminated by urban elites educated in European-style schools or schools which operated under Ottoman patronage. The Ottoman Tanzimat (literally 'reorganisations') – a period of major reforms 'from above' that began in 1839 and ended with the Ottoman First Constitutional era of 1876 – and their impact on Palestine and the wider Arab East have been given most scholarly attention. Yet the new evidence contradicts elitist, romantic Orientalist and biblicist approaches to modern Palestinian history. This evidence shows, first, that the start of modernities was in 18th century Palestine; second, that the Napoleonic invasion of Palestine and siege of Acre in 1799 followed rather than led the European material culture and commodities (including European textiles) which became widely available in much of urban and rural Palestine throughout the rules of al-'Umar and al-Jazzar (Baram 2007a, 2007b); third, that the 'new' economy and new agricultural tools of Palestine in the mid-18th century had already been significantly integrated within the modern international trade and European capitalist economy which had been ushered in by the British technological and industrial revolutions.

Although the European printing and educational revolutions did not catch up with Palestine until the late 19th century, the English Industrial Revolution of the 18th century and rise of European capitalism impacted on the economy of Palestine directly and profoundly. These new forces also contributed to the reorientation of Palestine towards Europe and creation of a new political economy and statehood in mid-18th century Palestine, a statehood that was effectively independent of the weakened Ottoman Empire, and which was headed by Palestinian leader Dhaher al-'Umar al-Zaydani (1689–1775). Natives of Safad, the Zaydanis would have been familiar with the local traditions and social memories of the province of Safad under the Mamluks: 'Kingdom of Safad' (مملكة صفد). Backed by a professional modern army and most of the Palestinian peasantry, the latter stood up to and defeated the Ottoman army and created a statehood which managed to impose its power and practical sovereignty on much of modern Palestine, despite being resented by many of the Palestinian urban elites of Nablus and Jerusalem.

The concept of formal sovereignty has undergone radical transformation in the modern era, from being historically derived from the sovereign (person or ruler) to being linked to the territorial concept of the modern nation-state. However, state, power and legitimacy remain central to the notion of sovereignty. In the 18th century the practical sovereignty of al-'Umar's regime was not derived from any modern notion of the nation-state, but from the ability of al-'Umar's regime to impose legitimate power on much of Palestine.

In view of these dramatic developments in Palestine, a history 'from below' and 'from within' approach can partly explain the rise of Dhaher al-'Umar al-Zaydani and early modernities in Palestine rather than theories of modernities which focus on metropolitan cultural elites in the 18th and 19th centuries or European missionary activities in late Ottoman Palestine, activities which centred on urban Palestine where the majority of the Palestinian Christians resided. Indeed al-'Umar can easily qualify as the founding father of early Palestinian modernities and social renewal, and the single most influential figure in the beginning of the modern reorientation of Palestine towards the Mediterranean region. In the 18th century the majority of the Palestinian population (predominantly Muslim) were peasants who lived in villages or small towns, with a few large urban trading centres. The term for 'modern' in 18th century Palestine was *jadid* (new) or *tajdid* (renewal, innovation), and it began in these small towns and villages of the Galilee. Powerful local leadership in 18th century Galilee and modernities manifested themselves in a variety of ways:

- The emergence of a new Palestine-based autonomous rule under both Dhaher al-'Umar and Ahmad Pasha al-Jazzar (1720–1804), a rule independent of both the Ottoman authorities and urban elites.
- New agricultural and technological innovations in Palestine which benefited the majority of Palestinian peasantry began in the 18th century – preceding and anticipating the rise of local urban Palestinian bourgeois 'nationalism' by at least a century – and deeply affected the agricultural production of Palestine. The considerable growth of international and regional export of Palestinian agricultural produce and urban products was shown in the export of Palestinian cotton, olive oil, wheat and soap.
- Palestinian state monopoly on the flourishing cotton, wheat and olive oil export to Europe and the international and regional export of

Palestinian produce and products generated much-needed new capital for investment in the country.

• The expansions of small towns and villages and construction of 'new' urban spaces in Palestine in the second half of the 18th century and the beginning of a distinction between the 'old spaces' and 'new spaces' (al-'Imarah al-Jadidah) was noted by several authors.

Inspired by the model of the neighbouring and autonomous Emirate of Mount Lebanon (1516–1841), al-'Umar's effective leadership, popular backing by much of the Palestinian peasantry and international trading relations with the French and British all brought about the creation of a *dawlah qutriyyah* in Palestine, a new state driven by and based on an indigenous agency, whose authority extended from Lebanon to Gaza, and whose modern capital was Acre. This Palestinian *dawlah qutriyyah* transformed Acre from a small village into a fortified and rich urban metropolitan centre. Throughout much of the 18th and early 19th centuries Acre, effectively and to all practical purposes, functioned as the second capital of modern Palestine. French cotton imports from Palestine and similar British imports following the Industrial Revolution and the rise of 'new' British technologies, with their insatiable demand for cotton, together with the new regional and international trade in cotton, olive oil, silk and textiles, all helped transform Palestinian agriculture and urban spaces in much of the country. New urban spaces and neighbourhoods were created in key cities such as Acre and Nablus, making these cities not only into the biggest and wealthiest centres in Palestine but also among the largest cities of al-Sham (Doumani 1995; Philipp 2001). The newly expanded port of Acre (together with the smaller port of Jaffa) remained the main international gateway to and from Palestine throughout much of the 18th and 19th centuries. After the decline of the Palestine cotton industry, coastal Acre and Nablus, together with al-Quds/Jerusalem, were still the three most important 'new' urban centres in Palestine and were central to the Ottoman administrative reorganisation of the country in the 1870s, as we shall see below, the Mutasarrifate of Noble Jerusalem and the Sanjaks of Acre and Nablus were central to the new (evolutionary) paradigm shift in the reconceptualisation of late Ottoman Palestine. The British industrial revolution also contributed indirectly to the emergence of the first modern Galilee-based 'state' in Palestine in the second half of the 18th century.

In Europe throughout the 18th century the perception of Palestine as a distinct 'country', separate from Syria, was widespread and the plethora of European maps of 'Palaestina/Palestina' produced in that century reflected this growing perception of Palestine. In 1747, in the London *Modern Gazetteer* (p. 65), Thomas Salmon, an English geography writer and author of *Modern History, or the Present State of all Nations* (1744–1746) – which provided 'a short view of the several nations of the world' – described Palestine as follows:

PALESTINE, a part of Asiatic Turkey, is sit.[uated] between 36 and 38 degrees of E. Lon.[gitude] and between 31 and 34 degrees of N. Lat.[itude], bounded by the mount Libanus, which divides it from Syria, on the N.[orth], by mount Hermon, which separates it from Arabia Deserta, on the E.[ast], by the mountains of Seir, and the deserts of Arabia Petraea, on the S.[outh], and by the Mediterranean Sea on the W.[est], so that it seems to have been extremely well secured against foreign invasions ... It is generally a fruitful country, producing plenty of corns, wine, and oil where it is cultivated.[2]

Crucially, political power and practical sovereignty in the Galilee in the 18th century was not the outcome of the imperial patron–client system of the urban leadership, nor did it derive from the central Ottoman authorities; in fact it evolved 'from within' and 'from below', and in defiance and actual military resistance to the Ottoman Empire. It was backed by many Palestinian peasants and resented by some of the Ottoman-backed urban elites. With the sharp decline of the Ottoman power, new technological and commercial developments in Europe and indigenous Palestinian struggle for autonomy emerged from within the Galilee countryside in the mid-18th century. Several factors contributed to this radical development. One of these was due to:

[new A]cre's exceptional status. Politically, it was an enclave – semi-autonomous, if not completely independent of the center of empire and its administration. This began when a local chieftain, Daher al-ʿUmar, established himself as an independent ruler in the city. His self-declared sovereignty was expanded and interpreted on an even broader scale by his successor, Jazzar Pasha. (Rosen-Ayalon 1998: 519–520)

The astonishing modern rise of the city and province of Acre represented more than anything else the dramatic reorientation of Palestine towards Europe in the 18th century – a reorientation which, unlike previous reorientations of the country by imperial dynasties including the Roman, Umayyad and Ayyubid/Mamluk, was engineered by a powerful indigenous Palestinian leader. Indeed, Acre became the capital of Dhaher al-ʿUmar al-Zaydani for nearly thirty years, from 1746 to 1775, and one of two most powerful trading cities in Palestine; the other one was Nablus. Not surprising, Acre also remained the capital of al-ʿUmar's successor, Ahmad Pasha al-Jazzar, Governor of the Ottoman Pashalik – in reality, a 'province' – of Acre from 1776 until his death in 1804. The dominance of Acre continued well into the early 19th century. After the death of al-Jazzar the Ottoman Governors of Acre, Suleiman Pasha al-ʿAdil (d. 1819) and ʿAbdullah Pasha (d. 1831) ruled much of Palestine and Lebanon and Damascus from their Palestinian capital of Acre.

The spectacular reorientation of modern Palestine towards the Mediterranean region/Europe and the dramatic rise of modern Acre in the 18th century began with the emergence and military successes of al-ʿUmar in Galilee, backed by the Palestinian peasantry. The latter's achievement of autonomous power in Palestine was spurred by revolutionary technological and industrial developments in Europe. The coastal port city of Acre had been a famous Crusade stronghold. In the centuries following the Crusades the city had slipped into oblivion and by the time of the Ottoman conquest old Acre had become a small fishing village (Philipp 2001: 1). Under the Mamluks and throughout the early Ottoman period the town of Safad replaced old Acre as the administrative capital of the Galilee. Yet in the middle of the 18th century modern Acre was the first of the major sites along Palestine's Mediterranean coast that quickly renewed its function as a 'new', dynamic, major port city following the sharp decline of the coastal cities in the post-Crusader period under both the Ayyubids and Mamluks

(Rosen-Ayalon 1998: 520; Philipp 2001: 1). But by 1785 modern Acre had become one of the largest cities in Palestine and the third largest city in al-Sham, after Damascus and Aleppo (Philipp 2001: 1).

HOURANI'S 'URBAN' ELITES PARADIGM?

Writing Palestine into the history of the 18th century, the idea of Palestinian social and economic autonomy under the Ottomans was masterfully explored by Beshara Doumani (1995) with special reference to the social history of 18th century Jabal Nablus. This was done within the framework of Albert Hourani's paradigm of the 'urban notables' (*a'ayan*): the political and economic elites in provincial Arab cities and towns that served as 'patrician' intermediaries between the imperial capital in Istanbul and provincial society and governed the provinces of the vast Ottoman Empire. The urban social elites of Palestine, as in the rest of the Arab East, sought to control regional and distant trade and dominate landownership in the countryside. However, in late Ottoman Palestine cities were relatively small and urban social elites were dependent on Ottoman patronage and interdependent with their surrounding villages and the mass peasantry of the countryside.

But the history of Ottoman Palestine cannot be confined to the politics of Hourani's urban notables or other forms of elite politics, whether this is centred on greedy feudal landlords who exploited the Palestine peasantry through the Ottoman *iltizan* land-cultivation system or on benevolent aristocratic patricians who set up remarkable charitable *waqf* foundations in the country. Although these urban elites resisted direct Ottoman rule in Palestine, they were drawn for the most part from the same social classes and their politics remained family-centred, fiercely competitive and deeply fractious (Mao'z 1968: 113) and, ultimately, ineffective. Also, the entire history of Palestine cannot be reduced to one paradigm: the imperial patron–client framework and elite politics. Crucially, this social autonomy of the urban '*ayans*' in Palestine cannot account for the dramatic emergence political autonomy 'from below' and 'from within' of an almost independent Palestinian entity in the 18th century, the al-'Dhaher al-'Umar state of Palestine, which was the closest Palestine got to a modern independent state. However, this elite paradigm of local 'urban notables' has influenced an entire generation of historians of the modern Middle East. Historians are often wary of challenging established paradigms and, with so many academic careers depending on them, this partly explains why al-'Umar's powerful state in Palestine, which lasted for nearly half a century, has been studied only marginally.

TAXATION, FRONTIER PROVINCES AND THE RISE OF AUTONOMOUS POWER IN 18TH CENTURY PALESTINE

Wolf-Dieter Hütteroth and Kamal Abdulfattah's (1977) seminal work on the Historical Geography of Palestine, Transjordan and Southern Syria in the Late 16th Century, based on a detailed Ottoman register (*mufassal defter*), describes these regions as 'frontier zones' under Ottoman rule. In 18th century Palestine, the *pashalik* of Safad (province of Safad) and Galilee as a whole were a case of 'frontier province' and a power base for a rising Palestinian local power under nominal Ottoman rule.

Appearing first under the Mamluks, the *Iltizam* taxation system was institutionalised by the Ottomans in the 15th century and was carried out by the farming of public tax revenues. The Ottoman state would outsource tax collection by auctioning taxation rights to the highest bidder (*mult-azim*), who would then profit, often profligately, from collecting the taxes locally, make payments to the state in fixed instalments, while keeping the profit. This outsourcing of the *Iltizam* tax system included the farming of land taxes and urban taxes, the production of certain goods such as wine and salt, and even the provision of certain public services. The outsourcing of the land Iltizam tax under the Ottomans, which resembled the *iqta'a* system under the Fatimids, gave rise to rich local elites and powerful local chieftains in Palestine and throughout the region. Formally abolished in the course of the reforms (*Tanzimat*) of 1856, but, in reality, continuing until the end of Ottoman rule in Palestine (Yazbak 1998: 72–73), the *Itizam* system was very profitable and highly exploitative and was for many centuries of great benefit to powerful local elites under the Mamluks and Ottomans (Abdul Rahmam and Nagata 1977).

Certain aspects of the impact of the Ottoman tax farming system, with the growth of local autonomy and rise of powerful chiefs in Palestine especially within the context of 'frontier provinces', can also be seen in the previous rise of the Ghassanid Arab *federate* kings (supreme phylarchs) of the 'frontier provinces' of Palaestina Secunda and Palaestina Tertia in the 6th and early 7th centuries and in the rise of the Jarrah leaders of the Bedouin tribes of Banu Tayy under the Fatimids, until their military defeat by Anushtakin al-Dizbari, the Military Governor of Palestine, in 1029 AD. The spectacular rise of Dhaher al-ʿUmar in Galilee in the 18th century is also a case in point. His ability to collect taxes efficiently, raise and command an army effectively, forge alliances successfully and enforce law and order, within the context of the 'frontier province' of the Galilee, were all part of the mix which explains his rise to power in 18th century Palestine.

The closest Palestine got to early modern independent statehood was a result of both commercial dynamism of Palestine and its legendary leader Dhaher al-ʿUmar and the continued neglect of the Ottomans. The Zaydani clan (*hamulah*) of Dhaher al-ʿUmar emerged from the Palestinian countryside and periphery of the country, from the *pashalik* of Safad, a 'frontier province' under both the Mamluks and Ottomans, not from the traditional major urban centres of the country or the generally pro-Ottoman urban social elites of Palestine. Born in the village of ʿArrabah in central Galilee, al-ʿUmar did not come from the traditional urban landowning aristocracy of Palestine and, unlike the local notables (*ʿayan*), he did not owe his legitimacy to the central Ottoman authorities. Al-ʿUmar's family members had served as local *multazims* (tax collectors) in the provincial towns of Tiberias and Safad in the *pashalik* of Safad and he himself had begun his career as a trader and tax farmer under the Ottoman *Iltizam* system (Krämer 2011: 60). But the Ottoman *Iltizam* land tax system in Palestine had been highly exploitative and oppressive towards the peasantry and, as we shall see below, al-ʿUmar's new taxation system and his socially enlightened regime were evidently popular among the Palestinian peasantry. He substantially reduced the power of the urban notables and 'predatory classes' that had fed upon vulnerable social groups, especially the peasants. Al-ʿUmar had received some formal education but he appears to have been largely self-taught and his early career, financial competence and practical experience as an efficient tax farmer were of critical value. But it was his political, military, economic, diplomatic and taxation skills which made him perhaps the most powerful leader in modern Palestinian history. His rise to power began in the Galilee countryside and his first headquarters was Tiberias in Eastern Galilee, not the traditional urban centres of the country: Nablus, Jerusalem and Gaza. After rebelling successfully against the Ottoman state and consolidating his regime, al-'Umar became effectively the sovereign ruler of much of Palestine. Following his military victory at Marj ibn 'Amer in 1735, thousands of local people, including many residents of Nazareth, joined his forces. Apparently among his Galilee supporters were many local Christians, including Christian women from Nazareth who provided his troops with food and water (Joudah 1987: 28–31). 'Over the next three decades Zahir al-Umar's stature became such that he found it possible to forge temporary alliances with the Russian government and to cooperate with the Mamluks in Egypt' (Doumani 1995: 42).

NOMINAL SOVEREIGNTY VERSUS PRACTICAL SOVEREIGNTY

Today there are many formally sovereign states in the Arab world, but not all of them are genuinely sovereign or independent when it comes to foreign policy. By contrast, al-'Umar's state in Palestine was sovereign in substance and reality, while nominally still part of the Ottoman Empire. However, al-'Umar's state was formally recognised by the Ottomans as an autonomous Emirate and at its peak in 1774 (a year before he was killed outside Acre) its territory extended from south Lebanon along the entire Palestinian coast to Gaza and included some regions in northern Transjordan. He also twice laid siege to the city of Nablus (Doumani 1995: 42). The headquarters of his administration shifted westwards, from his first capital in Tiberias to 'Araabah in central Galilee, then to Nazareth, then to Deir Hanna and finally to the port city of Acre in 1746. In the early 16th century Tiberias had become a city of refuge for Andalusian Arab-Jewish survivors of the Spanish Inquisition. These skilled Jewish migrants eventually contributed both to the expansion of the town's silk industry and the growth of Tiberias' role as a trade centre between Damascus and the Hijaz. Al-'Umar expanded and fortified Tiberias further, but now Acre was the capital of the Galilee and the centre of his lucrative international trade with Europe. Acre remained the centre of his regime for nearly three decades and subsequently became the capital of another autonomous regime in Palestine, that of Ahmad Pasha al-Jazzar (the 'Butcher'), who lived in the palace built by al-'Umar for another two decades from 1776 until 1804. Al-'Umar's regime would demonstrate once again the continuing interdependence of urban centres with their rural contexts in Palestine – a continuing feature of the history of Palestine, ancient, medieval and modern. With his Galilee-based Emirate or *dawlah qutriyyah*, al-'Umar became internationally known in the 18th century as 'King of Galilee' (Nasrallah 2015: x).

In the mid-18th century the deeply weakened Ottoman regime had to come to terms with the new power realities in Palestine, a country which remained only nominally part of the Ottoman Empire. In 1768 the Ottoman authorities were forced into a humiliating position of having to recognise al-'Umar's regime in Palestine in the way the Ottomans had been forced to recognise the emirate of Mount Lebanon and the regime of Emir Fakhr-al-Din II a century earlier. The Ottomans granted al-'Umar the title of 'Sheikh of Acre, Emir of Nazareth, Tiberias, Safed, and Sheikh of all Galilee' (Philipp 2015).

Al-'Umar's economic policies, which benefited the Palestinian peasantry, his military strategies and regional and international alliances (with the autonomous Druze Emirs of Mount Lebanon, Mamluk Egypt and Russia) were partly dictated by his struggle with the Ottoman Empire and partly by his monopolisation of the flourishing cotton and olive oil exports to Europe, especially raw cotton to England following its Industrial Revolution and the expanding British textile industry's demand for raw cotton from Palestine and the Near East. Al-'Umar's rise to power in the 18th century was facilitated by the considerable growth of cotton cultivation in Palestine and the export of this cash crop to France and England. The use of cotton for fabric is known to date back to prehistoric times and cotton had been cultivated in ancient Egypt and Persia, and it was also known to the Arabs since Antiquity. For many centuries since the Middle Ages Palestine and the Galilee had been a major area of cotton cultivation (Quataert

2002: 27; Le Strange 1890: 16–19; 2014: 18–19; al-Maqdisi 1994). Already in the 10th century AD Palestinian historian al-Maqdisi commented on the fact that cotton was one of the key agricultural products of Palestine (cited in Le Strange 2014: 18–19; also Le Strange 1890: 16–19; al-Maqdisi 1994).

Sizeable cotton cultivation and international trade with Palestine and al-Sham continued in the course of the Mamluk period but flourished in late Ottoman Palestine, especially in the 18th century. Today Suq al-Qattanin ('Market of the Cotton Merchants') – also known as Suq of Amir Tankaz al-Nasiri, the Mamluk ruler of Palestine and Syria – in the Old City of Jerusalem is a monumental and toponymic testament to the long history and significance of this Palestinian cotton industry. Suq al-Qattanin is located on the west side of the Haram al-Sharif. The market dates from 1336–1337 AD and contains some of the most exquisite and richest Islamic architecture in Jerusalem. In the middle of the Suq there is the signature of one of the craftsmen who worked on its construction. Written in Arabic *naskhi* script, the inscription reads: 'May God have mercy on him, the work of Muhammad bin Ahmad bin 'Alish. The Suq has two entrances, one to the west and the other to the east, called Bab al-Qattanin ('Gate of the Cotton Merchants'), which opens on to the west side of the Haram. Suq al-Qattanin is considered to be one of the most complete and beautiful medieval *suqs* not only in Palestine, but in the whole of the Near East (Burgoyne 1987; Burgoyne and Abu al-Hajj 1979: 128–129).[3]

From the time of the Crusades the Levant and north Palestine had supplied both regional and European textile markets via port cities such as Acre. The cultivation of cotton in Palestine was maintained throughout the Ottoman period but grew dramatically in the 18th century under the effective leadership of al-'Umar, who got involved in the world's most profitable commodity at the time: cotton. Al-'Umar's rise coincided with the rise of French and British demand for raw cotton following the Industrial Revolution in the 18th century. British capitalism and the manufacturing industries of Lancashire enabled Britain to emerge as the leading exporter of manufactured textiles. From the late 18th century onwards, the British city of Manchester acquired the nickname 'Cottonpolis' due to the cotton industry's predominance within the city, and Manchester's role at the heart of the regional and international cotton trade. Of course, the incorporation of Palestine into the modern European markets and British-dominated global capitalist system and import of textiles from Lancashire to Palestine posed a major challenge to the locally produced textiles in Palestine (Doumani 1995).

Al-'Umar's rule was of modern creation. His administration grew rich on foreign export of cotton and olive oil and his rule consolidated and expanded this lucrative trade with Europe and by the mid-18th century regional and global trade in cotton and textiles made his capital city of Acre and the Palestinian city of Nablus the biggest and the most prosperous cities in the country and among the largest cities of al-Sham (Doumani 1995; Philipp 2001). Despite the massive technological developments in Europe in the 19th century and subsequent decline of the cotton economy of the Galilee (Heyd 1942), even in the mid-19th century the British Consul in Jerusalem James Finn would recall his journeys in central Palestine and the Nablus–Jenin–Tulkarem triangle, and note that the cotton plantations he visited were 'beautifully clean and orderly' (Kamel 2015). In fact, as a consequence of al-'Umar's policies, for over a century between the 1730s and 1860s cotton would remain the main export from Palestine to Europe. Before 1852 Palestine exported its cotton mainly to the al-Sham region, Italy, France and, to a lesser extent, England. In 1859 it was reported by a British geographical gazetteer that

> Tobacco, lent[ils], olives, cotton and silk, are extensively produced in this pash.[lik of Acre] ['a part of Palestine'] ... The only manufactures are silk and cotton fabrics. The situation of this district is highly favourable to commerce. The exports from Acre and Beirut, its principal ports, are wool, cotton, silk, tobacco, gums, dried fruits, gallnuts, madder-root, and skins. The export trade is principally carried on with France and Italy ... This pash.[lik] is of modern creation. In 1749 it formed part of the pash.[lik] of Saida or Sidon, when Dhahir, son of Omar, an Arab Sheikh, having invaded Acre, succeeded in subduing the whole pash.[lik] to his way.[4]

However, after 1870 cotton lost its leading role as the key cash crop shipped to Europe, being replaced by the oranges of Palestine (the iconic

Jaffa oranges). Benefiting from new agricultural innovations and new tree grafting techniques, the Palestine Arab citrus industry became the number one produce exported to Europe throughout the last quarter of the 19th century (Lucas 2003: 21–22). During the second half of the 19th century modern cotton-spinning machinery was also imported into Palestine and a small-scale cotton-spinning industry continued into the 20th century.

Interestingly, in the 18th century the high quality of Palestinian and Levantine cotton seeds led to its transferral to the soils of the colonies of North America. But unlike the settler-colonialism of North America, in which cultivating and harvesting cotton became the leading occupation of slaves, the Palestine cotton plantations were cultivated by ordinary farmers. Yet 'still, canton production in the Levant during the late eighteenth century exceeded, by a factor of nearly thirty, that in the American colonies' (Quataert 2002: 27). The expanded port city of Acre became the first 'modern' Palestinian city in the 18th century to be directly affected by the new foreign trade, the British Industrial Revolution and England's demand for raw cotton.

For a century between 1730 and 1831 the export of highly profitable cash crops – first cotton and then grain – made Acre the largest centre of trade and political power on the Palestinian/Lebanese coast. The city also began to play a role in international politics in the last quarter of the 18th century (Philipp 2001: 3). First under al-'Umar and later under al-Jazzar – the Acre-based ruler from 1776 until his death in 1804:

> [Modern] Acre was the key to the first region in the eastern
> Mediterranean that was tied into modern economy ... an important
> fortified city of perhaps 25,000 inhabitants [which] was closely
> connected with the ever-rising demand for cotton in Europe.
> (Philipp 2001: 1)

Under the impact of international trade during the rule of both al-'Umar and al-Jazzar:

> [W]ithin a very short period of time, [modern] Acre bloomed into a
> city possessing several mosques ... caravansaries ... [public] baths and
> markets. It also boasted fortified walls and an aqueduct to ensure its

water supply. The [Galilee] villages further inland developed most of what was to become the basis of Palestine's agricultural economy. (Rosen-Ayalon 1998: 520)

Of modern creation, and perhaps the most monumental symbol of the culture of early modern Palestine is the White Mosque of modern Acre, famously known as al-Jazzar Mosque, which became the most powerful symbol of the modern capital of northern Palestine. Constructed in 1781, eighteen years before the Napoleonic invasion of Palestine, and influenced architecturally by the grand Ottoman mosques of Istanbul, its namesake (the White Mosque) evoked memories of the famous White Mosque of al-Ramla, the capital of Jund Filastin, the province of Palestine throughout early Islam. The compound of the White Mosque included an Islamic theological academy, the first college of its kind in Palestine. Modelled on the al-Azhar university college of Cairo, and departing from the traditional medieval Islamic schools (*madrasahs*) of Jerusalem, the mosque/college compound contained student lodging, an Islamic court and a major public library, all paid for by Palestinian local taxes and by the flourishing regional and international trade in cotton and other cash crops of Palestine. Spectacularly overlooking the Eastern Mediterranean Sea, al-Jazzar Mosque was also a statement of the reorientation of modern Palestine towards Europe under the impact of the international trade policies and the monumental building programmes pursued by the two powerful leaders, al-'Umar and al-Jazzar.

The encouragement of foreign trade, promotion of local agricultural innovations and export of profitable cash crops such as cotton, grain and olive oil to Europe, which began under al-'Umar in the 1730s, continued until 1830 and the legacy of this foreign trade stimulated the development in the Shamouti orange (which became internationally known as the Jaffa orange). Developed by Palestinian farmers in the mid-19th century, Shamouti oranges were an almost seedless variety of oranges with a tough skin that made them particularly suitable for international export (Issawi 2006: 127; Gerber 1982). Like the export of Palestine cotton and grain in the 18th and 19th centuries, much of the Shamouti orange crop was exported to France and England from the mid-19th century onwards.

Al-'Umar's powerful state ushered in a new dynamic era in Palestine, after a long period of Ottoman neglect, stagnation and rampant exploitation of the Palestinian peasantry, during which Palestine was turned into a frontier country and an imperial backwater. In this new dynastic period under al-'Umar, the Galilee and large parts of Palestine experienced effective and fair taxation, urban expansion and economic development. Many public buildings, fortresses, fortifications, warehouses, *khans* (caravanserais) – the most spectacular of which is the exquisitely-built *Khan al-Tujjar* of Acre; today the site is at the centre of Israeli Judaisation policies in the Arab city – and numerous places of worship were built throughout his domain. Many of these sites and monuments can still be seen today throughout the Galilee. Al-'Umar's state pursued religiously inclusive policies and encouraged the involvement of religious minorities (Christians, Jews and Shi'ites) in his administration, finance and economy. Statehood and early modernities in 18th century Palestine were intertwined:

> Under the leadership of Dhaher al-'Umar al-Zaidani (1730–75), a powerful and protective state was formed in northern Palestine that fostered development. Security was ensured for agricultural production, mainly wheat and cotton for export, particularly to France whose agents resided in the Zaidani capital and port of Acre. Peasants and religious minorities were protected and thus had a stake in the success of the state. In 1764–65, al-'Umar established a new town [Haifa] and secured it with walls. (Seikaly 2002b: 97)

The political stability and effective and fair taxation system provided by al-'Umar in northern Palestine and the expansion and transformation of historic urban centres such Acre, Tiberias and Safad also led to the founding of 'modern' Haifa' and the transformation of Nazareth from a small village into a major town in Palestine. Modern Haifa, or the 'new Haifa' (Haifa al-Jadidah), was founded by al-'Umar in 1764–1765. This was done by moving the 250 local inhabitants to the fortified village of Haifa 2.4 kilometres to the east of the old hamlet.[5] This 'new/modern' Palestinian Arab village became the nucleus of the modern town of Haifa (Yazbak 1998), today the third largest city in Israel. The new village was originally named in Arabic al-'Imarah al-Jadidah ('the New Construction'), a term applied to modern buildings in Palestine in the 18th century. Local Palestinians first called the village New Haifa and later simply Haifa. This new Arab village grew into an Arab town which in the 20th century developed into the modern city of Haifa (Seikaly 2002a, 2002b; Sharon 2013: 262; Mariti 1792: 318). In a similar vein, the 'new' era of al-'Umar's state symbolised the beginning of the modern history of Palestine.

The new agricultural economy and foreign trade of Palestine led to the transformation of Nazareth – al-Nasirah in Arabic, retaining the 'feminine' endings common to many Palestinian Arabic toponyms of Galilee – by al-'Umar's state from a small hamlet into a large town by encouraging immigration to it. The 'new town' of Nazareth played important economic, religious and strategic roles under al-'Umar's rule.

Al-'Umar's fourth capital was Nazareth and for this purpose he commissioned the construction of a new government house known as the Saraya (the 'Palace'). This historic building was constructed around 1740 and later in the 19th century served as the residence of the local Ottoman Governor of Nazareth and its subdistrict and subsequently as the city's municipal headquarters until 1991. While using Nazareth to secure his control over the hugely fertile agricultural lands of central Galilee (Yazbak 1998: 15) and Marj Ibn 'Amer, the rich granary of Palestine, al-'Umar encouraged religious toleration and protected the Christian communities in the town, which he also used to strengthen his international ties with France (Emmett 1995: 22). Al-'Umar also encouraged the Franciscans to purchase land and build a church in Nazareth in 1730, and enabled the Greek Orthodox community to build St Gabriel Church in 1767 (Emmett 1995: 220).

Beginning as a market town for the surrounding countryside under Dhaher al-'Umar, today Nazareth is the largest Palestinian city in Israel and the capital of the Palestinians inside Israel. Today the descendants of al-'Umar still live in Galilee and Nazareth and are known as the 'Dhawahri', in memory of Dhaher – along with the Fahoums, Zu'bis and 'Onallas, the Muslim families which constituted part of Nazareth's urban traditional Muslim land-owning elite which first rose under al-'Umar's rule and continued to dominate the city's politics throughout the late Ottoman and British Mandatory periods and under Israel since 1948 (Srouji 2003: 187).

Modern geo-political representations of Palestine are often located in the late Ottoman period or in 19th century Palestine and the actual historical links between the Palestinian 'statehood' created by al-'Umar and the modern conceptions of Palestine are complex. However, in history the line between fact and fiction or myth and reality is often blurred. The practically independent statehood in Palestine lasted nearly half a century from the late 1720s until 1775, far longer than the British Mandatory period in Palestine.

READING THE HISTORY OF MODERN PALESTINE THROUGH THE EYES OF THE INDIGENOUS PEOPLE

Reading the history of modern Palestine through the eyes of the indigenous people can shift the emphasis away from hegemonic Ottoman, British and Zionist gaze and chronologies and provide new indigenous perspectives. Modern (new) Acre can be a case study of this perspective. This beautiful and iconic capital of al-'Umar's state rose from the ashes to become one the most important modern Palestinian urban centres for nearly two centuries. This was less to do with imperial Ottoman calculations or the 'Ottoman heritage', and more the result of sheer indigenous determination and self-definition. However, by the end of the 19th century Acre's standing had declined to the advantage of the nearby coastal town of Haifa, as new powerful steam engines were developed in the West, powering bigger ships; new trade routes were opened up and the coast of Palestine became part of the regular route of the major European steamship companies (Seikaly 2002b: 97).

With the rise of anti-colonialist Palestinian nationalism, the emergence of new approaches to people's history and the decline of elite narratives, al-'Umar has emerged as a 'nationalist' hero among Palestinians today (Joudah 1987, 2015). Yet al-'Umar's self-governing entity should be seen within the context of his age; clearly his aims were dynastic not nationalist:

> Anxious to 'prove' a historical basis for Palestinian Independence, Palestinians often refer to the effort of the Palestinian leader Dhaher al-Umar to wrest control of much of Palestine from the Ottomans in the late eighteenth century ... But to attribute these challenges to

'national, territorially-based consciousness' is an altogether different and murky issue. (Abu Lughod 1988: 203)

Nevertheless, al-'Umar's emergence from a relatively humble background from 'within Palestine', his effective leadership, his popularity among the Palestinian peasantry for getting rid of the oppressive Ottoman Iltizam system – at least under his rule – his spectacular military successes, his effective resistance to Ottoman imperial direct rule in Palestine and his religiously tolerant policies towards Christians, Jews, Druze and Shiites all combined to give him a mythical status among Palestinians. Real and imagined, al-'Umar provided a role model for modern Palestinians. However, Palestinian *national* consciousness, as opposed to 18th century early modernities in Palestine, is a late Ottoman development and there is no historical evidence that a nationalist Palestinian ideology existed at the time of, or was developed by, al-'Umar. Evidently the 'nationalist' myth of Dhahir al-'Umar as the founder of the first modern 'Palestinian national state' is far more powerful and inspiring than the actual context of this powerful leader and his age. Yet the historical legacy of his self-fashioned and self-governing Palestinian entity and the lasting impact of its policies on modern Palestine are undeniable.

Also, crucially, for much of the 18th century the Galilee-based autonomous regimes of al-'Umar and al-Jazzar, with their close trade links and military alliances with European powers, Russia, Britain and France in particular, politically and physically linked the Galilee with the entire Palestinian coast from Lebanon to Gaza under a Palestine-based single administration. From the perspective of viewing Palestine as a single geo-political entity, the impact of this historic legacy of the 18th century would soon become evident in the way new representations of Palestine evolved in the 19th century.

European influences on the 'modernising' and enlightened administration of Dhaher al-'Umar were much in evidence. These early modernisation efforts were facilitated by the fact the conservative religious authority in the country, which rested with the *muftis* in the cities of Palestine, was always subordinate to the political authority. Italian antiquarian, scientist and traveller Giovanni Filippo Mariti, who arrived in Acre in

1760 and resided in the French quarter for two years, writes in *Travels Through Cyprus, Syria, and Palestine* about the influence of European ideas on the capital of Dhaher al-ʿUmar, Acre. He describes the swift response of the Governor of Acre to the then raging plague which was affecting not only Palestine but also Egypt and Syria. Large and small epidemics (occasionally combined with famine) had been a recurrent feature of medieval Palestine with devastating effects in terms of the high death toll in the country. Small epidemics also occurred in the Mediterranean port cities of Palestine during the First and Second World War. Yet in 1760 the enlightened al-ʿUmar acted decisively, brushing aside religious superstitions and imposing precautionary measures including a strict quarantine in Acre and measures affecting traders entering and leaving the city; these measures helped to minimise the effect of the epidemic on the crowded city and saved many lives:

> The governor of Acre checked the progress of this plague, by giving the inhabitants the means of withdrawing from its ravages; and these means, though contrary to the dogmas of the Mohametan religion, were eagerly embraced. The Europeans became their models; and the governor, after deriving them from every necessary information, shut himself up, after their example, together with his numerous family. The Muphti [*mufti*, top religious judge of Acre] alone, born the protector of the Mohametan law, cannot imitate a conduct which that law condemns. Instead of shutting himself up with silence in a prudent confinement, he thundered forth against this new method; reproached the governor for his conduct ... The governor, however, only laughed at this pious folly of the Muphti and sent a detachment of soldiers to impose a fine on him of two hundred and fifty sequins.[6] (Mariti 1792: 200–201, 203–204)

Al-ʿUmar, like Muhammad ʿAli of Egypt (1769–1849) and unlike the Palestinian Ottoman urban elites of Nablus and Jerusalem, was a rule-breaker and a ruler-maker, not a rule-taker, These urban elites were in a subordinate state of affairs where the power dynamic put them at a position of less influence, authority and significance than their imperial Ottoman 'rule-maker'. By contrast, al-'Umar's effectively independent regime was created in direct opposition and as a challenge to the authority of the Ottoman rule in Palestine, while nominally acknowledging the legitimacy of the Ottoman Caliph. Al-'Umar's authority operated within the context of Islamic legitimacy and power and Islamic history of Palestine produced a variety of notions of power, authority and legitimacy. Al-'Umar's state has been referred to by its detractors as a sheikhdom, while the late Albert Hourani referred to it as a 'little kingdom' (cited in Joudeh 2015), but it would be more appropriate to describe it as a sovereign 'frontier state' in most of Palestine for over a quarter of a century. However, it could be described as an emirate within the wider historical Islamic context of power and legitimacy. Historically an emirate was a geo-political entity or state that was ruled by a Muslim emir, sultan, sheikh, military commander, governor or prince. Etymologically emirate or amirate (Arabic: *imarah*) is the administration of territorial entity of an emir. The Arabic term could also imply principality. Under Islam, and until recently, emirates were a common form of governance and actual statehood. The variety of emirates included the famous Emirate of Córdoba, which was an independent state in Andalusia between 756 and 929, with Córdoba as its capital. Initially acknowledging the legitimacy of the Umayyad Caliphs in Damascus, in fact the Emirate of Córdoba not only grew in direct opposition to the Abbasid state and rejection of the Abbasid Caliphs in Baghdad, but also evolved and transformed itself into the Caliphate of Córdoba. With its capital in Córdoba, this state existed from 929 to 1031 and was at the time one of the most developed countries in the world. Also in Andalusia, the Emirate of Granada (also known as the Nasrid Kingdom of Granada; Spanish: Reino Nazarí de Granada), was established in 1248 and aligned with the Christian Kingdom of Castile, and remained a tributary state for the next 250 years. It was the last state in the Iberian Peninsula to be ruled by Muslims. Several centuries later, at the height of al-'Umar's power in Palestine in the mid-18th century, Kuwait became an emirate in the 1750s, headed by the Shaykh of Kuwait. In the late 19th century the Emirate of Kuwait became a British protectorate and it has since evolved into a modern state. Had al-'Umar's state survived the death of its founder in 1775 and persisted well into the 19th century, today the modern history of

Palestine would be read and written with the eyes of the indigenous people of Palestine, rather than through Ottoman, British or Zionist perspectives.

The lasting impact of al-'Umar's *dawlah qutriyyah* and al-Jazzar's powerful autonomous regime on both European and late Ottoman thinking as well as on the modern Palestinian psyche and memories can hardly be overstated. In the mid-18th century al-'Umar shifted the centre of power in Galilee from Safad (and the *Liwa* of Safad) to Acre, a town which al-'Umar transformed into one of the biggest, wealthiest and most well-fortified cities of the al-Sham region. It is hardly a coincidence, therefore, that in 1799 Napoleon Bonaparte sought but failed to conquer the city. Seventy years later, in the early 1870s – as we shall see in chapter nine – the Ottomans reorganised Palestine and created the *sanjak* of Acre as one of three administrative regions in the country. For nearly five centuries from 1266 until the early 18th century, Safad was the capital of the Galilee and after 1517 the Ottomans confirmed its administrative position in Galilee by creating the administrative *sanjak* of Safad. In view of the fact that the Safad had dominated the Galilee and northern Palestine for centuries under both the Mamluks and Ottomans, the creation of the *sanjak* of Acre in the late Ottoman period should also be counted as one the lasting legacies of 18th century Palestine under al-'Umar and al-Jazzar for the late Ottoman perception, and administrative reorganisation, of Palestine. Above all, al-'Umar's powerful regime provided an alternative model to the intermediary (patron–client) elite politics of Palestine and to the family-oriented, fiercely competitive and deeply fractious urban elite politics which bedevilled both late Ottoman and Mandatory Palestine until 1948.

Chapter 9

BEING PALESTINE, BECOMING PALESTINE

Rediscovery and new representations of modern Palestine and their impact on Palestinian national identity

We have on this earth what makes life worth living
the aroma of bread at dawn
a woman's opinion of men
the works of Aeschylus
the beginnings of love
grass on a stone
mothers who live on a flute's sigh
and the invaders' fear of memories
...
we have on this earth what makes life worth living
on this earth, the lady of earth
the mother of all beginnings
the mother of all endings
she was called Palestine
she came to be called Palestine
o lady, beause you are my lady
I am worthy of life
(Mahmoud Darwish, *On This Earth*[1])

NEW REPRESENTATIONS OF PALESTINE, 1805–1917

> For over two millennia, Palestine has been the destination of the three
> monotheisms. While some of these men and women offered sacrifices,
> collected relics, and prayed, others studied fought, preached, excavated
> or conquered. A rich granary in the Fertile Crescent, no land has
> been as much the focus of religious tourism and piety, pilgrimage and
> colonization as Palestine. (Matar 2013: 913)

Modern European travellers, pilgrims, writers, cartographers, geographers, biblical Orientalists and romance seekers had no historical, geographic or archaeological evidence or good reason to refer to modern Palestine as 'Cana'an'. They logically reproduced ancient maps of Palaestina, maps derived from more than a millennium and a half of Classical Antiquity and Byzantine Christianity. They also relied on the Hellenistic, Roman, early Christian, Byzantine and Arab Islamic toponymic memory and heritage of the country.

In the 17th and 18th centuries European romantic Orientalist and 'biblical geography' of Palestine increased phenomenally and voluminous publications on the historical geography of Palestine began to appear not only in Latin but in vernacular European languages. This included the works of Hadrianus Relandus (1676–1718), a prominent Dutch Orientalist, cartographer and philologist who made a lasting contribution to research on the scriptural geography of Palestine (Pailin 1984: 212). His work was mainly philological-theological in character and included *Antiquitates Sacrae veterum Hebraeorum* (1708) and *Palaestina ex monumentis Veteris illustrata* (1714), written in Latin, in which he sought to describe the geography of 'biblical Palestine'.

WESTERN TRAVELOGUES OF PALESTINE: THE DISTINCTION BETWEEN PALESTINE/ HOLY LAND AND SYRIA

For many decades in the 18th century the Galilee-based autonomous regime of Dhaher al-'Umar – with its increased trade links with France and Britain in particular – effectively linked the Galilee with the entire Palestinian coast from Lebanon to Gaza. It is not surprising, therefore, that throughout the 19th century the combined effect of European travelogues ('travels in Palestine'), guide books, religious treatises, novels, pilgrims' accounts and maps made a clear distinction between 'Palestine' and 'Syria' and treated historic Palestine/Holy Land for all practical purposes as a separate country. Moreover, throughout the 19th century for European and Russian travellers and pilgrims Palestine and the Holy Land were synonymous and interchangeable. This synonymy did not include Syria, which made Palestine sharply distinct from Syria to the north. In the 19th century religious revivalism, combined with feverish messianic nationalism, 'back to the Bible' movements and 'rediscovery' of Palestine, swept across Europe and Russia. Moreover, in European and Russian Orientalisms of the 19th century 'Palestine' and the 'Holy Land/ *Terra Sancta*/the land of Jesus' were interchangeable. This religio-political perception of Palestine, steeped in the stories of the New Testament, made Palestine/the Holy Land seem sharply distinct from Syria and Lebanon and made the Galilee (the birthplace of Jesus and the scene of many of the stories of the New Testament) inherently and closely linked with Jerusalem, Bethlehem, Hebron, Jaffa and Gaza, more than its traditionally close links under Islam with the vast al-Sham region.

The popularisation of the concept of Palestine was illustrated by the mountains of geographical literature on Palestine listed in the 1890 *Bibliotheca geographica Palaestinae* by Gustav Reinhold Röhricht, a German historian of the Crusades. Röhricht provided a census of 3515 print and manuscript accounts dedicated to Palestine literature between 333 AD and 1878 AD. The work also had a chronological list of maps relating to Palestine. Röhricht's survey of Palestine literature and publications shows the following:

(a)   333 to 1300 AD: 177 works
(b)   14th century: 97
(c)   15th century – with the invention of the printing press–: 279
(d)   16th century: 333
(e)   17th century: 390
(f)   18th century: 318

(g)   19th century (until 1878) – with the replacement of the hand-operated Gutenberg-style presses by steam-powered presses which allowed printing on an industrial scale –:1915 works. (Shalev 2012: 79)

However, this remarkable survey was far from being exhaustive. Western travelogues of Palestine in the 18th and 19th centuries included thousands of books, articles and other materials detailing accounts of the journeys of European, Russian and North American travellers to the Holy Land. Fuelled by modern capitalism, new printing technologies and new transport means, many of the travelogues on Palestine treated the country not so much as a land of living histories and shared memories of ordinary people but more of a memorial to Western Christianity – a Christianity in search of a new identity in the midst of the raging struggle between scientific rationalism and scepticism, on the one hand, and literalist evangelist fundamentalism, on the other. Typically, a Church of England journal, *The Church Quarterly Review* of 1891, described Röhricht's book as 'indispensable' to students of Palestinian geography. Röhricht's survey of Palestine literature is most revealing with regard to two particular periods: the Renaissance period and the 19th century. These two periods experienced two major European technological revolutions with considerable impact on the Palestine literature: first, the Renaissance printing revolution press from the late 15th century introduced the era of mass circulation of publications and second, in the 19th century the replacement of the hand-operated Gutenberg-style press by the steam-powered press allowed printing and publication on an industrial scale. This unprecedented industrial scale of production, circulation and consumption of Palestine/Holy Land knowledge was aided by the photographic revolution of the 1830s which began to produce masses of images of the Holy Land for the European, American and Russian markets.

A few examples of the large amounts of Palestine literature, including geographic publications on and 'travels in' Palestine in the 19th century, in several key European languages, include John Lewis Burckhardt's *Travels in Syria and the Holy Land* (1822); Thomas Wright's *Early Travels in Palestine* (1848), which consists of accounts of the early pilgrims to Palestine, and Leslie Porter's *A Handbook for Travellers in Syria and Palestine: Including an*

Account of the Geography, History, Antiquities, Inhabitants of these Countries,
Part 1 and 2 (1858, 1868), Vital Cuinet, Syrie, Liban et Palestine: *géographie administrative, statistique, descriptive et raisonnée* (1896); Titus Tobler's *Dritte Wanderung nach Palästina* (1859); and *Bibliographia Geographica Palestinae* (1867). John Murray, one of the most important and influential publishers in Britain, produced Porter's *A Handbook for Travellers in Syria and Palestine,* which treats Palestine as a separate country. This book describes Palestine in three major sections: Part I 'Palestine-Jerusalem' and 'Southern Palestine', which includes cities from Gaza to Jaffa, and Part 2 with two sections: (a) 'Northern Palestine', which included the Galilee and Damascus, and (b) 'Northern Syria'. In a similar vein, Joseph Meen's *Geography of Palestine: Historical and Descriptive* (1865) and Walter McLeod's *The Geography of Palestine, or, the Holy Land, Including Phoenicia and Philistia* (1856) were typical of the large number of books on the historical geography of Palestine published in Britain and Europe in the middle of the 19th century. These historical-geographic publications treated Palestine as a distinct country and a geo-political unit separate from Syria, Egypt and Arabia. It is also worth pointing out that the expression 'Southern Syria', which appeared briefly in the early 20th century, was never mentioned in these publications.

Crucially, in the second half of the 19th century translations of articles and books into Arabic began to distinguish clearly between Syria and Palestine. For instance, in 1883 George Edward Post's article 'Plants of Syria and Palestine' was published in the Arabic journal *al-Muqtataf* (1883), which was founded in 1876 at the Syrian Protestant College, today the American University of Beirut, before moving to Cairo in 1884. The same distinction is also found in the Arabic version of Post's *Nabat Suriyya wa-Filastin wa-al-Qatr al-Misri wa-Bawadiha (Flora of Syria and Palestine and Sinai: A Handbook of the Flowering Plants and Ferns Native and Naturalized from the Taurus to Ras Muhammad and from the Mediterranean Sea to the Syrian Desert)* (1896), an indication that by the 1880s European publications on Palestine geography and their translations into Arabic were beginning to have an impact on modern Arab perceptions of Palestine (Foster 2013) and the evolving notion that Palestine was a distinct geo-political unit.

The work of Guy Le Strange, a scholar of Arabic and Persian at Cambridge University, on the historical geography of Palestine under Islam in the Middle Ages, added another dimension to British preoccupation with Palestine in the second half of the 19th century. Guy Le Strange's *Palestine under the Moslems; A Description of Syria and the Holy Land from A.D. 650 to 1500. Translated from the Works of the Mediaeval Arab Geographers*, was published in London by the Committee of the Palestine Exploration Fund (PEF) in 1890. The PEF, founded in 1865, had already focused on Palestine/the Holy Land. Other antecedents to the PEF also focused on Palestine/the Holy Land and made a clear distinction between Palestine and Syria. This included the evangelical British Palestine Association, established sixty years before the PEF. The formation of the Palestine Association in the early 19th century had been spurred by the Napoleonic wars and the 1798–1801 French invasion and campaign in Egypt and Palestine. Napoleon's defeat at Acre in 1799 is one of the best-known episodes of modern world history. The collapse of his siege of Acre – the city known in Europe as the last capital of the Latin Crusader Kingdom of Jerusalem – in 1799 with the full support of British maritime power ushered in a new era in British direct involvement in the region and the beginnings of British religio-political distinction between Palestine and Syria. This became evident in a long romantic-evangelical poem from 1803, *Palestine*, which was composed by a clergyman, Reginald Heber, later known as Bishop of Calcutta, with the help of Sir Walter Scott. The popular poem was recited in London theatres and was later published, and set to music by the composer William Crotch, a professor of music at Oxford University. The increasing British evangelical involvement in Palestine also became evident in the renaming of the Palestine Association, which was established in 1805 shortly after the departure of the French from the region. This society had initially been founded in March 1805 under the name Syrian Society. A month later, on 24 April 1805, its founders decided that the Syrian Society 'shall henceforth be denominated The Palestine Association'. The Palestine Association was co-founded and led by William Richard Hamilton (1777–1859), a British diplomat, traveller, antiquarian and Egyptologist who later served as Under-Secretary for Foreign Affairs. The Association was formally disbanded in 1834 and incorporated into the Royal Geographical Society (Silberman 1982; Kark and Goren 2011).

Le Strange's *Palestine under the Moslems* (1890, 2010, 2014) placed the image of the Dome of the Rock on its cover and contained maps and illustrations. His work, which introduces 'the mass of information which lies buried in the Arabic texts of the Moslem geographers and travellers of the Middle Ages' (Le Strange 1890: Preface), provided vivid descriptions of Jund Filastin under Islam on the basis of the accounts of the 10th century Palestinian Jerusalemite historian and geographer al-Maqdisi and his work, *Ahsan al-Taqasim Fi Ma'rifat al-Aqalim* (*The Best Divisions for Knowledge of the Regions*) (al-Maqdisi 1994, 2002). Le Strange had already translated from Arabic into English and published in 1886 al-Maqdisi's famous work under the title *al-Mukaddasi's Description of Syria and Palestine*, and this title by Le Strange also underlines the sharp geo-political distinction between Palestine and Syria in European thinking in the 19th century.

The clear distinction between Palestine/the Holy Land, on the one hand, and Syria/al-Sham, on the other, was not exclusively European; as we have already seen, in the 17th century Palestinian Muslim author Salih ibn Ahmad al-Tumurtashi made that distinction in his work *The Complete Knowledge in Remembering the Holy Land and Its Boundaries and Remembering Palestine and its Boundaries and al-Sham* (1695–1696). Also, successive generations of medieval and modern Christian pilgrims referred to geographical subdivision of Palestine, Syria and Arabia. For educated local Palestinians, familiar with both classical Arab Islamic writings on Palestine and al-Sham and European publications on Palestine, and for ordinary Palestinians observing the caravans of European and Russian pilgrims at close quarters, this distinction between Palestine/the Holy Land and Syria would be taken for granted. Western-funded, Roman Catholic *Terra Sancta* schools based in the urban centres of Palestine where most Palestinian Christians resided began to appear in Nazareth, Jaffa, Bethlehem and Jerusalem, and for Palestinians educated in the European and Russian schools at home or abroad the production of the European 'knowledge' on the historical geography of Palestine/the Holy Land as well as the mushrooming of European consulates in Palestine would also be a matter of great interest and some concern. From the mid-19th century, with the improvement of communication and establishment of several European consulates in Palestine, the 'Grand Tour' of the 18th century – the traditional trip undertaken by mainly upper class European young men of means through Italian cities – was replaced by the 'Cook Tour' (organised by Thomas Cook): middle class early mass tourism and travels in 'Greece, Palestine and Egypt'. Thomas Cook arranged for the German Kaiser Wilhelm II to visit Palestine in 1898. The 'Cook's Tour' and Thomas Cook Holy Land Tourism also spawned numerous publications in many European languages on the 'geography of Palestine' and the Holy Land, many of which were also accessible to members of the educated Palestinian elite and Ottoman officials. On a popular level, European mass tourism in Palestine impacted on the Palestinian vernacular and, over time, intro-duced many French and Italian words into Palestinian Arabic – words such as hotel (otel), chauffeur, douche, beton (baton), mode (moda), canapé (canabai), salon, balcon (balconeh), billet (bolet), farmacia (farmashiyyah), souvenir, ascenseur, (ascensel), dossier (dusiyyeh), automobile, Benzina (banzin) and garage (karaj) still commonly in use today.

In the 19th century and early 20th century much of the European knowledge production on Palestine in books and travel diaries remained dominated by Biblical Studies, Scriptural Geography, Orientalism in which the Palestinian Arabs were portrayed as a 'simple appendix to the ancient Biblical [landscape] ... as "shadows" of the far-off past, "fossils" suspended in time' (Kamel 2014, 2015), while the Arab *fallahin* (peasants) of modern Palestine were viewed as symbols of the 'biblical Jews' (Gil, E. 2006). However, as early as the mid-19th century, biblical archaeologist and scriptural geographer Edward Robinson (1794–1863), writing in the early 1860s when travel by Europeans to the Levant became widespread, notes '*Palestine*, or *Palestina*, now the most common name for the Holy Land' (Robinson, E. 1865: 15; see also Robinson 1841; and Robinson et al. 1860).

This observation is also evident from Victor Guérin's seven-volume *Description géographique, historique et archéologique de la Palestine* (1868–1880; also Guérin 1881–1883). In the 1860s, the British had set up the Palestine Exploration Fund, which sponsored the *Survey of Western Palestine* and mounted geographical map-making expeditions in Palestine. The PEF was a typical example of the 'learned societies' founded in Britain and was responsible for processing the empire's notions and theories into pseudo-scientific Orientalist thinking and argumentation, leading to the shaping of British policy and intentionality which finds its apotheosis in the Balfour Declaration of 2 November 1917. One of the main political motives of the PEF was clear from its own publication: *Names and Places in the Old and New Testament and Apocrypha: With their Modern Identifications* (Palestine Exploration Fund 1889). The Palestine Exploration Fund listed more than 1150 place names related to the Old Testament and 162 related to the New Testament. British rule in Palestine formally began on 11 December 1917 when General Allenby officially entered the Old City of Jerusalem. Shortly after the British military occupation of Palestine, the British authorities set out to gather toponymic information from the local Palestinian inhabitants. The European preoccupation with 'biblical place names' and with Jerusalem, and the European and American growth of 'Bible Studies', had some impact on official Ottoman thinking and on the writings of some Palestinian nationalist authors. The latter sought to construct a counter-Zionist discourse by couching modern Palestinian nationalism in primordialist terms, rooted in Canaanite roots and the 'Land of Canaan' (see, for instance, Cattan 1969: 3–4).

PALESTINE-FOCUSED RUSSIAN ORIENTALISM IN THE LATE OTTOMAN PERIOD

> Branch from Palestine
> Tell me the Palestine branch:
> Where you grew up, where are you blooming?
> What kind of hills, some valleys
> Your decoration was?
> You were the pure waters of the Jordan
> East beam caressed you,
> Night is the wind in the mountains of Lebanon
> …
> You stand, the branch of Jerusalem,
> Shrine of the correct time!
> Transparent dusk beam lamps,
> And the ark of the cross, the symbol of the holy ...
> (Mikhail Yuryevich Lermontov 1837)[2]

Palm Sunday is a Christian feast before Easter which commemorates Jesus' triumphant entry into Jerusalem. The 1837 poem *Vetka Palestiny* (*The Palm Branch of Palestine*) by Mikhail Yuryevich Lermontov (1814–1841), a highly influential Russian Romantic poet also called 'the poet of the Caucasus' and the most important figure of Russian poetry after Alexander Pushkin's death in 1837, encapsulated Russian Orientalism and late Ottoman Palestine. With strong echoes of European Romanticism (1800–1850), the 1803 romantic poem by Reginald Heber, Lermontov's romantic-evangelical poem evokes the stories both of the Gospels and of Russian pilgrimage to Palestine in the 19th century, three-quarters of which pilgrimage took place at Easter (Hummel and Hummel 1995). This evangelising poetry was inspired by the religious imagination of the country the poet called 'Palestine', although Lermontov had never visited it (Merlo 2013). In the 19th century Russian Orientalist Orthodox representations of Palestine went hand in hand. Crucially, Russian writings on, and political activities in the country had a major impact on the perception, conception and actual events of late Ottoman Palestine.

Earlier in 1820 Dmitrij Daškov, a diplomat and the second counsellor of the Russian Embassy in Istanbul, was the first Russian writer who went to Palestine as a pilgrim. He also wrote an essay entitled on his travels (Merlo 2013). In fact, many of the Russian historical and literary representations of Palestine in the 19th century were actual descriptions and narrations of Russian pilgrims (Hopwood 1969: 10; Merlo 2013[3]). In 1848 Nikolai Gogol (1809–1852), the leading figure of Russian literary realism, went on a pilgrimage to Palestine. The romantic Orientalist representations of Palestine by Lermontov and other Russian Romantics of the 19th century also harked back to the history of early Christianity and of Palaestina under the Byzantines, a period in which, as we have seen in chapter four, the Palestine Orthodox Church became self-governing and emerged as one of the top five churches governing Christendom.

Lermontov's poem had also anticipated Russia's significantly increasing presence in Palestine, which began in 1844 with the arrival of the first Russian Orthodox Archimandrite in Palestine. Also in the 1840s, the Russians obtained permission to build a huge compound in Jerusalem. This was constructed after the Crimean War, in 1860–1864. Russian efforts culminated in the founding of the Russian Orthodox Palestine Society in

St Petersburg in 1882. In 1889 the word 'Imperial' was added to the name and the Society became known as the Imperial Russian Orthodox Palestine Society (Russian: Императорское православное палестинское общество; Turkish: Rus İmparatorluğu Ortodoks Filistin Cemiyeti; Arabic: الجمعية الإمبراطورية الأرثوذكسية الفلسطينية) (Hopwood 1969: 150–154) and to the Palestinian Orthodox community in Arabic as the Palestinian Orthodox Imperial Society (الجمعية الإمبراطورية الأرثوذكسية الفلسطينية). Spurred by the establishment of the British Palestine Exploration Fund in 1865, and its imperial, quasi-military, scientific expeditions to Palestine in the 1870s (see below), the Imperial Russian Orthodox Palestine Society was founded by politician and writer Vasili Nikolaevich Khitrovo (1834–1903), author of *Palestina i Sina* (2011), and chaired by the Grand Duke Sergei Alexandrovich who had visited Palestine in 1881. The Imperial Russian Orthodox Palestine Society was a scholarly, educational and social organisation. In addition to promoting and organising Russian pilgrimage to the Holy Land, it built schools and hospitals in Palestine and acted as a public body defending Russian interests (Stavrou 1961). The Society published its own research in two journals: *Soobsheniya Imperatorskovo Pravoslavnovo Palestinskovo Obshestva* (*Imperial Orthodox Palestinian Society Reports*) and the *Palestinskij Sbornik* (*Palestinian Collections*). It also established a translation and publishing house in Jerusalem partly in support of its extensive Arabic-language schools and secular teacher training seminaries in late Ottoman Palestine, the first of their kind in modern Palestine. These pioneering teacher training colleges paved the way for modern secular higher education in Palestine and for the Arab College (also known as the Government Arab College), a Jerusalem-based university college which existed throughout the Mandatory period from 1918 until 1948.

Following the 1905 Russian Revolution there was some decline in the budgets of the Imperial Orthodox Palestinian Society. After the Bolshevik Revolution of October 1917 the Society was renamed the Russian Palestine Society (Russian: Российское Палестинское Общество; Arabic: الجمعية الروسية الفلسطينية) and was attached to the Academy of Sciences of the USSR. During the Mandatory period, severe restrictions were imposed on the activities of the Society in Palestine by the British and after 1948 Israel confiscated much of its land and property. However, the original

19th century name of the Society, Imperial Russian Orthodox Palestine Society, was restored in 1992 following the dissolution of the Soviet Union in December 1991 and the creation of the Russian Federation. Furthermore, today the Society operates and runs projects in Palestine under its original 'Palestinian' Arabic name coined in the late 19th century: the Palestinian Orthodox Imperial Society.

The coat of arms of the Russian Empire, with its double-headed eagle, was formerly associated with the Byzantine Empire. The rulers of Russia had long held themselves to be the main protectors of Christian Orthodoxy, especially after most of the membership of the Greek Orthodox churches from 1460 until Greek rebellion of 1821 fell under the control of the Ottomans. In the 19th century imperial Russia continued to view itself as the 'Third Rome' and the successor to the Byzantine Empire. It continued to pose a serious geo-political threat to the Ottoman state. The latter sought alliances with other European powers, notably the British and French, to keep Russian ambitions in check. This led to the Crimean War of 1853–1856, whose immediate cause involved the European competition over Jerusalem and the rights of Orthodox Christian minorities in Palestine. The Orthodox Christians were the largest group among the Christian Palestinians. The Russians not only saw themselves as heirs to Orthodox Christianity and the Byzantine Empire in the East and protectors of the Orthodox community in Palestine, they were also concerned about the sharp decline in the proportion of the Orthodox among Palestinian Christians from 90 per cent in 1840 to about two-thirds in 1880 as a result of the proselyting activities of the Protestant and Roman Catholic churches.

In the second half of the 19th century Russia, competing for influence in Palestine with other European powers, took practical steps aimed at consolidating the Russian presence. The Russian Consulate was established in Jerusalem in 1858. This was followed by the setting up of the Committee for Palestine (اللجنة الفلسطينية) (1858–1864), a body supported by the Russian Foreign Ministry, and in 1860 the Russian Palestine Society (RPS) was also founded. The RPS guided Russian pilgrims to Palestine, bought property and built hospices, churches and schools in Jerusalem and Nazareth. This led to the establishment of a Russian colony ('compound') in Jerusalem in the 1860s. In 1864 the Committee for Palestine was created in the

Department for Asia of the Ministry of Foreign Affairs (1864–1889) (Merlo 2013). In 1890 the imperial Russian government supported and approved the establishment of Hovevei Tzion, a registered Russian charity officially known as the Society for the Support of Jewish Farmers and Artisans in Syria and Palestine (Общество по поддержке еврейских фермеров и ремесленников в Сирию и Палестину).

Subsidised by the Russian government, and passing through Jaffa, by 1910 about 8000 Russian (predominately peasant) pilgrims visited Palestine every year,[4] and by the First World War the average annual number rose to about 14,000. Organised by the Imperial Russian Orthodox Palestine Society, this influx of Russian pilgrims had an impact on Ottoman administrative reorganisation of Palestine in the early 20th century. Russian writings on, and mass pilgrimage to, late Ottoman Palestine were very important for a variety of political reasons and had (intended and unintended) consequences:

- Russian writings on Palestine inspired early Zionist colonial-settlers: Hovevei Tzion ('Lovers of Zion') who began to arrive from the territories of the Russian Empire in the 1880s. In 1890 the establishment of Hovevei Tzion as a registered Russian charity was officially approved by the imperial Russian government as the Society for the Support of Jewish Farmers and Artisans in Syria and Palestine (Общество по поддержке еврейских фермеров и ремесленников в Сирию и Палестину), which came to be popularly known among Zionist settlers as the Odessa Committee. Arabic and French were the two key languages of the educated classes of late 19th century Palestine and the Russian Society soon came to be known as 'Société pour le soutien des agriculteurs et les artisans juifs en Syrie et en Palestine'. It was dedicated to the practical aspects of establishing agricultural colonies and its projects included help in the founding of the early Zionist colonies (*moshavot*) of Rehovot and Hadera.
- The Russian Zionists dominated the World Zionist Organisation created by Theodor Herzl in the late 19th century.[5]
- The ambitions of the Russian Empire posed the greatest threat to the Ottoman Empire throughout much of the 19th century.

- As we shall see below, the clergy of the Russian Orthodox Church in Palestine, although technically in communion with the Greek-dominated Orthodox Patriarchate of Jerusalem, openly championed the local Palestinian Arab Orthodox community. Backed by the Russian authorities, the social and educational activities of the Russian Orthodox Church in Palestine and, more crucially, the Russian Orthodox Palestine Society founded in 1882 – after 1889 known to Palestinians as the Palestinian Orthodox Imperial Society (see below) – attracted sympathy from local Palestinian Orthodox Christians as it championed the radical idea that local Arab clergy should have cultural autonomy and should be promoted to be bishops and leaders of the Orthodox Patriarchate of Jerusalem, instead of the latter importing senior clergy from Greece.[6] In late Ottoman Palestine this idea had a galvanising effect on educated local Palestinian Orthodox Christians, many of whom were to become leading cultural figures, and in the forefront of the Palestinian nationalist struggle.

- The flourishing cultural and public spaces of late Ottoman Jerusalem and the reimagining of Palestinian territorial identity and growth of territorial patriotism and proto-nationalism, promoted by Palestinian Orthodox Arab intellectuals such Khalil Beidas in the late 19th century (see below), encouraged Palestinian Arab Orthodox journalists 'Issa al-'Issa (1878–1950) and his cousin Yousef Hanna al-'Issa to set up the daily newspaper *Falastin* ('Palestine') in Jaffa in January 1911; with its distinctly vernacular name, it was based on modern perceptions of Palestine. In late Ottoman Palestine the construction of a two-tier, Palestinian Arab/Ottoman, identity based on Ottoman citizenship and equality for all inhabitants was attempted. As we shall see, the newspaper *Falastin* (1911–1967) would also become not only one of the most influential voices of modern indigenous Palestinian national identity; it would also fiercely oppose Zionist settler-colonisation. For decades *Falastin* would remain dedicated to the cause of Palestine, to Palestinian territorial nationalism and pan-Arab solidarity, and to the Arab Orthodox community in its struggle with the Greek-dominated Orthodox Patriarchate of Jerusalem.

STRATEGIC AMBITIONS AND THE BRITISH PEACEFUL
CRUSADE: SCIENCE, EMPIRE AND THE MAPPING OF
PALESTINE BY THE PALESTINE EXPLORATION FUND
(1865–1877)

> We have there [in Palestine] a land teeming with fertility and rich
> in history, but almost without an inhabitant – a country without
> a people, and look! Scattered over the world, a people without a
> country. (Lord Shaftesbury, Chairman of the Palestine Exploration
> Fund, *Palestine Exploration Fund, Quarterly Statement for 1875*,
> London, 1875, p. 116)

Central to the Victorian 'peaceful' Crusader revivalism of the 19th century
and the successful opening of the 'Holy Land' to Europe's geo-political and
cultural-religious penetration was the British Palestine Exploration Fund and
'Ordnance Survey of Western Palestine' between 1871 and 1877. British scientific and technological advances in cartography and cadastral mapping were
fully harnessed for empire and imperial expansionism in the Middle East.
Ordnance Survey (OS) is the national mapping agency of Britain and is one
of the largest producers of maps in the world. The British official agency's
name indicates its original military and strategic purposes and its origins go
back to the mapping of Scotland in the aftermath of the Jacobite uprising
of 1745 and the absence of military maps and detailed knowledge of the
Scottish Highlands. The British were not the first to conduct instrumental
strategic mapping of Palestine. The first modern maps of Palestine, based on
an instrumental survey and using the most developed scientific instruments
of the time, had already been produced by Colonel Pierre Jacotin, a French
map-maker and Director of the French Survey Military Corps during Napoleon's expedition in Egypt and Palestine, who in 1799, on Napoleon's orders,
prepared dozens of secret maps of Egypt, Sinai and Palestine. Six of those
maps show parts of Palestine, especially the parts of the country through
which Napoleon's army marched in February to June 1799. Jacotin continued
to work on these maps after he returned to France and they were eventually
published in 1826, and became widely known as the 'Jacotin Atlas', labelling
Palestine in French and Arabic as 'Palestine or Holy Land'/'land of al-Quds'

(فلسطين أو أرض قدس) (also Khatib 2003; Karmon 1960: 155–173, 244–253). This cartographer representation of Palestine by the French would also find strong echoes in the establishment and naming of the autonomous admin-istrative province of al-Quds: متصرفية القدس الشريف (Mutasarrifate of Noble Jerusalem) by the Ottomans fifty years later, in 1872 (see pp. 259-260). The *Jacotin Map of Palestine*, surveyed during Napoleon's campaign in 1799, was also later published by the Palestine Exploration Fund (Kallner 1944). British colonial ambitions in late 19th century Palestine and the lack of detailed British military maps of the area were two of the key factors behind the formation of the British Palestine Exploration Fund and 'British Ordnance Survey of Western Palestine' in the 1870s.

As we shall see in chapter ten, the Israeli toponymic projects in the post-1948 period had their foundations in the de-Arabisation activities of James Finn and the biblical explorations in the 1870s by members of the Palestine Exploration Fund whose work, *Names and Places in the Old and New Testament and Apocrypha: with their modern identifications* (compiled by George Armstrong; revised by Sir Charles W. Wilson and Major C. R. Conder 1889), was central to British colonial toponymic projects in Pales-tine in the late 19th and first half of the 20th century.

The systematic mapping, surveying and place-naming projects, which reached their peak with the British Ordnance Survey of Western Palestine between 1871 and 1877, were largely strategic. The sacredness of Palestine was not a sufficiently convincing reason for the British to organise and finance such surveys. The main motive for mapping the country as a whole was its strategic and geo-political importance for the British Empire, which was then engaged in international struggles over the Middle East (Goren 2002: 87–110). However, the surveys and mapping of the British Royal Engineering Corp in the 1870s led subsequently to the growth of proto-Jewish Zionism.

The British Palestine Exploration Fund was founded in 1865 by a group of biblical scholars, scriptural geographers, military and intelligence officers and Protestant clergymen, most notably the Dean of Westminster Abbey, Arthur P. Stanley. Its 'scientific exploration' was coordinated very closely with the British politico-military establishment and intelligence commu-nity anxious to penetrate Ottoman Palestine, a country ruled by the Muslim 'sick man of Europe'. With offices in central London, the PEF today is an active organisation which publishes an academic journal, the *Palestine Exploration Quarterly*. In addition, the PEF presents public lectures and funds research projects in the Near East. According to its website, 'Between 1867 and 1870 Captain Warren carried out the explorations in Palestine which form the basis for our knowledge of the topography of ancient Jerusalem and the archaeology of the Temple Mount/Haram al-Sherif [sic]'; 'In addition to his explorations on, under, and around the Temple Mount/ al-Haram al-Sherif, Warren surveyed the Plain of Philistia and carried out a very important [military] reconnaissance of central Jordan'.[7] Captain (later General Sir) Charles Warren (1840–1927) of the British Royal Engineers, one of the key officers of the PEF, who was sent to map the 'scriptural topography' of Jerusalem and investigate 'the site of the temple', noted: '[British] King Consul [James Finn] rules supreme, not over the natives of the city, but over strangers; but yet these strangers for the most part are the rightful owners, the natives, for the most part, are usurpers' (Shepherd 1987: 127–128). Both Warren and the (above-mentioned) long-serving and famous British Consul, Finn, who was a restorationist Christian Zionist involved with the 'Mission to the Jews' (Shepherd 1987: 110), apparently 'literally burrowed' beneath the Muslim shrines in Jerusalem to chart the 'original dimensions' of the 'Temple Mount'. The biblical archaeology and toponymic projects of Warren and the Royal Engineers have remained basic data for many Israeli archaeologists, geographers and strategic planners of today (Shepherd 1987: 195; Benvenisti 2002: 11–27).

Following in the footsteps of the PEF, the British Mandatory authorities in Palestine set out to gather toponymic information from the local Palestinian population. The British drive to present European colonialism as a continuation of an ancient Jewish ownership of the land meant that place names in Palestine became a site of fierce contest between the European Zionist settler-colonisers and the indigenous Palestinians. Palestinian Arab names were (and continued to be) 'unnamed' and Hebraicised by the Zionists using a colonising strategy based on Old Testament names. Local Palestinian place names were deemed 'redeemed' and liberated when they were rendered from Arabic into Hebrew (Slyomovics 1998, 2002). The genealogy of British colonial name commissions and the Zionist Hebrew renaming project, which began in the 19th century, lingered under the

British colonial system in Palestine (al-Shaikh 2010) and were accelerated dramatically after the Nakba and the expansion of biblical and archaeological departments at Israeli universities.

THE HISTORIC AND GEOGRAPHIC MAPS OF PALESTINE: THE NATIONAL GEOGRAPHIC

The long history and geography of Palestine (ancient, medieval and modern) are deeply ingrained in the social and cultural memory of Europe and the Arab world. In 1890 German historian Gustav Reinhold Röhricht, in *Bibliotheca Geographica Palestine*, listed 3515 books issued in many languages between 333 AD and 1878 AD which dealt with the geography of Palestine. Röhricht's work also contains a chronological list of maps relating to Palestine.

Preoccupation with the history, geography and cartography of Palestine was also evident in the publications of the *National Geographic*, formerly the *National Geographic Magazine*, the official magazine of the National Geographic Society, based in Washington, DC. The NGS is one of the largest non-profit scientific and educational institutions in the world. Its interests include geography, history, archaeology and natural sciences. The *National Geographic* has been published continuously since its first issue in 1888. The archives of the magazine show a huge focus on the cartography, history and archaeology of historic Palestine (ancient and modern). The historic 'Palestine Maps' (no mention of 'Maps of Canaan') of the *National Geographic* (not known to be particularly pro-Palestinian) produced the following titles: 'Impressions of Palestine', 1 March 1915 ('Former British Ambassador to the U.S., James Bryce, relates his impressions of a predominantly Muslim Palestine'); 'Jerusalem's Locust Plague: Being a Description of the Recent Locust Influx into Palestine, and Comparing Same with Ancient Locust Invasions as Narrated in the Old World's History Book, the Bible', 1 December 1915 ('John D. Whiting compares the recent invasion of locusts in Palestine and Syria with the ancient locust plagues described in the Bible'); 'Among the Bethlehem Shepherds: A Visit to the Valley Which David Probably Recalled When He Wrote the Twenty-third Psalm', 1 December 1926 ('Shepherd families of Palestine live much as their ancestors did; often the youngest boy tends the sheep, with flute and staff in hand'); 'Changing Palestine', 1 April 1934 ('Improved transportation and communication give Palestine growing room as the small but strategic land continues its role as a meeting place for East and West'); 'Bombs over Bible Lands', 1 August 1941 ('In Syria, Palestine, and Iraq, where Romans, Babylonians, and Assyrians once battled, Germany and Russia vie for control of the oil-rich nations, disrupting historic lands with bombs, planes, and tanks'); 'Palestine Today', 1 October 1946 ('Under the control of Great Britain, Palestine struggles to cope with immigration. Growing cities and farms make a strange mix in the ancient land'); 'An Archaeologist Looks at Palestine', 1 December 1947 ('The author encounters history at every turn, in an ancient land that has been a cockpit of unending conflict for many centuries').

PARADIGM SHIFT IN LATE OTTOMAN PALESTINE (1872–1917): HISTORICAL CONTINUITIES AND ADMINISTRATIVE DIVISION OF PALESTINE

'Abdul-Karim Rafeq, a distinguished Syrian historian who pioneered the use of sharia (Islamic law) court records (*sijillat*) as sources for social and especially urban history and wrote extensively on Ottoman Syria and Palestine, came across the Arabic term *Filastin* on a number of occasions (Rafeq 1990; Gerber 2008: 51). Among Rafeq's Arabic sources for late 19th century Palestine was an 1879 Arabic manuscript by Damascene author Nu'man al-Qasatli, entitled: 'al-Rawda al-Numaniyya in the Travelogue to Palestine and some Syrian Towns' (Rafeq 1990; Gerber 2008: 51), which provides an 1870s survey of Palestine. This increase in the use of the Arabic terminology of Falastin and Filastin in the second half of the 19th century and the growing perception (local, regional and international) that modern Palestine/Holy Land was distinct, if not separate, from modern Syria, were among the multiple indicators of the paradigm shift in the perception of late Ottoman Palestine. However, with reference to the textual 'usage' of the terms *Filastin, Filistin* and *Falastin* in indigenous 'literary-scholarly' sources in Arabic, the context of the predominantly pre-modern oral/aural culture of Palestine should always be kept in mind. Also, crucially, unlike the introduction of printing presses in Europe in the 15th century – which gradually led to mass literacy and mass publications – Palestine had its first printing presses five centuries later, in the late 19th century – and subsequently one famous printing press in Jaffa was called 'Palestine Press', 'مطبعة فلسطين'– therefore, inevitably the volume of 'literary-scholarly' output on Palestine in Arabic prior to the late 19th century (in comparison with the mountains of sources in European languages) was limited.

For a host of reasons (top of which was the European powers' scramble for, and actual penetration of, Palestine/Holy Land), the perception of the importance of Palestine by the rulers of the shrinking Ottoman Empire began to change radically in the second half of the 19th century. This was a gradual process and was also reflected in Ottoman Turkish–English dictionaries of the early and mid-19th century: the term 'Holy Land' was often rendered into 'Filastin'. One such original dictionary was produced in 1856 by Sir James Redhouse, An English and Turkish Dictionary, which was later used as the basis for many Turkish–English dictionaries, trans-lated the English term 'Holy Land' into the Arabic script as 'Dar Filastin' (دار فلسطين), or or 'land of Palestine'; Redhouse 1856.).[8] In Islamic termi-nology, with which both Redhouse and Ottoman officials were familiar, the Arabic singular form *dar* may mean 'house', 'place', 'land', 'country', 'region' or 'territory'. This dictionary was commissioned by the American Board of Commissioners for Foreign Missions, the largest and most important American missionary organisation in the 19th century. The Board started a new mission to Palestine in 1819. But Redhouse himself had worked for the Ottoman government for many years, first as a draftsman in the late 1820s before he returned to England in 1834 to publish his first Ottoman–English dictionary. In 1838 Redhouse returned to Istanbul to work for the Ottoman government as an interpreter to the Vezir-i Azam (effectively Prime Minister) and the Minister for Foreign Affairs. In 1840 Redhouse was transferred to the Ottoman Admiralty and became a member of the Ottoman Naval Council. In this capacity, he went to Syria-Palestine to help with communications between the British and Ottoman fleets which at the time were blockading the Egyptian forces in the Levant under the command of Ibrahim Pasha. After the end of Egyptian rule in Palestine and Syria in 1841 Redhouse received the Sultan's Imperial Order *Iftar Nisani* in 1941, one of the chivalric orders of the Ottoman Empire. He remained in Istanbul until 1853 before returning to London to work for the British Foreign Office.

Another key indicator of the shift in the perception of the country of Palestine/Holy Land was the Ottoman administrative reorganisation in Palestine – reforms which were partly instituted under growing pressure from the European allies who had backed the Ottoman Empire in its struggle against the Egyptian occupation of the Levant in 1831–1840 and during the Ottoman–Russian (Crimean) War of 1853–1858. The 'sick man of Europe' was also increasingly falling under the financial control of the European powers, whose penetration of Holy Land/Palestine was unstoppable. *Eyalets* (provinces or *pashaliks*) were a primary administrative divisions of the Ottoman Empire, a division which lasted from the mid-15th century until the 1860s, and were headed by senior officials known as *valis*, or general governor. In 1859, in *A Gazetter of the World. Or Dictionary of Geographical Knowledge* (Vol. 1), a member of the British Royal Geographic Society, described Acre as a *pashalik* of the Ottoman Empire and a part of Palestine. In the 1860s the greatly weakened Ottoman Empire replaced these *eyalets* with *vilayets* (Arabic: *wilayah*). Both the *eyalets* and *vilayets* were subdivided into *sanjaks* or *liwas*. The *sanjaks* were divided into *qadas*, which in turn were divided into *nahiyahs*. In the early 1870s the Ottomans also created a special administrative status for Jerusalem, together with four other sub-districts, called *mutasarrifiyyah* (Arabic) or *mutasarriflik* (Ottoman Turkish) (Büssow 2011: 5; Abu-Manneh 1999: 36). The administrative 'reforms' of the 1860s and 1870s were introduced under the impact of growing European influence and they followed the devastating Crimean War (1853–1856), which involved Russia, Britain, France and the weakened Ottoman Empire. The immediate cause of the war centred on the fierce struggle of European powers for Palestine and over the 'rights' of Christian minorities in the Holy Land. Combined with a power struggle for the Holy Land and Jerusalem, these cataclysmic events propelled Palestine to centre stage in both European and Ottoman thinking. The far-reaching Ottoman administrative changes of the 1860s and 1870s, combined with intense European rivalry over the Holy Land, not only produced administrative consequences for Palestine but also contributed to a profound shift in the way Palestine was perceived, reconfigured and experienced in the late Ottoman period.

The shift began with a change in the perception and reconceptualisation of Palestine in the course the late Ottoman period (Tamari 2011) and was embodied in the administrative and territorial reorganisation of the country. Inspired by the creation of the independent administrative Mutasarrifate of Mount Lebanon in 1861, the autonomous Mutasarrifate of Noble Jerusalem (Arabic: متصرفية القدس الشريف; Ottoman Turkish: Kudüs-i Şerif Mutasarrı-flığı) was established in 1872 and given the special administrative status of *mutasarrıflığı* or *mutasarriflik*. The shift in the perception of Palestine was partly reflected in the scale of the new Mutasarrifate of Noble Jerusalem. To begin with it was at least five times bigger than the *sanjaks* of Nablus and Acre put together. This very large Mutasarrifate was never intended to be a *sanjak* but rather a kind of super *sanjak*, practically a *wilayah*, an independent province completely separate and remarkably distinct from the historic Ottoman administrative divisions of al-Sham. Also, the political status of the Mutasarrifate of Noble Jerusalem was unique in another respect: it came under the direct authority of Istanbul (Büsso 2011; Khalidi, R. 1997: 174).

Crucially these radical and far-reaching administrative reorganisations in Palestine were carried out with the consent or active support of the influential local Palestinian elites (Foster 2016a). No local Palestinian opposition to administratively separating Jerusalem and much of Palestine from the al-Sham region was recorded. The Mutasarrifate of Noble Jerusalem consisted of, in addition to the district of Jerusalem, four other large districts (*qadas*): Jaffa, Gaza, al-Khalil (Hebron) and Beersheba. With its huge size, this made it effectively a new province, at the centre of which was the holy city of Jerusalem. The latter for many centuries had been central to Provincia Palaestina, Byzantine Palaestina Prima and the Arab province of Jund Filastin; it became the provincial capital of the Mutasarrifate of Noble Jerusalem, a new province which was often conflated or equated with 'Palestine'. In 1911–1912 the Governor of the Mutasarrifate of Jerusalem, Cevdet Bey, wrote a letter to the popular Jaffa-based newspaper *Falastin* (فلسطين) calling himself the 'Governor of Palestine' (Foster 2016b; also Kushner 1987).

In 1872 the Ottomans also created the administrative *sanjaks* of Nablus and Acre, both of which, together of the Mutasarrifate of Jerusalem, formed the territorial basis of Mandatory Palestine in 1917-18. However, historians failed to recognise that both the historical roots of Mandatory

Palestine and the territorial basis of the *sanjak* of Acre go back to the 18th century and to the fact that the province (*pashalik*) of Acre was not a traditional province created by the Ottoman authorities. The province of Acre was a modern creation of the mid-18th century. It was effectively imposed on the Ottoman Empire by Dhahir al-'Umar, who militarily defeated the Ottoman army, occupied Acre in 1749 and made it the capital of his Galilee-based emirate. The latter, in effect, had replaced the old Ottoman administrative province of Sidon. In fact, the weak Ottoman authorities were subsequently forced to recognise al-'Umar's regime in large parts of Palestine and he was officially granted by them the title of 'Sheikh of Acre, Emir of Nazareth, Tiberias, Safed, and Sheikh of all Galilee' (Philipp 2015). After al-'Umar's death, Ahmad Pasha al-Jazzar, now officially recognised as the Governor of the *pashalik* of Acre, continued to rule, as al-'Umar, from the same capital, Acre, from 1776 until his death in 1804. This modern regional, administrative and power legacy of the 18th century persisted well into the 19th century and formed the basis of the *sanjak* of Acre.

While the Ottomans, with the support of local Palestinian elites, sought to send a clear message by creating an important administrative distinction between *sanjak* (Acre and Nablus) and *mutasarriflik* (Mutasarrifate of Jerusalem), some otherwise perceptive authors continued to refer, rather inaccurately, to the Mutasarrifate of Jerusalem as the 'Sanjak of Jerusalem' (Abu-Manneh 1999). Clearly the naming, size and status of the Mutasarrifate of Jerusalem meant that it was consciously conceived as a 'super *sanjak*' with a particularly eminent status.

Ottoman administrative reorganisation of Palestine in the 1870s also provides us with some clues as to the unmistakable links between the politics and economy of 18th century Palestine and that of evolving late Ottoman Palestine. Acre and Nablus were Palestine's most powerful trade and manufacturing centres throughout most of the 18th and 19th centuries and both were central to Palestine's and al-Sham's global trade in cotton and textiles. Also, crucially, Acre had been the capital of two practically independent Palestine-based regimes, those of Dhaher al-'Umar and Ahmad Pasha al-Jazzar, for almost half a century from 1746 to 1804. Also, interestingly, when the two *sanjak*s of Nablus and Acre were established, they were initially placed under the political authority of the Mutasarrifate of Jerusalem, rather than that of

Damascus (al-Sham). This suggests the beginning of a new conceptualisation of Palestine based on the idea of a unified Holy Land – an idea which began to shape European thinking in the 19th century and a discourse with which both Ottoman officials in Palestine and local Palestinian elites were acutely aware – subject to direct rule from an Istanbul-appointed *mutasarrif*. The mutasarrifate and the two sanjaks of Acre and Nablus were commonly referred to locally and internationally as 'Palestine'.

Images and perceptions are always very powerful and the new south–north division of Palestine/Holy Land inadvertently echoed historic south–month divisions of the country under both the Byzantines (with originally Palaestina Prima and Palaestina Secunda) and early Islam (Jund Filastin and Jund al-Urdun). Paradoxically, however, although the *sanjaks* of Acre and Nablus were soon to be attached to the *wilayah* of Beirut, mainly in order to counter persistent Western intervention in the Holy Land/Palestine, the creation of the Mutasarrifate of Jerusalem (as well as the two *sanjaks* of Nablus and Acre) were perceived and actually referred to by the British consul in Jerusalem as the creation of 'Palestine into a separate *Eyalet*'[9] (Abu-Manneh 1999: 39). The boundaries of this distinct Palestine e*yalet*, or unified Holy Land, were (by and large) the territory which became known as Mandatory Palestine (Foster 2016b).

Officially the Ottoman authorities, deeply concerned about European interference in the 'Holy Land', sought to confine the geographic term Filastin to the Mutasarrifate of Noble Jerusalem and a 1913 Ottoman geography textbook (*Mekatib-i Ibtida'iye, Juğrafiya-i Osmani*, Matbaa-i 'Amire, 1332 [1913/1914], p. 193) had a map showing the Mutasarrifate of Jerusalem equated with فلسطين ('Palestine').[10] However, the combination of the *sanjaks* of Acre and Nablus with the province or Mutasarrifate of Noble Jerusalem produced a radically different perception of Palestine/Holy Land and the combination of the 'Three in One' administrative districts was referred to in the register of the Islamic Sharia Court of Jerusalem as 'Eyalet al-Quds' (the 'Province of Jerusalem') (Abu-Manneh 1999: 43).

Historical continuities in the geographic division of Palestine should be kept in mind. The three-way division of Ottoman Palestine from south (Mutasarrifate of Noble Jerusalem) to north (the sanjaks of Nablus and Acre respectively) echoes previous divisions of the country under both early Islam (Jund Filastin and Jund al-Urdun) and the Byzantines (Palaestina Prima, Palaestina Secunda and Palaestina Salutaris) (Rosen-Ayalon 2006: 15). Of course, perceptions are very powerful and with historical hindsight this perception of late Ottoman Palestine/Holy Land as 'Three in One' – 'One *mutasarriflik* and two *sanjaks* in one *eyalet*', centred on Jerusalem and led by the Mutasarrifate of Jerusalem – is not entirely unjustified or historically unprecedented. Historically, we have already seen this 'Three in One' representation of Provincia Palaestina under the Byzantines in Late Antiquity, during which period the notion of the Holy Land also emerged and was consolidated. Of course, the 'Three *sanjaks*' are equivalent to the 'Three Palestines' (Palaestina Prima, Palaestina Secunda, Palaestina Tertia); they are based on the creative analogy of 'Three in One'. The Ottomans were themselves direct heirs to Byzantium and would have been aware of Byzantine and Arab histories of the Near East and Palestine. After all, the autocephalous and independent 'All Palestine' Orthodox Church, based on the Church of Jerusalem, operated for centuries under the Ottomans and its Patriarchs were officially approved by the Ottoman government. But from British imperial or colonial perspectives, we can also see the 'Three in One' analogy in the way modern Iraq was constituted by the British after the First World War, and constructed from the three Ottoman provinces of Baghdad, Basra and Mosul, with the capital Baghdad providing the focal point for modern Iraq as well as the historical reference to the great Muslim capital under the Abbasids. In the case of Palestine, for the British (as well as for all European powers in the 19th century) Jerusalem provided the historical reference and focal point for the modern conception of Palestine.

Six important and closely related developments in the second half of the 19th and early 20th centuries contributed towards the 'unifying' factors of 'Three in One (Palestine) Eyalet'. These Palestine/Holy Land developments deeply affected the Ottoman reorganisation and actual administration of Palestine. These developments were:

- Large-scale pilgrimage and mass tourism in Palestine.
- The construction of new road systems to accommodate the influx of Christian pilgrims.

- The establishment of Palestine/Holy Land missions, both diplomatic and ecclesiastical.
- The new Palestine/Holy Land photography produced mountains of images and played a unifying factor.
- Holy Land knowledge production (scriptural mapping, ordinance surveys and archaeological excavations).
- Palestine archaeology and famous archaeological discoveries related to the extent and splendour of Byzantine Palaestina, such as the Madaba Mosaic Floor Map, discovered in 1884.

The town of Nazareth became very important at the end of the 19th century as the first modern carriage roads were built to serve the influx of Christian pilgrims and the main road was constructed in lower Galilee to connect the Christian holy places of Nazareth, Kafr Kanna and Tiberias (Karmon 1960: 251). The influx of Christian pilgrims and European tourists to Palestine linked the Galilee very closely with the rest of Palestine. And this can be seen in the construction of seven European-style clock towers at the heart of the public spaces of key cities of late Ottoman Palestine (Jaffa, Haifa, Acre, Nazareth, Safad, al-Quds and Nablus), built between 1900 and 1903 at local initiatives and from stones quarried in Palestine. Designed to commemorate the silver Jubilee of the reign of the Ottoman Sultan 'Abd al-Hamid II, the clock towers served as new symbols of modern time-keeping and modernity. With the exception of the clock tower of al-Quds — which was blown up by the British in 1922 — these clock towers have remained key landmarks of Palestinian modernity. The impact of the industrial-scale pilgrimage and modern mass tourism on the administration of late Palestine can hardly be overstated. Consequently, and, perhaps not surprisingly, in 1906 the two districts of Nazareth and Tiberias in the Galilee were attached to the Mutasarrifate of Noble Jerusalem, mainly in order to accommodate the new mass pilgrimage and tourism from Russia, Europe and the US and facilitate the issuance of a single tourist visa to Christian pilgrims and travellers in Palestine (Bussow 2011: 70; Kark 1994: 131).

Not only had they reinforced the links between, and 'unity' of, the Christian holy sites of Jerusalem and those of the Galilee (Nazareth and Tiberias included). They also began to have a major impact on the political economy and the new geographical perceptions of the country – perceptions, as we shall see below, shared by European and Ottoman officials in Palestine as well as local Palestinians.

Of course, throughout the second half of the 19th century Ottoman officials in Palestine were determined to resist European intervention in the Holy Land, while making concessions to European powers either under intense pressures or due to shifting Ottoman alliances with European powers. From the perspective of the changes in late Ottoman Palestine, the perception of the Ottoman administrative rearrangement of Palestine as a 'Three in One' province, consisting of two administrative *sanjaks* and *mutasarriflik* and centred on the Mutasarrifate of Noble Jerusalem, evidently had a major impact on British imperial thinking during the First World War but especially after 1918. For instance, in 1921 the first British High Commissioner for Palestine, Sir Herbert Samuel, established the Supreme Muslim Council which consisted of a president and four members, two of whom were to represent the former Mutasarrifate of Noble Jerusalem and the remaining two to represent the former *sanjaks* of Nablus and Acre. These two *sanjaks* and one *mutasarriflik* corresponded to the three administrative districts of late Ottoman Palestine (Dumper 1994).

Central to the paradigm shift in late Ottoman Palestine was the perception throughout the late 19th century that the Mutasarrifate of Jerusalem, together with the *sanjaks* of Nablus and Acre, unified historic 'Palestine', or the Holy Land, into a distinct country. This was not confined to European and Palestinian authors. Politically and strategically this conception was also evident from an important Ottoman document, *Filastin Risalesi*, a military handbook issued for limited distribution to the officers of the Eighth Army Corps in Palestine at the beginning of the First World War. A demographic and geographic survey of the Palestine province, the manual included topographic maps, statistical tables and a geo-ethnography of Palestine. It also contained a general map of the country in which the boundaries of Palestine extended far beyond the frontiers of the Mutasarrifate of Jerusalem. In 1872 the boundaries of this *mutasarriflik*, with its five districts (*qadas*) of Jerusalem, Jafa, Gaza, Beersheba and al-Khalil, had analogies to both the Byzantine delineation of Palaestina Prima and the early Arab Islamic delineation of Jund Filastin. The northern borders of the *Filastin Risalesi* map included the Litani River and the city of Tyre. The map encompassed all of the Galilee and parts of southern Lebanon, as well as the *sanjaks* of Nablus and Acre (Tamari 2011).

THE REIMAGINING OF PALESTINIAN TERRITORIAL IDENTITY AND PROTO-NATIONALISM IN LATE OTTOMAN PALESTINE: KHALIL BEIDAS AND PALESTINIAN CULTURAL NATIONALISM

Palestinian territorial nationalism, like the idea of Palestine, has multiple beginnings and multiple sources. In *Palestinian Identity: The Construction of Modern National Consciousness* (1998), Rashid Khalidi argues that a distinct Palestinian national identity grounded in the land of Palestine emerged in the early 20th century. But, at the same time, Khalidi and several prominent historians of modern Palestine, including Beshara Doumani (1995), Ilan Pappe (1999), Baruch Kimmerling and Joel S. Migdal (1993, 2003), all suggested that before the appearance of political Zionism in the late 19th century, a local Palestinian national identity had been in the making (Pappe 1999: 3). This nascent positive Palestinian national territorial identity in late Ottoman Palestine was not connected to Zionism. However, although an incipient local Palestinian national movement preceded the advent of Zionism in Palestine, this movement was also spurred on by Zionist settlement and land-purchasing activities in the period prior to the First World War.

In late Ottoman Palestine, the population of the three Palestinian administrative districts (Jerusalem, Nablus and Acre) was overwhelmingly Muslim and Christian Arab. The Jewish minority numbered about 25,000; the majority was deeply religious and urban-based. Until the advent of European Zionism in the late 19th century relations among the Palestinians (Arabic-speaking Muslims, Christians and Jews) were peaceful and stable, forged by centuries of coexistence, shared history and shared country (Khalidi, W. 1984). The memoirs of Wasif Jawhariyyeh (1897–1972), a Palestinian Christian citizen of Jerusalem, *The Diaries of Wasif Jawhariyyeh*, provide compelling testimony to the emergence of a two-tier

Palestinian Ottoman territorial identity in late Ottoman Palestine and for the co-existence, cultural diversity and intermixing of Ottoman Jerusalem, a microcosm of late Ottoman modernity in Palestine. In the Palestinian world of Jawhariyyeh's youth, boundaries separating the lives of Palestinian Christians, Palestinian Jews and Palestinian Muslims were fluid.

> Jerusalem's modernity was a feature of internal dynamics in the Ottoman City and I propose that the social structure of the walled city was much more fluid than generally believed; further I suggest that the quarter system signalling the division of the Old City into confessional bounded domains was introduced and imposed retroactively on the city by British colonial regulations. (Tamari 2006: 28)

In Palestine the printing and publication revolution began in the late Ottoman period and developed on an industrial scale in the first half of the 20th century. This revolution was accompanied by the introduction of modern technologies, the growth in secular education and literacy and rapid urbanisation. Within a short period, and by 1948, more than one-third of Palestinian Arab society was urban-based. Together with the sharp rise in modern secular schools in the country, increased literacy broke the monopoly of the small, religiously minded, literate elites in the cities on education and learning and bolstered the emerging middle and professional classes in the cities. The increasing cultural self-awareness of educated people led to the rise of secular proto-nationalism in late Ottoman Palestine. Embryonic Palestinian cultural nationalism and territorial patriotism preceded Palestinian political nationalism and this was fostered in schools and teacher training seminaries in late Ottoman Palestine. In the second half of the 19th century the bilingual Russian Orthodox schools and teacher training centres in Palestine played an important role in promoting cultural renaissance in the country. These schools subsequently came to be among the best in the country, contributing to this national cultural awakening.

The works of Khalil Ibrahim Beidas, Ruhi al-Khalidi and Khalil al-Sakakini were the high end of the educational, cultural and literary revolution of late Ottoman Palestine – a modernist civic revolution which was dedicated to self-enlightenment, self-improvement, social empowerment and – politically speaking – self-representation, equal citizenship and regional autonomy within the Ottoman state. An intellectual and cultural pioneer, Beidas (1874–1949), was a Palestinian Christian scholar, educator, novelist and prolific translator of Russian literary works. Born in Nazareth, in the Galilee, in 1874, Beidas was educated in Russian-funded bilingual Orthodox schools in the Galilee and studied at the highly regarded Russian Teacher Training Seminary in Nazareth,[11] which was founded by the Imperial Russian Orthodox Palestine Society in 1886, and later housed in a building which became famously known to Palestinians throughout the Galilee as al-Maskubiyyah ('the Moscovite' compound). Other Russian compounds created in Palestine, including in Jerusalem and al-Khalil (Hebron), are still referred to by local Palestinians as al-Maskubiyyah. The most famous building constructed by the Society in Palestine was the Church of Mary Magdalene, on Mount of Olives in Jerusalem, built in 1886. Initially headquartered in Nazareth (between 1882 and 1884), the Society opened four schools in the Galilee and employed Orthodox Arab and Russian teachers and Arabic translators to translate school material from Russian to Arabic. By 1899 the Society had twenty-three modern 'Maskob Schools' in Palestine, and two Teacher Training Seminaries, including one for women in Beit Jala which opened in 1890; villages and towns were asked to provide the buildings, but all books, notebooks, pens and pencils, equipment, sport facilities, administration and teaching were free of charge.[12] Most schools were also co-educational, which added another dimension to the educational revolution introduced by the Palestinian Orthodox Imperial Society.

Soon after its arrival in Palestine in the early 1880s the Arabic rendition of the Russian name (Russian Orthodox Palestine Society) would have been taught in all Russian Orthodox schools in Palestine as Arabic was the instruction language while Russian was compulsory; other languages such as French, Turkish and Greek were voluntary. After 1889 the Arabic rendition of the Russian name became the Palestinian Orthodox Imperial Society . This Arabic version of the Society's name would have been used not only by Beidas throughout his primary and secondary schooling in Nazareth in the early 1890s, but has also continued to be used in publications by Palestinian Orthodox Christians for more than 135 years.[13]

Not only that. Eventually on 1 April 1902, after a period of negotiations between the Russian leaders of the Imperial Russian Orthodox Palestine Society and the Ottoman authorities, they recognised all thirty-seven schools and seminaries of the Society (the majority of which were in Palestine, with some in Syria and Lebanon) and the occasion was marked by public celebrations in Palestine, Syria and Russia.[14] The impact of this important official Ottoman recognition of the activities of the Palestinian Orthodox Imperial Society extended beyond education into the encouragement of Russian mass pilgrimage to Palestine, which was also organised by the same society. In the early 20th century Russian pilgrims constituted nearly 80 per cent of all foreign Christian pilgrims to the Holy Land. As we shall see below, this Russian mass pilgrimage forced the Ottoman authorities to make further administrative adjustments and in 1906 the districts of Nazareth and Tiberias were added to the Mutasarrifate of Noble Jerusalem, mainly to accommodate the new mass pilgrimage from Russia and the West in facilitating the issuance of a single tourist visa to Christian pilgrims and travellers in Palestine.

Beidas was a product of the educational and intellectual awakening of late Ottoman Palestine. He was also utilising local and imperial resources such as those made available by the Russian Palestinian Orthodox Imperial Society to articulate a new sense of modern Palestinian identity. Indeed, many of Beidas' ideas were also radical and even revolutionary by the standards of late Ottoman Palestine. After graduating from the Teacher Training Seminary in Nazareth, Beidas moved to Jerusalem, then the Palestinian intellectual and cultural capital of late Ottoman Palestine. He worked as a senior Arabic teacher at the Anglican St George's School in Jerusalem and as a translator from Russian to Arabic for the Imperial Russian Orthodox Palestine Society. He also travelled in Russia in 1892.

Beidas' exceptional linguistic and cultural talents and translations from Russian into Arabic were influenced by the works of leading Russian novelists and poets, including Alexander Pushkin, Nikolai Gogol, Dostoevsky, Leon Tolstoy and Maxim Gorky. Some of these authors had developed radical critiques of autocracy, popular approaches to history, identification with the lives of ordinary people and emphasis on freedom and social justice. Tolstoy had an idealistic view of the Russian countryside and Russian peasantry and this had an impact on Beidas' positive views of the Palestinian countryside and peasantry. Beidas had already translated into Arabic and published in Beirut in 1898 Pushkin's historical novel *The Captain's Daughter*. Beidas' weekly periodical, *al-Nafais al-'Asriyyah* (*Modern Gems*) was founded ten years later in 1908 in Haifa and it began by serialising the Russian classic novels Beidas was translating. Beidas is considered to be the 'pioneer of the Palestinian short story' (*Raid al-Qissah al-Filastiniyyah*) (Mazza 2015: 188) and in 1909 he published *The Conditions of Tyranny* (*Ahwal al-Istibdad*), one of the earliest critical accounts of tyrannical rule to appear in the Arabic language. Edward Said, a close relative of Beidas, astutely observed that Beidas' essays, short stories, historical novels and works of translation in the pre- and post-war periods played an important role in the construction of early modern Palestinian national identity (Moore-Gilbert 2009: 182).

The great flowering of Palestinian and Arab literature and poetry, of novel translations, journalism, educational experiments and private library collections during the late Ottoman period created a living memory of the period in Palestine, one much stronger in living Arab culture, than that of the mediaval al-Andalus period, for example. Beidas' own personal Jerusalem library of more than 6000 books was plundered, together with other Palestinian private libraries owned by Khalil Sakakini and other Palestinian Jerusalemites, by the Israelis during the 1948 Nakba and the episode was documented in *The Great Book Robbery*.[15] Beidas' and other Palestinian library collections can shed a great deal of light on the Palestinian intellectual renaissance and national consciousness in the late Ottoman period. An illustration of this new consciousness is found in the 1898 geographic Preface to Beidas' translation of Akim Aleksyeevich Olesnitsky's *A Description of the Holy Land*, Vol. 1 (also Foster 2016c) – the original version appeared in Russian in 1875[16] – by the Imperial Russian Orthodox Palestine Society. Beidas describes this as a publication of the Palestinian Orthodox Imperial Society. Bei Beidas also talks about the inadequate geographical works available in Arabic on his country 'Palestine' and about the indigenous 'sons and daughters of Palestine' (*Abnaa Filastin*, أبناء فلسطين) and 'their need for an extensive geographic work on their country'. Writing to local Palestinian audiences, Beidas knew that many Palestinians would be closely familiar with the indigenous connotations of the term أبناء فلسطين. Beidas describes Olesnitsky's work as follows: 'an extensive book which describes the country of Palestine with its places, rivers, lakes, mountains and valleys'. He also talks about his use of idiomatic Arabic and his choice of 'the simple expression which is closely related to [our] minds'.

Beidas' work and activities present a landmark in the emergence of modern Palestinian nationalism for a variety of reasons. Nine factors distinguish the scholarly, cultural and geographic contribution of Beidas to the modern notion of Palestine and the emergence of new a territorial national consciousness in late 19th century Palestine:

- Beidas, a native of the Galilee, was working from a modern wider concept of Palestine – and not just from medieval Arab Islamic social memory associated with the historic province of Jund Filastin.
- Beidas uses the terms *Palestinian* and *Palestine* simultaneously and interchangeably, which is a hallmark of modern Palestinian writing.
- The two-page Preface begins with the Arabic expression *al-Hamdu Lillah* ('Praise be to Allah', the Arabic word for 'God'), an expression frequently invoked by Muslims due to its centrality to the first chapter of the Quran and the name and sayings of the Prophet Muhammad. This expression is also used by Arabic-speaking Christians. But the implication is that work is aimed at all Arabic-speaking Palestinians.
- The complete absence of any reference to Zionism – in contrast with Palestinian national writings a decade later, the most famous examples of which are the newspaper *Falastin* (1911) and the writings of Ruhi al-Khalidi (1913) (see below) – and this points to the emergence of a two-tier *Palestinian Ottoman* identity and the beginnings of the Palestinian cultural renaissance in late Ottoman Palestine – a renaissance which preceded the subsequent national preoccupation with Zionism.
- The ease with which Beisas uses the terms 'Palestine' and 'our country' and the 'Palestinian Orthodox Imperial Society' without the need to define or explain these terms or introduce this Society. This suggests two things: (1) Beisas thought that his Arab readers would be familiar with these terms and have a full understanding of what he meant; (2) these terms and this Arabic name of the Society were already commonly used and understood.

- The Palestinian Orthodox Imperial Society ran a translation and publishing house in Jerusalem and after 1889 it operated in Palestine throughout the 1890s under the Arabic name: الجمعية الإمبراطورية الأرثوذكسية الفلسطينية, the name Beidas uses in his 1898 Preface.

- This late 19th century modern geographic (territorial) concept of Filastin advanced by someone educated in the modern schools of Galilee departed from the traditional regional Islamic concept of Palestine described or referred to by the Muslim scholars al-Maqdisi, Mujir al-Din, Khair al-Din al-Ramli and Salih ibn Ahmad al-Tumurtashiin in the 10th, 15th and 17th centuries respectively. The conception of Palestine understood by these four Muslim writers and *qadis* was derived from the medieval Muslim province of Jund Filastin, whose capital was al-Ramla, but whose territory did not include the Galilee.

- Historically, names of distinguished individuals before and under Islam in Palestine were augmented by adding town names to individual names: examples of prominent or distinguished Palestinians discussed above included:
  - Antiochus of Ascalon, in 2nd century BC Philistia.
  - Jesus of Nazareth, in the 1st century AD.
  - Eusebius of Caesarea Maritima, in 4th century Palaestina Prima.
  - Prokopios of Caesarea Maritima, in 6th century Palaestina Prima.
  - Al-Maqdisi (of 'al-Quds', the 'Jerusalemite') in the 10th century province of Filastin.
  - Muhammad al-Yazuri: Muhammad Hassan ibn Ali al-Yazuri, from Yazur, a town east of Jaffa in the Fatimid province of Jund Filastin, also vizier of the Fatimid state from 1050 to 1058.
  - Ibn Hajar al-'Asqalani (1372–1449), a leading medieval Shafi'i Sunni scholar whose family originated in 'Asqalan, Mamluk Palestine.
  - Kkair al-Din al-Ramli, 'of al-Ramla', in 17th century Ottoman Palestine.

- On a popular Palestinian level, individual names were also linked to their home towns, such as 'ibn Akka', 'son of Acre', or after their clan: for example, Dhaher al-'Umar al-Zaydani 'of the Zaydani clan'. The traditional forms of identification (whether 'Jesus of Nazareth' or 'Julian of Norwich', c. 1342–c. 1416) were common throughout the world. In his 1898 Preface, the Galilee-born Beidas talks about the 'sons of Palestine', a generic term for the 'people of Palestine'. This distinct territorial form of identification in the late 19th century is a radical departure from all other traditional forms of identification. In the 20th century the traditional forms of identification did not disappear completely, but they were augmented by this new form of territorial identification and patriotic consciousness (the 'sons of Palestine'). In the early decades of the 20th century the collective 'sons of Palestine' (أبناء فلسطين) also became known as *Sha'b Filastin* (شعب فلسطين, 'people of Palestine') and the 'Palestinian people' (الشعب الفلسطيني). But the roots of this new territorial national consciousness are found in the late 19th century.

- Today the Society operates publicly and runs various social and educational projects in Palestine and the Near East under the Arabic rendition of the name cited by Bedas in his 1898 Preface: الجمعية الإمبراطورية الأرثوذكسية الفلسطينية. In June and July 2012, to mark the 130th anniversary of the Society's foundation and start of its operation in 1882 in Palestine, the Society opened the Russian Centre for Science and Culture in Bethlehem and staged various celebrations in Moscow sponsored by the Russian government. Two years later, on 3 September 2014, a Galilee branch of the Imperial Russian Orthodox Palestinian Society was officially launched at the Arab Orthodox Centre in Nazareth which, despite the change in the circumstances of Nazareth, kept the 132-year-old 'Palestinian' name intact. Speakers at this official Nazareth ceremony included Russian official representatives and Hanna Abu Hanna, of Haifa – author of a recent work in Arabic on The Beginnings of the Palestinian Renaissance – who lectured on the seminal cultural activities of the Society in late Ottoman Palestine. It is also worth noting that a significant number of Palestinians educated in 'al-Maskob schools' in late Ottoman Palestine later joined Palestinian national parties during the British Mandatory period; some also joined the Palestine Communist Party (PCP) during the same period.

'BEING PALESTINE, BECOMING PALESTINE' IN MAHMOUD DARWISH'S POETRY

> I was born close to the sea to a Palestinian mother / and an Aramaic father, to a Palestinian mother and a Moabite father, to a Palestinian mother / and Arab father. (Darwish 1994: 69)

Palestinian 'national' poet Mahmoud Darwish (1941–2008) was inspired by the incredibly rich social and cultural memories of historic Palestine. His poetry gave a deep sense of such questions of Palestinian identity and its continued formation and transformation. While many modern Arab nationalists strive for uniqueness and exclusivity and continuously search for purity and clarity in constructing their nationalist identities, Darwish, by contrast, searched for the subtle, mixed and subdued forms of identity represented by an appreciation of the shadowy and inclusive heritage of Palestine. This subtle and rich heritage was woven into the fabric of modern Palestinian national identity and the way this identity was particularly framed by Darwish. The latter was brought up an internal refugee in the Galilee after his village, al-Birwa, was destroyed by Israel in 1948. He later lived much of his adult life in exile. Like many modern Palestinian intellectuals, Darwish did not emerge from the urban metropolitan elite or aristocratic families of the country, but came from the countryside and the periphery of Palestine (Galilee). However, Darwish became the embodiment of multi-tiered Palestinian national identity and the most celebrated producer of linguistic and cultural memory in modern Palestine. For Darwish, the multi-layered conception of Palestinian identity is evident by the fact that it is the product of all the powerful cultures that have passed through the land of Palestine: the Hellenistic, the Persian, the Roman, the Byzantine, the Aramaic, the Arab, the Jewish, the Muslim, the Arab Jewish, the Ottoman, the British.

However, the oral history and visual and material heritage of Palestine and their natural settings have also figured hugely in Darwish's 'national' poetry. For Darwish, modern representations of Palestinian Arab identity were deeply rooted in the history, geography and natural boundaries of the country, the toponymy and Arabic language and cultures of Palestine and its evolution within the wider Arab environs. According to a key historian of modern nationalism, Benedict Anderson (1991), European vernacular languages (replacing Latin) and the mass circulation of images by the press and in print capitalism played important roles in the way the 'modern nation' as an imagined community has been constructed and spread in Europe.

In the case of modern Palestine, the introduction of print capitalism in the late 19th century, the spread modern education, linguistic, cultural and religious memories, standard Arabic and vernacular (colloquial) Palestinian Arabic all became markers of a distinct identity. Perhaps it is not surprising that the most influential Palestinian national newspaper of the modern era was called *Falastin* (1911–1967) – not *Filastin* – emphasising the local colloquial Arabic name for the country, Falastin, as a way of forging a distinct or separate Palestinian national identity. In addition to the vernacularisation of a nascent national identity, the experience of distinct geography, living history and cultural, linguistic and religious memories of modern Palestine were central to the construction of modern Palestinian national identity. The Palestinian vernacular was certainly important in the visualisation of modern Palestine. In 1909 a *Manual of Palestinian Arabic, for Self-instruction* was published by H. H. Spoer (Fellow of the American School of Archaeology and Oriental Research in Jerusalem) and E. Nasrallah Haddad (teacher of Arabic at the Teacher Training Seminary at the Syrisches Waisenhaus in Jerusalem,[17] also known as the Schneller Orphanage). This incipient local nationalism was coupled with vernacularisation and interest in local Palestinian folklore, and this was particularly evident in the pioneering work of Tawfiq Cana'an (1882–1964), a physician, ethnographer, anthropologist, prolific author and Palestinian nationalist. Born in Beit Jala, Cana'an served as a medical officer in the Ottoman army during the First World War and would later serve as the first President of the Palestine Arab Medical Association founded in 1944.

Of course, by the 19th century Palestine had been for many centuries under Islam an Arab land and an Arab country (*balad, bilad*) with Arabic (vernacular and standard) being a key marker of its cultural identity. Under the impact of modernisation, vernacularisation and cultural awakening in late Ottoman Palestine during the second half of the 19th century, literary Arabic also went through updating and simplification in the curricula of some schools. In 1909, Palestinian educator Khalil Sakakini (1878–1953) founded the Dusturiyyah School in Jerusalem and pioneered a modern progressive education system which not only made the primary language of instruction Arabic instead of Turkish but also introduced new methods of teaching Arabic by updating Arabic grammar and simplifying its basic general rules (Tamari 2003). Later this progressive tradition of simplifying, updating and bringing literary Arabic closer to vernacular Palestinian Arabic continued in the 'national' poetry of Mahmoud Darwish.

Echoing the Heideggerean notion of the 'becoming of being', self-representation and the 'becoming of being Palestinian', according to Darwish, are related in some sense to the way modern Palestinian identity was progressively being uncovered, experienced, visualised and reconfigured.[18] For Darwish, the Arabic language and poetry and collective and social memories of Palestine, in particular, were fundamental to the uncovering and construction of local Palestinian identity. The metres of the rhythmical Arabic poetry are known in Arabic as 'seas' (*buhur*). Darwish's highly evocative poetry also visualised modern Palestine as a space between the (Mediterranean) Sea and the (Arabian) Desert, an idea which is deeply rooted in the medieval Arab Islamic conception and social memories of Palestine. But for Darwish the 'Hinterland of Palestine' (*bar Filastin*) and the 'Sea of Palestine' (*bahr Filastin*) – symbolised literally and metaphorically by the Mediterranean Sea and the Arabian Desert –represent Palestine as a whole. They are also spaces of experiences, of inner consciousness and subconsciousness and of consciously unveiled personal and collective identities.

VERNACULARISATION, INDIGENEITY AND MODERN REPRESENTATIONS OF PALESTINE IN THE PALESTINIAN ARAB PRESS: THE NEWSPAPER FALASTIN (1911–1967)

It is widely recognised that the geo-political conception of Palestine evolved significantly from the experiences of late Ottoman Palestine to those of the British Mandatory period, or from the notion of the 'sea to the desert' to the modern boundaries of the 'sea to the river'. In addition, resistance to Zionist immigration and settler projects from the late Ottoman period onwards played a large part in the national conceptualisation of modern Palestine. Palestinian national opposition to Zionism began to crystallise around Zionist-settler activities in Palestine in the years before the First World War.

It is widely recognised that education, print capitalism and the modern press played a major role in the formation of modern national identities (Anderson 1991). This was also true in the case of the growth of Palestinian education and the emergence of the Palestinian press in late Ottoman urban Palestine (Beška 2016b). In January 1911 Palestinian Arab Orthodox journalists 'Issa al-'Issa and his cousin Yousef al-'Issa set up in Jaffa (in the Mutasarrifiyyah of Jerusalem of late Ottoman Palestine) the daily newspaper *Falastin*. Why would one of the earliest modern Arabic national newspapers in Palestine be called *Falastin*, the colloquial (used daily) name for the country, not the standard or literary medieval Arabic names for the country: Filastin or Filistin.

Why vernacularise and use the vernacular Arabic form for Palestine for a leading *nationalist* newspaper, *Falastin*, rather than using Filastin or Filistin, the traditional standard Arabic names for the country – names which go all the way back to early Islam? Not only were these literary Arabic forms, Filastin or Filistin, remembered in the 19th century; in fact they were used in Palestinian and Arab writings and were synonymous with an administrative geographic unit (Abd al-Hadi 1923: 32). Moreover, the standard form of Filastin was used by Khair al-Din al-Ramli in the 17th century, the Islamic Sharia Court of Jerusalem in the 18th century and Khalil Beidas in the 1890s. In the absence of an explanation by the founding editors themselves, the answer to the adoption of the vernacular form of Falastin is likely to be multi-faceted and contextual: (a) in modern times, vernacularisation, 'nation-ness' and the need to establish a distinctive national identity can be seen again and again in early modern Europe, in modern Russia, Turkey, Japan and a whole range of countries across Asia; (b) vernacularisation was seen in late Ottoman Palestine as key to a distinct (and even separate) national identity marker; (c) naming a *national* newspaper 'from below', the editors adopted the form Falastin as the common, most widely spoken and most popularly used term by local Palestinians and on the streets of Palestine, as opposed to Filastin, which was largely confined to the writings in Arabic of the educated and cultural elites of the country. Clearly, the editors and journalists of *Falastin* were intent on popularising Palestinian nationalism 'from below' and among ordinary people and not just confining it to educated local elites.

Falastin was also founded in Jaffa, away from the prying eyes of the Ottoman authorities in Jerusalem, of which early Palestinian nationalists were deeply suspicious. Both Jaffa and Haifa – which were closely linked to the Ottoman Hejaz Railway and the rising Palestinian middle classes, and began to eclipse the historically powerful port city of Acre from the late 19th century onwards – emerged as major economic and cultural centres in late Ottoman Palestine, competing with the traditionally most powerful cultural centre in the country: al-Quds al-Sharif (Jerusalem). This three-way competition and the dynamic cultural awakening of late Ottoman Palestine would ultimately ensure the emergence of an amazingly rich and culturally diverse but fairly unified predominantly Arab country by the First World War.

In Haifa in December 1908, three years before the founding of *Falastin* in Jaffa, Palestinian journalist Najib Nassar (1865–1947) – who had worked as a pharmacist for the Scottish Hospital in Tiberias, Galilee – founded and edited *al-Karmel* (named for Mount Carmel in the Haifa district), the first Palestinian anti-colonial weekly newspaper in Arabic (Beška 2011).[19] These early Palestinian newspapers of the coastal cities of Jaffa and Haifa played an important role in the visualisation and textual reconstruction of modern Palestinian identity in the late Ottoman period (Beška 2011, 2016b). However, it should always be kept in mind that in the conception of modern Palestinian Arab identity the growth of Palestinian nationalism and the growing sense of local Palestinian territorial patriotism were always intertwined with deep-rooted identification with the surrounding Arab political and cultural environment (Bracy 2005, 2011).[20]

As we have already shown, indigenous social memory ('memory of memories') of historic Palestine was preserved in the writings of Muslim authors such as Khair al-Din al-Ramli (1585–1671) and in the archives of the Islamic Sharia Court of Jerusalem in the 18th century (Rood 2004), as well as in the local form of the name, 'Falastin'. Furthermore, based on indigenous social memory and Palestinian colloquialism, the choice of the vernacular Palestinian name *Falastin* for the Jaffa newspaper by the two Palestinian Arab Greek Orthodox journalists, the al-'Issas, reproduced the medieval Arab Muslim designation for the country, Falastin and Filastin. In an extraordinary leading article, Yousef Hanna al-'Issa echoes local social memories of historic Filastin.

The combative anti-Zionist newspaper *Falastin* (1911–1967) contributed significantly to the forging of a new (distinct and separate) Palestinian identity (Tamari 2014). *Falastin*'s editorial policy was also 'progressive' as it defended the Palestinian *fallah* on the land question and fought against religious fanaticism, sectarianism and ignorance (Tamari 2014; Beška 2016b: 3). The cultural geography of the editors of *Falastin* espoused secular Ottoman citizenship and equality combined with local Palestinian patriotism. They also promoted autonomous cultural-linguistic nationalism which embraced the Arab religious and cultural heritage of Islam. As for the political geography of Palestine, al-'Issa wrote in January 1912 that the boundaries of his 'homeland' (*watan*) extends 'from the borders of Egypt to the Balqa[21] and from the mountains of Moab [on the eastern shores of the Dead Sea] to the Mediterranean'.[22] Contrast this late Ottoman Palestinian nationalist perception of Palestine, which clearly draws inspiration from the memories of historic Palestine, including greater Palaestina under the Byzantines and the Arab province of Jund Filastin, with post-First World War Palestinian nationalist representations of the country which have since then stuck symbolically to the boundaries of British Mandatory Palestine (1917–1948).

It is not entirely clear whether Orthodox Yousef al-'Issa's geo-political representations of historic Falastin in 1912 was based on Palestinian Arab Orthodox Christian social and cultural memories which were linked to the independent All Palestine Orthodox Church of Jerusalem whose ecclesiastical jurisdiction had been widely recognised and exercised over greater Palestine (the 'Three Palestines', 4th–7th centuries AD) since the mid-5th century AD. This ecclesiastical jurisdiction, which would have been known to all educated Orthodox Palestine Christians in the early 20th century, has continued until today and it includes the whole of present-day Palestine/Israel and Jordan. In this ecclesiastical context, the remarkable discovery of the Byzantine Madaba Floor Mosaic Map in 1884 (discussed in chapter four), covering the area between Egypt to Lebanon and between the Mediterranean Sea and Eastern Arabia desert, and with the name Palaestina in its Greek inscriptions, and the growing involvement of the Greek Orthodox

Patriarchate in Jerusalem in the study of, and local and international publicity surrounding the discovery of, the map in the period between the early 1890s and 1906,[23] may be of some relevance to the way Yousef al-ʿIssa described the boundaries of Palestine in 1912. As for the Madaba Map itself, the first known representation of the map was, in fact, created at the Franciscan Printing Press in Jerusalem in 1897, with assistance from the Greek Orthodox Patriarchate in Jerusalem. Moreover, since the late 19th century the Palestine Arab Orthodox community had been involved in a struggle over the Arabisation of the Palestine Orthodox Church and the promotion of Arab bishops and senior hierarchs in the Greek-dominated Orthodox Patriarchate of Jerusalem. In fact for decades under the editorship of the al-ʿIssa cousins, *Falastin* would remain dedicated not only to Palestinian territorial nationalism within pan-Arab solidarity, but also to the Palestine Arab Orthodox community in its struggle with the Greek-dominated Orthodox Patriarchate of Jerusalem. Therefore, the ecclesiastical Orthodox memories of greater Palestine under the Byzantines cannot be ruled out since it has survived in the rhetoric of the Orthodox Patriarchate of Jerusalem until today. In any event, one thing is clear: historically, and according to Palestine Muslim geographers and writers, the 'Balqa region' – mentioned by al-ʿIssa – which is located north-west of ʿAmman, present-day Jordan's capital, was not part of the province of Jund Filastin of the Middle Ages; in fact, al-Balqa was originally and historically part of, and throughout most of the Umayyad period subordinated to, the Islamic province Jund Dimashq (the Damascus province), a massive province which incorporated other territories east of the River Jordan (Le Strange 2010: 43–48; Blankinship 1994: 47–48, 292, note 7).

In any case, the newspaper *Falastin* became the most widely circulated and, consequently, most influential Arabic daily in Palestine during the British Mandate, powerfully shaping the discourse of the Palestine nationalist political movement as it struggled to resist two foreign forces: British imperialism and Zionist settler-colonisation (Khalaf 2011; Jeferey 2015: 173), while its discourse after 1918 focused on the geography of Mandatory Palestine. From its beginnings in late Ottoman Palestine *Falastin* also was the Arab country's fiercest and most consistent critic of European Zionist settler projects.

THE TERM FILASTIN IN RUHI AL-KHALIDI'S
UNPUBLISHED MANUSCRIPT

Another early Palestinian opponent of Zionism was Ruhi Bey al-Khalidi (1864–1913), a brilliant writer, liberal thinker, Lecturer in Islamic Studies at the Sorbonne University, diplomat and talented politician at the turn of the 20th century (Kasmieh 1992; Khalidi, W. 1984: 74; Beška 2016c). Al-Khalidi also served as Consul-General of the Ottoman state in Bordeaux, France, from 1898 to 1908, while at the same time publishing articles in *al-Hilal* and *al-Manar* in Cairo under the pen name al-Maqdisi (the Jerusalemite) (Beška 2016c: 181). In 1900 al-Khalidi was a co-founder of the family (Islamic waqf) library, al-Khalidiyyah Library, in the Old City of Jerusalem. It is one of the largest and most important Muslim family libraries in the world and a living landmark to Palestine and the Palestinian people. Ruhi al-Khalidi was a nephew of the mayor of Jerusalem, Yusuf Diya al-Din Pasha al-Khalidi, and in 1908 he was one of three delegates elected to represent Jerusalem in the new Ottoman government, later becoming the deputy to the head of the Ottoman parliament (in 1911). Al-Khalidi was a close friend of Khalil al-Sakakini, a Jerusalemite progressive pedagogue and one of the most influential Palestinian educationalists and literary thinkers of the modern era.

Al-Khalidi's work was an example of the emergence of a distinct Palestinian territorial national identity among the educated urban elites in the country at the turn of the 20th century. Commenting on his Arab country of Palestine shortly before his untimely death in 1913, Ruhi al-Khalidi had this to say: 'It is noteworthy that whenever the name of the country appears, it is always Palestine, never southern Syria or anything else' (Ruhi al-Khaldi's unpublished manuscript, 'Zionism or the Zionist Question', al-Khalidiyyah Library, Jerusalem, cited in Gerber 1998a).[24]

Today al-Khalidiyyah Library houses a large collection of Islamic historical and *fiqh* manuscripts, a local collection built by Palestinians, and a unique Arabic manuscript about the history of political Zionism written by Ruhi al-Khalidi in the late Ottoman period. Al-Khalidi's undated manuscript, in his beautiful handwritten Arabic, was composed many months, perhaps several years, before his death in 1913. I had the chance of examining the text at the Khalidiyyah Library on 22 April 2017. The extraordinary manuscript looks like unfinished draft book which Ruhi al-Khalidi appeared to have been working on long before his death. Crucially, throughout the text repeatedly he uses the terms *Filastin* (فلسطين) and *turab Filastin* ('soil of Palestine', تراب فلسطين) to describe Zionist ambitions and settler-colonisation in his own country of Palestine. The manuscript also contains a list of Zionist colonies in Palestine, with their Hebrew names and with the local Palestinian Arabic names they had either replaced or were named after. Interestingly, there is no mention in the manuscript of *Suriyyah al-Janubiyyah* ('Southern Syria') as an alternative way of describing Ottoman Palestine. Instead Ruhi al-Khalidi mentions 'Roman Palestine' and refers to Filastin under the Ottomans. The manuscript was clearly intended for publication and overall it gives the impression that the Arabic term Filastin had been used by Ruhi al-Khalidi and his compatriot for decades.

Muslims coexisted with Christian Arabs and Arab Jews in Muslim-majority Palestine for centuries and Ruhi al-Khalidi was naturally sympathetic to the idea of Jewish religious attachment to Jerusalem. But he was highly critical of Zionism as a political project and saw Western Zionist colonisation schemes as a major threat to the indigenous people of Palestine. In an interview with the Hebrew periodical *ha-Tzvi* on 1 November 1909, al-Khalidi, then a member of the Ottoman parliament, expressed concern that Zionist settler-colonisation 'would inevitably lead to the expulsion of Arabs from the places they had inhabited for centuries' (Beška 2016c: 183).

Like Ruhi al-Khalidi, former Mayor of Jerusalem Yusuf Diya al-Din al-Khalidi (1829–1907) had strongly objected to the Zionist project in Palestine. Representing Jerusalem in the Ottoman parliament in the 1870s, al-Khalidi had earlier attended an English school in Malta where he studied English and French, and then continued to study Semitic languages in the Oriental Academy of Vienna. In a well-known letter to Zadok Kahn, the Chief Rabbi of France and an associate of Theodor Herzl, in early 1899, al-Khalidi suggested that the Zionists should find another place for the implementation of their political project:

> In theory, Zionism is an absolutely natural and just idea on how to solve the Jewish question. Yet it is impossible to overlook the actual reality, which must be taken into account. Palestine is an integral part

of the Ottoman Empire and today it is inhabited by non-Jews. This country is held in esteem by more than 390 million Christians and 300 million Muslims. By what right do the Jews want it for themselves? Jewish money will not be able to buy Palestine. The only way to take it is by force using cannons and warships. Turks and Arabs in general sympathize with Jews. But some of them were affected by the fever of hatred for Jews, as it happened to the most advanced of the [European] civilized nations. Also the Christian Arabs, especially the Catholic and Orthodox, hate Jews very much. Even if Herzl obtained the approval of the Sultan Abdiilhamit II for the Zionist plan, he should not think that a day will come when Zionists will become masters of this country ...

It is therefore necessary, to ensure the safety of the Jews in the Ottoman Empire, that the Zionist Movement, in the geographic sense of the word, stops ... Good Lord, the world is vast enough, there are still uninhabited countries where one could settle millions of [European] poor Jews who may perhaps become happy there and one day constitute a nation. That would perhaps be the best, the most rational solution to the [European] Jewish question. But in the name of God, let Palestine be left in peace. (Quoted in Beška 2007: 28–29)[25]

Around the same time, important developments in Arab opposition to Zionism centred on Zionist land purchasing activities in Palestine. Against the background of Arab (Palestinian, Syrian, Lebanese and Iraqi) desire for autonomy, equal citizenship, decentralisation and political reforms (not complete independence or sovereignty) within the Ottoman state, the sale of land to, and settler-colonisation by, European Zionists in Palestine was seen as a real threat to the indigenous people. The international Zionist movement and Zionist settlers in Palestine (in sharp contrast to the then German Templar settlers) made it clear that their ultimate objective was the establishment of a Jewish state in Palestine. According to Charles Smith (1996: 34), in 1897 'an Arab commission was formed in Jerusalem, headed by the mufti, to examine the issue of land sales to Jews, and its protests led to the cessation of such sales for several years'. In reality, however, land sales in Palestine never ceased. Zionist land purchasing activities in the Esdraelon plain and eastern Galilee continued and centred on some of the most fertile land in the country. These activities included the sale of lands of the Arab village of al-Fulah in the Nazareth sub-district to the Jewish National Fund in 1910. The lands of al-Fulah belonged to Elias Sursuq, a Greek Orthodox banker and absentee landlord from Beirut, who in 1910 reached a deal on their sale with the Zionists. According to Neville Mandel, this was 'some of the best agricultural land in Palestine' (cited in Bracy 2011: 45).

When the local Palestinian peasants refused to vacate their village and petitioned the Ottoman authorities, they were backed in their resistance by Shukri al-'Asali (1878–1916), the *qaimmaqam* (district governor) of Nazareth in Galilee and later a deputy in the Ottoman parliament, who became their key supporter in many of his articles in the Arabic press, including the newspaper *Falastin*. For al-'Asali, who wrote under a pseudonym, that of the legendary Salah al-Din who defeated the Latin Crusaders in the Battle of Hattin[26] in eastern Galilee in 1187, the Galilee was integral to Palestine. Entitled 'Letter of Salah al-Din al-Ayyubi to the Commander of the [Ottoman] Expedition to Hauran Sami Pasha al-Faruqi', one of his 1910 articles pleaded with the Ottoman Governor of Hauran to stand up to Zionist plans in Palestine:

> I beg you … to hurry and repel the Zionist threat from Palestine, whose soil is soaked with the blood of the Prophet's companions and with the blood of my armies and for the retrieval of which I have sacrificed [the lives] of my brothers, my people and commanders.[27]

The al-Fulah affair 'became the subject of an intensive newspaper campaign which had a powerful impact' on local Arab public opinion (Beška 2016b: 4). Echoing the political discourses, terminology and resistance literature (*Adab al-Muqawamah*) of early Palestinian journalism, the geo-political term Filastin, popularised initially by the newspaper *Falastin*, continued to be wedded to the Palestinian national recovery and nation-building in the post-Nakba period. The terminological continuities were evident in the Palestinian journalistic publications which paved the way for the emergence of the resistance movement in the late 1950s and founding of the Palestine Liberation Organisation (PLO) in the early 1960s. The first underground magazine of Fateh (*Harakat al-Tahrir al-Watani al-Filas-tini*; 'Palestinian National Liberation Movement'), which began to appear monthly in 1959 – under the editorship of Khalil al-Wazir (1935–1988), a Palestinian refugee from al-Ramla, the old capital of Jund Filastin – was called *Filastinuna, Nida al-Hayat* ('Our Palestine, the Call to Life'). Also, *Filastin* was the weekly supplement of the pro-Nasserist newspaper *al-Mu-harrir* (meaning the Liberator or the Editor), published in Beirut and edited by Ghassan Kanafani (1936–1972), a Palestinian refugee from Acre, a journalist, novelist and later a leading member of the Popular Front for the Liberation of Palestine (PFLP) (Rabbani 2005: 275).

HISTORIC CONTINUITIES AND COLONIAL TRANSFORMATION: PALESTINE AS A SINGLE OFFICIAL ADMINISTRATIVE AND TERRITORIAL ENTITY UNDER THE BRITISH (1918–MAY 1948)

Jerusalem was occupied by British forces in December 1917. The League of Nations formally awarded Britain a Mandate over Palestine in 1922. Under the British, Palestine was once again a distinct political and administrative entity for the first time in centuries. The sense of continuity between the ancient, medieval and modern political geography and naming traditions of Palestine eventually came into play in the designation of the British Mandatory Government of Palestine (1918–1948). This 'official' designation of the country as Palestine was universally accepted by the League of Nations, which came into existence in 1920, and by the United Nations which was founded in 1945.

Following the Palestine Exploration Fund, the British Mandatory authorities after 1918 assumed that the Palestinian Arabs (Muslims, Christians and Arab Jews) had also preserved knowledge of the ancient place names which could help identify archaeological sites. Furthermore, in the modern era, and especially during the British Mandate of Palestine, the term 'Palestinian' was used to refer to all people residing in Palestine, regardless of religion or ethnicity, including those European Jewish settlers granted citizenship by the British Mandatory authorities.

Fully aware of the destabilising effects of its pro-Zionist commitments and the need to maintain political stability in the country, in the 1920s the British Mandatory authorities in Palestine sought to preserve some of the continuities of late Ottoman Palestine in the Mandatory system. The British authorities decided not only to link the local name of the country, Filastin, to all the official institutions, units and documents produced by the British Mandatory Government of Palestine (1918–1948), they also linked some of the institutions they had helped create in the 1920s with the administrative structure and districts of late Ottoman Palestine. These official Palestine institutions and documents included:

- *The Supreme Muslim Council in Palestine (al-Majlis al-Islamic al-A'ala bi-Filastin)*: the SMC was established in 1923 with the support of the British Mandatory authorities and with authority over all the Muslim *waqfs* and sharia courts in Palestine. The composition of the SMC effectively linked the administrative districts of late 19th century Palestine with the administration of Muslim-majority Mandatory Palestine. The SMC consisted of five members: a president and four members, two of whom were to represent the autonomous administrative Mutasarrifate of Jerusalem and the remaining two to represent the late Ottoman *sanjaks* of Acre and Nablus.

- *Palestine Archaeological Museum*: continuities of late Ottoman Palestine and Mandatory Palestine are also found in the creation and collections of the Palestine Archaeological Museum. In 1918, almost immediately after the occupation of Jerusalem, the British Military Governor Sir Ronald Storrs took the decision to establish the Palestine Archaeological Museum in Jerusalem. The cornerstone of the Palestine Archaeological Museum was laid on 19 June 1930. The museum opened in 1938 as a 'national' (not biblical) museum and was modelled on modern European museums. The Palestine Archaeological Museum (renamed by Israel after 1967 as the 'Rockefeller Museum') contains historical artefacts, jewels and mosaics from the Neolithic through the Byzantine periods, and through the medieval Islamic and modern periods. Together with ancient Neolithic artefacts, the museum has the remains of 8th-century wooden beams from the al-Aqsa Mosque, and an elaborately carved lintel from the Church of the Holy Sepulchre, from the time of the Latin Crusaders. The Neolithic, ancient, medieval and modern heritage of Palestine is all encapsulated in this museum. The Palestine Archaeological Museum absorbed the collections of the Ottoman Imperial Museum of Antiquities in Jerusalem, the first archaeological museum to be set up in late Ottoman Palestine, which was founded in 1890 and existed until 1930. The latter's collections continued first with the British Palestine Museum of Antiquities (1921–1930) and then with the Palestine Archaeological Museum. That a 1910 handwritten Ottoman Catalogue of the Imperial Museum of Antiquities in Jerusalem has survived in the library of the Rockefeller Museum, where it is called the 'Pre-War Catalogue of the Palestine Archaeological Museum' (St Laurent with Taşkömürl 2013: 22–23).

- *Palestine Passport, Palestine Currency and Palestine Stamps*: the British Mandatory Government of Palestine (with its administrative capital in Jerusalem) produced Palestine passports, Palestine currency and Palestine stamps. The stamps were in three languages, with the imprint Palestine, فلسطين, פלשתינה, showcasing images of ancient and medieval Palestinian holy sites such as the Dome of the Rock in Jerusalem and the Nativity Church in Bethlehem. Interestingly, in 1970 the Palestinian National Liberation Movement, headed by Yasir 'Arafat, issued a commemorative stamp on the fifth anniversary of its foundation, which also reproduced the British Mandatory stamps with their imprints in Arabic, English and Hebrew.

- *The Palestine Pound and the Palestine Currency Board*: the British Mandatory Government of Palestine also issued the Palestine Pound (Arabic: *Junyeh Filastini*, جنيه فلسطيني; Hebrew: פּוּנְט פַּלְשֶׁתִינָאִי). Equal in value to the pound sterling, it was the currency of the British Mandate in Palestine from 1927 to 14 May 1948. The currency of the State of Israel between 15 May 1948 and August 1948 and between 1948 and 1952 the Palestine Pound continued to be legal tender in Israel. The Palestine Pound was also the currency of Transjordan until 1949 and remained in usage in the West Bank until 1950. In the Gaza Strip the Palestine Pound circulated until April 1951, when it was replaced by the Egyptian Pound.

- *The Palestine Police Force*: set up as a colonial police service established in Palestine 1920 and operated until 1948.

- *The Palestine Railways*: a government-owned railway company that ran all public railways in Palestine from 1920 until 1948.
- *The Palestinian Citizenship Order in Council*: a law of Mandatory Palestine governing citizenship in the country. It came into effect on 1 August 1925.
- *The Arab Palestine Sport Federation (al-Ittihad al-Riadi al-ʿArabi al-Filastini)*: a government body operating between 1931 and 1937 and between 1944 and 1948. It organised a variety of sports activities, including football, boxing and weight-lifting (Khalidi, I. 2006, 2014).
- *The Palestine Broadcasting Service*: it began radio transmissions from the new transmitter in Ramallah, with offices in Jerusalem. Staff were recruited for five hours of daily broadcasts in three languages, English, Arabic and Hebrew, and training was given by the BBC. In 1942, the transmissions were split into two stations: for English/Arabic (Radio al Quds) and English/Hebrew (Kol Yerushalayim).
- *The Palestine Citrus Marketing Board*: set up by the Mandatory government of Palestine to regulate all citrus exports from Palestine. In October 1956, a group of former Palestinian citrus farmers, who had become refugees in the West Bank in 1948, sued Barclays Bank in a Jordanian court in Jerusalem for £1 million. The amount represented the total value of the citrus crop exported collectively by this group in 1947.
- *Palestine Airways:* founded by Pinhas Rutenberg in Mandatory Palestine in the mid-1930s; operated under the aegis of British Imperial Airways from 1937 until 1940 until it was taken over by the British Royal Air Force as part of the British war effort.

SELF-DETERMINATION AND THE PROLIFERATION OF PALESTINIAN NATIONALIST ORGANISATIONS: THE PALESTINIAN NATIONAL MOVEMENT DURING THE MANDATORY PERIOD

As we have already seen above, Palestinian national consciousness did not emerge out of the blue in the early 20th century. It emerged gradually across decades and through momentous developments which affected Palestine and the wider region in the second half of the 19th century. However the overall goals of Palestinian nationalism in the post-First World War period shifted radically from autonomy and equal citizenship under the Ottomans to anti-colonial struggle, liberation and independence during the British Mandatory period.[28]

Crucially, active resistance to the existential threat posed by Zionist immigration to and settler-colonialism of Palestine during the Mandatory period became central to the Palestinian nationalist struggle. The context of post-First World War Palestine had changed radically. The British, who occupied Palestine in 1917–1918, had committed themselves to Zionist settler goals as framed in the Balfour Declaration of November 1917. In 1920 the San Remo Conference of the four Principal Allied Powers of the First World War decided to include the words of the Belfour Declaration in the text of the British Mandate over Palestine. In coming face to face with the existential threat of the pro-Zionist Balfour Declaration's commitments, the Palestinian nationalist movement, early on, had to grapple with what was to become a perennial dilemma: whether to emphasise the territorial Palestinian or pan-Arabist dimensions of Palestinian Arab identity. This dilemma bedevilled Palestinian nationalist politics throughout the first half of the 20th century and was carried forward well into the post-Nakba period.

In the post-First World War period, Palestinian nationalist resistance organisations began to proliferate. The Palestinian Revival Society (al-Nahdah al-Filistiniyyah), a Palestinian nationalist organisation, was founded in Damascus in March 1919. Its first president was Salim al-Tibi, who went from Jerusalem to Damascus in the anticipation of the formation of Emir Faisal's administration in the city. Al-Tibi had been a senior officer in the Arab Army of Emir Faisal and his father was the *mufti* of Tulkarem. He was later replaced as a president of the society by Salman 'Abdel-Rahman, the son of the mayor of Tulkarem (Tauber 2007: 95). Other leaders of the society were Muhammad 'Izzat Darwazah from Nablus, 'Abd al-Qader al-Muzaffar and Rushdi al-Shawa from Gaza. Al-Shawa travelled frequently between Damascus, Jerusalem, Jaffa and Gaza, accompanying al-Muzaffar on his trips to Palestine, smuggling arms and encouraging an uprising against the British. In 1919 it was reported he took 100 pistols from Damascus to Jerusalem for the members of al-Fida'iyyah (Tauber 2007: 94).

Also in the early days of the Mandatory period the Palestinian Arab national leadership convened the Palestine Arab Congress (al-Mutamar al-'Arabi al-Filastini), a series of national congresses organised by a nationwide network of committees and local Palestinian Muslim and Christian associations; between 1919 and 1928 seven congresses were held in Jerusalem, Haifa, Jaffa and Nablus (Porath 1974). From 1920 until 1934 the national Executive Committee of the Congress, which coordinated Palestinian opposition to the Balfour Declaration and British pro-Zionist policies in Palestine, was headed by Musa Kazim al-Husayni, Mayor of Jerusalem between 1918 and 1920. The Executive Committee and its local committees commanded widespread public support but they were never officially recognised by the British authorities. The resolutions of the Third Palestine Arab Congress held in Haifa on 4–14 December 1920, which were subsequently presented to British Colonial Secretary Winston Churchill in early 1921, were summarised by Ilan Pappe as follows:

> The slogan of the conference was 'Equality with the Mandate of Iraq'.
> The text of Iraq's mandate stipulated that it would have a parliament
> elected on the democratic principle of one citizen, one vote. It
> acknowledged Iraq as a *watani* (national entity) that would eventually
> become independent. [Sheikh Suleiman al-Taji al-Faruqi] explained
> to those gathered that these were the most elementary demands,
> yet they had been denied to the Palestinians because of the Balfour
> Declaration. (Pappe 2010: 208)

This Third Palestine Arab Congress:

> can be seen as the conceptive venue of the Palestine Arab national
> movement, meeting in Haifa in mid-December 1920, called on
> the new British rulers to establish a government 'to be chosen by
> the Arabic-speaking people who had lived in Palestine before the
> beginning of the [world] war'. It completely, flatly rejected [Zionist]
> Jewish claims to Palestine. (Morris 2009: 88)

Continuities in modern Palestinian national thinking can be seen in some of the institutionalised aspects of the Palestinian national struggle in the pre-Nakba period which re-emerged in the post-Nakba era. For instance, in 1930, following the 1929 'al-Burraq Uprising' (*Habbat al-Buraq*) in Muslim-majority Palestine, the Palestinian leadership set up the Palestine Arab National Fund (PANF). Established by the Palestine Arab Executive and led by Fouad Saba, a Palestinian activist and accountant born in Acre, the PANF took some practical financial steps to discourage land sales to Zionist national institutions in Palestine. The PANF was the antecedent to the much larger and more multi-purpose Palestine National Fund (PNF) set up by the PLO in 1964 (see below).

Understandably, during the Mandatory (colonial) period some leading Palestinian personalities continued to view Palestinian identity as part of wider Arab identity of the al-Sham region and/or pan-Arab identities. But pan-Arab or al-Sham identities as a whole cannot be understood in isolation from their constituent and particular (Palestinian, Lebanese, Syrian and Jordanian) identities. Furthermore pan-Arab or al-Sham ideologies cannot negate the existence of historic Palestine or the deeply rooted, distinct and particular Palestinian identity.

THE SHORT-LIVED NEWSPAPER *SURIYYA AL-JANUBIYYAH* (1919–1920)

Palestinian nationalism since 1918 has focused largely on the boundaries of Mandatory Palestine. However, the emergence of modern nationalism in the Arab East in the late 19th century spawned the creation of new ideas and several myths including that of Syrian Qawmi identity and the idea of 'Suriyya al-Janubiyyah', or 'Southern Syria', as a way of describing a particular modern Palestinian identity which began to emerge in the late Ottoman period. However, although the name Syria is as ancient as the name Palestine and the modern term Syria should not be conflated automatically with the traditional Islamic term of al-Sham, there is no evidence that a Syrian Qawmi identity or a distinct Suriyya al-Janubiyyah identity had existed or been used by Palestinians before the late 19th century.

At the same time the rise of modern nationalism in the Arab world has, in fact, resulted the creation of a two-tier Watani/Qawmi nationalism in the Arab East with two distinct and mutually complementary terms: *wataniyyah* and *qawmiyyah*, the former referring to country-based territorial nationalism (for instance, Palestine) and the latter to the wider pan-Arab solidarity and unity schemes. This wider context had direct implications for Palestine, and in the post-Ottoman period Palestinian nationalists sought to promote a dyadic form of secular nationalism which combined a Palestine-based *wataniyyah* (local patriotic nationalism) with *qawmiyyah 'arabiyyah*, a form of pan-Arab solidarity. Some Palestinian intellectuals also experimented for a short period after the First World War with Syrian Qawmi nationalism, but this political ideology is today largely extinct.

The short-lived Palestinian newspaper *Suriyya al-Janubiyyah* was a case in point. Further the invention of new terms, such as Suriyya al-Janubiyyah, often reflect multiple factors and the creation of the name of the newspaper *Suriyya al-Janubiyyas* ('Southern Syria') is a classic case in point. The term Suriyya al-Janubiyyah reflected the convergence of four political and cultural currents: (a) the Arab cultural and linguistic dimensions of modern Palestinian identity which were always strong; (b) the invention and propagation of a late 19th century Syrian nationalist ideology; (c) the anti-colonial nature of the modern Palestinian national struggle, a struggle shared with neighbouring Arab peoples; and (d) the particular circumstances surrounding the hurried formation of the pan-Arab nationalist regime in Damascus in 1919–1920 headed by Emir Faisal. Both the term Suriyyah al-Janubiyyah and Faisal's administration in Damascus were short-lived. Syrian nationalism – like Palestinian nationalism and Arab nationalism – is a modern ideology and Syria as a 'national, territorially based idea' was invented in the late 19th century by Arab writers such as Butrus al-Bustani (1819–1883), a Lebanese Maronite convert to Protestantism and a key figure in the Arab cultural awakening of his age, who is considered the intellectual founder of Syrian Qawmi nationhood (Sheehi 2011). The label Suriyya al-Janubiyyah was a short-lived politically-driven construct manufactured in the early 20th century as a by-product of the emergence of the Syrian nationalist (Qawmi) ideology of the period. Al-Bustani and some Arab figures in the Arab Renaissance of the late 19th century propagated the idea of 'greater Syria', partly in response to the bloody 1860 Druze–Maronite Civil War of Mount Lebanon which spread to Damascus and other Syrian and Lebanese cities with devastating consequences.

The Palestinian Arab newspaper *Suriyya al-Janubiyyah*, founded in Jerusalem in September 1919, does not testify to the weakness of the idea of Palestine after the First World War but rather points to the strength and close relations that had existed under Islam for centuries between Palestine and al-Sham. More specifically, this episode should be seen within the context of the political activities of the short-lived regime of Emir Faisal in Damascus in 1919–1920. The newspaper only operated for a few months until its final closure by the British in April 1920, shortly before Faisal's regime was removed by the French military. The newspaper was an organ of the al-Nadi al-'Arabi (the Arab Club), founded in Damascus in 1919, and supported Palestinian–Syrian unity under Emir Faisal's leadership in Damascus. It was published by a Palestinian lawyer, Muhammad Hasan al-Budayri, and edited by 'Arif al-'Arif with contributions from, inter alia, Haj Amin al-Husayni. Although the term Suriyyah al-Janubiyyah has almost vanished from Arab and collective consciousness or discourse, it is occasionally resurrected by pan-Arab intellectuals as a way of denying the existence of the Palestinian people.[29]

The term Suriyya al-Janubiyyah itself was propagated during and in the aftermath of this brief episode, but it was largely the outcome of the circumstances surrounding the formation of the short-lived pan-Arab administration of Faisal in Damascus and the concurrent debate about joint Palestinian–Syrian statehood. However, this episode also spawned a certain amount of literature on 'Southern Syria' and a great deal of confusion among historians, especially those who failed to understand the context and contingencies surrounding this new term. Some historians added more confusion by beginning to conflate a new label, Suriyya al-Janubiyyah, with al-Sham, an old term associated with the Islamic history of the wider Levant. Other historians also began to translate al-Sham automatically into 'greater Syria', thus adding more confusion and little understanding as to the origin of the term Suriyya al-Janubiyyah.

Yet, in contrast to al-Sham, Suriyya al-Janubiyyah was neither rooted in the history of Palestine nor found among Palestinians before the First World

War. Also, crucially, the setting up of a newspaper under the name *Suriyya al-Janubiyyah* for several months in Jerusalem is not in itself evidence that the term 'Southern Syria' encapsulated the whole spirit of the age or the lack of a 'Palestinian national identity' in 1919. On the contrary, from the 1920s onwards both Haj Amin al-Husayni and 'Arif al-'Arif emerged as highly influential figures in Palestinian nationalism and the term Suriyya al-Janubiyyah was not used by either of them after Faisal's fall in 1920.

Pan-Syrianism was a relatively short-lived ideological phenomenon. Moreover, during its brief existence, the newspaper *Suriyya al-Janubiyyah* advocated Palestinian–Syrian–Arab unity schemes with a strong commitment to Palestinian nationalism and strong opposition to Zionist settler-colonisation. At the time these political positions were perceived to be complementary rather than contradictory. However, with the overthrow of Faisal's administration in Damascus by the French in 1920, the idea of Suriyya al-Janubiyyah declined sharply and in the 1930s Palestinian political parties often combined strong commitments to Palestinian nationalism with pan-Arab – rather than pan-Syrian – unity schemes.

One influential current of Palestinian nationalism continued to advocate Palestinian *wataniyyah* – Palestine-based patriotic nationalism – closely allied with ideologies of pan-Arab *qawmiyyah* persisted throughout the British Mandatory period. This current strongly argued against the British pro-Zionist policy of detaching Palestine from its Arab history and environment. Well-known representatives of this current were leaders of the Istiqlal party: 'Awni 'Abd al-Hadi (1889–1970)[30] and Muhammad Izzat Darwazh (1888–1984), who had been one of the leaders of the Palestinian Revival Society (al-Nahdah al-Filistiniyyah), a Palestinian nationalist organisation founded in Damascus in 1919. 'Abd al-Hadi belonged to a landowning family in the Jenin (Nablus) area and Darwazah came from a middle class family of merchants from Nablus that had long been involved in textiles and had extensive trade relationships with the Arab merchants of Damascus and Beirut (Doumani 1995: 59–61). Both 'Abd al-Hadi and Darwazah had been educated in the Ottoman period and had been personally involved in radical pan-Arab political activities during the pre-Mandatory period. 'Abd al-Hadi had been educated in Beirut, Istanbul and at the Sorbonne University in Paris and Darwazah, a self-taught intellectual (Muslih 1991: 178), had served in the local Ottoman administration as a clerk in the Department of Telegraphic and Postal Services in Nablus and later as Director of Postal Services in Beirut. In the early 1930s the Istiqlal party became 'the only mass-based pan-Arabist party, [which] began to mobilize Palestinian Arabs around an anti-Zionist and anti-imperialist program' (Tamari 2008: 6–7). Furthermore, both 'Abd al-Hadi and Darwazah 'continued to believe in Palestine's identity as a component of the greater Syrian [Bilad al-Sham] homeland' (Tamari 2008: 7). The Istiqlal party sought independence for Palestine within Arab unity schemes – pan-Arab schemes which at the time were conceived as a way of empowering the Palestinian national struggle and resisting Zionist settler-colonisation. In fact, the leaders of the Istiqlal party saw no contradiction between the advocacy of pan-Arabism and their active involvement in the Palestinian national liberation movement. On the contrary, for them the two objectives were complementary. Also, opposition to Zionist national claims to Palestine and opposition to the Mandatory (colonial) system in the Middle East, which was the main obstacle to Arab self-determination, were perceived as intertwined: 'If the [British] Mandate fell, then the Zionist project would also collapse' (Krämer 2011: 256).

'Abd al-Hadi understood the close linkage at the time between local Palestinian identity, Arabism and opposition to settler-colonialism in Palestine. In his passionate quest to refute the Zionist claims to Palestine, 'Abd al-Hadi testified before the British Peel Commission in January 1937, while rejecting British policies which sought to detach Palestine from the rest of al-Sham in line with the commitments of the Balfour Declaration of 1917, which stated: 'His Majesty's Government view with favour the establishment in Palestine of a national home for the Jewish people'.

'Abd al-Hadi was, at the same time, a Palestinian Arab nationalist and a key figure in, and one of the chief spokesmen of, the Palestinian Arab nationalist movement during the Mandatory period. He served as secretary of the Executive Committee of the Palestine Arab Congress in 1928. He was also appointed general secretary of the Arab Higher Committee, which was formed in April 1936 to coordinate the general strike among Palestinians. The Istiqlal party took part in the Palestinian uprising in 1936–1939 and called for an Indian Congress Party-style boycott of the British (Khalidi, R. 2001: 25). The Istiqlal party was subsequently banned by the British.

As a shrewd countermove to the pan-Arabist orientation of the Istiqlal party, Haj Amin al-Husayni, the *mufti* of Jerusalem and head of the Supreme Muslim Council, and his supporters formed the Palestinian Arab Party (al-Hizb al-ʿArabi al-Filastini), which included key Palestinian Muslim and Christian leaders (Krämer 2011: 258). This party, which emphasised the Palestinian agency in, and Palestinian dimensions of, the national struggle in Palestine and dominated the Arab Higher Committee in the period 1936–1948, would subsequently inspire the emergence of the Palestinian National Liberation Movement (Harakat al-Tahrir al-Watani al-Filastini or Fateh) in the post-Nakba period.

The Palestinian Arab collective agency and Palestinian Arab national dimensions of the struggle in Palestine were also emphasised by another party created in the 1930s: the Palestine Arab Reform Party (Hizb al-Islah al-ʿArabi al-Filastin), established by members of the Khalidi family of Jerusalem in June 1935 (Krämer 2011: 258).

The Palestinian uprising of 1936–1939 had a major impact on the consolidation of the particular components of Palestine's national identity and national struggle in Palestine. This can be best illustrated and symbolised by the nationalist poem *Mawtini* ('My Homeland'), perhaps the most famous and influential Palestinian poem of all time. It was written by Ibrahim Tuqan (1905–1941) in 1934 and became a rallying cry against British colonialism and Zionism in Palestine during the great uprising in the 1930s (Jayyusi and Tingley 1977). Tuqan belonged to a notable Nablus family that had, under the Ottomans, dominated the politics of the city for much of the 18th and 19th centuries. He had been educated in Nablus, Jerusalem and at the American University of Beirut from 1923 to 1929. He later worked as a professor at the American University in Beirut and a sub-director of the Jerusalem-based Palestine Broadcasting Service. An excerpt from the poem, which has since then embodied that indomitable Palestinian national struggle for self-determination, reads as follows:

The sword and the pen
Not talking or quarrelling
Are our symbols
Our glory and covenant

And a duty to fulfil it
Shake us
Our honour
Is an honourable cause
A raised flag
O, your beauty
In your eminence
Victorious over your enemies
My homeland
My homeland.

FROM PALESTINE TO THE LAND OF ISRAEL: THE PALESTINE COMMUNIST PARTY (PALESTINISHE KOMUNISTISHE PARTEI)

The Israeli Communist Party began as an exclusively Jewish Ashkenazi party in Palestine in 1923. With Yiddish being the historical and literally the 'mother language' (*mame-loshn*) of the Ashkenazi Jews and being a language spoken by many East European Jews, the Communist Party was called in Yiddish: Palestinishe Komunistishe Partei. With the 'new Hebrew' being in ascendancy, the party became eventually known in Israel by its Hebrew name: Ha-Miflaga Ha-Komunistit Ha-Yisraelit. In Mandatory Palestine, however, its Arabic name was the Palestine Communist Party (al-Hizb al-Shuyu'i al-Filastini). In 1923, the PCP was born as a coalition of left-wing Zionist settlers and non-Zionist communists among the East European Jewish immigrants to Palestine. At its foundation and in its early years the party was predominantly Jewish and it remained small but overwhelmingly composed of East European Jews during much of Mandatory Palestine (Younis 2000: 117).

Dominated by Stalinists throughout much of the Mandatory period, in late 1947, following the Soviet Union's support for the UN Partition Resolution, the party embraced a Zionist designation for the country, 'Eretz Yisrael' (instead of Palestine) and were instrumental in securing military assistance from Czechoslovakia for the State of Israel during the toughest stages of the 1948 war.[31] Also in 1948 the leader of the party, Meir Vilner, was a signatory to the Israeli Zionist 'Independence Charter' (Megilat ha-'Atzmaut), which repeatedly described the country as the Land of Israel (Hebrew: Eretz Yisrael). In the post-Nakba period the party promoted a collective memory which contributed to the Israelification of the Palestinian citizens of Israel, the so-called 'Israeli Arabs'.

At the same time, during this early Mandatory period, the Palestinian Arabs created a labour movement and set up the Palestine Arab Workers Society (Jam'iyyat al-'Ummal al-'Arabiyyah al-Filastiniyyah), the main Palestinian Arab labour organisation, established in 1925 with headquarters in Haifa, and branches in Nazareth, Jaffa and Majdal 'Asqalan. From 1937 to 1947 its general secretary was Sami Taha (1916–1947) – born in 'Arrabah, a town near Jenin, his family later moved to Haifa – who was the main Palestinian Arab labour leader during the Mandatory period (Lockman 1996: 259). He was assassinated in Haifa on 12 September 1947. Throughout the 1920s and 1930s the Palestine Jewish communists maintained close relations with the Palestine Arab Workers Society.

In the middle of the Second World War, in 1943, the Palestine Communist Party, under pressure to accommodate the Middle Eastern policies of Stalinist Russia, came into conflict with the key aims of the Palestinian national movement. The party split with the more radical anti-Zionist Palestinian Arab members, who formed the National Liberation League in 1944. Coming under Zionist left-wing influences, and endorsing the Soviet notion that Zionism was a form of bourgeois nationalism, the PCP changed its name to MAKEY, the Communist Party of Eretz Yisrael ('the Communist Party of the Land of Israel') – after endorsing the UN Partition Resolution of November 1947 – embracing a term central to Zionist thinking. This was the first time the Palestine communists had used the Zionist term Eretz Yisrael ('Land of Israel'). Furthermore, the leader of MAKEY, Meir Vilner-Kovner, was one of the signatories of the Israeli Declaration of Independence of May 1948, a document whose Hebrew text does not mention the term Palestine and talks only about Eretz Yisrael. The document begins with rehashing some of the founding myths of Zionism:

[The Land of Israel] was the birthplace of the Jewish people.
Here their spiritual, religious and political identity was shaped.

Here they first attained statehood, created cultural values of national and universal significance and gave to the world the eternal Book of Books.[32]

Also, crucially, the party was involved in arms shipments from Czechoslovakia to the Zionist military organisations in 1948–1949 – deliveries which radically altered the military balance on the ground in Palestine in 1948 and proved significant for the establishment of the Israeli state. Since 1948 the Jewish members of the party have also served in the Israeli army.

Bedevilled by contradictory tendencies, after 1948 the party took part in Israeli parliamentary politics and became known as MAKEY. After another internal split in 1965, the main parliamentary faction became known as Rakah, an acronym for the New Communist List (Hebrew: Reshima Komunistit Hadasha). By this stage the party was a predominantly Palestinian Arab party within the Green Line with representation in the Israeli Knesset (parliament). Historically, and in particular since 1948, the party's political platform largely focused on equality and civil rights for the Palestinians within Israel. Today the party is known as Hadash, a Hebrew acronym for Ha-Hazit Ha-Demokratit Le-Shalom (Democratic Front for Peace and Equality; Arabic: al-Jabhah ad-Dimuqratiyyah lis-Salam wal-Musawah), with a political platform committed to the two-state solution.

PALESTINIAN NATIONAL INSTITUTIONS AND ORGANISATIONS IN THE POST-NAKBA PERIOD: THE REVOLUTIONARY POLITICS OF THE PLO

In the post-Nakba period a large number of Palestinian anti-colonial organisations and secular institutions were established. Several of these revolutionary bodies predated and anticipated the founding of the PLO in 1964 and these included the Palestinian Student Union in Cairo (1952), the General Union of Palestinian Students (1959), the first group of Fateh (Palestinian National Liberation Movement), founded in 1959 around an organ called *Filastinuna* (Our Palestine), the Palestinian Women's League (1963) and the General Union of Palestinian Workers (1963).

The national bodies created in the post-Nakba period included:

- All-Palestine Government (Hukumat 'Umum Filastin') in Gaza on 1 October 1948.
- The Palestinian Student Union set up in Cairo in the early 1950s, led by Yasir Arafat.
- Fateh (Harakat al-Tahrir al-Watani al-Filastini; Palestinian National Liberation Movement) was founded in 1959. Its first underground magazine which began to appear monthly in 1959 – under the editorship of Khalil al-Wazir (1935–1988), a refugee from al-Ramla – was called *Filastinuna, Nida al-Hayat* (*Our Palestine, the Call to Life*).
- The General Union of Palestinian Students (GUPS), established in Cairo in 1959, becoming part of the PLO in 1969.
- The Palestinian Women's League was established in Cairo in 1963; later in 1965 absorbed into the General Union of Palestinian Women.
- The General Union of Palestinian Workers (GUPW) was established in Hilwan in Egypt in 1963, becoming part of the newly created PLO in 1965.
- The first Palestinian National Council (PNC) met in (East) Jerusalem on 2 June 1964 and formally founded the PLO. The PNC became the legislative body of the PLO.
- The Palestine Liberation Organisation was established in June 1964.
- The Palestinian National Charter (al-Mithaq al-Watani al-Filastini) of the PLO was first adopted in June 1964.
- The Palestinian National Fund was set up 1964 and conformed to Article 24 of the PLO to finance the activities of the PLO. The PNF is responsible for managing financial aid coming from a variety of sources: funds from Arab states, contributions from wealthy Palestinians and a 'liberation tax' levied on Palestinians working in Arab countries.
- The Palestine Liberation Movement (Fateh) was established in 1965 and took over the PLO in 1968; the official organ of the PLO, *Filastin al-Thawrah* (*Palestine of the Revolution*), was set up in Beirut in 1972.
- The General Union of Palestinian Women was established in 1965 as part of the PLO and with the goal of organising Palestinian women

and promoting an active role for them in Palestinian social, social, economic and political spheres.

- The Popular Front for the Liberation of Palestine (al-Jabhah al-Sha'biyyah li-Tahrir Filastin) is a secular Palestinian socialist organisation founded in 1967 by Dr George Habash (1926–2008), a Palestinian refugee from Lydda, Mandatory Palestine. It has been the second largest of the groups forming the PLO.

- The Union of Palestinian Women Committees was set up in 1980 to empower Palestinian women and to contribute to the Palestinian national struggle against the Israeli military occupation. Since 2001 the Union has been licensed by the Palestinian Interior Ministry.

- The Palestinian National Authority was established following the Oslo Accords in 1993. Since then it has internally governed a small part of the occupied Palestinian territories.

- The Palestinian Broadcasting Corporation (PBC) was established in July 1994 within the jurisdiction of the newly formed Palestinian National Authority. The PBC has a subsidiary radio station, the Voice of Palestine, and a satellite channel, Palestinian Satellite Channel. The Palestinian TV channel first began broadcasting in 1996 in Gaza (Jamal 2005).

- The Palestinian Department of Antiquities and Cultural Heritage was created by the Palestinian National Authority in 1994. Its long-time head, Palestinian archaeologist Dr Hamdan Taha, saw it as a revival of the Palestine Department of Antiquities which was established in 1920 under the British Mandate (Taha 2010).

The revolutionary politics of the PLO experienced sharp decline after the departure of the PLO from Lebanon in 1982. Since then the PLO and its national institutions have become largely marginalised after the signing of the Oslo Accords in 1993, and especially since the creation of the Palestinian National Authority in 1994. However, the historic legacy, revolutionary politics and symbolic value of the PLO as a Palestinian national liberation movement, based on popular representation and enjoying significant support among anti-colonial movements in the Third World, go far beyond its current weak and dysfunctional organisational structures and virtual political paralysis.

STUDIA PALAESTINA: PALESTINE STUDIES AND THE PROLIFERATION OF MODERN RESEARCH SOCIETIES AND INSTITUTIONS

In modern times Palestine Studies as a scholarly discipline has grown phenomenally across several continents and has continued to expand in recent decades – although some of the recently founded centres focus largely on modern Palestine and the Arab–Israeli conflict. Furthermore, when referring to the ancient history of this region, modern European scholarship (and early Zionist scholarly societies such as the Jewish Palestine Exploration Society, founded in 1914) universally and unanimously talk about 'Palestine', even when referring to Jewish history.

The opening of the 'Holy Land' to Europe's political, cultural-religious penetration in the 19th century resulted in mountains of publications on Palestine. To cite some of the scholarly societies/centres/projects/museums/ journals relevant to Palestine Studies and the ancient history and heritage of Palestine:

- The Palestine Exploration Fund, founded in London in the 1860s with a focus on ancient Palestine; it published the *Palestine Exploration Quarterly*.
- The Palestine Pilgrims' Text Society: an organisation established in 1884, the society operated for eleven years and published translations of medieval texts relevant to the history of pilgrimage to the Holy Land. Particular attention was given to accounts containing geographical or topographical information in a variety of languages, including Greek, Latin, Arabic, Hebrew, Old French, Russian and German. Its publications included Guy Le Strange's translation from Arabic and annotation of al-Muqaddasi's (al-Maqdisi's) work under the title: *Description of Syria, including Palestine by Mukaddasi* (1986), Nasir-I-Khusrau's *Diary of a Journey Through Syria and Palestine* (1888).
- Deutscher Verein für die Erforschung Palästinas (German Society for the Exploration of Palestine). The Society's annual publication was *Zeitschrift des Deutschen Palästina-Vereins* (*Journal of the German Society for the Exploration of Palestine*).

- The Deutscher Verein zur Erforschung Palästinas (German Association for the Study of Palestine) was established in 1877 at the initiative of the Swiss geographer Carl Zimmermann's association for the promotion of Bible Studies and research on the history and culture of Palestine. From 1877 it regularly published Zimmermann's Zeitschrift.
- Imperial Orthodox Palestine Society (Russian: Императорское православное палестинское общество) was founded in 1882 as a scholarly and political organisation for the study of Palestine. Following the Bolshevik Revolution of 1917 the society was renamed the Russian Palestine Society (Russian: Российское Палестинское Общество) and was attached to the Academy of Sciences of the USSR. Its original Russian name was restored in 1992.
- *Zeitschrift des Deutschen Palästina-Vereins (Journal of the German Society for Exploration of Palestine)* is the official bulletin of the German Protestant Institute of Archaeology in the Holy Land (Deutsches Evangelisches Institut für Altertumswissenschaften des Heiligen Landes), founded in 1900. It covers topics such as archaeology, topography, iconography, religion, social anthropology, philology and literature.
- Palestine Archaeological Museum (al-Quds/Jerusalem), was initiated in 1918 and officially opened in 1938; it was renamed 'Rockefeller Museum' by Israel after the 1967 occupation.
- Palestine Folklore Museum (al-Quds/Jerusalem) was set up in al-Qala'a in the 1930s.
- Jewish Palestine Exploration Society was founded in 1914 with a focus on ancient Palestine; it was renamed after 1948 as the Israel Exploration Society.
- *The Journal of the Palestine Oriental Society* was published in Jerusalem by the Palestine Oriental Society from 1920 to 1948 and focused on ancient history and antiquities.
- The Institute for Palestine Studies, founded in Beirut in 1963, publishes the *Journal of Palestine Studies.*
- Palestine Research Centre was founded by the PLO in Beirut in 1965; it published a periodical entitled *Palestinian Affairs (Shu'un Filastiniyah).*
- *Journal of Holy Land and Palestine Studies* was founded in 2002; it is published by Edinburgh University Press.

- The European Centre for Palestine Studies, Exeter University was established in 2009.
- Center for Palestine Studies, Columbia University, New York.
- Centre for Palestine Studies (SOAS, London) was established in 2012.
- The Palestinian Museum opened in Birzeit in May 2016.

Chapter 10

SETTLER-COLONIALISM AND DISINHERITING THE PALESTINIANS

The appropriation of Palestinian place names by the Israeli state

> The four Great Powers are committed to Zionism. And Zionism, be it right or wrong, good or bad, is rooted in age-long traditions, in present needs, in future hopes, of far greater import than the desires and prejudices of the 700,000 [Palestine] Arabs who now inhabit that ancient land. (Arthur James Balfour, cited in Nutting 2013)

Zionist settler-colonialism is at the heart of the conflict in Palestine; settler-colonialism is a structure not an episode (Wolfe 2006). Zionist settler-colonialism is deeply rooted in European colonialism. Ignoring the existence and rights of indigenous peoples, British colonialists often saw large parts of the earth as *terra nullius*, 'nobody's land'. This (originally Roman legal) expression was used to describe territory which was not subject to the sovereignty of any European state – sovereignty over territory which is *terra nullius* may be acquired through occupation and/or settler-colonisation.

When in the late 19th century European 'Zionism nationalism' arose as a political force calling for the settler-colonisation of Palestine and the 'gathering of all Jews', little attention was paid to the fact that Palestine was already populated. Indeed, the Basel Programme adopted at the First Zionist Congress, which launched political Zionism in 1897, made no mention of a Palestinian indigenous population when it spelled out the movement's objective: 'the establishment of a publicly and legally secured home in Palestine for the Jewish people'.

Moreover, in the early years of their efforts to secure support for their enterprise, the Zionists propagated in the West the racist myth of 'a land without a people for a people without a land', a slogan popularised by Israel Zangwill, a prominent Anglo-Jewish writer often quoted in the British press as a spokesman for Zionism and one of the earliest organisers of the Zionist movement in Britain. Even as late as 1914, Chaim Weizmann, who was to become the first President of Israel and who, along with Theodor Herzl and David Ben-Gurion, was one of the three men most responsible for turning the Zionist dream into reality, stated:

> In its initial stage, Zionism was conceived by its pioneers as a
> movement wholly depending on mechanical factors: there is a country
> which happens to be called Palestine, a country without a people,
> and, on the other hand, there exists the Jewish people, and it has no
> country. What else is necessary, then, than to fit the gem into the ring,
> to unite this people with this country? The owners of the country [the
> Turks] must, therefore, be persuaded and convinced that this marriage
> is advantageous, not only for the [Jewish] people and for the country,
> but also for themselves.[1]

Neither Zangwill nor Weizmann intended these demographic assessments in a literal fashion. They did not mean that there were no people in Palestine, but that there were no people worth considering within the framework of the notions of racist European supremacy that then held sway. In this connection, a comment by Weizmann to Arthur Ruppin, the head of the colonisation department of the Jewish Agency, is particularly revealing. When asked by Ruppin about the indigenous Palestinian Arabs, Weizmann replied: 'The British told us that there are there some hundred thousand niggers [Hebrew: *kushim*, negroes] and for those there is no value.'[2]

In the English language, the word nigger is a White racist slur directed at Black and African people. Its derogatory connotations echo another pejorative English word, philistine, which White Britain borrowed from biblical prejudices and popularised in daily parlance. However, in the White racist colonial culture within which Weizmann and co. operated, the reference to the indigenous people of Palestine as nigger would have been instinctive and natural. Echoing Weizmann's demographic racism and Shaftesbury's biblical Orientalism, Zangwill himself spelled out the actual meaning of his slogan with admirable clarity in 1920:

> If Lord Shaftesbury was literally inexact in describing Palestine as a
> country without a people, he was essentially correct, for there is no
> Arab people living in intimate fusion with the country, utilising its
> resources and stamping it with a characteristic impress: there is at best
> an Arab encampment. (Zangwill 1920: 104; see also Kamel 2015)

The interplay between British domestic and imperial considerations, Jewish Zionist lobbyists (especially Chaim Weizmann, 1874–1952) and Christian Zionist prophetic politics would lead to the Balfour Declaration of 1917 which promised a 'Jewish homeland' in Palestine (Anderson, I. 2005: 1, 57–58). Then an imperial world power, Britain gave sanction for the first time to the Zionist campaign for possession of Palestine. This highly controversial document, dated 2 November, was issued by Foreign Secretary Arthur James Balfour (later Lord Balfour), in the form of a letter to a prominent British Jewish supporter of the Zionist movement, Lionel Walter (Lord) Rothschild, declaring British support for political Zionism:

> Her Majesty's Government views with favour the establishment
> in Palestine of a national home for the Jewish people, and will use
> their best endeavours to facilitate the achievement of this object, it
> being clearly understood that nothing shall be done to prejudice the
> civil and religious rights of the existing non-Jewish communities in
> Palestine, or the rights and political status enjoyed by Jews in any
> other country. (Quoted in Said 1980: 3)

Although the Zionist Jewish movement had already initiated a series of international congresses and established small Jewish colonies in the early 20th century Palestine, it was the sponsorship of Zionism by the leading imperial power of the age that would transform the Zionist project into a major European settler-colonial project in Palestine.

Balfour's legacy became inseparable from the pro-Zionist Declaration he issued in 1917. The reasons for the declaration were complex. Balfour's brand of Christian Zionism was driven by a great deal of Judeophobia, hyped perceptions of 'Zionist Jewish power' and of fears of mass immigration of Jews from Eastern Europe to Britain. As Prime Minister, Balfour had passed the 1905 Aliens Act, the main object of which was to restrict the entry into Britain of Jews from Eastern Europe. Brian Klug put it rather sceptically: 'Keeping Jews out of Britain and packing them off to Palestine were just two sides of the same antisemitic coin'.[3] Here Zionist historians often chose to ignore the distinction between drivers/motives and justification and seize upon Balfour's own post-war Christian Zionist rhetoric to justify his Declaration. Yet Balfour's strategic and nationalist domestic motives and concerns, especially his well-documented efforts and policies to stop the influx of Eastern European Jewry into the UK, must be taken into consideration in any attempt to assess the motives behind the Declaration as well as the long-term catastrophic consequences for Palestine of that Balfour commitment.

The religio-political roots of this British pro-Zionist commitment go all the way back to the Protestant Christian Zionist lobby which was established in London in the 1830s by Lord Shaftesbury (Anthony Ashley Cooper; 1801–1885). Shaftesbury came from the British aristocratic ruling elite and was for decades at the heart of the Victorian establishment. He also became well known for advocating socially reformist policies at the height of the Victorian era. Shaftesbury was a Tory member of the Commons, and later a member of the Lords, the upper house of Parliament in the United Kingdom. He was the nephew-in-law of Lord Melbourne (Prime Minister through most of the period from 1834 to 1841), and the stepson-in-law of Lord Palmerston (Foreign Minister for most of the 1840s and early 1850s, and then Prime Minister for most of the period 1855–1865) (Merkley 1998: 13). Palmerston (1784–1865) served twice as Prime Minister in the mid-19th century. For most of 1830 to 1865 he dominated British foreign policy when Britain was at the height of its imperialist power. Shaftesbury was offered positions of power by successive British governments, Palmerston encouraged and financially supported him and both men were instrumental in the establishment of the British Consulate in Jerusalem in 1838 – a Consulate which in the 19th century was dominated by Christian Zionists and was at the centre of British imperial schemes which led to the Balfour policy in Palestine (Schölch 1992).

In particular, crusading Protestant Christian Zionist Shaftesbury was the most ardent propagator and lobbyist of the restoration of 'God's ancient people', as he styled the Jews (Tuchman 1982). He and the influential circle he dominated were under the influence of the 'End of Times' prophetic politics – evangelising politics based on the Old Testament's Book of Daniel – which they believed would be fulfilled by the 'literal return' and 'Restoration' of the Jews to Palestine. As the demise of the Ottoman Empire appeared to be approaching, the Protestant advocacy of 'Jewish restorationism' and settler-colonisation of Palestine increased in the UK and was seen as highly beneficial to the expanding British Empire in the Middle East. In the mid-to-late 19th century Shaftesbury led the British Christian Zionist lobby which included establishment figures such as Lord Lindsay (Crawford 1847: 71), Lord Manchester, George Eliot, Holman Hunt and Hall Caine.

Epitomising Victorian Protestant imperialism, Bible-bashing Shaftesbury was also a myth-maker. He pushed zealously the myth of ubiquitous and perennial Jewish diaspora longing to 'return', and on 4 November 1840 he placed an advertisement in the *Times* (London):

RESTORATION OF THE JEWS: A memorandum has been addressed to the Protestant monarchs of Europe on the subject of the restoration of the Jewish people to the land of Palestine. The document in question, dictated by a peculiar conjunction of affairs in the East, and other striking 'signs of the times', reverts to the original covenant which secures that land to the [Jewish] descendant of Abraham. (Quoted in Wagner 1995: 91)

Shaftesbury was directly responsible for the propagandistic slogan 'A country without a nation for a nation without a country',[4] later to be become a key Zionist Jewish myth: 'A land without a people for a people without a land' (Masalha 1997; Hyamson 1950: 10, 12; Kamel 2015). Assessing the significance of his lobbying efforts on the fortunes of the Protestant Zionist movement in Britain, Donald Wagner writes:

> One cannot overstate the influence of Lord Shaftesbury on the British political elites, church leaders, and the average Christian layperson. His efforts and religious political thought may have set the tone for England's colonial approach to the Near East and in particular the holy land during the next one hundred years. He singularly translated the theological positions of Brightman, Henry Finch, and John Nelson Darby [the father of modern premillennial dispensationalism]:5 see below][5] into a political strategy. His high political connections, matched by his uncanny instincts, combined to advance the Christian Zionist vision. (Wagner 1995: 92)

In 1880 F. Laurence Oliphant (1829–1888), MP, novelist and evangelical Christian, a follower of Shaftesbury, published a book entitled *The Land of Gilead* (named after the biblical 'land of Gilead'),[6] in which he presented a plan of 'Jewish restoration' and a detailed project for Jewish settlement east of the River Jordan. He urged the British parliament to assist Jewish immigration from Russia and Eastern Europe to Palestine. Not surprisingly he also advocated that indigenous Palestinian Arabs be removed to reservations like those of the indigenous inhabitants of North America[7] (Sharif 1983: 68), or hinting at the Bantustan ideology later developed by South Africa (Sharif 1983: 68; Wagner 1995: 93).

A combination of Protestant religious and imperialist considerations drove some Britons to produce Christian Zionist novels, to set up exploration societies and to advocate the 'restoration of the Jews to Palestine' in public and in private.[8] Furthermore, a succession of archaeological discoveries in the Near East, military adventurism and the growing number of travelogues fired the imagination of Protestant missionaries, European officials and Arabist scholars and led to the direct involvement European powers in the Holy Land (Shepherd 1987; Osband 1989). This European obsession with the archaeological past was marked by a decided contempt for the indigenous people of Palestine and life in modern Palestinian villages and towns

At the height of the British Empire and the Victorian era prophetic politics of 'biblical restorationism' went hand in hand with increasing British colonial involvement in the 'Orient'. The Holy Land in the 19th century was an attractive target for several European nations which were flexing their colonial muscles around the globe. The region was ready for Western penetration, particularly while the Ottoman Empire was showing signs of political and economic disintegration. The race for a European national presence and colonial commercial interests in the East, and in the Holy Land in particular, was masked by scholarly activities and Oriental Studies (Said 1978). Coinciding with the European 'scramble for Palestine', various sectors of the Western academy, and most of the Western Christian churches, displayed an increasing interest in Palestine. Invariably foreign interest took the form of establishing Christian institutions – the Ottoman reforms after the Crimean War (1853–1856) granted equal rights, including property rights, to non-Muslims – thereby uniting Christian missionary endeavour with national influence. The interests of God and country ran in parallel. The British moved early,[9] and were soon emulated by the Russians,[10] Germans,[11] Austrians (Wrba 1996) and others, marking the beginning of extensive Western influence in Palestine, an influence which the Ottomans feared might be a prelude to attempting to recover Palestine as a Christian state.[12] Such was the degree of Western penetration that the Austrian consul, the Count de Caboga, reported in 1880 that Jerusalem had become a European city, and Captain (later General Sir) Charles Warren (1840–1927) of the British Royal Engineers and one of the key officers of the British Palestine Exploration Fund, who was sent to map the Old Testament topography of Jerusalem and investigate 'the site of the temple', noted: '[British] King Consul [James Finn] rules supreme, not over the natives of the city, but over strangers; but yet these strangers for the most part are the rightful owners, the natives, for the most part, are usurpers' (Shepherd 1987: 127–128).

Protestant Zionists and British imperialists believed that a 'Jewish Palestine' would be convenient for a British protectorate there along the main route to India. From the late 19th century to the middle of the 20th century three famous British prime ministers were closely associated with 'Gentile Zionism' in Britain: Benjamin Disraeli (1804–1881), who was successful in securing for imperial Britain control of the Suez Canal, David Lloyd George (1863–1945), whose government issued the Balfour Declaration of 1917, and Sir Winston Churchill, who for nearly half a century in and out of office was devoted to political Zionism and the British Empire (Sykes 1973: 45, 52, 207). Both Disraeli and Lloyd George were fascinated by the theories of amalgamation or affinity between Christianity and Judaism (Anderson, I. 2005: 60). Lloyd George, a Protestant Zionist, was once quoted as saying: 'I was taught far more history about the Jews than about the history of my own people' (quoted by Stein 1961: 142); and Disraeli was baptised a Protestant, but he remained fascinated by his Jewish background. Describing Protestant Christianity as 'completed Judaism', he – like many Christian Zionists – delighted in describing himself as the 'missing page' between the Old and New Testaments (Johnson, P. 1993: 324). Disraeli's civilising Christian imperialism combined patronising attitudes towards the Jews with imperialist foreign policies towards the Middle East, policies which he justified by invoking paternalistic and racist theories which saw imperialism as a manifestation of what Britain's imperial poet, Rudyard Kipling, would refer to as 'the white man's burden'.[13]

For centuries, and for more than eighty years of political Zionism, the Palestinian Arabs were an absolute majority in Palestine. Balfour was fully aware of this fact when, on 11 August 1919, he frankly expressed his typically colonialist views and wrote:

> Zionism, be it right or wrong, good or bad, is rooted in age-long traditions, in present needs, in future hopes, of far profounder import than the desires and prejudices of the 700,000 Arabs who now inhabit that ancient land ... The idea of planting a [European] minority of outsiders upon an indigenous majority population, without consulting it, was not calculated to horrify men who had worked with Cecil Rhodes or promoted European settlement in Kenya. (Quoted in Talmon 1965: 248, 250)

In 1925 Balfour visited Palestine and was a key guest of honour at the opening of the Hebrew University of Jerusalem. He was greeted enthusiastically by the leadership of the small European Zionist Yishuv (settlement) in Palestine, while the majority of indigenous inhabitants of Palestine welcomed him with black flags.

The key to understanding the contribution of Britain to the Palestinian Nakba (catastrophe) of the mid-20th century lies in the intensity with which some British Christian restorationists embraced the project of a 'Jewish homeland' in Palestine; the way in which the Bible and 'divine rights and divine promises' were seen by the likes of British Prime Minister Lloyd George and his Foreign Secretary Arthur James Balfour (who issued the Balfour Declaration); and generally the extraordinary appeal political Zionism had in the West. Although the Balfour Declaration was partly motivated by First World War calculations, it was not issued in an ideological vacuum. Its content reflected the Christian Zionist prophetic politics which became deeply rooted in 19th century imperialist Protestant Britain (Verete 1970).[14] This all meant that, from the beginning, the reality of Palestine and the Palestinians lay outside Western and Zionist representations of the 'Jewish homeland' in Palestine.

Furthermore, as Edward Said argued, the 'site of the Zionist struggle was only partially in Palestine'; the crucial site of the Zionist struggle remained until 1948 in the capital cities in the West, while the reality of Palestine and 'the native resistance to the Zionists was either played down or ignored in the West' (Said 1980: 22–23). By removing the struggle from the Middle East, the Palestinians (and Arabs) were prevented from representing themselves, and were deemed incapable of doing so: '[T]hey cannot represent themselves; they must be represented' (quoted in Said 1980).[15] In making the Zionist movement attractive to Western audiences, its leaders not only denied the existence of the Arabic-speaking people of Palestine; they represented the Arabs to the West as something that could be understood and managed in specific ways. Between Zionism and the West there was and still is a community of language and of ideology; Arabs were not part of this community. To a very great extent this community depends on a tradition in the West of enmity towards Islam in particular and the Orient in general (Said 1979: 25–26). A major success of the Christian and Jewish

Zionists has been their ability to occupy the space from which they were all to represent and explain the Arabs to the West:

> [The] Zionists took it upon themselves as a partially 'Eastern' people who had emancipated themselves from the worst Eastern excesses, to explain the Oriental Arabs to the West, to assume responsibility for expressing what the Arabs were really like and about, never to let the Arabs appear equally with them as existing in Palestine. This method allowed Zionism always to seem both involved in and superior to the native realties of Middle Eastern existence. (Said 1980: 26)

Despite such Christian and Jewish Zionist statements, however, the Zionist leaders from the outset were well aware that not only were there people on the land, but that people were there in large numbers. Zangwill, who had visited Palestine in 1897 and come face to face with the demographic reality, acknowledged in 1905 in a speech to a Zionist group in Manchester that 'Palestine proper has already its inhabitants. The pashalik of Jerusalem is already twice as thickly populated as the United States, having fifty-two souls to the square mile, and not 25 percent of them Jews' (Zangwill 1937: 210). Abundant references to the Palestinian population in early Zionist texts show clearly that from the beginning of Zionist settlement in Palestine, which Zionist historiography dates to the arrival of the members of the Russian Bilu Society in 1882, the Palestinian Arabs were far from being an 'unseen' or 'hidden' presence. Moreover, recent studies have shown that Zionist leaders were concerned with what they termed the 'Arab problem' (Hebrew: *Habe'ayah Ha'arvit*) or the 'Arab Question' (Hebrew: *Hashelah Ha'arvit*). As seen in their writings, the attitudes prevailing among the majority of the Zionist groups and settlers concerning the indigenous Palestinian population ranged from indifference and disregard to patronising superiority. A typical example can be found in the works of Moshe Smilansky, a Zionist writer and Labour leader who immigrated to Palestine in 1890:

> Let us not be too familiar with the Arab fellahin lest our children adopt their ways and learn from their ugly deeds. Let all those who are

loyal to the Torah avoid ugliness and that which resembles it and keep their distance from the fellahin and their base attributes.

There were, certainly, those who took exception to such attitudes. Ahad Ha'Am (Asher Zvi Ginzberg), a liberal Russian Jewish thinker who visited Palestine in 1891, published a series of articles in the Hebrew periodical *Hamelitz* that were sharply critical of the ethnocentricity of political Zionism as well as the exploitation of Palestinian peasantry by Zionist settler-colonists. Ahad Ha'Am, who sought to draw attention to the fact that Palestine was not an empty territory and that the presence of another people on the land posed problems, observed that the Zionist 'pioneers' believed that

> the only language that the Arabs understand is that of force ... [They] behave towards the Arabs with hostility and cruelty, trespass unjustly upon their boundaries, beat them shamefully without reason and even brag about it, and nobody stands to check this contemptible and dangerous tendency. (Cited in Masalha 1992: 7)

He cut to the heart of the matter when he ventured that the colonists' aggressive attitude towards the native peasants stemmed from their anger 'towards those who reminded them that there is still another people in the land of Israel that have been living there and does not intend to leave'.

Another early settler, Yitzhak Epstein, who arrived in Palestine from Russia in 1886, warned not only of the moral implications of Zionist colonisation but also of the political dangers inherent in the enterprise. In 1907, at a time when Zionist land purchases in the Galilee were stirring opposition among Palestinian peasants forced off land sold by absentee landlords, Epstein wrote a controversial article entitled 'The Hidden Question', in which he strongly criticised the methods by which Zionists had purchased Arab land. In his view, these methods entailing dispossession of Arab farmers were bound to cause political confrontation in the future. Reflected in the Zionist establishment's angry response to Epstein's article are two principal features of mainstream Zionist thought: the belief that Jewish acquisition of land took precedence over moral considerations, and the advocacy of a separatist and exclusionist Yishuv (colony) in Palestine.

Following in the footsteps of European settler-colonialists, before the First World War some Zionist leaders (notably Theodor Herzl in his Zionist novel *Altneuland*), conceived the reality of Palestine, and the material benefits European Jewish colonisation would bring to Palestine, to be similar to the supremacist ideology of the 'white man's burden'. During the Mandatory period, however, it became clear to the Zionist leadership that a systematic dislocation and 'transfer' of the indigenous inhabitants of Palestine was the *conditio sine qua non* of the Zionist enterprise (Wiemer 1983: 26; Masalha 1992).

In his seminal work, *Orientalism* (1978), Edward W. Said subjected Western 'Oriental Studies' to a devastating critique and exposed the underlying presumptions of the discipline. He also concluded that Biblical Studies were part of and an extension of the Western Orientalist discourse, which had been constructed without any 'Oriental'/Arab/Muslim reader in view. For Said, in this biblical Orientalist discourse the indigenous inhabitants of Palestine were presented as incapable of unified action and national consciousness. The biblical scholars, following in the footsteps of the Western Orientalists, concentrated on historical and archaeological questions. In *The Question of Palestine*, which came out two years after *Orientalism*, Said also tried to explain the erasure of Palestinians from history. For him, the deletion of the reality of Palestine centred on three key issues: first, understanding the representation of Palestine, the Palestinians and Islam in the West: Said's book *Covering Islam* (1981) should be treated as part of a trilogy which includes *Orientalism* (1978) and *The Question of Palestine* (Said 1980; Ashcroft and Ahluwalia 2001: 125). For Said, the representations of Islam in the West are an important part of the question of Palestine because they are used to silence the Palestinians, the majority of whom are Muslims (Said 1980; Ashcroft and Ahluwalia 2001: 128); second, understanding the 'contest between an affirmation and a denial'; third, understanding Western Orientalist attitudes towards Arabs and Islam; Western racial prejudices, and especially the Western narrative of a contest between the 'civilising' forces of the Zionist European settlers and the 'uncivilised', 'treacherous' and degenerate Oriental Arabs (Said 1980: 25–28). This biblically framed discourse entails (a) the shaping of history, 'so that this history now appears to confirm the validity of Zionist claims to Palestine, thereby denigrating Palestinians claims' (Said 1980: 8), and (b) the Zionist legitimisation of Zionist settler-colonisation in Palestine, a process that did not end with the creation of Israel in 1948.

HEBREWISATION: ANTECEDENTS TO ZIONIST TOPONYMY

The reinvention of both the Jewish past and modern Jewish nationhood in Zionist historiography and the creation of a modern Hebrew nationalist consciousness have received some scholarly attention (Myers 1995; Ram 1995: 91–124; Piterberg 2001; Raz-Krakotzkin 1993, 1994). Toponymic and remapping projects were also deployed extensively and destructively by the European colonial powers and European settler-colonial movements. In Palestine, the Zionist Hebrew renaming projects were critical to the ethnocisation of the European Jews and nationalisation of the Hebrew Bible. These projects were inspired by and followed closely British, French and American archaeological and geographical 'exploration' expeditions of the second half of the 19th and first half of the 20th centuries. In line with the reinventions of European ethno-romantic nationalisms, Zionist ideological archaeology and geography claimed to 'own' an exclusive 'national' inheritance in Palestine; the 'land of Israel' was invented and treated as a matter of exclusive ownership. This process of ethno-nationalisation and reinvention of the past intensified after the establishment of the Israeli state in 1948 as part of the general attempt to ethno-nationalise both Jews and the Hebrew Bible (Rabkin 2010: 130).

Since the rise of the Zionist settler movement in the late 19th century, and especially since the establishment of Israel in 1948, the struggle over toponymic memory and the renaming of sites has developed as an integral part of the political conflict in Palestine. The indigenous Palestinians have insisted on their own comprehensive set of Arabic place names through which they see their own social memory and deep-rootedness in the land of Palestine. On the other hand, since the ethnic cleansing of the 1948 Nakba and the creation of the Israeli state, a large number of Palestinian Arabic place names have been Judaised, Hebraicised. Indeed, since 1948 the Israeli army and Israeli state have sought systematically to replace Palestinian Arabic place names, claiming priority in chronology and using modern archaeology, map-making and place names as their proofs of Jewish roots in 'the land of Israel'. In Israel, the significance of place names lies in their potential to legitimise 'historical claims' asserted by the Zionist settler-colonial movement.

In her book *Bible and Sword: How the British came to Palestine* (1982), Barbara Tuchman shows how the two magnets, the Bible and the sword, have drawn countless British pilgrims, crusaders, missionaries, biblical archaeologists and conquerors of Palestine and ultimately led to the British conquest of Palestine in 1918. Central to this book is the assertion that the land conquest narrative of the Bible has been the key text that redeems the European settler-colonisation of Palestine. Outside the Middle East the Bible has redeemed European empires and European settler-colonialism, the conquest of the earth and even current American imperialism. As a fact of power, the authority of the biblical narrative has also been central to organised religion and collective memory. As organised memory, the authority of the Bible became critical to the political theologies of the Medieval Latin crusaders, Spanish *conquistadors*, in the struggle for colonial power in Latin America from 1492 until the 20th century, and a whole variety of settler-colonist projects. In fact, in modern times a range of Western settler-colonial enterprises have deployed the power politics of the biblical text and its 'famous' land conquest narrative very effectively and with devastating consequences for indigenous peoples. The narrative of Exodus has been widely deployed as a framing narrative for European settler-colonialism and the European *mission civilisatrice*, while other biblical texts have been appropriated and used to provide moral authority for European 'exploration' in, and settler-colonial conquests of, Africa, Asia, Australia and the Americas (Prior 1997, 1999).

FROM KARM AL-KHALILI TO KEREM AVRAHAM (1855): JAMES FINN'S COLONY

In the early modern period Palestinian place names contributed to the rise of biblical criticism. In the 17th century the rationalist Jewish philosopher

Baruch Spinoza of Amsterdam initiated a critical approach to Scriptural Studies by looking at place names in Palestine and the Bible. Using toponyms from Palestine as well as other arguments, he concluded that, contrary to the standard belief among Jews and Christians, Moses did not write the Pentateuch, the five books of the Hebrew Bible.

Palestinian place names attracted the attention of fundamentalist Christians and European imperialists in the 19th century. Toponymic projects and geographical replacing of place names in Palestine became powerful tools in the hands of the European powers which competed to penetrate the land of the Bible. The British were the first to recognise and exploit the power of state-sponsored explorations and began to link scriptural geography with 'restorationist' schemes, excavations and colonial penetration of Palestine. The first British colony of Kerem Avraham ('Abraham Vineyard') began as a small settlement founded in 1855 by the influential British Consul in Jerusalem James Finn, and his wife Elizabeth Anne Finn, the daughter of a noted English Hebrew scholar and herself a Hebrew speaker. James Finn, who served in Ottoman Jerusalem from 1846 to 1863, reigned supreme in the city and he became a central figure in the mid-19th century European penetration of Palestine. He also combined his British diplomatic job with Christian missionary activities. His activities paved the way for the biblical explorations and military mapping of Palestine by officers of the British Royal Engineering Corp on behalf of the London-based Palestine Exploration Fund.

James Finn combined biblical 'restorationist' ideology and missionary activities with official British civil service. He and his wife Elizabeth were originally members of the London Society for Promoting Christianity Amongst the Jews. Also, crucially, he was a close associate of Anthony Ashley Cooper, 7th Earl of Shaftesbury, a prominent Tory MP, a millennialist Protestant and a key contributor to Victorian Protestant Zionist 'restorationism', who invented the myth 'A land without people, for a people without a land'. In the early 1850s Finn had purchased Karm al-Khalili, Arabic for 'al-Khalili Vineyard', from a local Palestinian for £250. Al-Khalil is the indigenous Palestinian Arabic toponym for the (biblical) city of Hebron, a city which both local Palestinian Muslim and biblical traditions link to the Patriarch 'Ibrahim al-Khalil' (Abraham); thus Finn used an indigenous name to link firmly the toponym of the modern colony in Jerusalem to biblical traditions.

After the 1967 conquests, the Israeli state was bound to base its conception of Jerusalem upon a mythologised entity, 'Jerusalem of Gold', and to invoke abstract historical and ideological rights in the newly acquired territories, as well as resting its claim on territorial expansion and domination and the 'redemption of land' through settler-colonisation. The same process of appropriation and erasure of Palestinian heritage and the superimposition of a Zionist Hebrew colonising toponymy on Palestinian sites continued after 1967. Almost immediately after the conquest of East Jerusalem the Palestine Archaeological Museum, which represented the multicultural identity and shared heritage of Palestine, was renamed the Rockefeller Museum. Some items were taken to the Shrine of the Book (Hebrew: Hekhal Hasefer), a wing of the Israel Museum in West Jerusalem, which houses parts of the Dead Sea Scrolls discovered in 1947–1956 in the Qumran caves. The Palestine Archaeological Museum had been located on Karm al-Shakyh, the 'Vineyard' of Shaykh al-Khalili, a hill just outside the north-eastern corner of the Old City. The museum had been conceived and established during the Mandatory period, with financial support from the Rockefeller family. It was opened to the public in January 1938. The museum housed a large collection of artefacts unearthed in the excavations conducted in Palestine in 1890–1948. Also among the museum's prized possessions were historical artefacts from the al-Aqsa Mosque and 12th century (Crusader period) marble lintels from the Church of the Holy Sepulchre.

Until 1966 the museum was run by an international board of trustees; it was then taken over by the Jordanian state. Since 1967 the museum has been jointly managed by the Israel Museum and the Israel Department of Antiquities and Museums (later renamed Israel Antiquities Authority). The site is now the headquarters of the Israel Antiquity Authorities. While the Palestine Archaeological Museum of the Mandatory period still represented the positive diversity of religions and ethnicities that characterised Jerusalem and Palestine for many centuries, the Israel Museum and Shrine of the Book represent the single-minded determination by the Israel Antiquities Authority and Israel's heritage industry to Judaise and colonise both the ancient and modern histories of Palestine.

DISAPPEARING PALESTINIAN VILLAGES AND PLACE NAMES BEFORE 1948

During the pre-state period the Zionist Yishuv in Palestine developed four key strategies:

- The widespread use of the term Palestine in tandem with Eretz Israel in Zionism (late 19th century until 1948).
- Appropriation of Arab names, hybridisation of names of Jewish settlements and indigenisation of the settlers.
- Instrumentalisation of the myth-narratives of the Bible and 'restorationist' biblical archaeology: Hebrewisation and biblicisation of Palestinian Arabic toponyms.
- Utilisation of the toponymic lists of the Palestine Exploration Fund and the works of Western biblical archaeologists.

APPROPRIATION OF ARABIC PLACE NAMES, INDIGENISATION OF THE EUROPEAN SETTLERS AND HYBRIDISATION STRATEGIES

Subterfuge and the widespread use of the term Palestine in combination with Eretz Israel in Zionism (late 19th century until 1948)

The multi-cultural identity and diversity of Palestine was always in sharp contrast to the anachronism of mono-cultural Zionism, a latecomer European settler-colonial movement. A mono-culturalist ideology inspired by racialised and romantic 19th century European nationalism, Zionism originated in Central and Eastern Europe at the end of the 19th century. Therefore, it is hardly surprising that from its beginning in the late 19th century and until the creation of Israel in 1948 the Zionist leadership and institutions themselves frequently used the term Palestine in their official discourse and publications, This practice was in common with European and British official designation of the country as Palestine. However, during the Mandatory period the Zionists often employed this term Palestine in tandem with their imaginary construct of Eretz Israel, while, as I show in my 1992 work *Expulsion of the Palestinians: The Concept of Transfer in Zionist Political Thought, 1982–1948*, simultaneously planning to dismantle Palestine and ethnically cleanse the Palestinians (Masalha 1992).

Furthermore, the Zionist 'transfer' and ethnic cleansing strategies and toponymicidal practices sought to replace the heterogeneity and mixed space of Palestine with a 'pure' European colony, an Ashkenazi-dominated, mono-cultural space of the Zionist Yishuv until 1948 (Kimmerling 2003). In a microcosmic and typical fashion the heterogeneity of the thousands-of-years-old Jaffa was ethnically cleansed and culturally destroyed in 1948. This historic, culturally mixed Palestinian city was replaced after 1948 and subsumed by the European 'pure' Jewish city of neighbouring Tel Aviv, 'the capital of the pre-state Yishuv'/Colony, subsumed and subordinated ancient Jaffa under the post-1948 Hebrew designation of Tel Aviv-Yafo. This Zionist memoricidal and toponymicidal project was

> institutionally, cognitively, and emotionally built within an
> exclusionary Jewish 'bubble'. The plans for the new Jewish state
> were similarly exclusive. The Jewish state was supposed to be purely
> Jewish and no political and bureaucratic tools were prepared for
> the possibility, mentioned in all partition proposals, that large Arab
> minorities would remain within the boundaries of the Jewish state.
> (Kimmerling 2003: 22; see also Yiftachel 2006: 54; Shafir 1996a,
> 1996b, 1999)

During the Mandatory period the Zionist organisations in Palestine employed a variety of methods of subterfuge designed to conflate 'Palestine' with 'Eretz Yisrael'. One such example of concealment and subterfuge was the insertion of the Hebrew abbreviation of Eretz Yisrael (א״י), 'Land of Israel', after the Hebrew word for Palestine (פלשתינה) on the official Mandatory government stamps – stamps which would have been handled by tens of thousands of Arabs in Palestine and neighbouring countries, most of them not knowing Hebrew and unable to decipher the Zionist Hebrew abbreviation (א״י).

Although Palestinian leaders protested in the 1920s at this inclusion of 'Eretz Yisrael' in the official documents, stamps and currency of the British Mandatory Government of Palestine – a government which was committed to the pro-Zionist 'promise' of the 1917 Balfour Declaration – they were incapable of dissuading the Mandatory authorities from pursuing their pro-Zionist policies.

However, the extensive use of the official term Palestine by the Zionist organisations until 1948 is not surprising for two main reasons:

- All governments and millions of people across the world, and especially readers of European languages, identified the country as Palestine or the Holy Land – the only exceptions were the Zionist Jewish advocates, who also identified the country as Eretz Yisrael (Land of Israel):
- Following the pro-Zionist Balfour Declaration commitments of November 1917, the Zionist settler-colony in Palestine (the Yishuv) evolved both as 'settler-colonialism within British colonialism' and as a 'settler-colony with British colonialism'. This allowed the emerging European Yishuv to pursue a double strategy of (a) shadowing (and operating 'from within') the official terminology of British Mandatory system in Palestine; and (b) of creating a parallel autonomous Zionist Hebrew discourse.

Nonetheless, subterfuge (of Palestine-cum-Eretz Yisrael), euphemism ('transfer'), alternative facts, and new 'facts on the ground' were central to the newspeak and strategies of the Zionist colony ('Yishuv') in Palestine during the pre-state period and this is evident from the following examples:

- The Society for the Support of Jewish Farmers and Artisans in Syria and Palestine was a Hovevei Tzion organ established in 1890 with official support and encouragement of the Tsarist Russian government (Shafir 1996a: 46). The Society was dedicated to the practical aspects of establishing Jewish agricultural colonies in Palestine and its projects included help with the founding of the colonies of Rehovot and Hadera.
- The Jewish Agency for Palestine was founded in 1930, and played a central role in the founding of the Israeli state in 1948; the Chairman

325

of its Executive Committee from 1935 until May 1948 was David Ben-Gurion. Only after 1948 did it change its name to the Jewish Agency for Israel.

- The Palestine Office (German: Palästinaamt) was the name of a Zionist agency set up by the executive of the World Zionist Organisation in 1908 with its office in Jaffa. Headed by Arthur Ruppin (born in the German empire; 1876–1943), the Palestine Office served during the Ottoman period as the central agency for Zionist colonisation activities in Palestine, including land purchases and assisting Jewish immigration. After the First World War the Zionist name 'Palestine Offices' had a different connotation and applied to Zionist international missions charged with the mobilisation and organisation of Jewish immigration to Palestine. The Palestine Offices were subordinated to the Immigration Department of the Zionist Executive, which worked with the Jewish Agency for Palestine. The Palestine Offices were run by a Palestine Commission (Palaestinaamts kommission) composed of representatives of various Zionist parties.

- The Palestine Orchestra ('Israel Philharmonic Orchestra'; founded in Palestine 1936) and was continuously called the Palestine Orchestra until 1948.

- The Anglo-Palestine Bank: Israel's largest bank, Bank Leumi (National Bank) was originally founded in London as the Anglo Palestine Company. It was a subsidiary of the Jewish Colonial Trust which was founded by the Second Zionist Congress and incorporated in London in 1899. It subsequently became officially known as the Anglo-Palestine Bank and this name continued until 1948.

- The Palestine Electric Company was initially founded in 1923 by Pihnas Rotenberg as the Jaffa Electric Company. It was later incorporated in Mandatory Palestine as the Palestine Electricity, Corporation Limited. It only changed its name to the current one, the Israel Electric Corporation Limited, in 1961. Today it is one of the largest industrial companies in Israel.

- The *Palestine Post* was established in Jerusalem in 1932 as part of the Zionist movement and only changed its name in 1950 to the *Jerusalem Post*. The newspaper's targeted audiences were English readers in Palestine and neighbouring countries and Jewish readers abroad – British Mandate officials, local Jews and Arabs, tourists and Christian pilgrims. Zionist organisations considered the *Jerusalem Post* an effective medium for exerting influence on the British authorities in Palestine. During its first year the *Palestine Post* achieved a daily circulation of about 4000 copies and by 1944 its circulation reached 50,000 copies.[16]

- The Jewish Palestine Exploration Society was founded in 1914 with a focus on ancient Palestine; it was renamed after 1948 as the Israel Exploration Society.
- The Palestine Football Association was established in 1928 by Zionist Jewish football clubs; after 1948 it was renamed the Israel Football Association.
- The Palestine Potash Company was established in 1930. In 1951 the company was nationalised by the Israeli government and in 1953 it was renamed the Dead Sea Works.
- *Palestine Citrograph*, a monthly journal devoted to the citrus industry in Palestine, was published in Tel Aviv in the 1930s and 1940s by the Zionist Yishuv; the name was later changed to the Hebrew *Hadar*.
- The Palestine Economic Corporation (now the Israel Economic Corporation) was founded by American Zionist investors in 1922 as a public company and incorporated in the US. Initially it invested and operated through another American Zionist organisation, the Central Bank of Cooperative Institutions in Palestine and a string of Zionist 'Palestine' subsidiary companies including the Palestine Mortgage and Credit Bank Ltd and the Palestine Water Company. The Palestine Water Company itself became a subsidiary of the Palestine Economic Corporation in 1933 and in 1949 it was renamed Mekorot, the Israeli Water Company, a division of the Histadrut.
- Palestine Endowment Funds was created in 1922 by US Zionist leaders to enable the distribution of funds to selected and approved Zionist organisations in Palestine. Many years after Israel was established it was renamed Israel Endowment Funds. Its grants now total over $1 billion.
- The Palestine Automobile Corporation Ltd was founded in 1934 and began its activities as a Chevrolet dealer for Tel Aviv and Haifa. In 1937 the company took over the sole distributorship of Ford products,

marketing Ford cars and commercial vehicles manufactured in the US and in Europe. The company continued to operate under the 'Palestine' name for several years after the establishment of Israel.

- *Flora Palaestina* is a publication by the Israeli Academy of Sciences and Humanities, first appeared in 1966. It encompasses the *Palaestina* plant taxonomic and floristic data in the geo-botanical area between the Mediterranean coast in the west and the Transjordan deserts in the east, the mountains of Lebanon in the north and the desert of Sinai in the south. An updated version, *Distribution Atlas of Plants in the Flora Palaestina Area* by A. Danin, was published in 2004.

APPROPRIATION, HYBRIDISATION AND INDIGENISATION: THE APPROPRIATION OF PALESTINE PLACE NAMES BY EUROPEAN ZIONIST SETTLERS

From Mahlul to Nahlal

Palestinian place names began to be replaced by biblical and Hebrew-sounding names during the late Ottoman and Mandatory periods and small Palestinian villages began to disappear from the map, although local Palestinians continued to use the indigenous names for the new Zionist colonies. These practices of 'reclaiming by renaming', while displacing the indigenous names, were pivotal to the colonisation of the land of Palestine and as a language of creating an 'authentic' collective Zionist Hebrew identity rooted in the 'land of the Bible'. Referring candidly to the gradual replacement of Arabic place names (and of Palestinian villages) by Hebrew place names (and Jewish settlements) during the Mandatory period, Israeli Defence Minister Moshe Dayan – the author of *Living with the Hebrew Bible* (1978) – had this to say in an address in April 1969 to students at the Technion, Israel's prestigious Institute of Technology in Haifa:

> Jewish villages were built in the place of Arab villages. You do not even know the names of these villages, and I do not blame you because geography books no longer exist. Not only do the books not exist, the

Arab villages are not there either. Nahlal arose in the place of Mahlul; Kibbutz Gvat in the place of Jibta; Kibbutz Sarid in the place of Hunefis; and Kefar Yehoshua in the place of Tal al-Shuman. There is not a single place built in this country that didn't have a former Arab population.[17]

Dayan (1915–1981), who spoke Arabic, considered himself and was considered by his fellow European settlers as a typical *sabra*. He was born in Kibbutz Degania Alef in Palestine before his parents moved to Nahlal, founded in 1921. His father Shmuel Kitaigorodsky (who served in the first three sessions of the Israeli Knesset) was born in Zhashkov, modern-day Ukraine, immigrated to Palestine in 1908 and Hebraicised his name to Dayan, Hebrew for a judge in Jewish religious courts. According to Zionist propaganda the name Nahlal derived from a biblical village (Joshua 19:15). Yet Moshe Dayan knew and was prepared to acknowledge publicly that the name of his own settlement (*moshav*), Nahlal, was in fact a Hebrew rendering of the name of the Palestinian Arabic village name it had replaced, Mahlul; however, to give it a 'biblical authenticity', the Hebrew-sounding Nahlal was linked by the Zionists to a name mentioned in the Hebrew Bible. Also, Kibbutz Gvat, set up in 1926, was a Hebrew rendering of the former Arabic place name, the Palestinian village Jibta; Gvat also echoed the Aramaic name Gvata (meaning hill) and a biblical name in the Galilee.

Central to the construction of Zionist collective identity, and subsequently Israeli identity, based on 'biblical memory' was the Yishuv toponymic projects established in the 1920s to 'restore' biblical Hebrew or to create new biblical-sounding names of symbolic meaning to Zionist redemption of the land and colonisation of Palestine (Ra'ad 2010: 189). In the 1920s the Palestinian land of Wadi al-Hawarith[18] in the coastal region was purchased ('redeemed') by the Jewish National Fund from Arab absentee landlords, subsequently leading to the eviction of many Arab farmers. The Jewish settlement of Kfar Haro'e was established in 1934 on these lands. The Arabic name was rendered into the Hebrew-sounding Emek Hefer (the Hefer Valley). In some cases the Zionist Hebrew colonising toponymy simply translated Arabic names into Hebrew. In the 1920s a JNF Naming Committee was set up to name the newly established Jewish colonies in

Palestine to compete with the overwhelmingly Arabic map of the country; its renaming efforts were appreciated by the British Mandatory authorities and were incorporated into the Palestine government's official gazette (Benvenisti 2002: 26).

In the pre-1948 period many new Hebrew place names displaced the Arabic names: for instance, the first Zionist settlement in Palestine, Petah Tikva, was originally set up in 1878 (deserted and then re-established in 1882), on the lands of, and eventually replacing, the destroyed Palestinian village of Mlabbis. Petah Tikva is known in Zionist historiography as Im Hamoshavot – the 'Mother of the Colonies'. The Zionist religious founders stated that the name Petah Tikva came from the biblical prophecy of Hosea (2:17). The land of Petah Tikva was bought from two Arab absentee landlords based in Jaffa, Salim al-Kassar and Anton al-Tayyan. Six decades after the Nakba, Palestinian citizens of Israel still call the Jewish city of Petah Tikva 'Mlabbis'. The Zionist colony of Rehovot was founded in 1890 and was also called after a name mentioned in the Hebrew Bible, but which stood at a completely different location in the Negev Desert. Rehovot was set up by middle class Jewish businessmen and merchants on 10,000 *dunums* of land purchased from Arab landlords, displacing the Palestinian village of Khirbet Duran.

Secular Jewish Zionism was a classic case of the invention of a people in late 19th century Europe and a project for synthesising a nation. This invented tradition considered the Jews as a race and a biological group, and borrowed heavily from romantic nationalisms in Central and Eastern Europe. Political Zionism mobilised an imagined biblical narrative which was reworked in the late 19th century for the political purposes of a modern European movement intent on colonising the land of Palestine. As an invented late modern (European) tradition, Zionism was bound to be a synthesising project. As Israeli scholar Ronit Lentin has powerfully argued in *Israel and the Daughters of the Shoah: Reoccupying the Territories of Silence* (2000), the Israeli masculinised and militarised nationalism has been constructed in opposition to a 'feminised' Other. The founding fathers of Zionism reimagined the New Hebrew collectivity in total opposition to the despised Jewish diaspora unable to resist European anti-Semitism which led to the Holocaust. Zionism's contempt for diaspora Jews and rejection of a 'feminised' diaspora and its obsession with synthesising a nation is reflected in the fact that its symbols were an amalgam, chosen not only from the Jewish religion and the militant parts of the Hebrew Bible but also from diverse modern traditions and sources, symbols subsequently appropriated as 'Jewish nationalist', Zionist or 'Israeli': the music of Israel's national anthem, *ha-Tikva*, came from the Czech national musician, Smetana; much of the music used in nationalist Israeli songs originated in Russian folk-songs; even the term for an Israeli-born Jew free of all the 'maladies and abnormalities of exile' is in fact the Arabic word *sabar*, Hebraicised as (masculine and tough) *tzabar* or *sabra* (Bresheeth 1989: 131), the prickly pear grown in and around the hundreds of Palestinian villages destroyed by Israel in 1948. Even the 'national anthem of the Six Day War', No'ami Shemer's song 'Jerusalem of Gold', was a plagiarised copy of a Basque lullaby (Masalha 2007: 20, 39). Seeking to create an 'authentic, nativised' identity, the East European Jewish colonists claimed to represent an indigenous people returning to its homeland after 2000 years of absence; in fact Russian or Ukrainian nationals formed the hard core of Zionist activism.

From Palestinian Fuleh to Jewish Afula

Afula is an Israeli city in the northern district often known as the 'Capital of the Valley' due to its strategic location in the Jezreel Valley (Marj ibn 'Amer). It was founded in 1925 by Zionist settlers after the purchase of large tracts (60,000 *dunums*) of Arab land from the Arab absentee landlords of the Sursuk family in Beirut by Yehoshua Hankin (1864–1945), the Russian-born activist who was responsible for most of the major land purchases for the Jewish Colonial Association in late Ottoman Palestine and early Mandatory Palestine. These tracts became the site of numerous new Zionist colonies, including Dayan's Nahlal, Giva, Ein Harod, Kfar Yehezkel, Beit Alfa and Tel Yosef, settlements which replaced several Palestinian villages that disappeared from the map, some of which are mentioned by Dayan above.

The etymology of the Zionist settler toponym Afula is derived from the name of the Palestinian Arab village al-Fuleh, which in 1226 Arab geographer Yaqut al-Hamawi mentioned as being a town in the province of Jund Filastin. The Arabic toponym al-Fuleh is derived from the word *ful*, for fava beans, which are among the oldest food plant in the Middle East and were widely cultivated by local Palestinians in Marj Ibn 'Amer. The Palestinian village of al-Fuleh itself was depopulated during the Mandatory period. The 9500 *dunums* of land of al-Fuleh, which also became the site of the Jewish settlement of Merhavya, marked the beginning of a bitter struggle between the indigenous Palestinians and Zionist colonists over the rights of Palestine tenant farmers who had been evicted and eventually led to the eruption of the Palestrina peasant-based rebellion in 1936–1939. Reflecting on the internal Zionist 'transfer' debates, Berl Katznelson, one of the most popular and influential leaders of the dominant Mapai party, had this to say in a debate at the World Convention of Ihud Po'alei Tzion (the highest forum of the dominant Zionist world labour movement), in August 1937:

> The matter of population transfer has provoked a debate among us: Is it permitted or forbidden? My conscience is absolutely clear in this respect. A remote neighbour is better than a close enemy. They [the Palestinians] will not lose from it. In the final analysis, this is a political and settlement reform for the benefit of both parties. I have long been of the opinion that this is the best of all solutions ... I have always believed and still believe that they were destined to be transferred to Syria or Iraq. (Cited in Masalha 1992: 71)

A year later, at the Jewish Agency's Executive Committee of June 1938, Katznelson reiterated his support for a wholesale and 'compulsory transfer' of the Palestinians and added: 'Regarding the transfer of Arab individuals, we are always doing this' (cited in Masalha 1992: 114). In the early 1940s Katzelson reminded his colleagues in Mapai that the wholesale evacuation of the Palestinians was the continuation of a natural process that had begun when Zionist settlers had displaced Arab tenant farmers and residents with the establishment of Kibbutz Merhavya on the land of al-Fuleh which had led to a small-scale Arab 'transfer' (Masalha 1992: 130).

THE PURE ZIONIST SETTLER COLONY AND A MONOLINGUAL MINDSET: FROM PALESTINIAN ARAB MASHA AND SAJARA TO ISRAELI KFAR TAVOR AND ILANIYA

The Zionist settlement (*moshava*) of Kfar Tavor was founded in lower Galilee in 1909 by the Jewish Colonisation Association for a group of Ashkenazi settlers from Eastern Europe. The origin of the Hebrew name is neighbouring Mount Tabor (the name taken from Psalm 89:12). Throughout the Mandatory period this settlement was better known to the Zionist leadership of the Yishuv as Mescha, which was the Ashekenazi rendering of the Palestinian Arabic toponym, Masha. The nearby Zionist settlement Sejera (later renamed Ilaniya) was established a decade earlier, in 1900–1902, by the Zionist Colonisation Association. This too was an Ashkenazi rendering of the Palestinian Arabic name Sajara (Palestinian dialect for 'tree') for one of the earliest and most important Zionist settlements in Palestine.

The issue of Hebraicising Arabic toponyms such as Masha was not always a top priority of some of the fiercely secular early Zionist settler leaders in Palestine. The establishment of the Technikum in Haifa – now the Technion – by a secular German Zionist organisation at the beginning of the 20th century and the controversy about the language of instruction (German or Hebrew) marked the 'War of the Languages' (Margalit, S. 1994) in the Zionist colony (Yishuv) in Palestine. Some leaders of the left-wing secular Po'ale Tzion Zionist movement, such as Ya'akov Zerubavel (born Ya'akov Vitkin in the Ukraine, immigrated to Palestine in 1910), who was a Zionist writer, publisher and editor of a Yiddish newspaper, were strong proponents of Yiddish – a German dialect spoken by the Jewish communities of Central and Eastern Europe – shared the view of many left-wing secular Zionists that Hebrew was the language of only a few Jewish intellectuals and therefore not suitable for the party's goal of reaching the primarily Yiddish-speaking masses in Eastern Europe (Chaver 2004: 97). Yiddish is the historical and literally the 'mother language' (*mame-loshn*) of the Ashkenazi Jews, distinguishing it from the 'holy tongue' (*loshn koydesh*), meaning Hebrew and Aramaic. Yiddish takes most of its syntax and vocabulary from German but has loans from Slavic languages and Hebrew and Aramaic. However, for most early Zionist settler leaders Yiddish was closely associated with the despised and feminised diaspora Ashkenazi Judaism, while modern Hebrew represented the new masculinised settler-colonising Hebrew Man. Even Ya'akov Vitkin changed his family name to Ya'akov Zerubavel. Thus the 'War of the Languages' in the early Yishuv ended in victory for the 'new Hebrew', whose ascendancy was central to the formulation of the 'politico-social myths' of Zionism (Azaryahu 1995), of political Zionism and the construction of the militant Zionist Jewish 'national' identity of the Yishuv colony.

Among the early Zionist workers in Sejara was David Grün, who immigrated to Palestine from the Polish part of the Russian empire in 1906 and who later became known as David Ben-Gurion (1886–1973), the founding father of Israel and its first Prime Minister. The early Zionist settlers, workers and leaders of Sejara and Mescha, mostly Russian or East European nationals, created a Jewish defence organisation in Palestine: Hashmor (Hebrew for 'the Guard'), which was organised in 1909 by socialist Zionists. This was disbanded during the Mandatory period after the founding of the Haganah (Hebrew for 'defence') in 1920 from which the Israeli army emerged in mid-1948. The indigenising and nativising strategies of early settlers and leaders of Hashomer included dressing up like local Palestinian Arabs and cultivating an image of the Sabra, the 'new Jew' or the New Hebrew Man, rebranded as a 'native', self-reliant and armed Jew 'rooted' in the land of Palestine.

Throughout the British Mandatory period Sejara, like Mescha, remained better known to the settlers and the entire Zionist leadership of the Yishuv by its Arabic toponym (not its new Hebrew toponym Ilaniya), a place name which was based on the Arabic dialect of the adjacent Palestinian Arab village al-Sharaja ('tree' in Arabic). The Palestinian village al-Sharaja was subsequently destroyed by Haganah forces in 1948 and the Zionist colony of Sejara is known in Israel today as Ilaniya, which is also the Hebrew rendering of the Arabic toponym for 'tree'.

JUDAISATION, HEBRAICISATION AND
BIBLICISATION STRATEGIES

The Zionist colony of Gedera, located 13 kilometres south of Rehovot, was founded by Russian settlers in 1884, and like the colonies of Rehovot, Afula and Hadera, the purchase of its lands from Palestinian landlords involved Yehoshua Hankin. The Jewish Colonial Association gave Gedera a Hebrew-sounding name (Hebrew: 'wall') after a site supposedly mentioned in the Hebrew Bible. The name Hadera, on the other hand, clearly origi-nated from al-Khadra, and al-Khdeira in local Palestinian dialect, Arabic for 'green'. Although this key Zionist colony (today a major Israeli city) was given a Hebrew-sounding name, this Zionist name makes absolutely no sense in Hebrew (Bar On 1996: 38). The lands of the colony of Gedera had been purchased with the help of the French consul in Jaffa, Poliovierre. Local Palestinians of Qatra had been cultivating the land as tenant farmers when the Jewish settlers arrived, and they resented the intrusion onto what they still thought of as their land. Qatra was an ancient Palestinian centre of political and economic authority that along with thirty other urban sites in regions bordering the Mediterranean Sea had entered a period of decline in the late Bronze Age (Zevit 2003: 94) but flourished throughout the Islamic period. Archaeological excavations at Tel Qatra discovered a pottery workshop for the manufacture of Gaza jars.

Etymologically the naming of Gedera by early Zionist settlers closely followed Christian scriptural geography and biblical archaeology of the 19th century which worked from the narratives of the Bible. The 'biblical location' was first suggested by Victor Guérin (1868–1880, 1881–1883), a French biblical archaeologist and scriptural geographer who visited Pales-tine several times and whose works often referred to passages from the Hebrew Bible and Jewish sources such as the Mishna and Talmud as well as works by contemporary scriptural explorers such as Edward Robinson, who – like the medieval Crusaders and pilgrims in Maurice Halbwachs' *La Topographie légendaire des évangiles en terre sainte: étude de mémoire collective* (1941) – using the biblical narratives, decided, largely through speculation, that in more than a hundred biblical place names in Palestine, these were the origins of Arabic names used by the Palestinian *fallahin* (Robinson et al. 1860; Davis 2004: Macalister 1925). Guérin linked the name Gedera to the Palestinian village of Qatra (Fischer et al. 2008) which was depopulated and destroyed by Jewish forces in 1948. During the British Mandate of Palestine it was referred to by local Palestinians as Qatrat Islam to distinguish it from the Jewish colony of Qatrat Yahud (Jewish Qatra) or Gedera, as it was called by the Zionist settlers themselves. In the 1950s, a neighbourhood called Oriel (light of God) was established on the lands of Arab Qatra for new Jewish immigrants with visual impairments.

Central to the construction of Zionist collective memory – and subsequently Israeli identity – based on 'biblical memory' was the Yishuv's memorialising toponymy project which was established in the 1920s to 'restore' biblical Hebrew or to create new biblical-sounding names (Ra'ad 2010: 189). Both the JNF Naming Committee and the Israeli Governmental Names Committee of the 1950s were generally guided by the biblical geography of Victor Guérin (1868–1880, 1881–1883) and Edward Robinson's *Biblical Researches in Palestine, Mount Sinai and Arabia Petraea* (1841), in which he had argued that the place names of Palestinian villages and sites, seemingly Arab, were modern Arabic renderings of old Hebraic names. An important part of the 'New Hebrew' identity was the Zionist Hebrew toponymy and the Israeli maps which gradually replaced the Palestinian Arabic names (Cohen and Kliot 1981, 1992; Kliot 1989; Azaryahu and Golan 2001; Azaryahu and Kook 2002).

ZIONIST TOPONYMIC METHODS AND STRATEGIES IN THE POST-NAKBA PERIOD: KEY FEATURES OF THE ISRAELI PLACE NAMES PROJECTS

Until 1948 the Zionists were not in control of the toponymic processes in Palestine. Following the mass ethnic cleaning of the Nakba and the Israeli assumption of full control of nearly 80 per cent of historic Palestine, the cultural politics of naming was accelerated radically. State toponymic projects were now used as tools to ensure the effectiveness of the de-Arabisation of Palestine. One of these tools consisted of the official Israeli road signs, which are often in Hebrew, Arabic and English. But both the Arabic and the English are *transliterations* of the new Hebrew place names – rather than reflecting the original Palestinian Arabic name. Of course the overwhelming majority of Israelis cannot read Arabic; this is partly to remind the indigenous Palestinians inside Israel of the need to internalise the new Hebrew place names or perhaps to seek the express approval of the vanishing Palestinian Arab (Shohat 2010: 264), making Arabs complicit in the de-Arabisation of Palestine.

Key features and methods of Israeli Zionist renaming patterns and creation of new place name in the post-Nakba period included:

- The role of the Israeli Army: the Hebrew Names Committee of 1949 and indigenising of the European settlers.
- State-enforced projects: the Israeli Governmental Names Committee.
- The legendary toponymy of Zionist settlers and the medieval Crusaders.
- Toponymicide and the appropriation of Palestinian heritage; silencing of the Palestinian past: mimicry, the de-Arabisation of Palestinian place names and assertion of ownership.
- The creation of a usable past: the power/knowledge nexus.
- Judaisation strategies and the assertion of ownership: the superimposition of biblical, Talmudic and Mishnaic names.
- Fashioning a new European landscape as a site of amnesia and erasure.
- Transliteration of new Hebrew place names and road signs into English and Arabic, post-1967 occupation.

THE ISRAELI ARMY'S HEBREW NAMES COMMITTEE OF 1949: INDIGENISING THE EUROPEAN SETTLERS AND SELF-RENAMING

British Jewish historian Sir Lewis Bernstein Namier (1888–1960), who immigrated to the UK in 1907, was a long-time Zionist and a close friend and associate of Chaim Weizmann. He also worked as political secretary for the Jewish Agency in Palestine (1929–1931). Namier was born Ludwik Niemirowski in what is now part of Poland, and his devotion to Zionism did not prevent the Anglicisation of his name. While name changing among

British or American Zionist Jews who emigrated from Eastern Europe became part of the process of Anglicisation or Americanisation, name changing in Palestine among Zionist settlers began during the Mandatory period and became an integral part of the Hebrewisation and biblicisation of the immigrant settlers (Brisman 2000: 129). The initiative was begun by Yitzhak ben-Tzvi, the second President of Israel, and by a directive written by Ben-Gurion to army officers that it was their moral duty to Hebraicise their names as an example. As a result the Army set up a Hebrew Names Committee to propose Hebrew names to officers and soldiers in the Army. A booklet was compiled by Mordechai Nimtsa-Bi (1903–1949), the head of the Names Committee. The compilers offered four groups of suggested Hebrew name: family names, names of Taanim[19] and Amoraim,[20] biblical names and Hebrew personal names. A similar list was compiled a few years later by Yaakov Arikha under the title, *Behar likha shem mishpaha 'Ivri* (Select for yourself a Hebrew family name). The booklet, published in Jerusalem in 1954 by the Israeli Academy for the Hebrew Language (which had replaced the Hebrew language Committee of Eliezer Ben-Yehuda, see below) included advice on how to change family names, and lists of Hebrew names serving as an example (Brisman 2000: 129).

HYBRIDITY, HEBRAICISING AND THE MYTH OF RESTORATION: ELIEZER BEN-YEHUDA, THE COMMITTEE OF THE HEBREW LANGUAGE AND FOUNDING MYTHS OF MODERN HEBREW

Although Eastern European Jewish settlers claimed to represent an indigenous people returning to its homeland after 2000 years of absence, in fact Russian nationals formed the hard core of Zionist activism. This self-re-indigenisation and copying from the Arabic language and Palestinian Arab toponyms required a great deal of effort to create the mythological New Hebrew Sabra Man and construct a new Jewish identity. No wonder, for the early Zionist settlers were intent not only on 'inventing a Land, and inventing a Nation' (Rabkin 2010: 130), but also on inventing a new language and identity. Reinventing their own new,

Hebrew-imagined biblical identity, the post-1948 period saw top Zionist leaders, army commanders, biblical archaeologists and authors changing their names from Russian, Polish and German to 'authentic' Hebrew-sounding (biblical) names.

Despite the Semitisation of European Jews by linguistic and racial theorists in the second half of the 19th century, in fact modern Hebrew was invented by Ashkenazi Zionists in the early 20th century not as a Semitic language, but rather as a hybrid language, with European vocabulary and strong European connections, a cultural space with which new settlers of the Zionist colony (Yishuv) in Palestine felt at home. The Zionist Yishuv ('pure colony': Kimmerling 2003: 22) in Palestine became a new form of exile for which a new, strongly European, new Hebrew provided one of the key links to the old European cultural space.

However, for early European Zionist leaders, to build a new 'homeland'/ state in Palestine required the invention of a new language and the founding national myths and something altogether different – a new secular modern Ashkenazi Hebrew language. Many early Zionists called themselves 'New Hebrews' and not Jews, and, as we shall see below, deliberately changed their European Yiddish, Russian. Polish or German names to sound more Hebraic, more biblical; for a well-known example, David Grün initially became David Green after immigrating to Palestine, and subsequently David Ben-Gurion. However, the key inventor and 'father' of modern Hebrew was Eliezer Ben-Yehuda (formerly Lazar Perelman) (1858–1922), who became a legendary hero of Zionism on a par with the founding father of political Zionism, Theodor Herzl. As a cultural Zionist, Ben-Yehuda regarded 'modern Hebrew' and Zionism as symbiotic. He was hugely influential in the fashioning of a new Hebrew collective identity rooted in an invented 'ancient consciousness'. This was based on the transformation of liturgical Hebrew from a dormant (almost dead) language to a new language spoken today by millions of Israelis. Today Ben-Yehuda is revered in Israel as the instigator of the Hebrew language 'resurrection' and 'revival' and the creator of a modern Zionist vernacular. Today Rehov Ben-Yehuda (Ben-Yehuda Street), in central West Jerusalem, commemorates the creator of Israeli Hebrew.

But Ben-Yehuda was also the founding father of modern Hebrew and he was responsible for its two myths:

- The myth of Hebrew restoration.
- The myth that modern Hebrew is a Semitic language.

As we shall see below: modern Hebrew was in reality a new language: a Semi-to-European hybrid. Ben-Yehuda himself saw himself not only as the inventor of modern Hebrew but also as an inventor of the 'Jewish people'.[21] He wrote: 'There are two things without which the Jews will not become a people [*'am*]: the country [*ha-aretz*; i.e. Palestine] and the language [*ha-lashon*].'

HYBRIDISATION AND PATTERNS OF EARLY ZIONIST BORROWING FROM, AND MODELLING ON, ARABIC AND ARAMAIC

Believing that Arabic and Aramaic have preserved the ancient character of proto-Semitic language, Ben-Yehuda favoured a strong reliance upon Arabic and Aramaic in the creation of modern Hebrew in Palestine, although in reality modern Hebrew became a new Semito-European hybrid language borrowing many words from Yiddish, Arabic, Aramaic, Ladino, Latin, Greek, Polish, Russian, English and other European languages. However, the patterns pursued by Ben-Yehuda, of borrowing from and modelling on Arabic, built upon previous extensive Hebrew borrowings and morphological modelling on Arabic that took place during the golden age of Arab Islamic civilisation. Although the influence of Arabic on modern Hebrew cannot be attributed entirely to Ben-Yehuda or his Hebrew Language Committee,[22] many of the new words coined by Ben-Yehuda under the influence of Arabic became part of the standard Hebrew language of today.[23] Examples of the Hebrew words coined by Ben-Yehuda on the basis of Arabic words included *qattar* ('locomotive'), which he borrowed from the Arabic *qitar*; *taarikh* ('date'), from the Arabic *taarikh* ('history', 'dating'); and *adiv* ('polite'), which comes from the Arabic *adib* ('cultured').[24] Morphological patterns modelled on Arabic are found in the modern Hebrew greeting *boqer tov* ('good morning') and its refrain *boqer or* ('morning of light'), modelled after the Arabic *sabah al-khair* ('good morning') and *sabah an-nur* ('morning of light') (Shehadeh 1998: 60).

It should be borne in mind that the reference here is not only to patterns of direct borrowings from Arabic, but also to loan translation: words modelled closely after Arabic, consisting of the speech material of Arabic. As we will see below, this modelling on and loan translation from Arabic would subsequently have a major impact on the transformation of Palestinian Arab toponyms into Israeli Hebrew toponyms by the Israeli Names Committee.

Ben-Yehuda was born Lazar Perelman, in the Lithuanian village of Luzhky, and attended a Talmudic school in Belarus in the Russian Empire. A linguistic utopian and a secular linguistic Zionist, the most influential lexicographer of the Zionist vernacular also borrowed many words from literary and colloquial Arabic, Greek, Aramaic and other languages. A newspaper editor, Ben-Yehuda immigrated to Palestine in 1881 and became the driving spirit behind this Zionist vernacular revolution (Stavans 2008; Rabkin, 2006: 54–57; 2010: 132). At that time the Jews in Jerusalem spoke Arabic, Yiddish and French. Ben-Yehuda set out to resurrect and develop a new language that could replace Yiddish, in particular, and other languages spoken by the European Zionist colonists in Palestine. He had studied history and politics of the Middle East at the Sorbonne University in Paris and learned Palestinian colloquial Arabic. In the four years he spent at the Sorbonne he took Hebrew classes. It was this experience in Paris, and his exposure to the rise of French linguistic nationalism at the end of the 19th century, that inspired Ben-Yehuda (Perelman) to attempt the 'resurrection' of Hebrew as a practical and Zionist nationalist cultural project.

After arriving in Palestine in 1881, Lazar Perelman changed his name to Eliezer Ben-Yehuda ('Son of Judah') and became the first to use 'modern Hebrew' as a vernacular and transform it from a biblical language and a language of liturgy (*lashon hakodesh*) into a 'secular-nationalist' modern language. Ben-Yehuda's second wife Paula Beila took the Hebrew name Hemda, and he raised his son, Ben-Tzion ('son of Zion'), speaking only modern Hebrew by totally isolating him and refusing to let him be exposed to other languages during childhood.

Ben-Yehuda served as editor of a number of Hebrew-language newspapers, including *Ha-Tzvi* (*the Deer*). The latter was closed down for a year by the Ottoman authorities following fierce opposition from the Orthodox

Jewish community of Jerusalem, which viewed his work as sacrilegious. Jerusalem was a predominantly Arabic-speaking city, whose Jewish residents spoke both Arabic and Yiddish and objected to the use of the 'holy tongue' (*lashon hakodesh*), Hebrew, for everyday conversation. Other local Jews ridiculed the new Hebrew as a 'fabricated', hybrid language.

In Jerusalem Ben-Yehuda became a central figure in the establishment of the Hebrew Language Committee (*Va'ad Ha-lashon ha-'Ivrit*). It was initially set up in 1890, operated for one year, disbanded and then revived in 1904; Ben-Yehuda was its first president. Ben-Yeduda's linguistic efforts were crowned with success when the British colonial authorities in Palestine decided in 1922, under a Zionist Jewish High Commissioner, Herbert Samuels, to recognise modern Hebrew as one of the three official languages of British Mandatory Palestine, alongside Arabic and English.

Ben-Yehuda's committee was replaced by the Israeli Academy of the Hebrew Language, which was established following an Act of the Israeli Knesset, passed on 27 August 1953, as 'The Supreme Institute of the Hebrew Language' and located in the Hebrew University of Jerusalem. As modern Hebrew became more widely spoken among East European Zionist settlers in Palestine, the Hebrew Language Committee began to publish bulletins and dictionaries and coined thousands of words that are in everyday use today in Israel. The Committee's President, Ben-Yehuda, also compiled the first modern Hebrew dictionary. Ben-Yehuda argued that Arabic, a living fellow Semitic language, rather than European languages, should fill modern Hebrew *lacunae*, seeing Arabic as a major source for missing roots and new words in Hebrew (Shehadeh 1998: 61–62). Ben-Yehuda's claims, made in a 1914 article entitled 'Sources to Fill the *Lacunae* in our Language', echoed similar claims put forward by Western biblical archaeologists and scriptural geographers in the 19th century such as Edward Robinson and Victor Guérin. He wrote: 'the majority of the roots found in the Arabic vocabulary were once part of the Hebrew lexicon, and all of these roots are *not* foreign, *nor are Arabic*, but are *ours*, which we lost and have now found again' (Ben-Yehuda 1914: 9; see also Blau 1981: 32).

Ben-Yehuda, then head of the Jerusalem-based Committee of the Hebrew Language, insisted on the relevance of Arabic for reviving the dead language of Hebrew and reinventing modern (Ashkenazi) Hebrew.

Joshua Blau, Professor Emeritus of Arabic Languages and Literature at the Hebrew University of Jerusalem and President of the Israeli Academy of the Hebrew Language (1981–1993), writes that Ben-Yehuda insisted on the usefulness of living Arabic: 'In order to supplement the deficiencies of the Hebrew language, the Committee coins words according to the rules of grammar and linguistic analogy from Semitic roots: Aramaic and especially from Arabic roots' (Blau 1981: 33).

SELF-INVENTION, SELF-INDIGENISATION AND SELF-ANTIQUATION: PERSONAL NAME CHANGING BY MEMBERS OF THE PREDATORY ZIONIST ASHKENAZI ELITE OF ISRAEL

The change from a Yiddish family name such as Perelman, to a Hebrew family name such as Ben-Yehuda, provided many Zionist settlers in Palestine with a prototype for emulation in a process of self-invention and self-indigenisation. This process also inspired Prime Minister and Defence Minister David Ben-Gurion who used the Israeli army after 1948 to impose general Hebraicisation and purification procedures of family and personal names. Ben-Gurion himself was born David Grün in Russia; his mother was called Scheindel and his Russian-born wife was called Pauline Munweis when she met and married Ben-Gurion in New York (she later changed her name to Paula); after immigrating to Palestine David Grün became David Green; and he subsequently changed his family name to the biblical-sounding, and literally lionised and predatory, name David Ben-Gurion (literally 'son of the lion cub'). He also chose a biblical-sounding name for his daughter Geula ('redemption') and his son Amos, after a minor prophet in the Hebrew Bible.

For Ben-Gurion, the invention of a Hebrew tradition and the synthesising of a nation meant that the Hebrew Bible became not a religious document or a repository of theological assertions; it was reinvented as a nationalised and racialised sacred text central to the modern foundational myths of secular Zionism. As a primordialist ideology of secular nationalism, asserting the antiquity of Jewish nationalism (Smith, A. 1986,

343

1989: 340–367), and inspired by Eurocentric völkisch and racial ideologies, Ben-Gurion's Zionism viewed the Bible in an entirely functional way: the biblical language, narrative and place names functioned as a mobilising myth and as an 'historical account' of Jews' 'title to the land' – a claim not necessarily borne out by recent archaeological findings. For Ben-Gurion, it was not important whether the biblical narrative and place names were an objective and true record of actual historical events and the past. It is not entirely clear whether Ben-Gurion assumed that the ancient events the Israeli state was re-enacting had actually occurred. But, as he explains, 'It is not important whether the [biblical] story is a true record of an event or not. What is of importance is that this is what the Jews believed as far back as the period of the First Temple' (Pearlman 1965: 227; also Rose 2004: 9).

Like Ben-Gurion, many secular labour Zionists displayed from the outset a deeply ambivalent attitude towards religion. Although the movement's name is derived from the word 'Zion', which was originally the name of a fortress in Jerusalem, Zionism reinvented Judaism and translated Jewish themes into political action. Furthermore, Zionism had ambitions to create a new Hebrew society that would be different from Jewish life in the diaspora and did not see multi-religious and pluralistic Jerusalem as the appropriate place for the founding of such a new society. Not only was it full of aliens (native Palestinian Arabs), but it was also inhabited by the peaceful 'old Jewish Yishuv', whose members were part of the anti-Zionist ultra-Orthodox community. It is no wonder, therefore, that the Zionists preferred to build the new (and pure) Jewish city of Tel Aviv on the Mediterranean coast, just outside the Palestinian city of Jaffa. Tel Aviv was founded in 1910 in a region which, according to the Bible, was ruled by the Philistines (not the Israelites) from the 12th century BC onwards. It was named after a Babylonian city mentioned in Ezekiel (3:15). But the ethno-religious 'purity' of the European Hebrew colony, the New Yishuv, was best illustrated by the fact that during the Mandatory period its Zionist leaders preferred to live in the demographi-cally exclusive Tel Aviv rather than in multi-religious Jerusalem or Jaffa.

Those Zionist immigrants who chose to live in Jerusalem settled outside the historic city and built new Jewish neighbourhoods and the first Jewish university: the Hebrew University of Jerusalem. Tel Aviv remained home to the (Hebrew) Histadrut and all the Hebrew daily papers, and while Zionist leaders of the New Yishuv continued to swear by the name of Jerusalem, they did not live there and most of the Jewish immigrants to Palestine, about 80 per cent, settled along the Mediterranean coast, a region that (according to Avishai Margalit, of the Hebrew University) had never been the historic homeland of the Jewish people.[25]

The invention of a new masculine collective memory was based on hegemonic state power: the 'New Hebrew' language, the 'New Hebrew Man', a new and militarised society and an exclusively Jewish 'Hebrew City' (Tel Aviv), a 'New Yishuv' settler colony, and the new and armed Hebrew workers of the Histadrut, the General Federation of Hebrew Workers in the Land of Israel. Established in 1920, the militarised Histadrut and military service were central to the Zionist project of conquest. They represented that newly constructed muscular and militant national identity. The militarised Histadrut, in particular, dominated both the economic and military-security infrastructure of the Zionist Yishuv and played a major role in immigration, land settlement and colonisation, economic activities, labour employment and military organisation and defence (the Haganah), with trade union activity as only one part of its activities.[26] Palestinian citizens of Israel were not admitted as members until 1959. The Histadrut became central to this drive designed to create a 'New Settlement' of blood and common descent and redeem the 'biblical soil' by conquest. In the 1920s the Zionist Labour leadership also began to develop a boycott strategy in Palestine. Thus, in 1929, Ben-Gurion wrote of the need for an 'Iron Wall of [Zionist] workers' settlements surrounding every Hebrew city and town, land and human bridge that would link isolated points' and which would be capable of enforcing the doctrine of exclusive 'Hebrew labour' (*'avoda 'ivrit*) and 'Hebrew soil' (*adama 'ivrit*) (Masalha 1992: 24–25).

Although deeply secular, Ben-Gurion's Zionism instrumentally emphasised Jewish religion and Jewish 'ethnicity', promoted the cult and mythologies of ancient Israel and biblical battles, promoted the revival of a seemingly dead language, Hebrew, built up what became a powerful army, surrounded its 'ethnically' exclusive, 'pure' colony, the Yishuv, with an 'Iron Wall' (Shlaim 2000; Masalha 2000) and waged a bitter struggle for political independence and territorial expansion throughout the land of Palestine. In an article entitled: '(Re)naming the Landscape: The Formation of the Hebrew Map of Israel 1949–1960', Israeli political geographers Maoz Azaryahu and Arnon Golan write:

> The importance assigned to Hebrew as the language and culture of national revival was also manifest in the emphasis upon Hebrew purity and Hebraicization procedures. Hebraicization included the introduction of Hebrew nomenclatures in various fields of scientific knowledge e.g. botany or zoology. Of special political bearing and with far reaching personal consequences was the Hebraicization of family names of Jewish immigrants. This measure belonged to the construction of a new Hebrew identity. In the first years of Israeli independence, Ben-Gurion, the founding father of modern Israel, used his authority to promote Hebrew family names. In his capacity as a Defence Minister, he made the Hebraicization of family names obligatory for Israeli officials serving in representative positions e.g. high ranking army officers and diplomats. (Azaryahu and Golan 2001: 182)

Anthroponomastics (or anthroponymy) is the study of personal names. Zionist toponymic and anthroponymic projects were central to Zionist settler-colonisation strategies in Palestine and these included not only Hebrewisation, biblicisation and Judaisation of the country, but also self-indigenisation, self-antiquation. Personal names such Allon (oak; Arabic: ballut) and Aloni (my oak) became very popular in Zionist settlers' indigenising strategies. 'Palestine Oak' (بلوط فلسطين, Quercus Calliprinos) and Pistacia Palaestina are internationally famous, indigenous trees common to Palestine, the eastern Mediterranean region and the Levant (especially Palestine, Syria and Lebanon). 'Pistacia Palaestina' adds brilliant red to the Galilee landscape. Of the three species of oak found in modern Palestine, the 'prickly evergreen oak' (Quercus Coccifera) is the most abundant. It covers the rocky hills of Palestine with dense brushwood of trees. And for many centuries the traditional Palestinian plough, used in preparation for sowing seeds or to loosen or turn the soil, was made of oak wood. Like the Palestinian olive tree, 'Oak Palestine' is another key symbol of Palestine and Palestinian life. The oak tree of Palestine played a major part in Palestinian stories for children and generally in Palestinian cultural memory and folklore.

Within the Zionist strategies, there is a long list of Zionist leaders who formally changed their names from Russian and East European to Hebrew-sounding names. Many changed their names following Ben-Gurion's military directives after the establishment of Israel in 1948. While only a small minority of East European Jews who had migrated to the US or Britain chose voluntarily to anglicise their names, members of almost the entire Zionist elite of Israel were pressurised after May 1948 to change their European names to 'authentic'-sounding biblical ones. In fact this intense pressure was applied almost immediately after the establishment of Israel in May 1948. It was applied top down by Prime Minister and Defence Minister David Ben-Gurion, who effectively ordered all senior officers of the Israeli army to change their European surnames. Yigael Sukenik, chief of operations and acting chief of staff of the army in 1948, was the first to comply: 'On June 28, 1948, Ben-Gurion swore in the members of the IDF high command, insisting that each one adopted a Hebrew last name. Since most chose their Haganah code names, Yigael Sukenik became Yigael Yadin' (Pasachoff 1997: 220).

The following biblicisation list includes almost the entire political, military and intellectual Israeli elite, left, right and centre:

- David Ben-Gurion (1886–1973), Israeli Prime Minister and Defence Minister, used the Israeli army after 1948 to impose general Hebraicisation and purification of family and personal names. He was born David Grün in Russia; his mother was called Scheindel and his Russian-born wife was called Pauline Munweis when she met and married him in New York (she later changed her name to Paula).
- Moshe Sharett was born Moshe Shertok in Russia in 1894; he became Israel's Foreign Minister in 1948; he chose to Hebraicise his last name in 1949, following the creation of the State of Israel.
- Golda Meir was born Golda Mabovitch in Kiev in 1898; later called Golda Meyerson. Interestingly, she Hebraicised her last name only after she became Foreign Minister in 1956; she was Prime Minister 1969–1974.
- Yitzhak Shamir[27] was born Icchak Jeziernicky in Eastern Poland in 1915; he was Foreign Minister 1981–1982 and Prime Minister 1983–1984 and 1988–1992.

- Ariel Sharon was born Ariel Scheinermann in colonial Palestine in 1928 (to Shmuel and Vera, later Hebraicised to Dvora, immigrants to Palestine from Russia); he was Prime Minister 2001–2006.

- Yitzhak Ben-Tzvi was born in 1884 in the Ukraine as Yitzhak Shimshelevich, the son of Tzvi Shimshelevich, who later took the name Tzvi Shimshi; he was the second President of Israel.

- Yigal Allon, Commander of the Palmah in 1948 and later acting Prime Minister of Israel, was born Yigal Peikowitz in the settlement of Masha (Kfar Tavor). His father immigrated to Palestine from Eastern Europe in 1890.

- Menahem Begin, the founder of the current ruling Likud party and the sixth Prime Minister of Israel, was born in Brest-Liovsk, then part of the Russian Empire, as Mieczysław Biegun.

- Yitzhak Ben-Tzvi's wife, Rahel Yanait, born in the Ukraine as Golda Lishansky and immigrated to Palestine in 1908. She was a labour Zionist leader and a co-founder of the Greater Land of Israel Movement in 1967. Apparently she Hebraicised her name to Rahel Yanait in memory of the Hasmonean King Alexander Jannaeus (Hellenised name of Alexander Yannai) (126–76 BC), a territorial expansionist, who during a twenty-seven-year reign was almost constantly involved in military conflict and who enlarged the Hasmonean Kingdom. Her two sons, born during the British Mandatory period, were given biblical names: Amram, named after the father of Moses and Aaron, and Eli, named after the High Priest Eli.

- Levi Eshkol was born in the Ukraine in 1895 as Levi Skolnik; he was Israel's third Prime Minister, 1963–1999.

- Pinhas Lavon (1904–1976) was born Pinhas Lubianiker in what is now Ukraine and moved to Palestine in 1929; he was Defence Minister in 1954 and labour leader.

- Yitzhak Ben-Aharon (1906–2006) was an Israeli politician who became a general secretary of the Histadrut and held a cabinet post. He was born Yitzhak Nussenbaum in what is today Romania and immigrated to Palestine in 1928.

- Dov Yosef (1899–1980, an Israeli Labour politician who held ministerial positions in nine Israeli governments, was born Bernard Joseph in Montreal, Canada.

- David Remez was born David Drabkin in Belarus in 1886; he was Israel's first Minister of Transportation.
- Zalman Shazar, the third President of Israel (from 1963 to 1973), who immigrated to Palestine in 1921, was born in the Russian empire as Shneur Zalman Rubashov.
- Pinhas Rutenberg (1879–1942), a prominent Zionist leader and the founder of the Palestine Electric Company, which became the Israel Electric Corporation, was born in the Ukraine as Pyotr Moiseyevich Rutenberg.
- Avraham Granot (1890–1962), Director-General of the Jewish National Fund and later chairman of its board, was born in today's Moldova as Abraham Granovsky; he changed his name after 1948.
- Fayge Ilanit (1909–2002) was an Israeli Mapam politician born in the Russian Empire as Fayge Hindes, to Sharaga Hindes and Hannah Shkop. She immigrated to Palestine in 1929.
- Shimon Peres was born in Poland in 1923 as Szymon Perski; he was Israel's eighth Prime Minister and in 2007 was elected as its ninth President.
- Right-wing Russian Zionist leader Zeev Jabotinsky (1880–1940), the founder of Revisionist Zionism, changed his name from Vladimir Yevgenyevich Zhabotinsky during the Mandatory period, choosing a predatory name: Zeev ('wolf').
- Prominent Labour leader Haim Arlozoroff (1899–1933) was born Vitaly Arlozoroff.
- General Yigael Yadin (1917–1984), the army's second chief of staff and a founding father of Israeli biblical archaeology, was born Yigal Sukenik; he was ordered to change his surname by Ben-Gurion after May 1948.
- Eliahu Elat (1903–1990), an Israeli diplomat and Orientalist and the first Israeli ambassador to the United States, was born Eliahu Epstein in Russia and immigrated to Palestine in 1924.
- Yisrael Galili (1911–1986) was an Israeli government minister. Before 1948 he had served as chief of staff of the Haganah. He was born Yisrael Berchenko in today's Ukraine.
- Meir Amit (1921–2009) was an Israeli politician and cabinet minister and head of the Mossad from 1963 to 1968. He was born in Mandatory Palestine as Meir Slutsky to settler parents from Russia.
- Meir Argov (1905–1963), Israeli politician and a signatory of the Israeli Declaration of Independence, was born Meyer Grabovsky born in Moldova (then Russian empire) and changed his name after 1948.

- Pinhas Rosen (1887–1978), the first Israeli Minister of Justice and a signatory to the Israeli Declaration of Independence, was born in German as Felix Rosenbluth and changed his name after 1948.
- Abba Hushi (1898–1969), an Israeli politician and mayor of Haifa for eighteen years, was born Abba Schneller (also Aba Khoushy) in Poland and immigrated to Palestine in 1920.
- Mordechai Bentov (1900–1985) was a politician and cabinet minister. He was born in the Russian Empire as Mordechai Gutgeld and immigrated to Palestine in 1920.
- Peretz Bernstein (1890–1971) was a Zionist leader, Israeli politician and one of the signatories of the Israeli Declaration of Independence in 1948. He was born in Germany as Fritz Bernstein, immigrated to Palestine in 1936 and changed his name after the establishment of Israel.
- Avraham Granot (1890–1962), Israeli politician, chairman of the JNF Board of Directors and a signatory of the Israeli Declaration of Independence, was born in (today) Moldova as Abraham Granovsky; he immigrated to Palestine in 1924, and changed his name after 1948.
- Mordechai Bentov (1900–1985), Israeli journalist and politician, was born Mordechai Gutgeld in Poland and immigrated to Palestine in the Mandatory period.
- Herzl Vardi (1903–1991), Israeli politician, a signatory of the Israeli Declaration of Independence and editor of the Israeli daily *Yediot Aharonot*, was born Herzl Rosenblum in Lithuania and changed his name after 1948.
- Professor Benyamin Mazar, co-founder of Israeli biblical archaeology, was born Benyamin Maisler in Poland and was educated in Germany; he immigrated to colonial Palestine in 1929 and Hebraicised his name.
- Yitzhak Sadeh (1890–1952), commander of the Haganah's strike force, the Palmah, and one of the key army commanders in 1948, was born in Russia as Isaac Landsberg.
- General Yitzhak Rabin, the first native-born Israeli Prime Minister, 1974–1977 and 1992–1995, was born Nehemiah Rubitzov in Jerusalem to a Zionist settler from the Ukraine.
- General Yigal Allon (1918–1980), commander of the Palmah in 1948, government minister and acting Prime Minister of Israel, best known

as the architect of the Allon Plan, was born in Palestine as Yigal Paicovitch. His grandfather was one of the early East European settlers who immigrated to Palestine in the 1880s. After Israel was proclaimed in 1948 he changed his name to the Hebrew Allon ('oak' tree).

- Ephraim Katzir (1916–2009), the fourth President of Israel from 1973 to 1978, was born Efraim Katchalski, son of Yehuda and Tzila Katchalski, in Kiev and immigrated to Mandatory Palestine in 1925.
- Abba Eban (1915–2002), Israeli Foreign Minister and Deputy Prime Minister, was born Aubrey Solomon Meir Eban in Cape Town, South Africa, to Lithuanian Jewish parents; in 1947, after immigrating to Mandatory Palestine, he changed his first name to Abba (Hebrew: father) Solomon Meir Eban.
- General Tzvi Tzur (1923–2004), the Israeli army's sixth chief of staff, was born in the Zaslav in the Soviet Union as Czera Czertenko.
- General Haim Bar-Lev, army chief of staff in 1968–1971 and later a government minister, was born Haim Brotzlewsky in Vienna in 1924.
- Ben-Tzion Dinur (1884–1973), Israel's Minister of Education and Culture in the 1950s, was born Ben-Tzion Dinaburg in the Ukraine and immigrated to Palestine in 1921.
- General Moshe Ya'alon, former army chief of staff, was born in Israel in 1950 as Moshe Smilansky.
- Prominent Israeli author and journalist Amos Elon (1926–2009) was born in Vienna as Amos Sternbach.
- Yisrael Bar-Yehuda (1895–1965) was an Israeli labour politician who held a number of ministerial posts; he was born Yisrael Idelson in present-day Ukraine and immigrated to Palestine in 1926.
- Israel's leading novelist Amoz Oz was born in Mandatory Palestine in 1939 as Amos Klausner. His parents, Yehuda Klausner and Fania Mussman, were Zionist immigrants to Mandatory Palestine from Eastern Europe.
- Gershom Scholem, a German-born Jewish philosopher and historian and the founder of the modern academic study of Kabbalah (Jewish mysticism), was born Gerhard Scholem; he changed his name to Gershom Scholem after he emigrated to Mandatory Palestine in 1923.
- Moshe Kol (1911–1989), Israeli politician and a signatory of the Israeli

Declaration of Independence, was born Moshe Kolodny in Pinsk (Russian Empire) and changed his name after 1948.

- Avraham Nissan was a Zionist political figure in Mandatory Palestine and a signatory to the Israeli Independence Declaration in 1948: He was born Avraham Katznelson in 1888 in what is now Belarus and changed his name after 1948.

- Tzvi Shiloah (1911–2000), an Israeli Labour (Mapai) politician, who was one of the founders of the Whole Land of Israel Movement after 1967 and served as a member of the Knesset for Tehiya in the 1980s, was born Tzvi Langsam in the Ukraine and immigrated to Mandatory Palestine in 1932.

- Ben-Tzion Sternberg (1894–1962), a Zionist activist and a signatory to the Israeli Declaration of Independence, was born Benno Sternberg in the Austro-Hungarian empire.

- Yigal Tumarkin, a German-born Israeli artist known for his memorial sculpture of the Holocaust in Tel Aviv, was born in Dresden in 1993 as Peter Martin Gregor Heinrich Hellberg.

- Israel's greatest poet, Yehuda Amichai (1924–2000) (Hebrew for 'Praise my people alive'), was born in Germany as Ludwig Pfeuffer. He immigrated to colonial Palestine in 1935 and subsequently joined the Palmah and the Haganah. In 1947 he was still known as Yehuda Pfeuffer.

- Amos Kenan (1927–2009), an Israeli columnist and novelist, was born Amos Levine in Tel Aviv in 1927 and changed his family name after 1948.

- Peretz Bernstein (1890–1971), Israeli politician and one of the signatories of the Israeli Declaration of Independence in May 1948, was born in Germany as Fritz Bernstein and changed his name after 1948.

- Israeli Jewish communist leader, Meir Vilner (1918–2003), who began his political life as one of the leaders of the Zionist left-wing group Hashmer Hatzair and became a signatory to the Israeli Declaration of Independence in May 1948 under the name Meir Vilner-Kovner, was born Ber Kovner in Lithuania and immigrated to Palestine in the late 1930s.

- Abba Kovner, Meir Vilner-Kovner's cousin, was a well-known Israeli Zionist poet born in the Crimean city of Sevastopol. Abba Kovner's mother, Rosa Taubman changed her name to Rachel Kovner after immigrating to Palestine.

- Ya'akov Zerubavel, Zionist writer, publisher and one of the leaders of the Poale Tzion movement, was born Ya'akov Vitkin in the Ukraine.
- Historian Ben-Tzion Netanyahu, a Polish immigrant to the United States and the father of the current Israeli Prime Minister, Benyamin (Miliekowsky) Netanyahu, was born in Poland as Ben-Tzion ('son of Zion') Mileikowsky in 1910.
- Reuven Aloni (1919–1988), founder of the Israel Land Administration, an Israeli government authority responsible for managing land in Israel which manages 93% of the land in Israel, was born Reuven Rolanitzki. He was also the husband of Shulamit Aloni, born Shulamit Adler.
- Shulamit Aloni (1928–2014), born Shulamit Adler, was an Israeli politician and leader of the Meretz party and served as Education Minister from 1992 to 1993. Adler's father descended from a Polish family.
- Yosef Aharon Almogi (1910–1991), a Labour politician who served as a member of the Knesset between 1955 and 1977 and held several ministerial posts, was born Josef Karlenboim in the Russian Empire (today in Poland), and immigrated to Palestine in 1930.
- David Magen (born David Monsonego in 1945) is a former Israeli politician who held a number of ministerial posts in 1990s; he arrived from Morocco in 1949.
- Zalman Aran (1899–1970) was an Israeli politician. He was born Zalman Aharonowitz in the Ukraine and arrived in Palestine in 1926.
- Aharon Barak, President of the Israeli Supreme Court from 1995 to 2006 and the Attorney General of Israel (1975–1978), was born Aharon Brick in Lithuania in 1936. His father, Tzvi Brick, arrived in Palestine in 1947.
- Yitzhak Moda'i (1926–1998) was an politician and Knesset member; he was born Yitzhak Madzovitch in Mandatory Palestine.
- Yehuda Amital (1924–2010) was a Zionist Rabbi, cabinet minister and head of Yeshivat Har Etzion in the West Bank, established in 1968. He born Yehuda Klein in Romania and arrived in Palestine in 1944.
- Ehud Barak (born in 1942) is an Israeli politician who served as Prime Minister from 1999 to 2001 and earlier as chief of staff of the army. He was the son of Yisrael Mendel Brog (1910–2002), born to a family which immigrated from the Russian Empire. Ehud Brog Hebrewised his family name from Brog to Barak in 1972.

- Yosef (Joseph) 'Tommy' Lapid (1931–2008) was born Tomislav Lampel (Томислав Лампел) in Serbia. He was an Israeli journalist, politician and government minister.
- Naomi Chazan (born Naomi Harman in Mandatory Palestine in 1946) is an Israeli academic and politician. She is the daughter of Avraham Harman, an Israeli ambassador to the US. Harman was born in London and immigrated to Palestine in 1938.
- Rachel Cohen-Kagan (1888–1982) was an Israeli politician, and one of only two women to sign the Israeli Declaration of Independence in 1948. She was born Rachel Lubersky in today's Ukraine and immigrated to Palestine in 1919.
- Yehuda Karmon (1912–1995), Professor of Geography at the Hebrew University, was born Leopold Kaufman in Poland and moved to Palestine in 1938.
- Hanoch Bartov (died in 2016), a prominent Israeli author and journalist who also served as a cultural advisor in the Israeli embassy in London, was born Hanoch Helfgott in Palestine in 1926, a year after his parents immigrated from Poland.

Evidently many of these name changes took place around or shortly after 1948. During the Mandatory period, it was still advantageous for individuals to have their original European names.

The above list also shows senior officers and army chiefs of staffs (Hebrew: *rav alufs*) adopting Hebrew-sounding names in the post-1948 period. Ironically, although in the Hebrew Bible the Philistines are constructed as the Other and arch enemy of the Israelites, since 1948 a Philistine term such as *seren* (a lord) has been used by the Israeli army as a rank equivalent to captain. Also, the terms *aluf* and *rav aluf* (major general and lieutenant general, respectively), which have been used for the two highest ranks in the army, are apparently from the New Testament. In the New Testament *aluf* ('chief', the one who commands a 'thousand people') was a rank of nobility among the Idumites, identified by some scholars to be of Nabataean Arab origins, and often depicted as the Israelites' inveterate enemies whom the Hebrew prophets denounced violently.

Since 1948 the Israeli state has encouraged a conception of an ethno-centric identity on the basis of the traditions of land and conquest of the Hebrew Bible, especially the Book of Joshua, and those dealing with the biblical Israelites' origins that demanded the subjugation and destruction of other peoples. It is hardly surprising, therefore, that the Book of Joshua is required reading in Israeli schools. In fact, the Book of Joshua is a work of fiction and the Israelite'conquest' was not the'Blitzkrieg'it is made out to be in the Book of Joshua. But this book holds an important place in the Israeli school curricula and Israeli academic programmes partly because the founding fathers of Zionism viewed Joshua's narrative of conquest as a precedent for the establishment of Israel as a nation (Burge 2003: 82). Although the account of the Israelites' enslavement in ancient Egypt as described in the Book of Exodus is generally recognised as a myth, in Israeli schools and universities this is treated as actual history.

Furthermore, since 1948 Israeli academic institutions have continued the same colonialist tradition of intelligence gathering and data collection. The Israeli army and Israeli biblical academy, in particular, have always been intimately connected to and close partners in nation-building. Engagement in nationalist mobilisation, using the Bible and myth-making through spurious scholarly activity involves a large number of Israeli academics and social scientists, in particular archaeologists, political geographers and Orientalists. The involvement of Israeli academic institutions with the Governmental Names Committee (below), which has operated since the early 1950s, and continues to do so, from the Israeli Prime Minister's Office, is perhaps the best example of academic complicity in the production of knowledge through myth-making.

TOPONYMS 'FROM ABOVE' AND STATE-SUPERVISED PROJECTS: THE ISRAELI GOVERNMENTAL NAMES COMMITTEE

Post-1948 Zionist projects concentrated on the Hebraicisation/Judaisation of Palestinian geography and toponymy through the practice of renaming sites, places and events. The Hebraicisation project deployed renaming to construct new places and new geographic identities related to supposed biblical places. The 'new Hebrew' names embodied an ideological drive and political attributes that could be consciously mobilised by the Zionist hegemonic project. The official project began with the appointment of the Governmental Names Committee (Va'adat Hashemot Hamimshaltit) by Prime Minister Ben-Gurion in July 1949. Ben-Gurion had visited the Naqab/Negev in June and had been struck by the fact that no Hebrew names existed for geographical sites in the region. The 11 June 1949 entry for his War Diary reads: 'Eilat ... we drove through the open spaces of the Arava ... from 'Ein Husb ... to 'Ein Wahba ... We must give Hebrew names to these places – ancient names, if there are, and if not, new ones!' (Ben-Gurion 1982, Vol. 3: 989).

In the immediate post-Nakba period, Israeli archaeologists and members of the Israeli Exploration Society on the Governmental Names Committee concentrated their initial efforts on the creation of a new map for the newly occupied 'Negev' (Abu El-Haj 2001: 91–94). Commissioned to create Hebrew names for the newly occupied Palestinian landscape, throughout the documents produced by this committee were reported references to 'foreign names'. The Israeli public was called upon 'to uproot the foreign and existing names' and in their place 'to master' the new Hebrew names. Most existing names were Arabic. Charged with the task of erasing hundreds of Arabic place names and creating Hebrew names in the Negev, the committee held its first meeting on 18 July and subsequently met three times a month for a ten-month period and assigned Hebrew names to 561 different geographical features in the Negev – mountains, valleys, springs and waterholes – using the Bible as a resource. Despite the obliteration of many ancient Arabic names from the Negev landscape, some Arabic names became similar-sounding Hebrew names: for example, Seil 'Imran became Nahal Amram, apparently recalling the father of Moses and Aaron; the Arabic Jabal Haruf (Mount Haruf) became Har Harif (Sharp Mountain), Jabal Dibba (Hump Hill) became Har Dla'at (Mount Pumpkin). After rejecting the name Har Geshur, after the people to whom King David's third wife belonged, as a Hebrew appellation for the Arabic Jabal 'Ideid (Sprawling Mountain), the committee decided to call it Har Karkom (Mount Crocus), because crocuses grow in the Negev.[28] However, the sound of the Arabic name 'Ideid was retained for the nearby springs, which are now called Beerot Oded (the Wells of Oded), supposedly after the biblical prophet of the same name. In its report of March 1956 the Israeli Government Names Committee stated:

> In the summarised period 145 names were adopted for antiquities sites, ruins and tells [Arabic for hills or archaeological mounds]: eight names were determined on the basis of historical identification, 16 according to geographical names in the area, eight according to the meaning of the Arabic words, and the decisive majority of the names (113) were determined by mimicking the sounds of the Arabic words, a partial or complete mimicking, in order to give the new name a Hebrew character, following the [accepted] grammatical and voweling rules. (Quoted in Abu El-Haj 2001: 95)[29]

In *Hidden Histories*, Palestinian scholar Basem Ra'ad (2010), citing a 1988 study, *Toponymie Palestinienne: Plaine de St. Jean d'Acre et corridor de Jerusalem*, by Thomas Thompson, Francolino Goncalves and J. M. van Cangh, shows that the Israeli toponymy committees went far beyond their original mandates:

> There was simply not enough [biblical] tradition to go by, so [the project] could only continue by picking out Biblical or Jewish associations at random. It had to Hebrewise Arabic names, or in other cases translate Arabic to Hebrew to give the location an ideologically consistent identity. For example, some locations were rendered from Arabic into the Hebrew phonetic system: Minet el-Muserifa became Horvat Mishrafot Yam and Khirbet el Musherifa was changed to Horvat Masref. Sometimes, in this artificial process, the committees forgot about certain genuine Jewish traditions, as in the case of the total cancelling of the Arabic name Khirbet Hanuta, not recognising that it probably rendered the Talmudic Khanotah. This forced exercise of re-naming often even went against Biblical tradition, most notably in erasing the Arabic names Yalu and 'Imwas [after 1967]. Yalu became Ayallon, while 'Imwas, Western Emmaus,

associated with the Christ story, was one of the three villages, along with Beit Nuba, razed in 1967. The old stones from the villages were sold to Jewish contractors to lend local tradition and age to new buildings elsewhere, and the whole area was turned into the tragic Canada Park, made possible by millions from a Canadian donor. (Ra'ad 2010: 188–189; Thompson et al. 1988)

THE LEGENDARY TOPONYMY OF ZIONIST SETTLERS AND THE LATIN MEDIEVAL CRUSADERS

Israeli renaming committees followed the methods of Christian scriptural geographers and biblical archaeologists of the 19th century such as Victor Guérin and Edward Robinson who, like the Latin medieval Crusader pilgrims in Maurice Halbwachs' *La Topographie légendaire des évangiles en terre sainte: étude de mémoire collective* (1941), 'discovered', produced and reproduced particular place names from the myth narratives of the Bible, Talmud and Mishna.

Toponymicide, mimicry and de-Arabisation: appropriating Palestinian heritage, erasing the Palestinian past

The Palestinians share common experiences with other indigenous peoples who had their self-determination and narrative denied, their material culture destroyed and their histories erased, retold, reinvented or distorted by European white settlers and colonisers. In *The Invasion of America* (1975), Francis Jennings highlighted the hegemonic narratives of the European white settlers by pointing out that for generations historians wrote about the indigenous peoples of America from an attitude of cultural superiority that erased or distorted the actual history of the indigenous peoples and their relations with the European settlers. In *Decolonizing Methodologies: Research and Indigenous Peoples*, Maori scholar Linda Tuhiwai Smith argues that the impact of European settler-colonisation is continuing to hurt and destroy indigenous peoples; that the negation of indigenous views of history played a crucial role in asserting colonial ideology, partly because indigenous views were regarded as incorrect or primitive, but primarily because 'they challenged and resisted the mission of colonisation' (Smith, L. 1999: 29). She states:

> Under colonialism indigenous peoples have struggled against a Western view of history and yet been complicit with the view. We have often allowed our 'histories' to be told and have then become outsiders as we heard them being retold ... Maps of the world reinforced our place on the periphery of the world, although we were still considered part of the Empire. This included having to learn new names for our lands. Other symbols of our loyalty, such as the flag, were also an integral part of the imperial curriculum. Our orientation to the world was already being redefined as we were being excluded systematically from the writing of the history of our own lands.
> (Smith, L. 1999: 33)

Although continuing some of the pre-Nakba patterns, Zionist toponymic strategies in the post-Nakba period pursued more drastic memoricide and erasure and the detachment of the Palestinians from their history. With the physical destruction of hundreds of Palestinian villages and towns during and after 1948, the Israeli state now focused on the erasure of indigenous Palestinian toponymic memory from history and geography. The physical disappearance of Palestine in 1948, the deletion of the demographic and political realities of historic Palestine and the erasure of Palestinians from history centred on certain key issues, the most important of which is the contest between a 'denial' and an 'affirmation' (Said 1980; Abu-Lughod et al. 1991). The deletion of historic Palestine from maps and cartography was not only designed to strengthen the newly created state but also to consolidate the myth of the 'unbroken link' between the days of the 'biblical Israelites' and the modern Israeli state. Commenting on the systematic silencing of the Palestinian past, historian Ilan Pappe, in *The Ethnic Cleaning of Palestine*, deploys the doctrine of cultural memoricide, where he highlights the systematic scholarly, political and military attempt in post-1948 Israel to de-Arabise the Palestinian terrain, its names, spaces, religious sites, its villages, towns and cityscapes, and its cemeteries, fields, and olive and orange groves, and the fruit called Saber (cactus), the prickly pears famously grown in and around Arab villages and cultivated in Arab gardens in Palestine. Pappe conceives of a metaphorical palimpsest at work here, the erasure of the history of one people in order to write that of another people over it; the reduction of many layers to a single layer (Pappe 2006: 225–234).

In the post-Nakba period, some of the features of the Israeli renaming strategy closely followed pre-1948 practices of appropriation of Palestinian Arabic toponyms and mimicry. The historic Arabic names of geographical sites were replaced by evoked biblical or Talmudic names and newly coined Hebrew names, some of which vaguely resembled biblical names. It has already been shown that the replacement of Arabic places and the renaming of Palestine's geographical sites followed roughly the guidelines suggested in the 19th century by Edward Robinson (1841; Robinson et al. 1860). The obsession with biblical archaeology and scriptural geography transformed Palestinian Arabic place names, Palestinian geographical sites and the Palestinian landscape into subjects of Zionist mimicry and camouflaging (Yacobi 2009: 115). From the 19th century and throughout the first half of the 20th century Western colonialist imagination, biblical landscape painting, fantasy and exotic travel accounts, Orientalist biblical scholarship, Holy Land archaeology, cartography and scriptural geography have been critical to the success of the Western colonial enterprise in the Middle East, recreating the 'Biblelands', reinventing ahistorical-primordial Hebrew ethnicity, while at the same time silencing Palestinian history and de-Arabising Palestinian toponomy (Masalha 2007; Whitelam 1996; Long 1997, 2003).

Israel's biblical industry, with its Hebrew renaming projects, was embedded in this richly endowed and massively financed colonial tradition. Israeli historian Ilan Pappe remarks:

[In 1948–1949 the land] changed beyond recognition. The countryside, the rural heart of Palestine, with its colourful and picturesque villages, was ruined. Half the villages had been destroyed, flattened by Israeli bulldozers which had been at work since August 1948 when the government had decided to either turn them into cultivated land or to build new Jewish settlements on their remains.

A naming committee granted the new settlements Hebraized [sic] versions of the original Arab names: Lubya became Lavi, and Safuria [Saffuriyah] Zipori [Tzipori] … David Ben-Gurion explained that this was done as part of an attempt to prevent future claim to the villages. It was also supported by the Israeli archaeologists, who had authorized the names as returning the map to something resembling 'ancient Israel'. (Pappe 2004: 138–139)

Jewish settlements were established on the land of the depopulated and destroyed Palestinian villages. In many cases these settlements took the names of the original Palestinian villages and distorted them into Hebrew-sounding names. This massive appropriation of Palestinian heritage provided support for the European Jewish colonisers' claim to represent an indigenous people returning to its homeland after 2000 years of exile. For instance, the Jewish settlement that replaced the large and wealthy village of Beit Dajan (the Philistine 'House of Dagon'; with 5000 inhabitants in 1948) was named Beit Dagon; founded in 1948; Kibbutz Sa'sa' was built on Sa'sa' village; the cooperative *moshav* of 'Amka on the land of 'Amqa village (Wakim 2001a, 2001b; Boqa'i 2005: 73). Al-Kabri in the Galilee was renamed Kabri; al-Bassa village was renamed Batzat; al-Mujaydil village (near Nazareth) was renamed Migdal Haemek (Tower of the Valley). In the region of Tiberias alone there were twenty-seven Arab villages in the pre-1948 period; twenty-five of them, including Dalhamiya, Abu Shusha, Kafr Sabt, Lubya, al-Shajara, al-Majdal and Hittin, were destroyed by Israel. The name Hittin – where Saladin (in Arabic: Salah al-Din) famously defeated the Latin Crusaders in the Battle of Hattin in 1187, leading to the siege and defeat of the Crusaders who controlled Jerusalem – was changed to the Hebrew-sounding Kfar Hittim (Village of Wheat). In 2008 the Israel Land Authority, which controls Palestinian refugee property, gave some of the village's land to a new development project: a $150 million private golf resort, which was to have an eighteen-hole championship golf course, designed by the American Robert Trent Jones Jr. Nearby, the road to Tiberias was named the Menachem Begin Boulevard; heavy iron bars were placed over the entrance to Hittin's ruined mosque, and the staircase leading to its minaret was blocked (Levy 2004).

In Marj Ibn 'Amer (the Jezreel Valley) Kibbutz Ein Dor (Dor Spring) was founded in 1948 by members of the socialist Zionist Hashomer Hatza'ir (later Mapam) youth movement and settlers from Hungary and the United States. It was founded on the land of the depopulated and destroyed village of Indur, located 10 kilometres south-east of Nazareth. Whether or not the Arabic name preserved the ancient Indur, a Canaanite city, is not clear. After 1948 many of the inhabitants became internal refugees in Israel ('present absentees', according to Israeli law) and acquired Israeli citizenship, but were not allowed to return to Indur. In accordance with the common Zionist practice of bestowing biblical names on modern sites and communities, the atheist settlers of Hashomer Hatza'ir appropriated the Arabic name, claiming that Ein Dor was named after a village mentioned in Samuel (28:3–19). However, it is by no means certain that the kibbutz's location is anywhere near to where the 'biblical village' stood. An archaeological museum at the kibbutz contains prehistoric findings from the area.

In the centre of the country the once thriving ancient Palestinian town of Beit Jibrin, 20 kilometres north-west of the city of al-Khalil, was destroyed by the Israeli army in 1948. The city's Aramaic name was Beth Gabra, which translates as the 'house of [strong] men'; in Arabic Beir Jibrin also means 'house of the powerful', possibly reflecting its original Aramaic name; the Hebrew-sounding kibbutz of Beit Guvrin (House of Men), named after a Talmudic tradition, was established on Beit Jibrin's lands in 1949, by soldiers who left the Palmah and Israeli army. Today Byzantine and Crusader remains survive and are protected as an archaeological site under the Hebrew name of Beit Guvrin; the Arab Islamic heritage of the site is completely ignored.

Examples of appropriation of Arabic toponyms and mimicry
The influence of Palestinian Arabic toponyms on the Israeli toponyms are clear in loan Arabic place names, translations of Arabic place names and morphological patterns of renaming. Table 10.1 shows new Hebrew-sounding toponyms based on, derived from or modelled on the Arabic toponyms of Palestinian villages depopulated and destroyed before or in 1948.

Table 10.1 Examples of appropriation of Arabic toponyms

Palestinian villages and place names depopulated before or in 1948	Israeli settlements with toponyms derived from the names of destroyed Palestinian villages
Lubya; depopulated July 1948, Arabic: 'Bean'	Lavi (kibbutz); founded 1948; Hebrew: 'Lion'
Al-Kabri (in western Galilee); depopulated on 21 May 1948	Kabri (kibbutz); founded in 1949
'Alma (in the Sadad district); depopulated on 30 October 1948	'Alma (moshav); founded in 1949
Biriyya; depopulated on 2 May 1948	Birya (moshav); founded in 1971
'Amqa (in the Acre area); depopulated in October 1948	Amka (moshav); founded in 1949
Sajara (lower Galilee); depopulated July 1948, Arabic: 'Tree' 'Ayn Zaytun (western Galilee); depopulated; Arabic 'Spring of Olives'	Ilaniya; Hebrew: 'Tree' 'Ein Zeitim (kibbutz); Hebrew: 'Spring of Olives'; originally founded in 1891 north of the Arab village 'Ayn Zeitun; abandoned during the First World War; six Muslims and one Jew were recorded there in 1931, living in four houses; the Jewish settlement was re-established in 1946
Indur (Marj Ibn 'Amer); depopulated in 1948; Arabic toponym possibly preserves Canaanite site: Endor Fuleh; depopulated 1925; Arabic: 'Fava Bean' Tal al-'Adas; Arabic: 'Lentils Hill'	Ein Dor (kibbutz); founded 1948; Hebrew: 'Dor Spring' Afula (town); founded in 1925 Tel 'Adashim (moshav); established in 1923, Hebrew: 'Lentils Hill'
Al-Mujaydil (village); depopulated in July 1948	Migdal HaEmek (town); founded in 1952; Hebrew: 'Tower of the Valley'
'Ayn Hawd; depopulated in 1948; Arabic: 'Spring Basin'	'Ein Hod (Artists' colony); founded in 1953; Hebrew: 'Spring of Glory'1
'Eshwa, or 'Ishwa; depopulated in July 1948	Eshtaol (moshav); founded December 1949
'Aqir; depopulated on 6 May 1948	Kiryat 'Ekron (town); founded in 1948

Palestinian villages and place names depopulated before or in 1948	Israeli settlements with toponyms derived from the names of destroyed Palestinian villages
'Ayn Karim', or 'Ein Karim' (west of Jerusalem); depopulated in 1948; 'Generous Spring'	'Ein Karem (Jewish neighbourhood in West Jerusalem); Hebrew: 'Vine Spring'
Kafr Bir'im (northern Galilee); depopulated in October 1948; Arabic: 'Budding Village'	Bar'am (kibbutz); established in June 1949; Hebrew: 'Son of the People'
Mahlul; depopulated in the 1920s	Nahlal (moshav); founded in 1921
Jibta; depopulated in the 1920s	Gvat (kibbutz); founded in 1926
al-Bassa (western Galilee); depopulated on 14 May 1948	Batzat (nature reserve); renamed after 1948
Wadi al-Hawarith; Arabic: 'Valley of Ploughing'	'Emek Hefer; Hebrew: 'Valley of Digging' Ein Ha-Horesh (kibbutz); founded in 1931; was one of the first Zionist settlements in the northern part of Wadi al-Hawarith; Hebrew: 'the Plowman's Spring'; notable residents included Israeli historian Benny Morris
Wadi Sarar or Wadi Surar (west of Jerusalem); Arabic: 'Pebble Stream'	Nahal Sorek Nature Reserve created in 1965; Hebrew: 'Stream of Fruitless Tree' derived from the Arabic toponym made to sound like a name from the Midrash, the body of exegesis of the Torah
Seil 'Imran (Naqab); Arabic 'Stream of 'Imran'	Nahal Amram; Hebrew: 'Stream of Amram' recalling the biblical name of the father of Moses and Aaron
Jabal Haruf (Naqab); Arabic: 'Mount Haruf'	Har Harif; Hebrew: 'Sharp Mountain'
Jabal Dibba (Naqab); Arabic: 'Hump Hill'	Har Dla'at; Hebrew: 'Mount Pumpkin'
Tall as-Safi (north-west of al-Khalil); depopulated in July 1948; Arabic: 'the White Hill'	Tel Tzafit National Park

Palestinian villages and place names depopulated before or in 1948	Israeli settlements with toponyms derived from the names of destroyed Palestinian villages
Beit Dajan (south-east of Jaffa); depopulated in April 1948	Beit Dagon; founded in 1948; Hebrew: 'House of Grain'
Sa'sa' (upper Galilee); depopulated October 1948	Sasa; kibbutz; founded in January 1949
Hittin (eastern Galilee); depopulated in July 1948	Kfar Hittim (moshav); established in 1936; Hebrew: 'Village of Wheat'
Al-Khadra, or al-Khdeira (central Palestine); Arabic: 'Green'	Hadera; established in 1891 as a farming Zionist colony; today a major Israeli city; Israeli toponym makes no sense in Hebrew
Meiron or Mayrun (5 kilometres west of Safad); depopulated in 1948; the name is associated with the ancient Canaanite city of Merom or Maroma	Meron (moshav), founded in 1949
Al-Majdal (a coastal town in the south); depopulated between November and June 1950	Israeli city; renamed to the Hebrew-sounding Migdal 'Ad in 1949 and subsequently to the biblical sounding Ashkelon; Arabic 'Asqalan; Greek: Ascalon
Zir'in (village) in Marj Ibn 'Amer (Jezreel valley); depopulated in the summer of 1948; Arabic: sowing	Mizra (kibbutz) in the Jezreel valley, founded in 1923 (Hebrew: sowing); Mizra hosted the Palmah headquarters, until 1946 Yizre'el (kibbutz); established in August 1948 to the west of the remains of the depopulated Ziri'n
Yazur (town), 6 kilometres east of Jaffa; depopulated in spring 1948	Azor settlement; the historic Palestinian Muslim mosque/shrine was turned into a Jewish synagogue and renamed Sha'arey Tziyon, 'Gates of Zion'

Fifty-six years after the Nakba, in March 2004, Israeli journalist Gideon Levy wrote: 'The Zionist collective memory exists in both our cultural and physical landscape, yet the heavy price paid by the Palestinians – in lives, in the destruction of hundreds of villages, and in the continuing plight of the Palestinian refugees – receives little public recognition' (Levy 2004).

Levy adds:

> Look at this prickly pear plant. It's covering a mound of stones. This mound of stones was once a house, or a shed, or a sheep pen, or a school, or a stone fence. Once – until 56 years ago, a generation and a half ago – not that long ago. The cactus separated the houses and one lot from another, a living fence that is now also the only monument to the life that once was here. Take a look at the grove of pines around the prickly pear as well. Beneath it there was once a village. All of its 405 houses were destroyed in one day in 1948 and its 2,350 inhabitants scattered all over. No one ever told us about this. The pines were planted right afterward by the Jewish National Fund (JNF), to which we contributed in our childhood, every Friday, in order to cover the ruins, to cover the possibility of return and maybe also a little of the shame and the guilt. (Levy 2004)

A monumental 1992 study by a team of Palestinian field researchers and academics under the direction of Palestinian historian Walid Khalidi details the destruction of hundreds of villages falling inside the 1949 armistice lines. The study gives the circumstances of each village's occupation and depopulation, and a description of what remains. Khalidi's team visited all except fourteen sites, made comprehensive reports and took photographs. Of the 418 depopulated villages documented by Walid Khalidi (1992), 293 (70 per cent) were totally destroyed and ninety (22 per cent) were largely destroyed. Seven survived, including 'Ayn Karim (west of Jerusalem), but were taken over by Israeli settlers. A few of the quaint Arab villages and neighbourhoods have actually been largely preserved and gentrified. But they are empty of Palestinians (some of the former residents are internal refugees in Israel) and are designated as Jewish 'artistic colonies' (Benvenisti 1986: 25; Masalha 2005, 2012). While an observant traveller can still see some evidence of the destroyed Palestinian villages, in the main all that is left is a scattering of stones and rubble. But the new state also appropriated for itself both immovable assets, including urban residential quarters, transport infrastructure, police stations, railways, schools, libraries, churches and mosques, as well as books, archival and photo collections, and personal possessions, including silver, furniture, pictures and carpets (Khalidi, W. 1992).

'In many of the JNF sites', Pappe – who analyses several sites mentioned by the JNF website, including the Jerusalem Forest – observes:

> bustans – the fruit gardens Palestinian farmers would plant around their farm houses –appear as one of many mysteries the JNF promises the adventurous visitor. These clearly visible remnants of Palestinian villages are referred to as an inherent part of nature and her wonderful secrets. At one of the sites, it actually refers to the terraces you can find almost everywhere there as the proud creation of the JNF. Some of these were in fact rebuilt over the original ones, and go back centuries before the Zionist takeover. Thus, Palestinian bustans are attributed to nature and Palestine's history transported back to a Biblical and Talmudic past. Such is the fate of one of the best known villages, Ayn al-Zeitun, which was emptied in May 1948, during which many of its inhabitants were massacred. (Pappe 2006: 230)

In 1948 'Ayn Zaytun was an entirely Muslim farming community of 1000, cultivating olives, grain and fruit, especially grapes; the village name was the Arabic for 'Spring of Olives'; In 1992 Palestinian historian Walid Khalidi described the site as follows:

> The rubble of destroyed stone houses is scattered throughout the site, which is otherwise overgrown with olive trees and cactuses [cacti]. A few deserted houses remain, some with round arched entrances and tall windows with various arched designs. In one of the remaining houses, the smooth stone above the entrance arch is inscribed with Arabic calligraphy, a fixture of Palestinian architecture. The well and the village spring also remain. (Khalidi, W. 1992: 437)

Today the old stone mosque, parts of which are still standing, is not mentioned by the JNF website. In 2004 the mosque was turned into a milk farm; the Jewish owner removed the stone that indicated the founding date of the mosque and covered the walls with Hebrew graffiti (Pappe 2006: 217). Other mosques belonging to destroyed villages were turned into restaurants, in the case of the Palestinian town Al-Majdal (historic 'Asqalan) and the Palestinian village of Qaysariah (historic Caesarea-*Palaestina*; currently the archaeological, Roman–Crusader Theme Park of Caesarea which is part of the Israeli settler-colonial Heritage Industry); a shop in the case of Beersheba; part of a tourist resort in the case of al-Zeeb; a bar/restaurant (called 'Bonanza') and a tourist site in the case of 'Ayn Hawd (Pappe 2006: 217; Khalidi, W. 1992: 151).

In Eastern Galilee, Lavi, near Tiberias, a religious kibbutz founded in 1949 on the fertile lands of the Palestinian village of Lubya, depopulated during 1948 by the Haganah forces, is another example of the appropriation of Palestinian place names by Israel. Anyone can tell that the source of the Hebraicised name Lavi is the Palestinian village Lubya; the Zionists, however, claimed that Lavi comes from the ancient Jewish village that existed in the days of the Mishana and Talmud. Yet the appropriation of the Palestinian toponym and choice of the new Hebrew name Lavi (Lion) – rather than Levi, the ancient Jewish last name, and a Levite member of the priesthood – reflected the self-identity construction of the European Jewish colonists, the 'New Jews', and Zionism's new relationship to nature, political geography and tough masculinity (Massad 2006: 38). Moreover, at Lubya the JNF put up a sign: 'South Africa Forest. Parking. In Memory of Hans Riesenfeld, Rhodesia, Zimbabwe'. The South Africa Forest and the 'Rhodesia parking area' were created atop the ruins of Lubya, of whose existence not a trace was left.

Commenting on the gentrification of several former Palestinian villages (like 'Ayn Karim) and neighbourhoods (like those of Lydda and Safad) and their transformation into Jewish built environments, Israeli architect Haim Yacobi, of Ben-Gurion University, writes:

The Palestinian landscape is a subject of mimicry through which a symbolic indigenisation of the [Zionist] settlers takes place. As in other ethnocentric national projects, such mimicry may be described as 'an obsession with archeology', which makes use of historical remains to prove a sense of belonging ... The obsession with archeology and history, as well as with treating them as undisputable truths, is clearly evident in the texts that accompanied the design and construction of the gentrified Arab villages and neighborhoods. In this process, the indigenous landscape is uprooted from its political and historical context, redefined as local and replanted through a double act of mimicry into the 'build your own home' sites. (Yacobi 2009: 115)

THE CREATION OF A USABLE PAST: THE POWER/ KNOWLEDGE NEXUS

The creation of political 'facts on the ground' together with the instrumentalisation of cultural heritage is key to all modern settler-colonial projects. The treatment of the cultural heritage of Palestine as a tool for Zionist settler purposes is central to Israeli educational policies, the Israeli biblical academy and the Israeli government's renaming projects. The creation of a usable past (Peled-Elhanan 2012: 12) by the Israeli educational system and the Israeli biblical academy has been examined by several Israeli academics and authors, including Nurit Peled-Elhanan (2012: 12–47), Benjamin Beit-Hallahmi (1992), Shlomo Sand (2011), Meron Benvenisti (2002) and Gabriel Piterberg (2001, 2008). In *Original Sins: Reflections on the History of Zionism and Israel*, Beit-Hallahmi (of Haifa University) comments on Israel's biblical 'knowledge':

Most Israelis today, as a result of Israeli education, regard the Bible as a reliable source of historical information of a secular, political kind. The Zionist version of Jewish history accepts most Biblical legends about the beginning of Jewish history, minus divine intervention. Abraham, Isaac and Jacob are treated as historical figures. The descent into Egypt and the Exodus are phases in the secular history of a developing people, as is the conquest of Canaan by Joshua.

The Biblical order of events is accepted, but the interpretation is nationalist and secular.

The historicisation of the Bible is a national enterprise in Israel, carried out by hundreds of scholars at all universities. The starting point is Biblical chronology, then evidence (limited) and speculation (plentiful) are arranged accordingly. The Israeli Defence Ministry has even published a complete chronology of Biblical events, giving exact dates for the creation of the world ...

Claiming this ancient mythology as history is an essential part of Zionist secular nationalism, in its attempt to present a coherent account of the genesis of the Jewish people in ancient West Asia. It provides a focus of identification to counter the rabbinical, Diaspora traditions. Teaching the Bible as history to Israeli children creates the notion of continuity. It is Abraham ('the first Zionist', migrating to Palestine), Joshua and the conquest of Palestine (wiping out the Canaanites, just like today), King David's conquest of Jerusalem (just like today). (Beit-Hallahmi 1992: 119)

Reflecting on the tight state control and supervision of the history of Palestine and 'biblical knowledge' in the Israeli educational system, Shlomo Sand (of Tel Aviv University), further explains:

The teachings of the Bible, used more as a book of national history than sacred religious canons, also became a separate subject in primary and secondary education in the eyes of the first immigrant [pre-1948 Yishuv] community in Palestine. Each student in every level of the Hebrew school system studies the history of their collective past separately from universal history. It was logical that the development of the collective memory was completed by an adequate university education. The 'three-thousand years of Jewish nation' had the right to a separate field of pedagogy and research prohibited to 'unaccredited' historians who would presume to access it. One of the most striking results of this original approach was that from the 1930s to the 1990s, no teacher or researcher from the various departments of 'History of the Jewish People' in Israeli universities considered him- or herself to be a non-Zionist historian. Historians of general history whose Zionist identity was not always as confirmed had the freedom to treat questions dealing with Jewish history, but they were ineligible for budgets, scholarships, research institutes, chairs or directing doctoral theses relate to Jewish history. (Sand 2011: 159–160)

Commenting on the production, propagation and dissemination of biblical geographical and archaeological 'knowledge of the country', Meron Benvenisti, Israeli author and former deputy mayor of Jerusalem (from 1971 to 1978), explained that in the state school curriculum and in the army the subject of 'knowledge' of the land of the Bible (*yedi'at haaretz*) is obsessional. Furthermore, 'knowledge of the land' is both militarised and masculinised. This obsessive state-directed search for rootedness in the land by Israeli academia and often Western-funded Zionist research centres, and the treatment of the Bible as actual 'history', is conducted by predominantly secular Ashkenazi historians, nationalist archaeologists and biblical academics. Benvenisti writes:

> The Bible became a guidebook, taught by reference to the landscape, less for its humanistic and social message – and not for its divine authorship. There is nothing more romantic and at the same time more 'establishment' than to be connected in some fashion with this cult. Its priests are the *madrichim* – guides and youth leaders. An extensive institutional network sustained *yedi'at haaretz* [knowledge of the biblical country]: research institutes, field schools, the Society for the Preservation of Nature in Israel (SPNI), the Jewish National Fund, youth movements, paramilitary units, the army. (Benvenisti 1986: 20; also 2002)

In Zionism, the selective reconstruction of antiquity and manufactured 'biblical memory' was part of the historical mission of reviving the ancient national roots and spirit. '[Selective] Antiquity became both a source of legitimacy and an object of admiration' (Zerubavel 1995: 25). The American Israeli academic Selwyn Ilan Troen, of Brandeis University and Ben-Gurion University, under the subheading 'Reclaiming by Naming', remarks on the continuity of European Zionist colonisation of Palestine and 19th

century/early 20th century Western Christian archaeological excavations
and knowledge production:

> Zionism also set out to 're-imagine' and 're-constitute' the country's
> landscape. The process actually began with Christian explorers, and
> archaeologists and Bible scholars from Europe and the United States
> who visited Palestine from the mid-nineteenth century when the
> country was under Turkish rule. Contemporary Arab names were but
> adaptations or corruptions of ancient designations found in sacred
> texts or other historical sources. Zionist settlers continued the process,
> although for them it was not merely to recapture the Holy Land of
> Scriptures. Rather it was a deeply personal attempt to re-imagine
> themselves in the land of their ancestors. As a consequence, in
> renaming the land they consciously ignored or set aside many of
> the physical markers as well as the social and cultural ones of both
> Europe and the Arab neighbours ... Zionists celebrated the return
> to history of Biblical Rehovoth[30] and Ashkelon ['Asqalan] ... In
> addition, thousands of names were given to streets, public squares
> and the landscape, with signs in Hebrew everywhere. The total effect
> invited observers to appreciate that the settlements were the concrete
> manifestation of national revival by a people who could legitimately
> claim to be returning natives. (Troen 2008: 197)

ISRAELI BIBLICAL ARCHAEOLOGY AS A SECULAR RELIGION: JUDAISATION STRATEGIES AND THE ASSERTION OF OWNERSHIP: THE SUPERIMPOSITION OF BIBLICAL, TALMUDIC AND MISHNAIC NAMES

In present-day Israel, the claim is obsessively made that the Hebrew Bible is
materially realised thanks to secularising biblical archaeology, giving Jewish
history flesh and bones, recovering the ancient past, putting it in 'dynastic
order' and 'returning to the archival site of Jewish identity' (Said 2004: 46).
Biblical archaeology was always central to the construction of Israeli Jewish
identity and the perceived legitimacy of the Israeli state. The debate about

'ancient Israel', secularist and nationalist biblical scholarship and biblical archaeology is also a debate about the modern State of Israel, most crucially because in the eyes of many people in the West, the legitimacy of Zionist Jewish 'restorationism' depends on the credibility of the biblical portrait. One facet of that debate is the argument in the public domain over the use of the term 'Israel' to denote the land west of the Jordan, both in ancient and modern times. The inevitable outcome of the obsession with the Hebrew Bible in Western biblical scholarship, calling the land 'biblical' and with its exclusive interest in a small section of the history of the land, has resulted in focusing on the Israelite identity of a land that has actually been non-Jewish in terms of its indigenous population for the larger part of its recorded history (Whitelam 1996). This state of affairs would not exist in any other part of the planet; it is due to the Hebrew Bible and its influence in the West where an inherited Christian culture supported the notion that Palestine has always been somehow essentially 'the land of Israel'. Traditional biblical scholarship has been essentially 'Zionist' and has participated in the elimination of the Palestinian identity, as if 1400 years of Muslim occupation of this land meant nothing. This focus on a short period of history a long time ago participates in a kind of retrospective colonising of the past. It tends to regard modern Palestinians as trespassers or 'resident aliens' in someone else's territory.

The nationalist obsession with the sacred artefacts of secularising biblical archaeology has been central to the formation of Israeli secular-nationalist collective identity and Zionist nation-building since 1948. To present European Jewish identity as rooted in the land, after the establishment of Israel the science of archaeology was summoned to the task of constructing and consolidating that identity in secular times; the rabbis as well as the university scholars specialising in biblical archaeology were given sacred history as their domain (Said 2004: 45). Abu El-Haj's seminal work, *Facts on the Ground*, explores the centrality of selective biblical archaeology in the construction of Zionist Jewish collective identity before and after 1948. The work examined colonial archaeological exploration in Palestine, dating back to British work in the mid-19th century. Abu El-Haj focuses on the period after the establishment of Israel in 1948, linking the academic practice of archaeology with Zionist colonisation and with plans

373

for the Judaisation and repossession of the land through the renaming of Palestinian historic and geographic names. Much of this de-Arabisation of Palestine is given archaeological justification; the existence of Arab names is written over by newly coined Hebrew names. This 'epistemological strategy' prepares for the construction of an Israeli Jewish identity based on assembling archaeological fragments, scattered remnants of masonry, tables, bones and tombs, into a sort of special biography out of which the European colony of the Yishuv emerges 'visible and linguistically, as Jewish national home' (Abu El-Haj 2001: 74; Said 2004: 47–48; Bowersock 1988: 181–191).

A large number of Israeli experts on and practitioners of biblical excavations – from General Yigael Yadin and General Moshe Dayan to even General Ariel Sharon – have remarked that biblical archaeology is the 'privilege' Israeli science *par excellence* (Said 2004: 45–46; Kletter 2003). Magen Broshi, a leading Israeli archaeologist, and a current member of the Israeli Government Names Committee, noted:

> The Israeli phenomenon, a nation returning to its old–new land, is without parallel. It is a nation in the process of renewing its acquaintance with its own lands and here archaeology plays an important role. In this process archaeology is part of a larger system known as *Yedi'at haAretz*, knowledge of the land (the Hebrew term is derived most probably from the German *Landeskunde*) … The European immigrants found the country to which they felt, paradoxically, both kinship and strangeness. Archaeology in Israel, a *sui generis* state, served as a means to dispel the alienation of its new citizens. (Quoted in Said 2004: 46)

The Israeli historians, biblical scholars, archaeologists and geographers, Meron Benvenisti argues in *Sacred Landscape: The Buried History of the Holy Land since 1948*, have reinvented and reconstructed a history and chronology of ancient Palestine based on Israeli identity politics,

> so as to emphasise the Jewish connection to the land, adding designations such as the Biblical, Hasmonean, Mishnaic, and

Talmudic periods. From the 'early Muslim' period onward, however, they adopted the nomenclature of the 'conquerers' chronology', since in this way it was possible to divide the approximately 1,400 years of Muslim-Arab rule into units that were shorter than the period of Jewish rule over the Eretz Israel/Palestine (which lasted at most for 600 years), and especially to portray the history of the country as a long period of rule by a series of foreign powers who had robbed it from the Jews – a period that ended in 1948 with the reestablishment of Jewish sovereignty in Palestine. It was thus possible to obscure the fact that the indigenous Muslim Arab population was part and parcel of the ruling Muslim peoples and instead to depict the history of the local population – its internal wars, its provincial rulers, its contribution to the landscape – as matters lacking in importance, events associated with one or another dynasty of 'foreign occupiers'. (Benvenisti 2002: 300)

While the colonial attitudes of European and North American historians and social scientists towards former colonies of the West has begun to be re-evaluated critically since the 1960s, the Israelis have chosen to consolidate the colonial tradition and settler-colonial historiography in Palestine–Israel. In Israel, there has always been an obsession with 'biblical memory' and the convergence between biblical excavations and Jewish settler-colonisation has always loomed large, but became most pronounced after the post-1967 conquests. Furthermore, Israeli biblical archaeology has remained central to secular Zionist identity politics and Israeli settler activities – most Orthodox Jews in Israel were and still are indifferent to its findings (Elon 1997: 38). Meron Benvenisti observes that

British, American, and other academics engaged in the study of the archaeology and history of their former overseas colonies have begun to reevaluate the attitudes that prevailed during the colonial period. They have admitted grave distortions that were introduced into the history of the colonies as an outcome of Eurocentric attitudes, ignoring or erasing remaining traces of the natives' past and their material culture. In the wake of this evaluation, Amerindian,

Aborigine, and native African sites were studied and restored, and a new history was written, focusing on the organic chronicles of those regions, which had been a mere footnote in the history of the European peoples. The Israelis, by contrast, chose to maintain the colonial tradition with only minor changes ... The [Israeli] Antiquities Administration is aware of only two sites in Old Jaffa: the 'Biuim House' (the first home of this group of early Zionist pioneers in the country, in 1882) and the first building of the first [Zionist] Hebrew High School ('Gimnasiya Herzeliyya'), which have been declared 'antiquities' in accordance with Article 2 [of Israeli Antiquities Law of 1978]. Of course no structure 'of historical value' to the Palestinians has been declared as a protected antiquity under Israeli law. (Benvenisti 2002: 304–305)

Around Jerusalem thousands of acres of pine forests were planted by the Jewish National Fund, forests which are both intended to camouflage destroyed Palestinian villages and fashion a new pastoral 'biblical landscape', create a new collective memory and give the impression of an 'authentic' timeless biblical landscape in which trees have been standing forever. But this 'natural landscape' is a carefully constructed scene to camouflage the systematically expropriated land of Palestinian villages, the destruction of cultivated olive groves and the ethnic cleansing of the Nakba. The under-lying intention is to obscure the locations of the Palestinian villages and prevent any cultivation of the land by non-Jews. The Israeli architects Rafi Segal and Eyal Weizman, commenting on Israeli settlement and the creation of a pastoral biblical landscape, wrote:

In the ideal image of the pastoral landscape, integral to the perspective of colonial traditions, the admiration of the rustic panorama is always viewed through the window frames of modernity. The impulse to retreat from the city to the country reasserts the virtue of a simpler life close to nature ... the re-creation of the picturesque scenes of Biblical landscape becomes a testimony to an ancient claim on the land. The admiration of the landscape thus functions as a cultural practice, by which social and cultural identities are formed. Within this panorama, however, lies a cruel paradox: the very thing that renders the landscape 'Biblical' or 'pastoral', its traditional inhabitants and cultivation in terraces, olive orchards, stone buildings and the presence of livestock, is produced by the Palestinians, who the Jewish settlers came to replace. And yet, the very people who came to cultivate the 'green olive orchards' and render the landscape Biblical are themselves excluded from the panorama. The Palestinians are there to produce the scenery and then disappear ... The gaze that sees a 'pastoral Biblical landscape' does not register what it does not want to see, it is a visual exclusion that seeks a physical exclusion. Like a theatrical set, the panorama can be seen as an edited landscape put together by invisible stage hands ... What for the state is a supervision mechanism that seeks to observe the Palestinians is for the settlers a window on a pastoral landscape that seeks to erase them. The Jewish settlements superimpose another datum of latitudinal geography upon an existing landscape. Settlers can thus see only other settlements, avoid those of the Palestinian towns and villages, and feel that they have truly arrived 'as the people without land to the land with people'. (Segal and Weizman 2003: 92)

There are dozens of biblical and archaeological parks in Israel run by the Israel Nature and Parks Authority (Rashut Hateva' Vehaganim), a governmental organisation set up in 1998. Many of these archaeological (biblical and Crusader) 'national heritage' parks have been constructed on the ruins of Palestinian villages and towns destroyed in 1948. The negation of both the ancient Palestinian and Islamic heritage of the land by Israel's heritage industry of archaeological theme parks is very much in evidence today in Palestinian Saffuriyah (destroyed by Israel in 1948) – the heritage industry geared towards both the retrospective colonisation of the past and the fashioning of modern Israeli collective identity.

FROM PALESTINIAN MAJDAL-'ASQALAN TO BIBLICAL ASHKELON

In 1948 the towns and villages of southern Palestine, including the towns of Bir al-Sabi (Beersheba) and al-Majdal, were completely depopulated. Al-Majdal was established in the 16th century near the medieval Muslim city of 'Asqalan, a city that had a long history and a multi-layered identity dating back to the ancient Philistines. Its medieval Arab name, 'Asqalan, preserved its ancient Palestinian name, Ascalon. With one of the oldest and largest seaport in ancient Palestine, it was one of the five famous cities of the Philistines: Gaza, Gath, Ascalon, Ashdod (modern Arabic toponym: Isdud), Ekron ('Aqir). Al-Majdal/'Asqalan, on the eve of the 1948 war, had 10,000 (Muslim and Christian) inhabitants, and in October 1948 thousands more refugees from nearby villages joined them. Al-Majdal was conquered by the Israeli army on 4 November 1948 and many of its residents and refugees fled, leaving some 2700 inhabitants, mostly women and the elderly, behind. Orders in Hebrew and Yiddish were posted in the streets of the town, warning the soldiers to be aware of 'undesirable' behaviour on the part of the town's residents. 'As was customary in such instances', the Israeli intelligence officer wrote, 'the behaviour of the population was obsequious and adulatory' (Levy 2000). In December 1948, Israeli soldiers 'swept through' the town and deported some 500 of its remaining inhabitants. In 1949 the commanding officer of the Southern Command, Yigal Allon, 'demanded ... that the town be emptied of its Arabs' (Masalha 1997: 9). This was followed by an inter-ministerial committee decision to thin out the Palestinian population; another ministerial committee, 'on abandoned property', decided to settle al-Majdal with Jews; the town was being Judaised, and, with 2500 Jewish residents, it was named 'Migdal-Ad'. In December 1949, more Palestinians were deported to vacate more houses for Jewish settlers, this time for discharged Israeli soldiers. In the meantime, the Israeli army made the life of those Palestinians who remained a misery, hoping they would leave. The new commanding officer of the Southern Command, Moshe Dayan, returned to the proposal of Yigal Allon: 'I hope that perhaps in the coming years, there will be another opportunity to transfer these Arabs [170,000 Israeli Arabs] out of the Land of Israel', Dayan said at a meeting of the ruling

Mapai party on 18 June 1950. Dayan also submitted a detailed proposal for 'the evacuation of the Arab inhabitants of the town of Majdal'. Both the army chiefs of staff agreed, and Prime Minister Ben-Gurion authorised the plan on 19 June 1950 (Masalha 1997: 9).

In the summer of 1950, almost two years after the 1948 war, the Palestinian inhabitants of Majdal received expulsion orders and, over a period of a few weeks, were transported to the borders of Gaza. They were loaded onto trucks and dropped off at the border. The last delivery of 229 people left for Gaza on 21 October 1950. The Israeli officials distributed the 'abandoned' houses among new Jewish settlers. To this very day the Palestinian inhabitants of al-Majdal live in the shacks and shanties of the refugee camps in Gaza. In 1956, Migdal-Ad changed its name to the biblical-sounding Ashkelon (Levy 2000). Since then it has been kept as a purely Jewish city. Commenting on Israeli educational policies, Ismael Abu-Sa'ad, of Ben-Gurion University, writes:

> The education system is essential to making the displacement of indigenous history and presence 'official', through texts such as that quoted from the 6th grade geography curriculum in Israeli schools, which teaches Palestinian children that the history of the coastal plain began only a hundred years ago, with the advent of European Jewish settlement and their transformation of this previously 'abandoned area'. In the text, modern (Jewish) Tel Aviv overrides any mention of Arab Jaffa; modern (Jewish) Ashdod of (Arab) Isdud; modern (Jewish) Ashkelon of (Arab) al-Majdal[-'Asqalan]. Modern Jewish Rishon Litzion ('First in Zion') and Herzliya and numerous other new towns are superimposed upon an unacknowledged landscape of Palestinian villages emptied and demolished in 1948. The indigenous landscape is erased from the curriculum, while it is simultaneously being erased *by* the curriculum, because of its absence from the official historical and geographical materials being taught about the region. (Abu-Sa'ad 2008: 24–25)

The erasure of the heritage of Palestine and the Palestinians, physically and culturally, was summarised by Israeli political geographer Oren Yiftachel in 2008 as follows:

The act of erasure had been led, for many decades, by the Jewish state's apparatuses, those that aim to erase the remnants of the Arab-Palestinian society that lived in the country until 1948, and to deny the catastrophe that Zionism inflicted on this nation. The erasure that came after the violence, the flight, the expulsion and the demolition of the villages is visible in all discourses – in textbooks, the history that Zionist society tells itself, in the political discourse, in the media, in maps and now also in the names of the sites, roads, and junctions. Palestine, which lays under Israel, is disappearing from the Israeli-Jewish physical reality and discourse.[31]

THE NEW ISRAELI PLACE NAMES AND LANDSCAPE: FASHIONING A EUROPEAN LANDSCAPE AS A SITE OF AMNESIA AND ERASURE

In the first two decades of the state Israelis had a deep anxiety about the discovery of the truth about the 1948 Nakba and the 'nightmarish' prospect of Palestinian refugees returning to their towns and villages in what had become Israel. *Facing the Forests*, one of novelist A. B. Yehushua's first major works, was published in 1963. It opens with the destruction of a Palestinian village in 1948 and the planting of a JNF forest on its ruins. The novel recounts the story of an Israeli student who is 'obsessed' with the history of the Latin Crusaders. The student, looking for a break and solitude, finds a job as a forest ranger. When he arrives at the watch house in the JNF forest he finds an Arab man whose tongue had been cut out and the man's daughter. Shortly after his arrival the student begins to suffer from nightmares and he is constantly anticipating a catastrophe. As the summer continues the student begins to desire the man's daughter. The tension between the two escalates and suddenly the man sets fire to the forest and the whole forest burns down. At dawn the student 'turns his gaze to the fire-smoking hills, frowns. There out of the smoke and haze, the ruined village appears before his eyes; born anew, in its basic outlines as an abstract drawing, as all things past and buried'. While the student fails to see the truths unearthed by his research on the Latin Crusades, the fire reveals it. The novel ends with the destruction of the forest and the re-emergence of the Arab village (Yehoshua 1975: 385).

The JNF's forests, such as the Carmel National Park, became an icon of Zionist national revival in Israel and in Israeli Hebrew literature, symbolising the success of the European Zionist project in 'striking roots' in the ancient homeland and sacred landscape. Children were often named after trees and children's Hebrew literature described young trees as children (Zerubavel 1996). Names such as Ilan (tree), Oren (pine tree) Tomer and Tamar (male and female for palm tree), Amir (tree top), or Elon or Allon (oak tree) are very common in Israel. Natural woodlands of 'Palestine Oak' (بلوط فلسطين) covered many areas of historic Palestine, especially in upper Galilee, Mount Carmel, Mount Tabor (Arabic: Jabal al-Tur) and other hilly regions. Some local Palestinian Muslim traditions in Galilee have even attributed holiness to ancient oak trees. The ancient Palestine Oak tree and its leaves have been seen as a symbol of strength and endurance not only in Palestine but in many countries across the world. European pre-Christian and medieval Christian traditions of veneration of Palestine Oak trees are well known. The leaves of the oak were also traditionally an important part of German army regalia and symbolise ranks in the US army. In ancient Palestine, this tree had its own cult in local mythology, derived from local religious traditions; it is associated with life and is supposed to have grown since the beginning of the world (Niesiolowski-Spano 2011: 132–137).

But the worship of the JNF (European-style) forests in Israel has also become central to an invented Zionist secular collective memory. Israeli historian and journalist Amos Elon, who was born in Vienna as Amos Sternbach and immigrated to Palestine in 1933, changed his name to Amos Oak. In similar vein, General Yigal Allon, commander of the Palmah in 1948, was born Yigal Paicovitch and changed his name to the Hebrew-sounding Allon (oak tree). As we have seen above, this tradition of the 'ancient woods' and wood worship was derived from central European notions of romantic nationalism. In 2004 Amos Elon moved to Italy, citing disillusionment with developments in Israel since 1967. In *The Israelis: Founders and Sons*, Elon writes: '[F]ew things are as evocatively symbolic of the Zionist dream and rationale as a "Jewish National Fund Forest"' (Elon 1983: 200). Israel's European-style forests and reforestation policies enjoy Western support. Planting a European-style forest in the 'sacred soil' and 'sacred landscape' confirms the undeniable ethical value of Israel's (and by extension the West's) project in the East. Afforestation is also linked, materially and symbolically, to the European Holocaust, and thousands of trees have been planted in memory of the lost communities and individual victims (Elon 1983: 200). For Palestinians, however, few things better encapsulate the notorious role of the JNF since the Nakba (Jamjoum 2010).

FROM YERUSHALAYIM TO ORSHALIM: THE TRANSLITERATION OF NEW HEBREW TOPONYMS AND ROAD SIGNS INTO ENGLISH AND ARABIC

The official Judaisation, Hebraicisation and biblicisation schemes which began after 1948 continued into the post-1967 era. Israel began interfering with Arabic road signs and toponyms in occupied East Jerusalem immediately after June 1967. In that year it coined a new word, Orshalim, that was supposed to be the Arabic form of the Hebrew word for Jerusalem, Yerushalayim.[32] In recent years thousands of road signs became the latest front in Israel's battle of accelerating the erasure of the Palestinian Arab toponymic heritage of the land. The pattern, which began before 1967, included the transliteration of newly coined Hebrew toponyms and road signs into both English and Arabic. In July 2009, the Israeli Transport Minister Yisrael Katz announced a new road signs scheme for all major roads in Israel, occupied East Jerusalem and even parts of occupied West Bank to be 'standardised' by converting the original Arabic place names into straight transliterations of the new Hebrew name. Traditionally some road signs in Israel included names that were rendered in three languages top-to-bottom: Hebrew (first), English and Arabic. Under the 2009 scheme of the Transport Ministry, which was open about the political motivation behind its policy, Jerusalem, or al-Quds in Arabic, would be standardised throughout occupied East Jerusalem as Yerushalayim and transliterated into Arabic Orshalim; Nazareth, or al-Nasirah in Arabic, would be standardised into Natzrat; and Jaffa, the Palestinian port city after which Palestine's oranges became famous as Jaffa oranges, would be

Yafo. As for Palestinian Nablus, the ministry was also looking for ways to spell the Hebrew/biblical-sounding name Shechem in Arabic.[33] Today all major international airlines which fly to Ben-Gurion Airport (formerly Lydda airport, which was created in 1936 during the British Mandatory period and later renamed after Israel's first Prime Minister) use the Hebrew transliteration of the Arabic toponym Yafa (Jaffa) by drawing the attention of their passengers on arrival to weather in the Yafo-Tel Aviv region.

EPILOGUE: THE PALESTINIAN MULTI-LAYERED IDENTITY, TOPONYMIC MEMORY AND THE DIVERSE HERITAGE OF THE LAND

Palestinian responses to forced depopulation and ethnic cleansing from their villages and towns are 'discursively rich, complex and protean' (Slyomovics 2002). In recent decades novels, poems, films, plays, ethnographic and photographic documentation, maps, oral history archives, online websites, and a wide range of activities in exiled and internally displaced communities have been and are being produced, many with the aim of countering Israeli denial and correcting distortions of omission and commission that eradicate the Palestinian presence in the land. Also a large number of books have been produced both inside Israel and at Birzeit University, all dedicated to villages that have been depopulated and destroyed. These form part of a large historical and imaginative literature in which the destroyed Palestinian villages are 'revitalised and their existence celebrated' (Slyomovics 2002). In the post-1948 period Palestinians maintained the multiple meaning of their Arabic names and the multi-layered Palestinian identity embedded in ancient names (Ashrawi 1995: 132–134; Doumani 1995).

Palestinian nationalism (both secular and religious strands) however – like all other modern nationalisms – with its construction of national consciousness, is a modern phenomenon (Khalidi, R. 1998). But this must not be automatically conflated with the Palestinians' social, cultural and religious identities, which are deeply rooted in the land as well as in the ancient history and toponymic memory of Palestine. Furthermore, the

Palestinians, until the 1948 catastrophe, were predominantly peasants, deeply rooted in the physical and cultural landscapes of Palestine. The local dialect and the names of their villages and towns preserved the multi-layered and diverse cultural heritage of the country.

Today the Palestinians are culturally and linguistically Arab and largely but not exclusively Muslim. The Palestinian Muslim population was mainly descended from local Palestinian Christians and Jews who had converted to Islam after the Islamic conquest in the 7th century and inherited many of the social, cultural, religious and linguistic traditions of ancient Palestine, including those of the Israelites, Canaanites and Philistines (Shaban 1971: 25–161; Donner 1981; Nebel and Oppenheim 2000; Rose 2010; Esler 2011). Furthermore, the similarities between their Arabic language and Ugaritic suggests that Arabic was not a late intruder into Palestine from 638 AD onwards, following the Arab Muslim conquest (Ra'ad 2010). Also many Palestinians are Christian Arabs who have historic roots in Palestine and a long heritage in the land where Christ lived. Commenting on the multi-layered cultural identity and diverse heritage of the Palestinians, Palestinian sociologist Samih Farsoun (1937–2005) writes:

> Palestinians are descendants of an extensive mixing of local and regional peoples, including the Canaanites, Philistines, Hebrews, Samaritans, Hellenic Greeks, Romans, Nabatean Arabs, tribal nomadic Arabs, some Europeans from the Crusades, some Turks, and other minorities; after the Islamic conquests of the seventh century, however, they became overwhelmingly Arabs. Thus, this mixed-stock of people has developed an Arab-Islamic culture for at least fourteen centuries. (Farsoun 2004: 4)

The development of Palestinian nationalism in recent decades has brought with it a much greater awareness of critical archaeology and historical writing based on critical Biblical Studies and the question of the shared historical heritage of Palestine and the Palestinians (Thompson 2003: 1). Also, interestingly, Palestinian scholar Mazin Qumsiyeh has suggested, in his *Sharing the Land of Canaan*, a more realistic and less dichotomous approach to the debate on Canaanites–Israelites. He argued for coexistence in Palestine–Israel based on shared historical heritage and cultural and genetic affinities between the 'Canaanitic people': Mizrahi Jews and Palestinian Christians and Muslims (Qumsiyeh 2004: 28–30; see also Nebel and Oppenheim 2000).

Indeed, it would not be unreasonable to argue that the modern Palestinians are more likely to be the descendants of the ancient Philistines (and Israelites) than Ashkenazi Jews, many of whom were European converts to Judaism. Certainly historically, in contrast to the myth of 'exile and return', many of the original Jewish inhabitants of ancient Palestine remained in the country but had accepted Christianity and Islam many generations later. Today, however – in contrast to the mythologised Ashkenazi Zionist and Arab nationalist historiographies – more and more archaeologists and biblical scholars are convinced that the ancestors of the Israelites had never been in Egypt and that the biblical paradigm of a military conquest of Cana'an was completely fictional. Indeed, the archaeological evidence undermines, in particular, the Book of Joshua. If the Exodus from Egypt and the forty-year desert journey around Sinai could not have happened and the military conquest of the 'fortified cities' ancient Palestine (according to Deuteronomy 9:1: 'great cities with walls sky-high') were totally refuted by archaeology, who, then, were these Israelites, Philistines or Canaanites?

Palestinian digitally archived oral histories and toponymic memories of the hundreds of destroyed villages and towns have emerged in recent decades as a significant methodology not only for the construction of an alternative history of the Palestinian Nakba and memories of the lost historic Palestine but also for an ongoing indigenous life, living Palestinian practices and a sustained human ecology. In contrast with the Israeli settler-colonial heritage-style industry and a supremacist biblical archaeology, with its obsession with myth-narratives and assembling archaeological fragments, indigenous Palestinians have devoted much attention to the enormously rich sedimentations of village history and oral traditions as a reminder of the continuity of native life and living practices (Said 2004: 49; Masalha 2008: 123–156). Decolonising history and reclaiming and preserving the ancient heritage and material culture of Palestine and the Palestinians is vital. There is an urgent need to teach the ancient history of Palestine and the indigenous Palestinians (Muslims, Christians, Samaritans and Jews), including the production of new and critical Palestinian textbooks for schools, colleges and universities, as well as for the millions of exiled Palestinian refugees. This understanding and teaching should encompass the new critical archaeology scholarship of Palestine and the new critical understanding of the ancient history and memories of the land.

Bibliography

'Abd al-Hadi, Sabri Sharif (1923) *Jughrafiyat Suriyya wa Filastin al-Tabi'iyyah* [The Natural Geography of Syria and Palestine] (Cairo: al-Maktabah al-Ahliyyah) [Arabic].

Abdul Rahman, A., and Y. Nagata (1977) 'The Iltizam System in Egypt and Turkey', *Journal of Asian and African Studies* 14: 169–194.

Abu El-Haj, Nadia (1998) 'Translating Truths: Nationalism, Archaeological Practice and the Remaking of Past and Present in Contemporary Jerusalem', *American Ethnologist* 25(2): 166–118.

Abu El-Haj, Nadia (2001) *Facts on the Ground: Archaeological Practice and Territorial Self-fashioning in Israeli Society* (Chicago, IL: University of Chicago Press).

Abu Lughod, Ibrahim (1988) 'Territorially-based Nationalism and the Politics of Negation', in Edward W. Said and Christopher Hitchens (eds.) *Blaming the Victims: Spurious Scholarship and the Palestinian Question* (London: Verso): 193–206.

Abu-Lughod, Ibrahim, Roger Heacock and Khaled Nashef (eds.) (1991) *The Landscape of Palestine: Equivocal Poetry* (Birzeit, Palestine: Birzeit University Publications).

Abu-Manneh, Butrus (1999) *'The Rise of the Sanjak of Jerusalem in the Late Nineteenth Century'*, in Ilan Pappé (ed.) *The Israel/Palestine Question* (London: Routledge): 41–51.

Abu-Sa'ad, Ismael (2005) 'Forced Sedentarisation, Land Rights and Indigenous Resistance: The Palestinian Bedouin in the Negev', in Nur Masalha (ed.) *Catastrophe Remembered: Palestine–Israel and the Internal Refugees: Essays in Memory of Edward W. Said* (London: Zed Books): 113–141.

Abu-Sa'ad, Ismael (2008) 'Present Absentees: The Arab School Curriculum in Israel as a Tool for De-educating Indigenous Palestinians', *Holy Land Studies* 7(1): 17–43.

Abu-Sitta, Salman (2010) *Atlas of Palestine 1917–1966* (London: Palestine Land Society).

Adamec, Ludwig W. (2009) *Historical Dictionary of Islam* (Lanham, MD: Scarecrow Press).

Ahlström, Gösta W. (1993) *The History of Ancient Palestine from the Palaeolithic Period to Alexander's Conquest* (Sheffield: Sheffield Academic Press).

Al-Baladuri (2014) *Kitab Futuh al-Buldan* [Book of the Conquests of Lands], translated by Philip Hitti, *The Origins of the Islamic State* (1916; New York: Columbia University), Being a Translation from the Arabic, Accompanied with Annotations, Geographic and Historic Notes of *Kitab Futuh al-Buldan* (Charleston, SC: Nabu Press).

Album, Stephen (1998) *A Checklist of Islamic Coins*, 2nd edition (Santa Rosa, CA: S. Album).

Al-Dabbagh, Mustafa Murad (1965 and 1972–1986) *Biladuna Filastin* [Our Country, Palestine], 11 vols. (Beirut: Dar al-Taliah and Dar al-Huda).

Al-Farabi (1985) *On the Perfect State* [*Mabadia Ara' Ahl al-Madanat al-Faḍilah*], translated by R. Walzer (Oxford: Clarendon Press).

Al-Hamawi, Yaqut (1861) *Kitab Mu'jam al-Buldan* [Dictionary of Countries] (Leiden: Brill; originally published 1224–1228).

Al-Hut, Bayan N. (1981) *Al-Qiyadat al-Mu'assasat al-Siyasiyyah fi Filastin, 1917–1948* [Leadership of the Political Institutions in Palestine, 1917–1948] (Beirut: The Institute of Palestine Studies).

Al-Idrisi (1592) *De Geographia Universali: Kitab Nuzhat al-Mushtaq fi Dhikr al-Amsar wa-al-Aqtar wa-al-Buldan wa-al-Juzur wa-al-Madain wa-al-Afaq* [The Book of Pleasant Journeys into Faraway Lands] (Medici Press: Rome).

Al-Isfahani, Imad al-Din (1888) *Conquête de la Syrie et de la Palestine par Salâh ed-dîn* [Conquest of Syria and Palestine by Saladin], ed. Carlo Landberg (Leiden: Brill).

Al-Ju'beh, Nazmi (2008) 'Hebron Glass: A Centuries-old Tradition', *This Week in Palestine*, 25 January, at: http://archive.thisweekinpalestine.com/details.php?id=2133&edid=140

Al-Maqdisi (al-Muqaddasi/al-Mukaddasi), Muhammad ibn Ahmad Shams al-Din (1866) *Description of Syria, Including Palestine* (Bengal: Asiatic Society of Bengal).

Al-Maqdisi (al-Muqaddasi) (1994) *The Best Divisions for Knowledge of the Regions* [*Ahasan al-Taqasim Fi Ma'rifat al-Aqalim*], translated by Basil Anthony Collins (Reading: Garnet Publishing).

Al-Maqdisi (al-Muqaddasi), Shams al-Din Abi 'Abd Allah Muhammad ibn Ahmad (2002) *Ahsan al-Taqasim Fi Ma'rifat al-Aqalim* [The Best Divisions for Knowledge of the Regions] (Beirut: Dar al-Kutub al-'Ilmiyya).

Al-Turk, Sadiq Ahmad Ibrahim (1998) Study of Salih ibn Ahmad al-Tumurtashi's manuscript *Al-Khabar al-Tam for Dhikr al-Ard al-Muqaddasah wa-Hududiha wa-Dhikr Ard Filastin wa-Hududiha wa-Sham*. MA Dissertation, al-Najah University, Palestine.

Al-Shaikh, Abdul-Rahim (2010) 'Last Year in Jerusalem', *This Week in Palestine* 141 (January), at: http://www.thisweekinpalestine.com/details.php?id=2969&ed=177&edid=177

Al-Tumurtashi, Salih ibn Ahmad (1695–1696) *Al-Khabar al-Tam for Dhikr al-Ard al-Muqaddasah wa-Hududiha wa-Dhikr Ard Filastin wa-Hududiha wa-Sham* [The Complete Knowledge in Remembering the Holy Land and its Boundaries and Remembering Palestine and its Boundaries and al-Sham] (Abu Dis, Jerusalem: Markez Ihyai al-Turath al-Islami).

Al-'Ulaymi, Mujir al-Din (1973) *Al-Uns al-Jalil bi-Tarikh al-Quds wal-Khalil* [The Glorious History of Jerusalem and Hebron] (Amman).

Anderson, Benedict (1991) *Imagined Communities: Reflections on the Origin and Spread of Nationalism*, revised and extended edi (London and New York: Verso).

Anderson, Irvin H. (2005) *Biblical Interpretation and Middle East Policy: The Promised Land, America, and Israel* (Gainesville, FL: University Press of Florida).

Ammianus Marcellinus (c. 380) *The Roman History of Ammianus Marcellinus*: Book XIV, 8, 11, Tertullian.org, at: http://penelope.uchicago.edu/Thayer/E/Roman/Texts/Ammian/14*.html

Anabsi, Ghalib (1992) *From the 'Merits of the Holy Land' Literature*. MA dissertation, Tel Aviv University [Hebrew].

Arrian (2006) *Anabasis Alexandri* [The Journey of Alexander], Book VIII (Indica) (Sydney: Accessable Publishing Systems, Read How You Want).

Asali, K. J. (ed.) (1990) *Jerusalem in History* (New York: Olive Branch Press).

Ashcroft, Bill, and Pal Ahluwalia (2001) *Edward Said: Routledge Critical Thinkers*, paperback edition (London and New York: Routledge).

Asheri, David, Alan B. Lloyd and Aldo Corcella (2007) *A Commentary on Herodotus I–IV*. Edited by Oswyn Murray and Alfonso Moreno (Oxford: Oxford University Press).

Ashkelony, Brouria Bitton, and Arieh Kofsky (eds.) (2004) *Christian Gaza in Late Antiquity* (Leiden: Brill).

Ashrawi, Hanan Mikhail (1995) *This Side of Peace: A Personal Account* (New York: Simon & Schuster).

Ateek, Naim Stifan (1989) *Justice, and Only Justice: A Palestinian Theology of Liberation* (New York: Orbis).

Avni, Gideon (2014) *The Byzantine–Islamic Transition in Palestine: An Archaeological Approach* (Oxford: Oxford University Press).

Azaryahu, Maoz (1995) *State Rituals: Independence Celebrations and Memorials for the Fallen in Israel, 1948–1956* (Sde Boqer: Ben-Gurion Study Centre).

Azaryahu, Maoz (1996) 'The Power of Commemorative Street Names', *Environment and Planning D: Society and Space* 14: 311–330.

Azaryahu, Maoz (1997) 'German Reunification and the Politics of Street Names: The Case of East Berlin', *Political Geography* 16(6): 479–493.

Azaryahu, Maoz, and Arnon Golan (2001) '(Re)naming the Landscape: The Formation of the Hebrew Map of Israel 1949–1960', *Journal of Historical Geography*, 27(2): 178–195.

Azaryahu, M., and Kook, R. (2002) 'Mapping the Nation: Street Names and Arab-Palestinian Identity: Three Case Studies', *Nations and Nationalism* 8(2): 195–213.

Bagrow, Leo (2010) *History of Cartography*, revised by R. A. Skelton, 2nd edition (New Brunswick and London: Transaction Publishers).

Ball, Warwick (2000) *Rome in the East: The Transformation of an Empire* (London: Routledge).

Baram, Uzi (2007a) 'Archaeological Surveys, Excavations and Landscapes of the Ottoman Imperial Realm: An Agenda for the Archaeological Modernity of the Middle East', in Gelichi, Sauri, and Mauro Librenti (eds.) *Constructing Post-medieval Archaeology in Italy: A New Agenda* (Lorenzo: Edizioni All'Insegna del Giglio): 11–18.

Baram, Uzi (2007b) 'Filling a Gap in the Chronology: What Archaeology is Revealing about the Ottoman Past in Israel', in Sandy Sufian and Mark LeVine (eds.) *Reapproaching Borders: New Perspectives on the Study of Israel-Palestine* (Lanham, MD: Rowman & Littlefield): 17–40.

Barnes, Timothy D. (1981) *Constantine and Eusebius* (Cambridge, MA: Harvard University Press).

Bar On, Bat-Ami (1996) 'Meditations on National Identity', in Karen S. Warren and Duane L. Cady (eds.) *Bringing Peace Home: Feminism, Violence, and Nature* (Bloomington, IN: Indian University Press): 33–53.

Barsanuphius (2006) *The Fathers of the Church: Barsanuphius and John Letters*, Vol. 1, translated by John Chryssavgis (Washington, DC: The Catholic University of America Press).

Bassett, Thomas J. (1994) 'Cartography and Empire Building in Nineteenth-century West Africa', *Geographical Review* 84: 316–335.

Beheiry, Marwan R. (1981) 'The Agricultural Exports of Southern Palestine, 1885–1914', *Journal of Palestine Studies* 10(4): 61–81.

Beit-Hallahmi, Benjamin (1992) *Original Sins: Reflections on the History of Zionism and Israel* (London: Pluto Press).

Belayche, Nicole (2004) 'Pagan Festivals in Fourth-Century Gaza', in Brouria Bitton-Ashkelony and Aryeh Kofsky (eds.) *Christian Gaza in Late Antiquity* (Leiden and Boston: Brill): 5–22.

Ben-Dov, Meir (1977) 'Found After 1400 Years – The Magnificent Nea', *Biblical Archaeology Review* 3(4), December, at: https://www.biblicalarchaeology.org/daily/biblical-sites-places/jerusalem/found-after-1400-years-the-magnificent-nea/.

Ben-Gurion, David (1982) *Yoman Hamilhamah* [War Diary], vols. 1–3 (Tel Aviv: Misrad Habitahon Publications) [Hebrew].

Benvenisti, Meron (1986) *Conflicts and Contradictions* (New York: Villard).

Benvenisti, Meron (2002) *Sacred Landscape: The Buried History of the Holy Land since 1948* (Berkeley, CA: University of California Press).

Ben-Shlomo, David (2010) *Philistine Iconography: A Wealth of Styles and Symbolism* (Fribourg: Academic Press; Göttingen: Vandenhoeck & Ruprecht).

Ben-Yehuda, Eliezer (1914) 'Mekorot le Malle he-Haser bi-Leshonenu' [Sources to Fill the *Lacunae* in our Language], *Zichronot Wa'ad ha-Lashon* 4: 3–14 [Hebrew].

Ben-Zeev, Efrat (2014) *Remembering Palestine in 1948: Beyond National Narratives* (Cambridge: Cambridge University Press).

Berg, Lawrence D., and R. A. Kearns (1996) 'Naming as Norming: "Race", Gender, and the Identity Politics of Naming Places in Aotearoa/New Zealand', *Environment and Planning D: Society and Space* 14(1): 99–122.

Berg, Lawrence D., and J. Vuolteenhaho (eds.) (2009) *Critical Toponymies: The Contested Politics of Place Naming* (Burlington, VT: Ashgate Publishing Company).

Berlin, Andrea M. (1997) 'Archaeological Sources for the History of Palestine: Between Large Forces: Palestine in the Hellenistic Period', *The Biblical Archaeologist* 60(1): 2–51.

Beška, Emanuel (2007) 'Responses of Prominent Arabs towards Zionist Aspirations and Colonization Prior to 1908', *Asian and African Studies* 16 (1): 22–44.

Beška, Emanuel (2010) 'Shukri al-'Asali, an Extraordinary Anti-Zionist Activist', *Asian and African Studies* 19(2): 237–254.

Beška, Emanuel (2011) 'Anti-Zionist Journalistic Works of Najib al-Khuri Nassar in the newspaper Al-Karmel in 1914', *Asian and African Studies* 20(2): 167–192.

Beška, Emanuel (2012) 'Polemikos 'Isa al-'Isa and Printing Class: Too Much Borrowing?', *Jerusalem Quarterly* 50(Spring): 113–120.

Beška, Emanuel (2014a) 'Arabic Translations of Writings on Zionism Published before the First World War', *Asian and African Studies* 23(1): 154–172.

Beška, Emanuel (2014b) 'Political Opposition to Zionism in Palestine and Greater Syria: 1910–1911 as a Turning Point', *Jerusalem Quarterly* 59 (Summer): 54–67.

Beška, Emanuel (2015) 'Khalil al-Sakakini and Zionism before WWI', *Jerusalem Quarterly* (63/64): 40–53.

Beška, Emanuel (2016a) 'The Disgrace of the Twentieth Century: The Beilis Affair in *Filastin* Newspaper', *Jerusalem Quarterly* (66): 99–108.

Beška, Emanuel (2016b) *From Ambivalence to Hostility: The Arabic Newspaper Filastin and Zionism: 1911–1914* (Bratislava: Institute of Oriental Studies of the Slovak Academy of Sciences and Slovak Academic Press).

Beška, Emanuel (2016c) 'Anti-Zionist Attitudes and Activities of Ruhi al-Khalidi', in Zuzana Gažáková and Jaroslav Drobný (eds.) *Arabic and Islamic Studies in Honour of Ján Pauliny* (Bratislava: Univerzita Komenského v Bratislave): 181–203.

Biger, Gideon (1981) 'Where was Palestine? Pre-World War I Perception, AREA', *Journal of the Institute of British Geographers* 13(2): 153–160.

Birley, Anthony R. (1997) *Hadrian the Restless Emperor* (London and New York: Routledge).

Binns, John (1994) *Ascetics and Ambassadors of Christ: The Monasteries of Palestine 314–631* (Oxford: Clarendon Press).

Bitan, Hanan (1992) 'The Governmental Names Commission', *Eretz Israel: Studies in the Knowledge of the Land* 23: 367–370.

Bitan, Hanan (1998) *Sefer ha-Yishuvim veha-Meḳomot be-Yiśrael: Hamishim Shenot Hityashvut 1948* [Book of the Settlements and Sites in Israel: Fifty Years of Settlement] (Jerusalem: Ṿaʾadat ha-Shemot ha-Memshaltiyot, Miśrad Rosh ha-Memshalah) [Hebrew].

Bitton-Ashkelony, Brouria, and Aryeh Kofsky (2006) *The Monastic School of Gaza* (Leiden and Boston: Brill).

Blanc, H. (1954) 'The Growth of Israeli Hebrew', *Middle Eastern Affairs* 5: 285–392.

Blankinship, Khalid Yaya (1994) *The End of the Jihad State: The Reign of Hisham Ibn Abd Al-Malik and the Colla: Reign of Hisham Ibn 'Abd Al-Malik and the Collapse of the Umayyads* (New York: State University of New York Press).

Blau, Joshua (1981) *The Renaissance of Modern Hebrew and Modern Standard Arabic* (Berkeley, CA: University of California Press).

Boqa'i, Nihad (2005) 'Patterns of Internal Displacement, Social Adjustment and the Challenge of Return', in Nur Masalha (ed.) *Catastrophe Remembered: Palestine–Israel and the Internal Refugee: Essays in Memory of Edward W. Said* (London: Zed Books): 73–112.

Bowersock, Glen W. (1988) 'Palestine: Ancient History and Modern Politics', in Edward W. Said and Christopher Hitchens (eds.) *Blaming the Victims: Spurious Scholarship and the Palestinian Question* (London: Verso): 181–191.

Bowersock, Glen W. (1994) *Roman Arabia* (Cambridge, MA: Harvard University Press).

Bowersock, Glen W., Peter Brown and Oleg Grabar (eds.) (1999) *Late Antiquity: A Guide to the Postclassical World* (Cambridge, MA: Harvard University Press).

Bracy, R. Michael (2005) *Building Palestine: 'Isa Al-'Isa, 'Filastin', and the Textual Construction of National Identity, 1911–1931* (Fayetteville, AR: University of Arkansas Press).

Bracy, R. Michael (2011) *Printing Class: 'Isa Al-'Isa, Filastin and the Textual Construction of National Identity, 1911–1931* (Lanham, MD: University Press of America).

Breasted, James Henry (trans. and ed.) (2001) *Ancient Records of Egypt: The Twentieth through the Twenty-sixth Dynasties*, Vol. 4 (Urbana and Chicago: University of Illinois Press).

Bresheeth, Haim (1989) 'Self and Other in Zionism: Palestine and Israel in Recent Hebrew Literature', in *Palestine: Profile of an Occupation* (London and New Jersey: Zed Books): 120–52.

Brisman Shimeon (2000) *A History and Guide to Judaic Dictionaries and Concordances* (Hoboken, NJ: Ktav Publishing).

Broadbridge, Anne F. (1999) 'Academic Rivalry and the Patronage System in Fifteenth-Century Egypt', *Mamluk Studies Review* 3: 85–107.

Broshi, Magen (1987) 'Religion, Ideology and Politics and Their Impact on Palestinian Archaeology', *Israel Museum Journal* 6: 17–32.

Bruyère, Bernard (1929–1930) *Mert Seger à Deir el Médineh* [The Egyptian Deity Mertseger at al-Medina] (Cairo: Institut Français d'Archéologie Orientale).

Burckhardt, John Lewis (1822) *Travels in Syria and the Holy Land* (London: J. Murray).

Burge, Gary M. (2003) *Whose Land? Whose Promise?* (Cleveland: The Pilgrim Press)

Burgoyne, Michael Hamilton (1987) *Mamluk Jerusalem: An Architectural Study* (London: British School of Archaeology in Jerusalem and the World of Islam Festival Trust).

Burgoyne, Michael Hamilton, and Amal Abu al-Hajj (1979) 'Twenty-Four Medieval Arabic Inscriptions from Jerusalem', *Levant* no. 11: 128–129.

Burns, Thomas S., and John W. Eadie (eds.) (2001) *Urban Centers and Rural Contexts in Late Antiquity* (East Lansing, MI: Michigan State University Press).

Büssow, Johann (2011) *Hamidian Palestine: Politics and Society in the District of Jerusalem 1872–1908* (Leiden and Boston: Brill).

Butcher, Kevin (2003) *Roman Syria and the Near East* (Los Angeles, CA: Getty Publications).

Cannon, Garland, and Alan S. Kaye (1994) *The Arab Contributions to the English Language: A Historical Dictionary* (Wiesbaden: Harrassowitz Verlag).

Carriker, Andrew James (2003) *The Library of Eusebius of Caesarea* (Leiden: Brill).

Cattan, Henry (1969) *Palestine, the Arabs and Israel: The Search for Justice* (London: Longmans).

Champion, Michael W. (2014) *Explaining the Cosmos: Creation and Cultural Interaction in Late Antiquity Gaza* (Oxford: Oxford University Press).

Chaver, Yael (2004) *What Must Be Forgotten: The Survival of Yiddish Writing in Zionist Palestine* (Syracuse, NY: Syracuse University Press).

Chomsky, William Zev (1967) *Ha-Lashon ha-'Ivrit be-Darkhei Hitpathutah* [Ways of Development of the Hebrew Tongue], Sifriyyat Dani Le-Mada' ve-haskel 76 [Dani Library for Science and Enlightenment] (Jerusalem: Rubin Press).

Christensen, Peter (1993) *The Decline of Iranshahr: Irrigation and Environments in the History of the Middle East, 500 B.C. to A.D. 1500* (Copenhagen: Museum Tusculanum Press and University of Copenhagen).

Cohen, Getzel M. (2006) *The Hellenistic Settlements in Syria, the Red Sea Basin, and North Africa* (Berkeley and Los Angeles: University of California Press).

Cohen, Saul B., and Nurit Kliot (1981) 'Israel's Place Names as Reflection of Continuity and Change in Nation Building', *Names* 29: 227–248.

Cohen, Saul B., and Nurit Kliot (1992) 'Place Names in Israel's Ideological Struggle over the Administered Territories', *Annals of the Association of American Geographers* 82(4): 653–680.

Crawford, A. W. C. (Lord Lindsay) (1847) *Letters on Egypt, Edom and the Holy Land* (London: H. Colburn, V II).

Crown, Alan D. (1989) *The Samaritans* (Tübingen: Mohr Siebeck).

Cuinet, Vital (1896) *Syrie, Liban et Palestine: géographie administrative, statistique, descriptive et raisonnée* (Paris: Ernest Leroux).

Cyril of Scythopolis (1991) *The Lives of the Monks of Palestine* (Collegeville, MN: Cistercian Publications).

Darwish, Mahmoud (1994) 'In Praise of the High Shadow' ['*Madih al-Thil al-A'ali*'], *Diwan Mahmoud Darwish*, Vol. 2 (Beirut: Dar al-'Awdah): 69.

David, Ariel (2017) 'Ancient Egyptian Records Indicate Philistines Weren't Aegean Pirates After All', *Haaretz*, 23 July, at: http://www.haaretz.com/archaeology/1.802928

Davis, Thomas W. (2004) *Shifting Sands: The Rise and Fall of Biblical Archaeology* (New York: Oxford University Press).

Dayan, Moshe (1978) *Lehyot 'Im HaTanakh'* [Living With the Hebrew Bible] (Jerusalem: 'Edanim) [Hebrew]. Published in English as *Living With the Bible* (London: Weidenfeld & Nicolson).

De Villefosse, Antoine Héron (1897) 'Diplôme militaire de l'annee 139, découvert en Syrie. Note de M. Héron de Villefosse, membre de l'Académie', *Comptes rendus des séances de l'Académie des Inscriptions et Belles-Lettres* 41(3): 333–343.

De Vaux, Roland (1966) *The Cambridge Ancient History: Palestine in the Early Bronze Age*, Vol. 1, Part 15 (Cambridge: Cambridge University Press).

Dio Chrysostom (1951). *Discourses*, Vol. 5, translated by H. Lamar Crosby (Cambridge, MA: Harvard University Press, Loeb Classical Library Harvard University Press).

Donaldson, Terence L. (ed.) (2000) *Religious Rivalries and the Struggle for Success in Caesarea Maritima* (Waterloo, ON: Wilfrid Laurier University Press).

Donner, Fred McGraw (1981) *The Early Islamic Conquests* (Princeton, NJ: Princeton University Press).

Dothan, Trude (1992) *People of the Sea: The Search for the Philistines* (New York: Scribner).

Doumani, Beshara (1995) *Rediscovering Palestine: Merchants and Peasants in Jabal Nablus, 1700–1900* (Berkeley, Los Angeles and London: University of California Press).

Downey, Glanville (1958) 'The Christian Schools in Palestine: A Chapter in Literary History', *Harvard Library Bulletin* 12: 297–319.

Downey, Glanville (1963) *Gaza: In the Early Sixth Century* (Norman, OK: University of Oklahoma Press).

Downey, Glanville (1949) 'Paganism and Christianity in Procopius', *Church History* 18: 89–102.

Drijvers, Jan Willem (2004) *Cyril of Jerusalem: Bishop and City* (Leiden and Boston: Brill).

Drory, Joseph (2004) 'Founding a New Mamlaka: Some Remarks Concerning Safed and the Organization of the Region in the Mamluk Period', in Michael Winter and Amalia Levanoni (eds.) *The Mamluks in Egyptian and Syrian Politics and Society* (Leiden and Boston: Brill): 163–190.

Dumper, Michael (1994) *Islam and Israel: Muslim Religious Endowments and the Jewish State* (Washington, DC: Institute for Palestine Studies).

Du Pin, Louis Ellis, and William Wotton (2010) *A New History of Ecclesiastical Writers* (Detroit, MI: Gale ECCO, Print Editions; first published 1693).

Eban, Abba (1984) *Heritage, Civilisation and the Jews* (London: Weidenfeld and Nicolson).

Edson, Evelyn (2004) 'Reviving the Crusade: Sanudo's Schemes and Vesconti's Maps', in Rosamund Allen (ed.) *Eastward Bound: Travel and Travellers, 1050–1550* (Manchester and New York: Manchester University Press): 131–155.

Edson, Evelyn (2007) *The World Map, 1300–1492: The Persistence of Tradition and Transformation* (Baltimore, MD: The Johns Hopkins University Press).

Elad, Amikam (1992) 'Two Identical Inscriptions From Jund Filastin From the Reign of the Abbāsid Caliph, Al-Muqtadir', *Journal of the Economic and Social History of the Orient* 35 (4): 301–360.

Ellenblum, Ronnie (2003) 'Settlement and Society Formation in Crusader Palestine', in Thomas E. Levy (ed.) *The Archaeology of Society the Holy Land* (London and New York: Continuum): 502–511.

Elon, Amos (1997) 'Politics and Archaeology', in Neil Asher Silberman and David Small (eds.) *The Archaeology of Israel: Constructing the Past, Interpreting the Present* (Sheffield: Sheffield Academic Press): 35–47.

Elon, Amos (1983) *The Israelis: Founders and Sons*, revised edition (London: Penguin Books).

Emmett, Chad Fife (1995) *Beyond the Basilica: Christians and Muslims in Nazareth* (Chicago, IL: University of Chicago Press).

Esler, Philip F. (2011) *Sex, Wives, and Warriors: Reading Biblical Narrative with its Ancient Audience* (Eugene, OR: Cascade Books).

Eusebius (1861) *The History of the Martyrs in Palestine*, translated by William Cureton (London: Williams and Morgate), at: http://www.tertullian.org/fathers/euse-bius_martyrs.htm

Eusebius (1971) *Onomasticon* (*On the Place Names in Holy Scripture*) (Washington, DC: Catholic University of America Press).

Eusebius Pamphilus (2011) *The Ecclesiastical History of Pamphilus Eusebius*, translated by C. F. Cruse (Boulder, CO: Merchant Books).

Evian, Shirly Ben-Dor (2017) 'Ramesses III and the "Sea-peoples": Towards a New Philistine Paradigm', *Oxford Journal of Archaeology* (July): 267–285.

Falah, Ghazi (1996) 'The 1948 Israeli–Palestinian War and its Aftermath: The Transformation and De-signification of Palestine's Cultural Landscape', *Annals of the Association of American Geographers* 86: 256–285.

Farsoun, Samih K. (1997) *Palestine and the Palestinians* (Boulder, CO: Westview Press).

Farsoun, Samih K. (2004) *Culture and Customs of the Palestinians* (Westport, CT: Greenwood Press).

Feldman, Louis H. (1996) *Studies in Hellenistic Judaism* (Leiden: Brill).

Fetellus (Rorgo Fretellus) (1892) Vol. 19, translated by James Rose Macpherson (London: Palestine Pilgrims' Text Society; first published c. 1137/1138).

Fiema, Zbigniew T., Ahmad Al-Jallad, Michael C. A. Macdonald and Laïla Nehmé (2015) 'Provincia Arabia: Nabataea, the Emergence of Arabic as a Written Language, and Graeco-Arabica', in Greg Fisher (ed.) *Arabs and Empires before Islam* (Oxford: Oxford University Press): 373–433.

Fischer, Moshe, Itamar Taxel, David Amit (2008) 'Rural Settlement in the Vicinity of Yavneh in the Byzantine Period: A Religio-archaeological Perspective', *Bulletin of the American Schools of Oriental Research* (350): 7–35.

Folda, Jaroslav (2001) 'Art in the Latin East, 1098–1291', in Jonathan Riley-Smith (ed.) *The Oxford History of the Crusades* (Oxford: Oxford University Press): 141–159.

Foster, Zachary J. (2013) 'Ottoman and Arab Maps of Palestine, 1880s–1910s' (30 July), at: http://www.midafternoonmap.com/2013/07/ottoman-and-arab-maps-of-palestine.html

Foster, Zachary J. (2016a) 'Was Jerusalem Part of Palestine? The Forgotten City of Ramla, 900–1900', *British Journal of Middle Eastern Studies* 43 (2): 1–15.

Foster, Zachary J. (2016b) 'The Origins of Modern Palestine in Ottoman Documents', at: http://blog.palestine-studies.org/2016/02/09/the-origins-of-modern-palestine-in-ottoman-documents/

Foster, Zachary J. (2016c) 'Who Was the First Palestinian in Modern History?' *Palestine Square*, 18 February, at: http://www.academia.edu/22303943/Who_Was_the_First_Palestinian_in_Modern_History_Palestine_Square_

Foucault, Michel (1980) *Power/Knowledge* (New York: Pantheon).

Foucault, Michel (2002) *The Archaeology of Knowledge* (London: Routledge; first published 1969).

Furani, Khaled (2012) *Silencing the Sea: Secular Rhythms in Palestinian Poetry* (Stanford, CA: Stanford University Press).

Gallagher, William R. (1999) *Sennacherib's Campaign in Judah: New Studies* (Leiden: Brill).

Galor, Katharina, and Hanswulf Bloedhorn (2013) *The Archaeology of Jerusalem: From its Origins to the Ottomans* (New Haven, CT: Yale University Press).

Gann, Lewis (1981) *The Struggle for Zimbabwe* (New York: Praeger Publishers).

Gellner, Ernest (1983) *Nations and Nationalism* (London: Blackwell).

Gerber, Haim (1982) 'Modernization in Nineteenth-Century Palestine: The Role of Foreign Trade', *Middle Eastern Studies* 18 (3, July): 250–264.

Gerber, Haim (1998a) "Palestine' and Other Territorial Concepts in the 17th Century', *International Journal of Middle East Studies* 30: 563–572.

Gerber, Haim (1998b) 'Rigidity Versus Openness in Late Classical Islamic Law: The Case of the Seventeenth-Century Palestinian Mufti Khayr al-Din al-Ramli', *Islamic Law and Society* 5 (2): 165–195.

Gerber, Haim (2008) *Remembering and Imagining Palestine: Identity and Nationalism from the Crusades to the Present* (London: Palgrave Macmillan).

Gerson, Lloyd P. (2005) 'Antiochus of Ascalon', in Ted Honderich (ed.) *The Oxford Companion to Philosophy*, new edition (Oxford and New York: Oxford University Press).

Gibbon, Edward (1838) *The History of the Decline and Fall of the Roman Empire*, Vol. 1 (London: John Murray).

Gibbon, Edward (1840) *The History of the Decline and Fall of the Roman Empire*, Vol. 5 (Paris: Baudry's European Library).

Gil, Eyal (2006) *The Disenchantment of the Orient: Expertise in Arab Affairs and the Israeli State* (Stanford, CA: Stanford University Press).

Gil, Moshe (1996) 'The Political History of Jerusalem during the Early Muslim Period', in Joshua Prawer and Haggai Ben-Shammai (eds.) *The History of Jerusalem, the Early Muslim Period, 638–1099* (New York: New York University Press and Yad Izhak Ben-Zvi): 1–37.

Gil, Moshe (1997) *A History of Palestine, 634–1099* (Cambridge: Cambridge University Press).

Gilman, D. C., H. T. Thurston and F. M. Colby (eds.) (1905) 'Caesarea Palestinae', *New International Encyclopaedia,* 1st edition (New York: Dodd, Mead).

Gitler, Haim, and Oren Tal (2006) *The Coinage of Philistia of the Fifth and Fourth Centuries BC: A Study of the Earliest Coins of Palestine* (Milan: Edizioni ennerre. Materiali Studi Ricerche).

Glock, Albert E. (1999) 'Cultural Bias in Archaeology', in Tomis Kapitan (ed.) *Archaeology, History and Culture in Palestine and the Near East: Essays in Memory of Albert E. Glock* (Atlanta, GA: Scholars Press and American Schools of Oriental Research): 324–342.

Gnuse, Robert K. (1997) *No Other Gods: Emergent Monotheism in Israel* (Sheffield: Sheffield Academic Press).

Goitein, S. D. (1983) *A Mediterranean Society: Daily Life*, Vol. IV (Berkeley, CA: University of California Press).

Goodwin, Tony (2004) 'The Arab-Byzantine Coinage of Jund Filastin: A Potential Historical Source', *Byzantine and Modern Greek Studies* 28 (1): 1–12.

Goren, Haim (2002) 'Sacred, But Not Surveyed: Nineteenth-century Surveys of Palestine', *Imago Mundi: The International Journal for the History of Cartography* 54 (1): 87–110.

Gover, Yerach (1986) 'Were You There, or Was It a Dream? Militaristic Aspects of Israeli Society in Modern Hebrew Literature', *Social Text* 13/14 (Winter/Spring): 24–48.

Grainger, John D. (2016) *Syria: An Outline History* (Barnsley, South Yorkshire: Pen & Sword Books).

Grayson, A. Kirk (1996) *Assyrian Rulers of the Early First Millennium BC II (858–745 BC). (The Royal Inscriptions of Mesopotamia Assyrian Period)*, Vol. 3 (Toronto: University of Toronto Press).

Greatrex, Geoffrey and Samuel N. C. Lieu (eds.) (2002) *The Roman Eastern Frontier and the Persian Wars. Part II: AD 363–630. A Narrative Sourcebook* (London and New York: Routledge).

Greenstein, Ran (2014) *Zionism and its Discontents: A Century of Radical Dissent in Israel/Palestine* (London: Pluto Press).

Guérin, Victor (1868–1880) *Description géographique, historique et archéologique de la Palestine*, 7 vols. (Paris: Imprimé par autorisation de l'empereur à l'Impr. Impériale).

Guérin, Victor (1881–1883) *La Terre Sainte: Son histoire, ses souvenirs, ses sites, ses monuments*, 2 vols. (Paris: Imprimeurs-Éditeurs).

Guyot, S., and Seethal, C. (2007) 'Identity of Place, Places of Identities: Change of Place Names in Post-apartheid South Africa', *South African Geographical Review* 89 (1): 55–63.

Haddad, Gibril Fouad (2007) *The Four Imams and their Schools* (Cambridge: Muslim Academic Trust).

Hakim, Besim S. (2001) 'Julian of Ascalon's Treatise of Construction and Design Rules from Sixth-Century Palestine', *Journal of the Society of Architectural Historians* 60 (1, March): 4–25.

Halbwachs, Maurice (1925) *Les cadres sociaux de la mémoire* (Paris: Librairie Félix Alcan).

Halbwachs, Maurice (1941) *La Topographie légendaire des évangiles en terre sainte: étude de mémoire collective* (Paris: Presses Universitaires de France).

Halbwachs, Maurice (1980) *Collective Memory* [*Mémoire collective*, 1950] (New York: Harper and Row).

Halbwachs, Maurice (1992) *On Collective Memory* (Chicago and London: University of Chicago Press).

Hasel, Michael G. (2009) 'Pa-Canaan in the Egyptian New Kingdom: Canaan or

Gaza?', *Journal of Ancient Egyptian Interconnections* 1 (1): 8–17, at: https://journals.uair.arizona.edu/index.php/jaei/article/viewFile/5/7

Hawting, G. R. (2004) *The Idea of Idolatry and the Emergence of Islam: From Polemic to History* (Cambridge: Cambridge University Press).

Heidegger, Martin (2010) *Being and Time*, translated by Joan Stambaugh, revised by Dennis Schmidt (Albany, NY: State University of New York Press).

Heller, Yosef (1984) *Bamavak Lemedinah: Hamediniyut Hatziyonit Bashanim 1936–48* [The Struggle for the State: The Zionist Policy 1936–48] (Jerusalem: n.p.).

Heng, Gerladine (2015) 'Reinventing Race, Colonization, and Globalisms across Deep Time: Lessons from the *Longue Durée*', *PMLA* 130 (2, March): 358–366.

Herbert, Trevor (2006) *The Trombone* (New Haven, CT and London: Yale University Press).

Herodotus (1836) *History*, Vol. 1, Book II, translated by William Beloe (New York: Harper & Brothers).

Herodotus (1841) *Egypt of Herodotus*, with notes by John Kenrick (London: B. Fellowes).

Herodotus (1858) *The Histories (Book I to Book IX)*, translated by George Rawlinson, edited by E. H. Blakeney (London: J. M. Dent & Sons), at: https://archive.org/stream/herodotusooherouoft/herodotusooherouoft_djvu.txt

Herodotus (1860) *The History of Herodotus: A New English Version*, edited by George Rawlinson (New York: D. Appleton).

Herodotus (1987) *The History*, translated by David Grene (Chicago, IL: University of Chicago Press).

Herodotus (2014) *The Histories*, translated by Tom Holland (London: Penguin Books).

Herzog, Zeev (1999) 'Hatanach: Ein Mimtzaim Bashetah' [The Bible: There are no Findings on the Ground'; also often translated into English as 'Deconstructing the Walls of Jericho'], *Haaretz* magazine, 29 October: 6–8 [Hebrew].

Herzog, Zeev (2001) 'Deconstructing the Walls of Jericho: Biblical Myth and Archaeological Reality', *Prometheus* 4: 72–93.

Hevelone-Harper, Jennifer L. (2005) *Disciples of the Desert: Monks, Laity, and Spiritual Authority in Sixth-Century Gaza* (Baltimore, MD and London: The Johns Hopkins University Press).

Heyd, Uriel (1942) *Dahir al-Umar, Ruler of the Galilee in the 18th Century* (Jerusalem: Rubin. Mass) [Hebrew].

Hill, Donald (1984) *A History of Engineering in Classical and Medieval Times* (London and New York: Routledge).

Hill, George Francis (1914) *A Catalogue of the Greek Coins in the British Museum: Palestine (Galilee, Samaria and Judaea)* (London: British Museum and Longmans).

Hill, George Francis (2011) *Some Palestinian Cults in the Graeco-Roman Age* (Primary Sources, Historical Collections), Vol. 5 (London: British Academy and Oxford University Press).

Hillenbrand, R., and R. Auld (eds.) (2009) *Ayyubid Jerusalem: The Holy City in Context 1187–1250* (London: Al Tajir-World of Islam).

Hirschfeld, Yizhar (2004) 'The Monasteries of Gaza: An Archaeological Review', in Brouria Bitton-Ashkelony and Aryeh Kofsky (eds.) *Christian Gaza in Late Antiquity* (Leiden: Brill).

Hjelm, Ingrid (2016) 'Lost and Found? A Non-Jewish Israel from the Merneptah Stele to the Byzantine Period', in Ingrid Hjelm and Thomas Thomprosn (eds.) *History, Archaeology and the Bible Forty Years after 'Historicity': Changing Perspectives 6* (London: Routledge): 112–129.

Hjelm, Ingrid and Thomas L. Thompson (2016) *Biblical Interpretation beyond Historicity: Changing Perspectives 7* (London: Routledge).

Hobsbawm, Eric (1990) *Nations and Nationalism since 1780: Programme, Myth, Reality* (Cambridge: Cambridge University Press).

Hobsbawm, Eric, and Terence Ranger (1996) *The Invention of Tradition* (Cambridge: Cambridge University Press).

Hooks, Bell (1990) 'Marginality as a Site of Resistance', in Russell Ferguson et al. (eds.) *Out There: Marginalization and Contemporary Cultures* (Cambridge, MA: MIT): 241–243.

Hopkins, J. F. P., and N. Levtzion (eds.) (2000) *Corpus of Early Arabic Sources for West African History* (New York: Marcus Weiner Press).

Hopwood, Derek (1969) *The Russian Presence in Syria and Palestine. 1843–1914: Church and Politics in the Near East* (Oxford: Clarendon).

Houben, Hubert (2002) *Roger II of Sicily: A Ruler between East and West* (Cambridge: Cambridge University Press).

Humbert, Jean-Baptiste (2000) *Gaza Méditerranéenne: Histoire et archéologie en Palestine* (Paris: Editions Errance).

Hummel, Ruth, and Thomas Hummel (1995) *Patterns of the Sacred: English Protestant and Russian Orthodox Pilgrims of the Nineteenth Century* (London: Scorpion Cavendish).

Housel, Jacqueline A. (2009) 'Geographies of Whiteness: The Active Construction of Racialized Privilege in Buffalo, New York', *Social and Cultural Geography* 10 (2): 131–151.

Humphreys, Stephen R. (1977) *From Saladin to the Mongols: The Ayyubids of Damascus, 1193–1260* (Albany, NY: State University of New York Press).

Hütteroth, Wolf-Dieter, and Kamal Abdulfattah (1977) *Historical Geography of Palestine, Transjordan and Southern Syria in the Late 16th Century* (Erlanger: Vorstand der Fränkischen Geographischen Gesellschaft).

Hyamson, Albert M. (1950) *Palestine under the Mandate* (London: Methuen and Co.).

Ibn al-Ukhuwah, Muhammad b. Muhammad b. Ahmad al-Qurashi (1976) *Kitab*

Ma'alim al-Qurba fi Ahkam al-Hisba [Guide for the Enforcement of the Rules of Accounting] (Cairo: al-Hai'ah al-Misriyah).

Ibn Battuta (2005) *Travels in Asia and Africa 1325–1354*, translated and edited by H.A.R. Gibb (New Delhi and Chennai: Asian Educational Services).

Ibn Khordadbeh (1865) *Le Livre des Routes et Provinces* [Kitab al-Masalik was Mamalik, c. 870], translated by Charles Barbier de Meynard (Paris: Journal Asiatique).

Ibn Shaddad, Baha' ad-Din (2002) *The Rare and Excellent History of Saladin* [al-Nawadir al-Sultaniyyah wa'l-Mahasin al-Yusufiyyah by Baha' al-Din Ibn Shaddad], translated by D. S. Richards (Farnham, Surrey: Ashgate Publishing; first published 1228).

Irving, Sarah (2011) *Palestine* (The Vale, Chalfont St Peter: Bradt Travel Guides).

Isaac, Benjamin (2003) 'The Eastern Frontier', in Averil Cameron and Peter Garnsey (eds.) *The Cambridge Ancient History, Vol. XIII: The Late Empire A.D. 337–425* (Cambridge: Cambridge University Press): 437–460.

Islahi, Abdul Azim (2008) 'Works of Economic Interest in the Seventeenth Century Muslim World', *Thoughts on Economics* 18 (2, April): 35–50.

Issawi, Charles (2006) *An Economic History of the Middle East and North Africa*, reprint edition (London: Routledge).

Jacobson, David M. (1999) 'Palestine and Israel', *Bulletin of the American Schools of Oriental Research* (313, February): 65–74.

Jamal, Amal (2005) *Media Politics and Democracy in Palestine* (Brighton and Portland, OR: Sussex Academic Press).

Jamjoum, Hazem (2010) 'Challenging the Jewish National Fund', *The Electronic Intifada*, 21 July, at: http://electronicintifada.net/v2/article11406.shtml

Jansen, Willy (2006) 'Arab Women with a Mission: The Sisters of the Rosary', in Martin Tamcke and Michael Martin (eds.) *Christian Witness between Continuity and New Beginnings: Modern Historical Missions in the Middle East* (Münster: lit): 41–62.

Jayyusi, Salma Khadra, and Christopher Tingley (1977) *Trends and Movements in Modern Arabic Poetry* (Leiden: E. J. Brill).

Jeferey, John Barnes (2015) 'Visualizing the Emerging Nation: Jewish and Arab Editorial Cartoons in Paletsine, 1939–48', in Binita Mehta and Pia Mukherji (eds.) *Postcolonial Comics: Texts, Events, Identities* (New York and London: Routledge): 171–185.

Jennings, Francis (1975) *The Invasion of America: Indians, Colonialism, and the Cant of Conquest* (Chapel Hill: The University of North Carolina Press).

Johnson, Lee A. (2000) 'A Literary Guide to Caesaria Maritima', in Terence L. Donaldson (ed.) *Religious Rivalries and the Struggle for Success in Caesarea Maritima* (Waterloo, ON: Wilfrid Laurier University Press): 35–56.

Johnson, Paul (1993) *A History of the Jews* (London: Phoenix).

Josephus, Titus Flavius (1981) *The Jewish War* (London: Penguin Books).

Josephus, Titus Flavius (2004) *Antiquities of the Jews* (Boston MA: Digireads.com Publishing).

Josephus, Titus Flavius (2013) *Against Apion*, translated and commentary by John M. G. Barclay (Leiden: Brill).

Joudah, Ahmad Hasan (1987) *Revolt in Palestine in the Eighteenth Century: The Era of Shaykh Zahir Al-'Umar* (Princeton, NJ: Kingston Press).

Joudah, Ahmad Hasan (2015) 'Zahir al-'Umar and the First Autonomous Regime in Ottoman Palestine (1744–1775)', *Jerusalem Quarterly* (63–64): 72–86.

Kadman, Noga (2008) *Erased From Space and Consciousness: Depopulated Palestinian Villages in the Israeli-Zionist Discourse* (Jerusalem: November Books) [Hebrew].

Kadmon, Naftali (2004) 'Toponymy and Geopolitics: The Political Use – and Misuse – of Geographical Names', *The Cartographic Journal* 41: 85–87.

Kallner, D. H. (1944) 'The Jacotin Map of Palestine', *Quarterly Statement* (London: Palestine Exploration Fund) 76: 157–163.

Kamel, Lorenzo (2014) 'The Impact of "Biblical Orientalism" in Late Nineteenth and Early Twentieth Century Palestine', *New Middle Eastern Studies* 4: 1–5.

Kamel, Lorenzo (2015) *Imperial Perceptions of Palestine: British Influence and Power in Late Ottoman Times* (London: I. B. Tauris).

Kark, Ruth (1994) *American Consuls in the Holy Land, 1832–1914* (Detroit, MI: Wayne State University Press).

Kark, Ruth, and Haim Goren (2011) 'Pioneering British Exploration and Scriptural Geography: The Syrian Society/The Palestine Association', *The Geographical Journal* 177 (3): 264–274.

Karmon, Y. (1960) 'Analysis of Jacotin's Map of Palestine', *Israel Exploration Journal* 10 (3/4): 155–173; 244–253, at: http://jchp.ucla.edu/Bibliography/ Karmon,_Y_1960_Jacotin_Map_(IEJ_10).pdf

Kasmieh, Khairieh (1992) 'Ruhi al-Khalidi, 1864–1913: A Symbol of the Cultural Movement in Palestine Towards the End of Ottoman Rule', in Thomas Philipp (ed.) *The Syrian Land in the 18th and 19th Century: The Common and the Specific in the Historical Experience* (Stuttgart: F. Steiner): 123–146.

Katzenstein, H. Jacob (1982) 'Gaza in the Egyptian Texts of the New Kingdom', *Journal of the American Oriental Society* 102(1): 111–113.

Kazhdan, Alexander Petrovich (ed.) (1991) 'Cyril of Scythopolis', in *The Oxford Dictionary of Byzantium* (New York and Oxford: Oxford University Press).

Kearns, Robin A., and Lawrence D. Berg (2002) 'Proclaiming Place: Towards a Geography of Place Name Pronunciation', *Social and Cultural Geography* 3 (3): 283–302.

Kennedy, D. K (1980) 'Legio VI Ferrata. The Annexation and Early Garrison of Arabia', *Harvard Studies in Classical Philology* 84: 283–309.

Kennedy, George Alexander (1983) *Greek Rhetoric under Christian Emperors* (Princeton, NJ: Princeton University Press).

Kennedy, George Alexander (1994) *A New History of Classical Rhetoric* (Princeton, NJ: Princeton University Press).

Kennedy, George Alexander (2008) *Greek Rhetoric Under Christian Emperors* (Eugene, OR: Wipf and Stock Publishers).

Khalaf, Noha Tadros (2011) 'Falastin versus the British Mandate and Zionism (1921–1931): Between a Rock and a Hard Place', *Jerusalem Quarterly* 45 (Spring): 6–24, at: http://www.palestine-studies.org/sites/default/files/jq-articles/45_falastin_2.pdf

Khalidi, Issam (2006) 'Body and Ideology: Early Athletics in Palestine (1900–1948)', *Jerusalem Quarterly* 27: 44–58.

Khalidi, Issam (2014) 'Sports and Aspirations: Football in Palestine (1900–1948)', *Jerusalem Quarterly* 58: 74–88.

Khalidi, Rashid (1997) 'The Formation of Palestinian Identity: The Critical Years, 1917–1923', in James P. Jankowski, and Israel Gershoni (eds.) *Rethinking Nationalism in the Arab Middle East* (New York: Columbia University Press): 171–190.

Khalidi, Rashid (1998) *Palestinian Identity: The Construction of Modern National Consciousness* (New York: Columbia University Press).

Khalidi, Rashid (2001) 'The Palestinians and 1948: The Underlying Causes of Failure', in Eugene L. Rogan and Avi Shlaim (eds.) *The War for Palestine: Rewriting the History of 1948* (Cambridge: Cambridge University Press): 12–36.

Khalidi, Walid (1984) *Before Their Diaspora: A Photographic History of the Palestinians, 1876–1948* (Washington, DC: Institute for Palestine Studies).

Khalidi, Walid (1988) 'Kitab al-Sionism, aw al-Mas'ala al-Sihyuniyya li-Muhammad Ruhi al-Khalidi, al-Mutawafi Sanat 1913' [The Book *Zionism or the Zionist Question* by Muhammad Ruhi al-Khalidi], in Hisham Nashaheh (ed.) *Studia Palaestina: Studies in Honour of Constantine K. Zurayk* (Beirut: Institute for Palestine Studies): 37–81.

Khalidi, Walid (ed.) (1992) *All That Remains: The Palestinian Villages Occupied and Depopulated by Israel in 1948* (Washington, DC: Institute for Palestine Studies).

Khatib, Hisham (2003) *Palestine and Egypt under the Ottomans: Paintings, Books, Photographs, Maps and Manuscripts* (London: I. B. Tauris).

Khitrovo, Vasili Nikolaevich (2011) *Palestina i Sina* (Charleston, SC: Nabu Press; first published 1876).

Khusrau, Nasir (1888) *Diary of a Journey Through Syria and Palestine*, Vol. IV, translated from Persian and annotated by Guy Le Strange (London: Palestine Pilgrims' Text Society; first published 1047).

Kimmerling, Baruch (2003) *Politicide: Ariel Sharon's War against the Palestinians* (London and New York: Verso).

Kimmerling, Baruch, and Joel S. Migdal (1993) *Palestinians: The Making of a People* (New York: The Free Press).

Kimmerling, Baruch, and Joel S. Migdal (2003) *The Palestinian People: A History* (Cambridge, MA: Harvard University Press).

King, Margot (1989) *The Desert Mothers* (Toronto: Peregrina Publishing Co.).

Kliot, Nurit (1989) 'The Meaning of Arabic Settlement Names in the Land of Israel and their Comparison with Hebrew Settlement Names', *Ofakim Begeographia* 30: 71–79 [Hebrew].

Kletter, Raz (2003) 'A Very General Archaeologist: Moshe Dayan and Israeli Archaeology', *The Journal of Hebrew Scriptures* 4, at: http://www.academia.edu/1217256/2003_A_Very_General_Archaeologist_Moshe_Dayan_and_Israeli_Archaeology

Krämer, Gudrun (2011) *A History of Palestine: From the Ottoman Conquest to the Founding of the State of Israel* (Princeton, NJ: Princeton University Press).

Kushnner, David (1987) 'The Ottoman Governors of Palestine, 1864–1914', *Middle Eastern Studies* 23 (3): 274–290.

Lefebvre, Henri (2011) *The Production of Space* (Hoboken, NJ: Wiley-Blackwell).

Lemche, N. P. (1991) *The Canaanites and Their Land: The Tradition of the Canaanites* (Sheffield: Sheffield Academic Press).

Lemche, N. P. (1999) *The Canaanites and their Land*, published by the Journal for the Study of the Old Testament, Supplement no. 110 (Sheffield: Sheffield Academic Press).

Lentin, Ronit (2000) *Israel and the Daughters of the Shoah: Reoccupying the Territories of Silence* (New York and Oxford: Berghahn Books).

Le Strange, Guy (1886) *Description of Syria, including Palestine by Mukaddasi (Circa 985 A.D.* (London: Palestine Pilgrim's Text Society).

Le Strange, Guy (1890) *Palestine under the Moslems: The Description of Syria and the Holy Land from AD 650 to 1500.* Translated from the Works of the Medieval Arab Geographers (London: Alexander P. Watt for Committee of the Palestine Exploration Fund).

Le Strange, Guy (2010) *Palestine under the Moslems: A Description of Syria and the Holy Land from AD 650 to 1500* (New York: Cosimo Classics).

Le Strange, Guy (2014) *Collected Works of Guy Le Strange: Medieval Islamic World*, Vol. 1 (London and New York: I. B. Tauris).

Lev, Yaacov (2003) 'Turks in the Political and Military Life of Eleventh-Century Egypt and Syria', in Kuroki Hidemitsu (ed.) *The Influence of Human Mobility in Muslim Societies* (London: Paul Kegan): 43–62.

Lev, Yaacov (2006) 'Palestine', in Josef W. Meri (ed.) *Medieval Islamic Civilization: An Encyclopedia*, Vol. I (London and New York: Routledge): 590–592.

Levy, Gideon (2000) 'Exposing Israel's Original Sins', book review, *Haaretz*, 11 March.

Levy, Gideon (2004) 'Twilight Zone/Social Studies Lesson', *Haaretz*, 31 March.

Levy-Rubin, Milka (2000) 'New Evidence Relating to the Process of Islamization in Palestine in the Early Muslim Period – The Case of Samaria', *Journal of the Economic and Social History of the Orient*, 43(3): 257-276.

Lewandowski, Elizabeth J. (2011) *The Complete Costume Dictionary* (Lanham, MD: Scarecrow Press).

Lewin, Ariel (2005) *The Archaeology of Ancient Judea and Palestine* (Los Angeles, CA: J. Paul Getty Museum).

Litvinof, Barnet (ed.) (1983) *The Letters and Papers of Chaim Weizmann*, Vol. I, Series B (Jerusalem: Israel Universities Press).

Lockman, Zachary (1996) *Comrades and Enemies: Arab and Jewish Workers in Palestine, 1906–1948* (Berkeley, CA: University of California Press).

Long, Burke O. (1997) *Planting and Reaping Albright: Politics, Ideology, and Interpreting the Bible* (Philadelphia, PA: Penn State University Press).

Long, Burke O. (2003) *Imagining the Holy Land: Maps, Models and Fantasy Travels* (Bloomington, IN: Indiana University Press).

Lucas, Catherine (2003) *Palestine, la dernière colonie?* (Berchem: EPO).

Luckenbill, Daniel David (1924) *The Annals of Sennacherib*, Vol. II (Chicago: Oriental Institute Publications University of Chicago Press).

Luckenbill, Daniel David (1926) *Ancient Records of Assyria and Babylonia Volume 2: Historical Records of Assyria from Sargon to the End* (Chicago, IL: The University of Chicago Press).

Luz, Nimrod (2014) *The Mamluk City in the Middle East: History, Culture and the Urban* (Cambridge: Cambridge University Press).

Macalister, Robert Alexander Stewart (1925) *A Century of Excavation in Palestine* (New York: Fleming H. Revell Co.).

Magness, Jodi (2003) *The Archaeology of Early Islamic Settlement in Palestine* (Winona Lake, IN: Eisenbrauns).

Ma'oz, Moshe (1968) *Ottoman Reform in Syria and Palestine, 1840–1861: The Impact of the Tanzimat on Politics and Society* (Oxford: Clarendon Press).

Maqbul, Ahmad, S. (1992) 'The Cartography of al-Sharīf al-Idrīsī', in J. B. Harley and David Woodward (eds.) *The History of Cartography. Volume 2.1: Cartography in the Traditional Islamic and South Asian Societies* (Chicago, IL: The University of Chicago Press): 156–174.

Margalit, Avishai (1991) 'The Myth of Jerusalem', *The New York Review of Books* 38 (21), 19 December, at: http://www.nybooks.com/articles/1991/12/19/the-myth-of-jerusalem/

Margalit, Sheila (1994) 'The War of the Languages as a National Movement', *Cathedra*, no.74 (December): 87–119.

Mariti, Abbe (Giovanni) (1792) *Travels Through Cyprus, Syria, and Palestine; with a General History of the Levant*, Vol. I (Dublin: P. Byrne).

Martindale, John Robert (1980) *The Prosopography of the Later Roman Empire, Volume 2, A.D. 395–527* (Cambridge: Cambridge University Press).

Martindale, John Robert, Arnold Hugh Martin Jones and J. Morris (eds.) (1992) *Prosopography of the Later Roman Empire, Vol. III: A.D 527–641* (Cambridge: Cambridge University Press).

Masalha, Nur (1992) *Expulsion of the Palestinians: The Concept of 'Transfer' in Zionist Political Thought, 1882–1948* (Washington, DC: Institute for Palestine Studies).

Masalha, Nur (1997) *A Land Without a People* (London: Faber and Faber).

Masalha, Nur (2000) *Imperial Israel and the Palestinians: The Politics of Expansion* (London and Sterling, VA: Pluto Press).

Masalha, Nur (ed.) (2005) *Catastrophe Remembered: Palestine–Israel and the Internal Refugees: Essays in Memory of Edward W. Said* (London: Zed Books).

Masalha, Nur (2007) *The Bible and Zionism: Invented Traditions, Archaeology and Post-Colonialism in Palestine–Israel* (London: Zed Books).

Masalha, Nur (2008) 'Remembering the Palestinian Nakba: Commemoration, Oral History and Narratives of Memory', *Holy Land Studies: A Multidisciplinary Journal* 7(2): 123–156.

Masalha, Nur (2012) *The Palestine Nakba: Decolonising History, Narrating the Subaltern, Reclaiming Memory* (London: Zed Books).

Masalha, Nur (2013) *The Zionist Bible: Biblical Precedent, Colonialism and the Erasure of Memory* (Durham: Acumen).

Masalha, Nur, and Lisa Isherwood (ed.) (2014) *Theologies of Liberation in Palestine–Israel: Indigenous, Contextual, and Postcolonial Perspectives* (Eugene, OR: Wipf and Stock).

Massad, Joseph A. (2006) *The Persistence of the Palestine Question: Essays on Zionism and the Palestinians* (London: Routledge).

Matar, Nabil (2013) 'Palestine', in Jennifer Speake (ed.) *Literature of Travel and Exploration: An Encyclopedia*, Vol. 1 (London and New York: Routledge): 913–916.

Mazza, Roberto (2015) 'Transforming the Holy City: From Communal Clashes to Urban Violence, the Nebi Musa Riots in 1920', in Ulrike Freitag et al. (eds.) *Urban Violence in the Middle East: Changing Cityscapes in the Transition from Empire to Nation State* (Oxford: Berghahn Books): 179–195.

McDonagh, John (2004) 'The Philistines as Scapegoats: Narratives and Myths in the Invention of Ancient Israel and in Modern Critical Theory', *Holy Land Studies: A Multidisciplinary Journal* 3(1): 93–111.

McLeod, Walter (1856) *The Geography of Palestine, Or, The Holy Land, Including Phoenicia and Philistia* (London: Longman, Brown, Green, Longmans and Roberts).

Meen, Joseph A. (1865) *Geography of Palestine: Historical and Descriptive* (London: Sunday School Union).

Merkley, Paul C. (1998) *The Politics of Christian Zionism 1891–1948* (London: Routledge).

Merlo, Simona (2013) 'Travels of Russians to the Holy Land in the 19th Century', *Quest. Issues in Contemporary Jewish History. Journal of Fondazione CDEC*, No. 6, December, at: http://www.quest-cdecjournal.it/focus.php?id=339

Meyer, Martin (1907) *A History of the City of Gaza: From the Earliest Times to the Present Day.* Columbia University Oriental Studies, Vol. 5 (New York: The Columbia University Press).

Moore-Gilbert, Bart (2009) *Postcolonial Life-Writing: Culture, Politics, and Self-Representation* (London: Routledge).

Morris, Benny (2009) *One State, Two States* (New Haven, CT: Yale University Press).

North, Robert (1979) *A History of Biblical Map Making* (Wiesbaden: Reichert).

Murphy-O'Connor, Jerome (2008) *The Holy Land: An Oxford Archaeological Guide from Earliest Times to 1700*, 5th edition (New York: Oxford University Press).

Murphy-O'Connor, Jerome (2012) *Keys to Jerusalem: Collected Essays* (Oxford: Oxford University Press).

Muslih, Muhammad (1989) *The Origins of Palestinian Nationalism* (New York: Columbia University Press).

Muslih, Muhammad (1991) 'The Rise of Local Nationalism in the Arab East', in Rashid Khalidi, Lisa Anderson, Muhammad Muslih and Seeva S. Simon (eds.) *The Origins of Arab Nationalism* (New York: Columbia University Press).

Myers, David (1995) *Reinventing the Jewish Past: European Jewish Intellectuals and the Zionist Return to History* (New York: Oxford University Press).

Nash, Catherine (1999) 'Irish Placenames: Post-colonial Locations', *Transactions of the Institute of British Geographers* 24 (4): 457–480.

Nasir-I-Khusrau (1888) *Diary of a Journey Through Syria and Palestine*, translated from the Persian and annotated by Guy Le Strange (London: Palestine Pilgrims' Text Society,).

Nasrallah, Ibrahim (2015) *The Lanterns of the King of Galilee: A Novel of 18th Century Palestine* (Cairo: The American University in Cairo Press).

Nebel, Almut and Ariella Oppenheim (2000) 'High-resolution Y Chromosome Haplotypes of Israeli and Palestinian Arabs Reveal Geographic Substructure and Substantial Overlap With Haplotypes of Jews', *Human Genetics* 107(6): 630–641.

Nicolle, David (1996) *Medieval Warfare Source Book: Christian Europe and its Neighbours* (Leicester: Brockhampton Pres).

Niesiolowski, Lukasz (2016) *Goliath's Legacy: Philistines and Hebrews in Biblical Times* (Wiesbaden: Harrassowitz).

Niesiołowski-Spanò, Lukasz (2011) *Origin Myths and Holy Places in the Old Testament: A Study of Aetiological Narratives* (London: Equinox Publishing).

Nora, Pierre (ed.) (1996) *Realms of Memory*, Vol. I: *Conflicts and Divisions* (New York: Columbia University Press).

Nora, Pierre (ed.) (1997) *Realms of Memory*, Vol. II: *Traditions* (New York: Columbia University Press).

Nora, Pierre (ed.) (1998) *Realms of Memory*, Vol. III: *Symbols* (New York: Columbia University Press).

North, Robert (1979) *A History of Biblical Map Making* (Reichert: Wiesbaden).

Notley, R. Steven, and Zeev Safrai (2004) *Eusebius, Onomasticon* (Leiden: Brill Academic Publications).

Nutting, Anthony (2013) 'Balfour and Palestine, a Legacy of Deceit', posted on 8 July, at: http://www.balfourproject.org/balfour-and-palestine/

Nyangoni, Wellington (1978) *African Nationalism in Zimbabwe* (Washington, DC: University Press of America).

Ochsenwald, William, and Sydney Nettleton Fisher (2004) *The Middle East: A History*, 6th edition (New York: McGraw-Hill).

Origen (1966) *On First Principles*, translated by G.W. Butterworth (New York: Harper and Row).

Osband, Linda (1989) *Famous Travellers to the Holy Land* (London: Prion).

Pailin, David A. (1984) *Attitudes to Other Religions: Comparative Religion in Seventeenth- and Eighteenth-century Britain* (Manchester: Manchester University Press)

Palestine Exploration Fund (1889) *Names and Places in the Old and New Testament and Apocrypha: With their Modern Identifications*, compiled by George Armstrong; revised by Sir Charles W. Wilson and Major Conder (London: Alexander P. Watt for the Committee of the Palestine Exploration Fund).

Palmer, E. H. (1881) *The Survey of Western Palestine. Arabic and English Name Lists Collected during the Survey by Lieutenants Conder and Kitchener, R. E. Transliterated and Explained by E. H. Palmer* (London: Committee of the Palestine Exploration Fund).

Pappe, Ilan (1999) 'Introduction', in Ilan Pappe (ed.) *The Israel/Palestine Question: Rewriting Histories* (London and New York: Routledge): 1–7.

Pappe, Ilan (2004) *A History of Modern Palestine: One Land, Two Peoples* (Cambridge: Cambridge University Press).

Pappe, Ilan (2006) *The Ethnic Cleansing of Palestine* (Oxford: Oneworld Publications).

Pappe, Ilan (2010) *The Rise and Fall of a Palestinian Dynasty: The Husaynis 1700–1948* (London: Saqi Books).

Pasachoff, Naomi (1997) *Links in the Chain: Shaper of Jewish Tradition* (New York and Oxford: Oxford University Press).

Patrich, Joseph (1995) *Sabas, Leader of Palestinian Monasticism: A Comparative Study in Eastern Monasticism, Fourth to Seventh Centuries* (Washington, DC: Dumbarton Oaks).

Patrich, Joseph (2001) 'Urban Space in Caesarea Maritima, Israel', in Thomas S. Burns and John W. Eadie (eds.) *Urban Centers and Rural Contexts in Late Antiquity* (East Lansing, MI: Michigan State University Press): 77–110.

Patrich, Joseph (2011) *Studies in the Archaeology and History of Caesarea Maritima: Caput Judaeae. Metropolis Palaestinae* (Leiden and Boston: Brill).

Parvis, Paul (2008) 'Justin Martyr', *The Expository Times* 120(53, November): 53–61.

Pastor, Jack (1997) *Land and Economy in Ancient Palestine* (London and New York: Routledge).

Peled-Elhanan, Nurit (2012) *Palestine in Israeli School Books: Ideology and Propaganda in Education* (London: I. B. Tauris).

Pearlman, Moshe (1965) *Ben-Gurion Looks Back* (London: Weidenfeld and Nicholson).

Peters, Francis F. (1994) *Muhammad and the Origins of Islam* (New York: State University of New York Press).

Petersen, Andrew (ed.) (2002) *A Gazetteer of Buildings in Muslim Palestine*, Vol. I, British Academy Monographs in Archaeology (London: British Academy).

Petersen, Andrew (2005) *The Towns of Palestine under Muslim rule: AD 600–1600* (Ann Arbor, MI: University of Michigan Press).

Philipp, Thomas (2001) *Acre: The Rise and Fall of a Palestinian City, 1730–1831* (New York: Columbia University Press).

Philipp, Thomas (2015) 'Ẓāhir al-'Umar al-Zaydānī', *Encyclopaedia of Islam*, 2nd edition, edited by P. Bearman, Th. Bianquis, C. E. Bosworth, E. van Donzel and W. P. Heinrichs (BrillOnline), at: http://referenceworks.brillonline.com/entries/encyclopaedia-of-islam-2/zahir-al-umar-al-zaydani-SIM_8083?s.num=42&s.rows=100

Pinto, Karen (2006) 'Cartography', in Josef W. Meri (ed.) *Islamic Civilisation: An Encyclopaedia*, Vol. 1 (London: Routledge): 138–140.

Piterberg, Gabriel (2001) 'Erasures', *New Left Review* 10 (July–August): 31–46.

Piterberg, Gabriel (2008) *The Return of Zionism: Myths, Politics and Scholarship in Israel* (London: Verso).

Plett, Heinrich F. (2004) *Rhetoric and Renaissance Culture* (Berlin and New York: Walter de Gruyter & Co.).

Pliny the Elder (undated) *Natural History, Volume 1, Book V*: Chapter 13, at: http://penelope.uchicago.edu/Thayer/E/Roman/Texts/Pliny_the_Elder/home.html

Pliny the Elder (1949–1954) *Pliny's Natural History*, Vols. 1–10 (London: William Heinemann).

Pliny the Elder (1991) *Natural History*, translated and introduced by John Healey (London: Penguin Classics).

Porath, Yehoshua (1974) *The Emergence of the Palestinian-Arab National Movement, 1918–1929*, Vol. 1 (London: Frank Cass).

Porter, Leslie (1968) *A Handbook for Travellers in Syria and Palestine: Including an Account of the Geography, History, Antiquities, Inhabitants of these Countries*, Parts 1 and 2 (London: John Murray; first published 1858).

Post, George Edward (1883) 'Plants of Syria and Palestine', *Al-Muqtataf* 8: 81–83 [Arabic].

Post, George Edward (1896) *Nabat Suriya wa-Filastin wa-al-Qatr al-Misri wa-Bawadiha* [The Flora of Syria, Palestine, and the Egyptian Country and its Desert] (Beirut: Beirut: Syrian Protestant College).

Praetorius, Michael (1614–1620) *Syntagma Musicum* [Writings on Music], 3 vols. (Wittenberg: Wolfenbuttel).

Priestley, Jessica, and Vasiliki Zali (eds.) (2016) *Brill's Companion to the Reception of Herodotus in Antiquity and Beyond* (Leiden and Boston: Brill).

Prior, Michael (1997) *The Bible and Colonialism: A Moral Critique* (Sheffield: Sheffield Academic Press).

Prior, Michael (1999) 'The Bible and the Redeeming Idea of Colonialism', *Studies in World Christianity* 5 (2): 129–155.

Prokopios (Procopius) (2005) *History of the Wars*, Books I and II (of 8), translated by H. B. Dewing (Salt Lake City, UT: Project Gutenberg eBook; first published c. 560), at: http://www.gutenberg.org/files/16764/16764-h/16764-h.htm

Prokopios (Procopius) (2014) *The Wars of Justinian* (Cambridge, MA: Hackett Publishing Company; first published c. 560), at: https://sourcebooks.fordham.edu/ancient/arabia1.asp

Prummer, Reinhard (2002) *Early Christian Authors on Samaritans and Samaritanism: Texts, Translations and* Commentary (Tübingen: Mohr).

Qumsiyeh, Mazin B. (2004) *Sharing the Land of Canaan: Human Rights and Israel–Palestinian Struggle* (London: Pluto Press).

Quataert, Donald (2002) *Ottoman Manufacturing in the Age of the Industrial Revolution* (Cambridge: Cambridge University Press).

Ra'ad, L. Basem (2010) *Hidden Histories: Palestine and the Eastern Mediterranean* (London: Pluto Press).

Rabbani, Mouin (2005) 'Ghassan Kanafani', in Philip Mattar (ed.) *Encyclopedia of the Palestinians*, revised edition (New York: Facts on File): *275–276*.

Rabkin, Yakov M. (2006) *A Threat from Within: A Century of Jewish Opposition to Zionism* (London: Zed Books).

Rabkin, Yakov M. (2010) 'Language in Nationalism: Modern Hebrew in the Zionist Project', *Holy Land Studies: A Multidisciplinary Journal* 9(2, November): 129–145.

Rafeq, 'Abdul-Karim (1990) 'Filastin fi 'Ahd al-Uthmaniyin' [Palestine in the Ottoman Era], *al-Mawsu'ah al-Filistiniyyah*, Part 2, Special Studies, Vol. 2, Historical Studies (Beirut: Hay'at al-Mawsu'ah al-Filastiniyyah): 695–990.

Rainey, Anson F. (2001) 'Hereodotus' Description of the East Mediterranean Coast', *Bulletin of the American Schools of Oriental Research*, No. 321 (February): 57–63.

Ram, Uri (1995) 'Zionist Historiography and the Invention of Modern Jewish Nationhood: The Case of Benzion Dinur', *History and Memory* 7(1): 91–124.

Ramadan, Tareq (2010) 'The Standing Caliph Coins of Aylah Filastin', *Journal of the Oriental Numismatic Society* no. 203 (Spring): 3–6.

Ramadan, Tareq (2010a) 'An Umayyad Post-Reform Coin of Aylah, a Concise Commentary', *Journal of the Oriental Numismatic Society* no. 205 (Autumn): 10–12.

Rashed, Haifa, Damien Short and John Docker (2014) 'Nakba Memoricide: Genocide Studies and the Zionist/Israeli Genocide of Palestine', *Holy Land Studies* 13(1, May): 1–23.

Raz-Krakotzkin, Amnon (1993, 1994) 'Galut Betoch Ribonut: Lebikoret Shlilat Hagalut Batarbut Hayisraelit' [Exile Within Sovereignty: Toward a Critique of the 'Negation of Exile' in Israeli Culture], *Teurya Vi-Bikoret* [Theory and Criticism] 4: 23–56 and 5: 113–132 [Hebrew].

Redhouse, J. W. (1856) *An English and Turkish Dictionary* (London: Bernard Quaritch)

Reiter, Yitzhak (2010) 'The Waqf in Israel since 1965: The Case of Acre Reconsidered', in Marshall J. Breger, Yitzhak Reiter and Leonard Hammer (eds.) *Holy Places in the Israeli–Palestinian Conflict: Conformation and Co-existence* (London and New York: Routledge): 104–127.

Reland (Relandus) Adriaan (1714) *Palaestina ex Monumentis Veteribus Illustrata* [Palestine Illustrated from Ancient Monuments] (Utrecht: Willem Broedelet).

Riley-Smith, Jonathan (1977) 'The Survival in Latin Palestine of Muslim Administration', in P. M. Holt (ed.) *The Eastern Mediterranean Lands in the Period of the Crusades* (Warminster: Aris and Phillips): 9–22.

Riley-Smith, Jonathan (1978) 'Latin Titular Bishops in Palestine and Syria, 1137–1291', *Catholic Historical Review* 64: 1–15.

Riley-Smith, Jonathan (2005) *The Crusades: A History*, 2nd edition (London and New York: Continuum).

Robinson, Chase F. (2003) *Islamic Historiography* (Cambridge: Cambridge University Press).

Robinson, Edward (1841) *Biblical Researches in Palestine, Mount Sinai and Arabia Petraea: A Journal of Travels in the Year 1838* (London: J. Murray).

Robinson, Edward (1865) *Physical Geography of the Holy Land* (Boston: Crocker & Brewster).

Robinson, Edward, Eli Smith and others (1860) *Biblical Researches in Palestine and Adjacent Regions: A Journal of Travel in the Years 1838 & 1852* (Boston: Crocker and Brewster).

Roded, Ruth (1994) *Women in Islamic Biographical Collections: From Ibn Sa'd to Who's Who* (Boulder, CO and London: Lynne Rienner).

Röhricht, Gustav Reinhold (1890) *Bibliotheca geographica Palaestinae: Chronologisches Verzeichniss der auf die Geographie des Heiligen Landes Bezuglichen Literatur von 333 bis 1878* (Berlin: H. Reuther's Verlagsbuchhandlung).

Rogers, Randall (2002) *Latin Siege Warfare in the Twelfth Century* (Oxford: Clarendon Press).

Rokeah, David (2002) *Justin Martyr and the Jews* (Leiden and Boston: Brill).

Romer, Frank E (ed.) (1998) *Pomponius Mela's Description of the World*, 1st edition (Ann Arbor, MI: The University of Michigan Press).

Rood, Judith Mendelsohn (2004) *Sacred Law in the Holy City: The Khedival Challenge to the Ottomans as seen from Jerusalem, 1829–1841* (Leiden: Brill).

Room, Adrian (2006) *Placenames of the World: Origins and Meanings of the Names for 6,600 Countries, Cities, Territories, Natural Features and Historic Sites*, 2nd revised edition (Jefferson, NC and London: McFarland & Company).

Rose, John (2004) *The Myths of Zionism* (London: Pluto Press).

Rose, John (2010) 'In Praise of the Sun: Zodiac Sun-Gods in Galilee Synagogues and the Palestinian Heritage', *Holy Land Studies* 9(1): 25–49.

Rosen-Ayalon, Myriam (1998) 'Between Cairo and Damascus: Rural Life and Urban Economics in the Holy Land during the Ayyubid, Mamluk and Ottoman Periods', in Thomas Evan Levy (ed.) *Archaeology of Society in the Holy Land* (London and New York: Continuum): 512–523.

Rosen-Ayalon, Myriam (2006) *Islamic Art and Archaeology of Palestine* (Walnut Creek: CA: Left Coast Press).

Rotbard, Sharon (2015) *White City Black City: Architecture and War in Tel Aviv and Jaffa* (London: Pluto Press).

Saggs, Henry W. F. (ed.) (2001) *The Nimrud Letters, 1952. Cuneiform Texts from Nimrud V* (Trowbridge, Wiltshire: British School of Archaeology in Iraq and the Cromwell Press).

Said, Edward W. (1978) *Orientalism* (London: Routledge and Kegan Paul).

Said, Edward W. (1980) *The Question of Palestine* (London and Henly: Routledge and Kegan Paul).

Said, Edward W. (1981) *Covering Islam* (New York: Vintage).

Said, Edward W. (1999) 'Palestine: Memory, Invention and Space', in Ibrahim Abu-Lughod, Roger Heacock and Khaled Nashef (eds.) *The Landscape of Palestine: Equivocal Poetry* (Birzeit, Palestine: Birzeit University Publications): 3–20.

Said, Edward (2004) *Freud and the Non-European* (London: Verso, in association with the Freud Museum).

Salibi, Kamal S. (1993) *The Modern History of Jordan* (London: I. B. Tauris).

Sand, Shlomo (2009) *The Invention of the Jewish People* (London: Verso).

Sand, Shlomo (2011) *The Words and the Land: Israeli Intellectuals and the Nationalist Myth* (Los Angeles, CA: Semiotext(e)).

Sartre, Maurice (1988) 'La Syrie creuse n'existe pas', in G. L. Gatier, B. Helly and J.-P Rey-Coquais (eds.) *Géographie historique au proche-orient* (Paris: n.p.): 15–40.

Sartre, Maurice (2005) 'The Arabs and Desert Peoples', in Alan Bowman, Peter

Garnsey and Averil Cameron (eds.) *The Cambridge Ancient History: Volume 12, The Crisis of Empire, A.D. 193–337* (Cambridge: Cambridge University Press): 498–520.

Schiller, Jon (2009) *Internet View of the Arabic World* (Charleston, SC: Booksurge Publishing).

Schölch, Alexander (1992) 'Britain in Palestine, 1838–1882: The Roots of the Balfour Policy', *Journal of Palestine Studies* 22(1, Autumn): 39–56.

Schrader, Eberhard (2012) *Keilinschriften und Geschichtsforschung* [Cuneiform Inscriptions and Historical Research] (Charleston, SC: Nabu Press; first published 1878).

Scott, Samuel Parsons (1904) *History of the Moorish Empire in Europe*, Vol. 1 (Philadelphia and London: J. B. Lippinncott).

Scrivener, Frederick Henry Ambrose (1893) *Adversaria Critica Sacra: With a Short Explanatory Introduction* (Cambridge: Cambridge University Press).

Sedley, David (ed.) (2012) *The Philosophy of Antiochus* (Cambridge: Cambridge University Press).

Segal, Rafi, and Eyal Weizman (2003) 'The Mountain', in Rafi Segal, David Tartakover and Eyal Weizman (eds.) *A Civilian Occupation: The Politics of Israeli Architecture* (London: Verso): 79–96.

Segreteria di Stato Vaticano (2013) *Annuario Pontificio 2013* (Rome: Libreria Editrice Vaticana).

Seikaly, May (2002a) *Haifa: Transformation of an Arab Society 1918–1939* (London: I. B. Tauris).

Seikaly, May (2002b) 'Haifa at the Crossroads: An Outpost of New World Order', in Leila T. Fawaz, C. A. Bayly, with Robert Ilbert (eds.) *Modernity and Culture from the Mediterranean to the Indian Ocean* (New York: Colombia University Press): 96–111.

Shaban, M. A. (1971) *Islamic History: A New Interpretation, A.D. 600–750 (A.H. 132)* (Cambridge: Cambridge University Press).

Shahid, Irfan (1984) *Rome and the Arabs: A Prolegomenon to the Study of Byzantium and the Artabs* (Washington, DC: Dumbarton Oaks Research Library and Collection).

Shahid, Irfan (1986) 'The Jund System in Bilad al-Sham: Its Origins', in M. A. Bakhit and M. Asfour (eds.) *Proceedings of the Fourth International Conference on the History of Bilad al-Sham: Bilad al-Sham during the Byzantine Period*, Vol. 2 (Amman: University of Jordan / Yarmouk University): 45–52.

Shahid, Irfan (1989) *Byzantium and the Arabs in the Fifth Century* (Washington, DC: Dumbarton Oaks Research Library and Collection).

Shahid, Irfan (1995) *Byzantium and the Arabs in the Sixth Century*, Vol. 1 (Washington, DC: Dumbarton Oaks Research Library and Collection).

Shahid, Erfan (2002) *Byzantium and the Arabs in the Sixth Century*, Vol.2, Part. 1 (Washington, DC: Dumbarton Oaks Research Library and Collection).

Shahid, Irfan (2006a) *Byzantium and the Arabs in the Fifth Century* (Washington, DC: Dumbarton Oaks Research Library and Collection).

Shahid, Irfan (2006b) *Byzantium and the Arabs in Late Antiquity*, Vol. 3 (Washington, DC: Dumbarton Oaks Research Library and Collection).

Shahid, Irfan (2009) *Byzantium and the Arabs in the Sixth Century*, Vol. 2, Part 2 (Washington, DC: Dumbarton Oaks Research Library and Collection).

Shahid, Irfan (2010) *Byzantium and the Arabs in the Sixth Century*, Vol. 2, Part 2 (Cambridge, MA: Harvard University Press and Dumbarton Oaks Research Library and Collection).

Shahin, Mariam (2005) *Palestine: A Guide* (Northampton, MA: Interlink Books).

Shafir, Gershon (1996a) *Land, Labor and the Origins of the Israeli–Palestinian Conflict, 1882–1914* (Berkeley, CA: University of California Press).

Shafir, Gershon (1996b) 'Zionism and Colonialism: A Comparative Approach', in M. N. Barnett (ed.) *Israel in Comparative Perspectives: Challenging the Conventional Wisdom* (Albany, NY: State University of New York): 227–244.

Shafir, Gershon (1999) 'Zionism and Colonialism: A Comparative Approach', in Ilan Pappe (ed.) *The Israel/Palestine Question* (London: Routledge): 81–96.

Shalev, Zur (2012) *Sacred Words and Worlds: Geography, Religion, and Scholarship, 1550–1700* (Leiden and Boston: Brill).

Shamma, Samir (1969) 'The Ikhshidid Coins of Filastin', *Al-Abhath* 22 (3–4): 27–46.

Shamma, Samir (1980) *Al-Nuqud al-Islamiyyah Alati Duribat fi Filastin* [The Islamic Coins Struck in Palestine] (West Bank, Palestine: n.p.) [Arabic].

Sharif, Regina (1983) *Non-Jewish Zionism, Its Roots in Western History* (London: Zed Books).

Sharon, Moshe (1997–2013) *Corpus Inscriptionum Arabicarum Palaestinae* [A Collection of Arabic Inscriptions from Palestine], Vols. 1–5 (Leiden: Brill).

Sharon, Moshe (2013) *Corpus Inscriptionum Arabicarum Palaestinae*, H-1.5 (Leiden: Brill).

Sharon, Moshe (2003) 'The History of Palestine from the Arab Conquest until the Crusades (633–1099)', in Michael Avi-Yohah (ed.) *A History of Israel and the Holy Land* (Continuum: New York and London): 194–234.

Sheehi, Stephen (2011) 'Butrus al-Bustani: Syria's Ideologue of the Age', in Adel Bishara (ed.) *The Origins of Syrian Nationhood: Histories, Pioneers, and Identity* (London: Routledge): 57–78.

Shepherd, Naomi (1987) *The Zealous Intruders: The Western Rediscovery of Palestine* (London: William Collins Sons).

Shehadeh, Haseeb (1998) 'The Influence of Arabic on Modern Hebrew', in Christian-Bernard Amphoux, Albert Frey and Ursula Schattner-Riese (eds.) *Études sémitiques et samaritaines offertes à Jean Margain* (Lausanne: Éditions du Zèbre): 149–161.

Shlaim, Avi (2000) *The Iron Wall: Israel and the Arab World* (London: The Penguin Press).

Shohat, Ella (2010) *Israeli Cinema: East/West and the Politics of Representation* (London: I. B. Tauris).

Silberman, Neil Asher (1982) *Digging for God and Country: Exploration, Archaeology, and the Secret Struggle for the Holy Land 1799–1917* (New York: Alfred Knopf).

Silberman, Neil Asher, and David B. Small (1977) *The Archaeology of Israel: Constructing the Past, Interpreting the Present* (JSOTSS 237) (Sheffield: Sheffield Academic Press).

Sivan, Hagith (2008) *Palestine in Late Antiquity* (Oxford: Oxford University Press).

Slyomovics, Susan (1998) *The Object of Memory: Arab and Jew Narrate the Palestinian Village* (Philadelphia, PA: University of Pennsylvania Press).

Slyomovics, Susan (2002) 'The Gender of Transposed Space', *Palestine-Israel Journal of Politics, Economics and Culture* 9 (4), at: http://www.pij.org/details.php?id=114

Smith, Anthony D. (1971) *Theories of Nationalism* (London: Duckworth).

Smith, Anthony D. (1981) *The Ethnic Revival* (Cambridge: Cambridge University Press).

Smith, Anthony D. (1984) 'Ethnic Myths and Ethnic Revivals', *European Journal of Sociology* 22: 283–305.

Smith, Anthony D. (1986) *The Ethnic Origin of Nations* (London: Blackwell).

Smith, Anthony D. (1989) 'The Origins of Nations', *Ethnic and Racial Studies* 12(3): 340–367.

Smith, Anthony D. (1991) *National Identity* (London: Penguin).

Smith, Charles D. (1996) *Palestine and the Arab–Israeli Conflict* (New York: St. Martin's Press).

Smith, George (1875) *The Assyrian Eponym Canon* (London: Samuel Bagster and Sons).

Smith, Linda Tuhiwai (1999) *Decolonizing Methodologies: Research and Indigenous Peoples* (London: Zed Books).

Sokoloff, Michael (2003) *A Dictionary of Jewish Palestinian Aramaic of the Byzantine Period*, 2nd edition (Baltimore, MD: Johns Hopkins University Press).

Srouji, Elias S. (2003) *Cyclamens from Galilee: Memoirs of a Physician from Nazareth* (New York: iUniverse, Inc.).

St. Laurent, Beatric with Himmet Taşkömürl (2013) 'The Imperial Museum of Antiquities in Jerusalem, 1890–1930: An Alternate Narrative', *Jerusalem Quarterly* 55: 6–45, at: http://www.palestine-studies.org/sites/default/files/jq-articles/JQ%2055_The%20Imperial.pdf

Stein, Leonard (1961) *The Balfour Declaration* (Jerusalem: Magnes Press of the Hebrew University).

Suleiman, Yasir (2016) *Being Palestinian: Personal Reflections on Palestinian Identity in the Diaspora* (Edinburgh: Edinburgh University Press).

Stavans, Ilan (2008) *Resurrecting Hebrew* (Jerusalem: Schocken).

Stavrou Theofanis, George (1961) *The Russian Imperial Orthodox Palestine Society, 1882–1914*. PhD dissertation, Indiana University.

Sternhell, Zeev (1998) *The Founding Myths of Israel: Nationalism, Socialism, and the Making of the Jewish State* (Princeton, NJ: Princeton University Press).

Strabo (1917) *The Geography of Strabo*, with an English translation by Horace Leonard Jones, 8 Vols. (London: Heinemann).

Streeter, Burnett Hillman (1926) *The Four Gospels: A Study of Origins, Treating of the Manuscript Tradition, Sources, Authorship, & Dates*, 2nd edition (London: Macmillan; first published 1924).

Sturgis, Matthew (2001) *It Ain't Necessarily So: Investigating the Truth of the Biblical Past* (London: Headline Book Publishing).

Sykes, Christopher (1973) *Crossroads to Israel, 1917–1948* (Bloomington, IN and London: Indiana University Press).

Taha, Hamdan (2010) 'Two Decades of Archeology in Palestine', at: http://www.academia.edu/19771693/Two_Decades_of_Archeology_in_Palestine

Taha, Hamdan (2017) 'Palestine: A Fascinating History', *Palestine* no. 232 (August): 6–11.

Tal, Oren (2012) 'Greek Coinages in Palestine', in William E. Metcalf (ed.) *The Oxford Handbook of Greek and Tomean Coinage* (Oxford and New York: Oxford University Press): 252–274.

Talgam, Rina (2004) 'The Ekphrasis Eikonos of Procopius of Gaza: The Depiction of Mythological Themes in Palestine and Arabia during the Fifth and Sixth Centuries', in Brouria Bitton-Ashkelony and Aryeh Kofsky (eds.) *Christian Gaza in Late Antiquity* (Leiden and Boston: Brill): 209–234.

Talmon, Jacob L. (1965) 'Who Is a Jew?' *Encounter* XXIV (5, May) [cited in Georges Tamarin, *The Israeli Dilemma* (Rotterdam: Rotterdam University Press, 1973)].

Tamari, Salim (2003) 'A Miserable Year in Brooklyn: Khalil Sakakini in America, 1907–1908' *(Institute of Jerusalem Studies' 17 (*February), *at:* http://www.palestine-studies.org/jq/fulltext/77994

Tamari, Salim (2006) 'Wasif Jawhariyyeh, Popular Music and Modernity in Jerusalem', in Rebecca Stein and Ted Swedenberg (eds.) *Palestine, Israel, and the Politics of Popular Culture* (Durham, NC: Duke University Press).

Tamari, Salim (2008) *Mountain against the Sea: Essays in Palestinian Society and Culture* (Berkeley, Los Angeles and London: University of California Press).

Tamari, Salim (2011) 'Shifting Ottoman Conceptions of Palestine: Part 1: Filistin Risalesi and the Two Jamals', *Jerusalem Quarterly*, No. 47 (Fall): 28–38.

Tamari, Salim (2014) 'Issa al Issa's Unorthodox Orthodoxy: Banned in Jerusalem, Permitted in Jaffa', *Jerusalem Quarterly* 59: 16–36, at: http://www.palestine-studies.org/jq/fulltext/165351

Tarawneh, Taha Thalji (1982) *Mamlakat Safad fi 'Ahd al-Mamalik* [The Kingdom of Safad in the Era of Mamluks] (Beirut: Dar al-Afaq al-Jadidah).

Tauber, Eliezer (2007) *The Formation of Modern Syria and Iraq* (London: Routledge and Digital Printing; first published 1995).

The Encyclopaedia of Islam (1965) Vol. II, new edition (Leiden: E. J. Brill).

Thompson, Thomas L. (1979). *The Settlement of Palestine in the Bronze Age* (Wiesbaden: Reichert).

Thompson, Thomas L. (1987) 'The Origin Tradition of Ancient Israel I', *Journal for the Study of the Old Testament*, Supplementary Series 55 (Sheffield: Sheffield Academic Press; first published 1974).

Thompson, Thomas L. (1991) 'Text, Context and Referent in Israelite Historiography', in D. Edelman (ed.) *The Fabric of History: Text, Artifact and Israel's Past* (Sheffield: Sheffield Academic Press):65–92.

Thompson, Thomas L. (1992) *The Early History of the Israelite People From the Written and Archaeological Sources* (Leiden: Brill).

Thompson, Thomas L. (1998) 'Hidden Histories and the Problem of Ethnicity in Palestine', in Michael Prior (ed.) *Western Scholarship and the History of Palestine* (London: Melisende): 23–39.

Thompson, Thomas L. (1999) *The Bible in History: How Writers Create a Past* (London: Jonathan Cape).

Thompson, Thomas L. (2003) 'Is the Bible Historical? The Challenge of "Minimalism" for Biblical Scholars and Historians', *Holy Land Studies: A Multidisciplinary Journal* 3(1, May): 1–27.

Thompson, Thomas L. (2011) 'The Bible, Zionism and the Heritage of an Empty Land: Review Article', *Holy Land Studies: A Multidisciplinary Journal* 10(1, May): 97–108.

Thompson, Thomas L. (2016) 'Ethnicity and a Regional History of Palestine', in Ingrid Hjelm and Thomas L. Thompson (eds.) *History, Archaeology and the Bible Forty Years after 'Historicity': Changing Perspectives 6* (London: Routledge): 159–173.

Thompson, Thomas L., Maniragaba Balibutsa and Margaret M. Clarkson (1975) *The Settlement of Sinai and the Negev in the Bronze Age* (Wiesbaden: Reichert).

Thompson, Thomas L., F. J. Goncalves and J. M. van Cangh (1988) *Toponymie Palestinienne: Plaine de St. Jean d'Acre et corridor de Jerusalem* (Louvain-la-Neuve: de l'institut orientaliste de Louvain, Université catholique de Louvain).

Tobler, Titus (1859) *Dritte Wanderung nach Palästina im Jahre 1857* [Third Journey to Palestine in 1857], at: https://archive.org/details/titustoblersdri00toblgoog

Tobler, Titus (1867) *Bibliographia Geographica Palestinae* [Geographic Bibliography for Palestine] (Zurich), at: https://archive.org/details/Bibliographia GeographicaPalestinae

Tristram, Henry Baker (1884) *The Survey of Western Palestine: The Fauna and Flora of Palestine* (London: The Committee of the Palestine Exploration Fund).

Troen, Selwyn Ilan (2008) 'De-Judaizing the Homeland: Academic Politics in Rewriting the History of Palestine', in Philip Carl Salzman and Donna Robinson Divine (eds.) *Postcolonial Theory and the Arab–Israel Conflict* (London: Routledge): 195–207.

Tubingen Bible Atlas [*Tuebinger Bibelatlas*] (2001) (Wiesbaden: Reichert).

Tuchman, Barbara W. (1982) *Bible and Sword: How the British came to Palestine* (London: Macmillan; first published 1956).

Tucker, Judith E. (2002) 'Biography as History: The Exemplary Life of Khayr al-Din al-Ramli', in Mary Ann Fay (ed.) *Auto/Biography and the Construction of Identity in the Middle East* (New York: Palgrave Macmillan): 9–18.

Van Berchem, (1894) *Matériaux pour un Corpus inscriptionum Arabicarum* (Cairo: Institut français d'archéologie orientale du Cairo).

Verete, Mayir (1970) 'The Balfour Declaration and Its Makers', *Middle Eastern Studies* 6 (1): 48–76.

Von Suchem, Ludolph [Ludolf von Sudheim] (1971) *Ludolph Von Suchem's Description of the Holy Land, and of the Way Thither: Written in the Year A.D. 1350.* The library of the Palestine Pilgrims' Text Society, Vol. 12, Part 3, translated by Aubrey Stewart (New York: Ams Press).

Von Suchem, Ludolph [Ludolf von Sudheim] (2013) *Ludolph von Suchem's Description of the Holy Land and of the Way Thither: Written in the Year A.D. 1350*, edited and translated by Aubrey Stewart (Cambridge: Cambridge University Press).

Wagner, Donald (1992) 'Beyond Armageddon', *The Link* 25(4, October–November): 4.

Wagner, Donald (1995) *Anxious for Armageddon* (Scottdale, PA and Waterloo, Ontario: Herald Press).

Wakim, Wakim (2001a) *The Internally Displaced: Refugees in Their Homeland* (Cairo: Centre of Human Rights Studies) [Arabic].

Wakim, Wakim (2001b) 'Internally Displaced in their Homeland and the Main Stations', *Al-Ittihad*, special supplement for Land Day (March) [Arabic].

Wallace-Hadrill, D. S. (1982) *Christian Antioch: A Study of Early Christian Thought in the East* (Cambridge: Cambridge University Press).

Walmsley, Alan G. (1996) 'Byzantine Palestine and Arabia: Urban Prosperity in Late Antiquity', in N. Christie and S. T. Loseby (eds.) *Towns in Transition: Urban Evolution in Late Antiquity and the Early Middle Ages* (Brookfield, VT: Ashgate Publishing Company): 126–158.

Walmsley, Alan G. (2000) 'Production, Exchange and Regional Trade in the Islamic East Mediterranean: Old Structures, New Systems?', in Inge Lyse Hansen and Chris Wickham (eds.) *The Long Eighth Century: Production, Distribution and Demand* (Leiden: Brill): 265–343.

Ward, Walter David (2008) *From Provincia Arabia to Palaestinae Tertia: The Impact of Geography, Economy, and Religion on the Sedentary and Nomadic Communities in the later Roman Province of Third Palestine*. PhD dissertation, UCLA.

Weir, Shelagh (1994) *Palestinian Costume* (London: British Museum).

Westberg, David (2009) 'The Rite of Spring, Erotic Celebration in the Dialexeis and Ethopoiiai of Procopius of Gaza', in Ingela Nilsson (ed.) *Plotting with Eros: Essays on the Poetics of Love and the Erotics of Reading: Eros and the Poetics of Narrative* (Copenhagen: University of Copenhagen and Museum Tusculanum Press): 187–212.

Whitelam, Keith (1996) *The Invention of Ancient Israel: The Silencing of Palestinian History* (London and New York: Routledge).

Wiener, Noah (2016) 'Early Bronze Age: Megiddo's Great Temple and the Birth of Urban Culture in the Levant', *Bible History Daily, Biblical Archaeology Society*, 10 September, at: https://www.biblicalarchaeology.org/daily/ancient-cultures/ancient-israel/early-bronze-age-megiddos-great-temple-and-the-birth-of-urban-culture-in-the-levant/

Wiemer, Reinhard (1983) 'Zionism and the Arabs after the Establishment of the State of Israel', in Alexander Schölch (ed.) *Palestinians over the Green Line* (London: Ithaca Press): 26–63.

Wigram, William Anger (2004) *An Introduction to the History of the Assyrian Church* (Assyrian International News Agency; first published 1909), at: http://www.aina.org/books/itthotac/itthotac.htm

Wilkinson, J. (1975) 'The Streets of Jerusalem', *Levant* 7: 118–136.

Wilson, N. G. (1967) 'A Chapter in the History of Scholia', *Classical Quarterly* 61: 244–256.

Wilson, N. G. (1983) *Scholars of Byzantium* (Baltimore, MD: Johns Hopkins University Press).

Winckler, Hugo (1898) *Altorientalische Forschungen* (Leipzig: Eduard Pfeiffer).

Wittgenstein, Ludwig (2001) *Philosophical Investigations* (London: Blackwell Publishing; first published 1953).

Wolfe, Patrick (2006) 'Settler Colonialism and the Elimination of the Native', *Journal of Genocide Research* 8(4) (December): 387–409.

World Health Organisation (2007) *Male Circumcision: Global Trends and Determinants of Prevalence, Safety and Acceptability* (Geneva: World Health Organisation).

Wrba, Marian (ed.) (1996) *Austrian Presence in the Holy Land in the 19th and Early 20th Century. Proceedings of the Symposium in the Austrian Hospice in Jerusalem on 1–2 March 1995* (Tel Aviv: Austrian Embassy).

Wright, Thomas (1948) *Early Travels in Palestine* (London: Bohn's Antiquarian Library).

Yacobi, Haim (2009) *The Jewish-Arab City: Spacio-politics in a Mixed Community* (London and New York: Routledge).

Yazbak, Mahmoud (1998) *Haifa in the Late Ottoman Period, 1864–1914: A Muslim Town in Transition* (Leiden: Brill).

Yehoshua, A. B. (1975) 'Facing the Forests', in Robert Alter (ed.) *Modern Hebrew Literature* (New York: Behrman House; first published 1968): 351–392.

Yiftachel, Oren (2006) *Ethnocracy: Land and Identity Politics in Israel/Palestine* (Philadelphia, PA: University of Pennsylvania Press).

Younis, Mona N. (2000) *Liberation and Democratization: The South African and Palestinian National Movements* (Minneapolis, MN: University of Minnesota Press).

Zangwill, Israel (1920) *The Voice of Jerusalem* (London: William Heinemann).

Zangwill, Israel (1937) *Speeches, Articles and Letters* (London: Soncino Press).

Zeiner, Noelle K. (2005) *Nothing Ordinary Here: Statius as Creator of Distinction in the Silvae* (London and New York: Routledge).

Zerubavel, Yael (1995) *Recovered Roots: Collective Memory and the Making of Israeli National Tradition* (Chicago: University of Chicago Press).

Zerubavel, Yael (1996) 'The Forest as a National Icon: Literature, Politics and the Archaeology of Memory', *Israel Studies* 1(1, Spring): 60–99.

Zevit, Ziony (2003) *The Religions of Ancient Israel: A Synthesis of Parallactic Approaches* (London: Continuum International Publishing).

Notes

Introduction

1 Arabic: sing. balad; plural bilad.

2 *Biladuna Filastin* is also an eleven-volume work of reference on the historical geography of Palestine by Palestinian author Mustafa Murad al-Dabbagh (1965 and 1972–1986). This important encyclopaedia of Palestine is arranged by region and surveys the cities, towns and villages of Palestine from geographical, historical, archaeological, botanical and economic perspectives.

3 See, for instance, Ghalib Muhammad Samrin, *Qaryati Qaluniya: Al-ard wa-al-judhur: Filastinuna fi qissat qaryah* (1993 [Arabic]); Fateh's underground magazine which first appeared in 1959 was called *Filastinuna*.

4 'Azmi Beshara on the existence of a Palestinian People', at https://www.youtube.com/watch?v=EOqAGbpoDZc, posted 30 April 2009.

5 http://weekly.ahram.org.eg/Archive/1998/1948/378_said.htm

6 Monolatrism (Greek: monos: single and latreia: worship) was belief in the existence of many gods but with the worship of only one supreme deity. An example of monolatrism was the ancient Egyptian Pharaoh Amenhotep IV who installed himself as a supreme divinity ('God of gods') and officially changed his name to Akhenaten and introduced Atenism during his reign (1348/1346 BC). Under Akhenaten's successors, Egypt reverted to its traditional polytheism and Akhenaten himself came to be seen as a heretic.

7 Interview with William Montgomery Watt at: http://www.alastairmcintosh.com/articles/2000_watt.htm

8 Samaritanism is one the four distinct Abrahamic traditions of Palestine. The Samaritan tradition centres on the belief in the sanctity of Mount Gerizim (Arabic: Jabal Jarizim or Jabal al-Tur), one of the two mountains in the immediate vicinity of the Palestine city of Nablus. The mountain, which continues to be the centre of Samaritan religion to this day, is sacred to the Palestinian Samaritans who regard it, not Jerusalem, as having been the location of the holy temple. The Samaritan scripture is a text of five books written in the Samaritan alphabet. Some 6000 differences exist between the Samaritan Pentateuch and the Old Testament.

9 Classical Antiquity is a term broadly applied here to a long period of history (over a millennium) during which 'Classical culture' centred on the Mediterranean

421

region and comprised the intimate interaction of the civilisations of Ancient Greece, Ancient Rome with the 'Near East'. It is a period in which Greek and Roman cultural influences not only flourished but also wielded enormous influence throughout Southern Europe, South-Eastern Asia, the 'Near East' and North Africa.

10 Arnold Hugh Martin Jones, 'Palestine', *Encyclopaedia Britannica*, http://www.britannica.com/place/Palestine

11 Josephus (Hebrew: Yosef ben Matityahu).calls himself in Greek as Iōsēpos (Ἰώσηπος), son of Matthias.

12 The Palestinian village of Qaysariah was destroyed by Jewish forces in 1948.

Chapter 1

1 The Story of Sinuhe is considered one of the finest works of fiction of Ancient Egyptian literature. Its narrative is set in the aftermath of the death of Pharaoh Amenemhat I who founded the 12th Dynasty in the early 20th century BC. The popularity of this story is evident from the many surviving fragments. Egyptologists argue about its composition date; here we take the conservative date of the 14th century BC. It could be earlier, but it is not known to be.

2 Ramesses II is the most famous of the Pharaohs; in popular legendary imagination he has become the 'Pharaoh of the Exodus'.

3 The ancient Greek authors give to Africa the name of Libya.

4 The site most likely of Gath is Tell al-Safi, a Palestinian village 35 kilometres north-west of Hebron, depopulated by Israeli in 1948.

5 In Wadi al-Surar (modern Hebrew: Nahal Sorek).

6 Isdud was a large Palestinian village depopulated by Israel in 1948.

7 In 677/676 the Assyrian king Esarhaddon conquered Sidon and in 675 BC concluded a treaty with king Ba'al I of Tyre designed to neutralise the city in the Assyrian struggle with the Egyptians. Esarhaddon's Treaty with Ba'al is an Assyrian clay tablet inscription in Akkadian cuneiform describing a treaty between the Assyrian king Esarhaddon and King Ba'al I of Tyre. It was discovered in Nineveh in the Library of Ashurbanipal and fragments are currently in the British Museum. The treaty, published K 3500 + K 4444 + K 10235, was identified by Hugo Winckler in his Altorientalische Forschungen, II (Ancient Near Eastern Studies) in 1898. Under the terms of the treaty, Esarhaddon entrusted Baal with several settlements, including Acre, Dor and Byblos. The text includes: 'If a ship of Ba'al or of the people of ṣur-ri [Tyre] is shipwrecked off the coast of the land of pi-lis-ti [Pilistu] or anywhere on the borders of Assyrian territory, everything that is on the ship belongs to Esarhaddon ... These are the ports of trade and the trade roads which Esarhaddon, king of Assyria, granted to his servant Ba'al; toward a-ku [Acre], .du-u'-ri [Dor; Tantur], in the entire district of.pi-lis-te [Pilistu]'.

8   For an extensive discussion of the Palestine Nakba, see Masalha (1992, 1997, 2005, 2012) and Khalidi W. (1992).

Chapter 2

1   Herodotus (1858), at: https://archive.org/stream/herodotusooherouoft/herodo-tusooherouoft_djvu.txt

2   *Encyclopaedia Britannica*, at: https://www.britannica.com/biography/Aristotle/Political-theory

3   1st century BC Greek historian Diodorus Siculus (Diodorus of Sicily), in his multi-volume work *Bibliotheca Historica*, indicated that Coele-Syria stretched as far south as Joppa (Jaffa) in Palestine (Diodorus Siculus, *Bibliotheca Historica*, XIX, 93; XXIX, 29; translation by Charles Henry Oldfather.

Chapter 3

1   See for instance, Ovid, *Metamorphoses Book IV*, http://ovid.lib.virginia.edu/trans/Metamorph4.htm

2   Balsam, the name of the fragrant gum of the balsam tree, is derived from the Arabic Balasam; in Latin: balsamum; Greek: βάλσαμον; Hebrew: bosem.

3   *Appian of Alexandria, 'Preface of the Roman History', Livius.org*, http://www.livius.org/sources/content/appian/appian-preface-1/? Also in 150 AD Greco-Roman historian Arrianus of Nicomedia (modern Izmit, Turkey), in Anabasis Alexandri, which describes the campaigns of Alexander the Great, writes: 'On the right side of the Red Sea beyond Babylonia is the chief part of Arabia, and of this a part comes down to the sea of Phoenicia and *Palestinian* Syria' (Arrian 2006: 89).

4   http://www.newadvent.org/fathers/0126.htm

5   Pliny the Elder, *Natural History, Volume 1, Book V*: Chapter 13, http://penelope.uchicago.edu/Thayer/E/Roman/Texts/Pliny_the_Elder/home.html

6   Pomponius Mela, *De Chorographia Liber Primus, Thelatinlibrary.com*, http://www.thelatinlibrary.com/pomponius1.html

7   See also ibid.

8   'Philo Judaeus', in *Encyclopaedia Britannica*, http://www.britannica.com/biography/Philo-Judaeus

9   'Every Good Man is Free', XII.75.

10 In comparison, the total population of Pharisees, the forerunners of modern Rabbinic Judaism, were estimated by Josephus at 6000 (Flavius 2004).

11 'Early Jewish Writings', http://www.earlyjewishwritings.com/text/philo/book33.html

Chapter 4

1 Provincia Arabia, or the Roman Arabia Petraea, was the birth place of 'Philip the Arab', Roman Emperor from 244 to 249 AD. Philip went on to become a major figure in the Roman Empire (Bowersock 1994: 122).

2 Peraea (Greek: Περαία, 'the country beyond'), occupied the eastern side of the Jordan River valley. Subsequently the term was replaced by the Latin Transjordan.

3 The Romans promoted a regime of autonomous city-states in Palestine. A league of ten (or eleven) Hellenised cities in Eastern Palestine and Syria was formed after the Roman conquest in 63 BC; apart from Scythopolis (modern Beisan), all lay east of the Jordan River. The league survived until the 2nd century AD.

4 The Romans divided Arabia into three regions: Arabia Petraea, Arabia Deserta and Arabia Felix (Fertile Arabia), which included the Yemen.

5 Greek: Καισάρεια; the modern Palestinian village of Qaysariah; depopulated and destroyed by Israel in 1948.

6 Praeses (Latin: praesides), a term used under Constantine the Great (r. 306–337) to refer to specific class of provincial governors, the lowest after the consulares and the correctors.

7 Arnold Hugh Martin Jones, 'Palestine', *Encyclopaedia Britannica*, http://www.britannica.com/place/Palestine

8 In comparison, the total population of Palestine west of the River Jordan at the height of the Roman period did not exceed one million (Pastor 1997: 6)

9 Located on coastal dunes 10 kilometres south of Gaza city; the archaeological remains of what is known in Arabic as Tell Umm al-Amr; built by St. Hilarion (born in southern Gaza in 329 AD), the monk after whom it was named.

10 Miaphysites believe that the nature of Jesus, divine and human, are united in one. Although Chalcedonian Christianity considered Miaphysitism in general to be amenable to an orthodox interpretation, they nevertheless perceive it to be a form of Monophysitism.

11 'Bowl from Caesarea Palaestina', http://www.louvre.fr/en/oeuvre-notices/bowl-caesarea-Palaestinae and http://www.louvre.fr/oeuvre-notices/la-coupe-de-cesaree-de-palestine

12 'Caesarea Palaestina', *New Advent* (Catholic Encyclopaedia), http://www.newadvent.org/cathen/03134b.htm

13 The term for an edition of the Old Testament in six versions, an immense word-for-word comparison of the Greek Septuagint with Greek translations.

14 'Caesarea Palaestina', New Advent (Catholic Encyclopaedia), at: http://www.newadvent.org/cathen/03134b.htm

15 http://www.tertullian.org/fathers/eusebius_martyrs.htm. St Albina of Caesarea, who died in the 3rd century, is also listed in the Roman Catholic Martyrology.

16 http://www.newadvent.org/fathers/2504.htm

17 Originally the title 'titular see' applied to patribus infidelium ('in the lands of the unbelievers'). In 1882 the Catholic Church, seeking to improve relations with Orthodox Christians and avoid causing offence to Muslims, abolished the expression in partibus infidelium.

18 Bishop Antiochus represented the city of Capitolias, in Palaestinae Secunda, an ancient city east of the River Jordan and is identified with the modern village of Beit Ras in the Irbid region.

19 The Seven Ecumenical Councils, Christian Classics Ethereal Library, http://www.ccel.org/ccel/schaff/npnf214.xi.xv.html

20 The expression is derived from the Classical Greek ἐγκώμιον (enkomion) meaning 'the praise of a person or thing'.

21 Local farming in the Gaza region depended largely on the annual rain fall; today Gaza city enjoys 400 mm of annual rain fall, while the more arid region of Rafah, located 20 kilometres to the south, gets only 200 mm.

22 Ruth Webb, 'Rhetorical and Theatrical Fictions in Chorikios of Gaza', Center for Hellenic Studies, Harvard University, http://chs.harvard.edu/CHS/article/display/3259

23 Timothy W. Seid, 'Origins of Catena in Gaza', http://legacy.earlham.edu/~seidti/iam/catena.html

24 Le Stampa, 12 May 2015, http://www.lastampa.it/2015/05/12/esteri/vatican-insider/en/when-muslim-politicians-send-their-daughters-to-convent-schools-5xtR7LSxokCjnjuFLHwjAM/pagina.html

25 http://archmemory.blogspot.co.uk/2015/05/forgotten-as-if-you-never-were.html

26 Among the prominent Christian ascetics of the period was Barsanuphius of Palestine (died c. 540 AD). Born in Egypt, he lived in a Palestinian monastery in absolute seclusion for fifty years (Barsanuphius 2006).

27 St Anthony (251–356), a Coptic monk, became known as both the father and founder of desert monasticism. The Desert Mothers are less well known because the lives of the early saints were written by men for male monastic audiences (King 1989).

28 Coenobium is a communal monastery with a number of structures surrounded by a wall and the monks lived in a commune. This term is based on the Greek koinos (common) and bios (life).

29 In Sufi Islam, the *tariqah*, or 'path', metaphor is taken by the mystic towards the inner truth.

30 Sabbas' Life was written by one of his disciples, Cyril of Scythopolis (525–559) (modern Beisan) in Palaestinae Secunda, a Christian monk and historian of monastic life in Palestine in the early years of Christianity (Kazhdan 1991). His work known in English as *The Lives of the Monks of Palestine* is one of the main sources of monastic life in Byzantine Palestine.

31   Mar Saba Monastery is one of thirteen Palestinian sites included on the list submitted to UNESCO following the admission of Palestine to this organisation in 2011.

32   Al-Jazeera, 22 February 2010.

Chapter 6

1   The period of the Umayyad Marwanid Caliphs began with Marwan ibn al-Hakam in 684.

2   http://www.jewishvirtuallibrary.org/jerusalem-architecture-in-the-umayyad-period

3   This mixture of Islamic and Roman Byzantine styles is also found in the 'Hisham Palace'/Khirbat al-Mafjar, Jericho, and in al-Ramla and Tiberias (Khirbet al-Minyar). It is also found in the Arab Byzantine coinage minted in the towns of Jund Filastin in the 7th century.

4   This Palestinian town, located 15 kilometres south-west of al-Ramla, with a population of 5420 in 1948, was destroyed by Israel in 1948.

5   Via Maris is the modern name for an ancient trade and strategic rout dating from the Early Bronze Age. It connected Egypt with Syria and the Fertile Crescent and followed the coast of Palestine through the ancient cities of Gaza, 'Asqalan, Isdud, Jaffa and Tantur before turning east through Megiddo and the Esdraelon valley until it reached Tiberias, then through the Golan Heights to Damascus.

6   Arsuf was about 16 kilometres north of Jaffa and 34 kilometres south of Caesarea on the Mediterranean coast. Under the Byzantines in the 5th–6th centuries AD it was the second largest city in the coastal region of Palaestinae Prima, second only to Caesarea. It was populated by Samaritans and Christians and had a prosperous glass industry with products exported to Mediterranean countries. Under early Islam the city continued to prosper and large pottery production was developed (Hütteroth and Abdulfattah 1977: 140).

7   Le Strange commented that al-Maqdisi's 'description of Palestine, and especially of Jerusalem, his native city, is one of the best parts of the work. All that he wrote is the fruit of his own observation, and his descriptions of the manners and customs of the various countries, bear the stamp of a shrewd and observant mind, fortified by profound knowledge of both books and men' (Le Strange 1890: 5–6).

8   'Legio VI Ferrata', http://www.livius.org/articles/legion/legio-vi-ferrata/?; Kennedy (1980).

9   'Coin/Archives', http://www.coinarchives.com/w/results.php?search=fals+and+islamic

10   Aelia Capitolina was the official Roman and Byzantine name of Jerusalem until 638 AD when the Arabs occupied the city and initially kept the first part of the name as 'Ilya' (al-Maqdisi 2002: 43)

11   The collections of the Israeli Municipal Museum of al-Ramla contain a range of medieval Islamic coins including a hoard of 376 gold dinars and six gold bars discovered in 1964 in the vicinity of the White Mosque compound. See http://en.goramla.com/category/ramla-museum-1

12   This Palestinian town was depopulated and destroyed by Israel in 1948 and the Jewish settlement of Azor now stands on the lands of the Arab town.

13   'Al-Yazuri', *Encyclopaedia of Islam*, second edition, edited by P. Bearman, T. Bianqui, C. E. Bosworth, E. van Donzel, W. P. Heinrichs (Leiden: Brill Online).

Chapter 7

1   https://www.wdl.org/en/item/2892/

2   https://truthaholics.wordpress.com/2017/12/11/records-of-jerusalem-deeds-found-in-ottoman-archives-cause-israel-unease/ A similar proportion of waqf properties (20–25 per cent) also existed in the Palestinian city of Acre during the late Ottoman period (Reiter 2010: 110).

3   The Nea Church was destroyed during the Persian conquest of the city in 614, but its remains were further used as a source of building material by the Umayyads few decades later (Ben-Dov 1977).

4   The fair also exhibited the Illés Relief model of the Old city of Jerusalem, a model hand-crafted from molten zinc and is hand-painted. It was hand-crafted between 1864 and 1873 by Stephen Illés, a Hungarian Catholic who lived in Palestine.

Chapter 8

1   'The Palestinian People is a Colonial Invention', in Azmi Beshara on the existence of a Palestinian People, https://www.youtube.com/watch?v=EOqAGbpoDZc , posted 30 April 2009.

2   https://books.google.co.uk/books?id=lWcChegBF2sC&pg=RA1-PA65&redir_esc=y#v=onepage&q&f=false

3   Yusuf al-Natsheh, 'Suq al-Qattanin (Market of the Cotton Merchants)', in Discover Islamic Art, Museum With No Frontiers, 2016, http://www.discoverislamicart.org/database_item.php?id=monument;isl;pa;mon01;6;en

4   *A Gazetteer of the World. Or Dictionary of Geographical Knowledge.* Vol. 1 (Edinburgh and London: A. Fullarton and Co. 1959): 38–39.

5   The original small settlement was built on the slopes of Mount Carmel in in the late Bronze Age (14th century BC).

6   The sequin was a gold coin minted by the Republic of Venice from the 13th century until the takeover of Venice by Napoleon in 1797. Following the Venetian model, similar coins were used for centuries throughout the Mediterranean, in Palestine and throughout the Ottoman Empire.

Chapter 9

1   https://arablit.org/2013/01/15/we-have-on-this-earth-what-makes-life-worth-living/

2   http://www.all-poetry.ru/stih307.html

3   The first Russian writer who went to Palestine as a pilgrim was Dmitrij Daškov, a diplomat and the second counsellor of the Russian Embassy in Istanbul. He wrote an essay entitled 'Russkie poklonniki v Ierusalime. Otryvok iz putešestvija po Grecii i Palestine v 1820' (Merlo 2013).

4   'Jerusalem (After 1291)', *New Advent* (Catholic Encyclopedia), 1910, http://www.newadvent.org/cathen/08364a.htm; also Hummel and Hummel (1995). Other accounts put the figures at 15,000 in 1910 and 12,000 in 1913: http://www.joseph-zeitoun.com/2015/07/

5   The founding father of the Israeli state David Grun (later David Ben-Gurion) was born in the Russian Empire and immigrated to Palestine 1906. After the First World War broke out, Ben-Gurion, a Russian subject, was deported by the Ottoman authorities from Palestine and he returned to Palestine with occupying British forces in 1918.

6   'Jerusalem (After 1291)', New Advent (Catholic Encyclopedia), 1910, http://www.newadvent.org/cathen/08364a.htm

7   http://www.pef.org.uk/Pages/Warren.htm

8   https://books.google.co.uk/books?id=CydMAAAAYAAJ&pg=PA155&dq=filastin&hl=en&ei=XuBVTa-bEc-EhQfR36CoDA&sa=X&oi=book_result&ct=result&redir_esc=y#v=onepage&q=filastin&f=false

9   *The* province became known as vilayet in the late 1860s.

10 https://commons.wikimedia.org/wiki/File:1913_Ottoman_Geography_Textbook_Showing_the_Sanjak_of_Jerusalem_and_Palestine.jpeg

11 Mikhail Nu'aymah (1889–1988), a Lebanese author and well-known Arab poet, was also educated at the Russian teachers college in Nazareth in 1902–1906.

12 الجمعية الإمبراطورية الأرثوذكسية الفلسطينية, http://www.mansaf.org/orth_society.htm

13 See for example: ibid.

14 http://www.mansaf.org/orth_society.htm; https://arabic.rt.com/news/586864-130

15 http://www.aljazeera.com/programmes/witness/2012/05/20125915313256768.html (Masalha 2012).

16 'Святая земля: Отчет по командировке в Палестину и прилегающия к ней страны' [Holy Land: Report on a Business Trip to Palestine and Adjacent Countries] (Kiev: Kiev Theological Academy, 1875).

17 https://upload.wikimedia.org/wikipedia/commons/0/05/Manual_of_Palestinean_Arabic%2C_for_self-instruction_1909.png

18 The 'becoming of self' was often described in Darwish's poetry as the 'other self'.

However the term 'becoming of being' is based on the insight Martin Heidegger developed in *Being and Time* (2010). The conception assumes that the ontological truth of being's becoming (being in the world, being becomes progressively uncovered and articulated) is mediated by human thinking and action.

19   Nassar also published in 1911 the first book in Arabic on Zionism, entitled *Zionism: Its History, Objective and Importance*, in which he described Zionism as a settler-colonial movement seeking to displace the Palestinian Arabs in Palestine (Beška 2014a).

20   For a critique of Bracy's work, see Beška *(2012)*.

21   The historic name applies to the entire area of the eastern plateau of the Jordan valley including 'Amman, then part of the Nablus sanjak.

22   *Falastin*, 31 January 1912, p. 1.

23   Yiannis Meimaris, 'The Discovery of the Madaba Map: Mythology and Reality', at: http://198.62.75.1/www1/ofm/mad/articles/MeimarisMap.html

24   See aso Khalidi, W. (1988); Kasmieh (1992).

25   To this letter, he received a reply from Theodor Herzl (Beška 2007).

26   Imad al-Din al-Isfahani, a chronicler and advisor to Saladin, was present at the Battle of Hittin and the subsequent campaign to expel the Crusaders from the Holy Land (al-Isfahani 1888).

27   Shukri al-'Asali, 'Kitab min Salah al-Din al- Ayyubi ila qa'id al-hamla al-Haw-raniyya Sami Basha al-Faruqi', *al-Muqtabas*, 5 December 1910, cited in Beška (2014b).

28   For further discussion on the leadership and goals of the Palestinian national movement during the Mandatory period, see al-Hut (1981).

29   See, for instance, Azmi Beshara, 'The Palestinian People is a Colonial Invention', in Azmi Beshara on the existence of a Palestinian People, https://www.youtube.com/watch?v=EOqAGbpoDZc, posted 30 April 2009.

30   'Abd al-Hadi had been a founding member of the 1909 Paris-based underground al-Fatat (Jam'iyat al-'Arabiyah al-Fatat, 'the Young Arab Society'), an Arab nationalist organisation which was devoted to Arab cultural and administrative autonomy and unity within the Ottoman system. 'Abd al-Hadi had also served as private secretary of Amir Faisal at the Paris Peace Conference of 1919.

31   Aryeh Dayan, 'The Communists Who Saved the Jewish State', *Haaretz*, 9 May 2006, http://www.haaretz.com/print-edition/features/the-communists-who-saved-the-jewish-state-1.187221

32   Published in the Israeli Official Gazette, No. 1 of the 5th Iyar, 5708 (14 May 1948).

Chapter 10

1   A speech delivered at a meeting of the French Zionist Federation, Paris, 28 March 1914, in Litvinoff (1983, paper 24: 115–116).

2   See protocol of Ruppin's statement at the Jewish Agency Executive's meeting, 20 May 1936 (in Heller 1984: 140).

3   Brian Klug, 'The Other Arthur Balfour "PROTECTOR OF THE JEWS"', 8 July 2013, http://www.balfourproject.org/the-other-arthur-balfour-protector-of-the-jews/

4   Cited by Ami Isseroff, 'British Support for Jewish Restoration', http://www.mideastweb.org/britzion.htm; Masalha (1992, 1997, 2003).

5   J. N. Darby, *Letters of J. N. Darby*, Vol. 2 (London: G. Morrish, n.d.).

6   Numbers 32:1; Genesis 31:25; Genesis 37:25.

7   Cited by Ami Isseroff, 'British Support for Jewish Restoration', http://www.mideastweb.org/britzion.htm.

8   Ibid.

9   As early as 1821 the Anglican Church, through its Church Missionary Society and the London Jews Society (more properly, the Society for Promoting Christianity among the Jews, founded in 1808 to convert the Jews to Christianity), was considering the establishment of a post. The London Jews Society established the first permanent Anglican mission station in Jerusalem in 1833, two years after the crisis caused by the capture of the city by Muhammad 'Ali. In 1841, a Protestant bishopric in Jerusalem was established under joint British and Prussian auspices.

10 Russian interest in the Holy Land increased particularly after the Crimean War, as Russia availed itself of the opportunity of furthering Russian political concerns through protection of Orthodox interests in the Ottoman Empire. This was witnessed as early 1860 with the commencement of the building of a Russian cathedral and of a vast complex of hostels, offices and hospitals for the care for Russian pilgrims to Jerusalem.

11 German influence was reflected in the German Evangelical Church's administration of the hospital of the German deaconesses, the Syrian Protestant Orphanage, the Leper Hospital in the German colony, and the Lutheran Church of the Redeemer.

12 Not to be outdone, the Church of Scotland mission was established, which, in addition to St Andrew's in Jerusalem, provided medical and educational services in several centres in Palestine.

13 This famous poem was written by Kipling in 1899.

14 Cited by Isseroff, 'British Support for Jewish Restoration'.

15 Here Said uses Carl Marx's adage: 'they cannot represent themselves; they must be represented' in an epigraph to Orientalism.

16 http://web.nli.org.il/sites/JPress/English/Pages/Palestine-Post.aspx

17 Reported in Haaretz, 4 April 1969.

18 Wadi al-Hawarith was also the name of a Palestinian village depopulated in 1948.

19 Rabbinic sages whose views were recorded in the Mishnah.

20 Jewish Oral Torah scholars.

21 For further discussion of the invention of the Jewish people, see Masalha (2007) and Sand (2009).

22 Other key reasons behind the influence of Arabic on modern Hebrew include: (1) until the establishment of Israel in 1948 Arabic was spoken by the overwhelming majority of people in Palestine; (2) during the early stages of its revival Hebrew urgently needed new Semitic words and patterns and had to rely on a living Semitic language such as Arabic which the newly invented modern Hebrew found as a readily available rich resource to exploit; (3) Arabic is closest to Hebrew amongst the Semitic languages (Shehadeh 1998: 62; Chomsky 1967: 217).

23 Much of Israeli research has focused on the abundance of Arabic adjectives in Israeli Hebrew slang and on the significant impact of Arabic on the 'non-official', non-standard, colloquial Hebrew (Blanc 1954; Shehadeh 1998).

24 However, some words did not catch on. For instance, Ben-Yehuda's word for 'tomato' was badora, the Hebrew version of the Palestinian colloquial Arabic bandora; Ben-Yehuda failed to win this logistic battle and today Israeli Hebrew speakers use the word 'agvania (Balint 2008) – from the Hebrew root 'agav which means 'to love, to desire'. This also reflects the European (and vulgar) 'love apple' (Italian: pomo d'oro; French: pommes d'amour) for the Aztec fruit which was first brought to Italy from South America in the 16th century and to which the Europeans attributed aphrodisiac powers.

25 Avishai Margalit, 'The Myth of Jerusalem', *The New York Review of Books* 38(21), 19 December 1991.

26 Uri Davis, 'The Histadrut: Continuity and Change', paper submitted to the International Department, Norwegian Trade Union Federation, January 1999.

27 Shamir means flint. The Talmud contains the myth of King Solomon using Shamir in the construction of the first temple in the place of cutting tools.

28 Don C. Benjamin, 'Stories and Stones: Archaeology and the Bible, an introduction with CD Rom', 2006, http://www.doncbenjamin.com/pav/docs/archaeology_and_the_bible.pdf, note 78, p. 254.

29 Approximately one-quarter of all geographical names were derived from the Arabic names on the basis of the similarity of sounds.

30 Founded in 1890, the new Zionist settlement/city of Rehovot was named after a biblical town of a similar name, Rehoboth, which stood at a completely different location in the Negev Desert.

31 Oren Yiftachel's Introduction to Noga Kadman's Erased From Space and Consciousness (2008), p. 8, cited in Manar Makhoul, 'Un-erasing the Nakba: Palestinian Identity in Israel since the First Intifada', 13 March 2013, http://mondoweiss.net/2013/03/palestinian-identity-intifada/

32 Jonathan Cook, 'Israel's Plan to Wipe Arabic Names off the Map', The Electronic Intifada, 17 July 2009, http://electronicintifada.net/content/israels-plan-wipe-arabic-names-map/8351

33 Ibid.

Index

Note: Page numbers followed by *n* indicate an endnote with relevant number.